PORSCHE
911 in Racing

Vier Jahrzehnte im Motorsport
Four Decades of Motor Racing

gruppe C
motorsport verlag
gmbh

**Porsche 935 K3 turbo
Dick Barbour Racing
Winner IMSA GTX class
24 hours Le Mans 1980
Dick Barbour, Brian Redman,
John Fitzpatrick**

Text: Gustav Büsing
Michael Cotton
John Davenport
Wilfried Müller
Bill Oursler

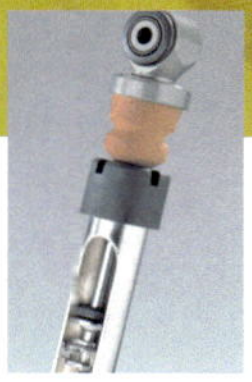

Hightech für den Motorsport

Die Renningenieure von ZF Sachs können bei ihrer Arbeit auf das exzellente Know-how aus dem Seriengeschäft und die Testeinrichtungen des Entwicklungszentrums zurückgreifen. Umgekehrt fließen die Erfahrungen aus dem Rennsport in die Entwicklungen für die Automobilindustrie ein und bringen so Vorteile für jeden Autofahrer.

www.zfsachs.com

Antriebs- und Fahrwerktechnik

Porsche 911 S 2,5 Coupe
Porsche Kremer Racing
Winner GT European Trophy
Hockenheim 1972: John Fitzpatrick

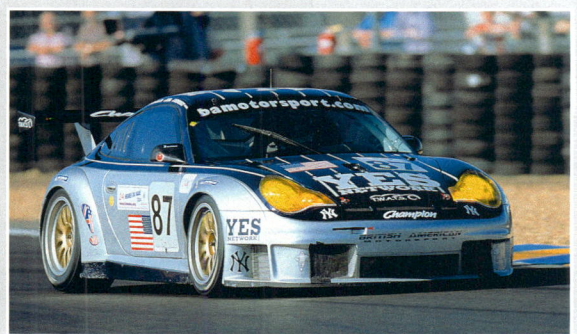

presented by

gruppe C
motorsport verlag
gmbh

Porsche 911 GT1
Champion Racing
12 hours Sebring 1999
Thierry Boutsen, Bob Wollek, Dirk Müller

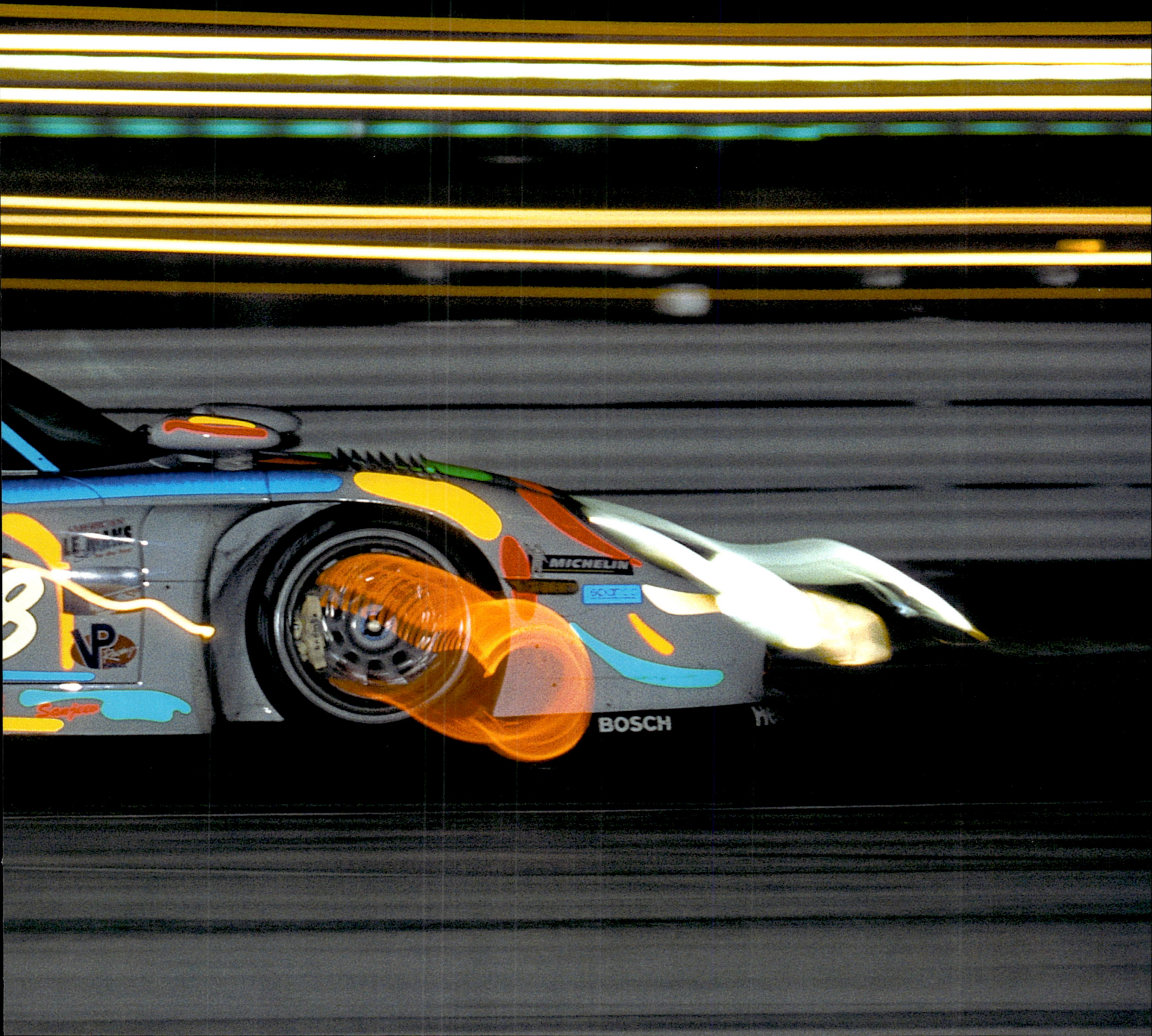

Der Verlag dankt der Abteilung Öffentlichkeitsarbeit und Presse der Porsche AG, Stuttgart, für die tatkräftige Hilfe und Unterstützung, ohne die ein Band wie dieser nicht hätte realisiert werden können.

Der persönliche Dank des Herausgebers gilt Klaus Parr und Dieter Gross, die mit ganz besonderer Liebenswürdigkeit und Kompetenz geholfen haben.

Und nicht zuletzt danken Herausgeber und Autoren den Herren Peter Falk, Herbert Linge, Hans Mezger und Norbert Singer für ihre Bereitschaft, sich in einem ausführlichen Gespräch an die frühen Jahre der 911-Sportgeschichte zu errinnern.

The publisher would like to express thanks to the Press and Public Relations department of Porsche AG in Stuttgart for their invaluable help and support, without which a publication like this could not have been produced.

Personal thanks and appreciation of the publisher go to Klaus Parr and Dieter Gross, who have been particularly helpful and efficient.

And not in the least, the publisher and the authors express their thanks to Messrs Peter Falk, Herbert Linge, Hans Mezger and Norbert Singer for their willingness to share their reminiscences of the early years of the 911's competition history in a lengthy conversation.

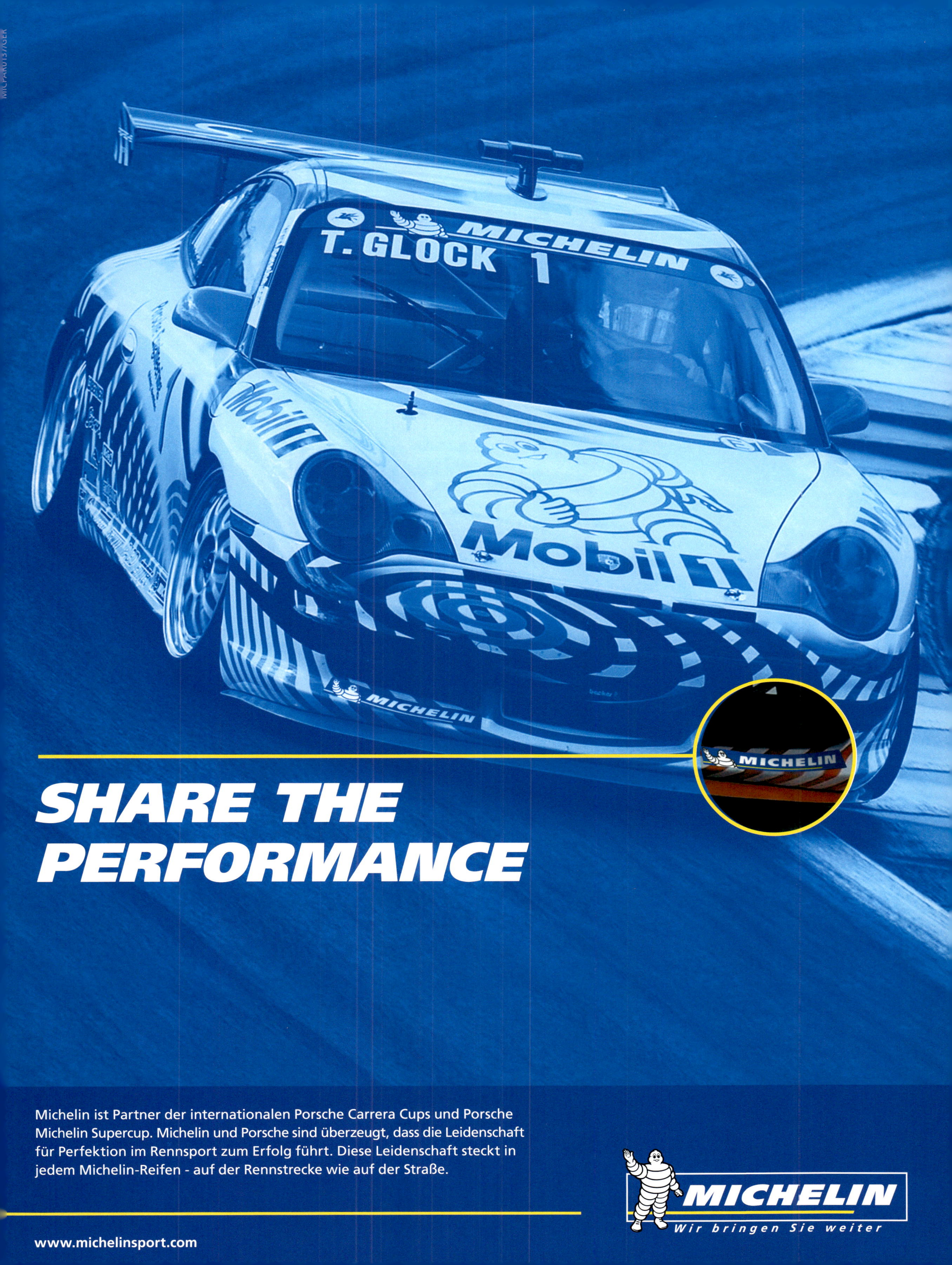

SHARE THE PERFORMANCE

Michelin ist Partner der internationalen Porsche Carrera Cups und Porsche Michelin Supercup. Michelin und Porsche sind überzeugt, dass die Leidenschaft für Perfektion im Rennsport zum Erfolg führt. Diese Leidenschaft steckt in jedem Michelin-Reifen - auf der Rennstrecke wie auf der Straße.

MICHELIN
Wir bringen Sie weiter

www.michelinsport.com

Herausgeber / Editor	Ulrich Upietz
Produktionsleitung / Production Manager	Tim Upietz
Autoren / Authors	Gustav Büsing, Michael Cotton, John Davenport, Wilfried Müller, Bill Oursler
Fotos / Photography	Porsche Presse Archiv, Bildagentur Kräling, McKlein, Bill Oursler, Ulli Upietz Photography
Übersetzung / Translation	Rene de Boer (Rebocar Automotive Productions), Deborah and Jörg-Richard Ufer
Ergebnisse und Statistik / Results and Statistics	Klaus Handermann
Reproduktion und Satz / Reproduction and design	LA CONCEPT GmbH, Jonas Hermanns - www.LA-CONCEPT.de
Papier / Paper	NOVATECH von Antalis - www.antalis.de
Produktion und Druck / Production and Printing	Heining & Müller GmbH, Klaus Schönenborn - www.hmb-print.de
Buchbinder / Bookbinder	Buchbinderei Terbeck - www.buchbinderei-terbeck.de
Copyright 2005 by	Gruppe C Motorsport Verlag GmbH - www.gruppec.de
ISBN 3-928540-44-0	Alle Rechte vorbehalten / All rights reserved - Printed in Germany

"Porsche" ist eine eingetragene Marke der Dr. Ing. h. c. F. Porsche AG; ihre Verwendung erfolgt mit freundlicher Gestattung der Porsche AG.

"Porsche" is a registered marque of Dr. Ing. h. c. F. Porsche AG; its use is made with the kind permission of Porsche AG.

Das Werk einschließlich aller seiner Teile ist urheberrechtlich geschützt. Jede urheberrechtswidrige Verwertung ist ohne Zustimmung des Verlages unzulässig und strafbar. Das gilt insbesonders für Vervielfältigungen, Übersetzungen, Nachahmungen, Mikroverfilmung und die Einspeicherung und Verarbeitung in elektronischen Systemen.

No part of this publication may be reproduced, stored in a retrieval system or transmitted, in any form or by any means, electronic, mechanical, photocopying, recording or otherwise, without prior permission in writing from the publisher.

An diesem Anblick können wir uns nicht sattsehen !

Wir gratulieren Porsche zu 40 Jahren 911.

Technik aus dem Motorsport

www.bbs.com

Porsche 911 GT3 RS
Land Motorsport PZ Koblenz
24 hours Nürburgring 2004
Marc Basseng, Franz Konrad,
Patrick Simon, Marino Franchitti

Hier erfahren Sie mehr – Porsche Online: Telefon 01805 356 - 911, Fax - 912 (EUR 0,12/min) oder www.porsche.de.

Wieder ein Beispiel dafür,
daß sich eine langfristige Anlage auszahlt.

Inhalt
Contents

18	Elfer-Väter erinnern sich / Sweet Memories
28	Die Handschrift des Technikers Norbert Singer / Engineered to success
40	Karriere eines Leistungssportlers / Four decades of development
144	Das Heimspiel fest im Griff / Popular on home Ground
170	In Top-Form auf jedem Geläuf / Superb in snow and mud
206	Reicher Lorbeer in Amerika / A battleground in Amerika
290	Porsche 911 - In Le Mans daheim / Porsche 911 forms fabric of Le Mans
318	Porsche 911-Markenpokale erobern den Globus / Porsche 911 one-make fascinates
336	Porsche Cup Poster 1972 - 2004 / Ergebnisse - Results
338	National and international championships won by Porsche 911
346	Overall wins by Porsche 911 in major national and international events
362	Technische Daten: 911 2.0 Monte - 911 GT3 RSR / Technical data: 911 2.0 Monte - 911 GT3 RSR

ELFER-VÄTER ERINNERN SICH

Peter Falk, Herbert Linge und Hans Mezger im Gespräch.

War es beim Modellwechsel vom 356 zum 911 von Beginn an klar, dass dieses neue Auto möglichst bald zum Wettbewerbseinsatz kommen sollte?
Falk: Ja, das war klar. Die Entwicklung des Motors – das kann Herr Mezger bestätigen – war darauf ausgelegt, ein sehr sportliches Auto als Nachfolger des 356 zu machen. Und auch die Möglichkeit, den 2-Liter-Motor nach und nach zu vergrößern, war schon einkalkuliert.

Die Hubraumvergrößerung war Bestandteil der Planung?
Mezger: Ja, aber natürlich nicht bis 3,6 oder sogar 3,8 Liter. Aber das ist eigentlich normal, weil wenn Porsche einen neuen Motor macht, dann kann man das nicht jedes Jahr machen. Deshalb muss einfach ein bisschen Reserve drin sein. Natürlich hat keiner gewusst – wir hätten das damals auch für unmöglich gehalten – wie weit das gehen würde. Denn das ist ja später auch nur mit anderen, besseren Materialien überhaupt möglich gewesen, auf diese Größenordnung und vor allem auf diese Leistung zu kommen. Das ist halt der technische Fortschritt im Verlauf von 40 Jahren.

Der erste Einsatz des 911 erfolgte schon ganz kurz nach dem Serienstart. Die Auslieferung begann im Herbst 1964 und als das Auto für die Monte vorbereitet wurde, waren die ersten Wagen gerade seit drei Monaten bei den Kunden.
Falk: Das Auto wurde erst Ende des Jahres homologiert. Wir sind das Training zwischen Weihnachten und Neujahr – wir waren vorher insgesamt zweimal da unten – noch mit einem Auto gefahren, das noch gar nicht homologiert war.

Die Modifikationen, verglichen mit der Serie, waren ja sehr gering.
Falk: Vom Motor her waren es praktisch nur die Weber- statt der Solex-Vergaser, weil die besser fahrbar waren, und vom Fahrwerk her waren es Koni-Stoßdämpfer, aber das war schon so ziemlich alles.

Und wie sind Sie beide, Peter Falk und Herbert Linge, dann zu der Ehre gekommen, diesen ersten Wettbewerbseinsatz zu fahren? War das praktisch ein Teil des verlängerten Versuchsprogramms?
Linge: Ja, wahrscheinlich war das mit ein Grund. Ich glaube, es hat aber auch noch einen anderen gehabt. In dieser Zeit gab es ja allgemein die Vorstellung, eine Rallye, vor allem eine Winter-Rallye, die kann nur ein Skandinavier fahren. Also Mitteleuropäer oder Deutsche sind unfähig, so eine Rallye zu fahren und sogar in der Spitze mitzugeigen. Das konnte sich einfach niemand vorstellen. Ich glaube, dass sich viele Leute gar nicht so sicher waren, was in diesem Auto steckt. Die Idee unseres damaligen Rennleiters von Hanstein war ja ursprünglich mal: Er wollte einfach dieses Auto in Monte Carlo präsentieren. Dazu hat er aber Leute gebraucht, bei denen er davon ausging, die bringen das Auto heil dorthin, damit man das dort vorzeigen kann. Von sportlichem Einsatz war nicht bei allen in der Firma die Rede, bei uns beiden aber schon ein bisschen. Bei uns gab es schon den Hintergedanken: So lässig werden wir das nicht angehen. Wir wollten da schon ein bisschen zeigen, was wir können und was das Auto kann.

Falk: Zur Ergänzung, weil Herbert gesagt hat, dass die Meinung bestand, dass nur die Skandinavier gewinnen können: Die Rallye Monte Carlo war ja früher nur eine sogenannte Uhren-Rallye. Da ging's ja wirklich nicht auf Dampf, sondern um genaues Fahren. Das war auch noch der Fall, als Mercedes 1960 diesen Eins-Zwei-Drei-Sieg errang. Das ging nur, weil es eine Uhren-Rallye war. Wenn es eine Rallye gewesen wäre so wie heute, dann wären die irgendwo hinten gelandet. Aber bei uns war es schon eine Rallye, wo es auf Dampf ging.

Wie war die Aufteilung im Auto? Sind beide gefahren oder gab es eine Arbeitsteilung in Fahrer und Navigator?
Falk: Die Rallye war ja damals sehr lang. Die ging für uns los in Frankfurt und die ganze Anfahrt über zwei Tage und eine Nacht oder so ähnlich. Da haben wir uns am Lenkrad abgewechselt. Aber die ganzen Sonderprüfungen, die hat nur Herbert gefahren.
Linge: Und das hatte natürlich auch einen Grund. Nicht, dass Peter das nicht hätte fahren können, sondern ich bin ein verdammt schlechter Beifahrer. Wenn ich daneben sitze, dann fahre ich trotzdem immer mit, und das ist nicht so gut. Er kann das viel besser.

Der Einsatz hat ja sicherlich Begehrlichkeiten bei den Sportfahrern geweckt. Wahrscheinlich gab es ja auch schon bald Leute, die mit dem 911 auf die Rundstrecke gehen wollten?
Linge: Ja, die Anfragen kamen natürlich prompt. Bei der Monte Carlo war für uns nicht alles so gelaufen, wie wir uns das vorgestellt hatten, aber im großen und ganzen waren schon alle unheimlich beeindruckt, was wir unter den Bedingungen, die da geherrscht haben, erreicht hatten. Vermutlich war's eine der schwierigsten Winter-Rallyes damals, soviel Schnee hat's nach meiner Erinnerung weder vorher noch nachher jemals gegeben. Du bist ja nur noch in den Schneewehen herumgefahren. Da kamen schon die Anfragen von unseren Kunden: Muss ich mir jetzt das Auto zulegen? Wir mussten die aber erst mal ein bisschen bremsen, denn wir hatten schon noch eine ganze Liste, was an dem Auto noch gemacht werden musste, um es wirklich noch wettbewerbsfähiger zu machen. Aber diese Monte Carlo hat schon die Begierde bei allen Porsche-Sportfahrern geweckt. Das war damals schon eine riesengroße Familie, man muss sich da nur mal die Starterfelder mit den 356 Carrera anschauen, wo jedes Wochenende 40 bis 50 Autos am Start standen. Die wollten natürlich schon alle das neueste Modell haben.

Was waren denn dann die ersten Entwicklungsschritte? Das Auto galt ja am Anfang als nicht ganz unproblematisch, um es vornehm auszudrücken.
Falk: Sehr vornehm ausgedrückt. Wir haben immer gesagt, das Auto war eine Schlange: Geradeauslauf verheerend, Windempfindlichkeit bis zum geht nicht mehr, Eindrehen in die Kurve, also Lastwechsel, verheerend. Man musste also schon sehr viel weiterentwickeln, bis das einigermaßen in Ordnung war. Wobei hauptsächlich die Änderungen an der Vorderachse mit anderen Gelenkgummis einen großen Fortschritt brachten. Auch das Gelenk am McPherson-Federbein unten wurde geändert und die Lenkung selber. Karosserieseitig gab es nicht viel, außer bei der Gewichtsverteilung.

Nun ist es ja oft so, dass ein Auto, das auf der Straße recht giftig und schwierig zu fahren ist, für den Sporteinsatz durchaus seine Vorteile hat.
Falk: Ja klar, es gab Fahrer, denen das Wurscht war, ob das Auto auf der Geraden hin und her ging. Das war denen völlig egal. Denen lag nur daran, dass man das Auto um die

Talking with Peter Falk, Herbert Linge and Hans Mezger
At the time of the switch from the 356 to the 911, was it clear from the very beginning that this car would be used for competition purposes as soon as possible?
Falk: Yes, it was. The development of the engine, as Mr. Mezger can confirm, has been focused on creating a very sporty car to become the successor of the 356. And the possibility to enlarge the two litre engine bit by bit hat been kept in mind, too.
So increasing the capacity had already been part of the planning?
Mezger: Yes, it had, but obviously not up to 3.6 or even 3.8 litres. But in fact, that is normal, because when Porsche is developing a new engine, they can't do so every year. Therefore, a little reserve just has to be there. Of course, no-one knew at the time how far things would go, and even we would have considered it impossible back then. After all, reaching this dimensions and especially this performance could only be achieved later with different, better materials. That is technical development in the course of 40 years.
The first competitive outing of the 911 already happened soon after series production had started. Delivery started in the autumn of 1964 and as the car was being prepared for the Monte, the first cars had been with the customers for only three months.
Falk: Homologation of the car came only at the end of the year. Prior to the event, we were in the South twice, but we did practice between Christmas and New Year with a car that hadn't even been homologated.
Compared to the production version, modifications were only very small.
Falk: Concerning the engine, we just put in Weber instead of Solex carburettors, because they were better to drive. And

SWEET MEMORIES THE FATHERS OF THE 911 REMEMBER

the suspension was fitted with Koni shock absorbers, but that was about it.
And how come that both of you, Peter Falk and Herbert Linge, got the honour to drive in this first competitive outing? Was it, in fact, part of the extended testing programme?
Linge: Yes, probably that was one of the reasons. But I think, there has been another one. Back then, people believed that only a Scandinavian could drive a rally, and especially a winter rally. So, central-Europeans, or Germans for that matter, were unable of driving such a rally, let alone be among the top contenders. No-one believed that. And I think that many people just didn't know what this car was up to. After all, our former motor sport boss, von Hanstein, had the original idea of just presenting the car in Monte Carlo. But to do so, he needed people whom he trusted to bring the car there in one piece, so that it could be shown. Not everybody

December 2004 (l.-r.): Hans Mezger, Peter Falk, Herbert Linge

Ecken herumschmeißen konnte. Und das konnte man. Die Rennfahrer, die haben diese Mängel überspielt. Die waren begeistert von der Leistung, waren trotz allem begeistert vom Fahrverhalten, weil sie damit zurecht kamen.

Linge: Aber es war am Anfang nur eine bestimmte Gruppe von Fahrern, die mit diesem Auto zurecht kamen. Ich kann mich noch erinnern, als der Carlo Abarth damals seine 750er und 1000er gemacht hat, da hat er bei internationalen Veranstaltungen grundsätzlich nur ehemalige Porsche-Fahrer auf seine Autos gesetzt. Da hat er zu mir gesagt: ‚Weisst du, das sind die einzigen, die mit so unmöglichen Autos umgehen können.' Seine Autos haben auch nur PS gehabt, aber von Straßenlage wussten die gar nichts. Aber es waren erfolgreiche Autos und er wusste, wen er drauf setzen musste.

Beim Elfer begann dann ja sehr bald die Aufrüstung. Motorseitig stieg die Leistung fast von Jahrgang zu Jahrgang. Der 911 S war dann das Auto, das man haben musste im Sport.

Falk: Der S war das erfolgreiche Rallye-Auto. Das ging los mit den drei Monte Carlo-Siegen hintereinander von 1968 bis 1970. Erst Elford, dann zweimal Waldegaard. Das war aber schon mit dem 2,2 Liter, glaube ich.

Stolz des Hauses: Der 911 2.0 erntet die bewundernden Blicke der Belegschaft in Zuffenhausen nach dem erfolgreichen Monte-Einsatz 1965.

Company's pride: The workforce at Zuffenhausen looking full of admiration at the 911 2.0 after its successful participation at Monte Carlo in 1965.

Linge: Also das Hauptproblem damals mit den ersten Autos war die Vergaser-Geschichte. Diese Dreifach-Vergaser von Solex, das war ein Drama ohne Ende. Die sind übergeschwappt, das Niveau hat sich nicht konstant halten lassen, und dann war das Gemisch zu mager. Ich kann mich gut erinnern, dass ich am Schluss, wo wir schon so richtig den Bogen raushatten mit dem Ding und auch richtig schnell waren, da hab ich Gas gegeben zu einem Zeitpunkt, wo man normalerweise sofort abfliegt, wenn man das macht. Aber der Motor kam mit so einer Verzögerung, dass du schon halb um die Kurve gefahren warst, bevor der Motor kam. Also hab ich schon vorher Gas gegeben, damit ich da hinten, wo ich's brauch, auch Leistung habe. Das kann man sich gar nicht vorstellen. Das war schon ein bisschen ein Glücksspiel, mit dem Auto wirklich schnell zu sein. Als das Problem mit dem Vergaser im Griff war, da hat es sofort ganz anders ausgesehen.

Mezger: Wir haben dann auch mit Weber Verbindung aufgenommen und später hat dann Solex einen nachgebauten Weber-Vergaser geliefert.

Falk: Der Solex hatte keinen Schwimmer. Das war eine neue Konstruktion für einen Vergaser. Die Pumpe pumpte rein und wenn das Ding voll war, dann ist die Kammer übergelaufen. Und bei jeder Kurve, bei jedem Bremsvorgang änderte sich das Niveau. Bei den Weber-Vergasern mit richtigem Schwimmer wurde das Niveau konstant gehalten.

Damals galt das Einstellen dieser Vergaser auch immer als eine Art Kunststück.

Mezger: Ich kann mich erinnern, da kam immer einer von Weber, der hat sich da drüber gebeugt und hat mit der Hand in die Steigrohre der Einspritzdüse ein kleines Löchlein reingebohrt, für den Übergang zwischen Leerlauf und Gas. Das dauerte zwar seine Zeit, aber dann ging's auch.

Linge: Mit dem war ich mal sechs Tage in Modena, da haben wir mit Weber-Vergaser Versuche gemacht. Da habe ich auch so gelächelt, wenn der mit einem 0,5 Millimeter Bohrer zu Werke ging. ‚Was soll der Quatsch, wie soll das Auto plötzlich gehen, wenn der da so kleine Löcher bohrt', habe ich gedacht. Doch der hat das super hingekriegt.

Mezger: Bei uns an den Rennmotoren war es der Eberhard Storz, der Senior, der die am besten einstellen konnte. Und bei den Bergrennen, da ist man halt halb den Berg hoch gefahren und hat dann dort die Vergaser eingestellt. Wobei man unten eine andere Einstellung brauchte als oben, wegen der Höhe.

Falk: So war's dann unten nicht gut und oben auch nicht, aber in der Mitte ging's prima.

Mezger: Aber immerhin halbwegs oben und unten. Wenn wir unten eingestellt hätten, wär's oben ganz schlecht gewesen und umgekehrt. Da sieht man mal, was man heute mit der Einspritzung hat.

Bis Ende 1969 hatte der 911 schon über 50 Landesmeisterschaften gewonnen und über 300 Siege in der GT-Klasse bis 2000 Kubikzentimeter erzielt.

Mezger: Der 911 war und ist eben ein unheimlich gutes Breitensport-Auto.

Linge: Das war aber auch lange Zeit eine Frage der Klasseneinteilung. Die Motorsport-Behörden haben ja dazu geneigt, immer wenn etwas gut lief, es sofort zu ändern, damit alles wieder durcheinander kommt. Das machen sie ja heut noch so. Konstanz hat es in den Reglements eigentlich immer nur für kurze Zeit gegeben. Das war natürlich auch mit der Grund, warum der Hubraum der Motoren geändert wurde. Als wir angefangen haben, war die 1600er-Klasse gut, dann waren es die Zweiliter. Dann ging die Klasse bis 2,5 Liter, also war dann der 2,2 Liter da. Aber wir waren immer wieder gezwungen, auf die Reglements einzugehen.

Falk: Wir haben in der Rennabteilung für den 911 überhaupt keine Zeit gehabt, denn wir waren mit den Typen 904, 906 und 910 beschäftigt. Der Elfer wurde mehr oder weniger bei Tunern oder Kunden oder wo auch immer – unter anderem in Zuffenhausen bei der Werksreparatur – betreut, aber eine

Einsatzbereit: Herbert Linge 1962 vor dem VW Bus der Rennabteilung.

Ready to go: Herbert Linge in front of the race department's Volkswagen bus in 1962.

in the company was talking about competition, but the two of us were. In the back of our minds, there was this thought: we are not going to take this easy. We wanted to show what we could do and what the car was up to.

Falk: Moreover, because Herbert has said, people believed that only Scandinavians could win: in the past, the Monte Carlo Rally was just a so-called time-rally. It wasn't about driving flat-out, it was rather about driving precisely. And that still was the case when Mercedes landed its triple victory in 1960. That could only happen, because it was a time-rally. Had it been a rally like it is nowadays, they would have been way, way behind. But when we competed, it was a rally in which we were pushing quite hard.

How were duties split up in the car? Did you drive both, or was there a driver and a co-driver?

Falk: Back then, the rally was very long. For us, it started in Frankfurt and then the entire way, something like two days and one night or so. We shared the driving. But only Herbert drove the special stages.

Linge: And there was a reason for that, of course. Not that Peter couldn't have been driving, but I am a very bad co-driver. When I sit alongside, I still drive myself, and that is not so good. He is much better at that.

The effort certainly caused interest among the sporting drivers. Probably, there were already people wanting to take the 911 to the race track pretty soon?

Linge: Yes, of course, requests came in right away. At the Monte Carlo, things didn't quite go as we had planned, but all in all, everybody was pretty much impressed of what we had achieved under those circumstances. Probably, it had been one of the most difficult winter rallies, because as far as I can remember, they never had that much snow, neither before nor after that year. We were only driving in snow storms. So, requests from our customers were coming in: do I have to buy that car now? But we had to slow them down, because we still had a list of things that had to be done on the car to make it really competitive. But this Monte Carlo Rally had sparked the interest among all Porsche drivers. Back then, it already was a huge fraternity. Just look at the starting grids with the 356 Carreras, with 40 to 50 cars in the race every weekend. Of course, they all wanted to have the latest model.

After that, what was the first step in development? After all, initially, the car had a reputation of being not quite without problems, to put it mildly.

Falk: That is very mildly. As we used to say, the car was a snake: horrible at a straight line, prone to side winds, all over the place when there was a load change in corners, just horrible. So there was a whole lot to develop to get it halfway right. Especially the changes on the front axle with different rubbers on the bearings were a big step forward. The bearing on the McPherson struts was changed, too, as was the steering itself. There wasn't that much to do on the body work, other than the weight distribution.

It often happen that a car that is quite tricky and difficult to drive on the road has its advantages in competition use.

Falk: Of course, there were drivers who didn't care whether the car was all over the place on the straights. They just didn't care. They just wanted to be able to throw the car around the corner. And they could. Racing drivers just drove around these problems. They were impressed by the power and they were impressed by the handling, no matter what, because they could cope with it.

Linge: But initially, only a selected group of drivers could cope with this car. I still remember that, when Carlo Abarth had made his 750s and 1000s, he would only put former Porsche drivers on his cars for international events. He told me: "You know, they are the only ones who are able to drive such impossible cars." (laughing) After all, his cars just had power, but they didn't know a thing about handling. Still, these cars were successful and he knew who to put in them.

For the 911, the development would start soon. The output of the engines increased almost every year. The 911 S became the car to have for competition.

Falk: The S was the successful rally car. It started with three Monte Carlo-wins on the trot from 1968 till 1970. First Elford, then Waldegaard twice. But, if I recall correctly, that was already with the 2.2 litre.

Linge: With the first car, the caburettor was the main problem. These Solex triple carburettors were a never-ending story. There was overflow, there was no way to keep the level, and then, the mixture wasn't good enough. I still remember vividly that at the end, when we finally had mastered the thing and we were pretty quick, too, I accelerated at a point where you usually would never make it, when you do so. But it took so much time before the engine picked up, that we were already halfway around the corner

Gute alte Zeit: Mit Hilfe einer Stechuhr errechnet Peter Falk bei den Langstrecken-Rennen in der Box die Rundenzeiten der eingesetzten Porsche-Fahrzeuge und der wichtigsten Konkurrenten.

Good old times: An attendance recorder in the pits helps Peter Falk at long distance events to calculate the Porsches' lap times as well as those of its most important competitors.

when it finally did. So I pushed the throttle already before, so that I would have power at the end, where I needed it. One can hardly imagine what it was like. Being really quick with that car was quite a bit of a gamble. But once the problem with the carburettor had been sorted, it was a different piece of cake right away.

Mezger: Then, we got in touch with Weber and later on, Solex provided a carburettor that had been built after the Weber.

Falk: The Solex didn't have a float. That was a new construction for a carburettor. The pump pumped in and when the thing was full, the chamber would overflow. And at every corner, every time you braked, the level changed. With the Weber carburettors, that had the right float, the level would be kept constant and that worked.

Back then, adjusting these carburettors always was a masterpiece.

Mezger: I remember, there was always somebody from Weber coming who bent over and drilled a tiny little hole in the tube of the injection nozzle for the transition between idle and when the throttle pedal was pushed down. It always took a while, but it worked after that.

Auf Rekordjagd: Im Oktober 1967 fuhr Porsche mit dem 911 R 2.0 in Monza über die Gesamtdistanz von 20.000 Kilometern mit einem Schnitt von 209, 20 km/h fünf Weltrekorde sowie elf Zeit- und Streckenrekorde. Einer der vier Piloten war der unvergessene Jo Siffert (im Auto und beim Einstieg).

Record hunt: With the 911 R 2.0, Porsche covered a distance of 20.000 kilometres at an average speed of 209,20 km/h at Monza in October 1967 resulting in five world records and eleven time and track records. Among the four drivers was the unforgotten Jo Siffert (in the car and entering the cockpit).

richtige Entwicklung in der Rennabteilung gab es damals nicht. Was aber auch wieder heißt, dass das Auto, so wie es produziert wurde, mit den entsprechenden Verbesserungen, die normal in die Serie einflossen, wettbewerbsfähig war.

Mezger: Mit den Motoren war es ähnlich. Wir haben uns um die großen Dinge gekümmert, und haben die Elfer-Motoren ohne viel Konstruktionsarbeit entweder in den Motorenversuch oder nach Zuffenhausen gegeben, und die haben ihn dann präpariert. Die haben dann so spezielle Filter oder Düsen statt der Serienteile obendrauf gemacht. Das wurde nicht in der Rennabteilung gemacht. So war der 911 in der Anfangsphase wirklich mehr Kundensport als Werkssport.

Linge: Richtig, da sind wir den 904-6 gefahren und die Kunden den 911.

Falk: Mit der Entwicklung des 911 in der Rennabteilung ging es erst los, als der 917 nicht mehr fahren durfte. Da lief erst noch das CanAm-Programm, aber ab 1973 begann dann die Entwicklung für die Carrera RS, RSR, 934 und 935.

Wie kam das eigentlich zustande, dass der Elfer in der Anfangsphase in zwei Kategorien einsetzbar war: als GT, aber auch als Tourenwagen?

Linge: Da hat man ein bisschen in die Trickkiste gegriffen. So ist die Sitzpolsterung zum Beispiel ziemlich dünn gewesen, denn damit erfüllte das Auto dann die Innenraumabmessungen für Tourenwagen und wurde entsprechend eingestuft. In der Normalversion haben zwischen Dach und Sitz ursprünglich 1,5 oder 2 Zentimeter gefehlt.

Mit dem Hubraum hatte das also überhaupt nichts zu tun?

Mezger: Nein, die Viersitzer sollten eigentlich Tourenwagen sein und die Zweisitzer GT. Und da haben sie im Reglement die Maße für einen echten Viersitzer vorgeschrieben und die hat man halt mit ein paar Tricks auch für den 911 erreicht.

Falk: Weil es so knapp war, hat man eben probiert, den 911 auch als Tourenwagen zu homologieren, was ja auch eine Zeitlang gelang. Später hat die FIA das dann abgelehnt, auch auf Druck anderer Hersteller. Und das Problem besteht bis heute fort.

Wir haben schon festgestellt, dass die Elfer-Entwicklung erst während der CanAm-Zeit so richtig begann.

Falk: Ich glaube, wir müssen noch was einschieben. Und zwar die Entwicklung des 911 R, den es ja ab 1968 gab. Da hat man mal versucht, diesen Viernockenwellen-Motor, den 916-Motor, zu installieren. Was am Anfang nicht ging, aber dann haben wir die Korsika-Rallye damit gefahren.

Was war das für ein Motor?

Mezger: Also, das war zu Piechs Zeiten und der Herr Piech hat sich damals vorgestellt, dass man den 911 generell in der Serie als Viernockenwellen-Version macht. Angefangen fast beim Dreizylinder, dann Vierzylinder, Sechszylinder und bis zum Achtzylinder für die Serie. Der erste Motor, den man als Viernockenwellen-Motor gemacht hat, war der Sechszylinder. Diesen Motor hat man dann in einem Rallye-Auto eingesetzt. Das ist damals, wenn ich mich richtig erinnere, daran gescheitert, weil man aus Gewichtsgründen Aluminiumschrauben für die Befestigung des Ölkühlers verwendet hat. Die sind abgerissen und dann ist das Öl ausgelaufen.

Falk: Wir hatten den Motor dann noch mal im 911 R in Mugello Ende Oktober 1967 drin. Da waren die Fahrer mit dem Ansprechverhalten überhaupt nicht zufrieden.

Mezger: Das Triebwerk sollte der künftige Basismotor werden für die Serie. Man hat da von einer Motorenfamilie gesprochen. Aber, das war dann glaube ich 1967, hat man ihn einfach um zwei Zylinder verlängert und hatte dann den Motor für den 908.

Falk: Noch ein weiterer Beweis für die Allround-Fähigkeit des Elfers: Der 911 R hat damals auch Weltrekorde gefahren, was nicht jedes Auto kann. Dass man Rallyes fährt und Rundstrecke fährt und dann auch noch Weltrekorde.

Für jeden Betrachter ist es aber vor allem sensationell, wie vielseitig dieses Auto über 40 Jahre einsetzbar blieb.

Mezger: Das hat man natürlich auch nicht gewusst, dass man damit so lange fahren kann. Es wurde ja schon Ende der 60er Jahre vom Ende gesprochen im Zusammenhang mit der Abgas-Gesetzgebung in Amerika, dass man große Motoren mit weniger Drehzahl machen müsse. Begonnen hatte es mit einem Sechszylinder Ende der 50er Jahre, dem sogenannten Typ 745. Der hatte noch Stößelstangen wie der alte Vierzylinder, der vom Käfer abstammte, und er hatte noch einen Nassumpf. Der wurde dann schnell - ich sage mal fast eingestampft - und es kam noch mal eine Zwischenlösung, das war dann der Typ 821. Der hatte schon obenliegende Nockenwellen. Ich glaube, das Auto, das in Frankfurt stand 1963, das hatte noch einen Nassumpfmotor drin, weil der Trockensumpf eigentlich erst im Jahr 1963 entwickelt wurde. Und erst dann hat man gesagt, so jetzt reicht es, jetzt ist es ein guter Serienmotor, der auch noch ein bisschen ausbaufähig ist für den Breitensport. Aber dass man dann natürlich fast alles an diesem Motor entwickeln konnte - die vier Ventile, die Wasserkühlung – das hat niemand geahnt. Selbst den Indy-Motor hat man draus gemacht. Der Motor hat eigentlich alles gekonnt, bis auf die Formel 1.

Sie haben die Wasserkühlung erwähnt, die es im Sport ja bereits lange vor der Serie gab. Wie kam es dazu?

Mezger: Der Auslöser war der Schaden, den wir 1977 in Le Mans hatten, wo der Jürgen Barth doch noch zu Ende gefahren ist mit fünf Zylindern. Wir wollten schon lange einen Vierventilmotor machen. Denn die Vorteile waren: besserer Brennraum, höhere Leistung, besserer Verbrauch und hö-

Linge: Once upon a time, I spent six days in Modena with him, testing with Weber carburettors. I was amused when he took his 0.5 millimetre drill out. "Now what is all that nonsense about, how can the car go all of a sudden when that guy is drilling such little holes in there", I thought. But he did a perfect job.

Mezger: Eberhard Storz, the elder, was the one who was best in adjusting our racing engines. And at hill climbs, we just went halfway up the hill and then adjusted the carburettors. However, at the bottom, we needed a different setting than at the top, because of the altitude.

Falk: So is wasn't good at the bottom and it wasn't good at the top either, but halfway, it was fine.

Mezger: Well, at the bottom and the top, it was at least more or less okay. Had we done the adjustment at the bottom, it would have been very bad at the top and vice versa. It shows how good things are today with injection.

By the end of 1969, the 911 had already won more than 50 national championship titles and it had scored over 300 wins in the GT class till 2000 cc.

Mezger: The 911 was an incredibly good car for club racing, and still is.

Linge: But for a long time, that was also due to the different categories. After all, motor sport authorities had a tendency to change everything immediately when things were going well, so that there would be chaos again. In fact, they still do so today. There has only been stability in the regulations for a short period of time. And of course, that was also one of the reasons why the capacity of the engines was changed. When we started, the 1600 cc class was good, then it was the two-litre category. Later on, it was 2.5 litres, so we came up with the 2.2 litre engine. But we were forced to respond to the regulations over and over again.

Falk: Talking about the many victories: in the racing department, we didn't have any time for the 911 back then, because we were involved with the model ranges 904, 906 and 910. The 911 was being taken care of more or less by tuners and customers or wherever else for that matter, among others in the factory workshop at Zuffenhausen, but there was no real development in the racing department. However, on the other hand, that also means that the car was competitive as it was built, with the according improvements that found their way into the regular production range.

Mezger: With the engines, it was likewise. We were taking care of the big things and gave the 911-engines without much construction work either to the engine test department or to Zuffenhausen, and they were the ones who prepared them. They mounted special filters or nozzles instead of the regular production parts. Thus, the 911 really was more about customer competition than works competition in its early stages.

Linge: That is right, we were competing with the 904-6 and the customers ran the 911.

Falk: The racing department only started development work on the 911 when the 917 wasn't allowed to race anymore. Then, we still had the CanAm-programme at first, but from 1973 onwards, development for the Carrera RS, RSR, 934 and 935 started.

Why did it happen that in its early days, the 911 could run in two categories, as a GT and as a touring car?

Linge: There were some tricks involved there. For instance, the seat upholstery was quite thin, because thus, the car had the interior dimensions for touring cars and was classified accordingly. In the normal version, 1.5 or 2 centimetres were missing between the roof and the seat.

So the engine capacity didn't play a role at all here?

Mezger: No, it didn't. The four-seaters were designated to be touring cars and the two-seaters to be GTs. So, the dimensions for a genuine four-seater were written in the regulations and with a few tricks, we achieved these with the 911 as well.

Falk: Because it was so close, we just tried to get the 911 homologated as a touring car as well, and we successfully did so for quite a while. Later on, the FIA said no, also because other manufacturers were putting them under pressure. And this problem still remains to the current day.

We already found out that development of the 911 only really started during the CanAm-era.

Falk: I think, we need to add something. And that is the development of the 911 R, that was available from 1968 onwards. In this car, we tried to put in the four-camshaft engine, the 916-engine. Initially, it didn't work, but then, we did the Corsica Rally with it.

What kind of engine was that?

Mezger: Well, that was at the time when Piech was in charge and Mr. Piech had the vision of turning the entire 911 model range into a four-camshaft version in mass production as well. Starting with the three-cylinder, then the four-cylinder, six-cylinder and so on, up to an eight-cylinder for regular production. The first engine to be built with four camshafts was the six-cylinder. And then, they put this engine into a rally car. If I recall correctly, this car failed because aluminium bolts had been used to mount the oil cooler in order to save weight. The bolts broke and the oil leaked out.

Falk: We had this engine once more in the 911 R at Mugello at the end of October, 1967. Drivers weren't satisfied at all with the throttle response.

Mezger: This engine would have become the future basis for regular production. There was talk about a family of engines. Then, they simply added two cylinders and thus, they had the engine for the 908. This was, I think, in 1967.

Falk: Another proof for the versatility of the 911: the 911 R established world records, back then. Something that you can't do with every car: compete in rallies, compete at circuits and establish world records, too.

But for anyone, the most sensational thing is, in how many different ways this car could be used for over 40 years.

Mezger: Of course, nobody knew that it would be out there that long. After all, there were already talks about the car reaching the end of its lifespan at the end of the 1960s, because exhaust gas regulations in America required bigger engines that did less revs. It all started at the end of the 1950s with a six-cylinder engine, the so-called Type 745. It still was a push-rod engine like the old four-cylinder that was derived from the Beetle, and it had wet-sump lubrication. But

1970:
Hans Mezger

here Verdichtung. Aber das ging einfach nicht mit der Luftkühlung, weil die Ventile dann nebeneinander statt hintereinander sitzen. Da gab's dann eine Sitzung nach Le Mans 1977 in Weissach, und da hat man beschlossen: Wir entwickeln eine Vierventilversion wassergekühlt. Was nicht einfach war, aus den Einzelköpfen eine wassergekühlte Version zu machen. Im Reglement stand: Der Zylinderblock muss aus der Serie stammen. Dann haben wir nachgefragt: Wir haben ja separate Zylinder, wie ist das bei unserem luftgekühlten Motor? Dann haben die Regelexperten gesagt, Zylinder gehören zum Zylinderblock, also das muss serienmäßig bleiben. Deswegen hat man dann damals diesen Motor gemacht mit wassergekühltem Zylinderköpfen und luftgekühlten Zylindern.

Setzen wir doch noch einmal da an, wo die 911-Weiterentwicklung begann, nachdem sich die Zeit mit dem 917 dem Ende zuneigte.
Falk: Die Rennabteilung hat dann auch mal Arbeit gebraucht, weil die CanAm-Geschichte lief ja drüben in Amerika, also ging's jetzt auf die 911-Geschichte los. Das wurde völlig in der Rennabteilung entwickelt. Und von dort gingen dann auch die Werkseinsätze los: Die Targa Florio, der RS mit dem Bürzel und dann anschließend der Turbo.

Turbo ist ein gutes Stichwort. Technisch war der Schritt zum Turbo eine große Zäsur in der 911-Rennsportgeschichte. Der erste 911 Turbo kam ja 1974. Können Sie die Schritte noch einmal nachvollziehen?
Mezger: Nachdem diese CanAm-Geschichte so erfolgreich war, wo Porsche ja Pionierarbeit geleistet hat, hat man hier überlegt, ob das nicht auch etwas für die angekündigte Produktionswagen-Weltmeisterschaft wäre. Dann kam der Vorschlag, man überträgt diese Technologie auf die Serie. Da gab's viele, viele Gespräche mit dem Vertrieb. Denn das Reglement verlangte 400 produzierte Autos als Basis. Das war während der Energiekrise, und der Verkauf hat gesagt, von dem Auto kann man keine 400 Stück verkaufen. Aber Professor Fuhrmann war damals derjenige, der einfach wollte, dass man das Auto baut. Letzten Endes hat man dann entschieden, ok, wir bauen die 400 Autos als Basisauto für die Weltmeisterschaft. So ist eigentlich der 911 Turbo letzten Endes entstanden im Hinblick auf dieses neue Reglement.

Die ersten Autos hatten ja noch ein fürchterliches Turboloch.
Mezger: Es gab ja den Turbo-May, und BMW hatte ja auch einen 2002 Turbo. Und die, sage ich heute, waren damals unfahrbar. Mit dem 911 Turbo konnte man schon rumfahren, Privatfahrer auch. Da gab es natürlich schon noch ein kleines Loch, aber da musste man sich halt dran gewöhnen.
Linge: Wobei man dazu sagen muss, dass Motoren, die für den Wettbewerb so ein bisschen frisiert wurden, die hatten auch dieses Loch. Da kam auch bei einer bestimmten Drehzahl die Leistung. Und wie es dann beim Turbo genauso war, hat man gesagt, das ist halt das Turboloch.

Haben wir noch etwas Wesentliches in der 911-Entwicklung vergessen?
Falk: Ich glaube, wir müssen noch über die Allrad-Entwicklung sprechen, denn das war auch noch einmal ein Entwicklungs-Sprung. Die Initialzündung dazu war der Audi Quattro, den wir im Versuch hatten. Wir hatten eines der drei gekauften Autos und waren von dem Ding so begeistert und freuten uns richtig auf Schnee. Ich war mit dem Herrn Bott auch einmal bei der Rallye Monte Carlo als Zuschauer mit dem Audi Quattro und das hat uns einfach dazu verleitet zu sagen: Wir müssen auch so etwas machen. Und damit begann die Entwicklung, den 911 Carrera 4 mit Allradantrieb zu bauen. Aus dem ja dann auch sehr schnell der 959 entstand und die Paris-Dakar-Autos.

Was war das Besondere an diesem Allrad-System?
Falk: Das erste Auto war der 964, der ein Differential hatte zwischen Vorder- und Hinterachse, das elektronisch mehr oder weniger gesperrt werden konnte, je nach Straßenzustand. Das war damals nicht gut, das war ziemlich schlecht, hauptsächlich deshalb, weil die Elektronik damals nicht so feinfühlig reagierte wie dies heute der Fall ist. Dieses Auto wurde bei einem Vergleich mit anderen Allrad-Autos in der Presse fürchterlich verrissen. Und aufgrund dieses Tests haben wir damals dann diese neue Version entwickelt. Also, das Schlechte bei dem Auto war, dass es fürchterlich über die Vorderachse schob und irgendwann kam's mal hinten. Es war also völlig unkontrollierbar und unvorhersehbar, was macht denn das Auto jetzt, wenn man mal so'n Berg hochfuhr bei Schnee. Das wurde erst besser durch das System, das heute noch in den Autos drin ist: Die Hinterachse starr angekuppelt ans Getriebe und die Vorderachse per Viscokupplung zugeschaltet, wenn es nötig ist. Der 959 hatte wieder ein anderes System. Der hatte auch die Hinterachse fest angebunden ans Getriebe und die Vorderachse mit einer Lamellenkupplung elektronisch zugeschaltet, was auch nicht so ganz sauber ging, weil die Elektronik nie so ganz genau wusste, was will der Fahrer jetzt. Das spielte nachher bei den Paris-Dakar-Autos überhaupt keine Rolle, weil da haben wir mehr oder weniger alles starr gefahren. Im Sand ging das ja und da ging's auch nur um Traktion und Vortrieb.
Linge: Der Spaß bei dem Auto war natürlich, dass man unheimlich schnell war auf Schnee und Eis. Ich werde nie vergessen, wie wir das erste Mal auf die Turracher Höhe gekommen sind, auf unsere Versuchsstrecke dort. Das Auto flog da hoch, wie wenn du im Trockenen bist. Ich sag: Das gibt's doch gar nicht. Was haben wir denn für Reifen? Na, die gleichen wie immer. Das war schon beeindruckend.
Falk: Das Problem war nur: Das Bremsen ging noch genauso schlecht.

So wurde der Elfer dann auch noch zum Wüsten-Auto.
Falk: Da gab's aber ja noch einen Zwischenschritt. Diese Paris-Dakar-Autos hatten vorne eben eine Doppelquerlenkerachse, was wir bis heute noch nicht in der Serie haben. Dagegen hat die Hinterachse, die wir damals für den 959 gemacht haben, in etwas anderer Form später auch Einzug in die Serie gehalten. Auch das war für den Elfer noch einmal ein großer Schritt.

1985:
Peter Falk

that one was, I would almost say, scrapped pretty quickly and we had an interim solution, which was the Type 821. It already had overhead camshafts. I think that the car that was on show in Frankfurt in 1963 still had a wet-sump engine, because in fact, dry-sump was only developed in 1963. And only then, they said: okay, that is it, now we have a good production engine, that has some potential for club racing, too. But no-one could expect that we could develop almost everything on that engine, the four valves, the water cooling. They even made the Indy-engine from this one. In fact, the engine could do everything, except Formula 1.

You mentioned water cooling, that was being used in competition long before it was in regular production. How did this come about?

Mezger: The thing that sparked it was the damage we had in Le Mans 1977, where Jürgen Barth still made it to the finish with five cylinders. We had wanted to build a four-valve engine for a long time anyway. After all, the advantages are obvious: better combustion, more power, better fuel consumption and higher compression. But it just couldn't be done with air cooling, because then, you have the valves next to each other rather than behind each other. So after Le Mans 1977, we had a meeting at Weissach, and there it was decided to develop a water-cooled four-valve version. Making a water-cooled version with the single heads wasn't easy. The regulations said that the cylinder block had to be from the production car. So we asked: we have separate cylinders, what is it like for our air-cooled engine. Then, the regulation experts said that the cylinders are part of the cylinder block, so that had to remain like it was in the production car. And that is why they made this engine with water-cooled cylinder heads and air-cooled cylinders at the time.

Let's get back to the point where development of the 911 started when the era with the 917 was coming to an end.

Falk: Well, the racing department needed something to do, because the CanAm-thing was far away in America, so it took care of the 911 project. The entire development took place in the racing department. And from that time on, there were the factory efforts: the Targa Florio, the RS with the ducktail and then the Turbo.

Apropos turbo. Technically, the step to the turbo was a significant milestone in the racing history of the 911. The first 911 Turbo came in 1974. Can you still recall the different steps?

Mezger: As the CanAm-project, where Porsche did a lot of innovation work, was so successful, people asked themselves here whether that could be something for the proposed world championship for production cars. Then, the proposal came to transfer this technology to the regular production models. There were many, many meetings with the sales department. Because regulations required a basis of 400 cars that had to be produced. It was at the time of the energy crises, and the sales department had said that there was no way to sell 400 cars like that. But professor Fuhrmann just wanted that car to be built. So finally, they said: Okay, let's build these 400 cars as the basis for the world championship. And that is how the 911 Turbo was conceived in the end with an eye on these new regulations.

The initial cars had a terrible turbo lag.

Mezger: There was a Turbo-May, and BMW had a 2002 Turbo as well. Today, I would say, those cars were undriveable back then. One could drive with the 911 Turbo, though, and privateer drivers could, too. Of course, there still was a slight lag, but you just had to get used to it.

Linge: Although it has to be said that the engines that were tuned a little bit for competition use also had this lag. These engines also had the power coming in at a certain number of

911 Carrera 2 Cup 1992: Herbert Linge

revs. And as it was just like that with the turbo, people said that this was the turbo lag.

Is there something important in the development of the 911 that we have forgotten?

Falk: Oh, I think, we still have to talk about four-wheel drive, as this was yet another step in the development process. The Audi Quattro that we had in the test department had sparked it. We had one of the three cars that had been bought and we were just excited by it, really looking forward to snow. With the Audi Quattro, I attended the Monte Carlo Rally as a spectator together with Mr. Bott and that just persuaded us to say: We must do something like that, too. And that is how development of the 911 Carrera 4 with four-wheel drive started. Which would lead to the 959 and the Paris-Dakar-cars pretty soon.

What was the special thing about this four-wheel drive system?

Falk: The first car was the 964, that had a differentia between the front and the rear axle that could be locked less or more electronically, depending on road conditions. At the time, it wasn't very good. In fact, it was quite bad, mainly because electronics didn't react as sensibly as it does today. This car was torn to pieces by the press when it was compared to other four-wheel driven cars. And because of these tests, we developed this new version. The bad thing about this car was that it was sliding over the front axle, and certainly, the rear axle would come. It was totally uncontrollable and unpredictable. You never knew what the car would be doing when you were driving up a hill in the snow. It would only get better when we had the system that is still being used in cars today: the rear axle in a solid connection with the gearbox and viscous coupling that brings in the front axle whenever it is required. The 959 had yet another system. It also had the rear axle in a solid connection with the gearbox, but the front axle was being connected electronically by means of a multi-plate clutch. That didn't work very precisely, because the electronics never really knew what the driver wanted at that moment. Later, with the Paris-Dakar-cars, this didn't matter at all, because we had everything more or less solid anyway. In the sand, we could do this, and the only things we needed were traction and torque anyway.

Linge: With that car, the funny thing was of course being incredibly fast on snow and ice. I will never forget the first time we got up the Turracher Höhe, to the test track we had there. The car would race up like in the dry. I said: This just can't be true. What tyres do we have, then? Well, the same as always. That was quite impressive indeed.

Falk: The only problem was: braking was as bad as ever.

So the 911 became a desert-car as well.

Falk: Yes, but there still was a step in between. These Paris-Dakar-cars had double wishbones up front, which we still don't have on normal production cars to date. However, the rear axle that we had made for the 959 later found its way into the production range in a slightly changed way. That was yet another big step for the 911.

THE FATHERS OF THE 911 REMEMBER   **25**

DIE HANDSCHRIFT DES TECHNIKERS NORBERT SINGER

Norbert Singer im Gespräch über seine Arbeit mit einigen Rennfahrzeugen aus der 911-Familie.

Nach Ihrem Einstieg bei Porsche Anfang 1970 vergingen noch rund zwei Jahr ehe Sie sich beruflich und intensiv mit einem Auto aus der 911-Familie beschäftigt haben.

Singer: Richtig. Ich habe den RSR als Projekt übernommen und hatte sozusagen meinen Einstieg über die Rallye Korsika. Anschließend ging es auf dem Rückweg bereits ernsthaft in Paul Ricard los, wo wir dran gearbeitet haben, aus dem Rallye-Auto ein Rundstreckenauto zu machen.

Warum machte Porsche den Schritt, werkseitig auf der Rundstrecke mit einer 911-Ableitung anzutreten?

Singer: Die Entscheidung fiel ja schon lange vorher, als man sich entschlossen hat, eine 200er-Serie vom Carrera RS zu bauen. Mit ein Grund war, dass die 911 an Gewicht heftig zugelegt hatten. Damals war es ja so, dass das Renngewicht das Homologationsgewicht war. Dadurch musste man leichte Straßenautos bauen, damit man dieses geringe Gewicht im Motorsport nutzen konnte. Deshalb die 200er-Serie, und die Autos lagen, wenn ich das noch richtig weiß, bei einer Größenordnung von 940 kg. Alle 200 Autos wurden auf der Zuffenhausener Stadtwaage gewogen. Bei der Homologation haben die Herren der FIA die offiziellen Wiegezettel angesehen und dann wurde das Gewicht mit 900 kg im Wagenpass eingetragen. Denn man durfte bestimmte Dinge abziehen, diese Komfortsitze und die Innenverkleidung und ähnliche Dinge.

Wir haben dann noch aerodynamisch ein bisschen was mit dem Bürzel gemacht. Der Heckmotor war eine etwas trickreiche Anordnung, gut für Traktion, aber in anderen Fällen nicht so toll. Ein 911er, das ist so, wenn Sie den leicht machen wollen, wird er zunächst einmal vorne leicht und hinten, wo die Antriebseinheit Motor/Getriebe ist, lastet das ganze Gewicht. Und nachdem der Motor nun hinter der Hinterachse sitzt, wird es natürlich mit der Gewichtsverteilung ganz schwierig. Mit diesem RSR ging es dann 1973 in die Werkseinsätze in der Marken-Weltmeisterschaft.

Sehr weit von der Serie war das Auto aber nicht entfernt?

Singer: Es hatte die üblichen Dinge, die erlaubt waren. Da gibt es ein bisschen Bugspoiler unterhalb der Stoßstange. Äußerlich konnte man sowieso nicht sehr viel tun. Der RSR hatte natürlich ein Mc-Pherson-Federbein mit Drehstäben hinten. Die Drehstäbe waren ein kritischer Punkt an diesem Auto: Die Drehstäbe gab es natürlich in verschiedenen Härten, nur irgendwann können Sie keinen dickeren Drehstab mehr rein tun. Aber das Reglement sah irgendwelche Zusatzfedern vor. Wir haben dann sehr schnell den Drehstab „einschlafen" lassen. Die waren nur noch zum Schein drin und wir haben alles über die Zusatzfeder abgestützt. Das klingt zwar jetzt sehr einfach. Aber die ganzen Dämpferaufnahmen waren ja nicht für diese Kräfte gemacht. Die Dämpferdome haben einen bestimmten Querschnitt und dann war Platz für den Dämpfer mit seiner Bewegung vom Lenker her. Wenn sie da plötzlich eine Feder rein bringen, dann war der Dämpferdom zu klein. Sie durften aber keinen anderen Dämpferdom dort rein tun, sonst wäre es eine Karosserieänderung, also hat man mit irgendwelchen Mitteln den Dämpferdom ein bisschen geweitet, denn unten ging es ja, aber oben hat es ein bisschen geklemmt. So hat man also Zug um Zug die Federn vergrößert und bei den Fahrversuchen sehr schnell gemerkt, dass man den Drehstab vergessen kann. Denn es ist furchtbar schwierig das Ding zu wechseln, wenn man an der Strecke mal eine härtere Feder einbauen will. So hat man den Dämpfer ausgebaut, hat die andere Feder durchgesteckt, hat ihn wieder eingebaut. Und dann konnten wir in einer Viertelstunde wieder fahren. Das war im Prinzip der erste große Schritt, das Auto mal auf Schraubenfedern zu stellen. Heute ist es selbstverständlich, aber das war damals überhaupt nicht so. Mir wurde im Haus von mehreren Seiten erklärt: Das haben schon so viele probiert, das geht nicht. Mir war klar, wenn sie mit der Abstimmung hier wirklich einen Schritt weiterkommen wollen, dann müssen sie irgendwann mal den Schritt tun und wir haben das so ein bisschen mit der Brechstange getan. Und schlussendlich hat es funktioniert.

Beim Rennen in Monza haben wir dann das Lager am Hinterachslenker – der bestand ja aus dieser Banane – geändert, und dieses Schwert war ja ursprünglich in einer Art

Leichtgewicht: Wagenpass des Carrera RSR aus dem März 1973. Aus der Rallye Version ist ein Spezial GT geworden, der fahrfertig 900 kg wiegt.

Light-weight: the vehicle pass of the Carrera RSR from march, 1973. The rally version has been converted to a special GT with a weight of 900 kg, ready to race.

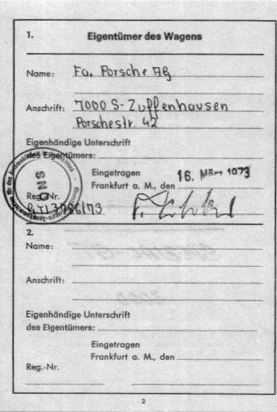

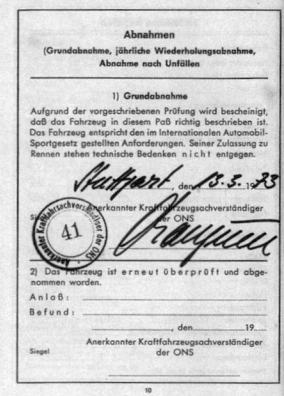

Norbert Singer talking about his work with some race cars from the 911 range.

When you joined Porsche at the beginning of 1970, it would still take some two years before you became professionally involved with a car from the 911 range.
Singer: That is right. I took over the RSR as a project and I started, so to say, with the Corsica Rally. Then, on the way back, things already started in earnest at Paul Ricard, where we worked hard on turning the rally car into a race car.
Why did Porsche make the step to a works commitment in circuit racing with a derivative of the 911?
Singer: The decision had been made long before, when they agreed upon producing a series of 200 cars of the Carrera RS. One of the reasons was that the 911 had put on quite a lot of weight. Back then, the race weight was the homologation weight. So therefore, one needed to build light cars for road use in order to be able to use this limited weight in motorsport. That was the reason to build the series of 200. If I recall it correctly, these cars had a weight of something like 940 kg. All 200 cars were being weighed on the city weighbridge of Zuffenhausen. At the time of homologation, the FIA people looked at the official weight certificates and then, the weight of 900 kg was written into the homologation papers. After all, it was allowed to deduct a few things, the comfort seats, the interior upholstery and the like.
From an aerodynamic point of view, we did a few things with the ducktail. The rear engine was a little bit tricky. It was good for traction, but not so great for all other aspects. When you want to make an 911 lighter, it will become lighter on the front axle first, while the entire weight is at the back, where the engine and the gearbox are. And because the engine is behind the rear axle, weight distribution becomes very delicate. With the RSR, we started our works effort in the 1973 world championship for manufacturers.

ENGINEERED TO SUCCESS
THE TECHNICIAN'S HANDWRITING NORBERT SINGER

But the car wasn't too far away from the production version, was it?
Singer: It had the usual things that were allowed. There was a little bit of a front spoiler underneath the fender. From the outside, we couldn't do much anyway. Of course, the RSR had McPherson-struts with torsion rods at the rear. These torsion rods were a critical point on this car: we had them at different levels of harshness, but suddenly, we came to the point where we could no longer put in a torsion rod that was even thicker. However, regulations included the possibility to mount some kind of additional springs. So we dropped the torsion rods pretty quickly. They were just in the car for good measure, but the additional springs did the job. This may sound very easy, but the working of the dampers wasn't meant to stand forces like that. The domes of the shock absorbers have a certain diameter and then, there was the space for the absorber with its usual travel from the suspension arm. When you suddenly put a spring in there, the dome of the shock absorbers would be too small. But you are not allowed to use a different dome, because that would involve a change of the bodywork, so the dome was widened a little bit, one way or the other. After all, it was all right in the lower part, it was just a little bit small in the upper part. So we made the springs larger bit by bit and during track tests, we found out pretty quickly that we could do without the torsion bar. After all, changing the thing is incredibly difficult when you want to build in a harder spring at the circuit. Now, we took the shock absorber out, put the spring in and build the shock absorber in again. And we were out on the track again after a quarter of an hour. Basically, putting the car on coil springs was the first big step. Today, that is normal, but back then, it wasn't. At the factory, several people told me: so many have tried before, that doesn't work. But I was certain that, if we wanted to make a step forward in set-up, we would have to go this way and we just forced it a little bit. And eventually, it worked out.
For the race in Monza, we changed the bearing on the suspension arm, which was this banana, that was mounted in some kind of rubber bearing. First of all, we replaced this

Gummilager gelagert. Dieses Lager haben wir zunächst durch ein Teflonlager ersetzt, was völlig regelkonform war. Und wir sind dann werkseitig noch weiter gegangen und haben ein Kugellager eingebaut. Mit diesem Kugellager hatten wir dann in Monza ein Problem bei der Abnahme. bzw. nach der Abnahme. Wir sind dann in die Prototypenklasse gewechselt. Was dann wiederum, wie soll ich es sagen, wegweisend war. Denn wir haben dann das Feld der GT-Klasse den Kunden überlassen. Während wir in der Prototypenklasse keine Chance hatten gegen den Matra, gegen Ferrari, aber völlig freie Hand in der Entwicklung. Und Professor Fuhrmann hat gesagt, das ist ganz toll, dann machen wir es einfach so, dann können wir bedingungslos, ohne Reglementprobleme zu bekommen, eine Entwicklung betreiben. Er hat zunächst natürlich an den Motor gedacht. Zuerst war es ein 2,8 Liter und dann hat man ihn auf 3,0 Liter gebracht. Aber jetzt gingen auch andere Dinge beim Fahrwerk und schlussendlich auch bei der Karosserie. So ist dieser „Maria-Stuart-Wagen" entstanden. Weil der End-Bürzel ist toll, aber wenn er breiter ist, ist er noch wirksamer.

War das nicht im Grunde genommen schon die Wegweisung in Richtung der Turboautos und des 935?

Singer: Ich bin mir nicht sicher, ob es 1973 schon klar war. Aber spätestens Ende 1973 war es so, wir kriegen ein neues Reglement, die Produktionswagen-Weltmeisterschaft. Deswegen ist dann 1974 der Turbo-Carrera entstanden, wo wir gesagt haben, es gibt zwar noch kein Reglement, aber wir bereiten uns darauf vor, speziell mit dem Turbomotor, haltbar für 24 Stunden. Das kommt ja auf uns zu. Lasst uns ein Jahr üben. Wiederum in der Prototypenklasse, da haben wir alle Freiheiten. Und so ist dieser Turbo-Carrera entstanden.

Noch einmal zurück ins Jahr 1973. Der erste Sieg eines 911-Werkswagen in Martin-Farben gelang Müller/van Lennep bei der Targa Florio. Sie waren beim Einsatz dabei und haben später den Bericht verfasst?

Markant: Der umlaufende Heckspoiler sorgte für die Bezeichnung „Maria-Stuart-Wagen".

Eye-catching: the wrapped around rear spoiler gave the car its nickname of "Mary Stuart".

Singer: Ja, ich war komplett von vorne bis hinten dabei. Und war Renningenieur, wenn Sie so wollen. Da gab es diese lustige Geschichte: Wir hatten damals mit meinem guten alten Freund Glotzbach von Dunlop ausgemacht, wir wechseln beim zweiten Stopp. Aufgrund des Verschleißes im Training hatten wir das festgelegt. Und dann kam Glotzbach im Rennen, kurz bevor also dieser Boxenstopp anstand, und sagte: Ich würde schon mal lieber gern das Rad anschauen, weil ich bin mir da gar nicht so sicher. Dann habe ich gesagt: O.K., wenn du unsicher bist, dann wechseln wir halt, ist ja kein Problem, ziehen wir halt den Boxenstopp vor. Wir haben also den Boxenstopp vorgezogen. Das ging auch ein bisschen länger, 1 Minute und 10 Sekunden. Damals war Räderwechseln und Tanken gleichzeitig möglich. Aber es gab noch keine Schnellheber und auch noch keinen Zentralverschluss. Nach dem Stopp kam dann Professor Fuhrmann und hat mich zur Sau gemacht: Sie, jetzt sind wir länger gestanden, so ein Blödsinn. Es war doch abgemacht. Er wusste das ja, er hat ja immer gefragt: Was machen wird denn? Nichts. Tanken und weiter. Und jetzt wechselt ihr das Rad. Warum und wozu? Jedenfalls in der Diskussion kam dann der Glotzbach zu uns und hat gesagt: Kommt mal mit, schaut mal. Hatten wir einen Plattfuß. Der Fuhrmann hat später gesagt: Gut habt ihr das gemacht. Und war ruhig. Und hat nie wieder was gesagt.

Wir hatten ja schon kurz über den Turbo gesprochen. Dieser Motor war doch ein ganz wichtiger Schritt?

Singer: Die Idee war ja, den Sechszylinder-Turbo für die Langstrecke, sprich Le Mans, tauglich zu machen. Ich weiss noch, als wir in Le Mans im ersten Nachttraining gefahren sind, da gab es bei uns einige Herren, die diese glühenden Auspuffrohre da unten drin im Auto gesehen haben: Das hält nie 24 Stunden. Das müssen wir ändern. Valentin Schäffer hat darauf gesagt: Wir können jetzt doch nicht anfangen, einen neuen Auspuff zu biegen. Dann habe ich gesagt: Das hat auf dem Prüfstand gehalten. Wir sind Rennen schon damit gefahren. Was soll da passieren? Dass die Rohre glühten, das haben wir halt nie gesehen. Aber jetzt in der Nacht sah man es halt. Am Prüfstand glühen sie doch auch. Es ging ja auch gut, wir wurden ja Zweiter 1974 in Le Mans. Ich erinnere mich aber auch noch an eine, heute würde man sagen Klausursitzung, bei Professor Fuhrmann. Der sagte also: Heute Abend kommt ihr zu mir in die Wohnung in Ludwigsburg. Da waren dann Falk, Mezger, Schäffer, Jantke, und ich war auch dabei. Sozusagen im Wohnzimmer gab es die Sitzung. Und dann hat Fuhrmann gesagt: Jetzt erklärt

DREHSTÄBE vorn:	19 mm ø	hinten:	26 mm ø
SCHRAUBENFEDERN vorn:	ROT-ROT-ROT-ROT	hinten:	ROT-ROT-ROT-GELB
DÄMPFER vorn:	V8 (160/160)	hinten:	H8 (180/170)
ANSCHLAGGUMMI vorn:	1	hinten:	2
STABILISATOREN vorn:	18 mm ø	hinten:	15 mm ø
VORDERACHSE:	SERIE	LENKER:	SERIE
STURZ: VL −1°50'	VR −1°50'	NACHLAUF:	6° 30'
VORSPUR:	0 gesamt	VORSPURÄNDERUNG:	0 (fein unter Lenkung)
HINTERACHSE:	SERIE	LENKER:	SERIE (LANG)
STURZ: HL −1°50'	HR −1°50'	VORSPUR:	1°10' gesamt
FELGEN vorn:	9 x 15"	hinten:	11 x 15"
REIFEN DUNLOP SLICKS			
vorn: 245/575-15 376 D15		atü:	1,6
hinten: 290/575-15 376 D15		atü:	1,8
BODENFREIHEIT vorn/hinten:	105 / 115 mm	MIT Benzin (VOLL) + Fahrer	
KAROSSERIE	SERIEN HECKSPOILER		
FZG.-GEWICHT:	mit 0 Benzin mit/ohne Fahrer	ca. 930 kg	
BEMERKUNGEN:	Zusatz Heckspoiler. (Blechteile) Kein Bugspoiler.		

R6 P — Dr.-Ing. h. c. F. Porsche KG Stuttgart-Zuffenhausen — Blatt - 2 -

WETTER BEIM START:	SONNENSCHEIN		
STRECKENBEDINGUNGEN:	TROCKEN	WIND:	KEINER
ÖLTEMPERATUR	ca. 100°C	ÖLDRUCK:	ca. 6,5 kg/cm²
BENZINVERBRAUCH:	38,4	ltr./100 km	
ÖLVERBRAUCH:	ca. 4,4	ltr./1000 km	
BREMSBELAG-VERSCHLEISS: vorn	9,7 mm/1000km	hinten	—
REIFEN-VERSCHLEISS: vorn	—	hinten	10,6 mm/1000km
SCHNELLSTE RUNDEN:			
TRAINING:	36' 52,1"	FAHRER:	VAN LENNEP
RENNEN:	36' 30"	FAHRER:	MÜLLER
N MAX IM 5. GANG:	8000 U/min	KM/H	268 (+7)
GEFAHRENE RUNDEN:			
TRAINING: + VORTR.	10 Rd.	720 km	
RENNEN:	11 Rd.	792 km	
AUSFALLURSACHE:	—		
BEMERKUNG: (defekte Teile)	—		

R6 P — Dr.-Ing. h. c. F. Porsche KG Stuttgart-Zuffenhausen — Blatt - 3 -

Dokumentiert: Bericht von Norbert Singer mit allen Details des Siegerfahrzeugs der Targa Florio 1973. Technisch bleiben keine Fragen offen.

Well-documented: Norbert Singer's report with all details about the winning car of the 1973 Targa Florio. Technically, no question remained unanswered.

bearing by a Teflon bearing, which was entirely according to the rules. And then, we went even further and we built in a ball bearing. With this ball bearing, we were having problems in scrutineering at Monza, or rather after scrutineering. So then, we changed into the prototype class. Which proved to be, how shall I say it, the way to go. Because after that, we left the GT-class to the customer teams. We had no chance against the Matras in the prototype class, but we were entirely free in development. And professor Fuhrmann said that it was great, that we would just do it that way, because we could work on development entirely free, without compromise, without getting problems with the regulations. Of course, he was thinking about the engine, Initially, it was a 2.8 litre engine, which was enlarged to 3.0 litres. But now, we could do other things as well, with the suspension and then also with the bodywork. This is how this "Mary Stuart car" came about. Because the ducktail was great, but it would be even more effective when we could make it wider.

Wasn't that, in fact, already the way towards the turbo cars and the 935?

Singer: I am not sure whether that was already so clear in 1973. But at the end of 1973, at the latest, it was clear that we would get new regulations, which would become the production car world championship. Therefore, the Turbo-Carrera came about in 1974. We said, there might be no regulations yet, but we are preparing for it, especially with the turbo engine that would last 24 hours. After all, that is what is coming. Let's rehearse for a year. Once more in the prototype class, because there, we have total freedom. And that is how the Turbo-Carrera came about.

Once again back to the year 1973. At the Targa Florio, Müller/van Lennep scored the first victory with a works-911

Gijs van Lennep and Norbert Singer

in Martini livery. You were there and wrote the report later on, didn't you?

Singer: Yes, I was there from the very beginning till the end. And I was race engineer, if you want to put it that way. There was a hilarious story: back then, we had agreed with my good old friend Dieter Glotzbach at Dunlop that we would change during the second stop. We had made that decision based upon the tyre wear in practice. And then Glotzbach came in the race, just before the pit stop, and said: I would rather have a look at that wheel, because I am not too sure. So I said: Okay, when you are not sure, we just change the tyre, no problem, we make an earlier stop. So we made an

THE TECHNICIAN'S HANDWRITING 31

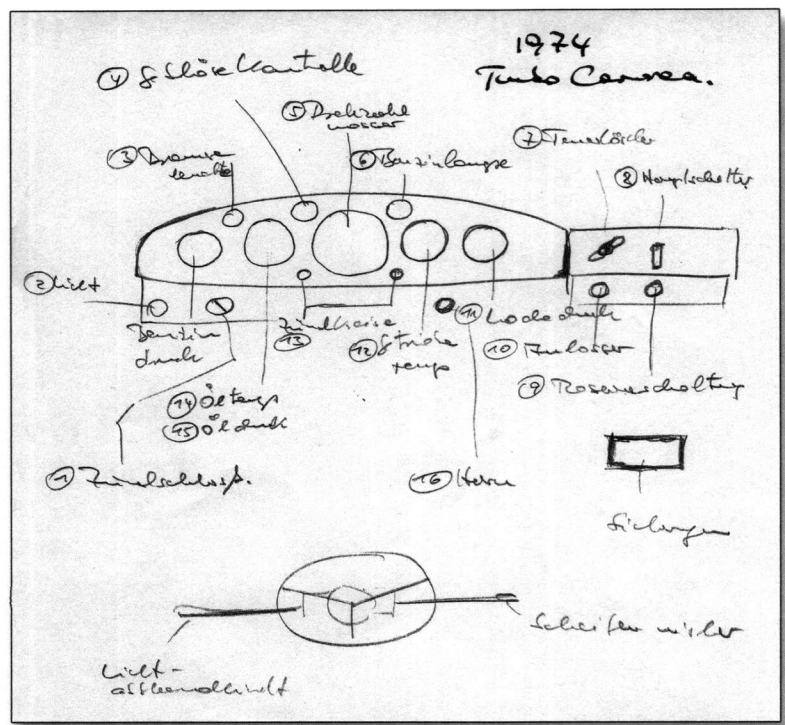

Entwurf: Erste Handskizze von Norbert Singer für den Instrumententräger des Turbo Carrera von 1974.

Design: First hand-drawn Sketch by Norbert Singer for The dashboard of the 1974 Turbo Carrera.

mal, wir haben die Leistung eines Matra, warum schlagen wir die Matra nicht? Ja, haben wir gesagt, Moment, da gibt es zunächst einmal das Gewicht. Wie schwer sind wir? Ja, so 800 kg. Und die Matra? 650. Also was müssen wir machen? 200 kg aus dem Auto rausbringen. Die Idee war, die Karosserie in ein Säurebad zu stecken und damit ganz dünn und leicht zu machen. Wir hatten auch einen gefunden, der sagte, das mache ich euch. Das kostet 80.000 oder 100.000 Mark. Um Gottes Willen, sind sie bekloppt? Dann hat er gesagt, ich muss alles anschaffen. Ich muss die Säure kaufen, das sind ein paar Kubikmeter. Ich muss eine Riesenwanne bauen. Das ist Edelstahl. Sonst fällt mir die Wanne schon zusammen, bevor das Auto drin ist. Das kostet halt soviel. Fuhrmann sagte: Nein, das ist zu teuer, das machen wir nicht. Also ist es unterblieben. Wir haben auch gesagt: Mittelmotorauto. Also vom Konzept her. Gewichtsverteilung, Schwerpunkthöhe usw. Der Matra war halt ein Prototyp vom ersten Federstrich an, der ja keine Basis hatte in der Serie. Und dummerweise einer der besten Prototypen seiner Zeit. Und wir kamen mit dem 911er und wollten den platt machen. Der Fuhrmann hat sich damit abgefunden und gesagt: O.K., dann fahren wir halt soweit vorne wie es geht. Jetzt sieht man da so ein bisschen die Evolution, wie das Auto halt zustande kam. Zunächst einmal seriennah, logischerweise. Das einzige, was er gekriegt hat waren die dicken Räder. Die waren damals, glaube ich, 15 Zoll breit. Die Felgen, die waren noch vom 917, da hatten wir schon Zentralverschluss gehabt. Dann haben wir auch 17 Zoll versucht. Das war natürlich der Überhammer.

Der Leistungszuwachs hat natürlich Folgen gehabt für das Gesamtfahrzeug?

Singer: Man muss sich das so vorstellen: Wir kamen von diesem Prototyp RSR von 1973, der in der Größenordnung 300 bis 310 PS hatte. Dann kam der Sprung auf die 400, 450 PS waren es dann schlussendlich. Die haben wir in dann erst in der Entwicklungsphase gehabt. Und da war klar, dass wir mal mit breiteren Rädern anfangen müssen. Gewicht reduzieren war auch klar. Aber es war noch alles sehr seriennah. Man hat dann irgendeinen Flügel darauf genagelt. Das Reglement gab eine maximale Breite vor. 2 Meter oder 2,10 Meter, wenn ich es richtig weiß. Die haben wir nicht ausgefüllt. Aber wir konnten das Auto dramatisch verbreitern. Dann hat man vorne Spoilerchen dran gesetzt. Denn Sie können nur hinten das drauf tun, was Sie an der Vorderachse können, sonst ist das Auto aus der Balance.

Ein wichtiger Punkt war sicher auch die Thermik?

Singer: Ja, unter der Haube hat ja alles geglüht. Das Abblasventil, diese Membranen am Abblasventil, wenn die zu heiß werden, gibt es Probleme. Dann war das Thema, wie kriegt der Turbo, der ja ganz unten sitzt, seine Luft. Deswegen der Aufsatz mit dem Schacht dahinter. War zwar ein langer Weg, aber er ließ sich vernünftig da runterführen. Dann haben wir einen Heckdeckel entwickelt, der zunächst ohne Ladeluftkühler war. Fuhrmann kam dann und sagte: Passt mal auf Freunde, ein Ladeluftkühler würde die Sache dramatisch verbessern. Damit kamen wir auf diese 450 PS. Jetzt: Wo macht man denn den Ladeluftkühler hin? Da hinten war schon alles ziemlich voll. Da haben wir dann den Ladeluftkühler in den Heckdeckel-Aufbau gesteckt. Da gibt es irgendwo ein Foto, das haben wir glaube ich das letzte Mal entdeckt, wo diese Ladeluft hier so rauf, unten den Kühler rein, dann durch und dann so.

Dann haben wir auch noch eine neue Hinterachse gemacht. Diese Banane und dieses Schwert, das ganze System war ja eigentlich Unsinn. Deswegen ist dann eine Neukonstruktion entstanden, mit schräg gestellten Dreieckslenkern. Da gab es natürlich auch ein paar Probleme. Das Ding ist uns zum Teil angerissen. Wir mussten dann auch noch eine hintere Bremsbelüftung erfinden. Durch mehr Leistung und höhere Geschwindigkeit musste auch mehr gebremst werden. So zieht sich das durch das ganze Fahrzeug. Mit ein paar PS mehr, das ist nur der Anfang, nicht das Ende.

Der nächste Schritt war dann der 934. Der hat zwar keine so große Rolle gespielt, aber wir sollten ihn nicht ganz unterschlagen.

Singer: Der 934 war im Prinzip der GT3 der damaligen Zeit. Das war dieser Turbo auf der Basis eines GT-Fahrzeugs, kostengünstig für die Kunden. Der 934 war ein tolles Auto. Er hatte ein Riesendrehmoment. Er hatte auch für die Klasse richtig Leistung, aber auch schmale Räder, die das Reglement vorschrieb. Darum war er nicht ganz leicht zu beherrschen. Zumal dieses Turboloch, dieser Turboversatz und

Dicke Backen: Als Turbo-Renner wuchsen dem Porsche 911 nicht nur gewaltige Kotflügel, sondern auch ein Ladeluftkühler und allerlei aerodynamisches Beiwerk.

Massive: As a turbo, the Porsche 911 not only had huge fenders, but also an intercooler and all kinds of aerodynamic add-on parts.

1000 km Österreichring: Gijs van Lennep, Herbert Müller (7) – Helmuth Koinigg, Manfred Schurti (8)

earlier stop. It was a little bit longer, too, 1 minute and 10 seconds. Back then, you could change tyres and refuel at the same time. But there were no fast jacks and no central wheel mounts.

After the stop, Professor Fuhrmann came up to me and was livid: Now, we were longer in the pits, such a shame. Didn't we agree. He knew, he would always ask: What are we going to do? Nothing. Just refuel and then continue. And now, you change the tyres. Why and what for? During that discussion, Glotzbach came up to us and said: Come along, have a look. And we had a puncture. Then, Fuhrmann said: You have done well. And he was silent. And didn't say a thing anymore.

We already briefly spoke about the turbo. This engine was quite an important step, wasn't it?

Singer: Well, the basic idea was to make the six-cylinder turbo suitable for endurance racing, in other words, for Le Mans. And I still remember that, when we went out for the first night practice session at Le Mans, some of our people saw these glowing exhaust pipes in the car and said: There is no way this will last for 24 hours. We must change them. Valentin Schäffer asked: We can't start constructing a new exhaust system here, can we? And then I said: It lasted on the dyno. We already raced with it. So what can go wrong? We just never saw that the pipes were glowing. But now, at night, one saw it. They also glow on the dyno. And after all,

things went well. In 1974, we came second at Le Mans.

I also remember a meeting at Professor Fuhrmann's. He said: Tonight, you are all coming to my house in Ludwigsburg. So, there we were: Falk, Mezger, Schäffer, Jantke, and myself. The meeting was in the living room, as a matter of fact. And Fuhrmann said: Okay, please tell me: we have the output of a Matra, so why don't we beat the Matras? Well, we said, first of all, there is the weight. How heavy are we? Well, some 800 kg. And the Matras? 650. So, what do we have to do? Get 200 kg out of the car. The idea was putting the bodywork in a bath filled with acid in order to make it very thin and light. We had even found somebody who had agreed to do that for us. But: it would cost 80,000 or 100,000 Marks. For heaven's sake, have you gone mad? Then, he told me, I had to buy everything. I had to buy the acid, a couple of cubic metres. I had to build such a huge bath tube. That is stainless steel. Otherwise, the tube will collapse even before the car is in it. And that just costs so and so much. Fuhrmann said: No, that is too expensive, we won't do that. So we left it at that. And we also said: mid-engined car. At least the concept. Weight distribution, centre of gravity and the like. The Matra had been built as a prototype from the first scratch that was put on paper, it had no production links. And unfortunately for us, it was one of the best prototypes of its era. And we turned up with the 911, wanting to beat it. Fuhrmann accepted the situation and said: Okay, then let's just try to get as close to the front as possible. That gives a little insight into the evolution, how the car was conceived. Initially still quite close to the production car, obviously. The only thing it got was bigger wheels. I think they were 15 inch wide at the time. The wheels were still the same as we used on the 917, we already had central wheel mounts. And then, we also tried 17 inch. That topped it all.

The increase in performance surely had its effect on the entire package?

Singer: You have to look at it like this: we came from the 1973 RSR prototype, that had something in the range of 300, 310 hp. Then, we stepped up to 400 and eventually, we even had 450 hp. But we only achieved this in the development stage. And then it became clear that we would have to put wider tyres on. And lay off weight, that was clear as well. But it was still very close to the production cars. Then, they just put some kind of wing on the car. Regulations only outlined a maximum width. 2 metres or 2.10 metres, if I recall correctly. Surely, we didn't get that far. But we could widen the car dramatically. And they put winglets at the front. Because you can only put something on the rear which you can also put on the front, otherwise, the car is out of balance.

Surely, thermal was an important aspect as well?

Singer: Yes, underneath the bonnet, everything was glowing. The pop-off valve, these membranes at the pop-off valve, when they are becoming too hot, you are in trouble.

THE TECHNICIAN'S HANDWRITING

934: Deutsche Rennsport-Meisterschaft 1976

dann das Einsetzen mit einem relativ heftigen Bums machte die Sache schwierig. Deswegen haben sich da auch nur solche Fahrer wie Stommelen, Schurti, Beltoise oder Wollek ausgezeichnet. Da haben sich die Männer von den Buben unterschieden.

Bei der Arbeit am 935 war doch viel Arbeit im Windkanal erforderlich, doch Porsche hatte damals gar keinen eigenen Windkanal. Wie haben Sie sich geholfen?

Singer: Wir sind als Gäste zu VW gegangen. Das waren immer so Unternehmungen mit der Brechstange, und das nur für einen Tag. VW war damals auch schon sehr straff organisiert. Maximal acht Stunden am Tag konnten wir arbeiten. Die acht Stunden begannen mit dem Betreten des Windkanalgebäudes und endeten mit dem Verlassen des Windkanalgebäudes mit Auto, Ausrüstung, Werkzeug und alles drum und dran. Dann haben wir mit viel List und Tücke eine versetzte Arbeitszeit durchsetzen können, so dass aus acht Stunden zehn Stunden wurden. Aber das war das äußerste der Gefühle. Insofern war unsere Windkanalzeit sehr limitiert. Man hatte natürlich ein Riesenprogramm, wenn man da hinfuhr.

Und dann das Problem mit den Terminen. Ich hab dann da oben den Mann, den ich gut kannte, angerufen und habe gesagt, wir sollten mit einem Rennauto messen, aber wir haben eigentlich nur ein Fenster von drei Tagen. Dann sagt er: Wann soll es denn sein? Na, in einer oder zwei Wochen, so ist es halt im Motorsport. Dann hat er gesagt: Das können Sie vergessen. Wir haben einen Dreischichtbetrieb. Und da geht überhaupt nichts. Sie können in drei Monaten vielleicht wieder anrufen. Dann kam Fuhrmann, dem haben wir das erzählt. Dann haben wir gesagt: Wir wollten in den Windkanal, aber es geht nicht. Wieso geht das nicht? Ich habe angerufen, drei Monate, keine Chance. Lassen Sie mich mal machen. Damals war bei VW ein anderer Österreicher als Entwicklungschef, der Professor Fiala. Das hat dann einen halben Tag gedauert, dann hat die Sekretärin vom Fuhrmann angerufen und hat gesagt: Der Herr Doktor hat mit dem Fiala gesprochen. Eine Stunde später hat Wolfsburg angerufen: Wann wollt ihr denn kommen? Montag, Dienstag oder Mittwoch? Dann haben wir gesagt: O.K. am Montag fahren wir hoch. Am Dienstag um 7.00 Uhr standen wir da. Und dann lief das ab. Später, wenn ich angerufen habe, haben sie bei VW gesagt: Sie kennen ja den kleinen Dienstweg. Das Büro Fuhrmann hat angerufen, bums, hatten wir den Termin.

Dennoch war die Zeit immer zu kurz. Man musste ja alle wesentlichen Dinge wie Flügel, Bodenfreiheit und solche Dinge durchfahren, bevor man in die Rennsaison geht. Da hat man natürlich bestimmte Dinge vorbereitet, wie zum Beispiel diesen Dellenkotflügel, der da irgendwo erschienen ist. Das hat man dann drauf gesteckt, das ging relativ schnell. Man musste auch Luftdurchsätze in den Bremsbelüftungen messen. Also, das passierte alles an diesem einen Tag. Das war also schrecklich. Die Leute bei VW haben dann schon immer das Kreuz gemacht, wenn wir gekommen sind: Jetzt kommen die Chaoten. Was wir da in einem Tag abgespult haben, da haben die mitunter eine Woche dran gebastelt.

Gut, das hätten Sie auch gerne gemacht?

Singer: Ja sicher. So eine Messung ging fünf bis sechs Minuten, was sehr kurz klingt. Aber wenn Sie 20 oder 30 Messungen machen wollen, dann ist das die reine Messzeit. Für die Umbauten blieb dann fast nichts mehr übrig. Jeder heutige Aerodynamiker würde die Hände über dem Kopf zusammenschlagen, bei dem Gedanken, wie wenig Zeit sie gehabt haben für diese Arbeiten. Aber auch der Prozess von der Skizze bis in den Windkanal war nach heutigen Maßstäben ungewöhnlich.

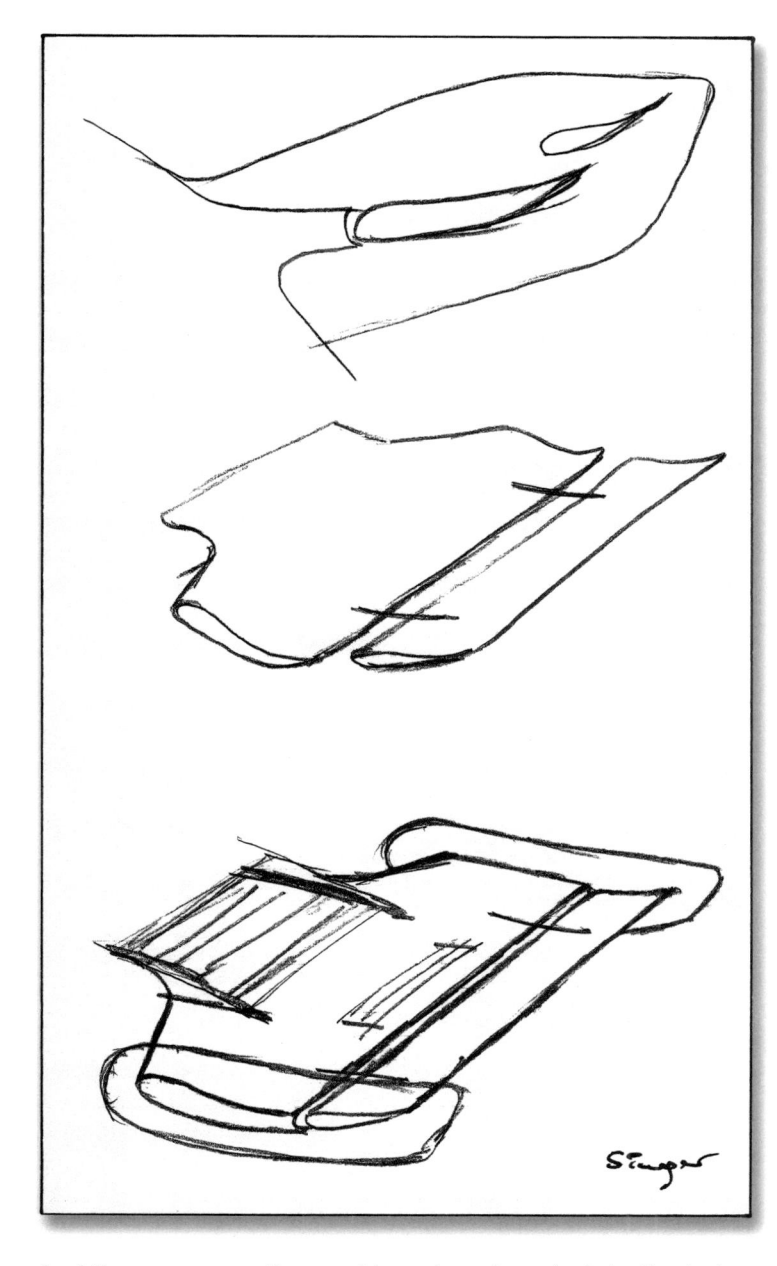

regulations required. Therefore, it wasn't particularly easy to handle. Especially the turbo lag and then the power coming in with quite a heavy bang made it difficult. Therefore, only drivers like Stommelen, Schurti, Beltoise or Wollek were able to shine with that car. It separated the men from the boys.

Work on the 935 required a lot of work in the wind tunnel, but back then, Porsche didn't have its own wind tunnel. How did you manage?

Singer: We went to Volkswagen as guests. These activities were always under a lot of time pressure, and only for one day. Back then, the organisation at Volkswagen was already very strict. We could work for a maximum of eight hours a day. And these eight hours started with entering the wind tunnel building and they ended with leaving the building with car, equipment, tools and everything. Then we managed to get permission to work with flexible hours, so that we could make ten hours out of eight hours. But that was as far as we could get. From that point of view, our time in the wind tunnel was strictly limited. Of course, we always had a huge workload when we went there.

And then, we always had problems getting a slot. So phoned somebody up there I knew very well and I said, in fact, we must do a test with a race car, but we only have three days. And then, he would say: when will that be? Well, in one or two weeks, the way things are in motor sport. He said: No way. We are working in three shifts. There is no time. Maybe you can call again in three months. Then, Fuhrmann arrived and we explained the situation to him. We said: We want to go into the wind tunnel, but we can't. Why can't you? I have phoned, three months, no chance. Let me give it a try. Back then, another Austrian was head of development at Volkswagen, Professor Fiala. So it took half a day, and then, Fuhrmann's secretary would call us and say: Herr Doktor has spoken with Fiala. One hour later, Wolfsburg would call: So, when would you like to come? On Monday, Tuesday or

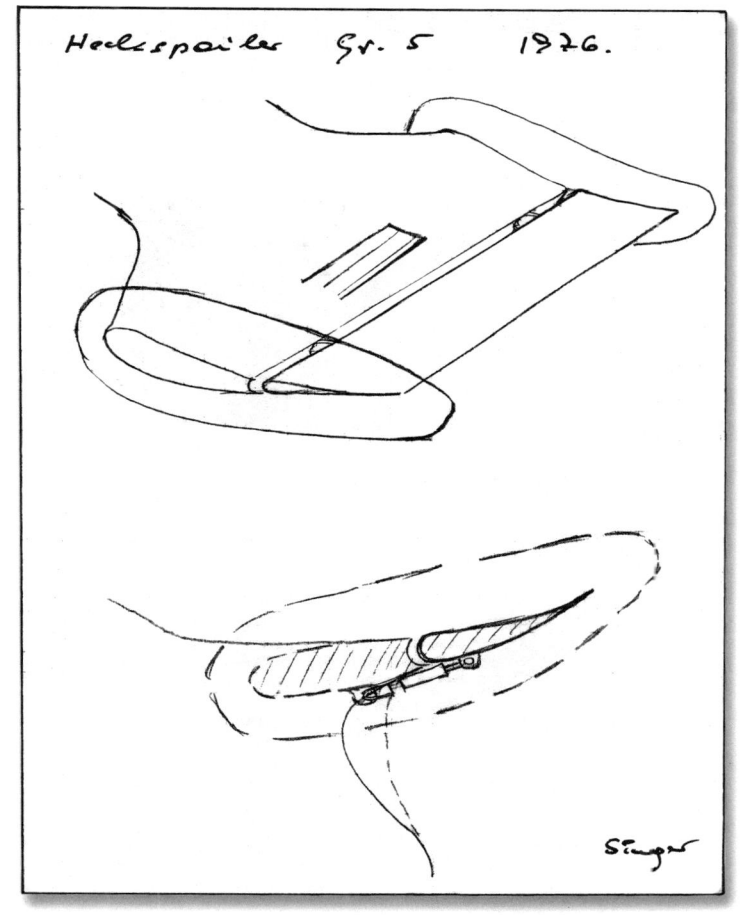

And there was another problem: how to get air to the turbo, that was placed very low. That was the reason for the big air intake with the duct behind it. It was a long way, but at least we could lead the air to the bottom. Then, we developed a rear lid that initially didn't include an intercooler. Then Fuhrmann came along and said: My dear friends, an intercooler would improve things dramatically. So this is how we reached the 450 hp. But: where did we have to put the intercooler? In the rear, everything was pretty much full already. So we put the intercooler in the construction on the rear lid. There is a picture, we discovered it recently, where you see the air flowing up here, then in underneath the cooler, then all the way through and so on.

Then, we also made a new rear axle. This banana and the sword, the whole system in fact didn't make sense. So that is why the new construction was put in place, with triangles at an angle. Of course, this would cause some problems as well. The thing would partly tear. And we also had to find a way to get airflow to cool the rear brakes. More power and higher speeds also meant more braking. So everything affected the whole car. It isn't just about a couple of more horsepower. That is only the beginning, not the end.

Then the next step was the 934. Admittedly, it didn't play such an important role, but we can't leave it out entirely.

Singer: Basically, the 934 was the GT3 of those days. It was a turbo based on a GT car, affordable for the customers. The 934 was a great car. It had loads of torque. And for its class, it had quite a lot of power, too, but also small wheels, as the

Ideen: Norbert Singers Skizzen für die Gestaltung des Heckspoilers des Porsche 935.

Ideas: Norbert Singer's sketches for the design of the rear wing of the Porsche 935.

Sie müssen bestimmte Dinge sich mal überlegen und dann: Wie könnte denn so etwas ausschauen? Dann gehen Sie mit der Skizze in die Werkstatt und sagen: Passt mal auf, ich stelle mir das so und so vor. Da haben wir irgendwo einen alten Deckel. Und den könnten wir nehmen und dann sägen wir das ab. Und das so anbauen und, so ist es halt entstanden. Aufgrund dieser Skizze eine Zeichnung zu machen, die dann in den Modellbau zu geben, das ist zwar der normale Entwicklungsweg. Aber in dem Fall soll es erstens schnell gehen und zum anderen, die Idee die Sie da haben, das kann gleich gehen, das kann auch überhaupt nicht gehen. Also diesen Aufwand zu betreiben und dann schlussendlich den ganzen Schmarr'n wegschmeißen, also einmal zu messen und zu sagen, alle Käse, vergesst das. Die Zeit und das Geld waren gar nicht da.

Was war das Besondere am 935? Was hat dieses Auto speziell ausgezeichnet? Das Auto war ja schon ein rechter Kraftprotz.

Singer: Das stimmt schon. Die Autos hatten, laut Leistungsdiagramm, alle 550 bis 600 PS. Was für den 911 schon sehr heftig ist. Zumal es diese Reifenlimitierung gab. Die 19-Zoll-Räder haben uns schon heftig geholfen, aber es war an der Grenze. Wenn sie sich die Gewichtsverteilung anschauen, die war ja auch nicht gerade so toll. Also wenn man da 35 Prozent auf der Vorderachse hatte, dann war das relativ gut. Dazu kamen noch 120 Liter Kraftstoff, das sind so zwischen 97 und 100 kg. Das heißt, ein Set-up war auch sehr spannend. Deswegen kam sofort der Schrei nach einem verstellbaren Stabi. Und musste man vorne verstellen und es hat nicht gereicht, dann musste man hinten verstellen. Damit waren schon zwei Hebel im Cockpit. Und diese verstellbaren Stabis, alle schön auf mechanischer Basis, die haben natürlich hin und wieder geklemmt. Die Autos hatten wahnsinnig Leistung, waren dann natürlich auch wahnsinnig schnell auf den Geraden. Sie hatten natürlich auch dieses Turboloch. Und Elektronik gab es noch keine. Das war eine mechanische Einspritzung, ein Gaspedal und das war es dann. Die Motorenleute haben natürlich von der maximalen Leistung geredet, haben auch ein maximales Drehmoment gehabt. Nur diese Leistung aus der Kurve heraus zu dosieren, das war ein recht langer Weg. Das war damals schon heftig.

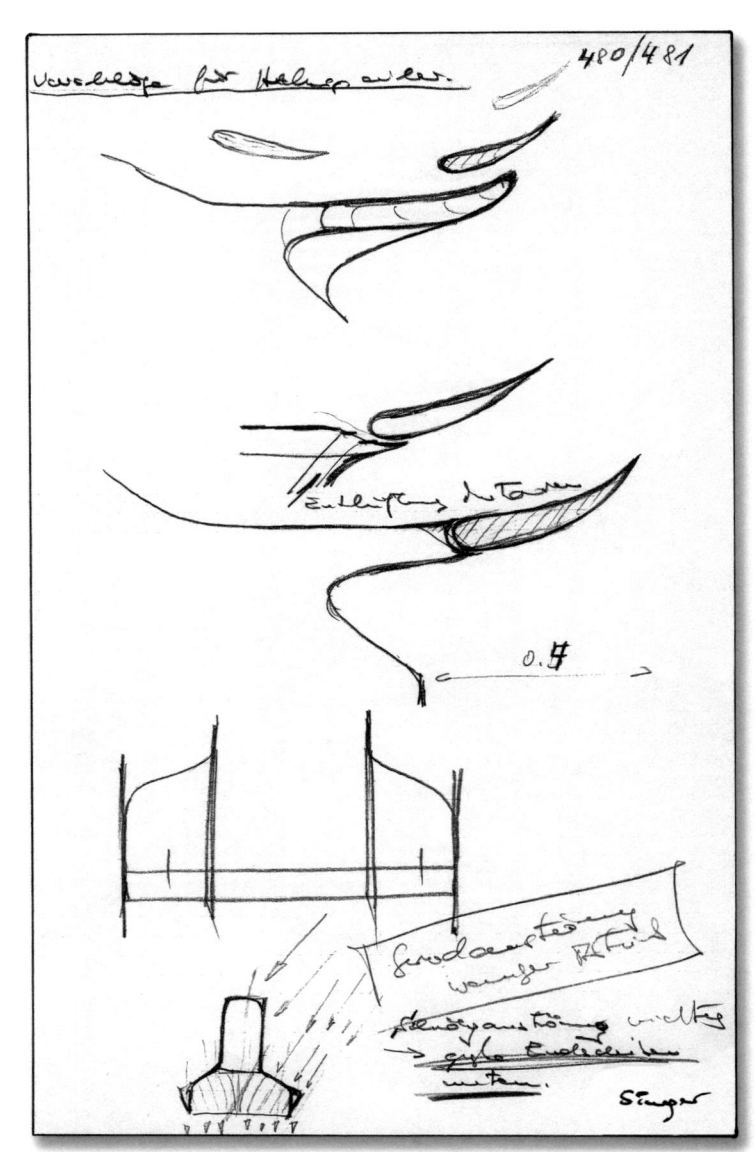

Erkenntnisse: „Schräganströmung wichtig" notierte Singer auf dieser Ideenskizze für Heckspoiler.

Insight: „Schräganströmung wichtig - the airflow at an angle is important", as Singer wrote on this sketch for a rear spoiler.

Eine spezielle Version des 935 war das sogenannte „Baby".
Singer: Das war eine ziemliche Nacht- und Nebelaktion, überhaupt mal dieses Auto fertig zu kriegen. Es war auch wieder so eine Fuhrmann'sche Idee zu sagen: Wir fahren in der kleinen Klasse. Da gab es die „bis 2,0 Liter" und „über 2,0 Liter". In der grossen Klasse haben die Porsche dominiert, weil da waren sie mehr oder weniger unter sich. Und in der kleinen Klasse gab es die Escorts und die 320 BMW. Also kam Fuhrmann und sagte: Passt auf, was können wir da machen. Wir können den Turbo, das war ein 1,4 Liter mal dem Turbofaktor, da kam das auf 2,0 Liter hin. Die Leistung, das war klar, dass wir die erreichen. Aber das Ansprechverhalten mit dem kleinen Motor war schon ein bißchen ein Elend. Man hat also eine 935 Karosserie genommen, und es war klar, das Mindestgewicht in der Klasse war, glaube ich, 730 kg. Die 935 wogen 900 bis 950 kg. Um auf 730 kg zu kommen mit einem ausgewachsenen 911, das war schon nicht ganz ohne. Dann hat man also das Ding wirklich ausgebeint. Die Mechaniker haben gesagt, wir machen sogar Erleichterungslöcher in die Drehzahlmessernadel. Wir haben das gemacht, ganz akribisch. Wir haben jedes Teil in die Hand genommen und haben gefragt: Geht's nicht leichter? So sind wir auf 710 kg gekommen. Das durfte keiner wissen. Das war ja so geheim. Die anderen haben alle mit diesen 730 kg gekämpft. Und wir stellen ein Auto hin, das ist unter-

Manfred Schurti and Norbert Singer

DIE HANDSCHRIFT DES TECHNIKERS

Wednesday? And then, we said: OK, let's go there on Monday. So on Tuesday at 7.00 am, we were there. And later, when I called, they said at Volkswagen: you know how to get things done. So Fuhrmann's office made the call, and we would get a slot right away.

Still, time was never enough. After all, we had to test all relevant things like wings, ground clearance and the like, before taking on the racing season. Of course, we had prepared a couple of things, like this fender with dimples that we had at a certain stage. We just put it on the car, that went relatively quickly. And we had to measure the airflow through the ventilation of the brakes. So we did all that on one day. It was horrible. The people at Volkswagen's wind tunnel crossed themselves when we turned up: oh, them again! Usually, it would take them a week to do all the things we did in one day.

Well, you would have liked to do it in one week as well, wouldn't you?
Singer: Yes, of course. Such a test would perhaps take five or six minutes, which sounds pretty quickly. But when you want to do 20 or 30 tests, it is only the time of the proper test. We would have hardly any time left to make the changes. Today, every aerodynamicist would be left speechless thinking of how little time you had to carry out all this work. But also the process from the initial drawing to the wind tunnel was unusual by today's standards.

We had to reflect on certain things and then ask: what could something like that actually look like? So, we would go into the workshop with a sketch and say: Listen, I see it like this or like that. We have an old lid somewhere. So we take that and cut it off here. And then we mount it here, and that is how it came about. Make a proper drawing based upon that sketch and give it into the construction department, that would be the normal way of development. But in such a case, firstly, things have to be done right away and secondly, the idea that you have might work immediately, but might also not work at all. So putting in all this effort and then finally discard the whole lot, so do a proper test and then saying: it's rubbish, forget it. We just didn't have the time and the money for that.

What was the particular thing about the 935? What made this car stand out? After all, it already had plenty of power.
Singer: That is right. All the cars had something in the range of 550 to 600 hp, according to the data sheets. Which is quite a lot for a 911. And even more so as we were having this tyre limit. The 19 inch wheels were quite helpful, but they were at the limit. And when you look at the weight distribution, that wasn't particularly great either. Having 35 percent on the front axle was already considered as quite good. Add to that 120 litres of fuel, so something between 97 and 100 kg. Which meant that finding the right set-up was quite an adventure. Therefore, there was immediate need for an adjustable stabiliser. And when you had to adjust at the front and it wasn't enough, you would adjust at the rear. So we already had two levers in the cockpit. And these adjustable stabilisers all were mechanical, so sometimes, one would get stuck. The cars had loads of power, were massively quick on the straights. And they had the turbo lag. And we didn't have any electronics. We had a mechanical injection, a throttle pedal, and that was it. The engine people were talking about maximum power output and they also had maximum torque. But to control this power accelerating out of a corner, that was quite a long way. That was pretty heavy back then.

The so-called "Baby" was a very special version of the 935.
Singer: Getting this car ready was a day- and night job. It was one of these ideas that Fuhrman would come up with, just saying: We are racing in the small class. We had classes up to two litres and above two litres. In the big class, Porsches dominated, because they hardly had any opposition. In the smaller class, there were the Escorts and the BMW 320s. So Fuhrmann came to us and said: What can we do there? We could run the turbo, which was a 1.4 litre engine at the time. With the turbo factor, that would be two litres. There was no doubt that we would have enough power. But the throttle response with the small engine would

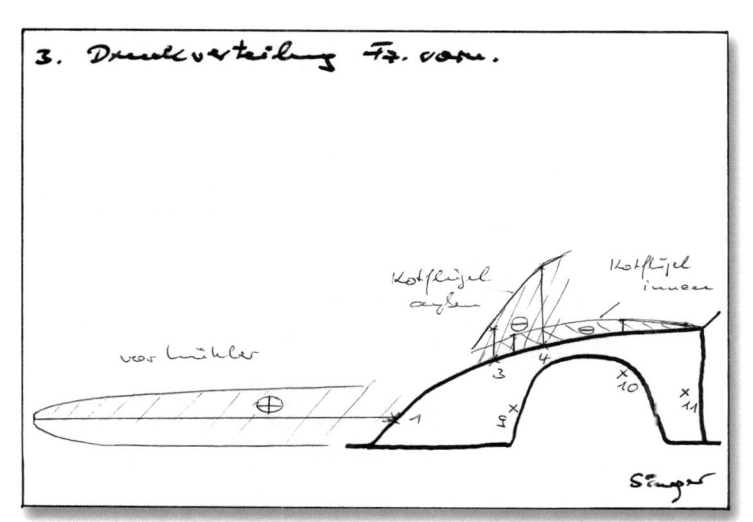

Ergebnisse: Nach Windkanalversuchen trug Singer die Druckverteilung in die Skizzen von Front und Heck des 935 ein.

Results: after wind tunnel tests, Singer would write down the distribution of the pressure on the sketches of the front and the rear of the 935.

gewichtig. Jetzt durfte keiner die Bleiplatten sehen, um Gottes Willen. Also haben wir den Zellen-Längsträger mit Blei ausgegossen.

Jetzt hatten wir am Norisring mit den blöden Spitzkehren ein bißchen ein Thema. Einmal ist das Auto dramatisch untersteuernd da rumgekommen, zum anderen hat der Turbo recht schlecht angesprochen. Heute geben die Motorenleute ein Kennfeld am Computer ein, das wurde damals über diese Raumnocken gemacht. Um einen Raumnocken herzustellen, musste auf dem Prüfstand erst einmal ein Kennfeld gefahren werden, das ging zwei, drei Wochen. Dann gingen die Daten zu Bosch oder Kugelfischer, und dann hat einer einen Raumnocken geschnitzt. Das ging noch einmal ein paar Wochen. Dann war das der Masternocken, und von dem wurde dann eine Kopie angefertigt und mit der konnten wir dann fahren. Wir sind halt aus den Ecken nicht richtig raus gekommen und insofern war das zunächst schon sehr enttäuschend. Wir hatten ein Seriengetriebe drin, da waren die Getriebeübersetzungen nicht so optimal. Auf jeden Fall, der Norisring war schon ein bisschen so na ja.

Norisring 1977: Jacky Ickx

Das Auto ist aber noch ein zweites Mal eingesetzt worden.
Singer: Zu Hause hat der Valentin Schäffer auf dem Prüfstand mal geschaut, dass er das Ansprechverhalten in die Reihe bringt, was ihm ganz gut gelungen ist. Wir haben am Auto geschaut und haben dann noch ein paar Versteifungsmaßnahmen eingeführt. Schlußendlich kam der Fuhrmann und sagte: Wisst ihr was, in Hockenheim fahren wir wieder. Dann habe ich gesagt: Bis dahin werden wir nicht fertig. Er hat gesagt: Wir fahren. Hockenheim kam von der Streckenführung her dem Turbo schon entgegen. Zum anderen war es kühl. Am Norisring war es heiss, das hat der Ickx sowieso nicht so arg mögen. Nach dem Training standen wir vorne. Dann haben wir das Ding sehr, sehr gut heimgefahren. Das war ein Bilderbuchrennen. Also vom Start weg. Zack, und wir haben das Ding gewonnen. Und die ganze Welt hat gestaunt: Wie hat Porsche das jetzt gemacht?
Ich kann mich noch erinnern, Manfred Jantke war dabei. Und der hat nach dem Rennen gesagt: Alle haben sich riesig gefreut, jetzt muß ich gleich den Alten anrufen, Fuhrmann. Dann habe ich noch zu ihm gesagt: Und sagen Sie ihm, er kann für mich Gehaltserhöhung einplanen. Nach einer Weile kam Jantke zurück. Fuhrmann war happy, Glückwunsch. Und zu Ihnen sagt er, berichtet der Jantke, Sie kriegen keine Gehaltserhöhung, denn Sie wollten gar nicht nach Hockenheim gehen. Ich müsste eine Gehaltserhöhung kriegen, hat der Fuhrmann gesagt.

Hockenheim 1977: Jacky Ickx, Jochen Mass

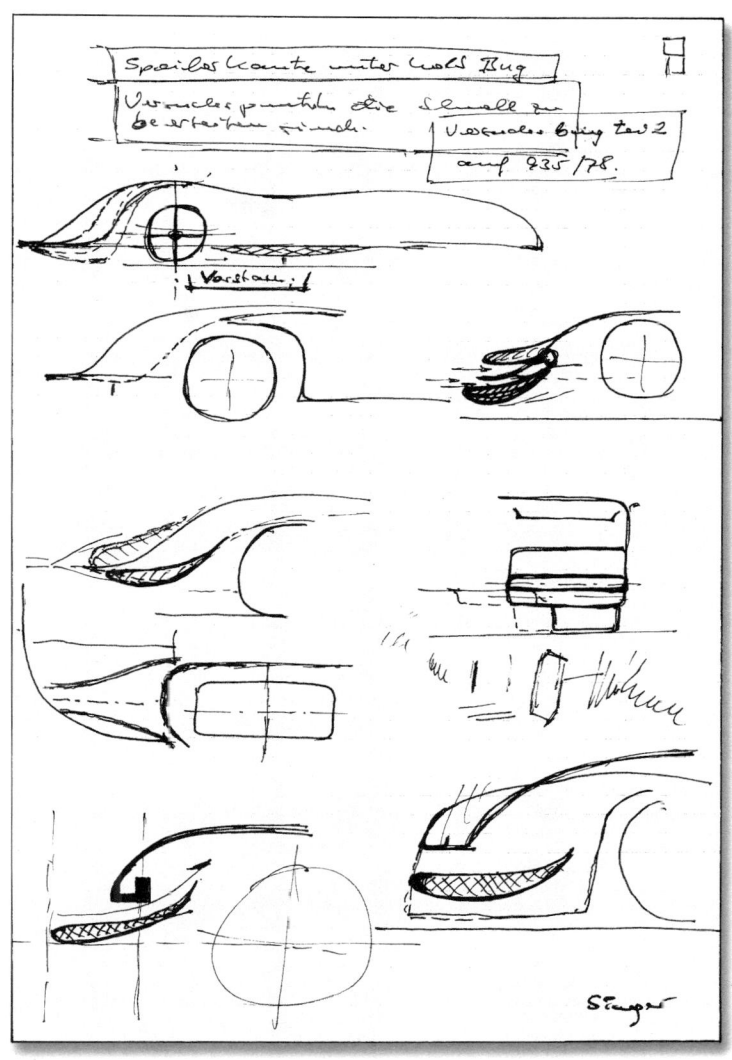

be something of a problem. So we took the bodywork of a 935 and it was clear. If I recall correctly, the minimum weight in the category was 730 kg. The 935s weighed 900 to 950 kg. In order to get down to 730 kg with such a big 911 was quite difficult. So we litterally took out everything we could. The mechanics said that we even made holes to make the needle of the speedometer lighter. We took every single part in our hands and asked: can't we make it lighter? That is how we got to 710 kg. Nobody was supposed to know this. It was a big secret. All the others had struggled to get to 830 kg. And we had a car that was underweight. Of course, nobody was allowed to see the sheets of lead that we had put in, for heaven's sake. So we filled the longitudinal structures of the cell with lead.

We had a little problem at the Norisring with its stupid hairpins. First of all, the car had dramatic understeer coming out of the corner and the response of the turbo was quite bad. Today, the engine people put a certain setting into the computer, but back then, we used these special cams. To make such a cam, we had to find the right value on the dyno first, which took two or three weeks. Then, the data went to Bosch or Kugelfischer, and they made that cam. That would take another couple of weeks. And then, we had the master cam and had a copy made of it which we used to drive. We just couldn't get out of the corners properly and it was very disappointing at first. We had a standard gearbox, the ratios weren't that good. In any case, the Norisring was a little bit so so.

But the car was being used a second time.
Singer: At home, Valentin Schäffer had worked on the dyno to get the response done, in which he succeeded quite well. We tried it on the car and put in a couple of things to make it stiffer. Finally, Fuhrmann would turn up and say: You know what, we will be racing again at Hockenheim. Then I said: We won't be ready in time before that. And he said: We are racing. The lay-out of the track at Hockenheim suited the turbo. And the weather was cool. At the Norisring, it had been hot and Ickx didn't particularly like that anyway. After qualifying, we were on top. And then, we claimed victory in a very, very beautiful way. It was a race like it should be. Right away from the start. We won it just like that. And all the world was astonished: how did Porsche do that?

I can still remember, Manfred Jantke was there. And after the race, he said: All were very happy, now, I have to phone the boss immediately, Fuhrmann. I said: Please, tell him, he can count my pay rise in. After a while, Jantke returned. Fuhrmann was happy, congratulations to all. And to you, Jantke reported, he said, you won't get a pay rise, because you didn't want to go to Hockenheim in the first place. Fuhrmann has said, it is me who should get a pay rise.

Jacky Ickx, Jochen Mass, Norbert Singer (r.)

KARRIERE EINES LEISTUNGS-SPORTLERS

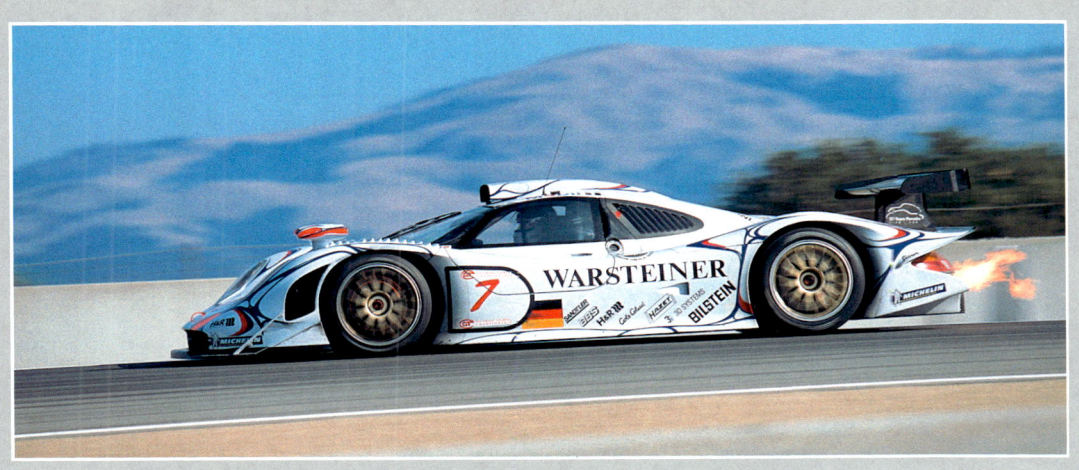

FOUR DECADES OF DEVELOPMENT

Author: Michael Cotton

41

VOM SCHOTTER AUF DIE PISTEN

Als 1965 der neue Porsche 911 seine Klasse bei der Monte Carlo Rallye gewann, wer hatte sich damals denken können, dass dieses Grand Turisme-Auto mit Heckmotor aus dem Stuttgarter Vorort Zuffenhausen in den folgenden vier Jahrzehnten große und kleine internationale Veranstaltungen gewinnen würde? Das der Sechszylindermotor, 40 Jahre nachdem das Modell in Frankfurt erstmals öffentlich gezeigt wurde, im gleichen Jahr Gesamtsiege sowohl beim 24 Stunden-Rennen von Daytona als auch beim 24 Stunden-Rennen von Spa einfahren würde?

Der 356, der ab 1949 produziert wurde, legte den Grundstein für den guten Ruf des Hauses Porsche, aber er hatte 1964 ausgedient. Fünfzehn Jahre an der Spitze, viele große Siege, aber dann wurde er von einem noch besseren Auto abgelöst. Der 911 hingegen wurde während seines Lebenszyklus ständig weiter entwickelt, und es gibt keine Anzeichen dass dieser Zyklus bald enden wird.

Er siegte viermal bei der Monte Carlo-Rallye, zweimal beim Marathon Paris-Dakar, er gewann die Targa Florio, das 12 Stunden-Rennen von Sebring.... die Liste geht weiter und weiter. In der Turboversion siegten 935 Sportwagen beim 24 Stunden-Rennen in Le Mans (1979) und räumte zwischen 1976 und 1981 immer wieder bei Langstreckenrennen zur FIA-Weltmeisterschaft und zur IMSA-Meisterschaft ab.

Die Leistung der Rennsportmodelle mit Saugmotoren nahm progessiv zu von 160 PS bis zu den 435 PS des heutigen Tages, eine erstaunliche Leistung für ein 3,6 Litermotor. Mit Turbo-Aufladung lieferte er ursprünglich 590 PS, während der Vierventilmotor in der 935/78-Ausführung nicht weniger als 750 PS leistete. Was auch immer gefragt war, Porsche fand immer die Motorleistung die für den Erfolg nötig war.

Was macht den Elfer so erfolgreich auf der Straße, bei Rallyes und auf der Rennstrecke? Ein hervorragender Entwurf war der erste Schritt. Die Nachfrage für den 911 blieb nahezu immer groß, und mit einer ständigen Weiterentwicklung ältert das Modell nie. Sogar in einem enttäuschenden Jahr, und davon gab es in den letzten vier Jahrzehnten einige, war und ist der 911 immer einer der meistverkauften Sportwagen weltweit, vielleicht nur geschlagen vom Chevrolet Corvette, der mehr für große Stückzahlen produziert wird. Hätte man die Lust am 911 verloren, hätte man sich satt gesehen an seiner Erscheinung und seiner Ausstrahlung, so würde das Modell im 21. Jahrhundert sicherlich nicht mehr bestehen und so wäre die Liste seiner Motorsporterfolge sicherlich schon abgeschlossen sein. Die Reaktion beim Publikum ist also der wichtigste Faktor.

Winner GT Targa Florio 1967: Jean-Claude Killy, Bernard Cahier

Targa Florio 1966: Jean-Pierre Nicholas, Jean-Loup Pellecuer

Winner GT 1000 km Nürburgring 1968: Malte Huth, Sepp Greger

RALLIES TO RACES

Who could have imagined, when the new Porsche 911 won its class in the 1965 Monte Carlo Rally, that the rear-engined Grand Touring car from the Zuffenhausen suburb of Stuttgart would win major and minor international events throughout the next four decades? That the flat-six engine would win the 24-Hours of Daytona and the 24-Hours of Spa outright in the same season, 40 years after the model was first exhibited in Frankfurt?

The 356, in production from 1949, established Porsche's fine reputation, but its job was done by 1964. Fifteen years at the top, many fine victories, and then it was replaced by something better. The 911, though, has been progressively developed throughout its lifespan, which shows no sign of coming to an end.

It has won the Monte Carlo Rally four times, the Paris-Dakar Raid twice, the Targa Florio, the Sebring 12-Hours... the list goes on and on. And then, in turbocharged form, the 935 race car has won the 24-Hours of Le Mans and swept the board in FIA World Championship and IMSA Championship endurance races repeatedly between 1976 and 1981.

In naturally aspirated form, the power of the competitions models has risen progressively from 160 horsepower to 450 horsepower today, a fabulous output for a 3.6 litre engine. In turbocharged form, the 935 model started out at 590 horsepower and went as high as 750 horsepower in the four-valve 935/78 model. Whatever the need, Porsche could always find the power to get the job done properly.

So what is it that makes the 911 model so successful, on the road, in rallies and on circuits? Superb design is the starting point. Public demand for the 911 has rarely flagged, and with constant development it shows no sign of age. Even in a disappointing year, and there have been a few in the last four decades, the 911 remains one of the world's best selling sports cars, second only, perhaps, to the Chevrolet Corvette which is produced for the mass market.

Had the public spurned the 911, got tired of its appearance and appeal, it would certainly not exist in the 21st century and the roll of competitions successes would have closed. So, public response is top of the list.

The 911 soon became an icon, an example of what all sports and Grand Touring cars should aspire to be. It was, and is, the choice of thousands of enthusiasts, year in and year out, whose ambition is to own a performance car which yields an immense amount of exhilaration and pure driving pleasure.

Jean-Pierre Gaban, "Pedro" (l.-r.): Winner 24 Hours Spa-Francorchamps 1967

Winner 24 Hours Spa-Francorchamps 1967: Jean-Pierre Gaban, "Pedro"

43

Der 911 wurde bald zur Ikone, zum Vorbild für alle Sportwagen und Gran Turismo-Fahrzeuge. Motorsport auf der Rundstrecke war in den sechziger Jahren sicherlich beliebt, aber gleiches galt für Rallyes und Bergrennen. Am Anfang war der 911 in der Vision von Dr. Ferry Porsche und seinen technischen Assistenten viel eher ein Rallyewagen als ein Auto für die Rennstrecke. Schließlich hatte Porsche mit dem Mittelmotor-Modell 904 ein Gran Turisme-Auto im Programm. Danach folgte eine ganze Reihe von Rennsportwagen, gekrönt vom mächtigen 917 im Jahre 1969.

Die ersten internationalen Rennsporterfolge des 911 kamen 1966 mit der S-Version, die 175 PS leistete. Die Amerikaner Jack Ryan und Art Benker gewannen die Zweiliter-GT-Klasse in Daytona, Sepp Greger und Carl-Gregor Auer siegten in der Zweiliter GT-Klasse beim 1000 km-Rennen auf dem Nürburgring und schließlich gewannen 'Franc' und Jean Kerguen auch noch die Zweiliter-GT-Klasse in Le Mans mit Platz 14 in der Gesamtwertung und einer zurückgelegten Distanz von 3.821 Kilometern bei einer Durchschnittgeschwindigkeit von 159,230 km/h.

Der 911 gewann Aufmerksamkeit und manche kauften das Auto wegen seiner Leistungen auf der Rennstrecke. Unüblich für die damalige Zeit waren die belüftete Bremsscheiben, die eine hervorragende Bremswirkung ermöglichten. Er verfügte serienmäßig über Stabilisatoren hinten und vorne und einstellbare Koni-Stoßdämpfer, so dass das Auto bei einem Gewicht von 1.030 kg verhältnismäßig starke Leistungen brachte. Je länger das Rennen, desto mehr Spaß hatten die Fahrer in ihren Porsche 911.

1000 km Nürburgring 1969: Hans Schuller, Edgar Herrmann

Winner GT 1000 km Spa-Francorchamps 1968: Dieter Glemser, Helmut Kelleners

1967 setzte sich die Legende fort, als der 911 Klassensiege in der GT-Klasse in Daytona, Sebring, Spa, der Targa Florio und auf dem Nürburgring einfuhr, also auf ganz unterschiedlichen Rennstrecken, von den Vollgas-Steilkurven auf dem Daytona International Speedway bis hin zu den holprigen und anspruchsvollen Straßen auf Sizilien, wo es schwierig ist, einen Schnitt von 100 km/h zu erreichen.

Journalist Bernard Cahier und Ski-Olympiasieger Jean-Claude Killy erreichten Platz sieben bei der Targa Florio 1967, Helmuth Kelleners und Jürgen Neuhaus wurden Elfte in der Gesamtwertung beim 1000 km-Rennen auf dem Nürburgring, wo der 910, ebenfalls mit dem Sechszylindermotor aus dem 911, die ersten vier Plätze belegten. Später gewannen Jean-Pierre Gaban und 'Pedro' das 24 Stunden-Rennen im belgischen Spa-Francorchamps, der erste von vielen Erfolge des Elfers bei 24 Stunden-Rennen.

Testfahrer Herbert Linge teilte sich in Le Mans einen 911S zusammen mit Robert Buchet. Ihre Durchschnittsgeschwindigkeit von 173,254 km/h für das ganze Rennen war beeindruckend. Das Duo erreichte den 14. Rang in der Gesamtwertung mit einer Distanz von 4.158 Kilometern.

Vic Elford machte sich einen grossen Namen in den frühen Jahren der 911-Geschichte. Zunächst als Rallyefahrer, als er 1967 die Rallye-Europameisterschaft gewann und bei der Monte Carlo Rallye 1968 den Gesamtsieg einfuhr, aber auch auf der Rundstrecke. Seine Leistungen im 911S des Importeurs AFN mit dem Kennzeichen GVB 911D begeisterte die Zuschauer bei den Rennen zur britischen Tourenwagenmeisterschaft, wo Elford gegen die Ford Falcons und Galaxies, Jaguars und gegen Jim Clark im Lotus Cortina antrat.

Unter der Führung von Ferdinand Piëch, dem Neffen von Dr. Ferry Porsche, arbeitete die Versuchsabteilung mit immer mehr Begeisterung an der Entwicklung des 911 für Sporteinsätze. Das Ergebnis war der 911R, der 1967 in kleiner Stückzahl produziert wurde. Das Auto war mit 800 kg erheblich leichter, während die Motorleistung mit einer speziellen Version des 911-Motors mit vier Nockenwellen auf 210 PS anstieg. Dieser Motor wurde auch schon im 906 eingesetzt. Der Motor war mit vier Nockenwellen vielleicht etwas komplizierter, aber er war leichter, mit einem Motorblock aus Magnesium, Pleuel aus Titan und lieferte außerdem 35 PS mehr. Die Leichtbaukarossen wurden vom Stuttgarter Spezialisten Karl Bauer angefertigt und hatten größere hintere Kotflügel für breitere Felgen. Die Türen, Kotflügel, Fronthaube und Heckklappe waren aus glasfaserverstärktem Kunststoff, die Scheiben waren aus Plastik. Das Leistungsgewicht wurde auf 260 PS pro 1000 kg erhöht.

Zunächst plante Porsche, den 911R in einer Stückzahl von 500 zu produzieren und eine Zulassung für die GT-Klasse zu beantragen. Aber der Markt war unsicher, der Motor war für den Straßenverkehr nicht optimal, und so entschloß sich Porsche zur Produktion von 24 Stück, die für ausgesuchte Sonderveranstaltungen eingesetzt wurden, gegebenermassen als Prototypen. Porsche behielt drei Stück und verkaufte 21, wobei das Gewicht auf 830 kg angestiegen war.

Einer der drei Werks-911R hatte ein halbautomatisches Sportomatic-Getriebe und siegte beim 84 Stunden-Rennen 'Marathon de la Route' auf dem Nürburgring mit Hans Herrmann, Vic Elford und Jochen Neerpasch. Diese Veranstaltung war nur ein schwacher Ersatz für den schweren Spa-Sofia-Lüttich-Marathon, der aufgrund der immer steigenden Verkehrsintensität in Mitteleuropa nicht mehr durchgeführt werden konnte.

Ein weiterer 911R, der bereits häufig von der Testabteilung benutzt wurde, wurde kurzerhand nach Monza gefahren und legte dort einen Hochgeschwindigkeits-Dauerlauf auf der gesamten Strecke, einer Kombination aus Steilkurven und dem normalen Streckenverlauf, zurück. Rico Steinemann, der kurz darauf Presse- und Sportchef bei Porsche wurde, Jo Siffert, Dieter Spoerry und Charles Vögele fuhren 96 Stunden am Stück Vollgas bei einer Durchschnittsgeschwindigkeit von 209,23 km/h. Sie setzten neue Rekordmarken bei 15.000 und 20.000 Kilometern.

Motor racing was certainly popular in the 1960s but so, too, were rallies and hill climbs. In the beginning the 911 was much more a rally car, in the eyes of Dr. Ferry Porsche and his technical assistants, than a racing car. After all, Porsche produced the mid-engined 904 as a Grand Touring model in 1964 followed by a whole raft of racing cars leading up to the omnipotent 917 model in 1969.

The earliest international racing successes of the 911 were achieved in 1966 by the S version, with 175 horsepower. This slight increase over the standard model's 160 horsepower was achieved with different chokes and jets on the Weber carburettors, and a through-flow exhaust system.

Americans Jack Ryan and Art Benker won the GT 2-litre class in the Daytona 24-Hour Continental, as the Florida event was then called, Sepp Greger and Auer won the GT 2-litre class at the Nurburgring 1,000 Kms and then, notably, 'Franc' and Jean Kerguen won the GT 2-litre class at Le Mans, finishing in 14th place overall and covering 3,821 kilometres at an average speed of 159.230 km/h.

People were beginning to take note of the Porsche 911, and some were buying it for its capabilities on the circuits. Unusually for its day, the 911S had ventilated disc brakes which gave it outstanding stopping power, it had front and rear anti-roll bars as standard and Koni adjustable dampers, so the overall level of performance in a car weighing 1,030 kg was quite high, making it capable of giant-killing acts. The longer the event the better the Porsche 911 drivers would like it!

The legend continued to grow in 1967 as the 911 won GT class victories at Daytona, Sebring, Spa, the Targa Florio and the Nurburgring, a wide variety of circuits ranging from the flat-out banking of the Daytona International Speedway to the rugged, bumpy and hazardous Sicilian route on which it is difficult to average 100 km/h even with a clear road.

Publicist Bernard Cahier and Olympic ski champion Jean-Claude Killy finished seventh overall in the 1967 Targa Florio, Helmuth Kelleners and Juergen Neuhaus were classified 11th overall at the Nurburg 1,000 Kms (Porsche 910/6 models, also with the 911's six-cylinder engine, claimed the top four places overall), then Jean-Pierre Gaban and 'Pedro' triumphed in the Spa 24-Hours at Francorchamps, Belgium, the first of many 'round the clock' successes for the 911.

Test driver Herbert Linge shared a 911S at Le Mans with Robert Buchet, and their average of 173.254 km/h for the entire duration was impressive. They finished 14th overall and covered 4,158 kilometres.

Vic Elford was a man who made a big name for himself in the early days of the 911, first as a rally driver, winning the 1967 European Rally Championship, and the 1968 Monte Carlo Rally outright, and on race tracks too. His exploits in the AFN importer's 911S, GVB 911D, drew spectators to the British Touring Car Championship where he scrapped with Ford Falcons and Galaxies, Jaguars, and notably Jim Clark in a Lotus Cortina.

Under the new direction of Ferdinand Piech, nephew of Dr Ferry Porsche, the experimental department began to take a fresh interest in developing the 911 as a competitions car. First off was the 911R, produced in low volume in 1967, substantially lightened to 800 kg and tuned up to 210 horsepower with a special four-camshaft version of the 911, already used in the 906 model.

The four-cam engine might have been a little more complex, but it was lighter with a magnesium block casting and titanium connecting rods and delivered another 35 horsepower. The lightweight bodies were made by Karl Bauer, a specialist in Stuttgart, with flared rear wheel arches to accommodate wider rims, glass fibre reinforced plastic doors, front wings, front lid and engine cover, and plastic windows; the doors were made of aluminium, and the power-to-weight ratio rose to 260 bhp per tonne.

At first, Porsche considered making 500 examples of the 911R and having the model homologated into the GT class. How the customers would have liked that! However the market was uncertain, the engine was rather inflexible for road use, and Porsche decided instead to make 24 and use them for special events necessarily entered as prototypes. Porsche kept three and sold 21, the weights of which crept up to 830 kg.

One of the three 'works' 911Rs was equipped with the new Sportomatic particle clutch semi-automatic transmission, and it won the 84-hour 'Marathon de la Route' on the Nurburgring in the hands of Hans Herrmann, Vic Elford and Jochen Neerpasch. This event was a poor substitute for the gruelling Spa-Sofia-Liege Marathon, which had to be abandoned in deference to increasing traffic densities in central Europe.

Another 911R, a well-used 'mule' from the test department, was driven to Monza at short notice and completed a high speed marathon on the full circuit, combining banking with the familiar road course. Rico Steinemann, soon to become Porsche's PR and Competitions manager, Jo Siffert, Dieter Spoerry and Charles Vogele completed 96 hours of flat-out motoring at an average of 209.23 km/h (130.01 mph) establishing records at 15,000 and 20,000 kilometres along the way.

Three drivers whose names would become synonymous with Porsche, Erwin Kremer, Willi Kauhsen and Helmut Kelleners, won the Spa 24-Hours in a 911S, the second major success in Belgium for the Porsche. Kelleners and Dieter Glemser also won the GT class in the Spa 1,000 Kilometre race, and again in the Monza 1,000 Kms. Greger and Huth won the GT class at the Nurburgring, Claude Haldi and Pierre Greub the GT class in the Targa Florio.

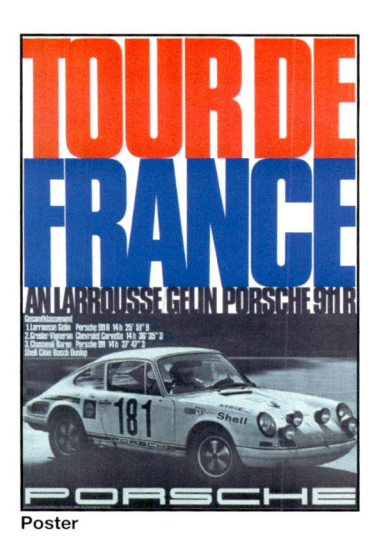

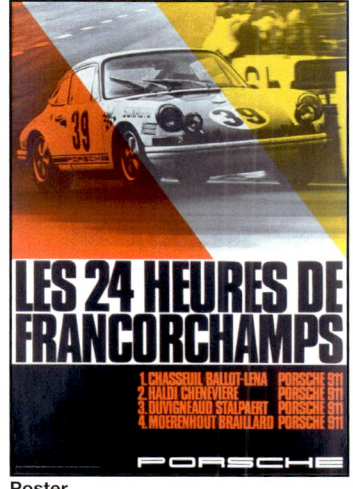

Winner GT 1000 km Nürburgring 1970: Dieter Fröhlich, Pauli Toivonen

Erwin Kremer, Willi Kauhsen und Helmut Kelleners, drei Fahrer, deren Namen fest mit Porsche verbunden waren, gewannen das 24 Stunden-Rennen von Spa mit einem 911S, der zweite große Erfolg in Belgien für den Porsche. Kelleners und Dieter Glemser gewannen auch die GT-Klasse beim 1000 km-Rennen in Spa sowie bei den 1000 km in Monza. Greger und Huth siegten in der GT-Klasse auf dem Nürburgring, Claude Haldi und Pierre Greub entschieden die GT-Klasse bei der Targa Florio für sich.

Eine merkwürdige Regel der FIA erlaubte Porsche den Einsatz des Basis-911 sowie des 911L in der Gruppe 2, die verbesserten Tourenwagen vorbehalten war, während der 911S und der 911T in der Gruppe 3 für Gran Turismo-Fahrzeuge zugelassen waren. Darüber hinaus wurde eine 930 kg leichte Version des 911T (das T stand für Touring) gebaut, die aber mit dem S-Motor mit 170 PS homologiert wurde.

So hatte Porsche Standbeine in zwei beliebten Fahrzeugklassen und manchmal gewann Porsche sie beide bei einer Veranstaltung, sehr zum Unmut der Teams die mit Ford Mustang, BMW 2000, Alfa Romeo GTA und dergleichen in der Gruppe 2 an den Start gingen.

Die belgischen Veranstalter sahen die Tourenwagen bei ihrer Veranstaltung vorzugsweise in der Hauptrolle und als Teams 1969 mit 911 die ersten vier Plätze in der Gesamtwertung belegten, mit Guy Chasseuil und Claude Ballot-Lena als Gesamtsiegern, entschloß sich die Organisation zu einer neuen Maßnahme. Auf ihrer Empfehlung änderte die FIA die Klasseneinteilung für 1970 und verbannte den 911 aus der Tourenwagenklasse. Somit kehrte wieder Ruhe ein, zumindest vorläufig, obwohl Porsche Jahre später erneut das Rennen gewinnen konnte, zunächst 1993 und dann erneut im Jahr 2003.

Im September 1969 bekam Porsche weitere Anfragen für den 911R, denn Gérard Larrousse wollte das Auto bei der Tour de France Automobile und bei der Tour de Corse fahren. Die Tour de France war eine neue Veranstaltung, offen für alle Autos mit Strassenzulassung. Innerhalb von sechs Tagen wurde auf 20 klassischen Rennstrecken und Bergrennstrecken in ganz Frankreich gefahren. Larrousse wollte gerne in der Tour mitfahren und überredete Porsche, ihm einen 911R zur Verfügung zu stellen. Zusammen mit Maurice Gelin feierte er auf diesem Auto den Gesamtsieg, mit weiteren Porsche-Teams auf den Plätzen drei, vier und fünf. Kurz darauf gewann Larrousse im gleichen Auto auch die Tour de Corse, womit er Vic Elfords Gesamtsieg aus dem Vorjahr wiederholte.

Die C-Serie des 911, die im September 1969 für das Modelljahr 1970 vorgestellt wurde, wies erhebliche Vorteile auf, die Rennfahrer nutzen konnten. Der Radstand wurde um 60 mm auf 2271 mm gestreckt, indem die Zugstreben verlängert und die Radkästen einfach weiter nach hinten platziert wurden. Dies trug zur besseren Gewichtsverteilung bei. Der Hubraum wurde auf 2195 ccm angehoben, indem der Hub von 80 mm auf 84 mm vergrößert wurde. Die Bohrung blieb mit 66 mm gleich, der serienmäßige 911 lieferte nun 180 PS. Fortan wurde das Kurbelgehäuse aus Magnesium angefertigt, womit an einer entscheidenden Stelle, nämlich am Getriebegehäuse, 10 kg eingespart werden konnte. Dies führte zu einer merkbaren Verbesserung im Fahrverhalten des 911. Mechanische Benzineinspritzung von Bosch kam anstelle von Vergasern und für den Wettbewerbs-Ausführungen wurde die Doppelzündung homologiert.

Jetzt war Porsche freilich nicht länger in der Zweiliterklasse, sondern in der 2,5-Literklasse. Deshalb wurde die Bohrung bei den Rennautos um einen weiteren Millimeter angehoben, so dass der Hubraum auf 2247 ccm vergrößert wurde. Die Motorleistung stieg um nicht weniger als 33 Prozent an, fortan lieferte der Motor 240 PS bei 7800 U./min. In dieser Form war der 911S in der Gruppe 3 für GT-Produktionsautos zugelassen, während eine extremere Version in der Gruppe 4 für GT-Spezialfahrzeuge eingestuft wurde. Insgesamt wurden 30 Autos für wichtige Kunden im Rennsport angefertigt. Diese konnten statt Bosch-Einspritzung auch Weber-Vergaser ordern, ohne dass dabei Leistung eingebusst wurde.

Die Gruppe 4-Version, intern ST genannt, war eine richtige Homologations-Spezialfertigung mit dünnerem Blechstahl für das Dach, für die hinteren Seitenteile und andere Teile die nicht belastet wurden. Im Innenraum wurde alles was nicht notwendig war, entfernt. Es gab keinen Unterbodenschutz und keine Schalldämmung. Sogar beim Lackieren wurde Gewicht eingespart, das zugelassene Gesamtgewicht wurde auf 840 kg reduziert.

Wie in einem anderen Kapitel beschrieben, hatte die Gruppe 4 Version einen hervorragenden Start im Jahr 1970, mit dem Doppelsieg bei der Monte Carlo-Rallye, der dritte Porsche-Sieg, mit Björn Waldegaard im Ziel vor Gérard Larrousse.

In jenem Jahr feierte Porsche auch den ersten Le Mans-Sieg mit dem Zwölfzylinder-Modell 917. Der Motor des 917 bestand tatsächlich aus zwei aneinander montierten 911-Triebwerken, wobei die Verbindung zum Getriebe in der Mitte der langen Kurbelwelle montiert wurde.

Mit den 917, unterstützt von 908, 910 und mit den Elfern, die in der GT-Klasse dominierten, belegte Porsche oftmals die Mehrzahl der Top 10-Platzierungen bei WM-Läufen. Man fragte sich, was wohl mit dem Langstreckensport passiert wäre, hätte Ferry Porsche keinen Interesse daran gehabt.

Die 2,3 Liter Porsche dominierten das 1000 km-Rennen auf dem Nürburgring im Mai, mit den ersten drei Plätzen in der GT-Klasse. Pauli Toivonen und Dieter Fröhlich kämpften während des gesamten Rennens (nicht weniger als sechs Stunden!) gegen Erwin Kremer und Georg Huber. Am Ende trennten die beiden Teams nur 0,2 Sekunden.

Winner 24 Hours Spa-Francorchamps 1969: Claude Ballot-Lena, Guy Chasseuil

1000 km Nürburgring 1970: Erwin Kremer, Günther Huber

Winner GT 1000 km Spa-Francorchamps 1971: Erwin Kremer, Günther Huber

It was an oddity in the FIA regulations that allowed Porsche to homologate the base 911 and the 911L in Group 2, reserved for modified touring cars, and the 911S and 911T in the Group 3 Grand Touring class. Furthermore, a lightweight version of the 911T (for Touring) was produced at 930 kg but was homologated with the S engine, with 170 horsepower.
Porsche got a foot-hold in two popular categories and sometimes won both of them in a single outing, to the chagrin of the teams running Group 2 Ford Mustangs, BMW 2000s, Alfa Romeo GTAs and the like.
The Belgian organisers preferred their event to be the domain of touring cars, and when 911 teams claimed the top four positions overall in 1969, led by Guy Chasseuil and Claude Ballot-Lena, they decided that enough was enough. At their prompting, the FIA altered the categories in 1970 and banished the 911 from the touring car category. Peace was restored, for the time being, although Porsche would return to win the 24-Hour race later in life, in 1993, and again in 2003.
Porsche had further requirements for the 911R in September 1969, for Gerard Larrousse to drive on the Tour de France Automobile and on the Tour de Corse. The Tour de France was a newly established "all comers" event visiting 20 classic circuits and hill climbs in France in the space of six days, open to all road-legal cars.
Larrousse was eager to take part in the Tour and persuaded Porsche to supply him with a 911R which he and Maurice Gelin drove to a fine victory, with other Porsches placed third, fourth and fifth. Soon afterwards Larrousse won the Tour de Corse outright in the same car, repeating Vic Elford's victory of the previous year.
The C-series 911 introduced in September 1969 for the 1970 model year offered significant advantages which competitions drivers were able to exploit. Notably, the wheelbase was lengthened by 60mm (to 2,271mm) simply by lengthening the rear trailing arms and moving the wheel arches backwards, thus improving the weight distribution, and the engine capacities across the range were increased to 2,195 cc by increasing the bore from 80mm to 84mm. The stroke remained at 66mm and the standard 911S now developed 180 horsepower.
Crank-cases were now made of magnesium, saving 10kg where it mattered most, also the gearbox cases, so there was an appreciable improvement in the 911's handling capabilities. Bosch mechanical petrol injection replaced carburettors and, for competitions models, twin-plug ignition was homologated.
Now, of course, Porsche was out of the 2-litre class and moved up to the 2.5 litre class so cars intended for racing had a further increase of 1mm on the bore, increasing the capacity to 2,247cc. Power was increased by no less than 33 per cent, to 240 horsepower at 7,800 rpm. In this form the 911S was homologated into the Group 3 production GT class, while a more extreme version was homologated into the Group 4 special GT class. A total of 30 cars were made for serious customers in racing, who could specify Weber carburettors instead of Bosch injection, with no sacrifice in power output.
The Group 4 version, known internally as the ST, was a real homologation special with thinner gauge sheet steel used in the roof, the rear side panels and other non-stressed areas, and the interior was stripped of all non-essentials. There was no underseal or sound-proofing, weight was even saved in the paint shop, and the homologated weight was reduced to 840 kg. As described in another chapter, the Group 4 version got the 1970 season off to a terrific start by claiming the top two positions in the Monte Carlo Rally, Porsche's hat-trick of victories, Bjorn Waldegaard finishing ahead of Gerard Larrousse.
This was the year of Porsche's first Le Mans victory, with the 12-cylinder 917 model, and it is worth noting again that the 917's engine was, effectively, two 911 motors joined together, and with the drive take-off located in the centre of the long crankshaft.
What with 917s, backed up by 908s and 910s, and 911s dominating the GT category, Porsches often occupied most of the top 10 positions in World Championship events. It made people wonder what state endurance racing would be in, had Dr Ferry Porsche not been interested in the sport!
The 2.3 litre 911 were out in force at the Nurburg 1,000 Kms in May, taking the top three positions in the GT category. Pauli Toivonen and Dieter Frohlich duelled for the entire distance (a marathon lasting six hours!) with Erwin Kremer and Georg Huber, eventually finishing 0.2 seconds apart. Kremer was angry about some tactics and gave Toivonen's car a push after the chequered flag! Third was another Porsche 2.3 driven by Hans Stuck, more usually associated with BMW in those days, and Clemens Schickentanz.

Winner Tour de France 1969: Gerard Larrousse, Maurice Gelin

RALLIES TO RACES

Kremer wurde jedoch schon bald entschädigt, denn er wurde im Kreis der "Magnificent Seven" für Le Mans aufgenommen. Im heftigen Regen feierte Porsche nicht nur den ersten Gesamtsieg, sondern belegte sogar die ersten drei Plätze. Der talentierte niederländische Fahrer Gijs van Lennep gewann den 1970 erstmals ausgeschriebenen Porsche Cup auf 917 und 908, eingeschrieben vom finnischen Porsche-Importeur Antti Arno-Wihuri. Van Lennep fuhr nicht im 911, aber ab 1971 ging der Porsche Cup ohne Ausnahme an Fahrer die mit dem 911 fuhren.

1971 gewann Erwin Kremer den Cup im 911, der von seinem eigenen Team vorbereitet wurde, mit GT-Klassensiegen auf dem Nürburgring, in Spa und in Monza und Rennsiegen im nicht zur Meisterschaft zählenden 500 km-Rennen auf dem Nürburgring sowie bei den 1000 km-Rennen von Barcelona und Paris und im 6 Stunden-Rennen von Jarama.

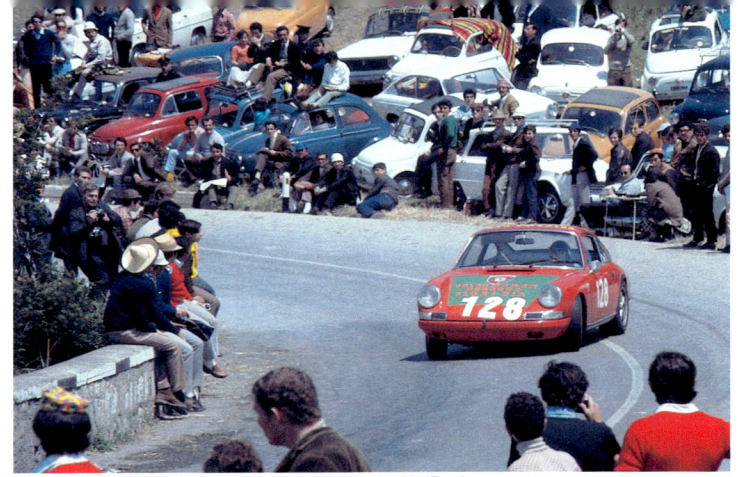

Targa Florio 1970: Ignazio Capuano, Giancarlo Barba

1000 km Nürburgring 1971: Leo Kinnunen, Björn Waldegaard

In den drei darauffolgenden Jahren wurde der Cup zweimal von John Fitzpatrick und einmal von Clemens Schickentanz gewonnen, jeweils mit Kremer-Porsche 911. Die Geschichte des Porsche-Cups weist neun Siege für Kremer Racing in den ersten zwölf Jahren von 1970 bis 1981 auf, mit Bob Wollek und Klaus Ludwig ebenfalls auf dem Ehrentafel.

Der Schweizer Fahrer Claude Haldi fuhr bei Läufen zur Sportwagen-WM regelmäßig in die Punkte. Mit Bernard Cheneviere gewann er die GT-Klasse beim ultraschnellen 1000 km-Rennen von Spa. Jo Siffert und Brian Redman gewannen dieses Rennen in der Rekordzeit von vier Stunden und neun Minuten bei einem Schnitt von 240,46 km/h und zeigten so das wahre Potenzial des 917. Haldis 911 hingegen absolvierte 55 Runden (749 Kilometer) bei einer Durchschnittsgeschwindigkeit von 186 km/h inklusive Boxenstopps, ein gutes Ergebnis für ein Produktionsauto.

Die letzte Veranstaltung für Porsche im Jahre 1970 war die Tour de France, bei der Gérard Larrousse erneut einen speziell angefertigten 911 zur Verfügung gestellt wurde. Es war eine 2,4 Literversion mit einer Leistung von 245 PS. Die Porsche-Techniker reagierten begeistert auf Larrousses Angebot von einer Kiste Champagner für jedes Kilo das den 911 leichter als 800 kg machte.

Larrousse mußte elf Kisten anschleppen, denn der Elfer wog nur 789 kg, der leichteste 911, mit viel Titanium, Plastik und Magnesium. Der Franzose hatte jedoch nicht damit gerechnet, dass Matra seine V12-Rennautos für die Straße umbauen ließ, und so wurde er nur Dritter, während zwei solcher Vollblut-Rennwagen die ersten zwei Plätze belegten.

Die Entwicklung ging weiter: Für das Modelljahr 1971 stellte Porsche den 2,4 Litermotor mit einem längeren Hub von 70,4 mm vor (die Bohrung betrug weiterhin 84 mm), was zu einem Hubraum von 2341 mm führte. Die Rennsportabteilung vergrößerte die Bohrung auf 86,7 mm, so daß der Hubraum auf 2380 ccm anstieg. Die Leistung wurde auf 275 PS erweitert. Dieser Motor war jedoch anfällig und es gab eine weitere Entwicklungsstufe mit Nikasil anstelle von Biral, so dass die Bohrung noch weiter auf 89 mm vergrößert werden konnte, während der Hub auf 66 mm zurückgestuft wurde. So kam man zu einem Hubraum von 2466 ccm und einer Leistung von 270 PS bei 8000 U./min.

Den Rennsportkunden wurde ein neues Getriebe "915" angeboten, mit einem größeren Drehmoment. Dieses Getriebe war mit einer im Gehäuse eingebauten Ölpumpe ausgefertigt. Es hatte jedoch einen Nachteil, denn es lieferte 7 PS weniger. Das war der Preis für Porsche-typische Zuverlässigkeit. Der erste Gang war nun links oben, statt ganz außen links unten, gegenüber dem Rückwärtsgang. Alle Kunden bevorzugten schon bald diese neue Anordnung. Die 911 der E-Serie hatten eine Frontschürze, die die Luftströmung unterhalb des Autos kontrollierte. Bilstein-Stoßdämpfer ersetzten Koni-Dämpfer.

Erwin Kremer und Günther Huber gewannen die GT-Klasse bei den 1000 km-Rennen von Spa und Monza. Kremer siegte auch auf dem Nürburgring, zusammen mit Jürgen Neuhaus. Schickentanz und Kersten gewannen das Rennen auf dem neuen Österreichring und die Schweizer Fahrer Bernard Cheneviere und Paul Keller gewannen die GT-Klasse bei der Targa Florio. Sie belegten den vierten Gesamtplatz und legten zehn der elf Runden des siegreichen Alfa Romeo T33 zurück. Die Elfer brachten eine gute Leistung in Le Mans, wo sie bis auf einen Platz alle Positionen zwischen den Rängen sechs und 13 belegten.

Der 911S hatte nun 86,7 mm Bohrung und 70,4 mm Hub und somit einen Hubraum von 2492 ccm. Die Motorleistung betrug 270 PS. Das war kaum ausreichend, aber die Porsche dominierten weiterhin in ihrem traditionellen Revier. Gottifredi und Pica gewannen die GT-Klasse bei der Targa Florio und belegten den fünften Gesamtrang, Kremer und Fitzpatrick feierten den GT-Klassensieg auf dem Nürburgring mit Gesamtplatz neun.

Am Ende der europäischen Saison, vor dem Finale in Watkins Glen, stand das 1000 km-Rennen auf dem Österreichring, in dem Testfahrer Günther Steckkönig und Rallyefahrer Björn Waldegaard Platz zehn belegten. Sie fuhren jedoch nicht in der GT-Klasse, denn sie hatten einige nicht zugelassene Aerodynamikteile am Auto, die schon einen Ausblick auf den nächsten Porsche gaben, den RS 2.7 Carrera.

1000 km Spa-Francorchamps 1971: Pierre Greub, Jean-Claude Gueri

Kremer soon had consolation, though, as he joined the 'Magnificent Seven' at Le Mans! Run in seriously wet weather conditions, Porsche not only claimed their first victory but occupied the top three positions overall.

Gijs van Lennep, the talented Dutch driver, became the first winner of the Porsche Cup in 1970 driving Porsche 917s and 908s entered by the Finnish Porsche importer, Antti Arno-Wihuri. Van Lennep did not race a 911, the model central to this book, but from 1971 onwards the Porsche Cup was invariably won by drivers of the 911.

In 1971 Erwin Kremer won the Cup in the 911 prepared by his own team, his record including GT class wins at the Nurburgring, Spa and Monza, victories in the non-championship Nurburg 500 Kilometre race, and 1,000 Kilometre races at Barcelona and Paris, also the 6-Hours of Jarama.

In the following three years the Cup was won twice by John Fitzpatrick and once by Clemens Schickentanz, always in Kremer Porsche 911s. The history of the Porsche Cup shows that Kremer Porsche Racing won the contest nine times in the first 12 years, between 1970 and 1981, with Bob Wollek and Klaus Ludwig joining the roll of honour.

The Swiss driver, Claude Haldi, was a regular points-scorer in the World Sports Car Championship, winning the GT class in the ultra-fast Spa 1,000 Kms with Bernard Cheneviere. Jo Siffert and Brian Redman won this event in record time, 4 hours and 9 minutes at an average of 240.46 km/h, really showing what the 917 was capable of. Haldi's 911, by contrast, completed 55 laps (749 kilometres) at an average speed of 186 km/h (115.57 mph), including stops, good going for a production car.

The last event that Porsche supported in 1970 was the Tour de France, again supplying Gerard Larrousse with a specially built 911. This was a 2.4 litre version of the 911ST, developing 245 bhp, and the factory engineers responded well to Larrousse's offer of a case of champagne for every kilo the car weighed below 800 kg.

1000 km Österreichring 1971: Erwin Kremer, Rudi Lins

Larrousse had to supply 11 cases because the lightweight car was down to 789 kg, the lightest 911 ever made with an extensive use of titanium, plastics and magnesium. The Frenchman had not reckoned on Matra making its V12 race cars suitable for road use, though, and two of these thoroughbreds claimed the first two positions overall, pushing him down to third overall.

Development continued apace as Porsche introduced the 2.4 litre engine for the 1971 model year with a longer, 70.4mm stroke (still with 84mm bore) resulted in a capacity of 2,341 cc. The racing department then further enlarged the bore to 86.7mm to yield a capacity of 2,380 cc; power rose to 275 horsepower. However this engine proved fragile, and there was a further development with Nikasil replacing Biral, making it possible to enlarge the bore still further to 89 mm while shortening the stroke back to 66mm. The resultant capacity was revised to 2,466 cc, and the power went up to 270 horsepower at 8,000 rpm.

A new gearbox, 915, with a higher torque rating was offered to racing customers, this having a dedicated oil pump incorporated in the housing. It had a drawback, though, of absorbing 7 bhp, a price that had to be paid for Porsche reliability. First gear was now left and up, opposite second, instead of being dog-leg left opposite reverse, and all customers soon preferred the new layout. The E-series 911s sported a front air dam which controlled the flow of air underneath the car, and Bilstein dampers replaced Koni.

As mentioned, Erwin Kremer and Gunther Huber won the GT category at the Spa and Monza 1,000 kilometre races (Kremer also won at the Nurburgring, with Jurgen Neuhaus). Schickentanz and Kersten won at the new Osterreichring, and Swiss drivers Bernard Cheneviere and Paul Keller won the GT category in the Targa Florio, finishing in fourth position overall and completing 10 of the 11 laps covered by the winning Alfa Romeo T33.

Porsche 911s finished well at Le Mans in 1971 occupying all but one of the positions between sixth and 13th (a 907 finished seventh).

The 911S now had a bore x stroke of 86.7 x 70.4mm for a capacity of 2,492 cc, and the power was quoted at 270 horsepower. It was barely enough, although Porsches shone in their traditional environments. Gottifredi and Pica won the GT class at the Targa Florio, fifth overall, Kremer and Fitzpatrick won GT at the Nurburgring, ninth overall, but at Le Mans the 911s had to concede to a quintet of Ferrari Daytonas, even a pair of Ford Capris which cleaned up in the 'Supertourisme' class. The first 911 home was that of Michael Keyser, Jurgen Barth and Sylvain Garant, in 13th place. Rounding off the season in Europe, before the finale at Watkins Glen, was the Austrian 1,000 Kms at the Osterreichring where factory test driver Gunther Steckkonig and rallyman Bjorn Waldegaard finished 10th. They were lifted out of the GT class, however, as they had some non-homologated aerodynamic features which gave a hint of the next great Porsche: the RS 2.7 Carrera.

Winner GT Targa Florio 1970: Libero Marchiolo, Antonio de Castro

RALLIES TO RACES   49

TURBOS MACHEN DRUCK

Winner Targa Florio 1973: Gijs van Lennep, Herbert Müller

Weil sich die Ära des 917 dem Ende zuneigte und weil die Entwicklungsarbeiten für den 917-10 und den 917-30 für die Can-Am-Serie abgeschlossen waren, widmete sich Porsche Ende 1972 wieder verstärkt der Weiterentwicklung des 911. Man vertraute weiterhin auf den bewährten luftgekühlten Sechszylindermotor mit zwei großen Ventilen pro Zylinder. Dadurch konnte Porsche nicht mithalten mit der neuesten Generation von Dreiliter-Prototypen wie der Matra V12, der Alfa Romeo V8 und Zwölfzylinder und die Autos von Lola und Mirage, die von einem Ford-Cosworth-V8-Motor angetrieben wurden. Dazu hätte man einen völlig neuen Dreilitermotor konstruieren müssen, womöglich sogar mit Wasserkühlung und Vierventil-Technik, und man hätte es mit jenen Firmen aufnehmen müssen, die direkt im Grand-Prix-Sport involviert waren.

Dr. Ernst Fuhrmann, der 1971 zum offiziellen Sprecher des Vorstandes benannt wurde, entschied sich zur Konzentration auf das Produktionsmodell, also den 911. Eine weise Entscheidung, wie sich heraus stellte. Norbert Singer, ein 33-jähriger Ingenieur mit Spezialisierung auf Aerodynamik, war fortan verantwortlich für die Entwicklung des 911 für den Rennsport. Seine neue Aufgabe kam gleichzeitig mit der Vorstellung des Carrera RS mit 2,7-Litermotor.

Die FIA hatte für 1973 eine Europameisterschaft für GT-Fahrzeuge ausgeschrieben, in der Autos, wie der Ferrari 365 GTB 'Daytona' und der De Tomaso Pantera, startberechtigt waren. Der Chevrolet Corvette und der Ford Mustang konnten auch fahren, sollten die Amerikaner Interesse zeigen, und freilich der allgegenwärtige Elfer, der in der Klasse bis 2500 ccm eingestuft wurde, weil der Hubraum des Produktionsmodell 2,4 Liter betrug.

Der neue Carrera RS 2.7, der Ende 1972 angekündigt wurde, entwickelte sich schnell zu einem der beliebtesten GT-Autos auf dem Markt, er wurde quasi über Nacht zum Klassiker. Der luftgekühlte Reihen-Sechszylinder war weitgehend neu. Der Motor hatte ein neues Kurbelgehäuse aus Aluminium statt aus Magnesium. Am hinteren Ende der Kurbelwelle wurde ein Dämpfer montiert, so dass die Welle kaum noch brechen konnte. Auf der Oberfläche wurden zusätzliche Rillen angebracht. Der Motor war zehn Kilo schwerer als der des 2.4, aber auch viel stärker. Die Bohrung wurde von 84 auf 90 mm vergrößert, während der Hub mit 70,4 mm unverändert blieb, der Motor leistete 210 PS.

Der Carrera RS war der erste Porsche mit einem Spoiler und einem Flügel auf der Heckklappe. Diese reduzierten den Auftrieb an der Hinterachse um 75 Prozent.

Obwohl er größere Räder und Bremsen hatte, wurde das Gewicht des Carrera RS 2.7 auf 900 kg reduziert, gegenüber 975 kg für den 911S. Diese Reduzierung war das Ergebnis von einfacher Verkleidung im Innenraum, weniger Schallisolation, der Anwendung von dünnerem Glas für die Frontscheibe, Glasfaser für die Stoßstangen und einem dünneren Stahl für die nichttragenden Karrosserieteile.

Für die Zulassung in der Gruppe 4 GT-Klasse musste der Carrera RS 2.7 in einer Stückzahl von mindestens 500 angefertigt werden. Weitere 55 Exemplare wurden nach RSR (Racing)-Spezifikation aufgebaut. Bei diesen Modellen wurde die Bohrung auf 92 mm erhöht, was den Hubraum auf 2808 ccm ansteigen ließ. Die Nockenwellen drehten sich in vier Lagern statt in drei. Eine mechanische Bosch-Einspritzung kam anstelle des K-Jetronic und der Diameter der Einlass- und Auspuffventile wurde vergrößert.

Durch diese Maßnahmen stieg die Motorleistung auf 310 PS oder 110 PS pro Liter an; ein hervorragender Wert für ein luftgekühltes Triebwerk mit großen Ventilen. Die Radkästen wurden um 5 cm vergrößert, so dass breitere Räder montiert werden konnten: 9 Zoll vorne und 11 Zoll hinten.

Außerdem wurden die belüfteten Bremsscheiben des 917 montiert, zusammen mit doppeltem Hauptbremszylinder und einem Bremskraftverteiler der vom Fahrer eingestellt werden konnte. Ebenso wurden ein größerer Spoiler vorne mit eingebautem Ölkühler und ein größerer Heckflügel montiert. Letzerer erzeugte bei einer Geschwindigkeit von 240 km/h einen Abtrieb von 27 kg.

Techniker Singer erlebte Oktober 1972 auf Korsika seine erste Rallye mit den Fahrern Gérard Larrousse und Bjorn Waldegard und zwei Mechanikern. Die neuen Carrera RSR waren nicht sehr erfolgreich: Waldegard hatte einen Unfall und Larrousse verlor viel Zeit wegen einer gebrochenen Antriebswelle. Von Korsika aus reiste das kleine Team direkt zur Rennstrecke in Paul Ricard, um das Auto weiter zu entwickeln. Es war ihr erster Test auf dieser Strecke.

Winner GT 1000 km Dijon 1973: Herbert Müller, Gijs van Lennep

TURBO ERA DAWNS

With the 917 era receding into history, and all the hard work completed on developing the 917-10 and 917-30 Can-Am cars, Porsche turned its attention to further development on the 911 model towards the end of 1972.

Relying on its trusty air-cooled flat-six engine, with two large valves per cylinder, Porsche could not compete with the new breed of 3-litre prototype cars, the Matra V12, the Alfa Romeo V8 and flat-12, and the Lola and Mirage powered by the Ford Cosworth V8 engine. To do so would involve the design of an entirely new 3-litre engine, perhaps with water cooling and four valves per cylinder, and entering a power race with companies directly involved in Grand Prix racing.

Dr Ernst Fuhrmann, appointed Spokesman for the Board in 1971, decided to focus the company's attention on the production model, the 911, an inspired choice as it turned out. Norbert Singer, a 33-year-old engineer specialising in aerodynamics, was put in charge of 911 development for competitions, an appointment that coincided with the launch of the 2.7 litre Carrera RS.

The FIA had decided to start a European Championship for GT cars in 1973 catering for such exciting cars as the Ferrari 365 GTB 'Daytona' and the De Tomaso Pantera. The Chevrolet Corvette and the Ford Mustang were eligible if the Americans cared to join the party, and of course the ubiquitous Porsche 911, which was limited to the up to 2,500 cc class, because the production engine capacity was 2.4 litres. The new Carrera RS 2.7, which was announced late in 1972, immediately because one of the most sought-after GT cars on the market, an "instant classic". The air cooled, flat-six engine was largely new, in particular having a new crankcase which reverted to aluminium alloy instead of magnesium. A damper was fitted to the rear of the crankshaft which virtually eliminated the possibility of breakage.

It had extra ribbing and was approximately 10 kg heavier than the 2.4 but much stronger, and it allowed the bore dimension to increase from 84 to 90mm, while the stroke remained at 70.4mm. The liners were made of Nikasil instead of Biral, and the power output was 210 bhp. The Carrera RS was the first Porsche to feature an air dam and a 'ducktail' wing on the engine cover, which reduced by 75 per cent the aerodynamic lift over the rear wheels.

Despite having bigger wheels and brakes, the Carrera RS 2.7 was down to 900 kg in weight, compared with 995 kg for the 911S, with simplified interior trim, the reduction or absence of sound-proofing, the use of thinner Glaverbel glass for the windscreen, glass-fibre for the bumpers, and thinner gauge steel for the unstressed panels.

1000 km Nürburgring 1973: Bengt Ekberg, Kurt Simonsen

"Der Umbau von Larrousses Auto für die Rennstrecke kostete uns einen Tag", erinnert sich Singer. "Das Fahrwerk wurde tiefer gelegt, es wurden breitere Kotflügel und breitere Räder montiert und so weiter. Wir hatten nicht viel Werkzeug im Lkw mit dabei, wir bauten das Auto einfach selber um. Wir testeten auf der langen Strecke, und das Auto fuhr Rundenzeiten von 2.13 oder 2.14 min. Dieter Glotzbach, der Dunlop-Reifentechniker, ein guter Freund von mir, sagte jedoch, dass die Ford Capri 2.10 min. fuhren."

"Ich hatte Angst, dass der Porsche drei oder vier Sekunden zu langsam war. Vielleicht sollten wir besser gehen, das Fahrwerk verbessern, mehr Leistung suchen. Aber zum Schluß fand Glotzbach drei weitere Reifensätze, und das Auto fuhr auf Anhieb 2.09 min. Ich fragte ihn, was passiert war. Er sagte, dass Ford genau diese Reifen benutzt hatte, als sie 2.10 min. fuhren. Damit war ich zufrieden."

Ein wichtiges Ergebnis aus diesem Test, der im Dezember mit Herbert Müller, Gijs van Lennep und Mark Donohue wiederholt wurde, war die höhere Anordnung der vorderen Achsschenkel an den Federbeinen. So konnte das Auto tiefer gelegt werden, während nach wie vor der volle Federweg zur Verfügung stand. In den Federbeinen wurden Schraubfedern montiert. Zusammen mit den ursprünglichen Drehstäben waren diese Hauptbestandteil der Aufhängung.

Daraufhin baute Porsche die ersten zwei Carrera RSR nach Gruppe 4-Reglement, mit breiteren Rädern und Kotflügeln, für den Einsatz beim 24 Stunden-Rennen von Daytona. Der Carrera von Roger Penske wurde von Mark Donohue und George Follmer gefahren. Sie schieden mit einem abgerissenen Schwungrad aus. Der Brumos-Racing-Carrera mit Peter Gregg und Hurley Haywood feierte dafür einen historischen Sieg.

Zugegebenermaßen waren alle Dreiliter-Prototypen ausgeschieden, aber nur wenige Monate später gewannen die gleichen Fahrer mit dem selben Auto auch die 12 Stunden von Sebring. Damit stellten sie eindeutig unter Beweis, dass der 911 von nun an ein potenzieller Rennsieger war. Je länger die Rennen, desto besser.

1000 km Nürburgring 1973: Herbert Müller, Gijs van Lennep

Die 55 RSR wurden schnell verkauft. Unter den namhaften Kunden waren Kremer Racing, Georg Loos, die Privatfahrer Claude Ballot-Lena und Claude Haldi und das Schweizer Haberthur-Team. Sie waren alle stark in den neun Rennen zur GT-Europameisterschaft, die meistens über eine Distanz von 500 Kilometern gingen. Auch in der Marken-WM, deren Rennen normalerweise über 1000 Kilometer gingen, waren die Porsche-Teams erfolgreich.

Die GT-Europameisterschaft startete mit zwei Läufen auf dem Nürburgring. Am Samstag und am Sonntag fand jeweils ein Rennen statt. John Fitzpatrick überdrehte den Motor seines Kremer Racing-RSR, und so ging der Sieg im ersten Lauf an Claude-Ballot Lena, der am Sonntag Platz zwei hinter Fitzpatrick belegte.

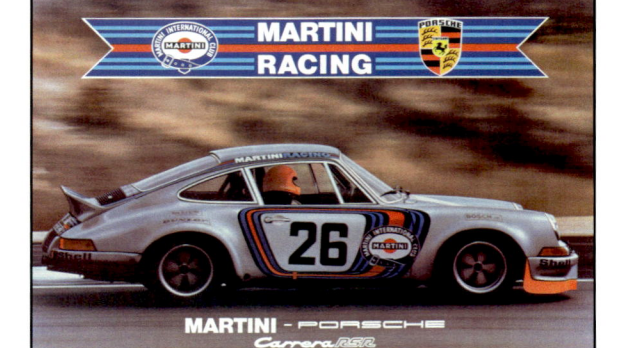

Ballot-Lena siegte erneut in Montlhéry, wo er Schickentanz auf dem Kremer Racing-Porsche schlug. Danach reiste die GT-Szene nach Imola, wo die Teams einen Schrecken erlebten, als Mike Parkes auf einem De Tomaso Pantera beide Läufe gewann, jeweils vor Schickentanz und Ballot-Lena.

Schickentanz gewann in Nivelles, auf der Strecke südlich von Brüssel. In Estoril kopierte Kremer erstmals das Martini Porsche-Werksteam, indem man Motoren mit einer Bohrung von 85 mm und einem Hubraum von 2993 ccm einsetzte.

Die Motorleistung änderte sich nur wenig, zu 315 PS (später in der Saison sorgte die Anwendung von Gasschiebern anstelle von Drosselklappen für eine Zunahme bis 330 PS). Dafür gab es aber mehr Drehmoment, und in der Meisterschaft mit einer solchen Leistungsdichte war dieser Unterschied entscheidend. Paul Keller gewann für das Kremer-Team den ersten Lauf in Estoril, Schickentanz siegte im zweiten Rennen.

Clay Regazzoni machte Porsche in Hockenheim einen Strich durch die Rechnung, indem er im De Tomaso Pantera, der vorher von Mike Parkes gefahren wurde, beide Rennen vor Schickentanz, Haldi und "Ballot" gewann.

Für den nächsten Lauf, das 6 Stunden-Rennen von Monza, wurden jeweils zwei Fahrer gebraucht. Schickentanz und Paul Keller siegten vor Erwin Kremer und Jürgen Neuhaus.

Poster

Poster

Poster

At least 500 examples had to be made to have the Carrera RS 2.7 homologated into the Group 4 GT category, and a further 55 were made to RSR (racing) specification. For these, the bore was further increased to 92mm, raising the capacity to 2,808cc. The camshafts ran in four bearings, instead of three, Bosch mechanical injection replaced K-Jetronic, and the inlet and exhaust valves were increased in diameter. The effect of this was to raise the power to 310 bhp, or 110 bhp per litre, an outstandingly high output for a big-valve, air cooled motor. The wheel arches were extended by 5cm so that wider wheels could be fitted, 9-inch wide rims at the front, 11-inch rims at the rear.

The 917's ventilated and cross-drilled brakes were adopted, complete with twin master cylinders and a driver-operated balance bar. A deeper air dam at the front, with a built-in oil cooler, was matched by a larger wing at the rear, inducing 27kg of downforce at a speed of 240 km/h.

Ing. Singer attended his first rally, in Corsica, in October 1972 with drivers Gerard Larrousse and Bjorn Waldegard and two mechanics. The new Carrera 2.7 RSRs did not fare well, Waldegaard having an accident and Larrousse delayed by a broken driveshaft, but straight from there the small team went to the Paul Ricard circuit (their first visit to the track) to carry out some development work.

"It took us a day to convert Larrousse's car to race trim" Singer recalls "with lowered suspension, wider fenders, wider wheels and so on. We did not have a lot of equipment in the truck, we modified the car ourselves. We tested on the long circuit and the car was doing 2:13s, 2:14s, but Dieter Glotzbach, the Dunlop engineer who is a good friend of mine, told me that the Ford Capris would run at 2m 10s.

"I was afraid that the Porsche was too slow by three or four seconds, we would have to go away and improve the suspension, find some more power, but right at the end Glotzbach produced three more sets of tyres and straight away the car would run at 2:09. I asked him, what happened? And he explained that these were the tyres that Ford used when they did 2:10, so I was happy."

A key development to come out of this test, which was repeated in December with Herbert Muller, Gijs van Lennep and Mark Donohue present, was to reposition the front stub axles higher on the struts in order to lower the car while still allowing full suspension travel. Coil springs were incorporated in the damper struts, becoming the principal method of suspension supplemented by the original torsion bars.

Porsche then built the first two Carrera RSRs to Group 4 specification, with wider wheels and fenders, to compete in the Daytona 24-Hours. Roger Penske's Carrera was driven by Mark Donohue and George Follmer, who had to retire with a loose flywheel, while the Brumos Racing example went on to record an historic victory in the hands of Peter Gregg and Hurley Haywood.

All the 3-litre prototypes had broken down, it had to be admitted, but a couple of months later the same drivers, with the same car, won the Sebring 12-Hours, reinforcing the message that Porsche's 911 was now a potential race winner. The longer the event, the better.

The 55 RSRs were soon sold, leading customers including Kremer Racing, Georg Loos, privateers Claude Ballot-Lena and Claude Haldi, and the Swiss Haberthur team, all of whom competed strongly in the nine-race European GT Championship, most of the races of 500 kilometre distance, and in the World Championship for Manufacturers which generally extended to 1,000 Kilometres.

The nine-round European GT contest began at the Nurburgring with two heats, one on Saturday and the other on Sunday afternoon. John Fitzpatrick over-revved the engine of his Kremer RSR and the first event was won by Claude Ballot-Lena, who finished second to Fitzpatrick in the Sunday race. "Ballot" won again at Montlhery, beating Clemens Schickentanz in the Kremer Racing Porsche, and the European GT circus then moved to Imola where the regular teams had a rude shock, as Mike Parkes won both heats in a de Tomaso Pantera, each time beating Schickentanz and Ballot-Lena.

Schickentanz won both heats at Nivelles, the featureless circuit south of Brussels, from Ballot-Lena, then at Estoril the Kremer Racing team was the first to copy the Martini Porsche factory team in the World Championship, running engines with an 85mm more and a capacity of 2,993 cc.

The power output was little changed, at 315 bhp (later in the season, the output rose to 330 bhp with the adoption of throttle slides instead of butterflies), but more torque was available, and the difference was decisive in this competitive championship. Paul Keller won the first heat at Estoril for the Kremer team, Schickentanz the second.

1000 km Nürburgring 1973: Georg Loos, Jürgen Barth

TURBO ERA DAWNS

1000 km Dijon 1973: John Fitzpatrick, Paul Keller

Ballot-Lena war nur Fünfter, und sein Ergebnis galt als Streichresultat für die Meisterschaft. So kam Schickentanz mit einem knappen Vorsprung an die Spitze der Tabelle und später wurde der deutsche Fahrer als erster Europäischer GT-Meister in der Fahrerwertung gekürt. Er startete nicht bei der Tour de France, während das Auto von Ballot-Lena, das zum größten Teil geführt hatte, vorzeitig ausfiel. So gewann ein Lancia Stratos vor einem Porsche Carrera, gefahren von Jacques Almeras und Jochen Mass. Schickentanz gewann auch den Porsche Cup mit einem privat eingesetzen Auto.

Das Porsche-Werksteam blieb der GT-Europameisterschaft fern, da diese Serie für Kundenteams ins Leben gerufen worden war. Martini & Rossi war Hauptsponsor des Werksteams, mit van Lennep und Herbert Müller als Fahrer. Die Saison startete verhalten, mit Platz neun im Gesamtklassement und einem Sieg in der GT-Klasse für Müller und van Lennep im 1000 km-Rennen von Dijon. Fitzpatrick und Keller kamen im Kremer-RSR auf Gesamtrang zehn ins Ziel, ein Platz vor den Schweizern Bernard Chenevière und Peter Zbinden. Claude Haldi wurde auf einem vom Schweizer Porsche-Händler Haberthur genannten Porsche 908/3 Achter.

Nach Dijon ging es nach Monza, wo die technischen Kommissare sich gegen das Martini & Rossi Carrera-Werksteam quer stellten. Sie beanstandeten eine Änderung an den Lagern der Hinterradaufhängung der beiden Fahrzeuge. Die ganze Aufhängung wurde am RSR vorher geändert, so dass die breiteren Hinterräder Platz hatten.

Ohne großen Worte zog Singer die Autos aus der Gruppe 4 zurück und schrieb sie in der Gruppe 5 bei den Prototypen ein. Gleichzeitig, quasi über Nacht, änderte er die Form des Heckflügels vom „Entenschwanz" zu einer viel breiteren Ausführung, die mehr Abtrieb gab.

Der Grund war zweierlei. Erstens wollte Porsche nicht gegen seine Kundenteams antreten, und man war froh, dass man die Gruppe 4 verlassen konnte. Zweitens gab die Gruppe 5 selbstverständlich viel mehr Freiraum für Experimente. „Wir wollten für die Autos in Martini-Farben mehr Möglichkeiten zur Weiterentwicklung haben", sagt Techniker Singer. „Wir machten uns ständig Sorgen: Ist dieses erlaubt? Ist jenes zugelassen? Mit einem Prototypen kann man machen, was man will." Keiner der beiden Martini-Porsche kam in Monza ins Ziel. Beide Autos fielen mit verbrannten Kolben aus. So belegten Kremer und Schickentanz den achten Gesamtplatz, vor Chenevière und Zbinden.

Für Spa entwickelte das Werk einen Dreilitermotor, der 315 PS leistete. Außerdem kamen 14 Zoll breite Hinterräder mit Zentralverschluß und Radnaben aus Titanium zum Einsatz. Natürlich wurden die Kotflügel entsprechend verbreitert. Die einstellbaren Federn wurden aus Titanium angefertigt. Die hinteren Schräglenker aus gegossenem Aluminium waren leichter und steifer als die herkömmlichen Lenker aus Stahl. Diese Komponenten aus Aluminium wurden 1974 auch für die Serienfahrzeuge des 911 übernommen.

Der 911 Carrera RSR sah nun völlig anders aus, mit Türen und Scheiben aus Kunststoff, was das Gesamtgewicht auf 850 kg senkte. Obwohl es nie den Speed der Matra, Ferrari und Gulf-Prototypen mitgehen konnte, erreichte das Auto immer gute Ergebnisse. In Spa zum Beispiel belegten van Lennep und Müller den fünften Gesamtrang im Rennen, das von Derek Bell und Mike Hailwood im Gulf-Mirage gewonnen wurde. Der nächste 911, ein Gruppe 4-Auto von Reinhold Joest, ebenfalls mit Dreilitermotor, kam mit Joest und Follmer auf Rang zehn ins Ziel.

Die 57. Targa Florio auf Sizilien stand dann auf dem Programm. Müller und van Lennep führten das Werksteam an, wie üblich mit einem weiteren Gruppe 5-Auto zur Unterstützung für Leo Kinnunen, den ehemaligen Werksfahrer und Halter des Streckenrekordes auf der „Madonie", zusammen mit Claude Haldi. Ein Gruppe 4-Auto mit 2,8 Litermotor wurde für Günther Steckkönig, den Testfahrer von Porsche und Baron Giulio Pucci eingeschrieben. Letzterer war der jüngere Sohn von Baron Antonio Pucci, der das Rennen neun Jahre zuvor auf einem 904 gewonnen hatte.

Er konnte die Erfolgstradition der Familie jedoch nicht fortsetzen, denn der junge Giulio verlor bei einer Testfahrt vor der Veranstaltung die Kontrolle über seinen Porsche und fuhr in der Hauptstraße von Campofelice einen Baum um. Sein RSR hatte danach die Form einer Banane, zum Glück passierte der Aufprall an der Beifahrerseite. Porsche verzieh ihm nicht nur, für das Rennen wurde sogar ein Ersatzauto bereitgestellt. Zusammen mit Steckkönig belegte er den sechsten Gesamtrang.

Das Matra-Team wollte seine Autos auf Sizilien nicht riskieren und blieb dem Rennen deshalb fern. So ruhten die Erwartungen auf den Werksteams von Ferrari und Alfa Romeo. Tatsächlich waren sie pro Runde fast drei Minuten schneller, aber ihr Aufgebot wurde bald dezimiert. Clay Regazzoni hatte im offiziellen Training einen massiven Abflug in einem der Zwölfzylinder-Alfa Romeo. Das Auto rollte einen Hang hinunter, Regazzoni blieb unverletzt. Der andere Alfa, mit Rolf Stommelen am Lenkrad, führte in den ersten drei Runden, aber Andrea de Adamich hatte auf seiner ersten Runde nach dem Fahrerwechsel einen Abflug und wurde danach nicht mehr gesichtet.

Arturo Merzarios Ferrari 312PB fiel mit Getriebeschaden in der dritten Runde aus, eine verspätete Folge eines Reifenschadens an der Hinterachse in Runde eins. Die Ferrari-Mannschaft war sehr enttäuscht, als Jacky Ickx auf einen Felsen prallte, der plötzlich auf der Idealline lag, und dann bei Collesano in die Leitplanke krachte. Damit war auch für ihn das Rennen beendet.

Nach der vierten von elf Runden hatte Herbert Müller einen beruhigenden Vorsprung, als er das Auto an van Lennep übergab. So setzten sie sich ab vom Lancia Stratos mit Sandro Munari und Claude Andruet. Im Ziel hatte der siegreiche

1000 km Dijon 1973: Bernard Cheneviere, Peter Zbinden

TURBOS MACHEN DRUCK

Start 1000 km Nürburgring 1973: George Follmer, Willy Kaushen (66)

Clay Regazzoni threw a spanner in Porsche's works at Hockenheim, winning both heats in the de Tomaso Pantera previously driven by Mike Parkes ahead of Schickentanz, Haldi and "Ballot".

Two drivers were needed for the next round, the Monza 6-Hours, which was won by Schickentanz and Paul Keller ahead of Erwin Kremer and Juergen Neuhaus.

Ballot-Lena was back in fifth place and had to drop his points, putting Schickentanz ahead by a narrow margin, and the German driver was later confirmed as the first European GT Champion driver. He did not contest the Tour de France and Ballot-Lena's car broke down, after leading for much of the distance, leaving victory to a Lancia Stratos ahead of a Porsche Carrera driven by Jacques Almeras and Jochen Mass. Schickentanz also won the Porsche Cup, for the best performances of the season in a privately run car.

Porsche's factory team kept well out of the European GT Championship, which was intended for customers, and had Martini & Rossi to sponsor the official team led by van Lennep and Herbert Muller. The season began quietly with Muller and van Lennep racing to ninth place overall in the Dijon 1,000 Kms, first in GT, Fitzpatrick and Keller 10th in their Kremer Porsche Carrera RSR, and Swiss Bernard Cheneviere and Peter Zbinden 11th. Claude Haldi, incidentally, finished eighth in a Porsche 908/3 entered by Haberthur, the Swiss Porsche dealership.

From Dijon to Monza, where the scrutineers objected to the factory's two-car Martini & Rossi Carrera team, pointing out a discrepancy on the rear suspension bearings, the whole suspension having been changed on the RSR to cater for the wider rear wheels.

With no further ado, Ing. Singer took his cars out of the Group 4 category and moved them into Group 5, with the Prototypes. At the same time, overnight in fact, he changed the shape of the rear wing from "ducktail" (burzel) to a much wider shape which gave more downforce, the prototype of the so-called "tea tray".

The reasoning was two-fold. Porsche did not want to compete against their customers, and were happy to leave Group 4 alone. Secondly, of course, Group 5 gave them far more freedom to experiment. "The idea was to have more room for development with the Martini sponsored cars" says Ing. Singer. "We were thinking, 'is this allowed?' 'Is this homologated?' As a Prototype, you can do anything you like."

Neither Martini Porsche finished at Monza, as it happened. Both cars suffered burned pistons, leaving Kremer and Schickentanz to finish eighth overall ahead of Cheneviere and Zbinden.

The factory's development for Spa was the full 3-litre engine, developing 315 bhp, and the installation of 14-inch wide rear rims (centre locking, on titanium hubs) with suitably widened fenders. The variable rate springs were changed to titanium, and the rear semi-trailing arms were made of cast aluminium, lighter and stiffer than the fabricated steel arms, and the aluminium components were adopted for the 911 production line cars in 1974.

1000 km Nürburgring 1973: Eberhard Sindel, Wilhelm Siegle

TURBO ERA DAWNS

Porsche einen Vorsprung von sechs Minuten auf dem Lancia. Kinnunen und Haldi belegten Rang drei, nachdem ihre beschädigte Hinterradaufhängung repariert worden war. Steckkönig und Pucci kamen auf Platz sechs ins Ziel.

Mit zwei Gesamtsiegen war Porsche nun auf Rang drei in der WM mit 62 Punkten, zwei Punkte hinter Matra und 13 Zähler hinter Ferrari.

Matra erlebte eine Katastrophe mit zwei Motorschäden auf dem Nürburgring, so dass Ferrari das 1000 km Rennen dominieren konnte. Haldi und Chenevière belegten Rang vier im Porsche 908/3, Müller und van Lennep kamen im Martini-RSR auf dem fünften Platz ins Ziel. So sicherte sich Porsche den zweiten Platz in der WM-Wertung mit 72 Punkten, hinter Ferrari, das 95 Punkte hatte.

Rang vier in Le Mans mit den Martini-RSR reichte problemlos für den Gewinn der Coupe d'Endurance, ein Pokal, der nach wie vor einen Ehrenplatz im Büro von Norbert Singer in Weissach hat. Er wurde überreicht für Leistungen in Spa, auf dem Nürburgring, bei der Targa Florio und in Le Mans. „Matra startete nicht bei der Targa Florio und Ferrari und sie nahmen sich gegenseitig die Punkte weg bei den restlichen Rennen. So sicherten wir uns den Pokal", so Singer.

Zwei Martini-Porsche bestritten den neunten Lauf der Weltmeisterschaft auf dem Österreichring. Das Rennen wurde dominiert von den Dreiliter-Prototypen. Die Porsche hatten ein neues Heck. Die Karrosserie hinter den Hinterrädern wurde angehoben, um Platz zu machen für einen größeren Heckflügel. Dieser gab mehr Abtrieb, während der Frontspoiler weiter nach innen gezogen wurde und sich um den Kotflügel wand. Im Frontbereich befanden sich ein größerer Luftkühler und Öffnungen für die Kühlung der Bremsen.

Müller und van Lennep belegten in Österreich Rang acht vor Helmuth Koinigg und Manfred Schurti. Es war erst Ende Juni, doch damit war bereits der europäische Teil der Weltmeisterschaft und auch der Werkseinsatz von Porsche beendet. Es blieb nur noch ein Rennen im Juli in Watkins Glen, wo die Teams von Penske und Brumos mit Gruppe 5-RSR die Porsche-Fahne hoch hielten. Hinter Prototypen belegten Mark Donohue und George Follmer den sechsten Platz, Gregg und Haywood kamen auf Rang sieben ins Ziel.

Turbo-Aufladung erwies sich auf Porsches Can-Am-Autos als sehr effektiv, und somit war das System, das auf Auspuffgas basierte, die logische Wahl für die von Martini & Rossi gesponserten Werksautos der Gruppe 5 für die Saison 1974. Hans Mezger war für die Motorentwicklung zuständig. Er war der Chefdenker, während Valentin Schäffer als Techniker die Theorie in die Praxis umsetzen musste.

Poster

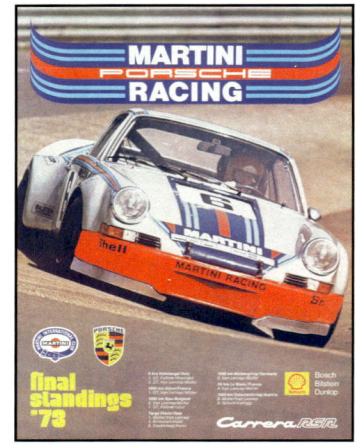

Poster

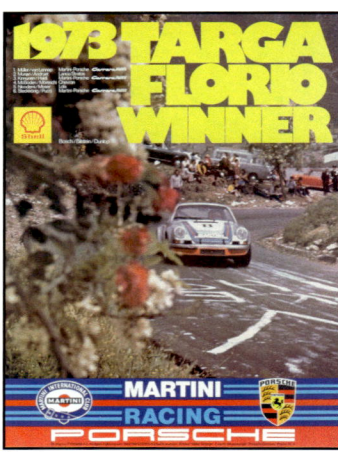

Poster

Es wurde erwartet, dass die FIA 1975 die Regeln für Langstreckenrennen ändern würde, um die Hersteller-WM zur Topklasse für Gruppe 5-Autos zu machen, abgeleitet von Produktionsmodellen, während die Gruppe 4 den Gran-Turismo-Fahrzeugen vorbehaten sein sollte. Später wurde die Gruppe 6 für offene Sport-Prototypen hinzugefügt. Porsche konnte auf die Entwicklung größerer Motoren verzichten, indem man die bestehenden Triebwerke mit Turbo-Aufladung versah. So wurde bei minimalem Hubraum maximale Leistung erzielt. Der Hubraum war wirklich minimal, weil die FIA einen Multiplikationsfaktor von 1,4 für aufgeladene Motoren ansetzte, sowohl mit mechanischem Kompressor als auch mit Turbolader. Wollte man also 1974 mit dem RSR Turbo in der Dreiliter-Sportwagenklasse fahren, so durfte der Hubraum nicht größer als 2143 ccm sein.

Das war genau der Hubraum des Turbomotors, den Porsche für den Einsatz vorbereitet hatte. Die Kurbelwelle des Zweiliters kam zum Einsatz, was zu einer Bohrung von 83 mm und einem Hub von 66 mm führte. Diese Abmessungen waren bekannt, aber jetzt in einer neuen Kombination. Sie führten zu einem Hubraum von 2142 ccm und einem rechnerischen Hubraum von 2999 ccm mit einem einzigen KKK Turbolader. Es wurde ein Luftkühler montiert, der die Temperatur der zusammengepressten Luft um 100 Grad reduzierte. Das Kühlgebläse wurde wie beim 917 waagerecht über dem Zylinderkopf angebracht. Der Inhalt des Ölbehälters wurde vergrößert, vom 908 wurde eine größere Ölpumpe übernommen.

Anfangs betrug die Motorleistung 480 PS bei einem Ladeluftdruck von 1,35 bar, aber nach Le Mans wurde der Druck auf 1,4 erhöht, was die Leistung auf 500 PS ansteigen ließ. Der Drehmoment betrug 460 Nm bei 7600 U/min. Für die Türen, Hauben und unbelasteten Karrosserieteile wurde ein leichter Kunststoff verwendet. Der Benzintank wurde von der Frontpartie in den Bereich des Rücksitzes gelegt, wo er näher am zentralen Schwerpunkt war. Aus Sicherheitsgründen musste der Tank jedoch in ein Gehäuse aus Stahl eingebaut werden, das mit der Karrosserie verschweisst wurde.

Die Frontpartie des 911 wurde steifer gemacht, die Aufhängung wurde geändert (die Federstäbe verschwanden komplett, Schraubfedern aus Titanium sorgten jetzt für die komplette Aufhängung), und das Gewicht der Rohkarosse sank massiv von 480 kg auf nur 409 kg.

1000 km Nürburgring 1973: Clemens Schickentanz, Paul Keller

1000 km Nürburgring 1973: Anton Fischhaber, Leopold von Bayern

The 911 Carrera RSR 'Martini' was now a very different looking car, with extensive use of plastic for doors and windows lowering the weight to 850 kg, and while it would never keep up with the Matra, Ferrari and Gulf prototypes, it was easily able to pick up good placings. At Spa, for instance, the race won by Derek Bell and Mike Hailwood in their Gulf-Mirage, van Lennep and Muller drove to fifth position overall. The next 911 along, a Group 4 car owned by Reinhold Joest, also with a 3-litre engine, finished 10th in the hands of Joest and George Follmer.

The best was yet to come, the 57th Targa Florio in Sicily. Muller and van Lennep led the team as usual backed by another Group 5 car for Leo Kinnunen, the former 'works' driver and Madonie lap record holder, with Claude Haldi, and a 2.8 litre Group 4 car for Gunther Steckkonig (the factory's test driver) and Baron Giulio Pucci, younger son of Baron Antonio Pucci who won the race nine years previously in a 904.

The family connection failed when young Giulio lost control of his Porsche during a pre-race test and felled a tree in the Campofelice high street, turning his RSR into a banana shape (passenger side, fortunately). Not only was he forgiven, but a T-car was prepared for the race and he drove with Steckkonig, to an eventual sixth place overall.

The Matra team was not prepared to dirty its cars in the Targa Florio, but the factory Ferrari and Alfa Romeo teams should have dominated, indeed they were nearly three minutes faster per lap, but their efforts were soon decimated. Clay Regazzoni had an enormous accident in one of the 12-cylinder Alfa Romeos during official practice, going end over end down a hillside, but was unhurt. The other Alfa, driven by Rolf Stommelen, led the first three laps, but Andrea de Adamich crashed on his 'out' lap and was not seen again.

Arturo Merzario's Ferrari 312PB retired with broken transmission on the third lap, a legacy of a punctured rear tyre on the opening lap, and then to the horror of the Ferrari team, Jacky Ickx hit a boulder that suddenly appeared on the racing line and hit a barrier at Collesano. He, too, was out.

Lap four, out of 11, and Herbert Muller had a healthy lead to hand over to van Lennep. These were professionals, their Porsche was made of stronger stuff, and they steadily drew away from the Lancia Stratos of Sandro Munari and Claude Andruet. In the end, the victorious Porsche had six minutes in hand over the Lancia. Kinnunen and Haldi were third, after having some rear suspension damage repaired, with Steckkonig and Pucci sixth.

At this point in the championship, and with two outright victories, Porsche lay third in the World Championship with 62 points, two points behind Matra and 13 behind Ferrari.

Matra had a disaster at the Nurburgring, with two engine failures, leaving Ferrari to dominate the 1,000 Kilometre race. Haldi and Cheneviere finished fourth in their Porsche 908/3, Muller and van Lennep fifth in their Martini Porsche RSR. Now Porsche moved into second place in the World Championship with 72 points, behind Ferrari on 95.

Fourth place at Le Mans for the Martini Porsche RSR was easily enough to earn the Coupe d'Endurance, a big trophy that still has pride of place in Ing. Singer's office at Weissach. It was awarded for performances at Spa, the Nurburgring, the Targa Florio and Le Mans. "Matra did not compete in the Targa Florio, and they and Ferrari took points off each other in the other races" says Singer. "The trophy was ours!"

Two Martini Porsches contested the ninth round of the World Championship at the Osterreichring, the event dominated by the 3-litre prototypes, and these had a new form of rear bodywork. The bodywork behind the rear wheels was elevated to support a swept back, larger rear wing, evidently giving greater down force, and the front air dam was made deeper and wrapped around the fenders, with a larger air cooler and bigger holes for brake ducting.

Muller and van Lennep finished eighth in Austria ahead of Helmuth Koinigg and Manfred Schurti. Although the month of June had another week to run, that was the end of the European end of the World Championship, and the conclusion of the Porsche factory effort.

1000 km Nürburgring 1974: Horst Godel, Dieter Franke

1000 km Österreichring 1974: Guillermo Rojas, Hector Rebaque

TURBO ERA DAWNS **57**

1000 km Nürburgring 1974: Horst Godel, Dieter Franke

750 km Paul Ricard 1974: Cyril Grandet, Guy Gentis

„Dr. Fuhrmann sagte, wir sollten Gewicht einsparen, indem wir eine neue Karosserie bauten", erinnert sich Norbert Singer. „Wir versuchten, die Karosserie leichter zu machen, indem wir sie in Säure eintauchten, aber es stellte sich heraus, dass dies sehr, sehr teuer war. Die Firma, die das machen sollte, hätte ein neues Bad bauen müssen, das groß genug war, um die Karosserie des 911 eintauchen zu können. Und die Flüssigkeit war so teuer, dass wir es so nicht machen konnten. Daher mussten wir ein spezielles Chassis bauen, bei dem wir einfach manches wegließen und leichtere Werkstoffe verwendeten." Dennoch konnte es der Gruppe 5-Porsche nicht gegen die Leichtbau-Prototypen aufnehmen, obwohl das Gewicht weiter auf 750 kg reduziert wurde. Er kam aber näher ran als der RSR 1973, der damals zwei überraschende Gesamtsiege einfuhr.

Die Ölkrise traf den Motorsport sehr hart, und alle Hersteller mussten ihre Programme neu überdenken. Ferrari zog sich komplett aus dem Langstreckensport zurück, um sich besser auf die Formel 1 konzentrieren zu können, aber Matra dominierte nach wie vor die Weltmeisterschaft mit Konkurrenz von Alfa Romeo, die den 33TT12 immer weiter entwickelte.

Daytona und Sebring, die traditionellen Rennen zur Eröffnung der Saison, wurden abgesagt, so dass die Weltmeisterschaft für Hersteller am 25. April in Monza begann, fast neun Monate nach dem Ende der Saison 1973. Beide Matra fielen mit Schäden an den V12-Triebwerken aus und die Alfa Romeo, angetrieben von Reihen-Zwölfzylindern, belegten auf ihrer Heimstrecke die ersten drei Plätze. Mario Andretti und Arturo Merzario sahen nach 1000 Kilometern als Erste die Zielflagge. Gijs van Lennep und Herbert Müller kamen im neuen 911 RSR Turbo auf Rang fünf ins Ziel, lediglich eine Runde hinter dem drittplatzierten Alfa und Derek Bells Gulf-Mirage. John Fitzpatrick, Georg Loos und Jürgen Neuhaus sicherten sich Rang neun im Gelo Racing-RSR und feierten den Klassensieg in der Gruppe 4.

Nur zehn Tage später fand in Belgien das 1000 km-Rennen von Spa statt, das von Jacky Ickx und Jean-Pierre Jarier auf Matra gewonnen wurde. Autodelta zog die Einschreibung des Alfa-Romeo-Teams wegen mangelnder Zeit zur Vorbereitung zurück. So belegten Bell und Mike Hailwood im Gulf-Mirage den zweiten Platz, während van Lennep und Müller im 911 RSR Turbo auf Rang drei ins Ziel fuhren.

Ein Podiumsplatz war ein gutes Ergebnis für das Werksteam. Diesmal folgten Fitzpatrick und Jürgen Barth direkt dahinter im Gelo Racing Porsche, vor Clemens Schickentanz und Willi Kauhsen im Kremer-Porsche.

Auf dem Nürburgring belegten Sport-Prototypen die ersten fünf Plätze. Diesmal folgten die zwei Martini 911 RSR Turbo den offenen Autos, Müller und van Lennep vor Helmut Koinigg und Manfred Schurti. Zuverlässigkeit war - wie schon 1973 - die Stärke des Werksteams und das System der Turbo-Auflandung entwickelte sich prächtig.

Das Ergebnis in Le Mans, Platz zwei in der Gesamtwertung, war ein erneuter Beweis für Porsches Turbo-Aufladung. Nach Le Mans ging die WM auf dem Österreichring weiter mit einem Schlagabtausch zwischen Matra, Alfa Romeo und Gulf-Mirage.

So blieben für Martini-Porsche nur noch die Ehrenplätze hinter fünf Sport-Prototypen. Van Lennep und Müller kamen auf Platz sechs ins Ziel. Paul Keller, Hans Heyer und Reine Wisell fuhren zwei Kremer-RSR im 6 Stunden-Rennen und belegten die Plätze neun und zehn in der Gesamtwertung.

Zu der Zeit war Porsche Zweiter hinter Matra-Simca in der WM-Wertung mit 70 Punkten, fünf mehr als Alfa Romeo. Die italienische Mannschaft um Technikchef Carlo Chiti war enttäuscht aufgrund mangelnder Zuverlässigkeit und zog sich zurück, um sich auf die Saison 1975 vorbereiten zu können.

58 TURBOS MACHEN DRUCK

One more event remained, at Watkins Glen in July, where the Penske and Brumos teams upheld Porsche's honour with full-specification Group 5 RSRs shipped out from Weissach. Mark Donohue and George Follmer were placed sixth, behind open prototypes, Gregg and Haywood seventh.

Turbocharging was working very well on Porsche's Can-Am cars, and the exhaust driven system was an obvious choice for the factory's Martini & Rossi sponsored Group 5 cars in 1974. Hans Mezger was in charge of engine design, the guru, and Valentin Schaeffer was the chief engineer, the man who put theory into practice.

The FIA was expected to rewrite the rules for endurance racing in 1975, making the World Championship for Manufacturers the top series for Group 5 cars, derived from the production line, and Group 4 for series Grand Touring machines. Only later was the Group 6 category added on, for open sports-prototypes.

Porsche, clearly, could avoid the need to develop larger engines by turbocharging existing units, extracting the maximum power from the minimum capacity. Minimum it was, too, as the FIA applied a multiplication factor of 1.4 for engines with forced induction, whether supercharging or turbo charging, which meant that if the Porsche RSR Turbo was to compete in the 3-litre sportscar formula in 1974, the volumetric capacity could not exceed 2,143 cc.

That was precisely the capacity of the turbocharged engine prepared by Porsche for the 1974 programme, using the crankshaft from the 2-litre engine, giving a stroke of 66mm, and a bore of 83mm. These were familiar dimensions in a new combination, yielding a capacity of 2,142cc and a calculated 2,999cc with a single KKK turbocharger applied.

An induction air cooler was fitted, air cooled, lowering the temperature of the compressed air by 100-degrees C, and the cooling fan was arranged horizontally over the flat-six, in the style of the 917's cooling fan. The oil capacity was increased, too, with a larger pump from the 908 model.

Initially, with a boost pressure of 1.35 bar, the power output was rated at 480 bhp, but after Le Mans this was lifted to 1.4 bar boost and 500 bhp. The initial torque figure was 46 mkg at 7,600 rpm. Further use was made of lightweight plastics for doors, lids and unstressed body panels, and the fuel tank

1000 km Nürburgring 1974: Bernard Cheneviere, Peter Zbinden

was moved from the front compartment to the rear seat area where it was close to the centre of gravity. However it had to be shielded by sheet steel, welded to the body, for safety reasons. The front end of the 911 was stiffened, the suspension modified (the torsion bars were eliminated altogether, titanium coil springs being the only method of suspension), and the weight of the 'body in white' was massively reduced from 480 kg to just 409 kg.

"Doctor Fuhrmann said we should save weight by making a new body shell" recalls Ing. Singer. "We investigated making the body lighter by dipping it in acid, but we found that this would be very, very expensive. The company that would do it would have to make a new vat big enough to take the 911 body shell. And the liquid was so expensive that we could not do it, so we had to make a special chassis by cutting things out and using lighter materials."

Still the Group 5 Porsche could not compete with the lightweight prototypes, despite being further lightened to 750 kg, but it was closer than the RSR had been in 1973, when two surprise victories were achieved.

The oil crisis hit motor sports very hard, and all the manufacturers were forced to review their programmes. Ferrari withdrew from endurance racing completely, better to concentrate on Formula One, but Matra continued to dominate the World Championship with competition from Alfa Romeo, still developing the 33TT12.

Daytona and Sebring, the traditional season-openers, were cancelled, so the World Championship for Manufacturers opened at Monza on April 25, almost nine months after the close of the 1973 season! Both Matras retired with broken V12 engines and the flat-12 powered Alfa Romeos claimed the top three positions on their 'home' circuit, with Mario Andretti and Merzario leading the way after 1,000 kilometres. Gijs van Lennep and Herbert Muller were placed fifth at the end in their new Porsche RSR Turbo, not disgraced as they finished one lap behind the third-placed Alfa and Derek Bell's Gulf Mirage. John Fitzpatrick, Georg Loos and Juergen Neuhaus finished ninth in the Gelo Racing Porsche RSR, winning the Group 4 category.

Just 10 days later the Spa 1,000 Kms was held in Belgium, and it was won by Jacky Ickx and Jean-Pierre Jarier in a Matra. Autodelta withdrew the Alfa Romeo team, citing lack of time for preparation, so the way was clear for Bell and Hailwood to finish second in their Mirage, on the lead lap, with van Lennep and Muller claiming third in their RSR Turbo.

A podium result was considered very good indeed for the

1000 km Nürburgring 1974: Herbert Müller, Gijs van Lennep

TURBO ERA DAWNS

Die FIA entschloss sich, die Einführung des neuen Reglements auf 1976 zu verschieben, was sämtliche Pläne im Hause Porsche durcheinander warf. Damit hatte das Team aus Weissach ein weiteres Jahr für die Vorbereitung der Fahrzeuge für die Gruppen 4 und 5, den 934 und den 935. Ein weiteres Jahr nach altem Reglement zu fahren, schien wenig Sinn zu machen.

Schließlich hatte Porsche bereits die bestmöglichen Ergebnisse erreicht: Platz zwei im Gesamtklassement in Le Mans und Watkins Glen sowie den dritten Gesamtrang in Spa. Sport-Prototypen belegten die Spitzenpositionen bei der neuen Veranstaltung in Paul Ricard sowie in Brands Hatch, während van Lennep und Müller in Frankreich Rang sieben und in Großbritannien Platz fünf heraus fuhren.

Das von Martini & Rossi unterstützte Werksteam hörte im September auf und verzichtete auf die Teilnahme am Rennen in Kyalami, das als Ersatz für Buenos Aires in den Kalender aufgenommen wurde. Man würde erst 1976 mit komplett neuen Autos wieder zurückkehren.

Die Entwicklung des 2,1 Liter-Turbomotors wurde im Heck der Porsche 908/3 fortgesetzt, die Spyder von Joest mit Unterstützung von Norbert Singer und von Dr. Dannesburger für van Lennep und Müller eingesetzt wurden.

Auf der Rennstrecke von Paul Ricard gewannen Rolf Stommelen und Tim Schenken die Gruppe 4 im Gelo Racing-RSR. Das Team von Georg Loos war auch in Brands Hatch und Kyalami erfolgreich.

John Fitzpatrick dominierte 1974 die GT-Europameisterschaft trotz seines Wechsels vom Kremer-Team zu Loos und dann wieder zurück zu Kremer. Er wurde auch der erste zweimalige Gewinner des Porsche Cups.

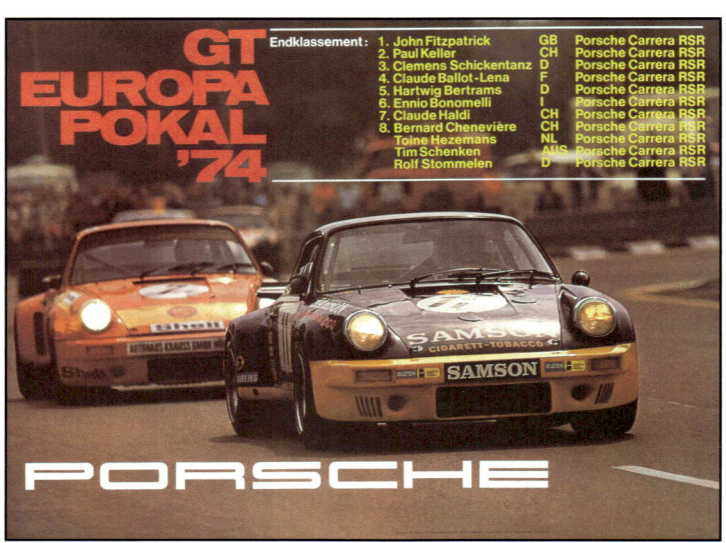

1000 km Nürburgring 1974: Herbert Müller, Gijs van Lennep

Der RSR von 1973 war ein hochentwickeltes Auto mit einem größeren Heckflügel und breiteren Hinterrädern, die ihm gegenüber den BMW 3.0 CLS und dem Ford Capri 3.0 einen Vorsprung verschafften. Fitzpatrick, der auf Ford Capri und Porsche Rennen fuhr, bevorzugte den 911 mit Abstand: "Er fährt sich viel besser", sagte er damals.

Fitzpatrick wurde von Kremer für das Fahren bezahlt, während Paul Keller dem Team zahlte, damit er das zweite Auto fahren durfte. Nach vier Rennen in der Weltmeisterschaft, der Europameisterschaft und der Deutschen Meisterschaft hatte der Brite jedoch keinen einzigen Punkt eingefahren, weshalb ihn Erwin Kremer entließ.

Zu allem Überfluss wechselte Fitzpatrick auch noch ins Lager des Immobilienmakler Georg Loos und er entwickelte sich bald zum regelmäßigen Sieger. Loos selber war jedoch ein ambitionierter Fahrer und er mochte es nicht, von seinen eigenen Teamkollegen geschlagen zu werden. So kam es, dass Fitzpatrick zur Saisonmitte zu Kremer zurückkehrte. Loos hatte es danach aber überraschenderweise satt, ständig von Fitzpatrick besiegt zu werden und holte ihn wieder zu sich, unter der Bedingung, dass Loos seine Karriere als Fahrer beenden und sich auf die Teamführung konzentrieren würde. „Danach war es viel besser", so Fitzpatrick. „Auch für die Saison 1975 blieb ich bei Loos."

Weil Fitzpatrick 1975 gleichzeitig für BMW Tourenwagenrennen fuhr, musste er einige Läufe der GT-Europameisterschaft auslassen. So ging der Titel an Hartwig Bertrams, der zusammen mit Schickentanz für das Tebernum-Team fuhr.

Fitzpatrick, Schenken und Toine Hezemans gingen für Loos an den Start, während Hans Heyer und Helmut Kelleners für Kremer fuhren. Letzteres Team hatte für seine RSR-Flotte spezielle Schrick-Nockenwellen anfertigen lassen, die die Motorleistung auf etwa 345 PS ansteigen ließen. Die Nocken hatten ein höheres Profil, aber die zusätzliche Leistung hatte ihre Auswirkung auf die Standfestigkeit: Die Motoren waren gut für kürzere Rennen, aber für 1000 km-Rennen waren sie nicht verlässlich.

Poster

1000 km Nürburgring 1974: Reinhardt Stenzel, Ove Andersson

factory team, this time with Fitzpatrick and Juergen Barth right behind in fourth place in the Gelo Racing Porsche, narrowly ahead of Clemens Schickentanz and Willi Kauhsen in a Kremer Racing Porsche.

Sports-prototypes claimed the top five positions at the Nurburgring and this time two Martini Porsche RSR turbos followed the open cars, Muller and van Lennep ahead of Helmut Koinigg and Manfred Schurti. As in 1973, reliability was the factory team's strong suit, and the system of turbo charging was developing in a very satisfactory manner.

The result of Le Mans, second place overall, was further proof of Porsche's system of turbo charging, told in another chapter, and from there the World Championship moved to the Osterreichring where there was a three-way battle between Matra, Alfa Romeo and Gulf Mirage.

That left Martini Porsche to pick up the pieces behind five sports-prototypes, van Lennep and Muller claiming sixth place. Paul Keller, Hans Heyer and Reine Wisell drove two Kremer Porsche RSRs in the 6-Hour race, which must have been a great feat of endurance, and picked up ninth and tenth positions overall!

At this point Martini Porsche lay second to Matra-Simca in the World Championship, with 70 points, five more than Alfa Romeo. The Italian team led by engineer Carlo Chiti became disillusioned with reliability problems and withdrew, to prepare better for the 1975 season.

The FIA decided at this point to delay the new regulations until 1976, an announcement that put all of Porsche's plans into disarray. It would give the Weissach team another year to prepare their Group 4 and Group 5 cars, the 934 and 935, thoroughly, but there seemed little point in pursuing another season of racing to old rules.

In fact Porsche had already claimed the best results available: second overall at Le Mans and Watkins Glen, third overall at Spa. Sports-Prototypes filled the leading positions at Paul Ricard (a new event) and at Brands Hatch, leaving van Lennep and Muller to claim seventh position in France and fifth in Britain.

Effectively the Martini & Rossi backed factory team closed down in September, passing up the opportunity to race at Kyalami (the South African event added to the calendar in place of Buenos Aires), and would reappear with entirely new cars in 1976. Development of the 2.1 litre turbo engine continued in the back of Porsche 908/3s run by Reinhold Joest, assisted by Ing. Singer, and by Dr Dannesburger for van Lennep and Muller.

Rolf Stommelen and Tim Schenken won the Group 4 category at the Paul Ricard circuit in a Gelo Racing Porsche RSR, and Georg Loos' team had further successes at Brands Hatch and Kyalami.

John Fitzpatrick dominated the European GT Championship in 1974 despite switching from the Kremer team to Loos, then back to Kremer, and he also became the first two-times winner of the Porsche Cup.

The 1974 RSR was a highly developed car with a bigger rear wing and wider rear wheels which gave it the edge on the BMW 3.0 CSL and Ford Capri 3.0. Fitz, who raced Ford Capris and Porsches, much preferred the 911: "it handles a lot better" he said at the time.

1000 km Spa-Francorchamps 1975: Claude Ballot-Lena, Jean-Claude Andruet

Poster

TURBO ERA DAWNS 61

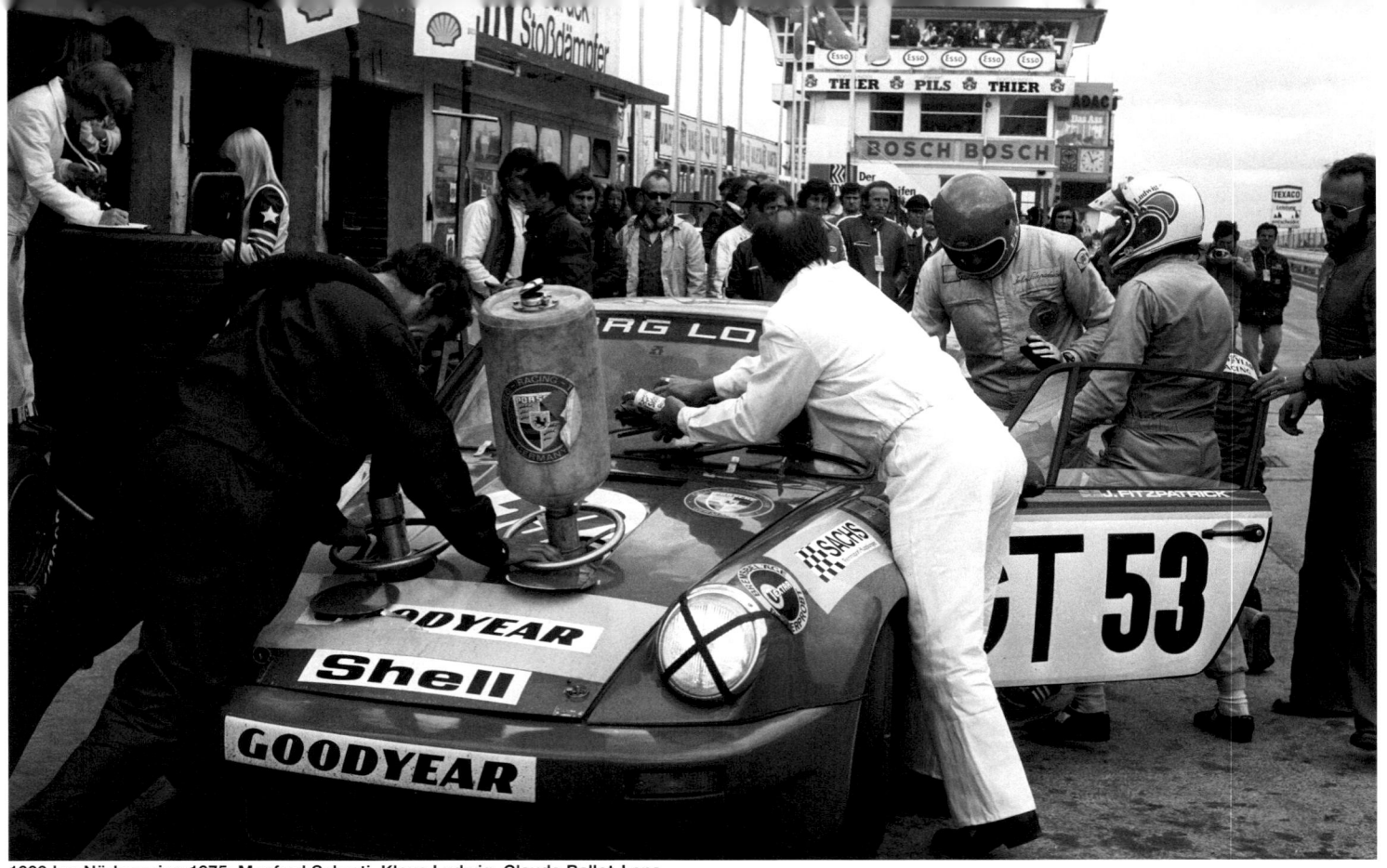

1000 km Nürburgring 1975: Manfred Schurti, Klaus Ludwig, Claude Ballot-Lena

Fitzpatrick gewann den Saisonauftakt, das 500 km-Rennen von Imola, vor Schickentanz, aber beide Autos scheiterten anschließend an den italienischen Kommissaren, weil die Führung der hinteren Bremsleitungen geändert worden war, um Überhitzung durch die Reifen zu vermeiden. So wurde Ballot-Lena vor Bertrams zum Sieger erklärt, obwohl von beiden die Autos nicht kontrolliert worden waren.

Die GT-Europameisterschaft war längst zur Spielwiese von Porsche geworden und obwohl sich die Serie großer Beliebtheit bei den Zuschauern erfreute, ließ das internationale Interesse nach. Auf dem Österreichring belegten Carrera RSR die ersten zwölf Plätze, mit Schickentanz an der Spitze vor Dieter Quester und Ballot-Lena.

Das Rennen auf dem Norisring ist traditionell eine der größten Motorsportveranstaltungen in Deutschland. Im Jahr 1975 war das Rennen mit 100.000 Besuchern ausverkauft. Sie sahen einen klaren Dreifachsieg für das Gelo Porsche-Team, mit Fitzpatrick vor Hezemans und Schenken.

Claude Haldi, der als Fahrer des Haberthur-Teams den Porsche Cup gewann, siegte im nächsten Rennen in Hockenheim, wo er von einem gut geplanten Boxenstopp profitierte. Als die Strecke abtrocknete, hatte er rechtzeigtig Slicks aufziehen lassen. In Misano gewann Schenken mit einer Sekunde Vorsprung auf Fitzpatrick, Bertrams wurde Dritter.

Das Tebernum-Team gewann das wichtige 6 Stunden-Rennen von Monza mit Bertrams, Schickentanz und Bengt Ekberg. Sie fuhren den Sieg nach Hause, nachdem der Gelo-Porsche, der nach fünf Stunden in Führung lag, einen Motorschaden hatte. Nur sieben Autos traten die Reise zum Saisonfinale in Jarama bei Madrid an. Dieses Rennen brachte einen weiteren Dreifachsieg für das Team von Georg Loos, mit Schenken vor Hezemans und Fitzpatrick.

Das Gelo-Team war ein ständiger Sieger in der Gruppe 4 der Hersteller-WM, mit Klassensiegen in Mugello (Fitzpatrick, Schurti und Hezemans, Gesamtrang neun), Dijon (Fitzpatrick und Hezemans, Gesamtrang fünf) und Monza, wo Fitzpatrick, Hezemans und Schurti den sechsten und siebten Platz belegten. Claude Haldi und Bernard Béguin erreichten im Haberthur-RS den vierten Platz in der Gesamtwertung beim 1000 km-Rennen von Spa. Auf der Rennstrecke von Enna auf Sizilien sicherten sich Bertrams, Schickentanz und Reine Wisell die Gesamtplätze vier und fünf mit ihren Porsche des Tebernum-Teams. Auf dem Nürburgring gewannen Helmut Kelleners, Hans Heyer und Bob Wollek die Gruppe 4 für Kremer-Porsche mit dem achten Platz im Gesamtergebnis. Es war passend, dass zwei Österreicher, Horst Felbermayr und Franz Doppler, die GT-Klasse beim letzten europäischen Rennen auf dem Österreichring gewannen.

Ein merkwürdiges Ergebnis ergab sich für Porsche mit dem Dreifachsieg in Zandvoort. Die niederländischen Veranstalter hatten sich entschieden, Autos der Gruppe 4 ohne Punkteberechtigung am Rennen zur Tourenwagen-EM teilnehmen zu lassen. Hezemans und Schenken gewannen das Rennen für Loos, vor van Lennep und Bob Wollek (Kremer) und Bertrams und Schickentanz (Tebernum). Das siegreiche Auto der Tourenwagen-EM, ein BMW 3.0 CSL, fand sich lediglich auf Platz vier ein.

Fitzpatrick was paid to drive for Kremer while Paul Keller paid the team to drive the second car, but after four races (in the World Championship, the European GT Championship and the German GT Championship) the British driver had scored no points at all, so Kremer cast him adrift.

At that, Fitz went off to drive for the newcomer, property developer Georg Loos, and started winning races on a regular basis. Loos, though, was an ambitious driver and hated being beaten by his own team-mates, so much so that Fitzpatrick rejoined Kremer for the middle part of the season. Then, surprisingly, Loos became disenchanted with being beaten by Fitzpatrick and lured him back on the basis that he, Loos, would give up driving and concentrate on team management. "It was a lot better after that" said Fitzpatrick. "In fact I stayed with Loos for the 1975 season as well." The fact that Fitzpatrick also drove for BMW in touring car races in 1975 meant that he missed some rounds of the European GT Championship, and the crown was passed to Hartwig Bertrams driving for the Tebernum team, with Schickentanz. Fitzpatrick, Schenken and Toine Hezemans drove for Loos, while Hans Heyer and Helmuth Kelleners drove for Kremer, who had special Schrick camshafts made for his fleet of RSRs raising the power to approximately 345 bhp. These had higher profiles, but the extra power came at the price of longevity; the engines were good for shorter duration races, but could not be relied upon for 1,000 kilometre events.

Fitzpatrick won the opening round, the Imola 500 Kms, ahead of Schickentanz, but both cars were then thrown out by the Italian scrutineers for having their rear brake pipes re-routed, to avoid them being chafed by the tyres. Ballot-Lena was then awarded the race ahead of Bertrams, although neither of their cars had been checked!

The European GT Championship had become a prototype of Porsche Cup racing, and while it drew big crowds it was falling in international recognition. Carrera RSRs filled the top 12 positions at the Osterreichring, where Schickentanz finished ahead of Dieter Quester and Ballot-Lena.

The Norisring is traditionally one of Germany's top motor sporting events and it drew a capacity crowd of 100,000 in 1975 to see the Gelo Porsche team sweep the board, with Fitzpatrick beating Hezemans and Schenken. Claude Haldi, who would win the Porsche Cup driving for the Haberthur team, won the next round at Hockenheim, benefiting from a well-judged pit stop for slick tyres when the circuit dried, then at Misano Schenken was the winner, finishing a second ahead of Fitzpatrick with Bertrams in third place.

Winner GT 1000 km Spa-Francorchamps 1975: Claude Haldi, Bernard Beguin

The Tebernum Porsche team won the key Monza 6-Hour race with Bertrams, Schickentanz and Bengt Ekberg sharing the victory after the Gelo Porsche blew its engine up while leading at the five-hour mark. Only seven cars went to Jarama, Madrid, for the final round which produced another clean sweep for Georg Loos's team, Schenken ahead of Hezemans and Fitzpatrick.

The Gelo team was a consistent winner of the Group 4 category in the World Championship for Makes, with class victories at Mugello (Fitzpatrick, Schurti and Hezemans, ninth overall), Dijon (Fitzpatrick and Hezemans, fifth overall), and Monza, where Fitzpatrick, Hezemans and Schurti managed to claim sixth and seventh positions.

Claude Haldi and Bernard Beguin drove their Haberthur Porsche RS to fourth place overall in the Spa 1,000 Kms, then at the Enna circuit in Sicily Bertrams, Schickentanz and Reine Wisell managed to be fourth and fifth overall in their Tebernum team Porsche.

At the Nurburgring it was the turn of Helmuth Kelleners, Hans Heyer and Bob Wollek to win the Group 4 class for Kremer Porsche Racing, eighth overall. Fittingly two Austrians, Horst Felbmayr and Franz Doppler, won the GT category in the final European round at the Osterreichring.

There was one very odd result for Porsche, with a clean sweep of the podium at Zandvoort where the Dutch organisers decided to allow Group 4 cars to compete without points in the European Touring Car Championship race. Hezemans and Schenken won that race for Loos ahead of van Lennep and Bob Wollek (Kremer) and Bertrams with Schickentanz (Tebernum), pushing a BMW 3.0 CSL ETCC car down to fourth.

1000 km Spa-Francorchamps 1975: Clemens Schickentanz, Hartwig Bertrams, Reine Wisell

ERFOLGE AM FLIESSBAND

6 Hours Mugello 1976: Toine Hezemans, Clemens Schickentanz

Das geänderte Reglement der FIA für Langstreckenrennen wurde 1976 eingeführt. Porsche nützte diese Gelegenheit und feierte Weltmeister-Titel sowie weitere Siege in Le Mans. Der Durchbruch der Turbomotoren im Rennsport, erstmals von BMW eingesetzt, aber in Weissach von den Porsche-Ingenieuren Hans Mezger und Valentin Schäffer weiterentwickelt, ermöglichte bisher unerhörte Leistungen aus luftgekühlten Reihensechzylindermotoren. 200 PS pro Liter war das Minimum, während der neue 911 Turbo sich als eine ideale Basis für Weltklasse-Rennsportwagen herausstellte.

Nach einer kurzen, erfolgreichen Rennsportsaison 1974 wurde der 911 Turbo im September 1974 auf der Motorshow in Paris vorgestellt. Auf Anweisung von Dr. Fuhrmann hatte das Auto eine komplette Ausstattung mit Leder, Klimaanlage und elektronischen Fensterhebern. Ein wahres Luxusauto, angetrieben von einem Dreilitermotor, der mit leichter Turbo-Aufladung eine Leistung von 260 PS brachte. Besser also, als die 210 PS des vielgeliebten Carrera RS 2.7.

Porsche setzte seine Dominanz der GT-Europameisterschaft mit dem abgeleiteten Gruppe 4-Auto, dem 934, fort. Nach einem unerfreulichen Kampf mit der FIA über die Interpretation der Regeln der Gruppe 5 in Bezug auf die Form der Motorabdeckung und des Heckflügels, dominierte Porsche auch die Marken-Weltmeisterschaft mit dem 935 in der Gruppe 5. Doch damit nicht genug, denn Porsche entwickelte in kürzester Zeit den 936, einen Rennsportwagen der Gruppe 6, womit man 1976, 1977 und 1981 die 24 Stunden von Le Mans gewann und 1976 die Krone in der Sportwagen-Weltmeisterschaft holte.

Diese drei Projekte wurden gleichzeitig unter der Leitung des bewährten Technikers Peter Falk durchgeführt, der später zum Sportchef ernannt wurde. 1965 fuhr Falk zusammen mit Herbert Linge beim Debüt des 911 die Monte-Carlo-Rallye.

Die drei Programme 1976 waren äußerst erfolgreich und brachten drei Meistertitel sowie einen wertvollen Sieg in Le Mans. Die Sponsorgelder kamen von Martini & Rossi und in diesen markanten Farben wurden Jochen Mass und Jacky Ickx zu den Helden der Saison. Sie holten sich mit ihrem Gruppe 5-Auto Gesamtsiege in Mugello, Vallelunga und Dijon-Prenois und gewannen mit dem Gruppe 6-Auto die Gesamtwertung in Monza, Imola und Dijon.

Darüber hinaus gewann Ickx zusammen mit Gijs van Lennep im 936 das 24 Stunden-Rennen von Le Mans. Mass siegte beim Sportwagenrennen in Enna mit Rolf Stommelen und nach einer Solofahrt auf dem Salzburgring.

All diese Rennen und Titel wurden mit verschiedenen Ausführungen des Sechzylindermotors des 911 gewonnen. Damit folgte man der Philosophie des Firmenchefs Dr. Fuhrmann, wonach der Rennsport benutzt werden sollte, um die Produkte des Hauses Porsche zu entwickeln und für diese zu werben. In ihrer Weisheit entschied die FIA, dass Gran-Turismo-Autos genau das sein sollten, was ihr Name verspricht. Schnelle, zweitürige Autos, mit denen man beispielsweise von Paris nach Marseille und zurück fahren kann, direkt von der Produktionslinie und nur leicht für den Einsatz im Rennsport angepasst, jedoch keineswegs zu stark modifiziert. Hohe Mindestgewichte wurden festgelegt, um den unnötigen Gebrauch von exotischen Leichtbaumaterialien zu unterbinden. Die Mindestgewichte wurden auf einer gleitenden Skala, abhängig vom Hubrum, bestimmt. Für ein Auto mit 4,2-Litermotor lag das Gewicht zum Beispiel bei 1120 kg. Das war weit mehr als die 900 kg, die der Porsche 3.0 RSR auf die Waage brachte, und der 934 war das erste Auto, das jemals mit elektrisch bedienbaren Fenstern in einem Rennen gefahren wurde, die außerdem aus Glas statt aus Plastik waren. Der Aufwand, der für das Entfernen der Elektromotoren notwendig gewesen wäre, hätte sich schlichtweg nicht gelohnt. Die FIA blieb bei der Faustregel von 1,4 als Multiplikationsfaktor für das Errechnen des effektiven Hubraums eines aufgeladenen Motors, sowohl für Triebwerke mit einem mechanischen Kompressor als auch für solche mit Turbolader. So wurde der 934 mit Dreilitermotor für den Sporteinsatz auf 4,2 Litern eingestuft. Weil die Version für den Straßenverkehr mit einem Gewicht von 1140 kg zugelassen war, mitsamt der ganzen Luxusausstattung, musste dort nicht viel eingespart werden. Es wurden ein Überrollkäfig aus Aluminium und ein Feuerlöscher montiert, aber das schwerste Einbauteil war der Zwischenkühler mit Wasserkühlung, der das Gesamtgewicht des 934 um 20 kg erhöhte. Im Gegensatz zum Martini-RSR-Turbo von 1974 hatte der 934 zwei Turbolader, nach wie vor von KKK. Mezger bevorzugte die Kühlung der Zwischenkühler mit Wasser, weil diese so kleiner ausfallen würden und unter der normalen Motorabdeckung platziert werden konnten, wie es das Reg-

Winner 6 Hours Vallelunga 1976: Jacky Ickx, Jochen Mass

SCALING THE HEIGHTS

The FIA's revision of endurance racing regulations came into force in 1976, and Porsche seized the opportunity to capture World Championship titles and further victories at Le Mans. The arrival of turbocharging in motor racing, pioneered by BMW in fact but developed by Porsche's engineers Hans Mezger and Valentin Schaeffer in Weissach, made it possible to extract unheard-of power levels from production based, air cooled, flat six cylinder engines, at least 200 bhp per litre, while the new 911 Turbo model proved to be an ideal base for world-class racing cars.

Following a short, but successful season of racing in 1974, the 911 Turbo model (code numbered 930) was announced at the Paris Show in September 1974. On Dr Fuhrmann's instructions it was fully equipped with leather upholstery, air conditioning and electric windows, a real luxury car, and was powered by a lightly turbocharged 3-litre engine developing 260 bhp, which compared favourably with the 210 bhp developed by the much-loved Carrera RS 2.7.

Porsche continued its domination of the European Grand Touring Car Championship with the derivative Group 4 car, the 934, and after a worrying tussle with the FIA over the interpretation of Group 5 regulations concerning the design and shape of the engine cover and rear wing, gained ascendancy in the World Championship of Makes with the Group 5 935. And, for good measure, Porsche rushed through the development of the Group 6 sports-racer, the 936, and used this to good effect to win the 24-Hours of Le Mans in 1976, 1977 and 1981, and to win the 1976 World Sportscar Championship.

All three of these simultaneous programmes were pursued under the direction of senior engineer Peter Falk, who would later be named as competitions director. It was Mr Falk, of course, who shared the 911's debut with Herbert Linge on the 1965 Monte Carlo Rally.

The three programmes in 1976 were hugely successful, capturing three titles and a coveted Le Mans victory. Sponsored to the hilt by the Italian vermouth company, Martini & Rossi, with very distinctive livery, Jochen Mass and Jacky Ickx were the heroes of the season with Group 5 outright victories at Mugello, Vallelunga and Dijon-Prenois, and Group 6 outright victories at Monza, Imola and Dijon.

Also, Ickx won the 24-Hours of Le Mans in a 936 shared with Gijs van Lennep, and Mass won sportscar races at Enna, with Rolf Stommelen, and in a solo drive at the Salzburgring. All of these races and titles were won with variations on the 911's six-cylinder engine, true to the ideals established by company chairman Dr Fuhrmann that racing was to be used to develop and promote Porsche's products.

Poster

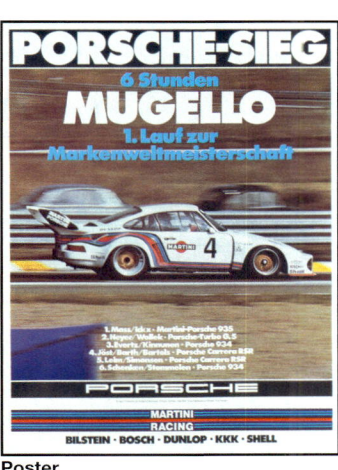

Poster

Winner GT 6 Hours Dijon 1976: Bob Wollek, Jürgen Barth, Reinhold Joest

Winner 6 Hours Vallelunga 1976: Jacky Ickx, Jochen Mass

lement vorschrieb. Das Gewicht spielte keine so große Rolle und hinter dem Frontspoiler wurden doppelte Wasserkühler montiert. Der Frontspoiler hatte auch Kühlöffnungen für die Zufuhr von Luft zum Ölkühler sowie zu den Bremsen.
Wolfgang Berger war als Techniker für das 934-Projekt verantwortlich. Porsche produzierte 30 Fahrzeuge, die an Kunden in Europa, sowie in den Vereinigten Staaten verkauft wurden, jeweils zu einem Preis von 108.000 DM. Die Kunden bekamen viel Auto fürs Geld, inklusive eines 485 PS-Motors mit 1,3 bar Ladeluftdruck. Teams steigerten die Leistung bald auf 580 PS, indem sie einfach den Druck auf 1,5 bar erhöhten. Das Reglement konnte sie nicht davon abhalten, und der Sechzylindermotor ließ es zu, wie sich herausstellte. Das K-Jetronic-System für Benzineinspritzung wurde beibehalten. Innerhalb des Motors wurden die Zylinderöffnungen vergrößert und die Profile der Nockenwellen erhöht. Die Zwischenkühler senkten die Temperatur der Ladeluft beträchtlich, von 150 auf 50 Grad. Wie beim „Turbo-Prototypen" im Jahre 1974 war das Kühlgebläse waagerecht über der Zylinderoberfläche montiert, um so eine bessere Verteilung der Luft zu bewirken.
Die Radaufhängung wurde mit einer Einheit aus Schraubfedern und Dämpfer versehen, die Räder hatten einen Zentralverschluss. Die Leichtmetallfelgen wurden in drei Teilen ausgeführt. Die Räder hatten einen Durchmesser von 16 statt 15 Zoll, so dass die Aufstandsfläche der Reifen vergrößert werden konnte. Die maximale Breite für die Hinterräder war auf 12,5 Zoll festgelegt worden. Wie zuvor wurden die Bremsen vom 917 übernommen, mit Innenbelüftung und Querrillen. Diese schweren Autos brauchten viel Bremskraft.
In Europa gehörten die Teams von Erwin und Manfred Kremer, Georg Loos und Max Moritz zu den erfolgreichsten Kunden. Sie fuhren nicht nur in der neuen GT-Europameisterschaft, sondern nahmen auch an den Läufen zur Marken-WM teil. Aufgrund der größeren Freizügigkeit des Gruppe 5-Reglements wurden ihre 934 bald mit breiteren Rädern, Kotflügelverbreiterungen und größeren zweiteiligen Heckflügeln ausgestattet.
Loos verpflichtete Toine Hezemans, Tim Schenken, Rolf Stommelen, Klaus Ludwig und Clemens Schickentanz als Fahrer, ein eindrucksvoller Kader. Egon Evertz, ein deutscher Industrieller, kaufte sich einen 934, den er sich mit Leo Kinnunen teilte. Die Gebrüder Kremer setzten Autos für Helmut Kelleners, Bob Wollek, Hans Heyer, Reinhardt Stenzel und Derek Bell ein.
Weder die Sportwagen-WM noch die FIA-GT-Meisterschaft zogen anfangs viele Teilnehmer an. So wurde aus den ge-

planten zwei Läufen zur Eröffnung beider Serien im April 1976 auf dem Nürburgring ein einziges Rennen über elf Runden auf der Nordschleife gefahren.
Das Rennen versprach ein Duell zwischen Rolf Stommelen im neuen Martini 936, unter der technischen Leitung von Helmut Flegl, und den turbogeladenen Alpine-Renault-Maschinen von Patrick Depailler und Jean-Pierre Jabouille. Aber zum Erstaunen und zur Verzweiflung der französischen Fans verlor Depailler in der zweiten Kurve hinter den Boxen bereits die Kontrolle auf der rutschigen Strecke und kollidierte mit seinem Teamkollegen, was für beide das Aus bedeutete. Stommelen fuhr eine einminütige Führung heraus, wurde dann aber langsamer durch Probleme mit dem Gaszug. Er verlor vier Minuten beim Boxenstopp und fiel auf Rang fünf zurück. Reinhold Joest übernahm im 908/3 Turbo die Spitze und gewann das Rennen, drei Minuten vor Hezemans im Loos 934. Der Niederländer gewann die GT-Wertung vor Kelleners, der seinen Kremer 934 auf den vierten Gesamtrang fuhr. Kelleners wiederum blieb vor Schenken (Gelo) und Stenzel (Kremer).
Erst zwei Monate später fand der zweite Lauf zur GT-Europameisterschaft auf dem Österreichring statt. Erneut siegte Hezemans, diesmal bis ins Ziel gefolgt von Bob Wollek (Kremer). Abgeschlagen auf Rang drei war Bertrams, der für das Gelo-Tebernum-Team fuhr. Bis auf Gianfranco Ricci, der im Lancia Stratos Fünfter wurde, räumten die 934 alles ab, während die älteren 3.0 RSR Rückendeckung gaben.
Hezemans gewann auch das dritte Rennen Ende Juni auf dem Nürnberger Norisring, das wie gewohnt sehr viele Zuschauer zum ehemaligen Reichsparteitagsgelände zog. Diesmal belegten Stenzel und Kelleners für Kremer die Plätze zwei und drei.
Der vierte Lauf in Misano war eher eine italienische Angelegenheit, weil die 934 von "Tambauto" und Angelo Pallavicini sich vom Ricci im Lancia Stratos absetzten. Tim Schenken fuhr im ersten Rennen die schnellste Runde, fiel aber danach aus und überließ schließlich den lokalen Teams den Kampf um die Ehrenplätze.

In their wisdom, the FIA decided that Grand Touring cars should be just that. Fast, two-door cars capable of being driven from Paris to Marseilles and back, taken from the production line and lightly modified for circuit work, but not to excess.

High minimum weights were established to prevent unnecessary use of lightweight, exotic materials. The minimum weights were established on a sliding scale, according to engine size, and for a 4.2 litre car, for instance, was 1,120 kg. This was far in excess of the 900 kg scaled by Porsche's 3.0 RSR, and the 934 model was the first ever to be raced with electrically power-operated windows, which had to be glass, not plastic. It just wasn't worth the bother of removing the electric motors!

The FIA still used the rule-of-thumb multiplication figure of 1.4 for calculating the effective capacity of a forced induction engine, be it with supercharging or turbocharging. Thus the 3-litre 934 was assessed as a 4.2 litre car for the purpose of racing, and since the production model was homologated at 1,140 kg complete with its luxury equipment, not much would have to be be discarded. An aluminium roll cage was installed, plus a plumbed-in fire extinguisher, but the heaviest item of equipment was the water cooled intercooler system which added 20 kg to the 934's weight.

Unlike the 1974 Martini Porsche RS Turbo, the 934 had a twin-turbocharger system, still KKK, and Mezger chose to cool the intercoolers with water because they would be smaller and would fit within the standard engine cover, a requirement of the regulations. The weight was not too important, and twin water radiators were located behind the air dam, which also had holes for ducting air to the oil cooler and the brakes.

Wolfgang Berger was the engineer in charge of the 934 project, and Porsche turned out 30 cars which were sold to leading customers in Europe and the USA, each priced at DM 108,000. They got a lot of car for their money, including a 485 horsepower motor, at 1.3 bar boost pressure, which the teams soon raised to approximately 580 horsepower

1000 km Nürburgring 1976: Gijs van Lennep, Hartwig Bertrams

simply by increasing the boost to 1.5 bar. There was nothing in the rules to stop them, and the six-cylinder engine proved remarkably tolerant.

The K-Jetronic fuel injection system was retained, and inside the engine the cylinder ports were enlarged and the camshaft profiles raised. The intercoolers reduced the temperature of the charged air considerably, from 150-degrees C down to 50-degrees. As on the 1974 'prototype' turbo, the cooling fan was installed horizontally above the cylinder barrels, for better distribution of air.

A coil spring/damper system was added to the torsion bar suspension, centre-lock hubs were installed, and the alloy wheels were in three pieces, the inner and outer sections bolted to the centres. The wheels were 16-inches in diameter, rather than 15-inches, in order to put a bigger tyre 'footprint' on the road, since the maximum width for the rear wheels was 12.5 inches.

The brakes, as before, were taken from the 917, internally vented and cross drilled. These heavy, very fast cars needed a lot of stopping!

In Europe the teams of Erwin and Manfred Kremer, Georg Loos (Gelo Racing) and Max Moritz were the principal and most successful customers who supported not only the new European GT Championship, but contested the World Championship for Manufacturers as well. Given the greater freedom of the the Group 5 regulations, their 934s were soon equipped with wider wheels, extensions to the fenders, and much larger two-tier rear wings.

Loos hired Toine Hezemans, Tim Schenken, Rolf Stommelen, Klaus Ludwig and Clemens Schickentanz to drive for him, an impressive squad of drivers. Egon Evertz, a German industrialist, bought a 934 which he shared with Leo Kinnunen, and the Kremer brothers ran cars for Helmut Kelleners, Bob Wollek, Hans Heyer, Reinhardt Stenzel and Derek Bell.

Neither the World Sportscar Championship nor the FIA GT Championship was well supported initially, so the planned double-header to open both series at the Nurburgring in April 1976 was turned into a single event, covering 11 laps of the Nordschleife, a distance of 250 kilometres.

The event promised a duel between Rolf Stommelen in the new Martini 936, engineered by Helmut Flegl, and the Alpine Renault turbocharged machines of Patrick Depailler and Jean-Pierre Jabouille. But to the amazement and despair of the French fans Depailler contrived to lose control at the second corner, behind the pits, on the greasy track and collide with his team-mate, putting both out of the contest.

6 Hours Österreichring 1976: Manfred Schurti, Jacky Ickx

Das traditionelle 1000 km-Rennen von Monza war der fünfte Lauf zur GT-Meisterschaft. Diesmal hatte Loos seine Starfahrer auf beiden Autos eingeschrieben. Hezemans, Schenken und Ludwig fuhren auf beiden Fahrzeugen und sicherten sich die Plätze eins und zwei in der Gesamtwertung. Die beiden 934 kamen fast zeitgleich über die Ziellinie, fast zwei Minuten vor dem Kremer 934, der von Kelleners, Bell und Stenzel gefahren wurde.

In Imola siegte Bob Wollek schließlich für Kremer Racing, nachdem Hezemans die schnellste Runde gefahren hatte und ausgefallen war. Heyer und Kelleners komplettierten den Dreifachsieg für die Kölner Rennschmiede.

Hezemans beendete die Saison mit seinem fünften Sieg in Hockenheim vor Schenken, Heyer und Wollek. Der Niederländer gewann ohne Probleme die Meisterschaft mit 100 Punkten vor Schenken und Kelleners mit je 57 Punkten und Wollek mit 45. Der Triumph für Porsche in der GT-Herstellermeisterschaft war noch überzeugender mit der maximalen Anzahl von 140 Punkten vor De Tomaso mit acht Punkten. In der Dreiliterklasse gab es eine etwas größere Leistungsdichte: Die Teams mit Porsche RSR fuhren 90 Punkte heraus, der Lancia Stratos hatte 70 Zähler.

Die Absage der GT-Europameisterschaft durch die FIA nach Saisonende kam keineswegs als eine Überraschung, da die deutsche Serie erfolgreich war und die Teams aus der internationalen Serie an sich zog.

6 Hours Mugello 1976: Bob Wollek, Hans Heyer

Winner 6 Hours Mugello 1976: Jacky Ickx, Jochen Mass

Die Ausschreibung für Le Mans beinhaltete nach wie vor eine Gruppe 4-Klasse. Die ambitiöseren Teams konnten ihre Autos aufwerten, wie es bereits einige getan hatten, und damit in der Gruppe 5 der Marken-WM fahren.

Der Automobil-Weltverband drohte außerdem, die Sportwagen-WM sterben zu lassen, es sei denn, die Saison 1977 würde besseren Sport bieten. Porsche entschloss sich zur Teilnahme mit dem 936 in Le Mans und verzichtete dafür auf alle anderen Renneinsätze. Renault traf mit dem Alpine A442 eine ähnliche Entscheidung, da ein Sieg in Le Mans das erklärte Ziel des französischen Herstellers war. So bestritt Alfa Romeo als einzige Marke die Sportwagen-WM, wobei der Name nicht hielt, was er versprach, denn die Serie war auf Europa beschränkt. Alfa gewann alle acht Rennen. Danach wurde die Serie eingestellt. Die Marken-WM überlebte aber.

Wenn es um internationale Siege in Le Mans, Daytona und Sebring, Titel in der WM, in der IMSA-Camel-GT-Meisterschaft und nationale Meisterschaften geht, dann ist der 935 das erfolgreichste Auto, das bisher von Porsche produziert wurde. Norbert Singer wurde mit dem 935-Projekt beauftragt, während Hans Mezger und Valentin Schäffer für den Turbomotor verantwortlich zeichneten. Gewichtsersparnis war wichtig, jedoch keine schwere Aufgabe, da die FIA auch in der Gruppe 5 eine gleitende Skala von Mindestgewichten eingeführt hatte. Es wurde beschlossen, den 935 in der Vierliterklasse fahren zu lassen, mit einem Mindestgewicht von 970 kg. Dazu bekam der Sechszylindermotor einen Hubraum von 2587 ccm mit einer Bohrung von 92,8 mm (statt 95 mm) und einem Hub von 70,4 mm.

Der Motor hatte ein waagerechtes Kühlergebläse, das mittlerweile Standard für Rennsportmotoren war, Doppelkerzenzündung, aber nur einen KKK Turbolader, der für beide Zylinderreihen arbeitete. K-Jetronic wurde durch mechanische Einspritzung von Bosch ersetzt und das einfache, aber starke Vierganggetriebe wurde beibehalten. Die Motorleistung betrug 590 PS bei 7900 U/Min., der Motor lieferte bei einem Ladedruck von 1,5 bar einen Drehmoment von 600 Nm bei 5.400 U/Min. Als 1977 der doppelte Turbolader eingeführt wurde, stieg die Leistung auf 630 PS an. Damit reagierte der 935 viel besser auf Bewegungen des Gaspedals, die Standfestigkeit wurde jedoch ein Problem. Die Zylinderkopfdichtungen waren anfällig und der Ladedruck konnte nicht weiter erhöht werden, um mehr Leistung zu erreichen, obwohl dies auch nicht wirklich nötig war.

Der 1975 gebaute Prototyp wog 900 kg, aber das war, bevor die FIA im Sommer die Mindestgewichte veröffentlichte. Singer hatte jetzt 70 kg, mit denen er spielen konnte. Er konnte die Gewichte genau dort platzieren, wo er sie haben wollte: in der Frontpartie des Autos und im Fußraum auf der Beifahrerseite. Der 120 Liter-Tank, der Öltank, die Batterie und der Feuerlöscher wurden alle im vorderen Bereich angeordnet, so dass 47 Prozent des Wagengewichts auf der Vorderachse ruhten. Der RSR Turbo 1974 hatte beispielsweise nur 30 Prozent seines Gewichts auf der Vorderachse.

Stommelen built up a lead of a minute, but then slowed with a stretched throttle cable, made a four minute pit stop and dropped to fifth position overall. Reinhold Joest then took the lead in his 908/3 turbo and duly won the race, finishing three minutes ahead of Hezemans in the Loos Porsche 934. The Dutchman was declared the winner of the GT race ahead of Kelleners, who was fourth overall in the Kremer Porsche 934, Schenken (Gelo) and Stenzel (Kremer).

Two months went by before the second round of the European GT Championship was held at the Osterreichring, and again Hezemans was the winner, this time chased to the line by Bob Wollek (Kremer), with Bertrams a distant third driving for the Gelo-Tebernum team. But for the presence of Gianfranco Ricci, who finished fifth in his Lancia Stratos, it would have been a clean sweep for the Porsche 934s with the older 3.0 RSRs playing a back-up role.

Hezemans won the third round, too, at the Nurnberg Norisring, the end-of-June race that attracts a huge crowd to the pre-war stadium. This time Stenzel and Kelleners were second and third for Kremer.

The fourth round at Misano was a more Italian affair as the Porsche 934s of 'Tambauto' and Angelo Pallavicini romped away from Ricci in his Lancia Stratos. Tim Schenken set the fastest lap in the first heat but then retired, leaving it to the local teams to finish the job.

The traditional Monza 1,000 Kms was the fifth round of the GT Championship and this time Loos had his star drivers playing the two-car trick, Hezemans, Schenken and Ludwig taking turns in both entries and finishing first and second overall, the two 934s almost level across the finishing line and nearly two minutes clear of the Kremer Porsche 934 shared by Kelleners, Bell and Stenzel.

Finally, Bob Wollek gave Kremer Racing a victory at Imola, after Hezemans had set the fastest lap and retired, with Heyer and Kelleners making it a clean sweep for the Cologne preparation shop.

Hezemans finished the season with his fifth victory, at Hockenheim, ahead of Schenken, Heyer and Wollek. The Dutchman won the championship with ease, with 100 points on the score-board, ahead of Schenken and Kelleners with 57 points apiece, Wollek with 45.

Porsche's victory in the GT Manufacturers Championship was even more convincing with a maximum of 140 points, ahead of de Tomaso on 8. It was a little closer in the 3-litre class where Porsche RSR teams had 90 points, and the Lancia Stratos accumulated 70.

It came as no surprise that the FIA cancelled the European GT Championship in the off-season, since the German championship was flourishing and taking entries away from the 'international' series.

A Group 4 category was still included in the Le Mans regulations, and the more ambitious teams could upgrade their cars (some had done so already) and run them in the Group 5 World Championship for Manufacturers.

There was also a threat from the governing body that the World Sportscar Championship would be cancelled unless the 1977 season provided better racing. Porsche decided to contest Le Mans, and no other race, with the 936 and Renault made a similar decision regarding the Alpine A442, a victory at Le Mans being the French company's top priority.

Therefore it was left to Alfa Romeo to contest the World Sportscar Championship (a misnomer, because it was confined to Europe) and win all eight rounds before this, too, was canned. The World Championship for Manufacturers was the survivor.

The 935 became the most successful racing car produced by Porsche so far in terms of international victories at Le Mans, Daytona and Sebring, World and IMSA Camel GT Championship successes, and scores of national championship titles.

Ing. Norbert Singer was given responsibility for the 935, with engineers Hans Mezger and Valentin Schaeffer providing the turbocharged engine. Weight saving was important but not onerous, since the FIA also applied a sliding scale of weights in Group 5.

It was decided to run the 935s in the 4-litre class, with a minimum weight of 970 kg, therefore the six-cylinder engine was given a swept capacity of 2,857 cc with a 92.8 mm bore (instead of 95 mm) and a stroke of 70.4 mm.

The engine had a horizontal cooling fan, which was now usual for racing units, twin-plug ignition, but had a single KKK turbocharger serving both banks of cylinders. Bosch mechanical injection replaced K-Jetronic and the simple, but strong 4-speed gearbox was retained. The differential was locked solid, 100 per cent in engineering terms compared with the 89 per cent locking factor on the 934's differential.

Poster

6 Hours Mugello 1976: Tim Schenken, Rolf Stommelen

6 Hours Vallelunga 1976: Bob Wollek, Hans Heyer

Anstelle der Stabfedern wurden Federn aus Titanium befestigt. Die Radnaben waren ebenfalls aus Titanium, so dass die Menge des unabgefederten Gewichts erheblich reduziert wurde. Die Räder waren aus Magnesium mit einer Breite von 11 Zoll und einem Durchmesser von 16 Zoll vorne und einer Breite von 14 Zoll (die reglementäre Maximalbreite) und einem Durchmesser von 19 Zoll hinten.

Kremer Racing startete in Köln ein ähnliches Projekt. Erwin und Manfred Kremer wollten gleich mit einem Auto in der Gruppe 5 fahren, während man zwei 934 in der GT-Europameisterschaft einsetzte. Der deutlichste Unterschied waren die 16 Zoll-Hinterräder, die beibehalten wurden, bis Goodyear zu Saisonmitte auch 19 Zoll-Reifen liefern konnte. Bob Wollek und Hans Heyer waren die Fahrer des Kremer 935. Nach den ersten beiden Rennen präsentierte Porsche die Martini-Werksautos mit einer völlig neuen Frontpartie, einer flachen Front, wobei die Scheinwerfer im Kotflügel vor den Rädern integriert waren. Es war ein Karrosserieteil, an dem die FIA-Kommissare nichts bemängeln konnten, weil das Reglement ausdrücklich sagte, dass „die Kotflügel frei sind".

„Der wahre Grund war, dass man mit den Verbreiterungen der Radhäuser spielen konnte, etwa 50 mm oder so", erklärt Norbert Singer. „Als wir den großen Schritt zu den 19 Zoll-Hinterrädern machten, mussten wir große Änderungen an den Kotflügeln durchführen. Weil der 911 ein besonderes Auto mit einem eigenen Erscheinungsbild ist, wollten wir die Scheinwerfer in die Kotflügel integrieren. Die Capri und BMW hatten sie bespielsweise im Kühlergrill."

„Wir präsentierten die zweite Version der Kotflügel mit den integrierten Scheinwerfern, und es gab einige Diskussionen mit der FIA-Kommission. Paul Frère war Mitglied dieser Kommission, ebenso Jabby Crombac. Wir fragten: „Wenn Euer Reglement sagt, dass der Kotflügel frei ist, was heißt das dann?" Sie stimmten zu, dass wir es machen konnten. Wenn es eine Lücke gibt, dann müssen wir sie nützen. Das gehört zum Spaß des Motorsports dazu!" Bald jedoch hatte die FIA-Kommission ihren eigenen Spaß und zwar mit schwerwiegenden Folgen. Nachdem Mass und Ickx in Mugello und Vallelunga die ersten beiden Rennen der Saison gewonnen hatten, und Singer im Kampf wegen der Anordnung der Scheinwerfer Recht bekommen hatte, griff die FIA ein und verlangte, dass der komplette Motor, inklusive Zwischenkühler, unter die serienmäßige Abdeckung passen musste. Obwohl die serienmäßige Abdeckung nicht verwendet wurde und durch eine völlig andere ersetzt worden war, müsste man sie zumindest montieren können. Dies war für Singer ein ziemlicher Schock. Aufgrund mangelnder mechanischer Zuverlässigkeit verlor Porsche dadurch drei Rennen, und es kostete der Firma eine halbe Million Mark. Soviel zum Thema Spaß.

Die Lösung war der Einsatz der schwereren, aber kompakteren wassergekühlten Zwischenkühler. Jeweils zwei davon brauchten einen Wasserkühler im Frontbereich. Nicht nur das, auch an der Luftzufuhr mussten Änderungen durchgeführt werden, der Motor musste neu abgestimmt werden, ein neues Gasgestänge wurde gebraucht, und die Anordnung der Einspritzpumpe wurde geändert.

BMW war ein starker Gegner. Die Firma aus München unterstützte nicht weniger als drei unabhängige Teams, welche Gruppe 5-Autos, basierend auf dem 3.5 CSL aus der amerikanischen IMSA-Serie einsetzten. Das Team Schnitzer hatte ein Auto, das abwechselnd von Ronnie Peterson, Brian Redman, Gunnar Nilsson und Dieter Quester gefahren wurde. Die Firma Alpina von Burkhard Bovensiepen setzte einen CSL für Sam Posey, Alain Peltier und Hugues de Fierlandt ein, während Shenton in Großbritannien ein Auto für Hermetite betreute, das von John Fitzpatrick und Tom Walkinshaw gefahren wurde. Porsche drückte der neuen Marken-WM seinen Stempel auf, indem es den Saisonauftakt in Mugello dominierte und die ersten sieben Plätze belegte. Brian Redman hatte auf Platz zwei liegend jedoch Pech, als der Motor seines Schnitzer-BMW in der letzten Runde des 6 Stunden-Rennens streikte. Da er die Zielflagge nicht sah, wurde er nicht gewertet. Mass und Ickx siegten, sechs Runden vor dem Kremer 935 von Wollek und Heyer. Egon Evertz und Leo Kinnunen fuhren in ihrem neuen 934 auf Platz drei, noch einmal sechs Runden zurück. Reinhold Joest, Jürgen Barth

6 Hours Vallelunga 1976: Kenneth Leim, Kurt Simonsen

70 ERFOLGE AM FLIESSBAND

Winner (l.-r.): Jacky Ickx and Jochen Mass

The power output was given at 590 bhp at 7,900 rpm, and the engine developed 60 mkg of torque at 5,400 rpm with 1.5 bar boost. In 1977, when the twin-turbocharger system was installed, power rose to 630 bhp and the 935 had much better response to throttle openings, but reliability became a concern. Cylinder head gaskets were prone to failure, and the boost pressure could not be increased in the quest for power (not that extra power was really needed!).

The working prototype built in 1975 was down to 900 kg, but this was before the FIA published the weight scale in the summer. With 70 kg to play with, Singer could position weights where he wanted them, in the nose of the car and in the passenger footwell. The 120 litre fuel tank, oil tank, battery and fire extinguisher were all located in the front compartment, putting an unusual 47 per cent of the car's weight on the front wheels. The 1974 RS Turbo, by comparison, had merely 30 per cent of its weight on the front wheels.

Titanium springs were fitted in place of torsion bars, and the wheel hubs were also made of titanium, saving a considerable amount of unsprung weight. The wheels were made of magnesium, 11 inches wide and 16 inches diameter at the front, 14 inches wide at the rear (the maximum permitted) and 19 inches diameter. As previously explained the larger diameter put a bigger tyre footprint on the road, as effective as racing with a wider tyre, and Dunlop provided special tyres for the job.

A similar project was undertaken by Kremer Racing in Cologne, with assistance from the factory. Erwin and Manfred Kremer wished to go straight into the Group 5 category with a single entry while running two new 934s in the European GT Championship, the most visible difference being the retention of 16-inch diameter rear wheels, until mid-season when Goodyear was able to supply 19-inch diameter tyres. Bob Wollek and Hans Heyer were the principal drivers of the Kremer Porsche 935.

After the first two races, Porsche presented the Martini 'works' car with a completely new frontal appearance, a 'droop snoot' with headlamps enclosed in the fairing ahead of the wheels. This was an "add on" panel which the FIA scrutineers could do nothing about, because their regulations stated specifically that "fenders are free".

"The real intention was that you could play with wheel arch extensions, just 50 mm or so" explains Ing. Singer. "When we made the big jump to 19-inch diameter rear wheels we had to make big changes to the fenders. And then, because the 911 is a special car with a distinctive appearance, we wanted to incorporate the headlamps in the fenders. The Capris and BMWs, for instance, had their headlamps incorporated in the grille.

"We presented the second type of fender with the headlamps incorporated, and there was some argument with the FIA Commission. Paul Frere was on the commission, and Jabby Crombac. We asked them, if your regulation says that the fender is free, what does it mean? Then they agreed that we could do it. "If there s a loophole we must take it. It is part of the fun of racing!"

Soon, though, the FIA Commission had some fun of its own, with serious consequences. After Mass and Ickx had won the first two races of the season, at Mugello and Vallelunga, and Singer had won his argument about the repositioning of the headlamps, the FIA stepped in and insisted that the complete engine, including the intercooler, had to fit inside the standard engine cover.

Although the standard engine cover had been thrown away, and replaced with something entirely different, it had to be interchangeable. This came as quite a shock to Singer. It would cause Porsche to lose three races to mechanical unreliability, and it would cost the company half a million D-marks, no laughing matter.

The solution was to instal the heavier, but more compact water cooled intercoolers, a pair of them needing radiators in the nose. Not only that, big changes had to be carried out to the induction system, the engine had to be remapped and retuned, a new throttle linkage designed, and a new space cam was designed for the injection pump.

Competition from BMW was strong, the Munich company supporting no fewer than three independent teams. Using Group 5 cars based on the 3.5 CSL (lightweight coupe) raced in the American IMSA series, Team Schnitzer ran one car driven, variously, by Ronnie Peterson, Brian Redman, Gunnar Nilsson and Dieter Quester. Burkhard Boversiepen's Alpina company ran a CSL for Sam Posey, Alain Peltier and Hugues de Fierlandt, while in Britain, Tivvy Shenton ran a car for Hermetite, driven by John Fitzpatrick and Tom Walkinshaw. Porsche made its mark on the new World Championship for Manufacturers by dominating the opening round, at Mugello, claiming the top seven places overall. Brian Redman was singularly unlucky, though, as his Schnitzer BMW blew up its six-cylinder engine on the final lap of the 6-hour race, while lying second, and was unclassified as he failed to take the flag.

Winner 6 Hours Vallelunga 1976: Jacky Ickx, Jochen Mass

SCALING THE HEIGHTS

6 Hours Watkins Glen 1976:
Jacky Ickx, Jochen Mass

Poster

und Willi Bartels belegten im Porsche 3.0 RSR Rang vier, zwei BMW CSL fuhren auf die Plätze acht und zehn.
In Vallelunga, wo der zweite Saisonlauf stattfand, war BMW bereits näher dran. Mass und Ickx siegten erneut, zehn Runden auf der 3,2 Kilometer langen Strecke vor dem BMW von Posey, de Fierlandt und Harald Grohs. Der Kremer 935 fiel in diesem Rennen aus, der dritte Platz ging an den RSR 3.0 von Kennerth Leim und Kurt Simonson, Fitzpatrick und Walkinshaw kamen auf Rang vier ins Ziel.
Danach wurde Porsches Siegesserie für eine gewisse Zeit unterbrochen. Jacky Ickx startete in Silverstone von der Pole-Position, aber verbrannte sich beim stehenden Start die Kupplung und rollte nach der Hälfte der ersten Runde aus. Später wurde der Martini-Porsche zurück ins Fahrerlager gebracht, so dass die Kupplung ausgetauscht werden konnte. Das Rennen war jedoch nur noch als Testeinsatz zu betrachten. Ronnie Peterson und Gunnar Nilsson fuhren in Silverstone den BMW CSL Turbo, dem eine Motorleistung von 800 PS nachgesagt wurde. Das Team startete aus der ersten Reihe neben Ickx und beim Start schien das Rennen bereits entschieden. Dann gab das Getriebe jedoch nach 40 Minuten den Geist auf. Heyer und Wollek kämpften daraufhin mit Walkinshaw und Fitzpatrick für die gesamte Dauer des 6 Stunden-Rennens. Walkinshaw startete im Hermetite-BMW und übergab das Lenkrad an Fitzpatrick für einen langen Schlussturn. Der BMW schlug den Kremer 935 nur um 1,18 Sekunden. Platz drei ging an Evertz und Kinnunen im 934 vor Grohs und de Fierlandt im Alpina-BMW.
Rolf Stommelen und Manfred Schurti fuhren den Martini 935 auf dem Nürburgring, während Mass und Ickx zur gleichen Zeit den Formel 1 Grand-Prix von Monaco bestritten. Der Porsche schied wegen eines gebrochenen Rotorarms aus, so dass die BMW den Sieg unter sich ausmachen konnten.
Auf dem Österreichring war die Zuverlässigkeit beim Martini 935 nach wie vor ein Thema. Ickx und Schurti fielen mit einem verzogenen Motorventil in der letzten Stunde aus. Quester und Nilsson gewannen das Rennen in der Steiermark vor Fitzpatrick und Walkinshaw. Der 934 von Claude Haldi und Peter Zbinden kam auf Rang drei ins Ziel.
BMW war von nun an im Kampf um den Weltmeistertitel ein ernsthafter Gegner für Porsche. Mit noch zwei 6 Stunden-Rennen in Watkins Glen und Dijon auf dem Programm betrug der Rückstand von BMW nur vier Punkte. Weil am Ende der Saison mehr Punkte gestrichen werden mussten, konnte sich Porsche bei keinem der zwei verbleibenden Rennen eine Niederlage erlauben. Deshalb setzte man einen zweiten Werks-935 für Stommelen und Schurti ein.

Wie sich herausstellte, wäre diese Maßnahme nicht wirklich notwendig gewesen. Die Porsche hatten ihre alte Zuverlässigkeit zurückgefunden, und die BMW waren nicht schnell genug. Stommelen und Schurti siegten in Watkins Glen, eine Runde vor dem 935 aus dem Team von Egon Evertz, gefahren von Kinnunen und Hezemans. Eigentlich war das Auto ein verbesserter 934. Mass und Ickx kamen auf Platz drei ins Ziel. Peter Gregg und Hurley Haywood belegten im BMW CSL Rang vier vor Peterson und Quester.
Porsche konnte sich noch nicht zurücklehnen. Man hatte zwar 102 Punkte, aber nach Abzug eines Streichresultats blieben nur 90 Punkte übrig, während BMW insgesamt 88 Punkte und nach Abzug immer noch 85 Zähler hatte. Der Unterschied war nach wie vor fünf Punkte, und der Sieger beim Saisonfinale in Dijon würde sich den Titel holen.
Erneut setzte Martini-Porsche zwei Autos ein, und erneut bestimmte BMW mit dem CSL Turbo für Peterson und Nilsson das Tempo. Eine Sekunde vor Trainingsschluss sicherten sich die beiden die Pole-Position und sie führten in den ersten 40 Minuten das Rennen an. Wieder einmal erwies sich das Getriebe als der wunde Punkt beim BMW.
Mass und Ickx, die am Samstag im 936 bereits das Rennen zur Sportwagen-WM gewonnen hatten, siegten am Sonntag im 935 erneut, eine Runde vor dem Kremer-935 von Wollek und Heyer. Platz drei ging an Stommelen und Schurti. Die BMW hatten keine Chance, sie kamen auf die Plätze sechs, sieben und neun ins Ziel.
Später zog sich BMW aus der Marken-WM zurück. Man bevorzugte die Entwicklung des 320i Turbo für Einsätze in der IMSA-Serie und sporadische Rennen in der WM. Ohne ernsthaften Gegner entwickelte Porsche die Werks-935 mit doppelten Turboladern. Die Motorleistung wurde auf 630 PS erhöht und die Fahrbarkeit des Autos erheblich verbessert. Es wurde eine Serie von 23 Autos für Kundenteams angefertigt, allesamt mit einfachem Turbo und 600 PS.

6 Hours Vallelunga 1976: Leo Kinnunen, Egon Evertz

6 Hours Watkins Glen 1976:
Toine Hezemans, Leo Kinnunen

ERFOLGE AM FLIESSBAND

Mass and Ickx won handsomely, six laps (32 kilometres) ahead of the Kremer 935 of Wollek and Heyer, followed a further six laps distant by Egon Evertz and Leo Kinnunen in their new Porsche 934. Reinhold Joest, Juergen Barth and Willi Bartels were fourth in a Porsche 3.0 RSR, and two BMW CSLs were placed eighth and tenth.

BMW was closer at Vallelunga, where the second round was held. Mass and Ickx won again, 10 laps of the 3.2 kilometre circuit ahead of the BMW of Posey, de Fierlandt and Harald Grohs. The Kremer 935 retired from this race and third place was claimed by the Porsche RSR 3.0 of Kennerth Liem and Kurt Simonson, with Fitzpatrick and Walkinshaw fourth.

After that, Porsche's bandwagon was halted for a while. Jacky Ickx started from pole position at Silverstone but burned out his clutch at the standing start, and rolled to a standstill halfway round the opening lap. Later the Martini Porsche was recovered to the paddock and the clutch was replaced, but its reappearance was only to serve as a test session.

Ronnie Peterson and Gunnar Nilsson drove the fantastic BMW turbocharged CSL at Silverstone, a car with a reputed 800 horsepower, and after starting from the front row of the grid, alongside Ickx, Peterson fairly ran away with the race until the transmission failed after 40 minutes.

Heyer and Wollek then duelled with Walkinshaw and Fitzpatrick throughout the six-hour race, Walkinshaw starting in the Hermetite BMW then leaving Fitzpatrick to complete a long final stint, and the BMW beat the Kremer Porsche 935 by a mere 1.18 seconds at the flag. Third were Evertz and Kinnunen in their Porsche 934, ahead of Grohs and de Fierlandt in the Alpina BMW.

Rolf Stommelen and Manfred Schurti drove the Martini Porsche 935 at the Nurburgring, while Mass and Ickx were competing in the Monaco Grand Prix, but retired with a broken rotor arm and that left the BMWs to fight for victory. Fitzpatrick's Hermetite CSL was leading at the 6-hour mark

Poster

Poster

300 km Nürburgring 1976: Helmut Kelleners

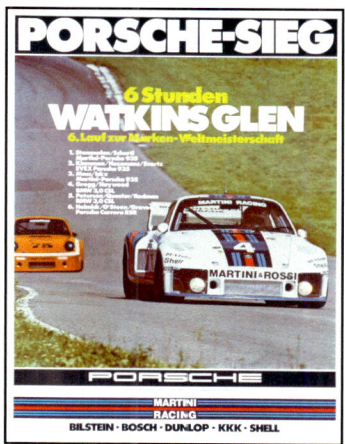

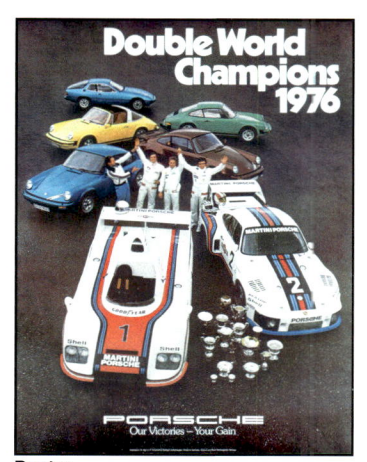

but slowed on the final lap with a fuel feed problem and let Quester and Albrecht Krebs through to win, ahead of the Loos Porsche 934 of Hezemans and Schenken, and the Kremer 934 of Bell, Stenzel and Kelleners.

Reliability was still an issue with the Martini Porsche 935 at the Osterreichring, where Ickx and Schurti retired with a bent valve in the engine in the last hour. Quester and Nilsson won the Austrian event from Fitzpatrick and Walkinshaw, with the Porsche 934 of Claude Haldi and Peter Zbinden placed third. BMW was now challenging Porsche seriously for the World Championship, just four points behind with two 6-hour races remaining, at Watkins Glen and Dijon-Prenois. With more points to be dropped at the end of the season Porsche could not afford to be beaten at either venue, and ran a second 'works' 935 in Martini colours for Stommelen and Schurti.

It was a case of overkill, as it transpired, the Porsches having regained their reliability and the BMWs being outpaced. Stommelen and Schurti won at Watkins Glen, a lap ahead of Egon Evertz's Porsche 935 (upgraded 934) with Kinnunen and Hezemans, with Mass and Ickx pushed down to third place. Peter Gregg and Hurley Haywood were fourth in their BMW CSL ahead of Peterson and Quester.

Still Porsche could not relax. The Stuttgart firm had 102 points gross but only 90 net, after dropping one result, while BMW had 88 gross and 85 net. The margin was still five points, and the winner of the final round at Dijon would claim the crown. Again Martini Porsche ran two cars, and again BMW rolled the dice with the turbocharged CSL for Peterson and Nilsson, who claimed pole position with half a second to spare and led for the first 40 minutes. Again, though, the transmission was the BMW's weakest link, and Porsche continued to dominate.

Mass and Ickx, who had won the World Sportscar Championship race on Saturday in their 936, became double winners with a fine success on Sunday afternoon in the 935, a lap ahead of the Kremer 935 of Wollek and Heyer, with Stommelen and Schurti placed third. The BMWs were outrun, finishing sixth, seventh and ninth.

With that, BMW virtually withdrew from the World Championship for Manufacturers, preferring to develop the 320i turbo model for IMSA racing and the odd foray into the World Championship. With little serious opposition, Porsche developed the factory 935s with twin turbochargers, pushing the power up to 630 bhp with better driveability, and produced a series of 23 customer cars, all with single turbo engines and 600 horsepower.

Kremer Racing, Georg Loos, Max Moritz, Jagermeister, Franz Konrad and Martino Finotto were among the customers who campaigned their 935s on a regular basis, and

Kremer Racing, Georg Loos, Max Moritz, Franz Konrad und Martino Finotto gehörten zu den Kundenteams, die ihre 935 regelmäßig einsetzten. Nach einem Jahr Abwesenheit, das er bei BMW verbrachte, kehrte John Fitzpatrick ins Kremer-Team zurück, wo er zusammen mit Bob Wollek fuhr.

Mass und Ickx, Stommelen und Schurti fuhren weiterhin im Werksteam. Das Martini-Team und Kundenteams gewannen alle neun Rennen zur Weltmeisterschaft. Veranstalter und Promoter machten sich Sorgen wegen fehlender Konkurrenz. Vier der zwölf geplanten Rennen wurden abgesagt, darunter zwei Rennen in Frankreich in Dijon und Le Castellet. Die Italiener organisierten dafür Ende Oktober ein extra Rennen in Vallelunga.

Das 24 Stunden-Rennen von Daytona zählte diesmal wieder zur Weltmeisterschaft. Porsche schickte also ein Martini-Auto nach Florida, ein 1976er 935 mit einfachem Turbo für Mass und Ickx. Zwei Reifenschäden zwangen das Duo zur Aufgabe. Kremers 935 verlor viel Zeit wegen Problemen mit der Kupplung und den Radlagern, so dass Wollek, Krebs und Joest auf Rang drei hinter den Amerikanern Hurley Haywood, John Graves und Dave Helmick zurückfielen. Sie blieben immerhin vor Finottos neuem 935.

Martini schrieb zwei 935 für den zweiten Saisonlauf in Mugello ein. Das Auto von 1976 für Schurti und Stommelen und den neuen 935/77 für Mass und Jürgen Barth. Der Werks-Mitarbeiter ersetzte Ickx, der krank war. Barth hatte ein Bremsproblem und in der ersten Kurve kam es zu einer Kollision mit dem Kremer-935, der von Bob Wollek gefahren wurde. Damit waren beide Autos aus dem Rennen. Der ältere Werks-935 von Stommelen und Schurti fuhr den Sieg nach Hause, sechs Runden vor Finotto, Carlo Facetti und Romeo Camathias.

Mass und Ickx feierten ihren ersten Saisonsieg in Silverstone, wo sie beim 6 Stunden-Rennen über die gesamte Distanz führten. Regen in der Schlussphase machte die Strecke rutschig, und so konnten Wollek und Fitzpatrick im Kremer-935 noch aufschließen, aber der Vorsprung von Mass und Ickx reichte. Stommelen und Hezemans holten Platz drei für Gelo Racing, während Peterson und Kelleners im BMW 320i, noch ohne Turbo, Rang vier belegten.

Auf dem Nürburgring regnete es. Das Wetter führte zu Problemen beim Werks-935/77. Mass und Ickx fielen durch Motoraussetzer aus. Schenken und Stommelen siegten im Gelo-Porsche vor Wollek und Fitzpatrick im Kremer-935. Diesmal ging der dritte Platz an Marc Surer und Manfred Winkelhock im 320i des BMW-Junior-Teams.

3 Hours Hockenheim 1977

Porsche entsandte nur ein Werksauto nach Watkins Glen, wo Mass und Ickx das 6 Stunden-Rennen gewannen. Im darauffolgenden Rennen in Mosport waren sie nicht so glücklich, denn nach zwei Stunden fielen sie mit einem defekten Kolben aus. Glücklicherweise siegten Peter Gregg und Bob Wollek mit einem 934.

Das Rennen in Brands Hatch stand wegen finanzieller Schwierigkeiten lange Zeit auf der Kippe, als es dann Ende September endlich stattfand, waren bis auf die Mannschaft von Georg Loos alle Teams da. Leider war der Regen so stark, dass das Rennen für einige Zeit unterbrochen werden musste, nachdem Stuck im neuen BMW 320i Turbo von der Strecke gekommen war. Das Rennen wurde wieder aufgenommen, mußte dann aber nach etwas weniger als drei Stunden endgültig abgebrochen werden. Erneut waren Mass und Ickx die klaren Sieger, vor Schurti und Edgar Dören. Franz Konrad war ein neues Gesicht auf dem Podium, er belegte mit Reinhold Joest und Bob Wollek den dritten Platz. Der WM-Lauf in Hockenheim bestand aus zwei Rennen zu je drei Stunden, eines am Samstag und eines am Sonntag. Ickx und Schurti fielen am Samstag mit einer kaputten Zylinderkopfdichtung aus. Damit konnten Bob Wollek und John Fitzpatrick ohne Probleme den Sieg für das Kremer-Team nach Hause fahren. Der Martini 935 revanchierte sich am Sonntag für den Ausfall und gewann das Rennen. Platz drei reichte für Wollek und Fitzpatrick zum Gesamtsieg.

Das Saisonfinale im Oktober in Vallelunga zog nur wenige Teilnehmer an. Das Starterfeld bestand zum Großteil aus italienischen Teams. Das Werksteam blieb daheim. Schon damals wollte man nicht gegen Kundenteams antreten, ausser wenn neue Komponenten getestet werden mussten. Auch die Kölner Teams Loos und Kremer traten die Reise nach Italien nicht an. Luigi Moreschi und "Dino" gewannen das Rennen im 935 vor "Victor" und Piero Monticone, ebenfalls im 935. Zur Abwechslung ging Rang drei an einen De Tomaso Pantera. Im Endstand der WM hatte Porsche mit 140 Punkten einen großen Vorsprung auf BMW mit 47,5 und De Tomaso mit 12 Zählern.

6 Hours Silverstone 1977: Bob Wollek, John Fitzpatrick

after a year out, with BMW, John Fitzpatrick rejoined the Kremer team to drive with Bob Wollek.

Mass and Ickx, Stommelen and Schurti were retained by the factory, and between them the Martini team, and the customer teams, won all of the nine qualifying rounds of the World Championship. Organisers and promoters were concerned by the lack of competition and four of the 12 scheduled rounds were cancelled, including two in France at Dijon and Le Castellet, but the Italians chipped in with an extra race, at Vallelunga at the end of October.

The Daytona 24-Hours was back in the World Championship so Porsche sent a Martini entry to Florida, a 1976 single-turbo 935 in fact, for Mass and Ickx, but two tyre failures caused their retirement. Kremer's 935 was badly delayed by clutch and wheel bearing problems, dropping Wollek, Krebs and Joest to third overall behind Americans Hurley Haywood, Graves and Helmick, ahead of Finotto's new 935.

Martini sent two 935s to the second round at Mugello, the 1976 car for Schurti and Stommelen and the new 935/77 for Mass with Juergen Barth, the factory employee standing-in for Ickx, who was unwell.

Barth, unfortunately, experienced brake failure on leaving the pits and collided heavily at the first corner with the Kremer 935 driven by Wollek, putting both cars out of the race. Victory went to the older 'works' 935 of Stommelen and Schurti, six laps ahead of Finotto, Facetti and Camathias

Mass and Ickx achieved their first win of the season at Silverstone, leading the 6-hour race from start to finish, with Wollek and Fitzpatrick closing in towards the finish in the Kremer 935 as rain made the track slippery. Stommelen and Hezemans were third for Gelo Racing, with Peterson and Kelleners taking a popular fourth place in a BMW 320i (not the turbocharged version, as yet).

It rained at the Nurburgring - never surprise, even in June! - and this caused the factory's 935/77 a problem as Mass and Ickx retired with a persistent misfire. Hezemans, Schenken and Stommelen won in the Gelo entry from Wollek and Fitzpatrick in the Kremer 935, and this time Surer and Winkelhock finished third in the BMW Junior Team 320i.

The factory sent a single entry to Watkins Glen, and Mass and Ickx duly won the 6-hour race. Their luck ran out at the Mosport round, which followed, as they retired after two hours with a piston failure. Surprisingly, Peter Gregg and Bob Wollek won in a 934.

The Brands Hatch round was an on-off-on affair, for financial reasons, but it was well supported by all but the Georg Loos teams when it was eventually held late in September. Unfortunately it rained so much that it had to be stopped for a while, when Hans Stuck crashed the new BMW 320i turbo, restarted, and eventually abandoned shortly before the three-hour mark. Mass and Ickx were the clear winners, once again, from Schurti and Edgar Doeren. Franz Konrad was a new visitor to the podium, third with Reinhold Joest and Bob Wollek.

Hockenheim staged its round of the World Championship as two three-hour events, one on Saturday and the other on Sunday. Ickx and Schurti retired from Saturday's event with a cylinder head gasket failure, leaving Wollek and Fitzpatrick to record an easy victory for the Kremer team. The Martini 935 made up for the failure by winning Sunday's 3-hour race despite being jammed in one gear, and third place was enough to secure an overall victory for Wollek and Fitzpatrick.

The final round, at Vallelunga on October 23, was poorly supported and featured mostly Italian teams. The factory team stayed at home, already putting into practice a policy of not racing against customers unless testing new components, and the Cologne based Loos and Kremer teams also failed to make the journey. Luigi Moreschi and "Dino" won that in a 935 ahead of "Victor" and Piero Monticone in a 935. Just for a change, a de Tomaso Pantera finished third.

3 Hours Hockenheim 1977: Rolf Stommelen, Toine Hezemans

3 Hours Hockenheim 1977: Claude Haldi, Bob Wollek, Werner Christmann

SCALING THE HEIGHTS 75

Poster Poster Poster Poster

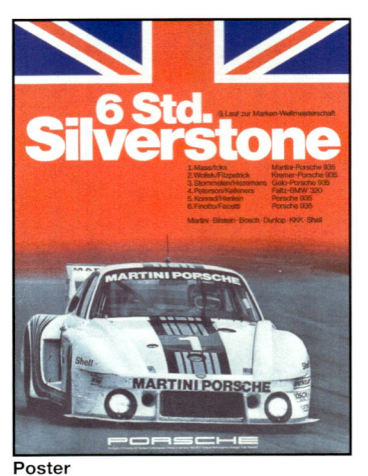

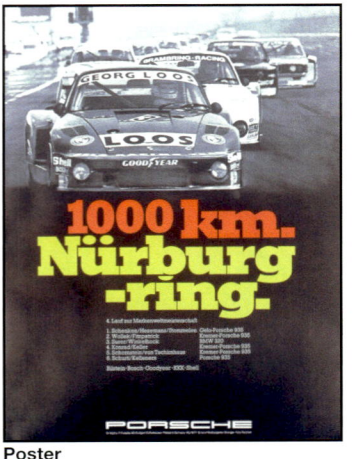

Nachdem man nicht mehr die komplette WM für Hersteller bestreiten musste, nahmen die Porsche-Techniker unter der Leitung von Norbert Singer 1977 zwei völlig neue Entwicklungsprojekte in Angriff, die jedoch eng mit einander verwandt waren. Das „Baby", das 1977 im Rennen eingesetzt wurde, war als Zweiliterauto für einige Rennen der Deutschen Meisterschaft konstruiert worden und formte danach die Basis für den 935-78. „Moby Dick" stieß im Rahmen des Reglements der Gruppe 5 in ungeahnte Dimensionen vor.

Der 934 und der 935 waren beide relativ schwergewichtige Autos. Die Techniker sehnten sich förmlich danach, wieder Super-Leichtbau-Konstruktionen zu realisieren.

Dr. Ernst Furhmann gab den Auftrag zur Produktion einer Sonderversion des 935 für den Einsatz bei den zwei wichtigsten Rennen zur Deutschen Rennsport-Meisterschaft (DRM), auf dem Norisring und im Rahmen des deutschen Formel 1 Grand-Prix in Hockenheim. Das Problem war jedoch, dass die DRM von Ford und BMW dominiert wurde und ausschließlich Zweiliterautos vorbehalten war.

Zunächst wurde der Hubraum des altbekannten Reihensechszylinders auf 1425 ccm reduziert, mit einer Bohrung von 71 mm und einem Hub von 60 mm. Mit dem Faktor 1,4 für turbogeladene Motoren ergab dies einen rechnerischen Hubraum von 1995 ccm. Mit einem KKK-Turbolader lieferte der Motor 370 PS, was in einem superleichten 911 hervorragende Leistungen versprach. Der Motor hatte jedoch wenig Drehmoment und das wäre eine Schwachstelle auf dem Norisring, dem Straßenkurs in Nürnberg mit seinen zwei Spitzkehren. Techniker Schäffer entwarf ein spezielles Turboladersystem, das er Jet-Intercooler nannte. Es bestand aus einem Niedrigdruck-Mantel um den wassergekühlten Turbo herum. Der Auspuff diente als Pumpe, indem er Luft aus dem luftgekühlten Zwischenkühler ansaugte und so eine bessere Wirkung erreichte. „Es war sehr clever", sagt Norbert Singer, der seine Auflage erfüllte, indem er einen 720 kg leichten 911 baute. Ein solches Gewicht war fast unglaublich: 15 kg Blei waren benötigt, um das Auto auf das vorgeschriebene Mindestgewicht zu bringen, das freilich von der Konkurrenz bei weitem überschritten wurde.

Ein Rohrrahmen aus Aluminium ersetzte den Unterboden aus Stahl, und auch die Front- und Heckstruktur wurden von Rohrrahmen ersetzt. Sämtliche Karrosserieteile wurden aus leichtem Kunststoff angefertigt. Räder mit einem Durchmesser von 16 Zoll kamen anstelle der 19-Zoll-Hinterräder, um die Übersetzungen zu reduzieren. Dennoch waren die Übersetzungen für das Norisringrennen völlig unbrauchbar.

Die Konzeption des „Baby" begann im März und das Auto wurde in vier Monaten fertig gestellt, aber der Einstand war kein Erfolg. Die Übersetzungen passten nicht, der Motor war nicht flexibel genug und außerdem litt Ickx extrem unter der Hitze im Cockpit. Er fuhr im Rennen vom 13. Startplatz auf Rang sechs vor, musste jedoch wegen Erschöpfung aufgeben. Dr. Fuhrmann ordnete daraufhin die Weiterentwicklung für einen Einsatz in Hockenheim, einen Monat später, an. Das Leistungsband des Motors war erheblich breiter, die Aufhängung wurde verbessert und die Übersetzungen neu angeordnet, so dass Ickx im Zeittraining 2,8 Sekunden schneller war als die Konkurrenz.

Die langen Geraden von Hockenheim waren wie gemacht für den "Baby-935". Ickx fuhr unangefochten den Sieg nach Hause. Im Ziel hatte er einen Vorsprung von 52 Sekunden. Danach durfte das „Baby" seinen Ruhestand im Porsche-Museum antreten.

Das Auto war die Basis für das nächste große Projekt von Porsche, der 935-78. Dieses Auto war keine Leichtbau-Konstruktion, weil das Reglement keine extreme Gewichtssparmaßnahmen erlaubte. Dennoch wies der 935-78 eine Reihe fortschrittlicher Innovationen auf.

So wurde der 935-78 von einem neuen Motor angetrieben. Nach wie vor mit sechs Zylindern, aber diesmal mit wassergekühlten Zylinderköpfen und vier Ventilen pro Zylinder. Der Motor drehte ohne Probleme bis 9.000 U/Min. Das Triebwerk wurde von Hans Mezger als 2,65 Liter-Motor für das bevorstehende Indycar-Programm entwickelt. In dieser Form hatte der Motor auch sechs Zylinder. Das Kühlergebläse war jedoch senkrecht montiert, da es nur die Zylinderoberfläche und nicht die Zylinderköpfe kühlen musste. Der Hubraum des 935-78 wurde auf 3211 ccm vergrößert (Bohrung x Hub 95,7 x 74,4 mm), was mit dem Multiplikationsfaktor von 1,4 einem rechnerischen Hubraum von 4495 ccm entsprach. Das Mindestgewicht von 1025 kg wurde einfach erreicht. Die Motorleistung wurde mit 750 PS bei 8.200 U/Min. und einem Ladedruck von 1,6 bar angegeben. Vereinzelt konnte der Druck auf 1,8 bar erhöht werden, so dass dem Fahrer über 800 PS zur Verfügung standen.

6 Hours Mugello 1977: Jochen Mass, Jacky Ickx

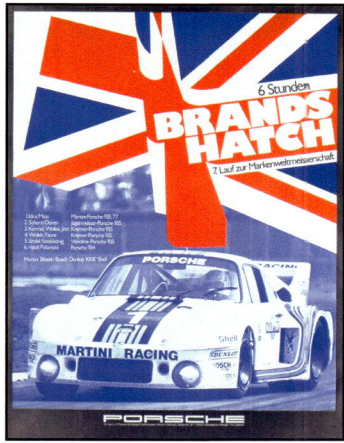

1000 km Nürburgring 1977: Edgar Dören, Jürgen Barth, Manfred Schurti

Poster

The final World Championship positions gave Porsche a huge lead, with 140 points (170 gross) ahead of BMW on 47.5 and de Tomaso on 12.

Freed from the constraints of full participation in the World Championship for Manufacturers, the factory team of engineers led by Ing. Singer started two entirely new lines of development in 1977, which were linked. The 'Baby', which raced in 1977, was prepared as a 2-litre car for a couple of appearances in the German Championship, and then formed the basis for the 935-78 'Moby Dick' took the Group 5 regulations to an altogether different plane.

The 934 and 934 were heavy cars, in comparitive terms, and the engineers hankered to make super lightweights again. Dr Ernst Fuhrmann gave the order to make a special version of the 935 to compete in the two most prestigious events in the German Championship, at the Norisring and supporting the German Grand Prix at Hockenheim. The problem was, the events were dominated by Ford and BMW, and were restricted to 2-litre cars.

First, the familiar flat-six engine was reduced in capacity to 1,425 cc with a bore and stroke of 71 x 60 mm. With the factor of 1.4 applied for a turbocharged engine, the capacity would be rated at 1,995 cc. With a single KKK turbocharger, the power output was 370 bhp, promising excellent performance in a super-light 911.

However the engine had poor torque, and that would hurt at the Norisring, the Nuremberg stadium which has two hairpin corners. Engineer Schaeffer designed a special turbocharger system which he called the jet intercooler, which comprised a low pressure jacket surrounding the water cooled turbo. The exhaust acted like a pump, sucking air out of the air cooled intercooler and making it much more efficient. "It was very clever" says Ing. Singer, who fulfilled his role by building a 911 down to 720 kg, an almost unbelievable figure; it needed 15 kg of lead to bring it up to the minimum weight, which rivals exceeded by a wide margin.

An aluminium tube frame replaced the steel floor, and tube frames replaced the front and rear structures too. All the panel work was made of lightweight plastics, and the 19-inch diameter rear wheels were replaced by 16-inch diameter wheels, to reduce the gearing. Even so, gear ratios were unsuitable for the Norisring race, held at the end of June.

The 'Baby' was conceived in March and was completed in four months, but its debut was not a success. The gearing was hopeless, the engine lacked flexibility (it had stationary power, not dynamic, according to Singer) and furthermore,

Ickx suffered very badly from heat exhaustion inside the cockpit. He moved up from 13th on the grid to sixth place, but was forced to retire from exhaustion. Dr. Fuhrmann then ordered further development for another appearance at Hockenheim, just a month later, and the result was quite different. The engine's power band had been widened, the suspension improved and the gearing revised, enabling Ickx to qualify 2.8 seconds faster than any rival.

Hockenheim's long straights suited the 'Baby' 935 ideally, and Ickx romped away to victory with 52 seconds in hand. With that, 'Baby' was retired with pride to the Porsche museum. It was the basis for Porsche's next major project, the 935-78, which was no lightweight (the regulations would not allow super weight-saving) but incorporated a number of advanced features.

Among other things, the 935-78 was powered by a new engine. Still with six cylinders, it had water cooled cylinder heads and four valves per cylinder, and could be taken safely to 9,000 rpm. The engine had been designed by Hans Mezger for the forthcoming Indycar programme, as a 2.65 litre unit, still with six cylinders but now with an upright cooling fan as it needed only to cool the cylinder barrels, not the heads. The capacity of the 935-78 was extended to 3,211 cc (bore and stroke, 95.7 x 74.4 mm) but 4,495 cc with the 1.4 multi-plication factor applied, and the minimum weight of 1,025 kg was easily attained. The power output was given as 750 bhp at 8,200 rpm with 1.6 bar boost, but 1.8 bar could be used sparingly, with over 800 bhp available to the driver.

The concept was planted in Singer's mind by the FIA decision to allow BMW and Ford to alter the floors of their cars,

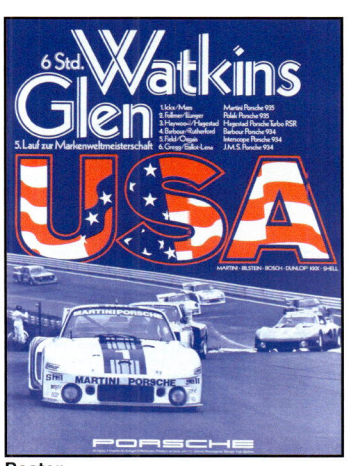

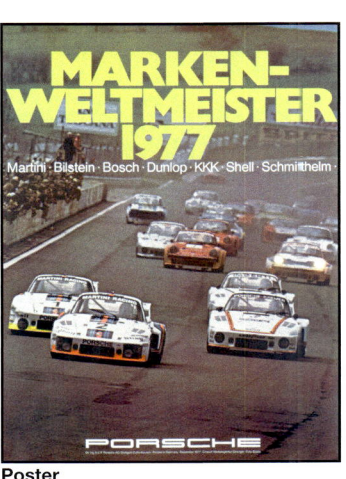

Poster

Poster

SCALING THE HEIGHTS

Diese Idee kam Singer durch die Entscheidung der FIA, die BMW und Ford erlaubte, den Unterboden ihrer Autos zu ändern, so dass die Auspuffröhre hinter den Türen platziert werden konnten. Martin Braungart von BMW hatte erklärt, Porsche habe einen Vorteil, weil der Motor des 911 im Heck lag, so dass der Auspuff genügend Freiraum hatte.

Mit Unterstützung von Thomas Amerschläger von Ford beantragte Braungart beim technischen Subkommittee der FIA die Genehmigung für das Einschneiden des Unterbodens. Diese Genehmigung wurde erteilt. „Ich sagte zu Barth, der mit mir da war, dass wir den ganzen Unterboden einschneiden konnten, wenn der Wortlaut so bleiben würde", erinnert sich Singer. „Der Regel wurde für Ford und BMW gemacht, weil sie die Motoren vorne hatten, aber niemand dachte daran, was Porsche machen könnte!"

Was Porsche machte, war ein neues Auto, basierend auf dem Konzept des "Babys". Die Mittelsektion aus Stahl wurde beibehalten, der Unterboden wurde aber herausgenommen und durch einen Unterboden aus Aluminium mit Wabenstruktur ersetzt. Dieser Unterboden wurde acht Zentimeter

Winner Silverstone 1978 (l.-r.): Jochen Mass, Norbert Singer, Jacky Ickx

6 Hours Mugello 1978: Bob Wollek, Henri Pescarolo

höher angeordnet, was die Karossie um die gleiche Höhe absinken ließ. Die Struktur wurde mit einem Überrollbügel aus Aluminium verstärkt. Sogar das Getriebe musste auf den Kopf gestellt werden, so dass die Antriebswellen in einer geraden Linie vom Differential zu den hinteren Radnaben drehen konnten. Die Karrosserie hatte eine flache Nase. Eine lange Heckpartie wurde aus Kunststoff angefertigt. So wurde das Erscheinungsbild des Autos nachhaltig geändert. Die Form der serienmäßigen Türen musste beibehalten werden, nicht jedoch die Türen selber. Das Auto war zwei Meter breit und hatte eine Länge von 4890 mm, während die Kundenautos des 935 nur 4680 mm lang waren.

„Von oben betrachtet gab es einen großen Unterschied zwischen den vorderen und den hinteren Kotflügel", erinnert sich Singer. „Ich sagte: OK, wir werden große NACA-Leitungen für die Zwischenkühler und die Zylinderköpfe einbauen, die ja schließlich wassergekühlt waren. „Als das Auto fertig war und erstmals auf seinen Rädern stand, war es komplett in weiß lackiert. Jeder schaute sich das Auto an und fragte: Ist das ein 911? Man sagte, das Auto sehe aus wie ein Walfisch, und vom ersten Tag an nannten wir es Moby Dick."

„Dann kam die FIA nach Weissach, um das Auto zu sehen, und sie sagten: Auf gar keinen Fall. Man fragte uns, was wir gemacht hatten. Das Auto war so niedrig und so breit, es sei kein 911. Es gab jede Menge Diskussion, lange Auseinandersetzungen. Schließlich gab man uns grünes Licht, die ursprüngliche Form der Türen musste aber beibehalten werden. Ich fragte, wo geschrieben stand, dass man sie nicht abdecken durfte. „Es war die gleiche Diskussion die wir ein Jahr zuvor hatten, als wir die ursprüngliche Heckscheibe haben mussten, so dass wir zum Schluß eine doppelte Heckscheibe hatten. Das war das gleiche Prinzip, und sie hatten es akzeptiert. Letztendlich stellten die Delegierten der FIA, Paul Frère und Kurt Schild, fest, dass das Auto dem Reglement entsprach und sie gaben grünes Licht. Sie nahmen eine Menge Fotos mit nach Paris. „Wenige Tage später bekamen wir ein Schreiben von der FIA, sie teilten uns mit, unser Auto sei illegal, man wolle keine solche Autos in der WM. Wir nahmen die Abdeckungen herunter, so dass man die Türen sehen konnte, und zogen die vorderen Kotflügel etwas mehr nach hinten durch, so dass wir einen aerodynamischen Vorteil haben würden.

Es gab nach wie vor Diskussionen, und wir meinten, dass die technischen Kommissare grünes Licht gegeben hatten. Schließlich bekamen wir ein Telex vom FIA-Präsidenten Pierre Ugeux. Er teilte mit, wenn die technischen Kommis-

1978: 935 Moby Dick

ERFOLGE AM FLIESSBAND

John Fitzpatrick

so that they could run the exhaust pipes out behind the doors. Martin Braungart, of BMW, argued that Porsche had an advantage because the 911's engine was at the back, so exhaust pipe clearance was not a problem.

Supported by Ford's Thomas Amerschlager, Braungart asked the FIA's technical sub-committee to allow the cutting of floors, and this was duly approved. "I said to Juergen Barth, who was with me, that if the wording stays like this we can cut the whole floor" Singer recalls. "The rule was written for Ford and BMW, with their engines at the front, but nobody thought what Porsche could do!"

What Porsche did was to base a new car on the 'Baby' concept. The steel centre section was retained but the floor was removed, replaced by a honeycomb aluminium floor which was positioned eight centimetres higher, effectively lowering the car by the same amount. The structure was reinforced by an aluminium roll cage, and aluminium subframes carried the front suspension, the powertrain and the rear suspension. Even the gearbox had to be turned upside down, so that the driveshafts could run in a straight line from the differential to the rear hubs.

'Flat front' bodywork was adopted, and a new longtail back section was made of plastic, utterly transforming the appearance of the car. The shape of the original doors had to be retained (but not the doors themselves), but in effect a new body was laid on top of the original, taking the width to two metres, and the overall length to 4,890 mm, compared with 4,680 mm for the 935 customer cars.

"When you looked from above there was quite a big step between the front and rear fenders" Ing. Singer recalls. "I said OK we will have big NACA ducts for the intercoolers and the cylinder heads, which were water cooled don't forget, and we had quick release fastenings so that you could see the original doors. "When it was built and lowered to the ground, it was all painted white, everyone looked at it and asked 'is this a 911?' They said it was like a whale, and from the first day we called it Moby Dick.

"Then the FIA came to Weissach to see the car, and they said 'NO WAY'! What were we doing? It was so low and so wide, it was not a 911. There was a lot of discussion, a lot of argument, and in the end they said OK, but you must have the original door shape. I asked them where it was written that you could not cover it.

"It was the same argument as we had the year before, we had to have the original rear window, so we finished up with a double rear window. That was the same principle, and they agreed it. In the end the FIA delegates, Paul Frere and Kurt Schild, said it complied with the regulations and it was OK, and they took a lot of pictures to Paris.

"Then we got a letter from the FIA saying that the car was illegal, they did not want these sort of cars running in the World Championship. We took off the covers so that you could see the doors, and extended the front fenders backwards a little way so that we had the aerodynamic benefit. There were still discussions, and we said that the scrutineers had given us the OK. In the end we got a tele-fax from the FIA president Pierre Ugeux who said that if the scrutineers had given their approval, then the technical sub-committee could not change it."

It was a close-run argument, and Singer knew that he had taken the regulations to the absolute limit, as he would do again with the Dauer Porsche LM in 1994. But as he said before, "if there is a loophole, we must take it".

Painted up in swoopy Martini & Rossi colours, the Porsche 935-78 caused a sensation when it appeared at Silverstone 6-Hours in May. The so-called 'silhouette formula' turned out to be nothing of the sort, and Jacky Ickx and Jochen Mass annihilated the sports car lap record on the British Grand Prix circuit, the German lopping 3.4 seconds off his own record set the previous year. He raised the best lap speed from 194.6 km/h to 202.514 km/h, and he and Ickx romped away to win by seven clear laps.

Bob Wollek and Henri Pescarolo were a distant second in the Kremer Porsche 935, none too pleased at being soundly beaten by Moby Dick. It was clear, though, that Porsche had no intention of contesting the full World Championship, and used Silverstone as a warm-up for Le Mans, where the 935-78 did not perform as well as expected, and finished eighth overall driven by Rolf Stommelen and Manfred Schurti. It misfired, it had an oil leak and it stopped 35 times for fuel, but in the early stages of the race it went every bit as fast as the prototypes!

Moby Dick's third appearance was at the Norisring at the end of June, a major German event but not a round of the World Championship, and there Ickx was able to make up for his difficult race in the 'Baby' 12 months previously.

Finally, Moby Dick raced once more at Vallelunga in the last round of the World Championship for Manufacturers, but Mass and Ickx had terrible problems with the handling. With a locked differential "it was under steering like hell" according to Singer, and defied all normal remedies. While the

6 Hours Dijon 1978: John Fitzpatrick, Hans Heyer, Toine Hezemans

SCALING THE HEIGHTS

6 Hours Mugello 1978: Martino Finotto, Carlo Facetti

sare zugestimmt haben, kann das Sub-Kommittee nicht mehr alles ändern." Es war ein Kampf auf der letzten Rille, und Singer wusste, das er bis an die äußerste Grenze des Reglements vorgestoßen war, wie er es viele Jahre später mit dem Dauer-Le Mans-GT machen würde.

Ausgeführt im Martini-Design war der 935-78 eine Sensation als er beim 6 Stunden-Rennen in Silverstone zum ersten Mal auftauchte. Jacky Ickx und Jochen Mass verbesserten den bestehenden Runderekord für Sportwagen. Der deutsche Fahrer unterbot seinen eigenen Rundenrekord um 3,4 Sekunden. Er ließ die Durchschnittsgeschwindigkeit für die schnellste Rennrunde von 194,6 auf 202,514 km/h ansteigen. Er und Ickx setzten sich sofort ab und gewannen klar mit einem Vorsprung von sieben Runden.

Mit erheblichem Rückstand fuhren Bob Wollek und Henri Pescarolo im Kremer 935 auf Rang zwei. Keiner von beiden war begeistert mit der klaren Niederlage gegen Moby Dick. Es war jedoch klar, dass Porsche keineswegs die Absicht hatte, die komplette WM zu bestreiten. Man nutzte das Rennen in Silverstone zur Vorbereitung für Le Mans, wo der 935-78 nicht so gut abschnitt als erwartet. Mit Rolf Stommelen und Manfred Schurti am Lenkrad fuhr das Auto auf den achten Gesamtplatz. Es gab Motoraussetzer, es gab einen Ölleck und das Auto kam nicht weniger als 35 Mal zum Nachtanken an die Box, aber in der Anfangsphase des Rennens war er nicht langsamer als die Prototypen.

Der dritte Auftritt von Moby Dick folgte auf dem Norisring, eine wichtige Veranstaltung in Deutschland, die aber nicht zur WM zählte. Hier konnte sich Ickx für sein schwieriges Rennen mit dem „Baby" ein Jahr zuvor revanchieren.

Zum Schluss fuhr Moby Dick noch einmal beim Finale der Hersteller-WM in Vallelunga. Hier litten Mass und Ickx unter massiven Problemen mit dem Fahrverhalten. Mit geschlossenem Differential war das Auto laut Singer „schrecklich zum Lenken". Alle normalen Maßnahmen zeigten keinerlei Wirkung. Während die Porsche von Kremer und Loos Rundenzeiten von 1.15 oder 1.16 hinlegten, hatte es der 935-78 schwer, die 1.17-Marke zu unterbieten. „Jeder konnte sehen, dass wir große Probleme hatten. Jacky kämpfte die ganze Zeit mit dem Auto und schließlich, nachdem wir die Feder, die Stabis und alles andere ausgetauscht hatten, änderten wir den Sturz der hinteren Räder. In den letzten Minuten fuhr er eine Rundenzeit von 1.13 und keiner konnte es glauben. Diese Zeit war einfach unglaublich."

Einmal mehr war der 935-78 in der Lage, die Kundenteams zu schlagen, hatte sogar Zeit für einen zusätzlichen Boxenstopp wegen des höheren Spritverbrauchs. Fünf Runden vor Schluss fuhr Ickx jedoch plötzlich mit einem Motorproblem an die Box. Der Riemen der die Benzin-Einspritzungspumpe betätigte, war gebrochen und das Werksteam hatte nicht mehr genügend Zeit für einen Wechsel. Das war eine Erleichterung für die Kundenteams. Wollek und Pescarolo siegten im Kremer 935.

Moby Dick fuhr kein Rennen mehr, fand seinen Platz im Porsche-Museum und inspirierte eine Reihe von Teams und Konstrukteure, allen voran Kremer Racing, einige seiner Merkmale zu kopieren. Die wassergekühlten Zylinderköpfe wurden allerdings auf keinen Fall zum Verkauf angeboten.

Porsche stellte dann die Entwicklung für den 935 ein. Man überließ es den Kundenteams, die Fahne mit einer Reihe von neu aufgebauten Autos hoch zu halten, 23 Exemplare wurden verkauft und rechtzeitig vor dem Start der Saison 1978 ausgeliefert.

Die Autos waren endlich allesamt mit den neuesten Doppelturbo-Motoren ausgestattet, die 600 PS lieferten. Auch 3,0 und 3,1-Litermotoren mit einer Leistung zwischen 675 und 720 PS standen zur Verfügung. Solche Ausführungen mussten jedoch in einer höheren Klasse mit einem Mindestgewicht von 1025 kg antreten, hatten also einen Extragewicht von 55 kg. Von der Dreiliter-Version mit 675 PS wurden die meisten Exemplare verkauft.

Georg Loos war ein wichtiger Kunde. Er kaufte sich drei Autos und zahlte eine grosse Summe für die personelle Werks-Unterstützung. Er war fest entschieden, mit seinem eigenen Team die WM zu gewinnen. Er hatte auch eine erstklassige Fahrerbesetzung mit Toine Hezemans, John Fitzpatrick, Klaus Ludwig und Hans Heyer. Peter Gregg startete für Loos in Daytona und in Watkins Glen, Rolf Stommelen fuhr auch in Daytona und Derek Bell verstärkte das Team in Silverstone sowie auf dem Nürburgring.

1000 km Nürburgring 1978: Manfred Schurti, Jacky Ickx

1000 km Nürburgring 1978: Herbert Müller, Claude Haldi

Poster

Kremer and Loos Porsches were running at 1:15 and 1:16, the 935/78 was struggling to break 1:17. "Everyone could see that we had big problems, Jacky was fighting the car all the time, and eventually when we had changed the springs, the bars and everything else, we altered the toe-in on the back wheels. In the last few minutes Jacky did a 1:13 and nobody could believe it, the time was impossible!"

Once again the 935-78 was able to outrun the customer teams, even having time for an extra pit stop on account of its consumption, but five laps from the end Ickx suddenly headed for the pits with the engine stopped. The belt serving the fuel injection pump had broken, and the Martini works team ran out of time to replace it.

That was a relief for the customers, anyway. Wollek and Pescarolo were the winners in their Kremer 935, ahead of two Gelo Racing Porsches, each with the same crew comprising Toine Hezemans, Klaus Ludwig and John Fitzpatrick.

Moby Dick did not race again, but took its place in the Porsche Museum and inspired a number of teams and constructors, most notably Kremer Racing, to copy some of its leading features. The water cooled cylinder heads were definitely not for sale, though.

The Porsche factory did no more development on the 935 once Moby Dick had been retired, leaving the customer teams to fly the flag with a new batch of cars, 23 in total, which were sold in time for the 1978 season.

All had the latest twin-turbo engines, at last, with a power output of 600 bhp, but 3.0 and 3.1 litre engines could be supplied developing between 675 and 720 bhp, although these cars had to run in a higher category with a minimum weight of 1,025 kg (an extra 55 kg, in other words). The 3-litre version was the most popular, with 675 bhp.

Georg Loos was the principal customer, buying three cars and even paying over the odds to have factory support, such was his determination to win the World Championship with his own team. He had a top driver line-up, too, including Toine Hezemans, John Fitzpatrick, Klaus Ludwig and Hans Heyer. Peter Gregg drove for Loos at Daytona and Watkins Glen, Rolf Stommelen at Daytona, and Derek Bell joined the team for Silverstone and the Nurburgring.

When Loos ran two 935s he had Heyer, Ludwig, Hezemans and Fitzpatrick seat-hopping between them, so that they got double results, and he employed six drivers when he ran his third car at Silverstone and the Nurburgring. Loos, however, entered only one of his 935s at Le Mans and it was the first to retire, with a broken piston.

The Kremer brothers bought two cars, selling one or to Dieter Schornstein and 'John Winter' (Louis Krages) and running it as their second team car. Bob Wollek and Henri Pescarolo drove the lead car very ably all season, the Frenchman bringing sponsorship from Adolphe Lafont.

Franz Konrad, "the young Austrian based in Germany" as the contemporary Autocourse annual described him, bought a 935 with asistance from Volkert Merl, the German oil dealer, and Joest also drove the car early in the season.

The Gelo team started the season as it meant to continue, with a strong victory in the Daytona 24-Hours thanks to Peter Gregg, Rolf Stommelen and Toine Hezemans. Second, but 30 laps behind, was another 935 driven by Dick Barbour, the car's owner, Johnny Rutherford and Manfred Schurti. Both the Kremer and Konrad teams were delayed by engine and turbocharger difficulties.

The Loos team claimed its second victory at Mugello, the red 935 driven by Hezemans, Fitzpatrick and Heyer taking the flag, but only after Pescarolo retired the Kremer Porsche from the lead with a holed piston. Konrad was second overall, with Merl and Joest, and only one lap down after six hours of racing.

SCALING THE HEIGHTS

Wenn Loos zwei 935 einsetzte, ließ er Heyer, Ludwig, Hezemans und Fitzpatrick abwechselnd auf beiden Autos fahren, so dass sie doppelte Ergebnisse einfuhren. Wenn er in Silverstone und auf dem Nürburgring sein drittes Auto einsetzte, hatte er sogar sechs Fahrer im Einsatz. Loos schrieb jedoch nur einen 935 in Le Mans ein und das Auto war das erste, das ausfiel. Die Ursache war ein gebrochener Kolben. Die Gebrüder Kremer kauften sich zwei Autos und verkauften eins an Dieter Schornstein und 'John Winter' (Louis Krages), das sie als zweites Auto ihres Teams einsetzten. Bob Wollek und Henri Pescarolo zeigten mit dem ersten Auto über die ganze Saison hinweg eine sehr gute Leistung. Der Franzose brachte Sponsorgelder von Adolphe Lafont.

Franz Konrad, der in Deutschland lebende Österreicher, wie ihn das Jahrbuch Autocourse aus jenem Jahr beschrieb, kaufte sich einen 935 mit Unterstützung von Volkert Merl, einem deutschen Ölhändler. Reinhold Joest fuhr am Anfang der Saison ebenfalls auf diesem Auto.

Das Gelo-Team begann die Saison nach Maß mit einem überlegenen Sieg im 24 Stunden-Rennen von Daytona für Peter Gregg, Rolf Stommelen und Toine Hezemans. Ein weiterer 935 mit Eigentümer Dick Barbour, Johnny Rutherford und Manfred Schurti belegte Rang zwei, jedoch mit 30 Runden Rückstand. Die Autos von Kremer und Konrad verloren viel Zeit mit Motor- und Turbo-Problemen.

Das Loos-Team holte sich den zweiten Sieg in Mugello. Der rote 935 mit Hezemans, Fitzpatrick und Heyer überquerte als Erster die Ziellinie, aber nur, nachdem Pescarolo im Kremer-Porsche wegen eines Kolbendefekts in Führung liegend ausgeschieden war. Konrad belegte zusammen mit Merl und Joest Rang zwei in der Gesamtwertung. Ihnen fehlten nach sechs Stunden lediglich eine Runde.

Das Kremer-Team schlug in Dijon mit einem ungefährdeten Sieg für Wollek und Pescarolo zurück. Fitzpatrick und Heyer sicherten sich den zweiten Platz mit drei Runden Rückstand wegen eines Lecks im Turbolader. Das Auto von Hezemans fiel mit gebrochener Antriebswelle aus, für Konrad führte eine kaputte Zylinderkopfdichtung zum vorzeitigen Ausfall.

In Silverstone ging es um den zweiten Platz hinter Moby Dick, und erneut hatte der Kremer-Porsche mit Wollek und Pescarolo die Nase vorn. Wollek hatte auch noch Zeit, das zweite Auto des Teams zu fahren. So verhalf er Schornstein und ‚Winter' zu Rang fünf hinter zwei BMW 320i. Das Gelo-Team, das drei Autos eingeschrieben hatte, erlebte ein Wochenende zum Vergessen: Hezemans beschädigte ein Auto nach einem Unfall und die beiden anderen fielen mit kleinen technischen Problemen aus.

Das 1000 km-Rennen auf dem Nürburgring war in zwei gleichen Teilen zu je 500 Kilometern aufgeteilt. Heyer und Ludwig gewannen das erste Rennen für das Gelo-Team vor Manfred Schurtis 935 in Jägermeister-Farben, den er zusammen mit Jacky Ickx fuhr. Pescarolo verlor Zeit nach einer Kollision und Hezemans fiel aus, ebenfalls nach einer Kollision mit einem langsameren Kontrahenten.

Wollek und Pescarolo gewannen das zweite Rennen. Sie schlugen Ludwig, Heyer und auch Hezemans, der zusätzlich ins Fahrerkader aufgenommen worden war. Schurti und Ickx belegten Rang drei. In der Addition beider Läufe siegten Ludwig, Heyer und Hezemans vor Schurti und Ickx. Platz drei ging an Pescarolo und Wollek, während Konrad, Merl und Ralf-Dieter Schreiber Rang vier belegten.

Wollek und Pescarolo feierten ihren zweiten bedeutenden Rennsieg des Jahres in Misano, weit vor dem 935 der italienischen Privatfahrer Vittorio Coggiola und Piero Monticone. Nach dem Ausfall der beiden Gelo-Porsche kamen Konrad und Merl auf Platz drei über die Ziellinie.

Winner 6 Hours Silverstone 1978: Jochen Mass, Jacky Ickx

In Watkins Glen gingen nur wenige europäische Teams an den Start. Auch Kremer verzichtete auf den Einsatz. Das Rennen brachte einen weiteren Sieg für Gelo Racing. Hezemans, Fitzpatrick und Gregg gewannen das Rennen vor Barbour, der zusammen mit Schurti und Stommelen fuhr.

Der achte und letzte Lauf zur Hersteller-WM 1978 fand in Vallelunga statt und brachte den dritten Saisonsieg für Kremer. Wollek und Pescarolo standen erneut ganz oben auf dem Treppchen.

Dieses Ergebnis kam jedoch nur durch den späten Ausfall von Moby Dick zustande. Dieser Ausfall war sicherlich kein politischer Rückzieher, wie es viele glaubten. Das Werksteam hatte einen einzigen WM-Lauf gewonnen, in Silverstone, während Gelo Racing vier Rennen gewonnen hatte.

Porsche beendete die WM-Saison mit 120 Punkten nach Abzug von zwei Streichresultaten, hatte jedoch eigentlich 160 Punkte eingefahren. BMW siegte in der Zweiliterklasse, ebenfalls mit 120 Punkten, hatte aber 140 Punkte vor Abzug der Streichresultate.

Die Sportwagen-Europameisterschaft (ehemals WM) erlebte 1978 ein schwieriges Jahr. Nach dem Rückzug des Porsche-Werksteam traf die FIA die mutige und richtige Entscheidung, die Gruppen 5 und 6 für die Saison 1979 zusammen zu legen. Diese Regelung wurde auch 1980 und 1981 beibehalten, mit einem starken Aufgebot von Lancia, während BMW so schnell wie möglich den M1 für den Einsatz in der Gruppe 5 entwickelte.

Winner 1000 km Nürburgring 1978: Klaus Ludwig, Hans Heyer, Toine Hezemans

ERFOLGE AM FLIESSBAND

1000 km Nürburgring 1978: Volkert Merl, Franz Konrad, Rolf-Dieter Schreiber

The Kremer team hit its stride at Dijon where Wollek and Pescarolo scored an easy victory, Fitzpatrick and Heyer finishing second, three laps behind, with a leaking turbocharger. Hezemans' 935 retired with a broken driveshaft, and Konrad's went out with a head gasket failure.

At Silverstone, the race was for second place behind Moby Dick, and again the Kremer Porsche came through in the hands of Wollek and Pescarolo. Wollek also found time to drive the team's second car, helping Schornstein and 'Winter' to fifth place behind a pair of BMW 320i. The Gelo team, which entered three cars, had a disastrous weekend as Hezemans crashed one car, and the other two retired with quite minor mechanical problems, a stripped wheel nut thread and an oil leak.

The Nurburgring 1,000 Kms was held in two equal parts, of 500 Kms. Ludwig and Heyer won the first for the Gelo team, from Schurti's Jagermeister sponsored 935 shared with Ickx, while Pescarolo was delayed by a clash with a backmarket and Hezemans retired, also after hitting a slower car.

Wollek and Pescarolo won the second race, beating Ludwig, Heyer and Hezemans who had been added to the line-up, with Schurti and Ickx placed third. On aggregate Ludwig, Heyer and Hezemans were the winners from Schurti and Ickx, with Pescarolo and Wollek third. In fourth place were Konrad, Merl and Ralf-Dieter Schreiber.

Wollek and Pescarolo scored their second main victory of the season at Misano, a long way ahead of the 935 of Italian privateers Vittorio Coggiola and Piero Monticone. Third were Konrad and Merl after the two Gelo Porsches retired, one having run out of petrol, the other with damaged piston rings. Watkins Glen, thinly supported by European teams and passed up by Kremer Racing, resulted in another victory for Gelo Racing, Hezemans, Fitzpatrick and Gregg taking the flag ahead of Barbour, racing with Schurti and Stommelen.

The eighth and final round of the 1978 World Championship for Manufacturers was held at Vallelunga, Italy, and rewarded Kremer Racing with their third victory of the season. Wollek and Pescarolo were again the winners, this time ahead of two Gelo Racing Porsches driven by Hezemans, Heyer and Fitzpatrick (second), and Ludwig, Fitzpatrick and Hezemans (third).

That result, as we know, came after Moby Dick's late retirement, which was definitely not a political withdrawal as many people believed. The factory team won a single World Championship race, at Silverstone, and Gelo Racing won four.

Porsche finished the World Championship with 120 points, but 160 gross after dropping two scores, while BMW won the 2-litre division also with 120 points, 140 gross.

The European Sportscar Championship (previously World) struggled through the 1978 season, and with the withdrawal of the Porsche factory team the FIA made a brave, and correct decision to combine Groups 5 and 6 for the 1979 season. The formula continued through 1980 and 1981, contested strongly by Lancia, while BMW hastened to develop the M1 for Group 5 racing.

Having achieved all that he set out to do, Georg Loos withdrew from the World Championship leaving his neighbours in Cologne, Erwin and Manfred Kremer, as the principal team representing Porsche. Klaus Ludwig joined the Kremer Racing team, and so crowned his career with a victory at Le Mans, and won the coveted Porsche Cup.

Kremer's K3 was the most extreme development of the 935 carried out by a private workshop, making full use of the 'boundary challenges' posed by Moby Dick, and reluctantly approved by the FIA. The interior roll cage extended forwards to the front suspension pickup points and rearwards to the rear suspension, effectively making this a space frame car within the centre part of the standard 911 bodyshell.

New bodywork, in plastic, covered the 911's familiar shape, making it far more aerodynamic, and the Kremers developed their own engines up to 3.2 litre capacity. The intercooler was cooled by air, saving the extra weight of the factory's water cooled system, and the ambient air was drawn through the intercooler by the engine cooling fan, which created low pressure. Clever.

Winner 6 Hours Vallelunga 1978: Bob Wollek, Henri Pescarolo

SCALING THE HEIGHTS

Nachdem er alles erreicht hatte, was er sich vorgenommen hatte, zog sich Georg Loos aus der WM zurück. Klaus Ludwig kam zum Kremer-Team und krönte seinen Laufbahn mit einem Sieg in Le Mans. Er gewann auch den begehrten Porsche Cup. Kremers K3 war die extremste Entwicklung des 935, die von einem Privatteam gemacht wurde. Jede Grenze des Reglements, die von Moby Dick aufgeweicht worden war, wurde gnadenlos ausgenützt, und die FIA gab zähneknirschend grünes Licht.

Neue Karrosserieteile aus Plastik verdeckten die bekannte Form des 911 und machten das Auto viel aerodynamischer. Die Kremer-Brüder entwickelten ihre eigenen Motoren mit Hubraum bis zu 3,2 Litern. Der Zwischenkühler wurde mit Luft gekühlt, so dass das Zusatzgewicht der vom Werksteam eingesetzten Wasserkühlung eingespart werden konnte. Die Außenluft wurde vom Kühlgebläse des Motors durch den Zwischenkühler geleitet. Eine kluge Lösung.

Der 3,2-Litermotor wurde nicht in Le Mans eingesetzt, kam dafür aber bei den 6 Stunden-Rennen zum Einsatz. Das Triebwerk lieferte 750 PS bei einem Ladedruck von 1,5 bar und 800 PS bei 1,7 bar. Porsche lieferte Verbesserungskits, so dass die Kundenteams ihre 935 auf den neuesten Stand bringen konnten.

Jacky Ickx

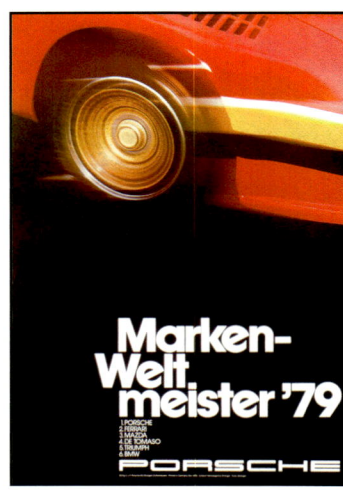

Poster

Kurz darauf folgte auf dem Nürburgring der dritte Sieg für Kremer mit Schurti, Fitzpatrick und Wollek. Rang zwei ging an den neuen K3 der Kremer-Brüder, eine innovative Entwicklung, inspiriert von Moby Dick. In diesem Auto hatten Ludwig und Plankenhorn nur elf Sekunden Rückstand auf ihren Teamkollegen. Pescarolo und Redman belegten Rang drei in einem weiteren Kremer 935. Zum ersten Mal sicherten sich die Brüder alle drei Plätze auf dem Podium.

Das Kremer-Team, zufrieden nach dem Sieg in Le Mans mit dem neuen K3, verzichtete auf die Teilnahme an den folgenden zwei WM-Läufen. Die Brüder Don und Bill Whittington gewannen das 6 Stunden-Rennen von Watkins Glen im eigenen 935/77A mit Unterstützung von Klaus Ludwig, der zur Verstärkung des Fahrerteams verpflichtet worden war.

Reinhold Joest siegte im August beim 6 Stunden-Rennen in Brands Hatch mit seinem 908/4, einmal mehr zusammen mit Volkert Merl. Er schlug den Kremer 935 K3 von Ludwig und Plankenhorn. Ein Chevron belegte Rang drei, Schornstein und Dören wurden Vierte. Das Saisonfinale 1979 wurde in Vallelunga ausgetragen, und erneut blieb die Kremer-Mannschaft in Köln. Porsche gewann wieder einmal die Hersteller-WM mit der maximalen Punktzahl von 120. Diesmal mussten keine Punkte gestrichen werden. Dieser Erfolg war in erster Linie dem Einsatz des Kremer-Teams zu verdanken.

1980 wurde die Hersteller-WM auf elf Rennen erweitert. Erneut wurden Sportwagen zugelassen, sie waren aber nicht punktberechtigt. Die wahre Herausforderung für die Porsche-Kundenteams waren die kleinen Lancia Beta Monte Carlo Coupé, extreme Gruppe 5-Autos, angetrieben von 1,4-Liter-Vierzylinder-Turbomotoren, von denen man sagte, dass sie mehr als 400 PS leisteten.

Die Lancia gewannen die Gesamtwertung in Brands Hatch, Mugello und Watkins Glen unter der Leitung von Cesare Fiorio. Die Fahrerbesetzung bestand aus Riccardo Patrese, Walter Röhrl, Michele Alboreto und Eddie Cheever.

Porsche 935 gewannen nur drei der elf WM-Läufe, fuhren aber reichlich Punkte in der Klasse über 2000 ccm ein. Diesmal musste Porsche den WM-Titel teilen. Insgesamt hatte man 210 Punkte eingefahren, nach Abzug von Streichresultaten blieben 160 Punkte übrig, da nur die acht besten Ergebnisse berücksichtigt wurden. Lancia hatte in der Zweiliterklasse insgesamt 200 Punkte eingefahren und hatte nach Abzug ebenfalls 160 Punkte.

Reinhold Joest gewann das 24 Stunden-Rennen von Daytona mit Stommelen und Merl im 935. In einem weiteren 935 belegten Al Holbert und John Paul Rang zwei.

Beim ersten europäischen Rennen der Saison in Brands Hatch war der bestplatzierte Porsche ein 935 K3, im Besitz

Winner 6 Hours Watkins Glen 1979: Klaus Ludwig, Don and Bill Whittington

Der Interscope 935 siegte 1979 beim 24 Stunden-Rennen von Daytona mit einer amerikanischen Fahrerbesetzung, die aus Eigentümer Ted Field sowie Danny Ongais und Hurley Haywood bestand. Danach wurde die WM in Europa fortgesetzt. Der nächste Lauf war in Mugello.

Dort feierte Kremer einen Doppelsieg mit Fitzpatrick, Schurti und Wollek vor Ickx, Wollek und Schurti. Platz drei ging an die Italiener Martino Finotto und Carlo Facetti im 935, die vom Osella-PA6-BMW mit Giorgio Francia und Lella Lombardi gejagt wurden.

Reinhold Joest gewann das 6 Stunden-Rennen von Dijon im eigenen 908/4 Turbo, wobei er den Kremer 935 von Schurti, Ickx und Wollek schlug. Platz drei ging an einen weiteren Kremer 935 mit Schornstein und Edgar Dören.

Im darauffolgenden 6 Stunden-Rennen von Silverstone holte sich das Kremer-Team den zweiten Saisonsieg mit Fitzpatrick, Wollek und Heyer. Der De-Cadenet-Sportwagen von Alain de Cadenet, basierend auf einem Lola, wurde Zweiter. Schornstein und Dören fuhren erneut auf Rang drei ein.

84 ERFOLGE AM FLIESSBAND

The 3.2 litre engine was not used at Le Mans but was introduced in 6-hour races, and developed 750 bhp on 1.5 bar boost and over 800 bhp on 1.7 bar boost. The Porsche factory introduced upgrade kits enabling customers to improve their 935s.

The Interscope Porsche 935 won the Daytona 24-Hours in 1979, an all American team comprising owner Ted Field, Danny Ongais and Hurley Haywood, then the World Championship moved to Europe, at Mugello.

There, the Kremer Racing team achieved a 1-2 success with Fitzpatrick, Schurti and Wollek ahead of Wollek, Ickx and Schurti. Third were the Italians, Martino Finotto and Carlo Facetti in their 935 chased by the Osella PA6 BMW of Giorgio Francia and Lella Lombardi.

Reinhold Joest won the Dijon 6-Hours in his Porsche 908/4 turbo, beating the Kremer Porsche 935 of Schurti, Ickx and Wollek. Third was another Kremer 935 driven by Schornstein and Edgar Doeren.

On, then, to the Silverstone 6-Hours where the Kremer team claimed its second victory of the season, with Fitzpatrick, Wollek and Heyer. Second was Alain de Cadenet's Lola based de Cadenet sports car, and again Schornstein and Doeren finished third.

Kremer's third win soon followed, at the Nurburgring, with Schurti, Fitzpatrick and Wollek in command. Second was an interesting Porsche, the Kremer brother's new K3, an advanced development inspired by Moby Dick, in which Klaus Ludwig and Axel Plankenhorn finished only 11 seconds behind their team-mates. Henri Pescarolo and Brian Redman were third in another Kremer Porsche 935, the first time that the brothers had occupied all three places on the podium.

The Kremer team, well satisfied with victory at Le Mans with the new K3, did not contest the next two rounds of the World Championship. The 6-Hour race at Enna was won by Lella Lombardi and Enrico Grimaldi in an Osella PA7 BMW, then the Whittington brothers, Don and Bill, won the Watkins Glen 6-Hours in their own Porsche 935/77A with Klaus Ludwig on the driver team.

Reinhold Joest wheeled out his Porsche 908/4 to win the Brands Hatch 6-Hours in August, again with Volkert Merl, beating the Kremer Porsche 935 K3 of Ludwig and Plankenhorn. A Chevron was placed third, Schornstein and Doeren fourth, and the Lancia Beta Monte Carlo 1.4 turbo of Riccardo Patrese and Walter Rohrl was fifth. That was a car that needed watching!

(l.-r.): Don Whittington, Klaus Ludwig, Bill Whittington, Manfred Kremer

1000 km Nürburgring 1979: Bob Wollek, John Fitzpatrick, Manfred Schurti

6 Hours Watkins Glen 1979: Rolf Stommelen, Dick Barbour, Paul Newman

The final round of the 1979 season was held at Vallelunga, and again the Kremers remained in Cologne. It was a clean sweep for the Osella sports car marque, Lombardi and Francia leading the way in their BMW powered PA7.

Again, Porsche won the World Championship for Manufacturers with a maximum of 120 points (none needed to be discarded), largely thanks to the efforts of Kremer Racing, well ahead of Lancia and BMW. The Osella marque was ineligible for points.

The World Championship for Manufacturers was expanded to 11 rounds in 1980 and allowed sports cars to take part although ineligible for points. The real challenge to the private Porsche teams came from the little Lancia Beta Monte Carlo coupes, extreme Group 5 cars powered by 1.4 litre, four-cylinder turbocharged engines said to develop over 400 bhp.

These proved outright winners at Brands Hatch, Mugello and Watkins Glen - in fact, the Lancia team directed by Cesare Fiorio claimed first and second positions in each of these 6-hour races, the drive team including Riccado Patrese, Walter Rohrl, Michele Alboreto and Eddie Cheever.

Porsche 935s won only three of the 11 rounds but picked up plenty of 'over 2,000 cc' placings and this time had to share the World Championship, with a gross score of 210 points and a net score of 160 (eight best). Lancia scored a gross of 200 points in the 2-litre division, and 160 points net (eight best) so it was a score-draw for the world championship title. Reinhold Joest won the Daytona 24-Hours with Stommelen and Merl sharing his 935, with Al Holbert and John Paul second in another 935.

SCALING THE HEIGHTS 85

1000 km Nürburgring 1980: John Fitzpatrick, Dick Barbour, Axel Plankenhorn

von Dudley Wood, der das Auto zusammen mit John Cooper und Peter Lovett fuhr. Das Team belegte den fünften Platz in der Gesamtwertung nach drei Lancia und dem De-Cadenet-Ford-DFV von Alain de Cadenet und Desiré Wilson. Immerhin fuhr Porsche die maximale Zahl von 20 Punkten ein.
Schlimmer war es in Mugello, wo die Lancia Beta Monte Carlo die Plätze eins, zwei und vier belegten. Ein BMW M1 gewann die Gruppe 5 und der beste Porsche war nur Achter mit Dany Snobeck und Paul Destic.
De Cadenet und Wilson gewannen das 6 Stunden-Rennen von Monza, indem sie den 935 von Henri Pescarolo und Jürgen Barth schlugen, immerhin noch vor dem Lancia von Patrese und Röhrl. Überraschenderweise gewannen de Cadenet und Desiré Wilson auch das 6 Stunden-Rennen von Silverstone, wobei sie nur knapp vor Siggi Bruns 908/4 blieben, in dem Barth als zweiter Fahrer fuhr. Diesmal fuhr der 935 K3 von Danny Ongais und Brian Redman auf den dritten Gesamtrang und sicherte sich damit die vollen 20 Punkte.
Stommelen und Barth gewannen das 1000 km-Rennen auf dem Nürburgring mit einem 908/4, nur 41 Sekunden vor Dick Barbours 935 K3, der Amerikaner zusammen mit Fitzpatrick und Plankenhorn fuhr. Das drittplatzierte Team, Hans Stuck und Nelson Piquet auf BMW M1, sorgten für etwas Abwechslung auf dem Siegerpodest.
Watkins Glen brachte einen weiteren Doppelsieg für die Lancia Beta Monte Carlo. Barbours 935 K3 belegte Rang drei mit Brian Redman und John Fitzpatrick, der den Gewinn des Porsche Cups ansteuerte. Mosport kam den leichten Lancia jedoch nicht entgegen. Diesmal holten sich Fitzpatrick und Redman den Gesamtsieg, vor John Paul Sr. und John Paul Jr. Kremers K3 belegte die Plätze eins bis drei.
Der zehnte Lauf in Vallelunga zog nur wenige Teilnehmer an. Es siegte der Osella-PA8-BMW von Giorgio Francia und Roberto Marazzai vor dem 908/4, den sich Siggi Brun mit Derek Bell teilten. Edgar Dören und Jürgen Lassig gewannen die Gruppe 5 im 935.
Das Finale dieser interessanten Saison ging in Dijon über die Bühne. Dort siegten Pescarolo und Barth im 935 klar vor Claude Haldi und Bernard Béguin, ebenfalls mit einem 935.
Die Hersteller-WM erlebte 1981 die letzte Saison, denn 1982 machte sie Platz für die Gruppe C. Um das Interesse an der Serie zu steigern, schrieb die FIA eine Fahrermeisterschaft aus, die vom Amerikaner Bob Garretson im 935 K3 gewonnen wurde. Es gab lediglich sechs Rennen. Diese waren Teil der 15 Rennen der Fahrermeisterschaft, mit sieben Veranstaltungen in Nordamerika. Lancia stellte das einzige Werksteam in der Serie mit Martini & Rossi als Sponsor. Man erwartete, dass Lancia die maximale Punktzahl in der Zweiliterklasse einfahren würde.

Porsche war durch Privatteams vertreten und war auch in der Lage, die maximale Punktzahl in der Klasse über zwei Liter einzufahren, aber vereinzelt musste man sich dem Kampf mit dem BMW M1 stellen.
Lancia hatte Schwierigkeiten in Daytona, wo ein Monte Carlo mit technischem Defekt ausfiel und der andere viel Zeit verlor. Der Sieg in der Zweiliterklasse wurde jedoch vom Jolly-Club-Lancia eingefahren, der auf dem siebten Rang ins Ziel kam und 20 Punkte kassierte. Der Sieg beim 24 Stunden-Rennen ging an Bob Garretson, dessen 935 K3 vom Cooke-Woods-Racing-Team eingesetzt wurde, mit Bobby Rahal und Brian Redman als Fahrerkollegen. Platz zwei ging an den 935 von Akin, der mit Derek Bell und Craig Siebert fuhr. Das 1000 km-Rennen von Monza wurde von Edgar Dören und Jürgen Lassig im Weralit-Team-935 gewonnen. Auch in diesem Regenrennen sah Lancia die Zielflagge nicht.
In Silverstone gab es einen neuen Sieger, der von Vegla gesponserte 935 von Harald Grohs, Dieter Schornstein und Walter Röhrl, dem ehemaligen Rallye-Weltmeister, der das Lager gewechselt hatte. Derek Bell hatte in Steve O'Rourkes BMW M1, den er sich mit dem Besitzer und David Hobbs teilte, neun Runden Rückstand. Zum dritten Mal in Folge fielen die Martini-Lancia aus. Ebenfalls zum dritten Mal fuhr jedoch ein privater Ex-Werks-Monte-Carlo auf Rang sieben ins Ziel und holte damit 20 WM-Punkte.
Nach drei Rennen hatten Porsche und Lancia je 60 Punkte. Der vierte Lauf wurde auf dem Nürburgring ausgetragen, wurde aber kurz vor Halbzeit abgebrochen, nachdem Herbert Müller einen schweren Unfall hatte. Er kam von der Strecke ab und fuhr in ein dort stehendes Auto, das vorher ausgefallen war. Müller kam beim Unfall ums Leben. Piquet und Stuck im BMW M1 wurden schließlich zu Siegern erklärt, Bob Wollek fuhr im Kremer 935 K3 auf Platz drei. Es gab nur die halbe Punktzahl. Porsche gewann somit 7,5 Punkte und fiel im WM-Stand hinter Lancia zurück.

1000 km Nürburgring 1980: Bob Wollek, Manfred Schurti

1000 km Nürburgring 1981: Bob Akin, Bobby Rahal

ERFOLGE AM FLIESSBAND

1000 km Nürburgring 1981

At Brands Hatch, the first event in Europe, the highest placed Porsche was the 935 K3 owned and driven by Dudley Wood, with John Cooper and Peter Lovett, in fifth position overall behind three Lancias and the de Cadenet Ford DFV of Alain de Cadenet and Desire Wilson. Never mind, Porsche got the full helping of 20 points.

Worse was to come at Mugello where the Lancia Beta Monte Carlos finished first, second and fourth. A BMW M1 won the Group 5 class and the best Porsche 935 was down in eighth place driven by Dany Snobeck and Paul Destic. Only 15 points for Porsche, not the full 20.

De Cadenet and Ms Wilson won the Monza 6-Hours, beating the Porsche 935 of Henri Pescarolo and Juergen Barth, who had the consolation of finishing ahead of the Lancia of Patrese and Rohrl. Dieter Schornstein and Harald Grohs were fourth in another 935. Surprisingly, de Cadenet and Desire Wilson also won the Silverstone 6-Hours, narrowly ahead of Siggi Brun's Porsche 908/4 co-driven by Juergen Barth. This time the Porsche 935 K3 of Danny Ongais and Brian Redman was third overall, picking up 20 points.

Stommelen and Barth won the Nurburgring 1,000 Kms in a 908/4, only 41 seconds ahead of Dick Barbour's 935 K3 which the big man drove with Fitzpatrick and Plankenhorn. Third was a BMW M1 raced by Hans Stuck and Piquet, putting some variety into the podium line-up.

Watkins Glen, another Lancia Beta Monte Carlo 1-2, with Barbour's 935 K3 third in the hands of Fitzpatrick, who was well on his way to winning the Porsche Cup, and Redman. Mosport, by contrast, did not suit the lightweight Lancias and this time Fitzpatrick and Redman achieved an outright victory ahead of John Paul Sr and John Paul Jr. Kremers' K3 model claimed the top three positions.

6 Hours Silverstone 1981: Preston Henn, Adrian Yates-Smith

The 10th round, at Vallelunga, was poorly supported. It was won by the Osella PA8 BMW of Giorgio Francia and Roberto Marazzai ahead of Siggi Brun's 908/4 with Derek Bell co-driving. Edgar Doeren and Juergen Lassig won the Group 5 class in their Porsche 935.

The final round of this interesting season was run at Dijon, where Pescarolo and Barth were the clear winners in a 935 ahead of another piloted by Haldi and Beguin.

The World Championship for Manufacturers entered its final season in 1981, preparing to make way for the fuel consumption controlled Group C in 1982, and to inject some more interest in the series the FIA inaugurated a Driver Championship, which was won by the American Bob Garretson in a Porsche 935 K3.

The championship for manufacturers comprised only six rounds, but these were included in the 15-round drivers championship which featured seven events in North America. Lancia had the only factory team in the championship, sponsored by Martini & Rossi (the Italian vermouth company had last been associated with Porsche in 1978, on Moby Dick), and could be expected to earn maximum points in the 2-litre division.

Porsche, represented by private teams, might also pick up maximum points in the over 2-litre division, although they had to contend with BMW's M1 on occasions.

Lancia's effort was humbled at Daytona, where one Monte Carlo broke down and the other was delayed, but still the 2-litre class was won by the Jolly Club's Lancia which finished seventh overall, and duly earned 20 points. The 24-Hours was won by Bob Garretson whose 935 K3 was run by the Cooke Woods Racing team, and co-driven by Bobby Rahal and Brian Redman. Second was Bob Akin's 935 co-driven by Derek Bell and Craig Siebert.

The Monza 1,000 Kms was won by Edgar Doeren and Juergen Lassig in their Weralit team 935 and again, in this wet race, the Lancia Martini team failed to finish. Fiorio was fortunate that a scruffy, ex-factory Montecarlo finished seventh, and won the 2-litre class.

Silverstone featured a new winner, the Vegla sponsored Porsche 935 of Harald Grohs, Dieter Schornstein and Walter Rohrl, the former World Rally Champion having switched his allegiance. Derek Bell was nine laps behind in Steve O'Rourke's BMW M1, shared with the owner and David Hobbs. For the third time in succession the Lancia Martinis failed to finish, but also for the third time in succession a privately run, ex-works Monte Carlo finished seventh and claimed 20 points.

Three rounds completed, three to go, and Porsche and Lancia were level on 60 points. The fourth round was held at the

SCALING THE HEIGHTS 87

Porsche und Lancia holten sich beide die maximale Punktzahl in Le Mans, wo der Charles-Ivey-Racing-K3 von Dudley Wood, John Cooper und Claude Bourgoignie auf den vierten Gesamtrang fuhr. Danach gab es nur noch ein Rennen in Watkins Glen. Die kleinen Lancia feierten einen Doppelsieg und holten sich ohne Probleme den letzten WM-Titel in der Gruppe 5. Bob Garretson fuhr im K3 zusammen mit Bobby Rahal und Rick Mears auf Platz drei.

Insgesamt startete Garretson mit seinem Porsche bei acht der 15 Läufe zur Fahrer-WM. Er bekam seinen Meistertitel keineswegs geschenkt. Nach dem Sieg beim 24 Stunden-Rennen von Daytona belegte er die Positionen vier in Riverside, sechs in Le Mans, drei in Watkins Glen, vier in Elkhart Lake und schließlich Rang zwei in Brands Hatch. Das letzte Ergebnis reichte ihm zum Titelgewinn.

Harald Grohs war ein verdienter Vizemeister. Er fuhr bei den fünf europäischen Rennen im Vegla-Porsche und startete bei vier Läufen in Nordamerika für das Andial-Meister-Team. Grohs feierte drei Siege, in Silverstone, Mosport und Elkhart Lake. Bobby Rahal, Dritter der Fahrerwertung, nahm an zehn Rennen teil, sowohl mit Garretson als auch mit Akin.

Es wird manchmal vergessen, dass die FIA 1982 zwei neue Kategorien für Gruppe B und Gruppe C-Fahrzeuge ausschrieb, in denen man nur für ein Jahr auch die alten Autos der Gruppen 4 und 5 sowie Sportwagen zuließ, um die Starterfelder etwas zu vergrößern. Lancia machte beim Versuch, 1982 den Fahrertitel zu gewinnen, von dieser Regelung gebrauch. Man schrieb „Barchettas", basierend auf dem Beta Monte Carlo ein. Die Fahrer waren punktberechtigt, der Hersteller war es nicht. Die Gruppe B erwies sich als Reinfall. Es wurde eine Mindeststückzahl von 200 Autos vorgeschrieben, das Reglement entsprach weitgehend dem der Rallye-WM. Nur ein Gruppe B-Auto ging an den Start, der Porsche 911 Turbo 3.0 von Georg Memminger und Fritz Müller. Ihr bestes Saisonergebnis war ein neunter Platz im Gesamtergebnis des 1000 km-Rennens auf dem Nürburgring.

6 Hours Silverstone 1982: John Cooper, Paul Smith (60) – Dieter Schornstein, Harald Grohs (63)

Porsche hatte für dieses Rennen nicht den neuen 956 gemeldet, obwohl es nach dem Debüt des Autos in Silverstone stattfand, und beanspruchte kurzerhand 15 Punkte für Memmingers Ergebnis. Die Regeln der FIA waren in diesem Punkt nicht eindeutig und erst Mitte Oktober wurde entschieden, dass nur Gruppe C-Autos Punkte für die Meisterschaft einfahren konnten.

Porsche und das Team von Jean Rondeau, das von Ford unterstützt wurde, waren ebenbürtig, aber das Rothmans-Porsche-Team sicherte sich den WM-Titel mit einem Doppelsieg im September in Spa. Memmingers Ergebnis vom Nürburgring machte keinen Unterschied, sein Auftritt in der Eifel führte jedoch zu vielen Diskussionen.

Der 935 zeigte sich auch 1982 gut in Form, obwohl er keine Punkte einfuhr. Ted Field und Rolf Stommelen belegten im Interscope 935 K3 den zweiten Gesamtplatz in Monza. Gianpiero Moretti und Mauro Baldi kamen im Momo-Auto in Silverstone auf Rang sieben ins Ziel und wiederholten dieses Ergebnis in Spa. Schornstein, Merl und Wollek waren Sechste im Gesamtergebnis von Mugello, Jim Adams und Ralph Kent-Cooke fuhren auf Platz sieben in Fuji.

Der letzte Auftritt des 935 in einem Lauf zur FIA-Weltmeisterschaft folgte in Brands Hatch, wo John Fitzpatrick, David Hobbs und Bob Wollek den dritten Gesamtplatz hinter dem 956 von Ickx und Bell und dem Lancia Barchetta von Fabi und Patrese belegten.

Winner Group B 1000 km Spa 1982: Georg Memminger, Fritz Müller

Winner Group 5 1000 km Spa 1982:
Gianpiero Moretti, Mauro Baldi

1000 km Spa 1982: Jürgen Lässig, Teddy Pilette, Jean-Paul Libert

1000 km Nürburgring 1983: Georg Memminger, Heinz Kuhn-Weiss

Nurburgring, but it was red-flagged shortly before half distance when Herbert Mueller had a major accident, running off the road and hitting a retired car, losing his life. Pit stops were due and there was a very confused situation, victory being awarded to the BMW M1 of Piquet and Stuck, with Bob Wollek third in a Kremer Porsche 935 K3. Half points were awarded but Porsche earned seven and a half, dropping behind Lancia in the title race.

Porsche and Lancia both claimed maximum points at Le Mans, where the Charles Ivey Racing K3 of Dudley Wood, John Cooper and Claude Bourgoignie finished fourth overall. One round then remained, at Watkins Glen, which was in danger of being cancelled for financial reasons. That would have suited Fiorio and the Lancia team, but the 6-Hours went ahead and the little Lancias scored a 1-2 victory, easily clinching the last World Championship title in Group 5. Garretson was third in his K3 with Bobby Rahal and Rick Mears. In total Garretson contested eight of the 15 Driver Championship races in his Porsche, and he earned his title the hard way. After winning the Daytona 24-Hours he finished fourth at Riverside, sixth at Le Mans, third at Watkins Glen, fourth at Elkhart Lake and, finally, second at Brands Hatch, the last result clinching the title.

Harald Grohs was the worthy runner-up, contesting the five European rounds in the Vegla Porsche and four in North America with the Andial Meister team. Grohs managed three victories at Silverstone, Mosport and Elkhart Lake. Bobby Rahal, third in the driver championship, competed in 10 rounds, both with Garretson and Bob Akin, winning at Daytona, while Akin and Derek Bell competed in 11 rounds. Edgar Doeren competed in nine rounds and was fourth in the driver championship.

It is sometimes forgotten that the FIA introduced two new categories in 1982 for Group B and Group C cars, also allowing the old Groups 4 and 5 cars, and sports cars, to make up the grids for one year only. Lancia made good use of this in an effort to win the 1982 Drivers Championship with its 'barchettas', open cars based on the Beta Monte Carlo. The drivers could score points but the manufacturer could not.

Group B proved to be a farce. It demanded a minimum production of 200 cars, production based and with regulations similar to those applying to World Championship rallies. Only one Group B car competed, a Porsche 911 Turbo 3.0 of Georg Memminger and Fritz Muller, and their best result of the season was ninth overall in the Nurburgring 1,000 Kms, and second in the combined Groups B and C.

Porsche did not enter the new 956 for this event, although it followed the Silverstone debut, and quickly claimed 15 points for Memminger's result. The FIA did not have a clear ruling on this aspect and it was not until mid-October that the decision was reached that the championship points were allocated only to Group C cars, and this was backed by a "clari-fi-cation". Porsche and Jean Rondeau's Ford backed team were evenly matched, but the Rothmans Porsche team clinched the World Championship with a 1-2 victory at Spa in September. Memminger's result at the Nurburgring made no difference, but his appearance at the Eifel track made waves. The 935s continued to give good service in 1982, although not scoring any points. Ted Field and Rolf Stommelen finished second overall at Monza in the Interscope 935 K3, Gianpiero Moretti and Mauro Baldi were seventh at Silverstone in the Momo entry, and were seventh again at Spa.

Schornstein, Merl and Wollek drove to sixth place overall at Mugello, Jim Adams and Ralph Kent-Cooke to seventh in the Fuji 6-Hours. The 935's final appearance in FIA World Championship racing was at Brands Hatch in October, where John Fitzpatrick, David Hobbs and Bob Wollek finished third overall behind the Ickx/Bell Rothmans-Porsche 956 and the Patrese/Fabi Lancia Barchetta.

1000 km Nürburgring 1982: Claude Haldi, Bernard Beguin

SCALING THE HEIGHTS

NEUBEGINN

Nach dem Wegfall der 3,5 Liter-Gruppe C im Jahre 1992 gewannen die klassischen Rennen wieder verstärkt an Bedeutung. So zum Beispiel Le Mans, das sehr gelitten hatte unter den Bestrebungen der FIA, die Privatteams aus der Sportwagen-Weltmeisterschaft zu jagen, das 24 Stunden-Rennen von Spa und das 1000 km-Rennen von Suzuka. Nationale GT-Meisterschaften sorgten in Deutschland, Großbritannien, Frankreich und Amerika für Aufschwung. Porsche wollte sich diesen neuen Herausforderungen stellen.

Das erste Auto das fertiggestellt wurde, war der 911 Carrera RSR, eine direkte Weiterentwicklung des Autos aus dem Carrera Cup (Typ 964) mit dem neuesten 3,8 Litermotor, der 325 PS leistete. Der 3,8 Litermotor war fast ein komplett neues Triebwerk. Zu den wesentlichsten Änderungen gehörten das Kurbelgehäuse, die Zylinderoberfläche, die Kolben, die hydraulischen Ventilstößel sowie die Einlass- und Auspuffkrümmer. Zudem wurde das neueste Bosch-Motronic 2.10 Steuergerät eingebaut. Es war ein kraftvoller Motor, der in der Saison 1993 und darüber hinaus sowohl für Profis als auch für Amateure genügend Leistung bringen sollte. Der RSR war leicht zu erkennen, denn er hatte die Breitbau-Kotflügel des Turbos und einen doppelten einstellbaren Heckflügel. Die Radaufhängung wurde geändert und es wurde ein weiterentwickeltes Bosch-ABS-System eingebaut, dass schneller reagierte.

Der RSR hatte einen Preis von DM 270.000 und konnte auf Anfrage mit einem 120 Liter-Benzintank sowie Speedline-Felgen mit einem Durchmesser von 18 Zoll und einer Breite von 9 Zoll vorne und 11 Zoll hinter geliefert werden. Das zugelassene Gewicht war 1120 kg, ein guter Wert für ein serienmäßiges GT-Auto mit Stahlkarrosse. Die Porsche-Techniker in Weissach wollten aber wieder in den Rennsport einsteigen, nicht mit dem RSR, der ausdrücklich nur den Kunden vorbehalten war. Stattdessen fiel ihr Auge auf den 911 Turbo S, die Straßenversion mit 3,2 Liter-Twinturbomotor. Man wollte ein ganz kleines Programm von auserwählten klassischen Rennen in Angriff nehmen.

Norbert Singer fing mit einer Rohkarrosse an, in die er zunächst einen kompletten Überrollkäfig installierte, der sich zu den Befestigungspunkten der vorderen und hinteren Radaufhängung ausstreckte. So wurde jene Steifigkeit erreicht, die es bereits zwei Jahrzehnte zuvor im 934 und im 935 gegeben hatte. Schraubfedern sorgten für die Radaufhängung, es wurden stabile Büchsen montiert und die Stabilisatoren konnten vom Cockpit aus verstellt werden. Die innenbelüfteten Bremsscheiben mit Querrillen, die bereits im 917 und im 935 benutzt wurden, hatten ABS zur Unterstützung.

Sebring 1993 (l.-r.): Hurley Haywood, Hans-Joachim Stuck, Walter Röhrl

Poster

24 Hours Nürburgring 1993: Harald Grohs, Jürgen von Gartzen, Jürgen Alzen, Walter Röhrl

Winner GT 12 Hours Sebring 1993: Hurley Haywood, Hans-Joachim Stuck, Walter Röhrl

STARTING AGAIN

Following the collapse of the 3.5 litre Group C formula in 1992, attention switched to the revival of the classic events such as Le Mans, which suffered badly from the FIA's misguided attempt to drive private teams out of the World Sportscar Championship, the Spa 24-Hours and the Suzuka 1,000 Kms. National GT championships were given a new lease of life in Germany, in Britain, in France and in America, and Porsche was ready to meet all the fresh challenges.

The first car to be prepared was the 911 Carrera RSR, which was a direct development of the Carrera Cup cars (type 964) and had the latest 3.8 litre engines with 325 bhp available. The 3.8 litre motor was an almost entirely new engine with a changed crankcase, cylinders barrels, pistons, hydraulic tappets, inlet and exhaust manifolds, and the latest Bosch Motronic 2.10 management system.

It was a powerful engine that would serve professional and amateur drivers well in 1993, and beyond. The RSR was easily identified in having the Turbo's 'wide body' wheel arches and a twin-deck adjustable rear wing. The suspensions were revised, with cross-bracing at the front, and a more advanced Bosch ABS5 system was adopted with faster responses. The RSR was priced at DM 270,000 and could be ordered with a 120 litre fuel tank, and 18-inch diameter Speedline wheels with 9J and 11J rim widths. Scrutineering weight was 1,120 kg, a good figure for a steel-bodied production GT car. Porsche's engineers at Weissach had a hankering to get back into racing, but not with the RSR which was strictly a customer car. Instead, they turned their attention to the 911 Turbo S, the 3.2 litre twin-turbo street model, planning a very limited programe of classic events.

Starting with a body-in-white, Norbert Singer first installed a full roll cage which extended to the front and rear suspension mounting points, providing the sort of stiffness seen in the 934-935 models nearly two decades previously. Coil springs formed the main method of suspension, solid mounted bushes were installed, and the anti-roll bars could be adjusted from the cockpit. The ventilated and cross-drilled brakes, dating back to the 917 and 935, had ABS assistance.

The Turbo S 3.2 litre engine was tuned up to 500 horsepower with two 34 mm inlet air restrictors applied, transmitting through a single-plate dry clutch and a five-speed type 950 gearbox. The oil radiator was mounted at the front, a vulnerable position it would prove to be.

Although this was a production based GT car Singer managed to incorporate a large bi-plane rear spoiler, similar to that of the 935, and a deep spoiler air dam under the nose. With the extensive use of lightweight materials, including Lexan for the side and rear windows and glass-fibre for the lids and doors, the weight came down to 1,050 kg.

24 Hours Nürburgring 1993: Georg Memminger, Jürgen Barth, Walter Röhrl, Fritz Müller

24 Hours Le Mans 1993: Hurley Haywood, Hans-Joachim Stuck, Walter Röhrl

Die Leistung des 3,2 Liter Turbo S Motors wurde auf 500 PS erhöht. Zwei Luftmengenbegrenzer mit einem Durchmesser von je 34 mm regelten den Lufteinlass. Das Fünfganggetriebe des Typs 950 hatte eine Einscheibentrockenkupplung. Der Ölkühler war vorne angebracht. Wie sich herausstellen sollte, ein gefährlicher Platz.

Obwohl dies ein serienmäßiges GT-Auto war, gelang es Singer, einen großen zweifachen Heckspoiler, ähnlich dem des 935, sowie einen großen Lufteinlass mit Frontspoiler einzubauen. Es wurden reichlich Leichtbau-Werkstoffe verwendet, wie Lexan für die Seiten- und Heckscheiben und Glasfaser für die Hauben und Türen. Dadurch wurde das Gewicht auf 1050 kg reduziert. „Die Form des Autos war bereits homologiert, also konnten wir nicht viel machen", erinnert sich Singer. „Wir hatten hinten einen neuen Flügel mit Lufteinlässen an der Seite, so dass mehr Luft zu den Turboladern strömen konnte. Wir mussten für diesen Flügel auch eine Strassenzulassung beantragen. Also gingen wir zum TÜV-Rheinland, weil wir herausgefunden hatten, dass die dort zuständige Person ein Rennsportfan war. Er gab die Zulassung."

Der 911 Turbo S LM GT erlebte 1993 lediglich zwei Einsätze. In Sebring ging er in Brumos-Farben an den Start. Hurley Haywood, Hans-Joachim Stuck und Walter Röhrl belegten den siebten Gesamtrang. In Le Mans schnitt das Auto sehr gut gegen die Jaguar XJ220C ab, bis Röhrl etwas unglücklich mit einem Debora-LMP2-Auto kollidierte und mit einem beschädigten Ölkühler ausfiel.

Walter Röhrl setzte im neuen RSR die schnellste Zeit eines Porsche im Qualifikationstraining für das 24 Stunden-Rennen auf dem Ring. Für die Pole-Position reichte es allerdings nicht, aufgrund der starken Konkurrenz von Opel und BMW. Am Sonntagmorgen fiel er jedoch zurück, als eine gebrochene Antriebswelle ausgetauscht werden musste.

Sechs 911 RS mit 310 PS starken Motoren gaben ein gutes Bild ab. Vier von ihnen belegten die ersten vier Plätze, allen voran das von Konrad Motorsport eingeschriebene Auto mit den Fahrern Franz Konrad, Ornulf Wirdheim, Frank Katthöfer und Antonio de Azevedo. Mit nur 53 Sekunden Rückstand belegte der Freisinger 911 mit Wolfgang Kaufmann, Michael Irmgartz und Edgar Dören den zweiten Platz.

Nicht weniger als 25 Porsche RS und RSR wurden für das 24 Stunden-Rennen von Spa-Francorchamps genannt, das eigentlich Tourenwagen vorbehalten war. Weil jedoch das Interesse von Teams mit rund 300 PS starken Zweiliter-Supertourenwagen nicht so groß war, entschieden sich die Veranstalter, beim Rennen von 1993 auch GT-Autos starten zu lassen. Man stellte bald fest, dass Porsche zurück war und den Sieg ins Auge gefasst hatte. Die Veranstalter wollten den GT-Autos kurzerhand ein Extragewicht von 100 kg aufbrummen (nicht nur für die Porsche, sondern auch für den Honda NSX, den Armin Hahne auf die Pole-Position gefahren hatte). Die Sportkommissare entschieden jedoch, dass das Reglement eine solche Maßnahme nicht zuließ.

Zwei Porsche RSR lieferten sich vom Start weg ein starkes Duell bis um sieben Uhr in der Früh das Rennen abgebrochen wurde, nachdem die Nachricht vom Tod des belgischen Königs Baudoin auch in Spa eingetroffen war. Der Honda NSX hatte durch Probleme mit dem Anlasser bereits in der Anfangsphase Zeit verloren. In der Nacht verabschiedete sich der Motor endgültig. Nach 15 Stunden trennten den Roock-Porsche von Jean-Pierre Jarier, Christian Fittipaldi und Uwe Alzen und den Paduwa-911 von Grohs, Dalmas und Bartels weniger als 150 Sekunden.

Drei Carrera RSR traten die lange Reise nach Suzuka für das Pokka 1000 km-Rennen an. Sie kehrten mit unterschiedlichen Ergebnissen heim. Dominique Dupuy hatte im Larbre-Auto bereits in der ersten Runde einen Abflug. Der Heico 911 fiel mit Jürgen Barth am Lenkrad wegen einer gebrochenen Antriebswelle aus, die in Spa siegreiche Roock-Mannschaft rettete jedoch die Ehre mit dem fünften Gesamtrang für Akihiko Nakaya, Dieter Koll und Philip Albara.

Jürgen Barth, Stéphane Ratel und der Pariser Journalist Patrick Peter formten gemeinsam die BPR Organisation, die 1994 die Global Endurance GT Series veranstaltete. Damit verschaffte man den Teams, die sich dem Langstreckensport verpflichtet hatten, eine Serie, die zwar von der FIA genehmigt werden musste, ansonsten jedoch keinerlei Bindung an die Motorsport-Behörde hatte. Die Serie erhielt keinen Meisterschaftsstatus, da sie sonst unter der Kontrolle der FIA hätte sein müssen. So wurden keine Punkte vergeben und am Ende der Saison gab es auch keinen Meister.

Poster

24 Hours Spa-Francorchamps 1993

1000 km Suzuka 1993: Dirk Ebeling, Jürgen Barth, Karl Wlazik

1000 km Suzuka 1993: Dieter Köll, Philippe Albera, Akihiko Nakaya

"The shape of the car was homologated so we could not do much about that" recalls Singer. "We had a new wing on the back with intakes at the sides to get more air to the turbochargers. We had to homologate that wing for the road, too, so we went to the Tuf in Rhineland where we found that the guy who was in charge was a racing fan, and he homologated it."

The 911 Turbo S LM-GT made but two appearances in 1993, at Sebring where it ran in Brumos colours. Hurley Haywood, Hans Stuck and Walter Rohrl finished seventh overall, and then at Le Mans where it performed very well indeed against the TWR Jaguar XJ220Cs, until Rohrl had an unfortunate collision with a Debora LMP2 car and retired with a damaged oil radiator.

Walter Rohrl set the fastest Porsche time in qualifying for the 24-Hours of the Nurburgring, driving the new RSR, although not pole position with stiff competition from Opels and BMWs, but dropped down the order on Sunday morning with a broken driveshaft which had to be replaced.

Six 911 RS models, with 310 bhp, made a good impression and four of them claimed the top four positions, led by the Konrad Motorsport entry driven by Franz Konrad, Ornulf Wirdheim, Frank Katthoefer and Antonio de Azevedo. Just 53 seconds behind at the finish was the Freisinger Motorsport 911 RS of Wolfgang Kaufmann, Michael Irmgartz and Edgar Doeren.

No fewer than 25 Porsche RS and RSRs were entered for the Spa 24-Hours, a race intended for touring cars. With the 2-litre, 300 bhp 'super touring' cars in short supply, the organisers decided to allow GT cars to compete in 1993, and soon realised that Porsche was back in business ... and their business is winning! The organisers tried to slap a 100 kg weight penalty on the GT cars (not only the Porsches, but the Honda NSX which Armin Hahne put on pole position), but the stewards decided that this was not allowed by the regulations.

Two of the Porsche RSRs had a ferocious duel right from the start of the race, until the premature showing of the red flag at seven o'clock in the morning following news of the death of the Belgian monarch, King Baudouin. The Honda NSX was delayed by a starter motor problem before the engine failed in the night.

After 15 hours of duelling, less than 150 seconds separated the Roock Racing Porsche of Jean-Pierre Jarier, Christian Fittipaldi and Uwe Alzen, and the Paduwa Racing 911 of Harald Grohs, Yannick Dalmas and Michael Bartels.

Three Carrera RSRs made the long trip to Suzuka for the Pokka 1,000 Kms, with varying success. Dominique Dupuy crashed the Larbre Competition entry on the opening lap, the Heico Motorsport entry broke a driveshaft while Juergen Barth was at the wheel, but Spa winners Roock Racing saved the day with fifth place overall for Akihiko Nakaya, Dieter Koll and Philip Albara.

Barth, Stephane Ratel and Parisian publicist Patrick Peter formed the BPR organisation to run the Global Endurance

Michel Delcourt, Robert Dierick, Stephane Meyers

STARTING AGAIN 93

Der Kalender umfasste acht Rennen auf interessanten Rennstrecken wie Le Castellet, Jarama, Dijon, Montlhéry, Vallelunga, Spa, Suzuka und das Finale auf dem Strassenkurs von Zhuhai im Süden Chinas.

Zahlreiche Porsche-Teams nahmen an der Serie Teil, einige mit dem aktuellen RSR, der auf dem 993 basierte. Die auffälligsten Merkmale waren die flachen Scheinwerfer und die breitere Karrosserie, der den 964 fast auf Anhieb altmodisch erscheinen ließ. Endlich hatte der 911 eine neue Hinterradaufhängung mit mehreren Streben. Die Aufhängung umfasste ansonsten Querlenker und Schraubfedern die auf einem Fahrschemel aus gegossenem Aluminium befestigt waren.

Der neue RSR hatte ein gleichmäßigeres Fahrverhalten. Die Leistung des 3,8 Litermotors wurde auf 350 PS angehoben und es wurde ein neues Sechsganggetriebe installiert. Walter Röhrl wurde mit der Abstimmung der Federn und Dämpfer beauftragt, die zweimal so hart als vorher waren. Das Auto war 20 Prozent steifer und erfahrene Fahrer stellten fest, dass der 911 nun eher ein Rennwagen als ein GT-Auto war. Wo man sie vergleichen konnte, waren die Rundenzeiten im Schnitt etwa zwei Sekunden schneller.

1000 km Paris 1994: Sandro Angelastri, Toni Seiler, Matteo Cassina

Winner 4 Hours Paul Ricard 1994: Bob Wollek, Jean-Pierre Jarier, Jesus Pareja

Porsche fertigte 100 Autos für den Renneinsatz, 55 RS-Fahrzeuge mit 310 PS für den Straßenverkehr, 49 für die Supercup-Serie, ebenfalls mit 310 PS und nur fünf RSR.

Die Porsche-Teams hatten reichlich Konkurrenz von den Ferrari F40, den Lotus und Venturi, Autos des französischen Spezialisten, den Ratel zum Rennsport gebracht hatte. Leconte war der Konkurrenz jedoch einen Schritt voraus, indem er den Ex-Werks-Turbo LM-GT erwarb und ihn bei ausgewählten Rennen für Jarier, Wollek und Pareja einsetzte.

Zur Vorbereitung schrieb Larbre Competition seinen neuen Turbo S Le Mans für das 24 Stunden-Rennen von Daytona ein. Man fuhr auf Rang zwei ins Ziel und gewann die GT-Klasse. Im Anschluß dominierte Larbre den ersten Lauf der BPR Global Endurance GT-Serie auf der Rennstrecke von Paul Ricard. Das Team gewann das Rennen mit zwei Runden Vorsprung auf den Freisinger 911 Biturbo von Edgar Dören und Michael Irmgartz.

Hinter diesen beiden Teams fuhr ein Trio von 911 RSR ins Ziel, angeführt von Leconte und Dominique Dupuy (Larbre), Konrad und Wirdheim (Konrad) und Lilian Keller, später bekannt als Bryner, sowie Enzo Calderari (Ecurie Biennoise). Nicht weniger als 38 Autos standen beim französischen Rennen am Start. 20 waren Fahrzeuge aus der Venturi Trophy, 14 Porsche (inklusive eines 944 und eines 968 Turbos), zwei Venturi in Le-Mans-Ausführung und zwei Lotus Esprit. Die Ferrari sollten später ins Geschehen eingreifen.

Ray Bellm, der einer der Schlüsselfiguren in der BPR-Serie werden sollte, kam mit einem Porsche RSR als Elfter ins Ziel, nachdem er viel Zeit verloren hatte aufgrund eines Problems mit der Ölversorgung.

Der zweite Lauf der BPR-Serie fand in Jarama nahe Madrid statt. Das von Repsol gesponserte Rennen zog 25.000 Zuschauer an. Viele wollten das Abschneiden von Prinz Alfonso d'Orleans, Neffe vom spanischen König Carlos, erleben. Er fuhr auf einem Ferrari, Porsche dominierte aber erneut.

Der 911 Turbo S Le Mans des Larbre-Teams siegte ohne Probleme beim 4 Stunden-Rennen mit der Fahrerbesetzung Jarier, Dupuy und Pareja. Die folgenden neun Autos im Ziel waren allesamt Porsche. Ray Bellm und Harry Nuttall belegten mit zwei Runden Rückstand auf dem Turbo S den zweiten Platz im Carrera RSR, das von Laurence Bristow gemeldet wurde, mit Michael Cane als Teammanager. Enzo und Lilian, wie man sie jahrelang kannte, fuhren im Carrera RSR der Ecurie Biennoise auf Rang drei.

Danach setzte das Larbre-Team den größten Teil der Saison aus, weil man sich auf den Porsche Supercup konzentrierte. Beim dritte Saisonlauf in Dijon-Prenois schlug Venturi zurück. Michel Ferté und Michel Neugarten gewannen das BPR-Rennen im Jacadi-Team-Venturi 600 LM mit einem 600 PS starken V6-Motor. Sie kamen zwei Runden vor Almo Copelli und Philippe Olczyk in einem gleichen Auto ins Ziel. Bellm und Nutall belegten Rang drei, erneut im Bristow-Carrera RSR.

Der nächste Lauf war das 1000 km-Rennen von Paris auf dem historischen Kurs von Montlhéry. Dort feierte Henri Pescarolo zusammen mit Jean-Claude Basso im Venturi 600 LM einen viel beachteten Sieg, 25 Jahre nach seinem ersten Erfolg in Montlhéry, damals auf Matra. Nach sieben Stunden kamen Bellm, Nuttall und Charles Rickett im RSR auf Platz drei ins Ziel, womit sie ihre bemerkenswerte Erfolgsserie fortsetzten. Hinter ihnen war der Mühlbauer-RSR mit Detlef Hübner, Ernst Palmberger und Danny Pfeil.

Die Fortsetzung folgte in Vallelunga. Ein sehr heißes Rennen mitten im Sommer, das mit dem Ferrari F40 des Indus-

GT Series in 1994, giving the teams loyal to endurance racing a series that had to be endorsed by the FIA, but had no allegiance to the controlling body. The series could not be called a championship, however, since the FIA's sanction would then be needed, so no points were awarded, and there was no 'champion' at the end of the season.

Eight rounds were arranged at interesting circuits including Le Castellet (Paul Ricard), Jarama, Dijon, Montlhery, Vallelunga, Spa, Suzuka, and finally, the colourful street circuit of Zhuhai in the south of China.

A large number of Porsche teams contested the series, some with the latest 993 based RSR. This was distinguished immediately by the laid-back headlamps and blended, more rounded body shell which made the 964 look obsolete almost straight away. At last it had a proper multi-link rear suspension with wishbones controlling the wheels, and coil springs mounted on a vacuum cast aluminium alloy sub-frame. The new RSR handled in a more even, predictable manner. The 3.8 litre engine was uprated to 350 bhp, and drive went through a new six-speed gearbox. Walter Rohrl was given the job of deciding the spring and damper rates, which proved to be twice as hard as before. The shell was 20 per cent stiffer, and experienced drivers reckoned that the 911 was now more like a racing car than a GT model. Lap times were improved by an average of two seconds, where comparisons could be made.

Porsche made 100 competition cars, 55 RS cars for street use with 310 bhp, 40 for the Supercup championship, also with 310 bhp, and just five RSRs.

The Porsche teams had plenty of competition from Ferrari F40s, Lotus and Venturi, the specialist French company which Ratel had introduced to racing. Jack Leconte kept one step ahead of the opposition, though, by acquiring the ex-factory Turbo S LM-GT and running it in selected events for Jarier, Wollek and Jesus Pareja. For a warm-up, Larbre Competition raced their new Turbo S Le Mans in the Daytona 24-Hours, finishing second overall and winning the GT category. From there, Larbre dominated the inaugural round of the BPR Global Endurance Championship at the Paul Ricard circuit (Le Castellet), winning the four-hour race with two laps to spare ahead of the Freisinger Motorsport Porsche bi-turbo of Edgar Doeren and Michael Irmgartz.

4 Hours Vallelunga 1994: Pietro Ferrero, Carlo Rossi

Following them were a trio of 911 RSRs led by Leconte and Dominique Dupuy (Larbre), Konrad and Wirdheim (Konrad) and Lilian Kelle (later known as Bryner) and Enzo Calderari (Ecurie Biennoise). No fewer than 38 cars started the French event, 20 of them Venturi Trophy machines, 14 Porsche (including a 944 and a 968 Turbo), two Venturi Le Mans specification cars, and two Lotus Esprits. The Ferraris would start their bid later, at Monza.

Ray Bellm, who would be a key figure in the BPR series, finished 11th in a Porsche RSR after a delay due to an oil breather problem.

The second round of the BPR series was held at Jarama, close to Madrid, and with sponsorship from Repsol drew a huge crowd, some said 25,000 strong. Some were interested in the progress of Prince Alfonso d'Orleans, nephew of King Carlos, driving a Ferrari 348, but Porsche again dominated the proceedings.

Larbre's 911 Turbo S Le Mans won the 4-Hour race with ease in the hands of Jarier, Dupuy and Pareja, and the next nine cars to cross the line were all Porsches! Ray Bellm and Harry Nuttall drove to second place, two laps behind the Turbo S, in their Carrera RSR entered by Laurence Bristow (Bristow Motorsport) and managed by Michael Cane, and third were 'Enzo and Lilian' as they have been for many years, in their Ecurie Biennoise Carrera RSR.

The Larbre team then missed the bulk of the season, needing to concentrate on the Porsche Supercup championship, and Venturi struck back at Dijon-Prenois, the switchback Burgundy circuit which hosted the third round. Michel Ferte

4 Hours Vallelunga 1994: Raymond Touroul, Eric van de Vyver

TECHNICAL DATA

GT1 - Same as ACO GT1, maximum 650 bhp, minimum 1,000 Kg, maximum rim width 14 in. fuel tank capacity 120 litres, no homologation needed, 1 example only. For instance, McLaren F1 GTR, Ferrari F40, Porsche GT2 Evo, Venturi LM600

GT2 - Same as FIA GT1, maximum 500 bhp, minimum 1,100 kg, maximum rim width 14 in. fuel tank capacity 100 litres, homologation 25 cars minimum. For instance, Porsche GT2, Callaway Corvette

GT3 - Same as ACO GT2, maximum 450 bhp, minimum 1,100 kg, maximum rim width 12 in. fuel tank capacity 120 litres, no homologation needed. For instance, 968 RS Turbo, Carrera RSR, Lotus Esprit S300

GT4 - Same as FIA GT2, maximum 350 bhp, minimum 1,100 kg, maximum rim width 12 in. fuel tank capacity 100 litres, 200 examples for homologation. For in-stance, Carrera RSR, Morgan Plus 8

GT5 - Reserved for Venturi Trophy cars

STARTING AGAIN

triellen Luciano della Noce aus Rom und Anders Olofsson einen neuen Sieger zeigte. Der lokale Renninstruktor Enrico Bertaggia belegte zusammen mit dem deutschen Computerexperten Andreas Fuchs im dröhnenden Callaway-Corvette Rang zwei, während Bellm und Nuttall erneut als Dritte über die Ziellinie fuhren.

In Spa schlug Venturi erneut zu. Nach einem spannenden Duell mit della Noce und Olofsson feierten Ferté und Neugarten im Jacadi 600 LM ihren zweiten Saisonsieg. Platz drei ging an den Callaway-Corvette, einem Auto aus der GT2-Klasse, das von Boris Said und Helmut Reis gefahren wurde. Der bestplatzierte Porsche war weit abgeschlagen auf Rang sechs. Einmal mehr kamen Bellm und Nuttall vor Enzo und Lilian ins Ziel.

Das Larbre Competition-Team kehrte beim 1000 km-Rennen von Suzuka in die Serie zurück. Die Veranstaltung fand Mitte August bei Sauna-Temperaturen statt. Einige der japanischen Spitzenteams, die man vorher schon in Le Mans gesehen hatte, ergänzten in Suzuka das Starterfeld. Das Rennen war ziemlich chaotisch und wurde von zahlreichen Unfällen und von einer roten Flagge gekennzeichnet. Es führte lange Zeit der SARD Gruppe C-Toyota, der in Le Mans Rang zwei belegt hatte. Schließlich kam Mauro Martini jedoch von der Strecke ab und beschädigte den Toyota, so dass der Larbre-Porsche Turbo S mit Jarier, Bob Wollek und Pareja den Sieg nach Hause fahren konnte.

Hinter zwei Honda NSX fuhr der Callaway-Corvette mit Said, Fuchs und Reis ins Ziel, gefolgt vom Freisinger-Porsche Biturbo mit Kaufmann und Ligonnet. Dirk Ebeling und Ulli Richter belegten im Heico RSR Rang acht.

Das Saisonfinale ging auf dem Straßenkurs in Zhuhai über die Bühne. Die Strecke war holprig und bestand hauptsächlich aus Rechtskurven zwischen Betonwänden. Für Fehler war kein Platz. Zugejubelt von 100.000 begeisterten Chinesen fuhren Jarier, Wollek und Jacques Laffitte den vierten Saisonsieg für Larbre nach Hause, nachdem sie die starke Callaway-Corvette geschlagen hatten.

Fuchs fiel im amerikanischen Auto nur zehn Minuten vor Schluss mit Getriebeschaden aus. Daraufhin erbte Franz Konrad den zweiten Platz im Porsche Biturbo, den er sich mit dem Briten Tiff Needell teilte. Der Heico-RSR fuhr mit Ebeling, Richter und Wlazik auf Platz drei vor dem Schweizer-Porsche von Olivier Haberthur und Laurent Lecuyer.

3 Hours Zhuhai 1994

Jack Leconte und Jean Chereau belegten den fünften Rang. Die erste Saison der BPR-Serie war ein großer Erfolg und die Zukunft des Langstreckensports schien wieder gesichert. Hätte es einen Meister gegeben, so wäre die Entscheidung gefallen zwischen Jean-Pierre Jarier, der im Turbo S Le Mans des Larbre-Teams vier Rennen gewonnen hatte und Ray Bellm sowie Harry Nuttall, die sich fünfmal gegen die starke Konkurrenz mit identischen Porsche durchsetzen konnten und die GT3-Klasse gewannen.

McLaren war seit Ende der sechziger Jahre als Konstrukteur in der Formel 1 und bei den Can Am-Sportwagen erfolgreich, aber war bis zum Start der Saison 1995 bei Langstreckenrennen weitgehend unbekannt. Gordon Murrays brilliantes Gran-Turismo-Auto, der ultimative Straßensportwagen mit drei Sitzen, wobei der Fahrer in der Mitte saß. Chassis und Karrosserie waren aus Kohlefaser, hinter dem Fahrer lag ein hervorragender Sechsliter V12-Motor.

Der McLaren F1 GTR hatte eindeutig das Potenzial, dem Langstreckensport seinen Stempel aufzudrücken. In der Strassenversion hatte das Auto eine Leistung von 627 PS und sogar mit den zwei von der FIA vorgeschriebenen Luftmengenbegrenzern vor dem Lufteinlass konnte man diese Leistung beibehalten. Was würde Porsche dem entgegenbringen können?

TECHNISCHE DATEN:

GT1: identisch mit ACO GT1, maximal 650 PS, minimal 1.000 kg, Räder maximal 14 Zoll breit, Benzintank maximal 120 Liter, keine Homologation erforderlich, Einzelfahrzeug genügt. Beispiele: McLaren F1 GTR, Ferrari F40, 911 GT2 Evo, Venturi 600 LM

GT2: identisch mit FIA GT1, maximal 500 PS, minimal 1.110 kg, Räder maximal 14 Zoll breit, Benzintank maximal 100 Liter, Homologation minimal 25 Autos. Beispiele: Porsche 911 GT2, Callaway-Corvette

GT3: identisch mit ACO GT2, maximal 450 PS, minimal 1.100 kg, Räder maximal 12 Zoll breit, Benzintank maximal 120 Liter, keine Homologation erforderlich. Beispiele: Carrera RSR, Lotus Esprit S300, 968 RS T.

GT4: identisch mit FIA GT2, maximal 350 PS, minimal 1.100 kg, Räder maximal 12 Zoll breit, Benzintank maximal 100 Liter, Homologation minimal 200 Fahrzeuge. Beispiele: Carrera RSR, Morgan Plus 8

GT5: Fahrzeuge aus der Venturi Trophy

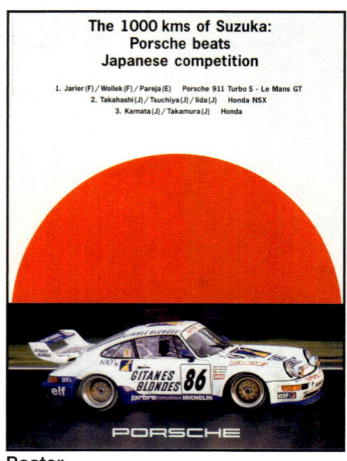

Poster

3 Hours Zhuhai 1994: Christian and Olivier Haberthur, Laurent Lecuyer

and Michel Neugarten won the BPR race in their Jacadi Team Venturi 600LM, a 600 horsepower V6, two laps clear of Almo Copelli and Philippe Olczyk in a similar car. Third were Bellm and Nuttall, again in their Bristow Motorsport Carrera RSR.

On then, to the 1,000 Kilometres of Paris at the historic circuit at Montlhery. There, Henri Pescarolo achieved a very popular victory in a Venturi 600 LM with Jean-Claude Basso, just 25 years after his first Montlhery success in a Matra. After seven hours of racing, Bellm, Nuttall and Charles Rickett were third in their RSR, maintaining a remarkable run of success, ahead of the Muhlbauer Motorsport RSR of Detlef Hubner, Ernst Palmberger and Danny Pfeil.

Vallelunga was the next stop, a very hot event in mid-summer, and a new winner, the Ferrari F40 of Rome industrialist Luciano della Noce with Anders Olofsson. Local racing instructor Enrico Bertaggia was second, with German computer whizz Andreas Fuchs, in the thundering Callaway Corvette, once again with Bellm and Nuttall giving chase in third position.

Venturi struck again at Spa, Ferte and Neugarten claiming their second success of the season in the Jacadi 600LM after a strong battle with della Noce and Olofsson. Third was the Callaway Corvette, a GT2 class car in the hands of Boris Said and Helmut Reis. The best Porsche was way down in sixth place, even beaten by a Ferrari 348, and again Bellm and Nuttall finished ahead of 'Enzo and Lilian'.

The Larbre Competition team was back in action for the Suzuka 1,000 Kms in August, the event held in sauna temperatures with the added attraction of some top Japanese teams previously in action at Le Mans. It was a chaotic race marred by crashes and breakdowns, even a red flag, and was dominated by a long time by the SARD Toyota Group C that finished second at Le Mans. Eventually Mauro Martini went off the road and damaged the Toyota, leaving the way clear for the Larbre Porsche Turbo S to win in the hands of Jarier, Bob Wollek and Pareja.

Behind two Honda NSX was the Callaway Corvette driven by Said, Fuchs and Reis, and then the Freisinger Motorsport Porsche bi-turbo of Kaufmann and Ligonnet. Eighth were Dirk Ebeling and Ulli Richter in their Heico Porsche RSR.

The season's finale took place in the streets of Zhuhai, a bumpy track comprising mainly right-angle bends between concrete walls, leaving no margin for mistakes. Cheered on by 100,000 excited Chinese, Jarier, Wollek and Jacques Laffitte achieved Larbre's fourth victory of the season after beating a strong challenge from the Callaway Corvette.

Fuchs retired the American car with broken transmission just 10 minutes from the end and Franz Konrad immediately claimed the runner-up position in his Porsche bi-turbo, with Briton Tiff Needell. Heico's RSR was third driven by Ebeling, Richter and Karl Wlazik, followed by the Swiss entered Porsche of Olivier Haberthur and Laurent Lecuyer, and Jack Leconte with Jean-Luc Chereau.

The first season of BPR racing was judged a huge success, restoring confidence in the tradition of endurance competition and allowing teams to build their strengths. If there was a champion, it would be a choice between Jarier who won four rounds in the Larbre team's Turbo S Le Mans, and Ray Bellm with Harry Nuttall, who on five occasions beat strong competition from similar Porsches to win the GT3 category.

McLaren has been a successful marque in Formula One since the late 1960s, and in Can-Am sports cars, but was quite unknown in endurance racing until the start of the 1995 season. Gordon Murray's brilliant Grand Touring car, the ultimate road-going high performance car, had three seats,

1000 km Suzuka 1994: Alfonso de Orleans Bourbon, Bert Ploeg

the driver in the centre, a carbon chassis, carbon body, and a superb BMW designed 6-litre V12 engine mounted in-line behind the driver.

Clearly, the McLaren F1 GTR had the potential to dominate endurance racing. It developed 627 bhp in street trim and could maintain this power even with the FIA's two inlet air restrictors installed. What sort of response could Porsche make? The RSR still had an important role, there was a class within the FIA and ACO regulations that suited it, but turbochargers were going to be needed to answer the challenge from McLaren.

Again, it fell to Ing. Singer and his team of engineers to develop a successor to the Turbo S Le Mans, and it was called the GT2 (appropriately, intended for the GT2 category). It was based on the current 993 chassis, a far better platform, and necessarily had an all-steel monocoque. The GT2 was introduced to the model range so that homologation could be completed, and no fewer than 42 special cars were produced for racing customers.

These used composites for the doors, luggage lid and rear lid, and fenders (32mm wider than standard) and acrylic side and rear windows. With twin KKK turbochargers and 3.6 litre flat-six engine yielded 480 bhp, with two 34mm inlet air restrictors applied, and some customers, notably Larbre, Konrad and Freisinger, opted to move into the GT1 category in a bid to get closer to the McLarens.

The Evo version was allowed bigger air restrictors, 40.4mm, which took the power to 550 bhp at 7,200 rpm. It ran with a larger rear wing, but it was soon realised that the 618 Nm torque figure was just too much for the transmission. The greater the downforce that was applied, the sooner the driveshafts and six-speed gearboxes would break.

1000 km Suzuka 1994: Jack Leconte, Jürgen Barth, Dominique Dupuy

Winner 4 Hours 1000 km Suzuka 1994: Bob Wollek, Jean-Pierre Jarier, Jesus Pareja

4 Hours Brands Hatch 1994: Karel Dolejsi, Peter Seikel, Peter Chambers

4 Hours Nogaro 1994: Jean-Pierre Jarier, Bob Wollek, Christophe Bouchut

4 Hours Nürburgring 1994: Toni Seiler, Wido Rössler, Franz Konrad

STARTING AGAIN

4 Hours Jarama 1995: Wolfgang Kaufmann, Bruno Giacomelli, Fulvio Ballabio

Der RSR spielte nach wie vor eine wichtige Rolle. In den Reglements der FIA und des ACO gab es eine Klasse die für den RSR passte. Turbolader waren jedoch gefragt, um es gegen den McLaren aufnehmen zu können.
Techniker Singer und seine Mannschaft bekamen den Auftrag, einen Nachfolger für den Turbo S Le Mans zu entwickeln. Das Auto wurde GT2 genannt und war für die GT2-Klasse bestimmt. Es basierte auf dem Chassis des aktuellen 993 und hatte dem Reglement entsprechend, ein Monocoque aus Stahl. Der GT2 wurde ins Modelprogramm aufgenommen, so dass die Straßenzulassung beantragt werden konnte. Nicht weniger als 42 Fahrzeuge wurden für Kunden aus dem Rennsportbereich produziert.
Für die Türen und Hauben sowie für die 32 mm breiteren Kotflügel wurde Kompositmaterial benutzt, die Seiten- und Heckscheiben wurden aus Acryl angefertigt. Dank zweier KKK-Turbolader lieferte der 3,6 Liter-Reihen-Sechszylindermotor mit zwei Luftmengenbegrenzern zu je 34 mm eine Leistung von 480 PS. Einige Kundenteams, allen voran Larbre, Konrad und Freisinger, bevorzugten den Aufstieg in die GT1-Klasse, um den McLaren näher kommen zu können.
Für die Evo-Version wurden größere Luftmengenbegrenzer von 40,4 mm zugelassen, was die Leistung auf 550 PS bei 7.200 U/Min. ansteigen liess. Das Auto hatte einen größeren Heckflügel. Bald stellte sich jedoch heraus, dass das Drehmoment von 618 Nm für das Getriebe einfach zu groß war. Je mehr Abtrieb erzielt wurde, desto schneller gingen die Antriebswellen und das Sechsganggetriebe zu Bruch.
Servolenkung kehrte in den Rennsport zurück. Die innenbelüfteten Bremsscheiben mit Querrillen wurden vom Turbo S übernommen, Bosch lieferte ein noch besseres ABS. Bremssattel mit vier Ventilen hatten eine 17 Prozent größere Kontaktfläche als beim serienmäßigen GT2. Das Gewicht wurde auf 1100 kg reduziert, der McLaren wog genauso wenig, also ergab sich hier keinen Vorteil.
Zu den Kunden für den GT2 gehörten Larbre Competiton, Konrad Motorsport, Kremer Racing, Manfred Freisinger, Haberthur Racing, Team Obermeier, Hans Mühlbauer, Peter Seikel, Paul Lanzanze und Paul Robe. Einige von ihnen setzten zusätzlich noch den RSR ein.
Larbre entschied sich bereits vor dem Start der Saison für die Evo-Version. Man behielt während der ersten Saisonhälfte den 480 PS-Motor bei, hatte aber die breiteren Räder und den größeren Heckflügel. Mit den schnellen Fahrern Jarier, Bouchut und Wollek, war das führende Auto des Larbre-Teams schlagkräftig und wurde somit zum ernsthaften Gegner für die McLaren-Teams.

Das erste Rennen fand in Jerez statt. Obwohl der Larbre-Porsche nur Vierter in der Startaufstellung war, hinter drei McLaren und 2,6 Sekunden von der Pole-Position-Zeit von Pierre-Henri Raphanel im Gulf-McLaren entfernt, war der 911 im 4 Stunden-Rennen ein starker Konkurrent. Nach zwei und nach drei Stunden führten Jarier und seine Teamkollegen das Feld an. Eine halbe Stunde vor Schluss jedoch überholte Ray Ballm den Larbre-GT2 und fuhr einen Vorsprung von 16 Sekunden heraus.
Zwei weitere McLaren hatten Kinderkrankheiten. Rang drei ging an die Schweizer Paarung von Enzo Calderari und Lilian Bryner im Stadler 911 GT2. Trotz eines Brandes im Motorraum während des Aufwärmtrainings am Sonntagvormittag kam der Repsol Kremer GT2 von Alfonso d'Orleans und Thomas Saldana auf Rang neun ins Ziel.
Vier McLaren und zwei Ferrari F40 belegten in Monza die vorderen Plätze in der Startaufstellung. Auch der ADA-De Tomaso Pantera war im Zeittraining schneller als der Larbre GT2 Evo. Der Kremer-Repsol-Porsche wurde von Alfonso d'Orleans im Training nachhaltig beschädigt. Das Larbre-Team war im Rennen jedoch stärker als im Training und führte einige Male das Feld an. Im Ziel fehlten Jarier, Wollek und Bouchut nur 16 Sekunden auf dem siegreichen McLaren von Thomas Bscher.
In Jarama erlebten zwei weitere McLaren ihren Einstand in der BPR Global-Endurance-Serie. Sie machten es noch schwieriger für Porsche im Zeittraining eine ordentliche Leistung zu zeigen. Seltener Gast in der Serie war Norbert Singer, der nach Spanien gereist war, um feststellen zu können, wie stark die McLaren geworden waren.
Wie üblich brachte das Larbre Competition-Team die beste Leistung mit dem dritten Gesamtrang für Jarier, Wollek und Bouchut. Sie kamen nach vier Stunden in der gleichen Runde wie die Sieger ins Ziel. Jürgen Lassig und Jürgen von Gartzen belegten den sechsten Platz in der Gesamtwertung. Enzo und Lilian kamen auf Rang sieben ins Ziel und gewannen im Stadler-Porsche die GT3-Klasse.
Larbre schickte auf den Nürburgring seinen 911 GT2 erstmals mit den größeren Luftmengenbegrenzern ins Rennen. Nun leistete der Motor 550 PS, stellte aber sofort die Schwachstelle des Evo heraus. Bei Jarier versagten in der zweiten Stunde die Bremsen und er verbrachte für die Reparatur viel Zeit an der Box. Danach schlitterte der Evo durchs Gras, nachdem eine Antriebswelle gebrochen war. Wollek war nur noch Passagier, bis das Auto zum Stillstand kam. McLaren belegten die Plätze eins bis fünf. Enzo und Lilian kamen auf Rang sechs ins Ziel vor dem Mühlbauer-GT2 von Detlef Hubner und Stefan Oberndorfer.

Winner GT2 1000 km Suzuka 1995 (l.-r.): Stephane Ratel, Lilian Bryner, Enzo Calderari

4 Hours Nogaro 1995

Power steering was re-introduced to the racing cars, the ventilated and cross-drilled brakes were from the Turbo S, with a still better Bosch ABS system, and four-piston calipers with a swept area 17 per cent greater than on the standard GT2. The weight was reduced to 1,100 kg, but so was the McLaren's, so no advantage there. Customers for the GT2 included Larbre Competition, Konrad Motorsport, Kremer Racing, Manfred Freisinger, Haberthur Racing, Team Obermeier, Hans Muhlbauer, Peter Seikel, Paul Lanzante and Paul Robe, some also running RSRs as a back-up.

Larbre went for the Evo version even before the start of the season, retaining the 480 bhp engine for the first half of the season but taking on the wider wheels and larger rear wing. In the right hands, those of Jarier, Bouchut and Wollek, the Larbre team's lead car was surprisingly effective and was able to give the McLaren teams some real competition.

The first contest was at Jerez, and although the Larbre Porsche was only fourth on the grid, behind three McLarens and 2.6 seconds off pole position (Pierre-Henri Raphanel, Gulf McLaren), it was a tenacious opponent in the four-hour race. Jarier and company were ahead of the field at the two-hour and three-hour marks, but Ray Bellm was able to pass the Larbre GT2 half an hour from the end and extend a lead of 16 seconds.

Two more McLarens encountered teething problems (Raphanel's had both front wheels fall off, after its first pit stop!), and third place was claimed by the irrepressible Swiss pair, Enzo Calderari and Lilian Bryner, in their Stadler Motorsport GT2. And despite a fire in the engine bay during the Sunday morning warm-up, the Repsol Kremer GT2 of Alfonso d'Orleans and Thomas Saldana was able to finish ninth.

Four McLarens and two Ferrari F40s dominated the grid at Monza, and even the ADA de Tomaso Pantera was able to out-qualify the Larbre GT2 Evo. The Kremer Repsol Porsche, unfortunately, was badly damaged by Alfonso d'Orleans in practice. The Larbre team raced more strongly than it qualified and got its nose ahead on occasions. At the finish Messrs Jarier, Wollek and Bouchut were just 16 seconds behind Thomas Bscher's McLaren, a very commendable result. Two more McLarens joined the BPR Global Endurance series at Jarama, making it all the more difficult for the Porsches to shine in the classification. A rare visitor to the series was Norbert Singer, who went to Spain to see for himself how formidable the McLarens had become, and to decide what needed to be done to arrest their progress.

As usual the Larbre Competition team came out best, third overall for Jarier, Wollek and Bouchut, still on the lead lap, too, after four hours. Juergen Lassig and Juergen von Gartzen were sixth overall in their HO Motorsport bi-turbo, and 'Enzo and Lilian' seventh, winners of the GT3 class in their Stadler Motorsport Porsche.

Larbre raced their GT2 with the larger inlet air restrictors for the first time at the Nurburgring, now with 550 horsepower, but it exposed the weakness of the Evo immediately. Jarier ran clean out of brakes in the second hour, and needed a long stop to repair the car, and then the Evo spun helplessly across the grass when a driveshaft broke, Wollek just a passenger until it stopped sliding. McLarens claimed the top five positions overall, with Enzo and Lilian sixth and the Muhlbauer GT2 seventh with Hubner and Oberndorfer.

Two poorly supported rounds followed, the BPR calendar apparently too crowded in the run-up to Le Mans. Larbre's GT2 Evo was an early retirement at Donington Park with a faulty gear selector shaft, and Matthias Stadler had two cars in the top six, those of Konig and Mastropietro, and Enzo and Lilian who had been delayed by a stop to check brakes. Only one McLaren appeared at Montlhery, that of Jean-Luc Maury-Laribiere, and it was an early retirement when saloon car man Marc Sourd collided with a slower car while lapping it. This made way for a Porsche clean sweep, and Hans Muhlbauer's team had the honour of being the only Porsche team to win a BPR round in 1995, driven by Hubner and Oberndorfer. Second was the Parr Motorsport GT2 of Bill Farmer, Robert Nearn and Paul Edwards.

Ferrari was the winner at Anderstorp, the airfield track in southern Sweden, and it was owned by series co-organiser Stephane Ratel. Michel Ferte and Olivier Thevenin were the drivers who got the best out of the F40's turbocharged engine on the runway straight, and McLarens claimed second and third positions.

3 Hours Zhuhai 1995: Lilian Bryner, Enzo Calderari

STARTING AGAIN 101

Es folgten zwei Rennen mit nur kleinen Starterfeldern. Der BPR-Kalender umfasste in den Wochen vor Le Mans offensichtlich zuviele Rennen. Der Larbre-GT2 fiel schon bald mit einem gebrochenen Schalthebel aus. Matthias Stadler hatte zwei Autos unter den ersten Sechs, das von Helmut König und Renato Mastropietro und den 911 von Enzo und Lilian, die bei einem zusätzlichen Boxenstopp zur Kontrolle der Bemsen Zeit verloren hatten.

In Montlhéry fuhr nur ein McLaren, das Auto von Jean-Luc Maury-Laribière. Es fiel schon früh aus, nachdem Tourenwagen-Fahrer Marc Sourd beim Überrunden mit einem langsameren Auto kollidiert war. So belegen Porsche-Teams die besten Plätze. Die Mannschaft von Hans Mühlbauer war das einzige Porsche-Team, das 1995 ein Rennen zur BPR-Serie gewinnen konnte. Die siegreichen Fahrer waren Hübner und Oberndorfer. Platz zwei ging an Bill Farmer, Robert Nearn und Paul Edwards im Parr 911 GT2.

3 Hours Zhuhai 1995: Christophe Bouchut, Jean-Pierre Jarier

Ferrari siegte auf dem Flugplatzkurs im südschwedischen Anderstorp. Das Auto gehörte Stéphane Ratel, einem der Organisatoren der Serie. Die Fahrer, die auf dem Rollfeld das beste aus dem Turbomotor des F40 holten, waren Ferté und Thevenin. McLaren belegten die Plätze zwei und drei. Danach folgten vier Porsche-Teams, angeführt vom Konrad-GT2 mit Franz Konrad, Toni Seiler und Marco Spinelli. Enzo und Lilian wurden Fünfte, das Elf-Haberthur-Auto mit Ferdinand de Lesseps, Charles Margueron und Philippe Charriol fuhr auf Rang sechs ins Ziel.

Das Rennen in Suzuka, Mitte August, wird allen Teilnehmern wegen der enormen Hitze und Luftfeuchtigkeit in Erinnerung bleiben. Die Bedingungen raubten allen die letzten Kräfte. Die Fahrer lieferten eine fast übermenschliche Leistung. Jack Leconte entsandte zwei Porsche nach Suzuka. Dupuy fiel jedoch schon bald aus, nachdem er in der ersten Runde in einer Kollision involviert war. Bouchut bestritt in Spa ein Formel 3000-Rennen, so dass Wollek und Jarier fast sieben Stunden nur zu zweit fahren mussten. Als Belohnung erreichten sie Platz vier in der Gesamtwertung. Ratel tat sich mit Enzo und Lilian zusammen. Alle drei freuten sich über den achten Gesamtrang und den Sieg in der GT3-Klasse vor Franz Konrad und Antonio Hermann.

Nach der Hitze in Suzuka folgte der Regen von Silverstone. Als die Strecke abtrocknete, kam Enzo Calderari frühzeitig zum Wechsel auf Pirelli-Intermediates an die Box. Zur Hälfte des Rennens setzte er sich an die Spitze und führte 20 Runden lang. Sein Einsatz war jedoch umsonst, weil der Schweizer die maximale Fahrzeit überschritten hatte. Lilian Bryner musste die Zeitstrafe von sechs langen Minuten in der Box absitzen und trommelte wütend aufs Lenkrad.

Lotus holte einen seltenen Erfolg: Alessandro Zanardi und Alex Portman belegten den vierten Gesamtrang im Esprit Turbo und gewannen die GT3-Klasse vor dem Lazante 911 GT3 von Burdell, Langton und Rössler.

Der elfte Lauf der Saison 1995 fand in Nogaro statt, die Rennstrecke im Süden Frankreichs mit Blick auf die schneebedeckten Pyrenäen. Wieder einmal ein Flugplatz, so dass die McLaren und Ferrari einen Vorteil hatten. Sie belegten die ersten sieben Plätze in der Startaufstellung. Der Larbre GT2-Evo stand nur in der vierten Reihe.

Obwohl sie ein Auge auf dem Temperaturanzeiger halten mussten, belegten Jarier, Wollek und Bouchut den sechsten Platz in der Gesamtwertung. Kelleners fiel im Roock GT2 mit Getriebeschaden aus. Rang sieben ging an Enzo und Lilian vor dem zweiten GT2-Evo von Larbre Racing mit Eric Helary, Pierre Yver und Jean-Luc Chereau.

Schließlich kehrte die Serie nach Zhuhai zurück. Man fuhr erneut auf dem Straßenkurs mit jeder Menge Prunk und wehenden Fahnen, die das Bild vom armen China in den Hintergrund verdrängten. Wollek freute sich über die überraschende Einladung, einmal Bellms McLaren zu fahren. Der Franzose wollte gerne mal das Auto der Konkurrenz ausprobieren, der Engländer wollte gerne mal das Urteil eines Profis über sein Auto hören. Keiner von beiden war jedoch sehr glücklich, als nach 76 Runden der Schalthebel brach, noch bevor Bellm überhaupt zum Fahren gekommen war.

Bouchut, der als Vierter gestartet war, machte einen seiner seltenen Fehler, als er sich in der Einführungsrunde drehte und in die Mauer fuhr. Die abtrocknende, aber noch rutschige Strecke hatte ihn überrascht. Der zweite Larbre GT2-Evo fiel aus, als sich Stéphane Ortelli drehte und eine Mauer touchierte. Dabei beschädigte er die Luftzufuhr zum Motor, worauf das Triebwerk überhitzte.

Platz vier ging an Enzo und Lilian im Stadler 911 GT2, die zweimal belohnt wurden für eine starke und konstante

Poster

4 Hours Donington Park 1995: Stefan Oberndorfer, Detlef Hübner, Andre Ahrle

Porsches filled the next four places led by the Konrad Motorsport GT2 of Konrad, Toni Seiler and Marco Spinelli, with Enzo and Lilian fifth and the Elf Haberthur entry sixth driven by Ferdinand de Lesseps, Charles Margueron and Philippe Charriol. Sadly though Detlef Hubner, winner at Montlhery, made a late decision to withdraw from racing, leaving Muhlbauer and co-driver Oberndorfer stranded mid-season.

Suzuka, the Japanese circuit visited in August, will be remembered by all the competitors for the intense heat and humidity, which sapped everyone's energy. It was hard enough working in the garages, and the drivers were superhuman to exert themselves in the airless cockpits, while dressed in two or three layers of Nomex.

Jack Leconte sent two Porsches to Suzuka, having bought a new one for Le Mans, but Dupuy was an early casualty, involved in a collision on the opening lap. Bouchut was competing in an F3000 race at Spa, leaving Wollek and Jarier to share nearly seven hours of driving, rewarded by fourth position overall. Ratel joined Enzo and Lilian, all three delighted with eighth place overall and winners of the GT3 class, ahead of Konrad and Antonio Hermann.

From the heat of Suzuka to the rains of Silverstone! Enzo Calderari made an early stop to fit Pirelli intermediate tyres as the track dried, temporarily, and burst into an overall lead midway through the race, for 20 glorious laps. It was in vain, though, as the Swiss exceeded the maximum time allowed at the wheel and Ms Bryner had to sit in the car, drumming her fingers, for six long minutes, a penalty imposed by the officials. Lotus made a rare visit to the leader board, Alessandro Zanardi and Alex Portman driving the Esprit Turbo to fourth overall, and the GT3 class victory, ahead of the Lanzante Motorsport GT2 of Burdell, Langton and Roessler.

Nogaro, the Gascony circuit with views of the snow-capped Pyrenees, was the venue for the 11th round of the 1995 series. Another airfield circuit which favoured the McLarens and Ferraris, claiming the first seven places on the grid, leaving Larbre's GT2 Evo on the fourth row.

Despite needing to drive with an eye on the temperature gauge, Jarier, Wollek and Bouchut finished in sixth place overall. Kelleners retired the Roock Racing GT2 with a broken gearbox, and seventh place was taken by Enzo and Lilian, with Larbre's second GT2 Evo eighth in the hands of Eric Helary, Pierre Yver and Jean-Luc Chereau.

Finally, a return to Zhuhai, again on the street circuit with pageantry and flag-waving that suspended all notions of "poor China". Wollek accepted a surprise invitation to drive Bellm's McLaren, the Frenchman keen to sample the competition, the Englishman to have a professional's opinion of his expensive car. Neither was particularly happy as the gear selectors broke after 76 laps, before Bellm had a chance to

4 Hours Anderstorp 1995: Giuseppe Quargentan, Raffaele Sangiuolo

1000 km Suzuka 1995: Wolfgang Kaufmann, Yukihiro Hane

compete. Bouchut, fourth on the grid, made a rare mistake as he slid and hit the wall on the parade lap, caught out by the slippery, drying track condition, and the second Larbre GT2 Evo retired when Stephane Ortelli slid and hit a wall, closing the ducting to the engine and causing it to overheat.

Fourth, then, were Enzo and Lilian in their Stadler Motorsport GT2, and they had two rewards for a supremely fast and consistent season: first, they were runners-up in the BPR series, behind 'champions' Thomas Bscher and John Nielsen, and secondly they shared the richly endowed Porsche Cup, awarded to the best privateer drivers worldwide.

Nobody could predict, at the start of the 1996 season, that it would be the final one for the Barth, Peter and Ratel organisation. It was hugely successful, to the point where grids were filled and competitors were being sent home! No fewer than 51 cars practised for the opening round at the Paul Ricard circuit, cold during the first weekend in March, but the grid was limited to 48 and included McLaren, Ferrari Porsches, Venturi, Callaway Corvette, Lotus, Alpine-Renault, Marcos and Morgan. This was going to be a season of GT racing at its best.

All the races, bar one at Anderstorp, were won by McLarens, and the Swedish event was again won by a Ferrari, this time the F40 of Luciano della Noce and Anders Olofsson. In the Porsche ranks, Jarier's services had been snapped up by Fabien and Michael Roock, who ran three GT2s (the lead car an Evo), Wollek joined Konrad's team, and Kelleners remained with Roock.

Jack Leconte, deciding to go with the GT2 and not the unreliable Evo, formed his Larbre Competition team around Patrice Goueslard and Andre Ahrle, backed by Jean-Luc Chereau who drove the second car. Bouchut went freelance, and drove a Venturi in the opening round. Lister Cars joined the series with the Storm GT, a Jaguar V12 powered 'special' which performed at a high level, and in 1996 Porsche's customer teams really were racing for class victories alone, sometimes out of the top six overall.

STARTING AGAIN 103

4 Hours Monza 1996: Robert Nearn, Stephane Ortelli

Saison. Erstens belegten sie den zweiten Platz in der Endwertung der BPR-Serie hinter den Meistern Thomas Bscher und John Nielsen. Zweitens gewannen sie zusammen den hochdotierten Porsche Cup, den Preis für die weltweit besten Privatfahrer.

Niemand konnte zu Beginn der Saison 1996 erahnen, dass diese die letzte Saison für die Organisation von Barth, Peter und Ratel sein sollte. Die Serie war sehr erfolgreich, sogar so sehr, dass auf manchen Strecken die maximale Größe des Starterfeldes erreicht wurde und Teams wieder nach Hause geschickt werden mussten. Nicht weniger als 51 Autos fuhren im Training in Paul Ricard am kalten ersten Märzwochenende. Nur 48 Autos durften im Rennen starten, darunter McLaren, Ferrari, Porsche, Venturi, Callaway-Corvette, Lotus, Alpine-Renault, Marcos und Morgan. Es sollte eine Saison mit GT-Rennsport vom Feinsten werden.

Alle Rennen bis auf Anderstorp wurden von McLaren-Teams gewonnen. In Schweden siegte erneut ein Ferrari, diesmal der F40 von Luciano della Noce und Anders Olofsson. Im Porsche-Lager wurde Jarier von Roock verpflichtet, die drei GT3 einsetzten, zusätzlich einen 911 GT2-Evo.

Jack Leconte entschied sich für den GT2 und gegen den Evo. Er formierte seine Larbre-Mannschaft um Patrice Goueslard und André Ahrle, mit Unterstützung von Jean-Luc Chereau, der das zweite Auto fuhr. Lister Cars erlebte seinen Einstand in der Serie mit dem Storm GT, einem Spezialfahrzeug mit Jaguar V12-Motor, der eine starke Leistung brachte. Porsche-Kundenteams kämpften 1996 lediglich noch um Klassensiege, manchmal sogar außerhalb der Top-Sechs in der Gesamtwertung.

Jarier, der seinem Namen als Spitzenfahrer gerecht wurde, konnte in Le Castellet mit den McLaren und Ferrari mithalten, hatte aber bald einen Bremsdefekt und fuhr dem Harrods McLaren am Ende der Mistral-Geraden seitlich ins Auto, als das gelbe Fahrzeug gerade in die schnelle Signes-Kurve einlenkte.

Porsche 911 GT2-Evo belegten im Ziel gute Platzierungen. Wollek und Konrad waren Vierte in der Gesamtwertung. Kaufmann und Mike Hezemans fuhren für das Freisinger-Team auf Rang fünf vor dem Roock-Porsche mit Eichmann, Kelleners und Ruch, die die GT2-Klasse gewannen.

Die Ferrari kamen in Monza beim zweiten BPR-Lauf der Saison nicht über die gesamte Renndistanz. Im Kampf um die Spitze beförderte Nielsen James Weaver, der Maurizio Sandro Sala in Bellms McLaren ersetzte, gekonnt ins Kiesbett.

Der Konrad GT2-Evo brauchte einen neuen Achsschenkel, Jariers Roock-Porsche hatte einen Motorschaden, ebenso der Repsol-Kremer-Porsche, der von Bouchut und Saldana gefahren wurde. Im Ziel belegten Eichmann, Kelleners und Ruch Rang drei für Roock Racing. Langton, Burdell und Stanley Dickens fuhren für Lanzante Motorsport auf den vierten Platz vor Goueslard und Ahrle im Larbre-Porsche.

Die Gebrüder Kremer hatten in Jarama nicht mehr Glück: Der Repsol GT2 Evo von Saldana und Alfonso d'Orleans fiel vor heimischem Publikum nach einer Kollision mit dem Larbre GT2 von Jesus Pareja aus. Es war eine rein spanische Angelegenheit, sehr zur Unfreude des Publikums, diesmal nicht weniger als 50.000 Zuschauer.

Eichmann fuhr schon früh an die Box, um die Hinterradaufhängung kontrollieren zu lassen. Jarier hatte erneut einen Motorschaden, Enzo und Lilian hatten ein gebrochenes Radlager und hinter fünf McLaren und Ferrari belegten Konrad und Wollek den sechsten Rang. Cor Euser gewann die GT2-Klasse im Marcos-Chevrolet.

Der Einstand der Bigazzi-McLaren mit Werks-Unterstützung von BMW sorgte dafür, dass die Porsche-Teams in der Startaufstellung von Silverstone noch weiter hinten standen. Wie üblich schnitten sie jedoch im Rennen besser ab als im Zeittraining. Am Ende der ersten Stunde waren Jarier und Wollek Elfter und Zwölfter. Das Roock-Team war jedoch sehr enttäuscht, als Ruch auf dem Weg in die Box ohne Benzin liegen blieb.

Jariers Evo fiel 35 Minuten vor Schluss wegen eines Getriebeschadens aus und der beste Porsche im Ziel war der 911 von Konrad und Wollek auf Rang neun der Gesamtwertung. Der fünfte Saisonlauf auf dem Nürburgring war für Porsche kein großartiges Rennen, da alle GT2-Evo ausfielen.

Das gleiche Bild in Anderstorp, wo Della Noce und Olofsson klar alle McLaren schlugen. Mike Hezemans und Alex Portman fuhren im Lotus Esprit Turbo auf Platz sechs. Eichmann, Ruch und Neugarten belegten Rang sieben und gewannen erneut die GT2-Klasse.

McLaren und Ferrari dominierten in Suzuka, wo sie die ersten sieben Plätze belegten. Der Kampf in der GT2-Klasse war viel spannender. Eichmann, Ruch und Ralf Kelleners holten sich den Klassensieg, fuhren aber nur 20 Sekunden vor Konrad, Wollek und Ortelli ins Ziel.

Es gab Meinungsunterschiede in Suzuka, was die einst so familiäre Atmosphäre in der BPR-Serie störte. Patrick Peter hatte Ärger mit Barth und Ratel und sie mit ihm. Ausserdem plante Porsche-Motorsport den Einsatz des neuen 911 GT1 mit Mittelmotor bei einigen Rennen am Ende der Saison einzusetzen.

Jarier, top driver as he was, got his Roock GT2 Evo among the McLarens and Ferraris at Le Castellet, but soon ran out of brakes and rammed the side of the Harrods McLaren at the end of the Mistral Straight, the yellow car just turning into the rapid curve at Signes.

Porsche's GT2 Evo machines were well placed at the finish, Wollek and Konrad placed fourth overall, Kaufmann and Hezemans fifth for Freisinger's team, then Eichmann, Kelleners and Ruch sixth for Roock, winners of the GT2 class.

The Ferraris failed to go the distance at Monza, the second BPR race of the season, and Nielsen expertly tipped James Weaver into a gravel trap while contesting the lead, Weaver replacing Maurizio Sandro Sala in Bellm's Gulf McLaren.

Konrad's GT2 Evo needed a new stub axle, Jarier's Roock Porsche had an engine failure, and so did the Repsol Kremer Porsche with Bouchut and Saldana on duty. When all the dust settled Eichmann, Kelleners and Ruch were third overall for Roock, Langton, Burdell and Stanley Dickens fourth for Lanzante Motorsport, and Goueslard and Ahrle fifth for Larbre.

The Kremer brother's luck did not improve at Jarama, the Repsol sponsored GT2 Evo driven by Saldana and Alfonso d'Orleans retiring, in front of the 'home' crowd, in a collision with Jesus Pareja's Larbre GT2. It was an all-Spanish affair, which did not please the crowd rated, this time, at 50,000.

Eichmann made an early stop to have his rear suspension checked, Jarier had another engine failure, Enzo and Lilian had a wheel bearing failure, and behind five McLarens and Ferraris Konrad and Wollek claimed sixth position. Cor Euser won GT2 in his Marcos, leaving von Gartzen and Patrick Huisman seventh in their Oberbayern Porsche GT2.

The appearance of the Bigazzi McLarens, with BMW backing, pushed the Porsche teams even further back on the grid at Silverstone, but as usual they raced better than they qualified. Jarier and Wollek were 11th and 12th at the end of the first hour, 8th and 10th after two hours (half distance), but the Roock team was thoroughly disappointed as Ruch ran out of fuel on his 'in' lap.

Jarier's Evo retired 35 min. from the end with a broken gearbox, and the best Porsche at the finish was that of Konrad and Wollek, ninth overall - despite breaking a driveshaft at the last corner! Euser's Marcos again won GT2, challenged by the Oberbayern GT2 of von Gartzen and Hezemans.

Round 5 at the Nurburgring was not a great race for Porsche, the Evos all breaking down. The Kremer Repsol Evo, unlucky again, had an engine failure, Roock and Konrad both had driveshaft failures. With McLarens and Ferraris dominating the top six positions, Eichmann, Ruch and Neu-

4 Hours Paul Ricard 1996: Lilian Bryner, Enzo Calderari

4 Hours Jarama 1996: Tomas Saldana, Christophe Bouchut

garten finished seventh for Roock, winning the GT2 class, Burdell and Largton eighth for Lanzante.

It was a similar story at Anderstorp, where della Noce and Olofsson handsomely beat all the McLarens, with Mike Hezemans and Alex Portman sixth in a Lotus Esprit Turbo. Seventh, and again winners of the GT2 category, were Eichmann, Ruch and Neugarten ahead of Seiler and Ortelli in a Konrad GT2. Now, support for the Evo model was waning, as repeated engine and transmission failures thwarted all attempts to obtain results.

While McLarens and Ferraris dominated at Suzuka, claiming the top seven positions, the race for the GT2 class was far more exciting. Eichmann, Ruch and Ralf Kelleners won the class, but were only 20 seconds ahead of Konrad, Wollek and Ortelli, driving a 480 bhp GT2 for a change. Euser had led at half distance, in his Marcos Chevrolet, but was delayed by an oil leak.

There was tension at Suzuka, spoiling the customary ambiance of the BPR series, which came to a head in the paddock chalet on Saturday night. Patrick Peter was at odds with Barth and Ratel, and they with him, and Porsche AG were planning to enter their new mid-engined GT1 model in late-season races.

The GT1 had shown what it could do at Le Mans, second and third overall, first and second in GT1, and the McLaren teams were most unhappy that this newcomer would burst in on championship. Specifically, they said, it was not in production and it was not homologated (but the ACO GT1 class allowed for this).

STARTING AGAIN 105

Der 911 GT1 hatte in Le Mans mit den Plätzen zwei und drei in der Gesamtwertung bereits sein Potenzial gezeigt. Die Mc Laren-Teams waren höchst unerfreut, dass dieser Neuling in die Meisterschaft eingreifen würde. Man beanstandete speziell die Tatsache, dass das Modell nicht in der Serie produziert wurde und keine Straßenzulassung hatte, obwohl die GT1-Klasse dieses erlaubte.

Bellm ging sogar so weit, dass er eine Vereinigung der Teams ins Leben rief, die mit der BPR verhandeln sollte. Er bekam schließlich die Zusage, dass der 911 GT1 keine Punkte einfahren konnte. Ansonsten hätte es Bellm möglicherweise den Titel in der BPR-Serie gekostet.

Der 911 GT1 erlebte seinen Einsand in Brands Hatch mit Stuck und Boutsen und er gewann mit deutlicher Überlegenheit. Es war ein überragendes GT-Auto, genau wie es Bellm und die anderen McLaren-Fahrer befürchtet hatten. Für Porsche jedoch brachte dieser 911 die lang ersehnte Rückkehr aufs Siegerpodest und zwar nicht in der GT2 und GT3-Klasse, sondern auf dem höchsten Treppchen im Gesamtklassement. Eusers gelber Marcos war ein starker Gegner in der GT2-Klasse. Franz Konrads 911 GT2 hatte allerdings am Ende die Nase vorn, als Konrad, Wollek und Ortelli mit zehn Sekunden Vorsprung auf Rang sechs die Ziellinie überquerten. Der Neu-Einsteiger der Serie, die Oreca-Chrysler Viper GTS-R von Olivier Beretta und Justin Bell, belegte den achten Platz. Das französische Team unter der Leitung von Hugues de Chaunac sollte in den darauffolgenden Jahren eine starke Leistung zeigen.

In Spa feierten Stuck und Boutsen im 911 GT1 einen noch überzeugenderen Sieg. Von den Porsche-Privatteams hatte Roock Racing ein hervorragendes Rennen, wobei am Ende Rang sieben in der Gesamtwertung herauskam. Eichmann, Ruch und Kelleners hängten Eusers Marcos-Chevrolet um eine Runde ab.

1000 km Suzuka 1996: Tomiko Yoshikawa, Guy Martinolle, Jean Lagniez

Porsche siegte beim 4 Stunden-Rennen von Zhuhai, der elfte und letzte Lauf der BPR-Serie. Collard und Kelleners, der die etablierten Teilnehmer mit seiner Pole-Position schockte, wurden auf dem 911 GT1 eingesetzt.

Eichmann und Ruch, die mit Ortelli fuhren, waren die Schnellsten in der GT2-Klasse und brauchten die Punkte zum Gewinn des Vizetitels in der nach wie vor inoffiziellen BPR-Fahrermeisterschaft, hinter Bellm und Weaver. Ein kaputter Turbolader warf das Roock-Team zurück auf Rang neun, was gerade zur Vizemeisterschaft reichte und Eichmann den Gesamtsieg im Porsche Cup brachte.

911 GT1 1996

Zhuhai 1996

Roock, Konrad und Larbre waren die stärksten GT2-Teams in Nogaro, wo der Marcos das Tempo nicht ganz mitgehen konnte. Nach vier Stunden fuhren Konrad und Wollek mit 43 Sekunden Vorsprung auf den Roock-Fahrern Eichmann, Ruch und Kelleners ins Ziel. Goueslard und Ahrle belegten für Larbre den dritten Platz.

In Zhuhai wurde eine neue permanente Rennstrecke eröffnet, die zwar nicht das Flair des Straßenkurses hatte. Kein Mensch, der bei den Feierlichkeiten zur Eröffnung dabei war, wird jemals den Löwentanz mit den Schlagzeugern und den gesamten Prunk der Veranstaltung vergessen.

Eusers Marcos siegte in der GT2-Klasse vor dem zweiten Roock-Porsche mit Hürtgen, Andy Pilgrim und Michel Ligonnet und dem Stadler-Porsche von Enzo und Lilian.

Obwohl es damals keiner wusste, war das Rennen in China die letzte Veranstaltung der BPR-Serie, die 1997 von der FIA übernommen wurde. Barth, Peter und Ratel verdienen grosses Lob, dass sie den Langstreckensport nach dem Untergang 1992 wieder auf die Räder gestellt hatten. Mehr noch, sie hatten ihn auf ein so hohes Niveau gebracht, dass die FIA sich gezwungen sah, die Kontrolle mit einer offiziellen Meisterschaft zu übernehmen.

Winner 4 Hours Spa-Francorchamps 1996: Thierry Boutsen, Hans-Joachim Stuck

Bellm went so far as to form an entrant's union which would negotiate with BPR, and succeeded in getting a decision that the Porsche GT1 would not be allowed to score points, and possibly deny him the chance to win the BPR series.

The 911 GT1 did make its appearance at Brands Hatch, in the hands of Stuck and Boutsen, and it did win with considerable ease. It was a superior GT car, just as Bellm and the other McLaren drivers feared. For Porsche, though, it was a long overdue return to the podium, not in the GT2 and GT3 categories, but on the top step overall.

Euser's yellow Marcos was a strong competitor in the GT2 class, but Franz Konrad's GT2 got its nose ahead at the finish, as Konrad, Wollek and Ortelli took the flag with 10 seconds to spare, in sixth place overall. Eighth overall were newcomers to the series, the Team Oreca Chrysler Viper GTS-R of Olivier Beretta and Justin Bell, and the French team headed by Hugues de Chaunac was destined to make a big impact in years to come.

Stuck and Boutsen achieved a still more decisive victory at Spa in the 911 GT1, and of Porsche's private teams Roock Racing had an outstanding race to finish seventh overall, Eichmann, Ruch and Kelleners managing to lap Euser's Marcos. Soames Langton and Paul Burdell were provisionally third in GT2 until the timekeepers figured that Langton had exceeded his maximum time at the wheel, unfortunate as it was the last race the Englishman completed.

Roock, Konrad and Larbre were the top GT2 contenders at Nogaro, where the Marcos was a little off the pace. Racing to their limit for four hours, Konrad and Wollek finished 43 seconds ahead of Roock men Eichmann, Ruch and Kelleners, with Goueslard and Ahrle third for Larbre.

Claudia Huertgen made her BPR debut at Nogaro with the Roock team, but was defeated by a broken driveshaft coupling when fourth.

Langton had a mystery accident in the Lanzante GT2 which left him in a vegetative state, the worst accident to befall any competitor in the BPR series. It was speculated that he had already lost consciousness before reaching a corner where he ploughed straight ahead into the protective banking without braking or steering.

A new, permanent circuit was opened at Zhuhai which lacked the charisma of the street circuit, but was more forgiving of driver errors. No-one who attended the opening ceremony will forget the fabulous Lion Dance performed with drums, and the sheer pageantry of the occasion.

Porsche won the Zhuhai 4-Hours, the 11th and final round of the BPR series, with the GT1 driven by new signings Ralf Kelleners, who shocked his elders by claiming pole position, and Emmanuel Collard.

Eichmann and Ruch, driving with Ortelli, were quickest in GT2 and needed points to claim second place in the (still unofficial) BPR driver championship, behind Bellm and Weaver. A broken turbocharger put the Roock team back to ninth in class, but it was just enough for them to claim the runner-up spot, and just as importantly, for Eichmann to win the Porsche Cup.

Euser's Marcos won GT2, though, ahead of Roock's second Porsche driven by Huertgen, Andy Pilgrim and Michel Ligonnet, and the Stadler Porsche of Enzo and Lilian.

The Chinese race, we did not know at the time, was the final event in the BPR series, which was 'claimed' by the FIA in 1997. Barth, Peter and Ratel deserved medals for putting endurance racing back on its wheels after the debacle of 1992, and raising it to such a high level that the FIA felt the need to take control with an official championship.

4 Hours Monza 1996: Patrice Gueslard, Andre Ahrle, Jack Leconte

DOMÄNE GT SPORT

Norbert Singer war klar, dass Porsche ein neues GT-Auto für den Rennsport benötigte. Sein Eindruck wurde durch den Besuch im Frühjahr 1995 in Jarama verstärkt und ebenfalls durch das eher mässige Abschneiden der Privatteams in der GT2-Klasse in Le Mans.

Sein Konzept war ein GT1-Auto mit Mittelmotor, basierend auf dem Monocoque des 911, jedoch mit dem zukünftigen wassergekühlten Motor unmittelbar hinter der Fahrgastzelle. Die Leistung sollte minimal bei 600 PS liegen. Nur mit einer solchen Maschine konnte Porsche überhaupt daran denken, die McLaren F1 GTR und die Ferrari F40 zu schlagen, oder etwa den F50, dessen Einstand in der BPR-Serie bald erwartet wurde.

Der Porsche-Vorstand gab am 24. Juli 1995 grünes Licht. Die ersten Zeichnungen wurden am 20. August angefertigt und im November wurden die ersten Blechteile geschnitten. Das Projekt wurde mit aller Kraft vorangetrieben. Die erste Rohkarrosse wurde am 2. Januar 1996 geliefert und Jürgen Barth fuhr das Auto zum ersten Mal am 14. März auf der Teststrecke in Weissach. Der Termin für die offizielle Premiere stand schon Monate zuvor fest, nämlich beim Testtag in Le Mans am 28. April. Dort wurden zwei rennfertige Autos für sechs Fahrer benötigt. Hans-Joachim Stuck sollte zusammen mit Thierry Boutsen und Bob Wollek fahren, Yannick Dalmas wurde mit Scott Goodyear und Karl Wendlinger eingeteilt. Selbstverständlich lief alles wie geplant.

Der 911 (993) Turbo war die Basis des GT1. Alles hinter dem Cockpit wurde jedoch entfernt und eine neue Wand wurde hinter dem Fahrer errichtet. Hinter dieser Spritzwand befand sich der wassergekühlte Motor. Mit einer Bohrung von 95 mm und einem Hub von 74,4 mm (bekannte Größen) hatte der 911 GT1 einen Hubraum von 3163 ccm. Jeder Zylinder hatte vier Ventile und die Leistung wurde mit 600 PS bei 7.200 U/Min. angegeben. Drehmoment betrug 650 Nm bei 5.500 U/Min. Es wurden doppelte KKK 27.2 Turbolader montiert. Die Gemischaufbereitung und die Zündung wurden von einem TAG 3.8 Motorsteuerungsgerät überwacht.

Im Dach des GT1 wurde ein großes Ansaugrohr montiert. Der Lufteinlass befand sich über der Mitte der Frontscheibe, die in der Mitte einen Knick hatte, um den Luftwiderstand zu reduzieren. Das synchronisierte Sechsganggetriebe wurde verstärkt und die Kraftübertragung erfolgte mittels einer Einscheibenkupplung. Die Aufhängung der Vorderräder umfasste Doppelquerlenker und senkrecht montierte Dämpfer mit Schraubfedern. Hinten wurden die innen montierten Feder-

Winner 4 Hours Spa-Francorchamps 1996: Thierry Boutsen, Hans-Joachim Stuck

4 Hours Zhuhai 1996

Test Paul Ricard 1996: 911 GT1

GRAND TOURERS

There was no doubt in Ing. Singer's mind that Porsche needed a new Grand Touring car for racing, the impression reinforced by his visit to Jarama in the Spring of 1995, and further by the poor performances of the private GT2 teams at Le Mans. His concept was a mid-engined GT1 car based on the 911's monocoque, but with the forthcoming water cooled engine immediately behind the cabin, and a minimum of 600 horsepower. Only with such a machine could Porsche hope to beat the McLaren F1 GTRs and the Ferrari F40s (and the F50 that was expected to join the BPR series shortly).

Porsche's board of management gave the go-ahead on July 24, 1995, drawings were started on August 20 and the first metal was cut in November. For expediency the carbon bodywork was to be made by Zakspeed Nitec in Niederzissen, and the project was pushed along at top speed. The first raw body was delivered on January 2, 1996 and Juergen Barth drove it for the first time on the Weissach test track on March 14. The public debut had been scheduled for months. It would be at the Le Mans test day on April 28, when two race-ready cars would be required for six drivers. Hans Stuck would team up with Thierry Boutsen and Bob Wollek, and Yannick Dalmas with Scott Goodyear and Karl Wendlinger. Needless to say, it all went like clockwork!

The 911 (993) Turbo was the base for the GT1, but everything behind the cockpit was cut away and a full-width bulkhead was constructed behind the driver. Aft of the bulkhead was a sub frame which carried the water cooled engine, similar to that which would power the Boxster and later, the 911/996. It was very much part of Porsche's philosophy to try out new ideas in the racing cars, and give them a pedigree before they reached production.

With a bore of 95 mm and a stroke of 74.4 mm (familiar dimensions!) the GT1's capacity was 3,163 cc. There were 4 valves per cylinder and the power was quoted at 600 bhp at 7,200 rpm, with 650 Nm of torque at 5,500 rpm. Twin KKK K27.2 turbochargers were fitted, and the two inlet air restrictors each had a diamater of 36.6 mm. TAG 3.8 engine management controlled the mixture and spark timing.

A large air scoop was mounted in the GT1's roof, the intake above the centre of the windscreen which had a depression in the centre so as to reduce the air resistance. The six-speed synchromesh gearbox was reinforced, and power went through a single-disc sintered clutch. The front suspension comprised double wishbone control arms and vertical dampers with coil springs, while at the rear pushrods ac-

Winner 4 Hours Brands Hatch 1996: Thierry Boutsen, Hans-Joachim Stuck

Dämpfereinheiten mittels Zugstreben aktiviert. BBS lieferte 18 Zoll-Räder mit Zentralverschluss, vorne 11 Zoll breit und hinten 13 Zoll breit. Es gab ein ABS von Bosch, während eine Servolenkung die Aufgabe der Fahrer erleichterte.

Mit seiner Höhe von 1173 mm lag der GT1 genau 110 mm tiefer als der Turbo in Straßenversion. Er war 4683 mm lang und 1946 mm breit. Die zwei Autos für Le Mans wogen bei der technischen Abnahme 1049 bzw. 1056 kg.

Für den Erwerb der Zulassung wurde der 911 GT1 mit dem luftgekühlten 3,6 Litermotor aus dem RSR bestückt. Turbolader konnten nachträglich montiert werden. Eine Version mit 300 PS wurde zum Verkauf angeboten. Hierfür gab es keine Kunden, dennoch wurden 1997 20 Stück mit einer 545 PS starken Version des Reihen-Sechsylinder-Turbomotors zu einem Preis von je 1,5 Millionen DM verkauft. Weitere 15 Exemplare wurden in einer leistungsstärkeren Ausführung für Rennteams angefertigt.

Die zwei Werks-Porsche erlebten einen hervorragenden Einstand in Le Mans, wo sie die Plätze eins und zwei in der GT-Klasse belegten. Im Gesamtklassement wurden sie Zweiter und Dritter hinter dem TWR-Porsche des Joest-Teams. So belegte Porsche alle Podiumsplätze.

4 Hours Brands Hatch 1996

Weissach 1996: 911 GT1

Stuck und Boutsen fuhren den Porsche bei seinem ersten Rennen auf britischem Boden in Brands Hatch. Stuck stellte sofort die Dominanz des Porsche unter Beweis, indem er sich die Pole-Position sicherte. Für ältere Teammitglieder aus Weissach wurden sofort schöne Erinnerungen wach: 1982 erlebte der 956 sein Debüt in Silverstone und die Entscheidung im Kampf um den Fahrertitel der Langstrecken-WM fiel in jener Saison beim Finale in Brands Hatch, wo sich Ickx knapp gegen Riccardo Patrese im Lancia durchsetzte.

Das BPR-Rennen bot wenig Abwechslung, da sich Stuck mit verhaltenem Tempo von den McLaren absetzte. Er und Boutsen fuhren bis zum Fallen der Zielflagge einen Vorsprung von einer Runde auf dem Harrods-McLaren von Wallace und Grouillard heraus.

Beim nächsten Lauf in Spa-Francorchamps war es eine andere Geschichte. Boutsen stellte einen neuen Trainingsrekord auf, indem er die Strecke in den Ardennen fast 13 Sekunden schneller als jedes GT-Auto zuvor umrundete. Und der vorherige Rekord war gar nicht so schlecht, zwei Jahre zuvor von Olofsson im Ferrari F40 aufgestellt. Boutsen jedoch setzte mit 2.13,857 Minuten eine neue Bestmarke. Olofsson war diesmal fast vier Sekunden langsamer und gab zu, dass der Porsche in jeglicher Hinsicht besser sei.

Boutsen fuhr bereits in der ersten Rennrunde einen Vorsprung von sieben Sekunden heraus und stellte in der zweiten Runde des Rennens wieder einen neuen Rundenrekord für GT-Fahrzeuge auf. Seine Bestzeit von 2.16,978 im Rennen war schneller als die beste Qualifikationszeit jedes einzelnen Konkurrenten. Erneut siegte der 911 GT1 mit einem Vorsprung von einer Runde auf die McLaren und Ferrari. Diesmal war es eine lange Runde von fast 7 Kilometern.

Der letzte Auftritt folgte auf der neuen permanenten Rennstrecke in Zhuhai. Für das Rennen wurden zwei Autos vorbereitet. Ralf Kelleners und Emmanuel Collard, beide Spitzenfahrer aus dem Supercup, wurden verpflichtet. Wollek und Dalmas wurden auf dem zweiten GT1 eingeschrieben. Die beiden jungen Fahrer hatten lediglich zwei Testfahrten zur Verfügung, bevor sie die Reise nach China antraten. Kelleners setzte sich auf Anhieb durch, denn er sicherte sich die Pole-Position, 17 Hundertstelsekunden schneller als Dalmas. Jean-Marc Gounon hatte im Ferrari F40 jedoch nur eine halbe Sekunden Rückstand.

Dalmas bestimmte das Tempo, sein Landsmann Collard überholte ihn jedoch ohne Probleme in der dritten Runde und behielt die Führung bis ins Ziel. Beim ersten Stopp gab es einen Fahrerwechsel und plötzlich kam Hektik auf, als Wollek den GT1 nicht mehr per Knopfdruck starten konnte. Er wurde angeschoben, was die Sportkommissare letztendlich dazu bewegte, nicht eine, sondern gleich zwei Strafen auszusprechen. Zunächst musste Wollek anhalten, den Motor ausschalten und per Knopfdruck wieder anlassen. Danach musste er abermals anhalten und vier Minuten als Strafe fürs Anschieben absitzen. Es war eine harte Bestrafung, die ihn drei Runden zurückwarf. Er kam letztendlich auf Platz fünf ins Ziel. Collard und Kelleners siegten mit zwei Runden Vorsprung vor dem Ferrari F40 von Gounon, Bernard und Belmondo und schrieben so die Erfolgsgeschichte des ersten Produktions-Porsche 911 mit Mittelmotor.

Was danach passierte, war für Porsche jedoch höchst unerfreulich. McLaren Cars forderte die FIA auf, die Kontrolle über die Serie zu übernehmen und wurde dabei von BMW Motorsport unterstützt, da BMW den Einsatz eines Werksteams plante. Auch Mercedes machte Druck bei der FIA, man möge doch die Serie übernehmen, da auch Mercedes überraschenderweise den Einstieg mit einem neuen Auto

tuated the inboard spring/damper units. BBS supplied the centre-locking wheels, 18-inch diameter, 11J at the front and 13J at the rear, and Brembo 8-piston callipers (front) took care of the braking, on carbon discs. Bosch ABS was installed, and power steering made life easier for the drivers. The GT1 stood 110 mm lower than the road-going Turbo at 1173 mm, was 4,683 mm in length and 1,946 mm high. The scrutineering weight was given as 1,000 kg, but the two cars scrutineered for Le Mans were 1,049 kg and 1,056 kg.

For the purpose of homologation the GT1 was offered with the 3.6 litre, air cooled RSR engine (turbochargers could be added later!) and in fact a 300 horsepower version was offered for sale. There were no customers, but 20 were sold to the public in 1997 at DM 1.5 million apiece, with a 545 bhp version of the flat-six turbo engine. Furthermore, 15 were made to a higher specification for race teams.

The two 'works' GT1s had an outstanding debut at Le Mans, where they finished first and second in the Grand Touring category, second and third overall behind the Joest Racing TWR Porsche, so making a clean sweep of the podium.

Hans Stuck and Thierry Boutsen gave the GT1 its debut race on British soil, at Brands Hatch, and the tall German immediately stamped Porsche's authority on the event by claiming pole position. There were plenty of good memories for senior personnel from Weissach, who recalled the debut of the 956 at Silverstone in 1982, and the climax of that season at Brands Hatch when Ickx narrowly beat Riccardo Patrese's Lancia for the WEC drivers championship title.

The BPR race did not offer much excitement, as Stuck pulled away from the McLarens at a gradual pace, careful not to make the task look too easy. He and Boutsen opened up a one-lap lead over the Harrods McLaren of Wallace and Grouillard at the finish.

It was a different story at Spa-Francorchamps, the next event in the series. This time Boutsen smashed the qualifying record, lapping the Ardennes circuit nearly 13 seconds inside the GT lap record … not a bad one, set two years before by Olofsson in a Ferrari F40, and created a new mark at 2m 13.857s. Olofsson was nearly four seconds slower, offering the opinion that the Porsche was "better in every department". Ing. Singer and Hartmut Kristen could not conceal their pleasure. Boutsen was able to put seven seconds between himself and his challengers, and in fact his second lap established a new GT record at 2m 16.978s, which was faster than anyone else had qualified. Again, the Porsche finished a lap ahead of the McLarens and Ferraris, but this was a long lap measuring almost seven kilometres.

The final appearance of the Porsche GT1 was at Zhuhai, on the new permanent circuit, and two cars were prepared for the event. Ralf Kelleners and Emmanuel Collard, top drivers in the Supercup series, and with nothing to prove in endurance racing, were engaged to drive one car, Wollek and Dalmas the other. The two youngsters had only two test sessions before setting off to China, and Kelleners immediately made his mark by claiming pole position, 17-hundredths of a second faster than Dalmas but with Jean-Marc Gounon only half a second slower in a Ferrari F40.

Dalmas set the pace, but his compatriot Collard calmly overtook him on the third lap, and maintained the lead. Drivers were changed at the first stop, and there was consternation when Wollek was unable to start his Porsche on the button.

The GT1 was given a push-start, which persuaded the stewards to impose not one, but two penalties. First, Wollek had to stop, turn off the engine and restart on the button, then he had to stop again and wait four minutes, the penalty for the push-start! It was a harsh punishment which dropped him three laps, to an eventual fifth position overall.

Collard and Kelleners won the race by two clear laps, ahead of the Ferrari F40 of Gounon, Eric Bernard and Paul Belmondo, and thus created a new legend about the first mid-engined, production Porsche 911.

The events which followed were distinctly unfavourable to Porsche, however. On the one hand, McLaren Cars lobbied the FIA to take control of the series, backed by BMW Motorsport which planned to run a factory team.

On the other hand, Mercedes were also pushing the FIA to take over, planning a surprise entry with a new car built by the subsidiary AMG. The DTM series was about to collapse with the withdrawal of Alfa Romeo, and Mercedes had big plans to return to endurance racing with a special V12 car, the CLK-GTR. Don Panoz had a surprise, too, the Panoz GTR designed by Adrian Reynard, powered by a forward mounted Ford V8 engine.

The FIA, which had the statutory right to do so, announced the official FIA Grand Touring Championship for 1997, and effectively stopped BPR in its tracks by denying it television rights for any races it might plan to run. Completing the coup, executive vice-president Bernie Ecclestone then recruited Stephane Ratel to organise the FIA GT Championship, and he in turn asked that Juergen Barth should help him with his duties. It was game, set and match to the FIA, leaving Patrick Peter angry and impotent.

Winner 4 Hours Zhuhai 1996:
Emmanuel Collard, Ralf Kelleners

4 Hours A 1 Ring 1997: Horst Jr. and Sr. Febermayr, Stefano Buttiero

plante, das von Tochterfirma AMG gebaut wurde. Die DTM-Serie stand nach dem Rückzug von Alfa Romeo vor dem Aus und Mercedes hatte große Pläne für die Rückkehr in den Langstreckensport mit einem speziellen Fahrzeug mit V12-Motor, dem CLK-GTR. Don Panoz hatte ebenfalls eine Überraschung, nämlich den von Adrian Reynard entworfenen Panoz GTR. Dieses Auto wurde von einem im Bug platzierten Ford V8-Motor angetrieben.

Die FIA schrieb für 1997 die offizielle FIA Grand Touring-Meisterschaft aus, wozu man freilich auch das Recht hatte. Die FIA stoppte außerdem die BPR in ihren Bestrebungen, indem man ihr sämtliche Fernsehrechte für die Rennen die sie eventuell veranstalten wollte, entnam. Um den Machtwechsel komplett zu machen, verpflichtete Vizepräsident Bernie Ecclestone daraufhin Stéphane Ratel für die Organisation der FIA GT-Meisterschaft. Dieser wiederum setzte durch, dass Jürgen Barth ihm bei dieser Aufgabe unterstützen konnte.

FIA-Präsident Max Mosley beteuerte, dass nur Autos die tatsächlich für den Straßenverkehr gebaut und verkauft worden sind, in die Meisterschaft zugelassen werden. Die für den Rennsport erlaubten Änderungen werden weiterhin sehr eingeschränkt sein. Diese Aussage wurde in einer Pressemitteilung wiederholt, die nach dem World Council am 6. Dezember 1996 in Monaco herausgegeben wurde. Eine zusätzliche Erklärung schwächte die Aussage jedoch wieder ab, denn es hiess weiter: Die FIA behält sich für die nahe Zukunft das Recht vor, einzelne von spezialisierten Herstellern gebaute Fahrzeuge, zur Teilnahme einzuladen.

Eine gravierende Änderung mit dem Ziel, künftig auch Mercedes und Panoz mit Autos, die keineswegs für den Strassenverkehr geeignet waren, fahren zu lassen. Jeder Hersteller baute ein Straßenauto, welches beim Saisonauftakt am 13. April 1997 zur Begutachtung im Fahrerlager stand. Die Hersteller bekamen die Auflage, das jeweilige Modell bis zum 31. Dezember zuzulassen und zum Verkauf anzubieten. Es war also eine Homologation mit rückwirkender Kraft und sämtliche Teilnehmer waren erstaunt, als AMG-Mercedes erstmals mit speziellen GT-Autos teilnahm, die den Bodenbelag berührten und auf den schnellen Geraden von Hockenheim Funken sprühten. Sogar Gordon Murray, der sich bei der Verbesserung des McLaren F1 GTR mit geändertem Fahrwerk, Karrosserie und einem neuen Unterboden wirklich viel Mühe gegeben hatte, gab zu, dass es niemals ein Straßenauto geben könnte, das so niedrig am Boden sei. Von Anfang an war Mercedes im Vorteil. Und was tat die FIA? Die Regelmacher beauftragten Porsche, den Lufteinlass um zehn Prozent zu verkleinern, so dass die Motorleistung von 640 PS auf 580 PS reduziert wurde. Obwohl man 15 Autos für den Rennsport rund um den Globus gebaut hatte, wovon fünf in der FIA GT-Meisterschaft eingeschrieben waren – womit Porsche wieder einmal das Fundament der Serie gelegt hatte – sollte Porsche also bestraft werden.

AMG-Mercedes gab die Leistung seines Sechsliter V12 Motor mit etwa 600 PS an. McLaren sprach auch von 600 PS, aber beide Zahlen wurden als sehr zurückhaltend bewertet. Die wahre Leistung wird für beide wohl 630 bis 640 PS gewesen sein. Die Straßenversionen hatten jedenfalls viel mehr Leistung: Ohne die Luftmengenbegrenzer der FIA lieferte der McLaren GTR-LM nicht weniger als 680 PS.

Nach zwei Rennen zur FIA GT-Meisterschaft wurde die FIA davon überzeugt, die Grösse der Lufteinlässe bei den Porsche wieder auf dem alten Niveau zu bringen. Somit war die Situation wieder gerecht.

Damit jedoch genug Politik. Porsche hatte sich entschieden, 1997 nur bei ausgewählten Rennen, den Klassikern, an den Start zu gehen. Man überließ den Kundenteams die Teilnahme an der Meisterschaft. Das gestiegene Ansehen der FIA-GT-Meisterschaft und die Teilnahme von Mercedes und BMW machte die Sache für Porsche jedoch zu wichtig, daran nur halbherzig heranzugehen. So wurde kurzerhand mit Unterstützung von Mobil, Warsteiner, Bilstein und Michelin ein Werksteam auf die Beine gestellt. Stuck und Boutsen wurden für die gesamte Saison als Fahrer verpflichtet. Nach Le Mans sollte ein zweites Auto für Wollek und Dalmas eingesetzt werden.

1000 km Suzuka 1997: Michel and Manuel Monteiro, Henri-Louis Maunoir

4 Hours Donington 1997: Magnus Wallinder, Geoff Lister, John Greasley

FIA president Max Mosley was insistent that "only cars which have been genuinely built and sold for road use will be admitted to the championship. Permitted modifications for racing will continue to be strictly limited." This statement was repeated in a press release issued after the World Motor Sport Council in Monaco on December 6, 1996, but it was diluted by the additional statement: "The FIA will reserve the right for the foreseeable future to invite certain cars built by specialist manufacturers to compete."

A big change there, with the purpose of allowing Mercedes and Panoz to compete with cars which were far from suitable for road use. Each manufacturer built a token road car which was available for inspection at the opening round, at Hockenheim on April 13, 1997, and was instructed to have the model homologated and on sale by December 31.

It would, in other words, be a retrospective homologation, and all the participants were shocked when AMG Mercedes competed for the first time with special GT cars that scraped the tarmac, and raised showers of sparks, at speed on Hockenheim's long straights. Even Gordon Murray, who had put a lot of effort into improving the McLaren F1 GTR with revised suspension, bodywork and underfloor venturi, reckoned there was "no way" that a road car could be made to run that close to the ground.

Advantage Mercedes, from Day 1. And what did the FIA then do? The rule-makers instructed Porsche to reduce the diameter of the inlet air venturi by 10 per cent, reducing the (up-rated) power output of 640 bhp down to 580 bhp. So, despite having made 15 cars for competitions around the world, and having five registered for the FIA GT Championship (and again forming the backbone of the series) Porsche was to be penalised. AMG Mercedes claimed "approximately 600 bhp" for their 6-litre V12 engine, and McLaren also claimed 600 bhp, although both were thought to be very conservative, and the true figures for both were likely to have been 630 to 640 bhp; the road cars were more powerful, McLaren's GTR-LM developing as much as 680 bhp without FIA restrictors.

After two rounds of the GT Championship the FIA was prevailed upon to restore the Porsches' air restrictor sizes, restore the 640 bhp, so justice was done.

Enough of the politics, though. Porsche had decided to contest selected races in 1997, the prestige events, and leave it to customers to fight for the championship, but the higher prestige of the FIA GT Championship, and the arrival of Mercedes and BMW, made it too important for Porsche to tackle half-heartedly. At short notice a full-scale factory team was put together with backing from Mobil, Warsteiner, Bilstein and Michelin, and the drivers hired for the full season were Stuck and Boutsen, with a second car to be added after Le Mans for Wollek and Dalmas.

The privately owned Porsche GT1s were raced by Roock Racing (Ralf Kelleners and Dalmas), JB Racing (Emmanuel Collard and Juergen von Gartzen), Kremer Racing (Christophe Bouchut and Carl Rosenblad, plus Klaus Ludwig, a late addition for the opening round), BMS Scuderia Italia (Christian Pescatori and Pier Luigi Martini) and Schuebel Engineering (Pedro Lamy and Bob Wollek).

From the top of the list, in GT1, Porsche faced three Gulf Team Davidoff McLarens, two more Colnbrook cars from BMW Motorsport (JJ Lehto and Steve Soper being the stronger pairing), two David Price Racing Panoz, two AMG Mercedes CLK GTR (Bernd Schneider and Marcel Tiemann in one, Alexander Wurz and Alessandro Nannini in the other), and three Lotus Elise GT1s which raced well on occasions.

Team Oreca's Chrysler Viper team presented formidable competition in the GT2 class, the American manufacturer having made a wise decision to leave the GT1s get on with their power-play, the two 8-litre, 10-cylinder cars driver by Olivier Beretta, Philippe Gache, Tommy Archer and Justin Bell. There were two Marcos LM600s on the grid, one for Cor Euser and Harald Becker, and the Callaway Corvette for Rocky Augusta and Almo Coppelli.

Half of the massive, 47 car grid was occupied by Porsches, seven in the GT1 category (one works car, five customer cars, and a GT2 Evo entered by Karl Augustin), and no

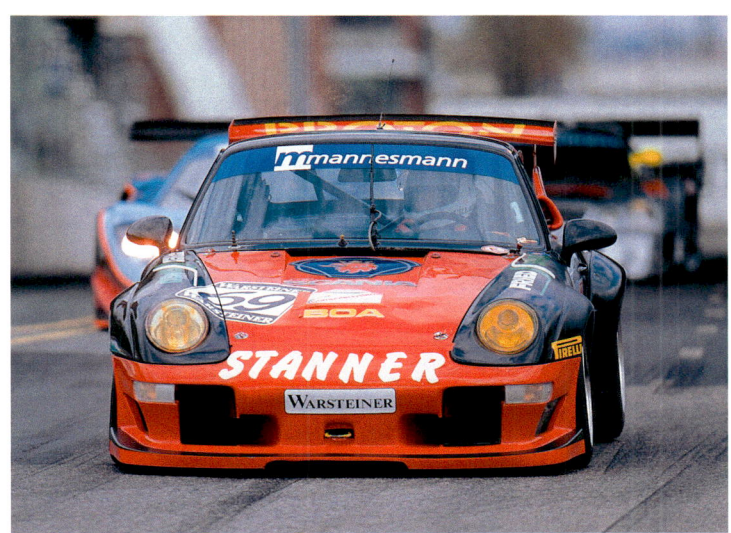

1000 km Suzuka 1997: Emmanuel Collard, Mauro Baldi, Alain Ferte

3 Hours Helsinki 1997: Cor Euser, Harald Becker

Die privaten 911 GT1 wurden eingesetzt von Roock Racing (Ralf Kelleners und Yannick Dalmas), JB Racing (Emmanuel Collard und Jürgen von Gartzen), Kremer Racing (Christophe Bouchut und Carl Rosenblad sowie Klaus Ludwig, der in letzter Minute für den Saisonauftakt verpflichtet wurde), BMS Scuderia Italia (Christian Pescatori und Pier Luigi Martini) sowie Schübel Engineering (Pedro Lamy und Bob Wollek). An der Spitze des GT1-Feldes nahm es Porsche gegen drei Gulf-Team-McLaren sowie zwei weiteren Fahrzeugen aus Colnbrook von BMW Motorsport auf. Außerdem fuhren zwei Panoz von David Price Raing, zwei AMG Mercedes CLK-GTR sowie drei Lotus Elise GT1.

Die Chrysler Viper des Team Oreca waren starke Gegner in der GT2-Klasse. Der amerikanische Hersteller hatte sich entschieden, nicht gegen die Werksteams anzutreten. Die zwei Autos mit Achtliter-Zehnzylindermotoren wurden von Beretta, Gachce, Archer und Bell gefahren. Das Starterfeld umfasste weiterhin zwei Marcos LM600 und eine Callaway-Corvette. Die Hälfte des starken Teilnehmerfeldes waren Porsche. Sieben in der GT1-Klasse und nicht weniger als 17 GT2, nach wie vor mit 480 PS.

Die wichtigsten Porsche-Teams in der GT2-Klasse waren Roock Racing mit zwei Autos (Claudia Hürtgen, Bruno Eichmann und Ni Amorim sowie Stéphane Ortelli, François Lafon und Jean-Marc Smadja), Stadler Motorsport mit zwei Autos (Enzo Calderari und Lilian Bryner sowie Uwe Sick, Dennis Lay und Axel Rohr), Konrad Motorsport mit zwei Autos (Franz Konrad, Uwe Alzen und Philipp Peter sowie Toni Seiler, Marco Spinelli und Michel Ligonnet). Einzelne 911 GT2 wurden eingesetzt von Karl Augustin (Helmut Reis, Wido Rössler und Hans-Jörg Hofer), Monteiro Racing (Manuel und Miguel Monteiro), Krauss Motorsport (Michael Trunk und Bernhard Müller), Kremer Racing (Thomas Saldana und Alfonso d'Orleans), Rudi Walch (Luca Riccitelli, Raffaele Sangiuolo und Leonardo Maddalena), Proton Competition (Gerold Ried, Patrick Vuillaume und Ernst Geschwender), Dellenbach Motorsport (Manfred Jurasz, Rainer Bonnetsmüller und Günther Blieninger), dem GT-Racing-Team (Luca Drudi und Luigino Pagotto), Elf Haberthur (Jean-Claude Lagniez, Guy Martinolle und Michel Neugarten) und Peter Seikel (Ruggero Grassi, Renato Mastropietro und Fred Rosterg).

Porsche hatte nun die zahlenmässig stärkste Vertretung im Langstreckensport seit dem Höhepunkt der Gruppe C Mitte der achziger Jahre. Einige Teams die beim ersten Rennen zur FIA GT-Meisterschaft an den Start gingen, blieben die ganze Zeit dabei und waren auch noch 2004 erfolgreich im Einsatz. Die Porsche-Teams mussten sich sowohl in der GT1- als auch in der GT2-Klasse den Erfolg jedoch hart erarbeiten.

3 Hours Helsinki 1997: Pierluigi Martini, Christian Pescatori

Hans-Joachim Stuck machte das schönste Statement in Hockenheim mit einem Cartoon auf der Seite des Heckflügels. Es zeigte einen FIA-Luftmengenbegrenzer, der ihm die Kehle zuschnürte, mit der Überschrift: „Entschuldigung, ich bin begrenzt". Stuck und Boutsen fehlten drei Sekunden zum Mercedes und sie standen in der vierten Startreihe. Hinter ihnen folgten die 911 GT1 von Collard/von Gartzen, Kelleners/Dalmas, Bouchut/Rosenblad/Ludwig, Martini/Pescatori und Lamy/Wollek.

Zu allem Überfluss fuhr Stuck in der ersten Kurve bereits ins Heck eines McLaren und drehte sich, worauf er bis ans Ende des Feldes zurückfiel. Ein Boxenstopp war notwendig, um eine neue Frontpartie montieren zu lassen. Danach starteten er und Boutsen eine fulminante Aufholjagd, die sie bis auf Rang vier nach vorne brachte. Beide Mercedes hatten technische Probleme und McLaren belegten die ersten drei Plätze. Alle Porsche waren standfest. Es fehlte ihnen jedoch eine oder zwei Runden auf den Siegern.

Beretta und Gache gewannen die GT2-Klasse und fuhren im Chrysler Viper auf Rang zehn in der Gesamtwertung. Der Roock-Porsche von Hürtgen, Eichmann und Amorim hatte jedoch nur 15 Sekunden Rückstand. Es folgte der Rest der Porsche-GT2-Armada. Kein schlechter Start für Porsche in der zweiten Division.

Meistens erwarteten Teams in Silverstone schlechtes Wetter und auch 1997 wurden sie in dieser Hinsicht nicht enttäuscht. Die Bedingungen wechselten von trocken bis zu starken Regenfällen. Diese Mischung sorgte dafür, dass die Reifentechniker während des gesamten Wochenendes

4 Hours Nürburgring 1997: Lilian Bryner, Enzo Calderari, Ulrich Richter

1000 km Suzuka 1997: Patrice Goueslard, Jean-Luc Chereau, Jack Leconte

DOMÄNE GT-SPORT

3 Hours Laguna Seca 1997: Hans-Joachim Stuck, Thierry Boutsen

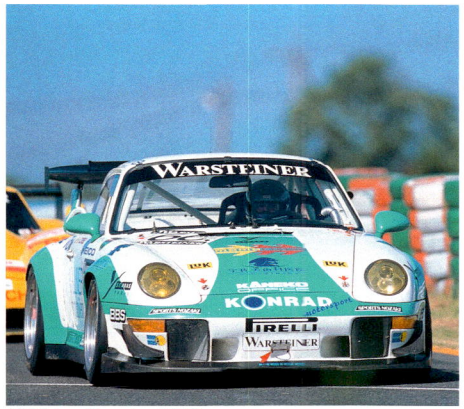

1000 km Suzuka 1997: Franz Konrad, Wolfgang Kaufmann, Seiichi Sodeyama

fewer than 17 GT2s, still with 480 bhp. The principal entrants were Roock Racing with two cars (Claudia Huertgen, Bruno Eichmann and Ni Amorim, and Stephane Ortelli, Francois Lafon and Jean-Marc Smadja), Stadler Motorsport with two cars (Enzo Calderari and Lilian Bryner, and Uwe Sick, Dennis Lay and Axel Rohr), Konrad Motorsport with two cars (Franz Konrad, Uwe Alzen and Philipp Peter, and Toni Seiler with Marco Spinelli and Michel Ligonnet).

There were single-car Porsche GT2 entries from Karl Augustin (Helmut Reis, Wido Roessler and Hans-Joerg Hofer), Monteiro Racing (Manuel and Michel Monteiro), Krauss Motorsport (Michael Trunk and Bernhard Muller), Kremer Racing (Tomas Saldana and Alfonso d'Orleans), Rudi Walch (Luca Riccitelli, Raffaele Sangiuolo and Wolfgang Muenster), Angelo Zadra (Zadra, Marco Brand and Leonardo Maddalena), Proton Competition (Gerold Reid, Patrick Vuillaume and Ernst Geschwender), Dellenbach Motorsport (Manfred Jurasz, Rainer Bonnetsmuller and Gunther Blieninger), the GT Racing Team (Luca Drudi and Luigino Pagotto), Elf Haberthur (Jean-Claude Lagniez, Guy Marti-nolle and Michel Neugarten) and last, but not least, Peter Seikel (Ruggero Grassi, Renato Mastropietro and Fred Rosterg).

Now, Porsche had the largest presence in endurance racing since the pinnacle of Group C racing in the mid-1980s, and some of the teams and drivers that competed in the opening round of the FIA GT Championship were there for the duration, still active and successful in 2004. Numerically strong, certainly, the Porsche teams both in GT1 and in GT2 would have to work very hard for their successes.

Hans Stuck made the most elegant statement at Hockenheim with a cartoon on his rear wing end-plate. 'Sorry, handicapped!' with an FIA air restrictor throttling his throat. This was before qualifying, a sorry affair in which Schneider captured pole position with the debutant Mercedes, three-quarters of a second faster than JJ Lehto in his BMW Motorsport McLaren. Stuck and Boutsen were three seconds off the pace of the Mercedes, occupying the fourth row of the grid, followed in line by the Porsche GT1s of Collard/von Gartzen, Kelleners/Dalmas, Bouchut/Rosenblad/Ludwig, Martini/Pescatori, and Lamy/Wollek. Making matters worse, Stuck ran into the back of a McLaren at the first corner and spun, going right to the tail of the field. A pit stop was needed for a new tail, then he and Boutsen began a heroic comeback which carried them to fourth position overall. Both the Mercedes had technical problems and McLarens took the top three positions, Lehto and Soper ahead of the Gulf Team Davidoff entries of Gounon/Raphanel and Nielsen/Bscher.

All the Porsches were completely reliable but one or two laps adrift of the winners, and behind Stuck and Boutsen in fourth place were Kelleners/Dalmas, Lamy/Wollek, Martini/Pescatori, Bouchut/Rosenblad/Ludwig, and Collard/von Gartzen.

Beretta and Gache won the GT2 class, 10th overall in their Chrysler Viper, but the Roock Racing Porsche of Ms Huertgen, Eichmann and Amorim was only 15 seconds behind at the finish, followed by the rest of the Porsche GT2 pack. It was not a bad start for Porsche in the second division.

Visiting teams had come to expect wet weather at Silverstone, and they were not disappointed in 1997. Conditions varied between dry but with rain threatening, heavy rain, then drying again, a mix that keeps tyre fitters on their toes all weekend. Schneider was on pole position for the second time, David Brabham was surprisingly alongside in the new Panoz, but for Porsche, Kelleners and Dalmas were back on the fourth row in the Roock GT1, Stuck and Boutsen were even further back, on the eighth row.

Boutsen soon made ground on the leaders, moving up to fifth position after covering 10 laps on a drying track, and after the confusion of the first pit stops Pedro Lamy snatched the lead in the Schuebel Porsche. It was a happy moment for the Portuguese, who had suffered terrible injuries while testing his Formula One Lotus at the Northampton track three years previously.

Pit stops done, the race developed into the usual battle between Mercedes and McLaren, with Stuck and Boutsen chasing in fifth position. After two hours and 40 minutes, though,

4 Hours Hockenheim 1997: Tomas Saldana, Alfonso de Orleans Bourbon

GRAND TOURERS **115**

4 Hours Mugello 1997: Uwe Sick, Axel Rohr, Denis Lay

4 Hours A 1 Ring 1997: Yannick Dalmas, Allan McNish

3 Hours Helsinki 1997: Ralf Kelleners, Stephane Ortelli

3 Hours Laguna Seca 1997: Michael Trunk, Bernhard Müller

kaum eine ruhige Minute hatten. Schneider fuhr zum zweiten Mal auf die Pole-Position, neben ihm stand David Brabham im neuen Panoz. Kelleners und Dalmas standen im Roock-GT1 nur in der vierten Reihe, während Stuck und Boutsen in Reihe acht noch weiter abgeschlagen waren.

Boutsen schloss bald zu den Führenden auf, indem er in den ersten zehn Runden auf trockener Strecke auf Rang fünf vorfuhr. Nach dem Durcheinander bei den ersten Boxenstopps schnappte sich Pedro Lamy im Schübel-Porsche die Führung. Es war ein schöner Moment für den Portugiesen, der sich drei Jahre zuvor auf der gleichen Strecke beim Test im Lotus-Formel 1 schwere Verletzungen zugezogen hatte. Nachdem die Boxenstopps abgeschlossen waren, entwickelte sich das Rennen zum üblichen Kampf zwischen Mercedes und McLaren, während Stuck und Boutsen auf Rang fünf das Nachsehen hatten. Nach zwei Stunden und 40 Minuten setzte sintflutartiger Regenfall den Grand-Prix-Kurs komplett unter Wasser. 40 Minuten lang rollte das Feld hinter dem Führungsfahrzeug. Kurz nach dem Neustart musste das Rennen mit der roten Flagge abgebrochen werden. Kox und Ravaglia wurden im BMW-Motorsport-McLaren zu Siegern erklärt vor Schneider und Wurz.

4 Hours Donington Park 1997: Nigel Barrett, Koit Veertee

Porsche musste sich mit Rang fünf sowie dem siebten Platz für Wollek und Lamy zufrieden geben. Chrysler siegte erneut in der GT2-Klasse, während Hürtgen, Eichmann und Amorim für Roock Racing einmal mehr den zweiten Platz belegten.

Wie das Rennen in Zhuhai fand auch die neue Veranstaltung in Helskini auf einem holprigen Straßenkurs statt. Rund um die Strecke standen Betonwände, die jeden noch so kleinen Fehler sofort bestraften. Lokalmatador Lehto erfreute seine Fans mit einer atemberaubenden Pole-Position.

Porsche hatte einen Rückschlag erlebt, als Dalmas beim Test in Spa aufgrund eines Reifenschadens einen schweren Unfall hatte. Der Fahrer brach sich zwei Finger und das Werksteam entschied sich, auf die Reise nach Finnland zu verzichten, denn das Rennen war nur drei Wochen vor Le Mans. Man glaubte, dass dies keine Strafen seitens der FIA zur Folge haben sollte. Team Oreca ließ seine Chrysler Viper aus der GT2-Klasse ebenfalls zuhause. Beide Teams waren entsetzt, als der World Council die Sache gar nicht so leicht nahm und die fehlenden Teams bestrafte.

In der GT1-Klasse wurde Porsche von drei Teams vertreten. Roock fuhr mit Kelleners und Ortelli. Für den Franzosen war er der erste Einsatz in der großen Klasse. Scuderia Italia fuhr wie üblich mit Pescatori und Martini und Franz Konrad teilte sich seinen GT1 mit Mauro Baldi. Die Porsche-Teams waren dankbar, dass sie ihre größere Luftmengenbegrenzer wieder verwenden durften, hatten dann aber Schwierigkeiten, die 640 PS auf der holprigen und schmutzigen Strecke zu nützen. Man stellte bald fest, dass Motoren ohne Turbo hier einen Vorteil hatten. Lehto und Soper siegten beim drei Stunden-Rennen von Helsinki, mit drei Runden Vorsprung, während Kelleners und Ortelli im Roock-Porsche für Platz zwei hart kämpfen mussten. Scuderia Italia belegte Rang sechs, Konrad war Siebter. Hinter ihnen fuhren Hürtgen, Eichmann und Amorim auf den neunten Gesamtrang ins Ziel und gewannen die GT2-Klasse.

Eine kaputte Ölleitung brachte Porsche um die Chance, mit dem 911 GT1 den Gesamtsieg in Le Mans zu holen. Einmal mehr rettete Joest Racing jedoch mit dem TWR-Porsche die Ehre. Während die Spitzenteams in Frankreich im Einsatz waren, testete AMG-Mercedes ausführlich auf dem Nürburgring, wo der nächste Lauf der FIA GT-Meisterschaft stattfand. Der Einsatz machte sich für Mercedes bezahlt, denn man holte sich dort einen Doppelsieg. Hinter den beiden Mercedes liefen fünf McLaren ein. Mit vier Runden Rückstand belegten Collard und von Gartzen den achten Platz. Bouchut und Rosenblad fuhren auf Rang neun, Stuck und Boutsen belegten nach Problemen mit der Benzinversorgung Position zehn.

Den einzige Lichtblick brachten Hürtgen, Eichmann und Amorim, die für das Roock-Team einmal mehr die GT2-Klasse für sich entscheiden konnten. Chrysler führte zwar in der Teamwertung der GT2, die Roock-Fahrer hatten jedoch einen komfortablen Vorsprung in der Fahrerwertung.

In Spa zeigte sich für Porsche ein Aufwärtstrend. 1996 hatte der GT1 dort ohne Probleme gewonnen und diesmal kämpften Wollek und Dalmas hart für einen Podiumsplatz, Rang drei in der Gesamtwertung hinter Lehtos McLaren und Schneiders Mercedes. Thierry Boutsen, der im Werks-Porsche GT1 schon frühzeitig mit einer defekten Servolenkung ausgefallen war, fuhr dann zusammen mit Wollek und Dalmas. Kelleners und Pedro Chaves fuhren im Roock-GT1 auf Rang sieben, Pescatori und Martini belegten den zehnten Platz. Die Roock-Siegesserie in der GT2-Klasse wurde jedoch unterbrochen, als Claudia Hürtgen unglücklicherweise mit Kox im McLaren kollidierte und dabei die Lenkung beschädigte. Sie kam zusammen mit Eichmann und Amorim noch auf Platz fünf in der GT-Klasse ins Ziel.

a torrential rainstorm turned the Grand Prix circuit into a lake and pace cars were deployed for 40 minutes. Soon after the resumption the race had to be stopped with red flags, and the race was awarded to Kox and Ravaglia in their BMW Motorsport McLaren, ahead of Schneider and Wurz.

Porsche had to be content with fifth place for Stuck and Boutsen, seventh for Wollek and Lamy. Chrysler again won the GT2 category, again with Ms Huertgen, Eichmann and Amorim second for Roock Racing.

Like Zhuhai, the new event at Helsinki was run on bumpy road lined by concrete walls, ready to punish the slightest mistake. Lehto, the local hero, made his fans happy with a heart-stopping pole position ("I am sorry I have scratched the car" he told team manager Charly Lamm, surveying grazes on both flanks of the McLaren) ahead of the two Mercedes.

Porsche AG had suffered a setback, a major crash for Dalmas while testing at Spa, the result of a tyre failure. The driver suffered two broken fingers and the factory team decided against the trip to Finland, as they believed, without any sanction from the FIA because the race was only three weeks before Le Mans. Team Oreca failed to send the Chrysler Vipers to contest the GT2 class, and all were dismayed when the World Council took a serious view and penalised the abstainers

Three teams represented Porsche in the GT1 class, Roock Racing taking Kelleners and Ortelli (the Frenchman's first outing in the top class), Scuderia Italia running Pescatori and Martini as usual, and Franz Konrad sharing his Porsche with Mauro Baldi. The Porsche teams were thankful to get back their larger air restrictors, but then had difficulty in putting 640 bhp to the dusty, bumpy road and realised that the naturally aspirated engines had an advantage. Lehto and Soper won the Helsinki 3-hour "Thunder Race" in style, with three laps to spare, while Kelleners and Ortelli worked hard to claim second place overall for the Roock team. Scuderia Italia was sixth, Konrad seventh, and right behind them Ms Huertgen, Eichmann and Amorim were ninth overall, winning the GT2 class and making the Roock brothers the happiest pair in Finland.

A broken oil line thwarted Porsche's chances of winning Le Mans with the GT1 model, though once again Joest Racing saved the day with the TWR Porsche WSC, and while the top teams were busy in France, AMG Mercedes did some serious testing at the Nurburgring, where the next round of the FIA GT Championship would be held.

The effort paid off handsomely for Mercedes with their first victory of the season, a 1-2 result in fact, and behind them five McLarens locked out the top seven positions. It was the worst outing of the season for Porsche's GT1, as Collard and von Gartzen were four laps down in eighth position, Bouchut and Rosenblad ninth, Stuck and Boutsen tenth with fuel feed difficulties. Gerd Ruch dropped Konrad's GT1 into the gravel, and this was the last straw for the Austrian entrant who vowed to switch back to the GT2 division for the remainder of the season. If there was one ray of sunshine, it beamed on Ms Hurtgen, Eichmann and Amorim who once again won the GT2 category for the Roock team, beating Justin Bell and Marc Duez in a Team Oreca Viper. Chrysler led the GT2 teams championship, but Roock's drivers were comfortably ahead in the GT2 drivers championship.

If the Nurburgring was the lowest point in Porsche's season, the next round at Spa marked an upturn. The GT1 had won the race with ease in 1996, and this time Wollek and Dalmas fought hard to earn a podium result, third overall behind Lehto's McLaren and Schneider's Mercedes. They were joined by Thierry Boutsen, whose factory entered Porsche GT1 had a power steering failure early in the race.

Revisions to the GT1, including a wider front track and smoother bodywork, suited the factory cars, and the nature of the track was better for the turbocharged Porsches which suffered from throttle lag from slow corners.

Kelleners and Pedro Chaves drove well to seventh place in the Roock GT1, Pescatori and Martini to 10th, but Roock Racing's golden run was spoiled when Claudia Huertgen had an unfortunate collision with Peter Kox's McLaren, and damaged the steering. She, Eichmann and Amorim struggled home to fifth place in GT2, but behind two Chrysler Vipers, Euser's Marcos, and the British G-Force team's GT2 driven by John Greasley, Geoff Lister and Magnus Wallinder.

AMG Mercedes sent three cars to the A1-Ring in Austria, and made a good job of the race with first, second and fourth positions overall. Lehto and Soper were third in their McLaren, but their lead in the FIA championship was slipping away. Porsche AG brought the Scot, Allan McNish, into the factory team with Dalmas and, after an unscheduled brake pad change, they finished seventh overall behind the sister-car of Wollek and Boutsen. Pescatori and Martini were eighth for Scuderia Italia, and in GT2 Ortelli laid the ground-

1000 km Suzuka 1997: Christophe Bouchut, Carl Rosenblad, Ralf Kelleners

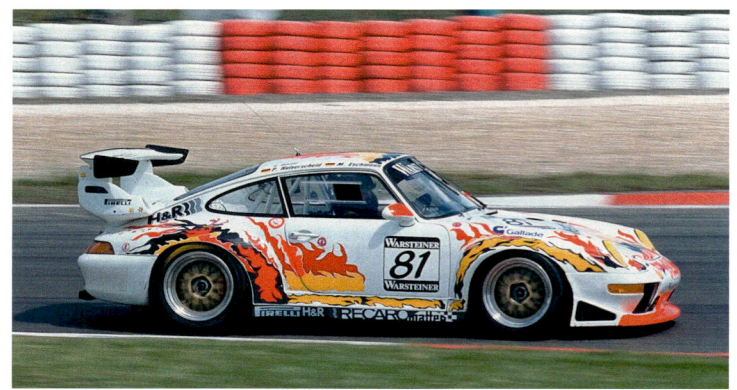

4 Hours Nürburgring 1997: Paul Hulverscheid, Michael Eschmann, Gunther Döbler

Winner GT2 3 Hours Laguna Seca 1997: Bruno Eichmann, Stephane Ortelli (56)

AMG-Mercedes entsandte drei Autos zum A1-Ring in Österreich und belegten die Gesamtpositionen eins, zwei und vier. Porsche-Motorsport liess den Schotten Allan McNish zusammen mit Dalmas im Werksteam fahren. Sie fuhren nach einem unplanmäßigen Boxenstopp auf Rang sieben hinter dem Schwesterauto von Boutsen und Wollek ins Ziel. Pescatori und Martini belegten für die Scuderia Italia den achten Platz. In der GT2-Klasse legte Ortelli für Claudia Hürtgen und Bruno Eichmann den Grundstein zum Klassensieg, womit sie den ersten Platz im Zwischenstand der Fahrerwertung zurückeroberten. Zur Erleichterung der Roock-Mannschaft erlaubte das Reglement jedoch, dass Fahrer nachträglich auf ein anderes Auto genannt werden konnten.

Mit der Erfahrung von grosser Hitze und extremer Luftfeuchtigkeit in Suzuka aus früheren Jahren brachte Porsche sechs Fahrer zum 1000 km-Rennen, Ende August auf dem japanischen Kurs. Stuck, Boutsen und Wollek fuhren ein Auto. Der zweite GT1, der mit neuem sequentiellen Getriebe ausgestattet war, wurde von Dalmas, McNish und Lamy gefahren, nachdem sich das Schübel-Team aus der Meisterschaft zurückgezogen hatte. Konrad hatte sich bereits aus der GT1-Klasse verabschiedet, so dass lediglich noch drei Privatteams übrig blieben.

Dalmas stellte den Wert des sequentiellen Getriebes unter Beweis, indem er vor den Teams von AMG-Mercedes und BMW Motorsport die Pole-Position eroberte. Norbert Singer erklärte jedoch, dass dieses System nur ein bis zwei Zehntelsekunden brachte. Mercedes setzte sich im Rennen bald an die Spitze, während Dalmas Platz drei gegen JJ Lehto verteidigen musste. Später erlebte der Werks-Porsche einen seltenen Ausfall, als der Schalthebel abbrach. Die Reparatur kostete dem Team sechs Runden. Schließlich kamen Stuck, Boutsen und Wollek mit zwei Runden Rückstand auf Rang fünf ins Ziel. McNish und Lamy belegten Position zehn.

Beretta und Gache gewannen für Chrysler die GT2-Klasse. Sie fuhren eine Runde vor dem Roock-GT2 von Pedro Chaves, Robert Nearn und Hisashi Wada ins Ziel.

Donington Park war wahrscheinlich die schlechteste Strecke für Porsche im Kalender der FIA, mit zwei Haarnadelkurven und verschiedenen langsamen Kurven, wo das Leistungsloch der Turbolader ein richtiger Nachteil war. Drei Mercedes standen in der Startaufstellung vor den beiden BMW-Motorsport-McLaren. Dalmas stand in der dritten Startreihe.

Beide 911 GT1 hatten nun das sequentielle Getriebe. Die Mercedes-Mannschaft war in Bestform und feierte einen wieteren Doppelsieg, mit dem man erstmals die Führung in der FIA-GT-Meisterschaft übernahm, Pescatori und Martini gewannen das interne Rennen der Porsche auf dem zehnten Gesamtplatz vor Stuck und Boutsen. Beretta und Gache gewannen für Chrysler erneut die GT2-Klasse, eine Runde vor Eichmann, Ortelli und Hürtgen im Roock-Porsche.

Mugello brachte ein viel besseres Ergebnis für Porsche. Schneiders Mercedes wurde nach einer Kollision aus dem Rennen geworfen war und das Auto von Ludwig musste mit defekter Servolenkung aufgeben. Lehto und Soper feierten den Sieg. Der dritte Podiumplatz ging an Dalmas und Wollek. Bell und Drudi gewannen im Chrysler Viper die Klasse GT2 vor zwei Roock-Porsche. Schneider und Ludwig machten einen Schritt in Richtung Meistertitel mit dem Sieg im Oktober in Sebring beim ersten FIA-Langstreckenrennen in Amerika seit 1981. Lehtos McLaren wurde 20 Minuten vor Schluss durch einen Brand stark beschädigt.

Brabham und Perry McCarthy fuhren erstmals aufs Podium für das Team von Don Panoz. Sie belegten hinter dem McLaren von Kox und Ravaglia den dritten Platz. Wollek und Dalmas fuhren auf Position vier, Stuck und Boutsen kamen auf Rang sechs ins Ziel.

Die Viper des Team Oreca stürmten auf die Plätze eins und zwei in der GT2-Klasse, während der normalerweise zuverlässige Roock-Porsche von Eichmann und Hürtgen mit einem defekten Kühlgebläse ausfiel. Amorim und Uwe Alzen fuhren den zweiten Roock-Porsche auf Rang drei.

Ein Sieg für Schneider und Ludwig beim Saisonfinale in Laguna Seca brachte AMG-Mercedes und Bernd Schneider die Meistertitel für Teams und Fahrer. Porsche erlebte einen äußerst versöhnlichen Abschluss der Saison mit den Plätzen zwei, drei und fünf im Gesamtergebnis. Porsche beendete die Saison mit dem vierten Platz in der Teamwertung hinter AMG Mercedes, BMW Motorsport und dem Gulf Team Davidoff. Roock Racing sicherte sich Rang fünf. Bob Wollek war der bestplatzierte Porsche-Fahrer im Endstand der Fahrermeisterschaft auf Rang zwölf. In der GT2-Klasse sicherte sich das Viper Team Oreca vor Roock Racing und Konrad Motorsport den Titel in der Teamwertung. Eichmann belegte hinter Bell Rang zwei in der Fahrerwertung. Ihm fehlte nur ein Punkt zum Titelgewinn.

DOMÄNE GT-SPORT

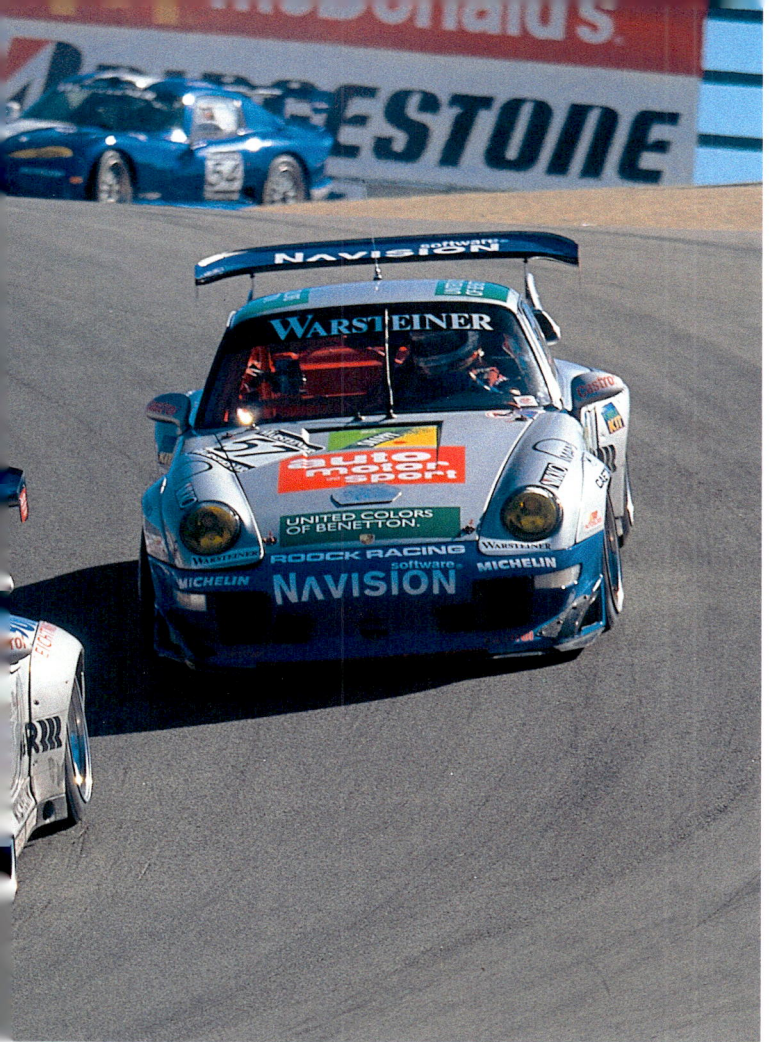

Uwe Alzen, Claudia Hürtgen, Ni Amorim (57)

work for Eichmann and Ms Huertgen to win the category, and return to the lead of the drivers championship. Earlier, Eichmann had collided with Euser's Marcos, but the rules allowed driver switching, to the Roock team's relief.

Mindful of the high temperatures and humidity experienced at Suzuka, Porsche AG took six drivers to Japan for the Pokka 1,000 kilometre race at the end of August. Stuck, Boutsen and Wollek drove one car, and the second, with a new sequential gearbox, was crewed by Dalmas, McNish and Lamy (the Schuebel team had withdrawn from the championship, as did Konrad from the GT1 class, leaving just three private teams). Dalmas seemingly proved the worth of the sequential transmission by claiming pole position ahead of the AMG Mercedes and BMW Motorsport teams, although Ing. Singer maintained that the system was worth "only one or two tenths of a second". The drivers thought differently, though, the Frenchman saying that it was now much easier to change gear while the car was turning, something that happens a lot at Suzuka. Mercedes quickly forged ahead in the race, leaving Dalmas to defend third position from JJ Lehto. Later the works Porsche had an unusual breakage as the gear lever broke free at floor level while McNish was driving, losing the team six laps.

At the end Stuck, Boutsen and Wollek were fifth, two laps behind the Mercedes team, Dalmas, McNish and Lamy 10th. Beretta and Gache won the GT2 division for Chrysler, a lap ahead of the Roock Racing GT2 of Pedro Chaves, Robert Nearn and Hisashi Wada.

Donington Park is possibly the worst circuit for Porsche in the FIA calendar, with two hairpin bends and several more slow corners where the lag of the turbochargers was a real handicap. Three Mercedes lined up for the grid ahead of the two BMW Motorsport McLarens, with Dalmas qualifying on the third row. Both the Porsche GT1s now had sequential transmissions. The Mercedes team was at its imperious best, claiming another 1-2 victory and going ahead for the first time in the FIA GT Championship, despite the third place result for Lehto and Soper (their seventh podium in eight races). Even the Panoz team finished ahead of the Porsches, Pescatori and Martini winning the 'Porsche race' in 10th position ahead of Stuck and Boutsen.

Beretta and Gache won GT2 for Chrysler, a lap ahead of Ortelli, Eichmann, and Ms Huertgen in their Roock Porsche.

Mugello provided Porsche with a much better result, but only after Schneider's Mercedes was eliminated by a back-marker accident and Ludwig's by a power steering failure. Lehto and Soper gained a much-needed victory ahead of Nannini and Tiemann in their Mercedes, with Dalmas and Wollek on the podium, in third place, ahead of Boutsen and Kelleners. Justin Bell and Luca Drudi won GT2 in their Chrysler Viper, ahead of two Roock Racing GT2s, those of Ortelli (running out of fuel on the last lap), Eichmann and Huertgen, ahead of Goueslard, Amorim and Chaves.

Schneider and Ludwig closed on the FIA GT Championship titles as they won the Sebring round in October - the first FIA endurance race to be held on American soil since 1981 - while Lehto's McLaren was badly damaged by fire just 20 minutes from the end. "A terrible day for us" is how the Finn described the disaster, who now had only a slight chance of seizing the title at Laguna Seca a week later.

Brabham and Perry McCarthy claimed their first podium result for Don Panoz's team, third behind the McLaren of Kox and Ravaglia, with Wollek and Dalmas fourth overall, Stuck and Boutsen sixth. It was not a great result for Porsche AG, but it was respectable. Team Oreca's Vipers romped to a 1-2 victory in GT2, while the usually reliable Roock Porsche of Eichmann and Huertgen was sidelined by a cooling fan failure. Amorim and Uwe Alzen stepped into third place in Roock's second Porsche, though stationary with a broken turbocharger.

A final victory for Schneider and Ludwig at Laguna Seca ensured that AMG Mercedes and Schneider would claim the FIA GT Championships for teams and drivers, while Porsche AG finished the season on a very high note with second, third and fifth positions overall. In their wake, Bruno Eichmann and Stephane Ortelli achieved a fine GT2 class victory for the Roock Racing team, although Justin Bell squeeked through to win the Drivers championship a single point ahead of Eichmann, and Viper Team Oreca finished well ahead in the Teams championship.

4 Hours Donington 1997: Patrice Goueslard, Michel Neugarten, Luigiano Pagotto

GRAND TOURERS

Für die Saison 1998 wurde ein neues Auto benötigt, denn der auf dem Produktionsmodell basierende GT1 war nicht in der Lage, dem komplett aus Kohlefaser angefertigten AMG-Mercedes CLK-GTR Paroli zu bieten. Herbert Ampferer und Horst Marchart, Leiter Forschung und Entwicklung, überzeugten Dr. Wiedeking für ein neuen Rennwagen, den 911 GT1-98. Das Auto musste logischerweise 911 heissen, denn es wurde vom gleichen serienmäßigen Sechszylinder-Turbomotor angetrieben, hatte jedoch ein komplett neues Chassis aus Kohlefaser, eine neue und niedrigere Karrosserie und ein neues Fahrwerk. Es war ein richtiges Rennauto, dass kaum den Anspruch hatte, auch für den Einsatz auf der Strasse geeignet zu sein.

Der Antriebsstrang entsprach dem des 97er-Modells. Die FIA bestrafte Porsche jedoch erneut, indem man die Luftmengenbegrenzer wieder einmal verkleinerte, von 35,7 mm auf 33,9 mm. So wurde die Motorleistung auf 550 PS bei 7.200 U/Min. reduziert. Erneut protestierte Porsche ohne Erfolg bei der FIA. Ein positiver Punkt: Das Mindestgewicht für den GT1-98 wurde auf 940 kg heruntergesetzt, obwohl beide Autos bei der technischen Abnahme in Le Mans 967 kg wogen. Es ist wichtig zu erwähnen, dass die FIA in wichtigen Angelegenheiten gegen Porsche zu arbeiten schien, der ACO aber vernünftiger war, denn er schrieb für den GT1-98 Begrenzer mit einem Durchmesser von 34,8 mm vor, die eine Leistung von 600 PS ermöglichten. Auch war der ACO toleranter, was die Platzierung der Luftmengenbegrenzer für die Lufteinlässe betraf.

„Im Motorsport zählen nur Siege", sagte Dr. Wiedeking, der damit die enttäuschende Saison 1997 abschloss und gleichzeitig kein Mißverständnis darüber aufkommen liess, dass für 1998 bessere Ergebnisse erwartet wurden.

500 km Hungaroring 1998

500 km Oschersleben 1998: Michael Bartels, Armin Hahne, Alexander Grau

500 km Laguna Seca 1998: Jean-Luc Chereau, Patrice Gouesland, Jack Leconte

BMW Motorsport zog sich aus der FIA GT-Meisterschaft zurück. Direktor Karl-Heinz Kalbfell erklärte am Ende der Saison 1997, dass „wir den GT-Teil der Meisterschaft gewonnen haben" und äußerte so sein Missfallen am Spezialfahrzeug von AMG-Mercedes. Gulf Oil zog sich ebenfalls zurück. Die Anzahl der Teilnehmer schrumpfte, die Qualität nahm jedoch zu. Porsche Motorsport setzte zwei Autos mit Michelin-Bereifung für Yannick Dalmas und Allan McNish sowie für Uwe Alzen und Jörg Müller ein. Für Le Mans und einige Rennen zu Saisonmitte blieben auch Bob Wollek und Stéphane Ortelli im Team. Porsche wurde darüber hinaus verpflichtet, zwei Fahrzeuge an das Zakspeed-Team zu verleasen, wo man Michael Bartels, Armin Hahne, Andreas Scheld, Sandy Grau und Max Angelelli unter Vertrag hatte. Zakspeed war an Pirelli gebunden.

AMG-Mercedes ließ den Australier Mark Webber zusammen mit Bernd Schneider fahren, während Ricardo Zonta mit Klaus Ludwig fuhr. Ausserdem wurden zwei CLK-GTR aus 1997 dem Persson-Motorsport-Team anvertraut, wo Jean-Marc Gounon, Marcel Tiemann, Christophe Bouchut und Bernd Mayländer im Einsatz waren. Alle vier Autos fuhren auf Bridgestone-Reifen, so dass der Reifenkrieg genauso wichtig war wie der Kampf der Automobilhersteller.

Für die Saison 1998 führte Porsche einige Verbesserungen am GT2 durch, der aber nach wie vor auf dem Modell 993 mit luftgekühltem Motor statt auf dem neuen 996 mit Wasserkühlung basierte. Erstmals wurde Doppelkerzenzündung verwendet und es kam ein neues System für die Regelung des Ladedruck zum Einsatz, das eine präzisere Dosierung ermöglichte. Die Motorleistung der Strassenversion stieg an von 430 auf 450 PS, die Rennversion lieferte trotz Luftmengenbegrenzer von 33,9 mm nun 485 PS.

Allan McNish was able to set the fourth fastest qualifying time in the Porsche badly damaged during qualifying at Sebring, and the Scotsman then gave the GT1 its best performance of the entire season as he led the three Mercedes, and all the McLarens, for the first hour of the race.

Porsche's GT1 was, at last, racing the way it was supposed to go all season, but the advantage was thrown away by a bad pit stop, on account of a jammed wheel nut.

BMW Motorsport switched its pairings so that Lehto's last chance to win the drivers championship would be shared with Peter Kox, and Soper's with Ravaglia. Lehto's McLaren leaked its water away in the early laps, and retired, and Ravaglia spun and was hit by another car, so the BMW Motorsport finished the season with no additional points.

On-form at last, but too late to influence the championship, Dalmas and Wollek were second overall for Porsche, Mc Nish and Ralf Kelleners third, still on the lead lap, Stuck and Boutsen fifth. Porsche AG finished the season in fourth position in the Teams Championship behind AMG Mercedes, BMW Motorsport and Gulf Team Davidoff, with Roock Racing fifth. Bob Wollek was the best-placed Porsche driver, down in 12th position.

In GT2, Viper Team Oreca won the Teams Championship ahead of Roock Racing and Konrad Motorsport. Eichmann was second to Bell in the Drivers Championship, by a single point, with Claudia Huertgen fifth and Ni Amorim sixth.

A new car would be needed for the 1998 season, as the production based GT1 model was simply not up to the task of competing against the all-carbon AMG Mercedes CLK GTR. Herbert Ampferer made his case to R&D director Horst Marchart, and he to Dr Wiedeking, gaining support for a new Porsche model, the 911 GT1-98.

It would necessarily be called 911, since it was powered by the same, production based six-cylinder turbo engine, but it had an entirely new chassis made of carbon composite materials, new and lower bodywork, and new inboard suspensions. It was, in short, a proper racing car making almost no pretence to be suitable for road purposes.

The power train was similar to that in the '97 model, but the FIA stung Porsche AG again by reducing the size of the inlet air restrictors, again, to 33.9mm instead of 35.7mm, thus reducing the power to a quoted 550 bhp at 7,200 rpm.

And again, Ampferer protested to the FIA without success, also maintaining that in the case of the turbocharged engine, the inlet air restrictors had to be located too close to the turbochargers, resulting in the air hitting the turbines at supersonic speed, thus reducing efficiency. On the positive side, the GT1-98 was reduced to 940 kg, although both entries at Le Mans were weighed at 967 kg. It is important to note that while the FIA seemed to work against Porsche at critical junctures, the ACO was more enlighted, allowing the GT1-98 to race with 34.8 mm inlet air restrictors and to develop 600 bhp. Also, the ACO was more lenient in the positioning of the inlet air restrictors, so Porsche's best opportunities of the season were likely to be realised at Le Mans.

"Only victory counts in motor racing" said Dr Wiedeking grimly, writing-off the disappointing season in 1997 and serving a warning that better things were expected in 1998.

BMW Motorsport withdrew from the FIA GT Championship, director Karl-Heinz Kalbfell remarking pointedly that "we won the GT part of the championship" at the end of the 1997 season, in protest against AMG Mercedes' "special" car that had to undergo fundamental changes in the suspension and steering before homologation could be granted retrospectively. Gulf Oil withdrew, too, but Thomas Bscher soldiered on with his now uncompetitive McLaren F1 GTR.

Numbers were down but quality was up, and the 1998 season polarised. Porsche AG ran two cars, on Michelin tyres, for Yannick Dalmas and Allan McNish, and Uwe Alzen with Joerg Muller, with Bob Wollek and Stephane Ortelli retained for Le Mans and some mid-season events. Porsche was obliged to lease two cars to the Zakspeed team which employed Michael Bartels, Armin Hahne, Andreas Scheld, Sandy Grau and Max Angelelli. Zakspeed was contracted to Pirelli. AMG Mercedes brought in the Australian driver, Mark Webber, to drive with Bernd Schneider, and Ricardo Zonta to drive with Klaus Ludwig. In addition, two of the 1997 model CLK GTRs were leased to the Persson Motorsport team which employed Jean-Marc Gounon, Marcel Tiemann, Christophe Bouchut and Bernd Maylaender. All four cars raced on Bridgestone tyres, so the 'tyre war' was just as important as the contest between rival makes.

1000 km Suzuka 1998: Nigel Smith, Takaji Suzuki, Gerhard Marchner

GRAND TOURERS

In Silverstone holte sich McNish die Pole-Position. Der Schotte führte in den ersten zwölf Runden des Rennens, bis ein seltener Motorschaden am Porsche-Reihensechszylinder auftrat. Alzen wurde mit einer 30 Sekunden-Zeitstrafe belegt, weil er den Panoz von David Brabham ins Kiesbett befördert hatte. Er kam mit nur acht Sekunden Rückstand auf Schneider und Webber ins Ziel. Beretta und Lamy siegten in der GT2-Klasse vor dem Elf-Haberthur-Porsche von Neugarten, Ruch und Spinelli. Uwe Sick und Jochen Rohr belegten für Stadler Motorsport den dritten Platz.

Das Porsche-Werksteam gewann zum 16. Mal das 24 Stunden-Rennen von Le Mans. Der Sieg kam zeitgleich mit den Feierlichkeiten zum 50-jährigen Firmenjubiläum in Stuttgart. Zwei Wochen später wurden die beiden gleichen Autos zum dritten Saisonlauf der FIA GT-Meisterschaft nach Hockenheim transportiert, erneut mit kleineren Luftmengenbegrenzern. Die Fahrer beklagten sich über das Fahrverhalten und dass sie auf den Geraden nicht schnell genug waren. Sogar die Persson-Motorsport-CLK-GTR schlugen die 911 GT1-98. Für Porsche-Fans bot die Startaufstellung einen tristen Anblick, mit zwei AMG-Mercedes CLK-LM in der ersten Reihe, zwei CLK-GTR in der zweiten Reihe und zwei Werks-Porsche in der dritten Reihe. Bernard qualifizierte den DAMS-Panoz auf Rang sieben vor den beiden Zakspeed-GT1.

Die Porsche-Fahrer taten sich schwer, dem Tempo zu folgen. Dalmas wollte in der zweiten Schikane Wendlinger in der Viper überrunden, drehte sich dabei und verlor zwei Runden als er aus dem Kiesbett gezogen werden musste. In der Schlussphase des Rennens hatte Alzen in der zweiten

500 km Dijon 1998: Eric Graham, Herve Poulain, David Smadja

Ein neuer, leichterer Frontspoiler ermöglichte eine bessere Anströmung der Ölkühler, die kleiner und leichter waren. Auch die Form des Heckflügels wurde geändert. Gemäss dem neuesten FIA-Reglement musste das ABS ausgebaut werden. Die Strassenversion wog 1370 kg, die Rennsport-Ausführung etwas mehr als 1100 kg.

Roock Racing (Eichmann, Ortelli, Ahrle und Maassen), Konrad Motorsport (Konrad, Toni Seiler und verschiedene andere Fahrer), Elf Haberthur (Neugarten, Ruch und Spinelli) und Krauss Race Sports (Michael Trunk und Bernhard Müller) waren die führenden Einsatzteams, zusammen mit Proton Competition und Stadler Motorsport.

Zahlenmässig war Porsche in der GT2-Klasse stark vertreten. Die Teams mussten es jedoch gegen das Team Oreca aufnehmen, das die dritte Saison mit den Chrysler Vipern bestritt, nun mit einer Leistung von 600 PS, trotz Luftmengenbegrenzer. Das Team unter der Leitung von Hugues de Chaunac war fast unschlagbar. Man gewann neun von zehn Rennen, fünfmal sogar mit Doppelsieg.

Insgesamt hatte Porsche am Anfang der Saison die besten Chancen, sie wurden aufgrund von Anfangsschwierigkeiten mit dem neuen Auto jedoch nicht genutzt. In Oschersleben, wo der Saisonauftakt über die Bühne ging, sicherte sich Jörg Müller die Pole-Position und er führte in der Anfangsphase des Rennens, womit er zeigte, dass der neue 911 GT1-98 wirklich ein überragendes Auto war. Danach gab es jedoch an beiden Autos Probleme mit dem Unterboden und beide fielen später aus. Daraufhin konnten Ludwig und Zonta ohne Probleme den Sieg nach Hause fahren. Die Viper belegten die ersten zwei Plätze in der GT2-Klasse. Eichmann und Maassen kamen auf Rang drei ins Ziel, wurden aber disqualifiziert, nachdem die technischen Kommissare den Heckflügel ihres Porsche als illegal betrachteten. So erbten Konrad und Nick Ham den dritten Platz.

1000 km Suzuka 1998: Yannick Dalmas, Allan McNish, Stephane Ortelli

124 DOMÄNE GT-SPORT

Porsche introduced some improvements to the GT2 model for the 1998 season, but it was still based on the air-cooled 993 model and not the new, water cooled 996. It had dual ignition for the first time, with twin spark plugs, and a new and more accurate boost pressure control system. The power of the road version went up from 430 to 450 bhp, and that of the racing version to 485 bhp on 33.9 mm inlet air restrictors. A new, lighter front apron allowed better air flow to the oil coolers, which were smaller and lighter, and the rear wing was modified. ABS had to be deleted, to meet the latest FIA regulations. The road version weighed 1,370 kg, and the racers a little over 1,100 kg.

Roock Racing (Eichmann, Ortelli, Ahrle and Maassen), Konrad Motorsport (Konrad, Toni Seiler and various co-drivers), Elf Haberthur (Neugarten, Ruch and Spinelli) and Krauss Race Sports (Michael Trunk and Bernhard Muller) were the principal runners, along with Proton Competition and Stadler. Numerically Porsche was strongly represented in the GT2 division, but the private teams were up against Team Oreca entering its third season with the Chrysler Vipers, which now boasted 600 bhp even with inlet air restrictors. The team directed by Hugues de Chaunac was almost invincible, winning nine of the ten contests, five times with 1-2 results.

Overall, Porsche's best opportunities came early in the season, but they were not taken, on account of new-car teething difficulties. At Oschersleben, where the opening round was staged, Joerg Muller claimed pole position and led the early stages of the race, demonstrating that the new Porsche GT1-98 really was a superior car. Both cars, then, had un-

500 km Hungaroring 1998: Patrick Vuillaume, Gerold Ried

dertray problems and expired with rear suspension breakages, clearing the way for Ludwig and Zonta to score an easy victory, 50 seconds ahead of Gounon and Tiemann Vipers were first and second in GT2, Olivier Beretta and Pedro Lamy ahead of Wendlinger and Donohue, but Eichmann and Maassen were disqualified from third position when the scrutineers deemed their rear wing to be illegal. The third place was then awarded to Konrad and Nick Ham. It was McNish's turn to claim pole position at Silverstone, home ground, and the Scot led the first dozen laps before a rare failure struck the Porsche flat-six engine. Alzen was awarded a 30-second penalty for tipping David Brabham's Panoz into the gravel, and finished just eight seconds behind Schneider and Weber.

Beretta and Lamy again won GT2, ahead of the Elf Haberthur Porsche of Neugarten, Ruch and Spinelli, with Stadler Motorsport's Uwe Sick and Jochen Rohr third. Ortelli and Huertgen retired with an oil pressure failure.

These were Porsche's best chances in GT1, and they were not taken. The reality of the situation became clear at the Le Mans test weekend when AMG Mercedes presented an entirely new car, the CLK-LM, powered by a naturally aspirated V8 engine based on the former DTM V6. It was powerful, it was reliable, and it would make the "old V12", as Mercedes would begin to call it, look obsolete.

Happily, the Porsche AG team was able to win the 24-Hours of Le Mans for the 16th time, the success coinciding with the company's 50th birthday celebrations in Stuttgart, but after that the team came back to earth with a bump.

A fortnight later the same two cars were taken to Hockenheim for the third round of the FIA GT Championship, again with smaller inlet air restrictors, and they did not perform well. Drivers complained that they were not riding well over the bumps, they lacked straight-line speed, and even the Persson CLK-GTRs out-performed the 911 GT1-98s.

The grid looked depressing for Porsche fans, with two AMG Mercedes CLK-LMs on the front row, two CLK-GTRs on the second row and two Porsche 'works' cars on the third, Muller ahead of Dalmas. Eric Bernard qualified the DAMS Panoz seventh, ahead of the two Zakspeed GT1s. Nor was the GT2 grid any better for Porsche, with two Team Oreca Vipers and Cor Euser's Marcos ahead of the two Roock Racing Porsches, Ortelli ahead of Maassen.

Porsche's drivers were struggling for pace, and paid the price on race day. Dalmas made an ambitious move to lap Wendlinger's Viper at the second chicane, spun and lost two laps being extracted from the gravel, and late in the contest Alzen crashed his GT1 heavily, also at the second chicane, when he went off-line to pass a Porsche GT2. Later, a mechanical failure was blamed for the accident. An oil line rup-

500 km A 1 Ring 1998: Uwe Sick, Axel Rohr

500 km Donington Park 1998: Michael Bartels, Massimiliano Angelelli

500 km Homestead 1998: Jörg Müller, Uwe Alzen

500 km Donington Park 1998: Bruno Eichmann, Mike Hezemans, Andre Ahrle

GRAND TOURERS 127

Schikane einen schweren Abflug. Später stellte sich ein technischer Defekt als Ursache für den Unfall heraus. Porsche rettete noch den sechsten und den siebten Platz ins Ziel mit Dalmas und McNish vor Bartels und Hahne im Zakspeed-GT1. In der GT2-Klasse kamen die beiden Oreca-Viper mit zwei Runden Vorsprung vor den beiden Roock-Porsche von Eichmann und Maassen sowie Ortelli und Hürtgen ins Ziel.

Dijon-Prenois war die nächste Strecke im Kalender. Manche erinnerten sich, wie Porsche dort 1989 das Sauber-Mercedes-Team geschlagen hatte. Die Mercedes CLK-LM belegten erneut die erste Startreihe, diesmal jedoch war Alzen Drittschnellster. Dalmas qualifizierte sich auf Rang fünf.

„Wir haben uns dieses Wochenende um 10 Prozent verbessert. Um die Mercedes schlagen zu können, müssen wir uns jedoch um 40 Prozent verbessern", sagte Dalmas mit einer Deutlichkeit, die im Porsche-Team wenig Begeisterung fand. Ludwig und Zonta führten das Feld an und fuhren bis zum Fallen der Zielflagge einen Vorsprung von 62 Sekunden auf Dalmas und McNish heraus. An vierter Stelle liegend fielen Alzen und Müller kurz nach Beginn der dritten Stunde des Rennens mit einem Getriebeschaden aus. Mit erheblichem Rückstand von drei Runden belegte das Zakspeed-Team den sechsten und siebten Platz in der Gesamtwertung.

500 km Dijon 1998: Patrice Goueslard, Carl Rosenblad, Bob Wollek

500 km Hungaroring 1998: Michel Neugarten, Gerd Ruch, Marco Spinelli

500 km Laguna Seca 1998: Michael Trunk, Bernhard Müller

Das Team Oreca feierte einen weiteren GT2-Sieg. Während die Teams von Roock und Konrad mit kleinen Problemen zu kämpfen hatten, belegte Jean Pierre Jarier den dritten Rang. Er fuhr zusammen mit François Lafon den Sonauto-GT2.

Die Viper dominierten dermassen, dass die FIA den 911 GT2-Teams erlaubte, größere Luftmengenbegrenzer zu verwenden. Der Vorteil war allerdings relativ, da die zusätzliche Leistung auch das Getriebe und die Antriebswellen stärker belastete. Die Situation hatte es vorher schon beim Evo gegeben: Die Zuverlässigkeit wurde beeinträchtigt. Die GT2-Teams bevorzugten es, ihre Autos leichter zu machen, statt extra Motorleistung zu haben.

Das heisseste Rennen des Jahres fand in Ungarn statt. Die Mercedes CLK-LM dominierten erneut. In der GT2-Klasse fiel ein Auto nach dem anderen aus. Am Ende waren Eichmann und Maassen die verdienten Sieger im Roock-Porsche. Ihr Sieg war heiss umkämpft: Mit 32 Grad Lufttemperatur, 48 Grad Asphalttemperatur und über 50 Grad Hitze im Cockpit. Dalmas und McNish fuhren aufs Podium. Hinter den beiden CLK-LM fuhren sie auf Rang drei ins Ziel. Sie hatten nur 54 Sekunden Rückstand auf Schneider und Webber. Wollek, der Uwe Alzen ersetzte, fuhr mit Müller auf Platz vier, dahinter folgten Bartels und Hahne.

Eichmann und Maassen profitierten von ihrer Zwei-Stopp-Strategie und schlugen so Beretta und Ortelli um 24 Sekunden. Der Marcos lief auf Rang drei ein, der Elf-Haberthur-Porsche wurde Vierter. Es war für Porsche der einzige Sieg in der FIA GT-Meisterschaft 1998.

Das 1000 km-Rennen in Suzuka war das längste Rennen der Saison. Wie üblich sicherten sich Schneider und Ludwig die Plätze in der ersten Startreihe. McNish und Müller belegten Reihe zwei, die Persson-Motorsport-Mercedes standen in der dritten Reihe. Diesmal jedoch konnte sich Schneider beim Start nicht einfach so absetzen. McNish überholte schon bald Zonta und setzte Schneider unter Druck. Als aber Hoffnung aufkam, dass der Schotte bald die Führung übernehmen könnte, verbremste sich Zonta vor der zweiten Degna-Kurve und fuhr dem Porsche ins Heck. Beide Autos landeten inm Kiesbett und Zontas Mercedes wurde als erstes herausgezogen. Zonta sagte, er hätte die Kontrolle über

tured and started a fire, which would be an expensive repair before the next race. Porsche salvaged sixth and seventh positions overall, Dalmas and McNish ahead of Zakspeed's Bartels and Hahne, while in GT2 the two Oreca Vipers finished two laps ahead of the two Roock Porsches, Eichmann and Maassen ahead of Ortelli and Huertgen, who had recovered from a front tyre failure.

Dijon-Prenois was the next venue on the calendar, and our minds switched back to Porsche's surprise defeat of the Sauber Mercedes team in 1989. The Porsche GT1s were much more competitive, but would they be good enough to spring a surprise? Mercedes CLK-LMs again claimed the front row but this time Alzen was third quickest and Dalmas fifth. "We have made a 10 per cent improvement this weekend, but we need to make a 40 per cent improvement to beat the Mercedes" said Dalmas with a clarity that did not please the Porsche team. Although Schneider and Webber dominated the race their CLK-LM failed to reach the finish, after a rear tyre deflated and caused an accident. A stone had got trapped between the caliper and the rim, causing loss of pressure through the wheel itself.

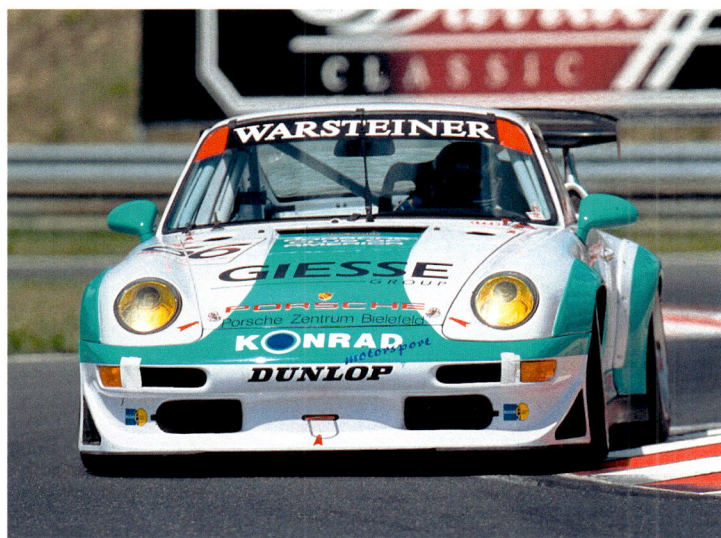

500 km Hungaroring 1998: Franz Konrad, Altfrid Heger, Nick Ham

Ludwig and Zonta were then at the head of the field, easing out a 62 second lead over Dalmas and McNish at the finish. Alzen and Muller retired with a broken gearbox just into the third hour, when fourth, and the Zakspeed team finished a distant sixth and seventh overall, three laps behind.

Team Oreca again led GT2 with a 1-2 finish, and with minor problems afflicting the Roock and Konrad teams third position went to the old warrior, Jean-Pierre Jarier, sharing the Sonauto Porsche GT2 with Francois Lafon.

So dominant had the Vipers become, the FIA allowed the Porsche GT2 teams to instal larger inlet air restrictors, but gratitude was limited as the extra power put more strain on the gearboxes and driveshafts, creating a new 'Evo' dilemma and a bout of unreliability. Where possible, the GT2 teams preferred to lighten the cars rather than use the extra power. Hungary was the setting for the hottest race of the year, in which the Mercedes CLK-LMs were again dominant but GT2 was like a game of musical chairs, at the end of which Eichmann and Maassen were the hot and worthy winners in their Roock Porsche. With an ambient temperature of 32 degrees, a track temperature of 48 degrees and cockpit temperatures in excess of 50 degrees, all the survivors deserved medals! Dalmas and McNish earned their podium result, third behind the two CLK-LMs and just 54 seconds behind Schneider and Webber at the end. Behind them were Wollek, replacing Alzen, and Muller, then Bartels and Hahne.

Sixth, and winners of GT2, were Eichmann and Maassen, the latter totally exhausted after his last stint and in need of hospital treatment. The Marcos was the early pace-setter, set back by a 10-second stop-go penalty, and both the Vipers suffered from heat induced fuel pressure problems. Wendlinger's retired with a differential failure, Ortelli was sidelined by a start-line accident but, on a two-stop strategy which paid dividends, Eichmann and Maassen were able to beat Beretta and Lamy by 24 seconds, with the Marcos third and the Elf Haberthur Porsche fourth. It was Porsche's one victory of the 1998 FIA GT season, sad to say.

The Pokka 1,000 Kms race at Suzuka was the longest of the season and offered Porsche another chance to shine. As usual, Schneider and Ludwig claimed the front row, McNish and Muller the second and the Persson Motorsport Mercedes the third, but this time Schneider did not pull away effortlessly at the start.

McNish soon passed Zonta and put pressure on Schneider, something quite unexpected, but when hopes were rising that the Scot would snatch the lead, Zonta appeared to miss his braking point at the second Degna curve, by the overbridge, and slammed into the back of the Porsche. Both cars finished up in the gravel, and Zonta's Mercedes was towed out first, giving him an advantage on the track.

Zonta said that he lost downforce and steering control behind McNish and offered a full apology, which the Scotsman was reluctant to accept. Claudia Huertgen, caught up in the same accident, described Zonta as a "lunatic".

Schneider and Webber claimed their usual victory, AMG Mercedes now closing on the FIA title, Ludwig and Zonta recovered to second overall, McNish and Dalmas to third. Team Oreca finished first and second in GT2, with Euser third, Konrad fourth.

Donington was the circuit that best suited the Mercedes CLK-LM, and the AMG team again finished first and second, visibly pulling away from the works Porsches out of the two hairpin bends. The FIA imposed a 50 kg weight penalty on the V8 Mercedes for the rest of the season, but the silver cars maintained their superiority. McNish led the 500 kilometre race for 10 memorable laps by virtue of jumping the

500 km Dijon 1998: Jörg Müller, Uwe Alzen

Trotz dreier mechanisch bedingten Ausfälle und einem sechsten Platz in Hockenheim fuhren Dalmas und McNish auch sechs Podiumsplätze in Folge nach Hause: Ein zweiter Platz und fünf dritte Plätze verhalfen ihnen zum geteilten fünften Rang im Endstand der Fahrerwertung, hinter Ludwig und Zonta, Schneider und Webber. Müller belegte Rang sieben, Alzen wurde Achter. Das Zakspeed-Team verbesserte in der zweiten Saisonhälfte seine Leistung, nachdem Pirelli bei der Reifenentwicklung nachgelegt hatte. Die Saisonbilanz war bescheiden, abgesehen vom Sieg in Le Mans.

Herr Singer, was war das Problem? „Meiner Meinung nach gab es verschiedene Faktoren. Der Turbomotor war ein Teil des Problems. Besonders mit den Luftmengenbegrenzern war er nicht so effizient wie ein Saugmotor. Beim Herausbeschleunigen aus langsamen Kurven verloren wir pro Runde fast eine Sekunde, zum Beispiel in den Haarnadelkurven in Donington. Manche sahen das Problem beim Motor, manche eher bei der Aerodynamik. Das ist eine normale Diskussion. Besonders dann, wenn man nicht gewinnt. Für mich war die Regelung des Turbos nicht optimal. Außerdem war Michelin nicht auf dem gleichen Niveau wie Bridgestone. Auf einigen Strecken konnten wir die gleichen Rundenzeiten fahren, aber sie blieben konstanter. Im Rennen waren die Bridgestone-Reifen viel besser. Mercedes hatte den Sechslitermotor, der sehr stark war und ein besseres Ansprechverhalten hatte. Darüber hinaus konnten ihre Reifen die Leistung umsetzen, sie waren beim Beschleunigen sehr stark." Im De-

das Fahrzeug verloren, als er hinter McNish fuhr, und er entschuldigte sich förmlich, was der Schotte nur zögerlich akzeptierte. Schneider und Webber sicherten sich ihren üblichen Sieg, AMG-Mercedes hatte den FIA-Titel schon fast sicher. Ludwig und Zonta holten auf und belegten Rang zwei, McNish und Dalmas kamen auf Platz drei ins Ziel. Das Team Oreca belegte die Plätze eins und zwei in der GT2-Klasse. Euser wurde Dritter, Konrad Vierter.

Donington war die Strecke, die den Mercedes CLK-LM am besten entgegenkam. Das AMG-Team feierte einen weiteren Doppelsieg. Beim Herausbeschleunigen aus den beiden Spitzkehren konnten sich die Mercedes jedesmal deutlich von den Werks-Porsche absetzen. Die FIA belegte den Mercedes mit V8-Motoren für die restlichen Rennen der Saison mit 50 kg Zusatzgewicht. Die silbernen Autos hielten jedoch ihre Dominanz aufrecht. McNish führte nach einem Frühstart zehn Runden lang das 500 km-Rennen an, wurde aber dann mit der schwarzen Flagge zum Rennleiter zitiert und musste in der Boxengasse eine Zehn-Sekundenstrafe absitzen. Beretta und Lamy gewannen die GT2-Klasse. Becker und Euser belegten im Marcos Rang zwei, Konrad und Altfrid Heger kamen im Porsche auf Platz drei ins Ziel.

Die drei verbleibenden Rennen der Meisterschaft in Österreich, Homestead (Miami) und Laguna Seca brachten alle das gleiche Ergebnis: Einen überlegenen Sieg für das AMG-Mercedes-Team. Überraschenderweise gewannen Routinier Klaus Ludwig und Youngster Ricardo Zonta die drei letzten Rennen und sicherten sich so den Fahrertitel in der FIA-GT-Meisterschaft.

Es gab einen weiteren Podiumsplatz für die Porsche, als Müller und Alzen in Laguna Seca auf Rang drei ins Ziel fuhren. Die Hochgeschwindigkeitsstrecke kam dem 911 GT1-98 entgegen. McNish zeigte erneut eine gute Leistung. Er überholte Schneider im Kampf um Rang zwei und folgte Ludwig wie ein Schatten, wurde aber von einem Kupplungsdefekt aus dem Rennen geworfen.

500 km Hockenheim 1999: Wolfgang Kaufmann, Michel Ligonnet

500 km Dijon 1998: Michael Bartels, Armin Hahne

130 DOMÄNE GT-SPORT

start, but was black flagged and had to serve a 10-second penalty in the pit-lane. He claimed that the Mercedes were slow in accelerating to the green light and he drove between them, believing that he was not ahead at the start-line, "but the stewards said I was, and I can't argue".

Beretta and Lamy won GT2 in eighth position overall, with Euser and Becker second in their Marcos, Konrad and Altfrid Heger third in their Porsche.

Austria, Homestead (Miami) and Laguna Seca, the three remaining rounds of the one-sided contest, went the same way, sweeping victories for the AMG Mercedes CLK-LM team. Curiously, veteran driver Klaus Ludwig and youngster Ricardo Zonta won the last three races and claimed the FIA GT Driver Championship title, lifting it from under the noses of Scheider and Webber who'd had a retirement and a couple of unlucky races to handicap their effort.

There was one more podium position for Porsche AG when Muller and Alzen finished third at Laguna Seca, a high speed track that suited the GT1-98 well. McNish had excelled again, passing Schneider for second place and shadowing Ludwig, but without warning the clutch pedal went to the floor and left him without gears.

Despite three retirements for mechanical reasons and a sixth place at Hockenheim, after visiting the gravel trap, Dalmas and McNish also earned six successive podium results (a second place, and five third positions), to finish equal fifth in the championship behind Ludwig and Zonta, Schneider and

500 km Hockenheim 1999: Mauro Casadei, Stefano Bucci

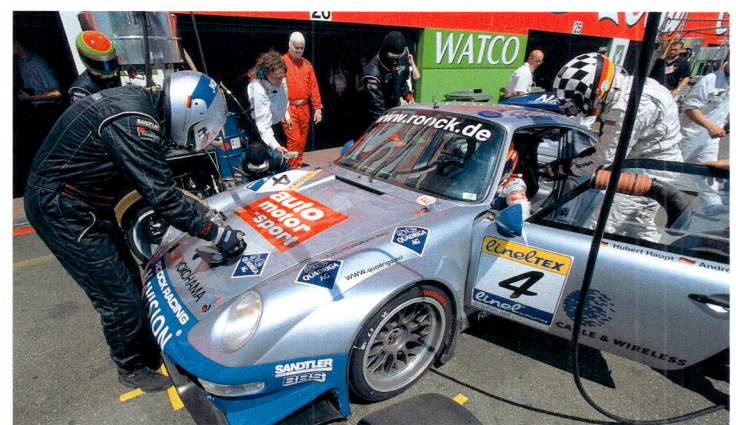

500 km Zolder 1999: Hubert Haupt, Andre Ahrle, Claudia Hürtgen

Webber. Muller was seventh, Alzen (who missed a race) eighth, and the Zakspeed team improved its performances in the latter half of the season, when Pirelli stepped up development of its tyres.

The analysis of the season was bleak, saved only by the Le Mans victory which must never be under-estimated. Ten victories for Mercedes, nil for Porsche, a dreadful score-line.

So what went wrong, Mr Singer? "In my opinion, there were several factors. It was a little bit the turbo engine, especially with the restrictors in the way, it was not as efficient as a naturally aspirated engine. Especially accelerating out of slow corners, we lost nearly a second a lap in those two slow corners at Donington. "Some people blamed the engine, some blamed the aerodynamics, this is a normal discussion, especially when you are not winning. For me, the turbo control was not right. "Then, Michelin was not on the same level as Bridgestone. In some places we could match their lap times but they had more stability through the stint. In race conditions, the Bridgestone tyres were much better. Mercedes had the 6-litre engine which was very strong, very responsive, and they had the tyres to cope with the traction, they could accelerate very well."

Herbert Ampferer, who retained his position as head of engine development, had no doubt that restrictions imposed by the FIA, particularly, on Porsche's turbocharged engines put the flat-six under an unfair handicap. Why this should have happened, nobody knew. "With a naturally aspirated engine" he argued, "we would be in the same position as Mercedes, as Panoz and BMW."

Dr Wiedeking gave the order to disband the Porsche AG racing team in order to concentrate the minds of all his engineers on developing the forthcoming Cayenne SUV.

The Porsche 911 would continue to play a leading role in endurance racing, of course, as the GT2 continued to contest the top group and, from 1999 onwards, the GT3 would become the car to beat in the new made-to-measure N-GT category for near standard production cars.

Beretta and Lamy finished their 1998 season in style with three more victories, amassing more than double the points of their team-mate Karl Wendlinger. Roock Racing were second in the GT2 Teams Championship, lead driver Bruno Eichmann fourth in the Drivers Championship, and Franz Konrad deservedly claimed third place in the Teams Championship, fifth in the Drivers series.

Porsche's withdrawal from the FIA GT Championship left AMG Mercedes out on a limb, without competition, since BMW, Nissan and Toyota wanted only to race at Le Mans. Mercedes therefore built a new car for Le Mans - it flew! - and Stephane Ratel closed down the GT1 class (which had become a sham for GT prototypes) and promoted the GT2s to the top division.

zember gab Dr. Wiedeking den Auftrag, das Rennteam Porsche Motorsport aufzulösen, so dass sich alle Techniker auf der Entwicklung des neuen Cayenne konzentrieren konnten. Der Elfer sollte selbstverständlich weiterhin eine grosse Rolle im Langstreckensport spielen, da der 911 GT2 in der Spitzenklasse fuhr und ab der Saison 1999 das Mass aller Dinge in der neuen N-GT-Klasse für seriennahen Autos werden sollte. Roock Racing belegte Rang zwei in der GT2-Teamwertung. Ihr Spitzenfahrer Bruno Eichmann war Vierter in der Fahrerwertung. Franz Konrad wurde verdient Dritter in der Teamwertung und Fünfter bei den Fahrern.

Nach Porsches Ausstieg aus der Meisterschaft stand AMG-Mercedes ohne Gegner da, weil BMW, Nissan und Toyota nur in Le Mans fahren wollten. Mercedes baute deswegen ein neues Auto für Le Mans – es flog! – und Stéphane Ratel stellte die GT1-Klasse ein, da sie längst zur Spielwiese für GT-Prototypen geworden war. Die GT2 formten fortan die Spitzenklasse.

Für die Saison 1999 und danach beinhaltete die GT-Klasse Fahrzeuge, die auch für die Strasse zugelassen waren, wie Chrysler Viper, Porsche GT2, Lister Storm und der neue Ferrari 550 Maranello.

500 km Hockenheim 1999: Sascha Maassen, Paul Hulverscheid, Michael Eschmann

Nahezu unvermeidlich dominierten die starken Chrysler Viper die FIA GT-Meisterschaft vier Jahre lang, obwohl sie Konkurrenz bekamen vom Lister Storm und später vom Ferrari 550 Maranello, der bei Prodrive entwickelt wurde. Porsche stellte die Entwicklung am 911 GT2 ein und konzentrierte sich auf den neuen 911 GT3 mit Saugmotor, der 1999 in Le Mans seine Premiere erlebte.

Wolfgang Kaufmann und Michel Ligonnet belegten beim Saisonauftakt in Monza den dritten Gesamtrang im Freisinger-GT2. Damit brachen sie die Phalanx der Viper und verhinderten so einen Sechsfachsieg der amerikanischen Marke. Beide belegten in Silverstone Platz sechs, wurden dort aber geschlagen von Stéphane Ortelli und Claudia Hürtgen, die im Roock-Porsche auf der fünften Position ins Ziel fuhren. Im Juni in Hockenheim durfte Franz Konrad zusammen mit Bob Wollek aufs Podium steigen. Kaufmann und Ligonnet wurden Fünfte, Hubert Haupt und André Ahrle belegten für Roock Rang sechs. Konrad und Wollek setzten ihre Serie fort mit einem weiteren dritten Platz auf dem Hungaroring, nur eine Runde hinter den beiden Viper des Team Oreca.

Als die FIA GT-Meisterschaft sich zum fünften Saisonlauf in Zolder einfand, hatten die Viper des Team Oreca bereits eine Menge Zusatzgewicht von bis zu 100 kg für die eingefahrenen Erfolge an Bord. Die Porsche-Teams hingegen durften mit größeren Luftmengenbegrenzern fahren. Ortelli und Maassen taten sich für den sechsten Saisonlauf in Oschersleben mit Paul Hulverscheid zusammen. Dort holte Ortelli für Porsche die einzige Pole-Position der Saison.

Maassen führte das Rennen an. Wendlinger fand keinen Weg an ihn vorbei und Hulverscheid fuhr zu Mitte des Rennens sehr stark. Danach übergab er das Lenkrad an Ortelli, der das Rennen zu Ende fuhr. Die Oreca-Viper waren in der letzten Stunde vorne. Ortelli setzte im Kampf um Rang zwei jedoch Jean-Philippe Belloc unter Druck, bis sich eine halbe Stunde vor Schluss das Differential verabschiedete.

Maassen und Konrad fuhren im September in Donington Park den vierten und letzten Podiumsplatz der Saison für Porsche ein. Manfred Freisingers Team war mit Kaufmann als Spitzenfahrer die erfolgreichste Mannschaft. Nur einmal in Donington kam das Team nicht unter die ersten Sechs im Gesamtergebnis. Die fünfjährige Zusammenarbeit mit Michael Ligonnet endete jedoch in Homestead, wo sich Bob Wollek für die restlichen Rennen der Saison dem Team anschloss. Sie beendeten die Meisterschaft als das bestplatzierte Porsche-Team: Fünfter in Homestead, Vierter in Watkins Glen und erneut Vierter in Zhuhai.

Der 911 GT2 war zweifelsohne am Ende seiner Laufbahn. Im Jahre 2000 war der alte Haudegen dennoch gut für einen Sieg. Manfred Freisinger und Franz Konrad setzten weiterhin das Twin-Turbo-Modell gegen die immer stärker werdende Konkurrenz ein. Die Anzahl der Chrysler Viper im Starterfeld nahm ständig zu. Sie fuhren im Laufe der Saison nicht weniger als achtmal unter die ersten Sechs. Das überraschendste Ergebnis des Jahres kam auf dem Lausitzring, wo Kaufmann und Haupt die gesamte Konkurrenz schlugen und ganz oben aufs Podium steigen durften.

Es war der erste wichtige Erfolg für Freisinger und der erste GT2-Sieg für Porsche seit dem Rennen in Ungarn 1998. Es war auch der erste Sieg für Porsche bei einem Lauf zu einer FIA-Meisterschaft seit Bob Wollek und Frank Jelinski 1989 in Dijon die Mercedes-Gruppe-C-Mannschaft besiegten.

Der Porsche GT2 verabschiedete sich aus der internationalen Szene, nachdem sich alle führenden Porsche-Teams für die Saison 2000 auf den 911 GT3 konzentrierten. Schließlich war dieser fast genauso schnell wie der GT2, sparsamer, zuverlässiger und fast unbesiegbar in der N-GT-Klasse.

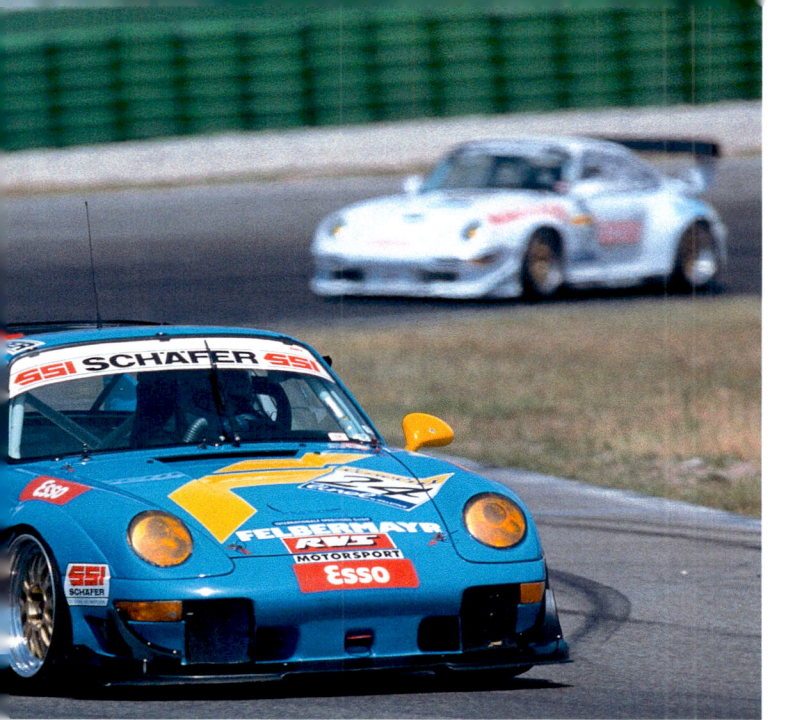

500 km Hockenheim 1999: Horst Felbermayr Jr. and Sr.

In 1999, and beyond, the new GT top class for production line cars would comprise Chrysler Vipers, Porsche GT2, Lister Storm, and the new Ferrari 550 Maranello which started its career in 2000. Almost inevitably, the 600 bhp Chrysler Vipers dominated the FIA GT Championship for four seasons, though challenged by Lister Storm and latterly, by the Prodrive developed Ferrari 550s. Porsche put no more development into the GT2 model, concentrating on bringing the naturally aspirated GT3 into the world at Le Mans in 1999 so the teams run by the Roock brothers, Franz Konrad and Manfred Freisinger were looking for crumbs on the floor, and the occa-sional podium position.

Only once in 1999 did Chrysler not finish first and second overall, and that was when Julian Bailey, Andy Wallace and William Hewland finished second to Beretta and Wendlinger at Donington Park in September, driving Laurence Pearce's Lister Storm.

Wolfgang Kaufmann and Michel Ligonnet drove the Freisinger Motorsport GT2 to third place overall at Monza, the opening round of the series, splitting a solid wall of Vipers in the top six positions. The same pairing finished sixth at Silverstone, but were beaten by Stephane Ortelli and Claudia Huertgen who were fifth overall for Roock Racing.

Then it was Franz Konrad's turn to step up on the podium, with Bob Wollek, at Hockenheim in June, where Kaufmann and Ligonnet were fifth, Hubert Haupt and Andre Ahrle sixth for Roock Racing. Konrad and Wollek made it a double success with another third place at the Hungaroring, only one lap down on the two Team Oreca Vipers.

By the time the FIA GT Championship teams reached Zolder for the fifth round in July, the Team Oreca Vipers were suffering from weight handicaps, up to 100 kg for continuing success, and the Porsche teams were again allowed to run larger inlet air restrictors, a mixed blessing. The Roock brothers withdrew from the championship, but on a high note as Hubert Haupt put his GT2 on the front row of the grid, alongside the Lister Storm.

Haupt retired, unfortunately, leaving Kaufmann and Ligonnet to lead the Porsche teams home in fourth position, with Konrad and Heger sixth. Ortelli and Maassen teamed up with Paul Hulverscheid for the sixth round, at Oschersleben and Ortelli claimed Porsche's one pole position of the season.

Maassen led the race stylishly, Wendlinger failing to find a way past, and Hulverscheid put in a strong middle stint on soft compound tyres, handing the Porsche to Ortelli for the third stint. The Oreca Vipers were ahead in the final hour, but Ortelli was challenging Jean-Philippe Belloc for second place until his differential failed in the final half-hour.

Maassen and Konrad earned Porsche's fourth (and final) podium result of the season, third overall at Donington Park in September, yet at the end of the season Konrad, who had won the Porsche Cup in 1997 and again in 1998, counted it as one of the least lucky in his career, as his season ended with gearbox and other problems in the late season rounds in Homestead and Watkins Glen. Manfred Freisinger's team led by Kaufmann was the most successful, failing to be classified in the top six overall only once, at Donington Park, although a five-year association with Michel Ligonnet came to an end at Homestead when Bob Wollek joined the team for the remainder of the season. They finished the series as the top Porsche team, fifth at Homestead, fourth at Watkins Glen and fourth again at Zhuhai.

The Porsche GT2 was undoubtedly near the end of its life, but there was one more victory left in the old warrior in 2000. Manfred Freisinger and Franz Konrad continued to campaign the twin-turbo model against increasingly long odds, as the number of Chrysler Vipers increased on the grids, and they finished in the top six overall on no fewer than eight occasions during the season.

500 km Hockenheim 1999: Franz Konrad, Bob Wollek

The most surprising result of the year was at the Lausitzring, where Kaufmann and Haupt beat all the competition to mount the top step of the podium. The pair drove fast and sensibly as rain hit the banked circuit, overcame confusion in the pit-lane and took the chequered flag, as surprised as any in the stadium. It was the Freisinger team's first major victory, Porsche's first since the GT2 success in Hungary in 1988, and (one for the historians!) Porsche's first victory in an FIA championship race since Wollek and Jelinski trounced the Mercedes Group C team at Dijon in 1989.

Konrad and von Gartzen never finished higher than fifth all season, another disappointing performance in the Austrian's opinion. Apart from the odd appearance, the GT2 retired from the international arena as all the top Porsche teams turned their attention to the 911 GT3 model in 2000. It was, after all, practically as fast as the GT2, more economical, more reliable, and was almost unbeatable in the newly created N-GT class.

GRAND TOURERS 133

DER GT3 BEHERRSCHT DAS FELD

Als der Automobile Club de l'Ouest 1999 in Le Mans eine neue Kategorie für serienmässige GT-Fahrzeuge ankündigte, war es auch für Porsche eine neue Chance. „Die Autos dürfen für den Renneinsatz angepasst werden, hauptsächlich im Bereich der Sicherheit und des Fahrwerks", erklärte Alain Bertaut, Sportdirektor des ACO, als er die neue GT-Kategorie ankündigte. „Ich würde sagen, dass die Autos mindestens zu 80 Prozent original sein müssen."

Es mussten mindestens 50 Fahrzeuge produziert werden, jedoch ohne einen zeitlichen Rahmen. Das Mindestgewicht lag bei 1100 kg und der maximale Tankinhalt wurde auf 100 Liter festgesetzt. Turbolader oder mechanische Auflading wurden erlaubt, Porsche entschied sich jedoch, die Supercup-Ausführung des 911, basierend auf der Modellreihe 996, weiter zu entwickeln, zusammen mit dem wassergekühlten 3,6 Liter-Saugmotor mit vier Ventilen pro Zylinder.

Der GT3 Supercup hatte eine Motorleistung von 380 PS, während der GT3 R 410 PS leistete. Sequentielle Gangschaltung war nicht erlaubt und auch Bremsen aus Kohlefaser waren verboten. Alle herausnehmbaren Teile, wie Türen und Hauben, durften jedoch leichter gemacht werden. Bald stellte sich heraus, dass ein schneller GT3 R aufgrund des günstigeren Spritverbrauchs einen 911 GT2 über die Distanz schlagen konnte. Bei einem Preis von 180.000 Euro bei der Markteinführung war der R klar im Vorteil. Die Porsche-Kundenteams standen Schlange für den GT3 R, darunter Larbre Competition, Haberthur, RWS, GTC Motorsport, G-Force, PK Sport, Perspective Racing, MAC Racing und ART Engineering, die sich allesamt in der FIA GT-Meisterschaft engagieren wollten und manche auch in Le Mans.

Die FIA GT-Meisterschaft erlebte 1999 ein Übergangsjahr, nachdem die exotischen GT1-Fahrzeuge von Porsche und Mercedes nicht mehr starteten. Die Einführung der GT3-Klasse im Jahr 2000 sorgte für neues Leben in dieser Serie. Teilweise bot die N-GT-Klasse, wie sie die FIA nannte, eine große Leistungsdichte und spannenden Rennsport. Christophe Bouchut und Patrice Goueslard brachten 2000 für das Larbre-Competition-Team eine glänzende Leistung. Sie gewannen mit fünf Klassensiegen in zehn Rennen den Titel.

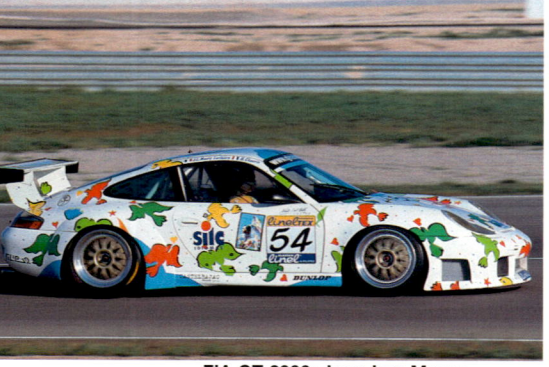

FIA GT 2000: Nigel Smith, Robert Nearn

FIA GT 2000: Jean-Luc Maury-Laribiere, Bernard Chauvin

Winner 24 Hours Nürburgring 2000: Michael Bartels, Uwe Alzen, Altfrid Heger, Bernd Mayländer

Winner FIA N-GT 2000: Christophe Bouchut, Patrice Gueslard

GT3 DOMINATES 'SHOWROOM' CLASS

When the Automobile Club de l'Ouest announced a new category at Le Mans, for near standard Grand Touring cars in 1999, it was a golden opportunity for Porsche to return to its roots. "The cars will be modified to be suitable for the track, in the areas of safety and suspension mainly" said Alain Bertaut, the ACO's sporting director, when he announced the new category. "I would say that these must be at least 80 per cent original."

At least 50 cars must be made (but without a time limit), the minimum weight would be 1,100 kg, and the maximum fuel tank capacity would be 100 litres. Turbo or supercharging would be allowed, but Porsche decided to develop the 996 Supercup model 911 with its naturally aspirated, water cooled 3.6 litre engine with four valves per cylinder.

The GT3 Supercup developed 380 bhp, while the 'international' GT3 RS developed 410 bhp. Sequential gearbox operation was banned, along with carbon brakes, but any detachable panels (such as doors, engine cover and front lid) could be lightened. It soon became clear that a well driven GT3 R could beat a GT2 over a distance, with better fuel economy, and at the equivalent of 180,000 Euro at the introduction, the case for the R was clear-cut.

Porsche's customers were queuing up for the GT3 R, among them Larbre Competition, Haberthur, RWS, GTC Motorsport, G-Force, PK Sport, Perspective Racing, MAC Racing and ART Engineering, all with plans to contest the FIA GT Championship and, in some cases, Le Mans.

The FIA GT Championship went through a transition stage in 1999, with the elimination of the exotic Porsche and Mercedes GT1 cars, and the introduction of the GT3 class in 2000 brought some fresh air to the series. Some of the closest and best racing was to be seen in the N-GT class, as the FIA called it. Christophe Bouchut and Patrice Goueslard performed brilliantly for the Larbre Competition team in 2000, winning the championship with five class wins in 10 appearances, their GT3 R sponsored by Jean-Luc Chereau's specialist commercial vehicle company. They were never out of the points and won the championship at the eighth round, at the Lausitzring.

Luca Riccitelli, who had been selected by the factory for the GT3 R's debut at Le Mans in 1999, often seemed to need the same piece of track as Bouchut, and the two had a very public clash at the Osterreichring which resulted in the Frenchman being found at fault for the accident, and fined. Riccitelli drove for Rudi Walch's RWS Red Bull team which was second in the Teams championship, the Italian placed third in the Drivers championship.

FIA GT 2000: Luca Riccitelli, Dieter Quester

ELMS Silverstone 2000: Randy Pobst, Bruno Lambert

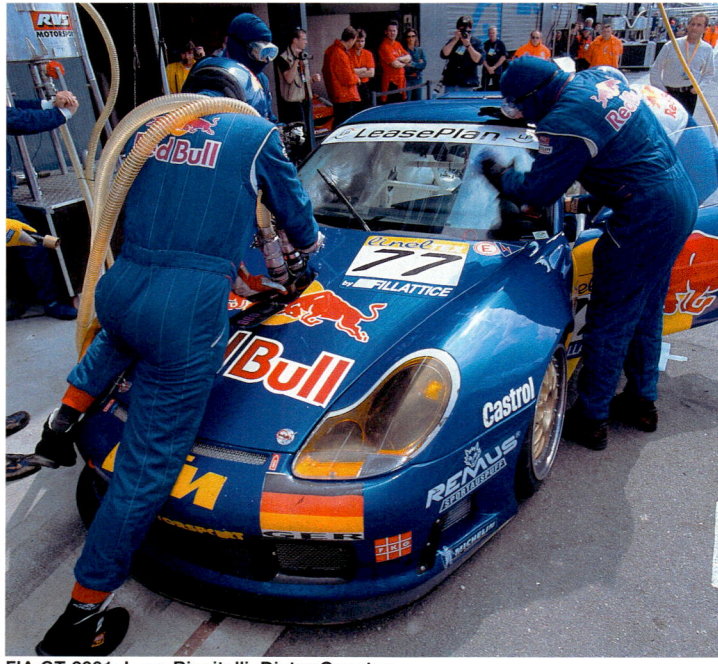

FIA GT 2001: Luca Riccitelli, Dieter Quester

FIA GT 2001: Nikolaj Fomenko, Alex Vassiliev

Luca Riccitelli, der vom Werk für das Debüt des 911 GT3 R 1999 in Le Mans verpflichtet wurde, fuhr für das RWS Red Bull-Team von Rudi Walch, das Rang zwei im Endstand der Meisterschaft bei den Teams belegte. Der Italiener sicherte sich den dritten Platz in der Fahrerwertung. John Greasleys Team war Dritter in der Teamwertung vor dem EMKA-Team von Steve O'Rourke und dem österreichischen ART Engineering-Team. Freisinger Motorsport erlebte auf dem Lausitzring sein Debüt in der N-GT-Klasse mit zwei russischen Fahrern, Nikolaj Fomenko und Alex Vasiliev, die erstmals auf internationalem Niveau fuhren.

Der GT3 R holte sich den ersten Gesamtsieg im Jahre 2000, beim 24 Stunden-Rennen auf dem Nürburgring, wo Michael Bartels, Uwe Alzen, Altfrid Heger und Bernd Mayländer die große Konkurrenz mit sehr unterschiedlichen Fahrzeugen besiegten.

Porsche war stark in den GT- und N-GT-Klassen der FIA-GT-Meisterschaft 2001, gewann aber in keiner der beiden Klassen den Titel. In der N-GT-Klasse gewann das JMB Ferrari 360-Team ganz knapp den Titel mit den Fahrern Christian Pescatori und David Terrien. Das Ferrari-Team konnte sich erst den Titel sichern, nachdem Luca Riccitelli beim Saionfinale in Estoril aus dem Rennen war. Antonio Garcia und Riccitelli waren im Startunfall beteiligt. Man verlor zehn Runden an der Box, um einen neuen Kühler zu wechseln. So fehlte ihm sogar der einzige Punkt, der ihm bereits zum Titelgewinn gereicht hätte.

Porsche lieferte auch den Hauptteil des Starterfeldes der neuen European Le Mans-Serie (ELMS). Die beiden ersten Läufe dieser Serie, jeweils vor und nach den 24 Stunden von Le Mans, zählten ebenfalls zur American Le Mans-Serie (ALMS). Porsches Kampf mit den BMW M3 GTR V8 wurde in Donington zugunsten von Alex Job Racing entschieden, als Sascha Maassen und Lucas Luhr die LM GT-Klasse gewannen. Das BMW-Team schlug in Jarama jedoch mit einem überlegenen Doppelsieg zurück. Die BMW waren nicht unumstritten, da nur drei Autos gebaut wurden und es fraglich war, ob dieses Modell in der Produktionsklasse gehörte. Die Serie von fünf Rennen setzte sich fort, nachdem sich die Amerikaner wieder auf die Heimreise gemacht hatten. Robin Liddell und Mike Youles gewannen im PK Sport GT3 mit einem Sieg und einem zweiten Platz den LM GT-Titel. Liddell erreichte einen zweiten Platz in Donington Park zusammen mit Stéphane Ortelli im Freisinger-Team. Romain Dumas und Xavier Pompidou fuhren dann den Freisinger-Porsche zum Sieg in Estoril.

Porsche eroberte in der Saison 2002 den Platz an der Spitze in der N-GT-Klasse zurück. Mit acht Siegen aus zehn Rennen war man Ferrari deutlich überlegen. Stéphane Ortelli gewann im Freisinger GT3 RS sieben Rennen, zusammen mit den Teamkollegen: Sascha Maassen, Marc Lieb und Emmanuel Collard. Philipp Peter und Toto Wolff fuhren für das Autorlando-Team in Oschersleben einen weiteren Sieg ein, nachdem Ortelli und Maassen aufgeben mussten.

Ortelli gewann auch das 24 Stunden-Rennen von Spa, das doppelte Punkte einbrachte. Dort fuhr er zusammen mit Romain Dumas und Emmanuel Collard. Das Autorlando-Team beendete die Meisterschaft auf Rang drei in der Teamwertung. Die RWS-Mannschaft von Rudi Walch schloss, entgegen den Erwartungen, die Saison mit dem vierten Rang in der Meisterschaft ab. Der Österreicher startete die Saison mit Luca Riccitelli und Dieter Quester.

Manfred Freisingers Team triumphierte 2003 erneut in der N-GT-Klasse der FIA-Meisterschaft. Die Konkurrenz bestand diesmal nicht nur aus dem JMB Ferrari 360 von Fabrizio de Simone und Andrea Bertolini, sondern auch aus dem Mara-

DER GT3 BEHERRSCHT DAS FELD

John Greasley's Pennzoil Quaker State G-Force team was third in the Teams Championship, ahead of Steve O'Rourke's EMKA/GTC team and the Austrian ART Engineering team. Michel Neugarten was fourth in the Drivers championship, competing for Perspective Racing, and fifth was Nigel Smith who competed for G-Force. Freisinger Motorsport made its N-GT debut at the Lausitzring with two Russian drivers making their international debut, Nikolai Fomenko and Alex Vasiliev.

The GT3 R model scored its first outright victory in 2000, appropriately in the 24-Hours of the Nurburgring where Uwe Alzen, Michael Bartels, Altfrid Heger and Bernd Maylaender triumphed over a large and varied entry.

Porsche raced strongly in the GT and N-GT categories in the 2001 FIA GT Championship, but won neither. Jack Leconte switched his loyalty to the Chrysler Viper GTS-R in GT, taking Bouchut and Jean-Philippe Belloc to the top class and the outright championship. Their season included victory in the inaugural FIA GT Spa 24-Hours, worth double points.

In N-GT, Jean-Michel Bouresche's JMB Ferrari 360 team narrowly claimed the title with drivers Christian Pescatori and David Terrien, who won five of the 11 rounds. The title went to the Ferrari team only after Luca Riccitelli was effectively taken out of the final round at Estoril, where Anthony Kumpen made an over-ambitious start in Paul Belmondo's Viper and crashed into Philipp Peter's Redolfi Orlando Porsche, pushing it into the wall.

Antonio Garcia and Riccitelli were also involved, the RWS Red Bull team driver losing 10 laps in the pits having a new radiator installed, and forfeiting even the single point that would have given him the championship. Despite winning N-GT at Spa, for double points, Riccitelli finished level on points with Pescatori and Terrien, who took the title by virtue of having five victories.

Riccitelli, who raced with Dieter Quester, had won only twice for RWS, while Philipp Peter and Johnny Cecotto also won the opening two rounds in their Redolfi Orlando Porsche. Thierry Perrier and Michel Neugarten won the final round at Estoril in their Perspective Racing Porsche.

Winner 24 Hours Spa 2002 (l.-r.): Stephane Ortelli, Romain Dumas, Emmanuel Collard

Porsche also provided the backbone to the new European Le Mans Series, the first two rounds of which were also rounds of the American Le Mans Series, either side of the Le Mans 24-Hours. Porsche's battle against the BMW M3 GTR V8 went in favour of Alex Job Racing at Donington, where Maassen and Luhr won the LM-GT class, but the BMW team turned the tables at Jarama with a convincing 1-2 victory

The BMWs were certainly controversial, since no more than three had been built and it was doubtful if they belonged in the "showroom" category, but they were colourful and crowd-appealing.

The five-race series continued when the Americans had returned home, and Robin Liddell and Mike Youles were able to take the LM-GT title in the PK Sport GT3 with a victory and a second place to their credit. Liddell's second place was at Donington Park, raising an invitation from Manfred Freisinger to join his Porsche team for a couple of races, sharing with Stephane Ortelli. Wolfgang Kaufmann had been displaced from the Freisinger team, but he soon joined forces with the Spaniard, Paco Orti, for the final rounds.

Romain Dumas and Xavier Pompidou drove the Freisinger Porsche to a lucky victory at Estoril, their engine failing. A full course caution enabled Pompidou to reach the flag just before the engine blew! Magnus Wallinder joined Peter Seikel's team at Estoril, sharing with Geoff Lister, but when the German team elected to miss Estoril, in favour of the ALMS race at Laguna Seca, Wallinder jointed former motorcycle champion Terry Rymer in the Harlow Motorsport Porsche.

Porsche re-established itself at the head of the FIA GT Championship's N-GT category in 2002 with a dominant performance against Ferrari, taking eight victories from 10 rounds. Stephane Ortelli won seven rounds in the Freisinger Motorsport Porsche GT3 RS, with a variety of factory supplied co-drivers including Sascha Maassen, Marc Lieb and Emmanuel Collard. Philipp Peter and Toto Wolff delivered the remaining victory for the Autorlando Porsche team, at Oschersleben, when Ortelli and Maassen were forced to retire with a broken wheel rim.

The season began badly for Ortelli. He and Ni Amorim won the opening round at Magny Cours, but their car was protested by the JMB Ferrari team and was found to have a slightly oversize fuel tank. JMB was then declared the winner, and again at Silverstone after Amorim put the Freisinger Porsche off the track.

FIA GT 2001: Steve O'Rourke, Tim Sugden

FIA GT 2001: Johnny Ceccoto, Philipp Peter

24 Hours Spa 2003: Andrea Chiesa, Alex Caffi, Gabrio Rosa, Luca Drudi

Winner 24 Hours Spa 2003: Stephane Ortelli, Romain Dumas, Marc Lieb

24 Hours Spa 2003 (l.-r.): Stephane Ortelli, Norbert Singer, Romain Dumas

FIA GT 2003: Mike Jordan, Mark Sumpter

FIA GT 2003: Walter Lechner Jr., Stephane Daoudi

nello-Concessionaires-Ferrari-Team aus England, das zwei Autos für Jamie Davies, Tim Mullen und Darren Turner einsetzte. Marc Lieb fuhr die ganze Saison zusammen mit Ortelli. Er kam zum Saisonauftakt nach Barcelona mit der rechten Hand im Gips. Die Ärzte erteilten ihm ein Startverbot, so dass Lieb zusammen mit Maassen fuhr. Letzterer kollidierte mit einem langsamen Fahrer und beschädigte den Kühler. So brachte er Lieb um die Chance, sich in der Meisterschaft einen Vorteil gegenüber Ortelli zu verschaffen. Ortelli und Lieb blieben in Enna ebenfalls punktlos, siegten dafür aber überzeugend in Brünn, Donington und Spa, wo es doppelte Punkte gab, sowie in Anderstorp.

Das 24 Stunden-Rennen von Spa war ein besonderer Sieg für Porsche, denn der Freisinger GT3 fuhr ein nahezu fehlerfreies Rennen mit Ortelli, Lieb und Dumas, vor den ehemals dominierenden Chrysler Viper und Ferrari 550 Maranello. Das belgische Rennen fand zum größten Teil im Regen statt, was den Porsche in der N-GT-Klasse einen kleinen Vorteil brachte, denn den Geschwindigkeitsnachteil gegenüber den schnelleren Autos gab es nicht mehr. Der Sieg wurde von Norbert Singer beobachtet, der seine Urlaubstage unterbrach. Der Porsche von Peter Seikel belegte mit Gabrio Rosa, Alex Caffi und Andrea Chiesa den dritten Rang.

JMB Racing und Maranello Concessionaires erwiesen sich in der Schlussphase der Saison als starke Konkurrenten für Freisinger. Das EMKA-Team von Steve O'Rourke belegte den vierten Platz in der Endwertung. RWS und das Team Eurotech teilten sich den fünften Rang in der Endwertung.

Die Saison 2004 zeigte ein eher mässig besetztes Starterfeld in der N-GT-Klasse. Das von Yukos gesponserte Freisinger-Team wurde auf drei Autos aufgestockt und hatte nur wenige Gegner.

In der LMES fuhren unterdessen die meisten N-GT-Teams. Es erwies sich für sie als einfacher, Sponsorgelder für vier 1000 km-Rennen aufzutreiben, als für die elf Rennen zur FIA GT-Meisterschaft, mit kostspieligen Veranstaltungen in Dubai und Zhuhai zum Saisonabschluss.

Stéphane Ortelli, der Meister der Jahren 2002 und 2003, fuhr zusammen mit Emmanuel Collard. Sascha Maassen und Lucas Luhr, die in dieser Serie zurückkehrten, teilten sich ebenfalls ein Auto, während der dritte 911 den Russen Alexei Vasiliev und Nikolai Fomenko anvertraut wurde. Weil man vier Werksfahrer einsetzte, wechselte das Freisinger-Team auf Michelin-Reifen.

Das neue Team von Gian Paolo Coppi setzte einen Ferrari 360 für Christian Pescatori ein. Er fuhr meistens zusammen mit Fabrizio de Simone. Als Team gewannen sie jedoch nur

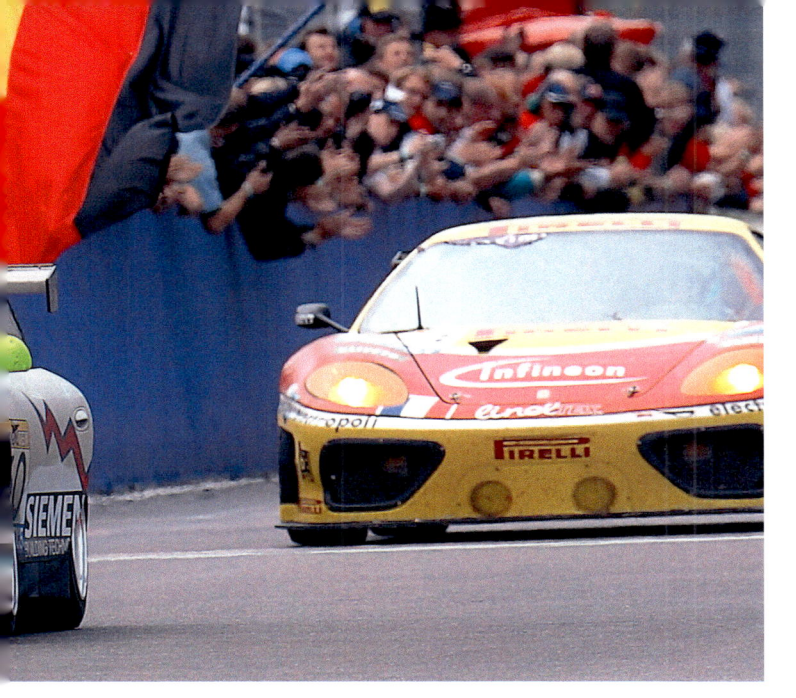

From nil points after two races, Ortelli and his professional co-drivers then won seven of the next eight, including the double points Spa 24-Hours when Romain Dumas joined him and Collard. They raced on Dunlop tyres, and at Estoril Ortelli lapped as much as five seconds a lap faster than all his opponents on a damp, drying track.

The Autorlando Porsche team finished third in the N-GT championship, Wolff sixth in the drivers championship and Peter 10th after missing two rounds (one when he was invited to drive a works Audi at Le Mans, and had a priority at the Trials which clashed with the Silverstone round). He was replaced at Silverstone by Johnny Mowlem, who claimed second position with Wolff, one of the Autorlando team's four podium positions.

Rudi Walch's RWS team defied the odds to finish fourth in the championship after a turbulent season. The Austrian started the season with Luca Riccitelli and Dieter Quester, but despite leading briefly at Silverstone the partnership ended in June, when Quester took his Red Bull sponsorship to a Ferrari GT team (something that he would soon regret).

Manfred Freisinger's GT3 team triumphed again in the FIA GT Championship N-GT category in 2003, against stronger competition not only from the JMB Racing Ferrari 360 of Fabrizio de Simone and Andrea Bertolini, but the two-car Maranello Concessionaires Ferrari team from Britain with Jamie Davies, Tim Mullen and Darren Turner.

Marc Lieb was paired with Ortelli for the full season, the strongest combination available, but again Ortelli started the season badly. He turned up at Barcelona, for the opening round, with a plaster cast on his right hand, having broken a bone while training. The medics would not allow him to drive, so Lieb drove with Maassen … who hit a back-marker and broke the radiator, depriving Lieb of the chance to make a head-start on Ortelli in the championship! Ortelli and Lieb also failed to score points at Enna, but they won convincingly at Brno, at Donington, at Spa where double points were scored, and at Anderstorp.

The Spa 24-Hours was a special triumph for Porsche since the Freisinger Motorsport GT3 had a near faultless race in the hands of Ortelli, Lieb and Romain Dumas, ahead of the once dominant Chrysler Vipers and Ferrari 550 Maranellos. The Belgian round was partly wet, which gave the N-GT Porsche a certain advantage (or rather, eliminated the speed advantage of the faster cars), and superior fuel consumption won the day in difficult circumstances. Their victory was master-minded by Ing. Norbert Singer, who takes vacation in strange ways.

Second, and well beaten at Spa, was a Care Racing Ferrari 550 Maranello driven by old friends of Porsche, Enzo Calderari and Lilian Bryner, and third overall was the excellent entry of Peter Seikel driven by Gabrio Rosa, Alex Caffi and Andrea Chiesa

JMB Racing and Maranello Concessionaires gave Freisinger Motorsport a good fight to the end of the championship, leaving Steve O'Rourke's EMKA Racing Porsche team in fourth place, and RWS Yukos and Team Eurotech tied in fifth place. Tim Sugden, driving for EMKA, sneaked into the driver championship in sixth place, thanks in part to his N-GT victory at Enna, with Martin Short.

The 2004 FIA GT Championship season, by contrast, was very poor indeed in the N-GT class, where Freisinger's Yukos sponsored team was expanded to three cars with little competition. The Maranello Concessionaires Ferrari team was not seen again, backer Sam Li switching his attention to the Audi Sport UK Team Veloqx R8s at Le Mans, and in the revived Le Mans Endurance Series.

It was the LMES that attracted most of the N-GT teams, often under-funded and finding it easier to raise sponsorship for four 1,000 kilometre races, in which they could run three paying drivers, than for the 11 rounds of the FIA GT Championship, which ended with 'fly away' rounds at Dubai and Zhuhai. Stephane Ortelli, champion in 2002 and 2003, drove with Emmanuel Collard, while homecomers Sascha Maassen and Lucas Luhr shared another, and Russians Alexei Vasiliev and Nikolai Fomenko the third. Freisinger's team switched to Michelin tyres as part of the deal for having four factory drivers, and the faltering Russian oil giant Yukos funded the whole effort, "money in the bank before the start of the season" as Freisinger confided.

Gian Paolo Coppi's new team ran the sole Ferrari 360 for Christian Pescatori, usually with Fabrizio de Simone, but they won only a single round together, at Hockenheim in May. Pescatori also won the 11th and final round at Zhuhai, China, with Jamie Melo.

Gerold and Christian Reid, two of the most faithful Porsche customers, supported the show with their Proton Competition 911 GT3 and were immediately rewarded with a podium position, third, in the opening round at Monza.

Luhr crashed over a kerb at Monza and broke a radiator, leaving Ortelli and Collard to claim the first victory of the season, but he and Maassen fought back to win the next three rounds, and finish second on two occasions, before the big event at Spa on July 31. Luhr again had an unfortunate 'off' which needed a long stop for a new front splitter, so Ortelli

FIA GT 2003: Gabriele Gardel, Bert Longin

GT3 DOMINATES 'SHOWROOM' CLASS **139**

ein Rennen in Hockenheim. Gerold und Christian Ried, zwei der treuesten Porsche-Kunden, verstärkten das Starterfeld im Proton Competition 911 GT3 und wurden auf Anhieb mit einem Podiumsplatz belohnt: Sie belegten beim Saisonauftakt in Monza die dritte Position.

Luhr fuhr in Monza über einen Randstein und beschädigte dabei den Kühler, so dass Ortelli und Collard den ersten Saisonsieg einfahren konnten. Luhr und Maassen gewannen aber die drei darauffolgenden Rennen und fuhren zweimal auf Rang zwei vor dem großen Rennen in Spa. Luhr hatte erneut einen unglücklichen Abflug und verlor viel Zeit, da ein neuer Frontsplitter montiert werden musste. So verschafften sich Ortelli und Collard einen Vorsprung in der Meisterschaft, nachdem sie zusammen mit Romain Dumas hinter zwei Ferrari Maranello auf Rang drei ins Ziel fuhren. Sie kassierten die maximale Punktzahl in der N-GT-Klasse, während die Freisinger-Porsche auch die Positionen vier und fünf im Gesamtklassement belegten. Vasiliev erreichte zusammen mit Timo Bernhard und Jörg Bergmeister den vierten Rang, Luhr wurde mit Maassen und Lieb Fünfter.

Nach dem neunten Saisonlauf in Oschersleben, wo Luhr und Maassen erneut Ortelli und Collard besiegten, war der Titelkampf nach wie vor sehr ausgeglichen. Ortelli und Collard hatten 82 Punkte, Maassen und Luhr 75,5 Punkte. Die FIA GT-Meisterschaft 2004 umfasste zum Schluss zwei Rennen ausserhalb Europas, in Dubai und Zhuhai. Das Rennen in den arabischen Emiraten fand auf einer völlig neuen Rennstrecke mitten in der Wüste statt. Bei extrem hohen Temperaturen belegten Maassen und Luhr den siebten Platz im Gesamtergebnis und gewannen die N-GT-Klasse, nur elf Sekunden vor Ortelli und Collard. Für Maassen und Luhr war es der sechste Klassensieg der Saison und sie verkürzten den Rückstand in der Meisterschaft auf 4,5 Punkten.

Ortelli brauchte seine Teamkollegen nicht schlagen um seinen dritten Titel in Folge nach Hause zu fahren. Er brauchte nur ins Ziel zu kommen. In China jedoch fehlte ihm jegliches Glück. Der Ferrari 360 von Pescatori und Melo lief gut und siegte in der N-GT-Klasse über Maassen und Luhr. Ortelli und Collard fielen zum ersten Mal in der Saison aus. Der Grund war ein defektes Getriebe. „Sascha und ich fahren schon vier Jahre zusammen, dies ist unser dritter gemeinsamer Titel", sagte Luhr zum Schluss. „Ich denke, das ist eine recht ordentliche Leistung." Die Partnerschaft war tatsächlich sehr erfolgreich: Drei Titel in Amerika und danach der Gewinn der FIA GT-Meisterschaft.

FIA GT 2004: Antonio de Castro, Renato Premoli, Bruno Barbaro

FIA GT 2004: Stephane Ortelli, Emmanuel Collard

Die Le Mans Endurance-Serie (LMES), eine gemeinsame Initiative des Automobile Club de l'Ouest und der SRO von Stéphane Ratel, umfasste lediglich vier klassische 1000 km-Rennen in Monza, auf dem Nürburgring, in Silverstone und in Spa. Die Serie war ein großer Erfolg mit vollen Starterfeldern und spannendem Rennsport. Freisinger Motorsport setzte einen Porsche ein. Es gab aber drei verschiedenen Sieger in der LM-GT-Klasse und der Titel ging an das Sebah-Team, das einen vier Jahre alten GT3 eingeschrieben hatte und kein einziges Rennen gewinnen konnte.

Stéphane Ortelli und Romain Dumas gewannen beim Saisonauftakt in Monza. Sie fuhren nur 50 Sekunden vor dem Ferrari 360 von Rusinoff, Daoudi und Melo ins Ziel. Platz drei ging an den Racers Group-Porsche von Patrick Long, Lars Eric Nielsen und Thorkild Thyrring, auf Platz vier fuhr der Sebah-Porsche von Bart Hayden und Piers Maserati ins Ziel. Der Cirtek-Porsche von Sascha Maassen und Adam Jones gewann auf dem Nürburgring die N-GT-Klasse. Der Vorsprung auf den Sebah-Porsche mit Xavier Pompidou und Marino Franchitti betrug drei Runden. Auf Rang drei diesmal der japanische Choroq-Porsche mit Kazuyuki Nishizawa, Haruki Kurosawa und Manabu Orido.

Der dritte Lauf fand in Silverstone statt und diesmal siegte der JMB-Ferrari. Pompidou und Maserati belegten im Sebah-Porsche erneut Rang zwei, während Long, Nielsen und Thyrring auf Platz drei ins Ziel fuhren in Nielsens Porsche, der diesmal von Farnbacher eingesetzt wurde.

Nach dem Sieg beim Saisonauftakt der LMES gewann Freisinger Motorsport auch das letzte Rennen. Ortelli und Collard siegten ohne Probleme, ihr Vorsprung auf Adam Jones und Maassen im Cirtek-Porsche betrug zwei Runden. Platz drei ging an Pompidou und Marc Lieb. Dieses Ergebnis brachte Sebah den Titel bei den Teams. Ferrari-Fahrer Rusinov gewann mit nur einem Punkt Vorsprung auf Ortelli den Titel in der Fahrerwertung.

Winner FIA GT 2004: Lucas Luhr, Sascha Maassen

and Collard forged ahead in the championship by finishing third overall, with Romain Dumas, behind a pair of Ferrari Maranellos. They scored top points in N-GT, with Freisinger's Porsches also claiming fourth and fifth positions overall, Vasiliev fourth with Timo Bernhard and Joerg Bergmeister, and Luhr fifth with Maassen and Lieb.

Mike Jordan's JWR (Jordan Warnock Racing) Porsche GT3 finished eighth, Jordan driving with twins David and Godfrey Jones, with the Proton Porsche ninth driven by two father-and-son pairings, Reid and Felbermayr.

With nine rounds completed at Oschersleben, and another victory for Maassen and Luhr over Ortelli and Collard, the championship was still finely balanced, Ortelli and Collard with 82 points, Massen and Luhr with 75.5 points, then Vasiliev on 45.

The 2004 FIA GT Championship season ended with two 'fly-away' events at Dubai and Zhuhai, the Middle East race on a completely new track built in barren desert. In extremely hot conditions, Maassen and Luhr finished in seventh place overall, winners of the N-GT category, just 11 seconds ahead of Ortelli and Collard. It was the sixth class victory of the season for Maassen and Luhr and narrowed the gap to 4.5 points. Ortelli did not need to beat his team-mates to win the title for the third year in succession, but he needed to finish safely, and his luck ran out in China. The Ferrari 360 of Pescatori and Melo raced well and won N-GT, beating Maassen and Luhr, while Ortelli and Collard posted their first retirement of the season with a broken gearbox. "Sascha and I have been driving together for four years, and this is our third title together" said Luhr at the end. "I think that this is a pretty good result."

Theirs has been an outstanding partnership, with three titles in America followed by the FIA GT Championship victory. Ortelli and Collard were runners-up in the championship, with Pescatori placed fifth on points, Yukos man Alexei Vasiliev sixth. Czech drivers Jan Vonka and Miro Konopka claimed the third podium position at Zhuhai in their Vonka Racing 911 GT3 RS, "not the fastest car" Konopka remarked, "but reliable."

LMES 2004: Xavier Pompidou, Marc Lieb

LMES 2004: Haruki Kurosowa, Kazuyuki Nishizawa

The Le Mans Endurance Series, a joint effort by the Automobile Club de l'Ouest and Stephane Ratel's SRO, comprised just four "classic" 1,000 kilometre races at Monza, the Nurburgring, Silverstone and Spa, and was judged a great success with full grids and exciting racing. Freisinger Motorsport supported the series with a single Porsche, back on Dunlop tyres, but there were three different winners in the LM-GT class and the 'title' went to the Sebah Automotive team, with a four-year-old GT3, which won none of them!

Stephane Ortelli and Romain Dumas won LM-GT in the opener, at Monza, finishing just 50 seconds ahead of the JMB Racing Ferrari 360 of Roman Rusinoff, Stephane Daoudi and Jaime Melo. Third was the Racers Group Porsche (Patrick Long, Lars Eric Nielsen and Thorkild Thyrring), fourth the Sebah Porsche of Bart Hayden and Piers Masarati, and fifth the Cirtek Porsche of Adam Jones and Sascha Maassen. That was an interesting mix, and it was the Cirtek Porsche of Jones and Maassen that won N-GT at the Nurburgring, a very strong effort in mostly wet conditions, finishing three laps ahead of the Sebah Porsche of Xavier Pompidou and Marino Franchitti. Third in class, this time, was the Japanese Choroq Racing Team Porsche of Kazuyuki Nishizawa, Haruki Kurosawa and Manabu Orido.

Ortelli and Collard did enough to win the LM-GT class at the Nurburgring, but due to a misunderstanding Collard entered the pit-lane before the chequered flag, and was the wrong side of the wall. It was an expensive mistake which took the Freisinger Porsche out of the classification.

The third round was at Silverstone and this time it was the JMB Ferrari's turn to win, Stephane Daoudi and Roman Rusinov sharing the five and a half hour drive, with Pompidou and Masarati again finishing second in the elderly Sebah Porsche, and Long, Nielsen and Thyrring third in Nielsen's Porsche, this time entered by Farnbacher. Collard and Ortelli could only manage fifth in class at Silverstone after having a power steering failure attended to.

Having won the first round of the LMES, Freisinger Motorsport then won the last as Ortelli and Collard cruised to a comfortable victory two laps ahead of Adam Jones and Maassen in the Cirtek Porsche. Third were Pompidou and Marc Lieb, a super line-up in the old GT3, a result that gave Sebah the teams title. Ferrari driver Rusinov claimed the drivers title by a single point from Ortelli, with Pompidou third.

LMES 2004: Tony Burgess, Philip Collin

LMES 2004: Adam Jones, Sascha Maassen

GT3 DOMINATES 'SHOWROOM' CLASS 141

Sieger fahr

1993 24h-Rennen Nürburgring

1994 Super-Cup

1996 24h-Rennen LeMans

1986 Paris – Dakar

1976 Markenweltmeisterschaft

1971 GT-Rennen

Ob Erstausrüstung, Motorsport, Tuning oder Serienersatz – BILSTEIN ist das Synonym für Spitzenqualität und Höchstleistung im Fahrwerkbau. Die Anforderungen unserer Kunden und das Engagement im Motorsport sind für BILSTEIN der Antrieb für Entwicklung und Innovation. Alle Mercedes-Benz Teams der DTM sowie viele andere Rennserien und mehr als die Hälfte aller Teams des 24h-Rennens auf dem Nürburgring nutzen die leistungsfähige BILSTEIN-Einrohrtechnologie.

en BILSTEIN.

996 Super-Cup

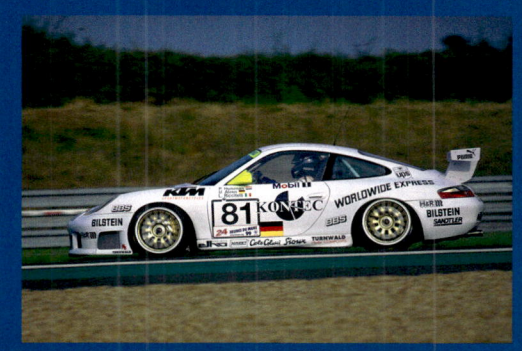

1999 24h-Rennen LeMans

2000 24h-Rennen LeMans

2000 Super-Cup

2003 24h-Rennen Nürburgring

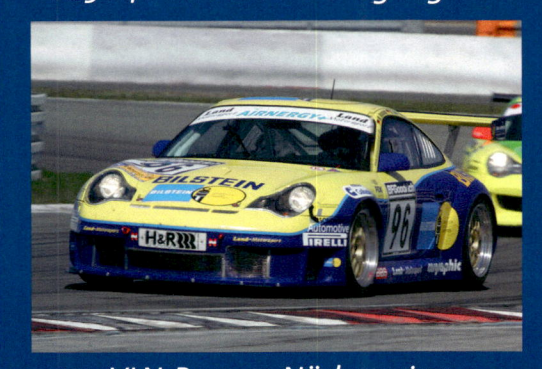

2005 VLN-Rennen Nürburgring

BILSTEIN – Fahrwerktechnik in Perfektion

+49 (0) 2333.791-4588
bilstein.de

BILSTEIN®
GASDRUCK STOSS DÄMPFER

DAS HEIMSPIEL FEST IM GRIFF

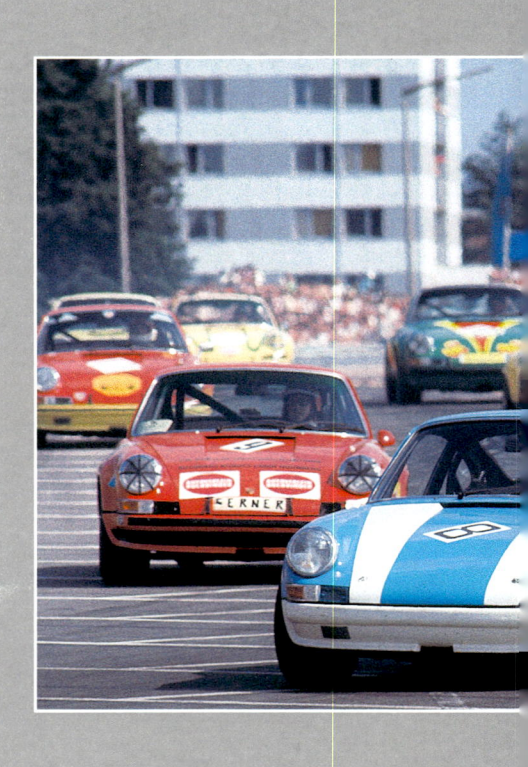

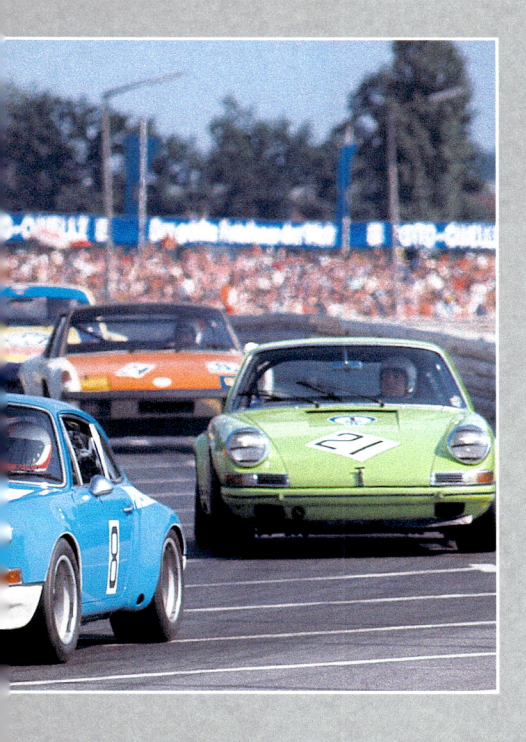

POPULAR ON HOME GROUND

Author: Gustav Büsing

Norisring 1966: GT winner Hans Kater

So wie der Modellwechsel im Hause Porsche vom 356 zum 911 einen fast nahtlosen Übergang bildete, so gelang auch die Stabübergabe im Rundstreckensport fast übergangslos. Nachdem zahlreichen Privatfahrern mit dem 356 schöne Erfolge gelungen waren, übte das Nachfolgemodell schon angesichts seiner Leistungsdaten einen besonderen Reiz aus. Bei einem Hubraum von 1991 ccm und mit einer Leistung von 130 PS bei 6.100 U/min übertraf der Neue in der Serienversion den zuletzt gebauten 356 C beim Hubvolumen um 25 Prozent und bei der Leistung gar um 40 Prozent. Das reichte für eine Geschwindigkeit von 211 km/h, die Beschleunigung von 0 auf 100 km/h dauerte 8,8 Sekunden. Vollgetankt betrug das Gewicht 1080 Kilogramm, woraus sich das Leistungsgewicht von 8,3 kg/PS errechnete – allesamt Werte, die sich auch 40 Jahre später noch sehen lassen können. Und es sollte auch nicht lange dabei bleiben.

Die ersten Rundstrecken-Elfer in Deutschland präsentierten sich außerordentlich brav. Zulassungsschilder waren normal, lediglich die entfernten Radkappen und die Startnummern auf Türen und Fronthaube machten ihre Rolle als Teilnehmer-Fahrzeuge deutlich. In der GT-Klasse bis 2000 ccm wiesen die Ergebnislisten von 1966 „Hans Kater" als den erfolgreichsten der 911-Rundstrecken-Piloten aus. Ob Rennstrecken Trier, Norisring oder die Flugplatzrennen in Mainz-Finthen und Wunstorf, stets siegte der Mann mit dem Pseudonym, meist vor dem Mainzer Carl Gregor Auer. Was da noch auf die Sportwelt zukommen sollte, ließ vor allem das Ergebnis am Norisring ahnen: Fünf 911-Piloten teilten sich die ersten fünf Ränge.

1967 setzte sich die Siegesserie ungebremst fort. Mit drei feinen, aber bedeutsamen Unterschieden: Es griffen jetzt auch prominentere Piloten ins 911-Lenkrad, wie zum Beispiel Jürgen Neuhaus oder Udo Schütz, die beim Flugplatzrennen in Mainz-Finthen die beiden obersten Stufen des Treppchens in der GT-Klasse bis 2000 ccm besetzten. Außerdem räumte der Elfer nun auch in der Tourenwagen-Klasse bis 2000 ccm die Pokale ab. Die Tourenwagen-Definition des Reglements, die sich der Innenraum-Abmessungen bediente, machte es möglich. Ein paar Zentimeter dünnere Rücksitzpolster ließen den Elfer so zu einem mehr als konkurrenzfähigen Tourenwagen werden, zum nicht geringen Verdruss der Konkurrenz. Klassensiege in Hockenheim, Mainz-Finthen, Avus, Nürburgring und Wunstorf zusätzlich zu den GT-Erfolgen füllten das Erfolgskonto der noch jungen Porsche-Kreation. Schließlich tauchten in den Ergebnislisten unter den Erfolgreichen am 911-Lenkrad Namen auf, die in den nächsten Jahrzehnten Rennsportgeschichte schreiben sollten: Erwin Kremer und Reinhold Joest, die beispielsweise in dieser Reihenfolge am 27. August 1967 Platz 1 und 2 beim Flugplatzrennen Mainz-Finthen bei den Tourenwagen über 1600 ccm belegten.

Der bedeutendste Erfolg der Saison 1967 gelang der Porsche-Mannschaft beim 84-Stunden-Rennen auf dem Nürburgring. Die Kombination von Nord- und Südschleife diente bei diesem Marathon als Ersatz für die traditionsreiche Rallye Lüttich-Sofia-Lüttich, die wegen zunehmender Verkehrsdichte nicht mehr durchgeführt werden konnte. Mit den erfahrenen Piloten Vic Elford, Jochen Neerpasch und Hans Herrmann holte Porsche den Gesamtsieg bei dieser materialmordenden Veranstaltung, die zeitweise von dichtem Nebel und kräftigem Regen begleitet wurde. Nur 13 der insgesamt 43 gestarteten Teams, die ihre Ruhepausen in Wohnwagen unmittelbar an der Gegengeraden verbrachten, erreichten das Ziel in Wertung. Der 210 PS starke Siegerwagen war mit der „Sportomatic" ausgerüstet, der Porsche mit diesem Einsatz zu größerer Popularität verhelfen wollte.

International Touring Car Race Trier 1966

Winner Marathon de la Route 1967: Vic Elford, Jochen Neerpasch, Hans Herrmann

Just as Porsche's model change from the 356 to the 911 was an almost seamless transition, the process in circuit racing also went smoothly. Following the many good results achieved by numerous privateer drivers with the 356, the successor model already looked attractive because of its performance figures. With an engine capacity of 1991 cc and an output of 130 hp at 6100 rpm, the production version of the 911 exceeded the capacity of the 356 C in its final guise by 25 percent and its output by as much as 40 percent. This was enough for a top speed of 211 km/h, and acceleration from 0-100 km/h took 8.8 seconds. With the fuel tank topped up, the car weighed in at 1080 kg, so the performance/-weight ratio was 8.3 hp/kg. All these were values that still would make quite a good impression 40 years later. And they weren't to remain at their initial level.

The first 911s used for circuit racing in Germany were extraordinarily tame. Licence plate were a common sight, only the removed wheel covers and the starting numbers on the doors and the front lid identified them as competition vehicles. In the GT-class up to 2000 cc, the result lists of the 1966 season show "Hans Kater" as the most successful 911-circuit racer. Both on street courses like Trier and the Norisring and at airfield tracks like Mainz-Finthen and Wunstorf, victory always went to the man with the pseudonym, usually ahead of Carl Gregor Auer from Mainz. The result at the Norisring especially gave a little hint of things still to come for the motorsport world: the first five places were taken by drivers with a Porsche 911.

In 1967, the winning streak went on. Three small, yet important differences: now, there were also quite well-known drivers competing with the 911, like Jürgen Neuhaus or Udo Schütz, who claimed the top two places in the GT-class up to 2000 cc in the airfield race in Mainz-Finthen. Moreover, the 911 also collected silverware in the touring car category up to 2000 cc. The touring car definition in the regulations, that used the interior dimensions of the car as the main criterion, allowed this. A somewhat thinner upholstery for the rear seat was used to turn the 911 into a highly competitive touring car. The opposition was anything but pleased.

Class wins at Hockenheim, Mainz-Finthen, Avus, Nürburgring and Wunstorf along with the successes achieved in the GT-class were added to the result list of the still young Porsche-creation. And finally, there were drivers competing with the 911 who would be writing racing history in the decades to come: Erwin Kremer and Reinhold Joest, who, as an example, occupied first and second places in this order in the over 1600 cc touring car category in the airfield race at Mainz-Finthen on August 27, 1967.

But the most significant success of the 1967 season was achieved by the Porsche works-team in the 84-hour race at the Nürburgring. At this marathon event, the combination of the Nord- and Südschleife (lap distance 28.2 kilometres) replaced the traditional rally Liege-Sofia-Liege, that could no longer be organised due to increasing traffic density. With experienced drivers Vic Elford, Jochen Neerpasch and Hans Herrmann, Porsche claimed the overall win in this machine-killing event that was, typically for the Eifel, partly held in thick fog and torrential rain. Only 13 of the 43 teams that had taken the start made it all the way through to be classified at the finish. Drivers could take their breaks in caravans that were parked at the back stretch. The 210 hp winning car featured "Sportomatic", a system that Porsche wanted to promote by virtue of this race.

At the end of 1967, Porsche produced a small series for customers based on the winning car of the Nürburgring. Baptised 911 R, with the R for Racing, this version was a

Trier 1966: GT winner Karl Gregor Auer

POPULAR ON HOME GROUND 147

Ende 1967 legte Porsche für seine Kunden auf der Basis des Siegerwagens vom Nürburgring eine Serie auf. Das 911 R getaufte Modell – das R stand für Racing – war ein auf dem Serien-Coupé aufgebauter Prototyp, der dank vieler Kunststoffteile und einer extremen Magerausstattung nur 830 Kilogramm wog. Angetrieben wurde das Leichtgewicht von einem Carrera 6-Motor der 210 PS leistete. Der 911 R war ausschließlich für den rennsportlichen Einsatz bestimmt und kostete in der Grundausstattung 45.000 Mark. Vielen Privatfahrern war das zu teuer. Sie blieben deshalb bei serienmäßigen oder leicht frisierten Serien-911, die als L/T-Modelle 130 PS (oft als Tourenwagen homologiert) und als S-Modell 160 PS leisteten. Vom 911 R wurden 19 Exemplare an Kunden verkauft, drei Autos blieben im Werk.

In der Deutschen Rundstrecken-Meisterschaft ging es zu wie immer: viele Klassen, großes Durcheinander und wenig Übersicht fürs interessierte Publikum. Porsche 911 beherrschten die Tourenwagen-Klasse bis 2 Liter Hubraum ebenso wie die GT-Klasse bis 2 Liter Hubraum. Für Unterhaltung war jedoch gesorgt, wie der Original-Bericht der „auto, motor und sport"-Ausgabe Nr. 20 von 1968 vom Flugplatzrennen in Ulm beweist: „Zum ereignisreichsten Rennen des Tages wurde der Lauf der Tourenwagen bis 2000 ccm. Die Porsche 911-Fahrer Stenzel, Kaiser, Dongus und Bayer lieferten sich einen harten Kampf. Stenzel und Dongus führten die Vierergruppe abwechselnd an, während Bayer sich drehte und zurückfiel. Auch dem schnellen Stuttgarter Kaiser unterlief ein Fehler, als er Stenzel ausbremsen wollte und dabei in der Wiese landete." Bei gleicher Gelegenheit ging der Sieg in der GT-Klasse an den Garmischer Ernst Kraus, jedoch erst nachdem Ferfried Prinz von Hohenzollern mit seinem 911 T wegen Frühstarts eine Strafminute gefangen hatte.

1000 km Nürburgring 1969: Reinhardt Stenzel, Erwin Kremer

1000 km Nürburgring 1968: Hans-Dieter Blatzheim, Alan Hamilton

1000 km Nürburgring 1968: Jean-Claude Killy, Jean Guichet

Absolutes Highlight der Tourenwagen-Rennen in Deutschland war alljährlich das 6-Stunden-Rennen auf dem Nürburgring, der „Große Preis der Tourenwagen." Obwohl hier auch eine Menge Prestige im Spiel war, konzentrierte sich Porsche auf die Sportwagen-Rennen und überließ den Kunden das Feld gegen die Armada der Werkswagen von BMW, Ford und Alfa. 1968 erwiesen sich die Werks-2002, gefahren von Hahne/Quester und Quester/Ahrens als zu stark für die 911-Armada. Immerhin gelang dem Duo Gunnarsson/Rothfeld mit ihrem 911 ein hervorragender dritter Rang vor den Markenkollegen Fröhlich und Pon, die nur wenige Sekunden dahinter und auch noch in der selben Runde wie die Sieger einliefen. Eine prominente Besatzung errang den sechsten Platz: Kremer und Kauhsen, und auf Rang 8 wurde das Duo Klocke und Braun geführt. Die schnellste Runde fuhr Helmut Kelleners auf seinem 911 mit 9.36,6 Minuten.

1969 gelang den Porsche-Piloten der begehrte Sieg: Das Duo Hezemans und van Lennep gewann das Gesamtklassement mit einem vom Holländer Ben Pon vorbereiteten 911, dem 235 PS nachgesagt wurden. In ihrer Klasse belegten Kremer und Gall den dritten Rang. Zum Favoritenkreis hatte auch Rolf Stommelen gezählt, der mit einem 911 unterwegs war, der 1967 noch mit dem Freiherrn von Wendt am Steuer den Tourenwagen-Europapokal gewonnen hatte. Als Handikap galt in den Augen der Berichterstatter jedoch Fahrzeug-Besitzer Georg Loos, der sich mit Stommelen das Lenkrad teilte und als zu langsam galt, um den Porsche-Werksfahrer erfolgversprechend unterstützen zu können. Die Sache hatte sich allerdings erledigt, als Stommelen in der 14. Runde im schnellen Bergaufstück vom Kesselchen zum Karussell beim Überrunden eines Fiat 124 von der Piste gedrängt wurde, einen respektablen Baum fällte und sich mehrfach überschlug – zum Glück ohne Verletzungen davonzutragen.

DAS HEIMSPIEL FEST IM GRIFF

prototype built from the coupé production car with a weight of only 830 kg, a result of the use of many plastic parts. The light-weight vehicle was powered by a 210 hp Carrera 6-engine. The 911 R was exclusively meant for competition purposes and was sold at 45,000 DM in its basic version. For many customers, this was too expensive. Therefore, they remained loyal to their standard or slightly modified 911 production cars with an output of 130 hp for the L/T-models (often homologated as touring cars) and 160 hp for the S-models. Of the 911 R, 19 cars were sold to customers, three remained in the factory.

In the German circuit racing championship, the situation was as ever: many classes, much confusion and no overview for spectators. Porsche 911s dominated in the touring car category up to 2 litres, just as they did in the GT-class up to 2 litres. There was plenty of entertainment, though, as reported in "auto, motor und sport" nr. 20 of 1968 about the airfield race in Ulm: "The race for touring cars up to 2000 cc was the most eventful race of the day. The Porsche 911-drivers Stenzel, Kaiser, Dongus and Bayer had a fierce battle. Stenzel and Dongus alternated in the lead of the group of four, while Bayer spun and dropped back. Fast driver Kaiser from Stuttgart also made a mistake while attempting to outbrake Reinhard Stenzel, after which he landed in the grass." At the same event, victory in the GT-class went to Ernst Kraus from Garmisch, but only after Ferfried Prinz von Hohenzollern had been given a one minute time penalty for jumping the start with his 911 T.

The annual highlight in German touring car racing undisputedly was the six-hour race at the Nürburgring, the "Großer Preis der Tourenwagen". Although there was a lot of prestige at stake here as well, Porsche concentrated on sports car racing and left it to its customers to take up the battle against the armada of works-cars entered by BMW, Ford and Alfa. In 1968, the works-2002s, driven by Hahne/Quester and Quester/Ahrens, turned out to be too strong for the 911s. Still, the Gunnarsson/Rothfeld-pairing scored a fine third place with their 911 ahead of fellow-Porsche-drivers Fröhlich/Pon, who made it to the finish only a few seconds down and still on the same lap as the winners. Two well-known drivers occupied sixth place: Kremer/Kauhsen, with Klocke/Braun in eighth position. The fastest lap time was set by Helmut Kelleners with his 911 in 9.36.6 minutes.

In 1969, Porsche-drivers claimed the coveted victory: the duo Hezemans/van Lennep won the race with a 911, prepared by Dutchman Ben Pon. Reportedly, its engine had an output of 235 hp. Kremer/Gall finished third in class. Driving a 911, Rolf Stommelen had also been one of the favourites, having won the Europa Cup for touring cars together with Freiherr von Wendt in 1967. But, according to reporters, his handicap was car owner Georg Loos, who shared driving duties with Stommelen and was considered too slow to be an adequate team-mate for the Porsche works-driver. But this didn't matter anyway, as Stommelen was pushed off the track on lap 14 while trying to overtake a Fiat 124 in the fast uphill-section from Kesselchen to the Karussell. He knocked-down a massive tree and barrel-rolled his car several times, but luckily walked away unscathed.

From 1970 onwards, it was over with the confusion about the 911 as both a touring car and a GT car. Now, the Porsche 911 fitted either in the GT class up to 2 litres (older cars) or above 2 litres (911 S from 1969 onwards, delivering 180 hp in its standard production version). The variety of classes in the German circuit racing championship with a total of eleven capacity-based categories for touring cars and GT cars and a complicated points scoring system was confusing enough in itself.

Among the Porsche-drivers in the smaller category, top positions were usually being taken by Leopold Prinz von Bayern. Now, he had to cope more and more with internal opposition from various Porsche 914/6s. Georg Loos from Cologne was another race winner who would be writing Porsche racing history in years to come.

With the 2.2 litre 911 S, heavyweight Dieter Fröhlich, driving the yellow Chiquita-Porsche, and Clemens Schickentanz from Willich usually dominated proceedings in their class. Sometimes, they had to take on American muscle cars with engine capacities of up to 7 litres (!), that had the upper hand over the Porsches as far as engine power was concerned, but failed to match the cars from Zuffenhausen when it came to road-holding and reliability.

International Solitude Race 1969: Hans-Dieter Weigel

Deutsche Rennsport Meisterschaft Hockenheim 1970

Ab 1970 war es vorbei mit dem Durcheinander von Elfern als Tourenwagen und GT-Fahrzeug. Der Porsche 911 gehörte nun entweder in die GT-Klasse bis 2 Liter Hubraum (ältere Modelle) oder über 2 Liter Hubraum (911 S ab Modelljahr 1969, der serienmäßig mit 180 PS ausgeliefert wurde). Dafür war die Klassenvielfalt in der Deutschen Rundstrecken-Meisterschaft mit insgesamt elf Hubraumklassen für Tourenwagen und GT und einer komplizierten Punktwertung immer noch verwirrend genug.

Bei den „Porsche-Tretern" der kleineren Hubraumklasse war es zumeist Leopold Prinz von Bayern, der sich die Spitzen-Platzierungen sichern konnte. Er hatte es jetzt vermehrt mit hausgemachter Konkurrenz in Form von einigen Porsche 914/6 zu tun. In den Siegerlisten fand sich mit Georg Loos aus Köln ein weiterer Name, der später noch Porsche-Rennsportgeschichte schreiben sollte.

Mit dem 2,2 Liter-911 S beherrschten Dieter Fröhlich aus Essen mit seinem gelben Chiquita-Porsche und Clemens Schickentanz aus Willich normalerweise ihre Klasse. Sie mussten sich gelegentlich auch mit einigen amerikanischen Exoten mit bis zu 7 Liter Hubraum auseinander setzen, die den Elfern in Sachen Motorleistung zwar klar überlegen waren, aber in Sachen Straßenlage und Zuverlässigkeit nicht an das Zuffenhausener Produkt heranreichten.

Für die zahlreichen Privatfahrer hatte sich das Werk etwas Neues ausgedacht: An die Stelle der bisher üblichen Rabatte auf Ersatzteile trat 1970 erstmals der bis heute existierende "Porsche-Cup". Punktberechtigt war jeder Fahrer, der national oder international mit einem Porsche in Wettbewerben startete, nicht gewertet wurden allerdings Werkseinsätze. Außerdem wurden die jeweiligen Meisterschaften nach ihrer sportlichen Bedeutung gewichtet. 1970 betrug die Gesamtpreissumme 200.000 Mark, wobei an den Erstplatzierten allein 50.000 Mark gingen. Erster Porsche-Cup-Gewinner wurde Gijs van Lennep.

In der Saison 1971 änderte sich an den Gegebenheiten in der deutschen Rundstrecken-Szene nur wenig. Während zwischen Alfa, BMW und Ford in den Meisterschaftsverdächtigen Tourenwagen-Klassen auf der Strecke wie auch am grünen Tisch die Fetzen flogen, änderten sich in den für Porsche-Fahrer interessanten GT-Klassen eigentlich nur die Namen der erfolgreichen Piloten. Helmut Hinse und Eckart Gutowski hielten die 911-Fahnen in der Klasse bis 2 Liter Hubraum hoch, was gegen die starken Porsche 914/6 zunehmend schwieriger wurde. In der Klasse über 2 Liter Hubraum fehlte Dieter Fröhlich, der auf einen Opel Commodore umgestiegen war. Neben Clemens Schickentanz gaben jetzt Frank Gerlach und Helmut Henzler den Ton an.

Weil mangels eines Seriensiegers gegen die meist werksunterstützte Tourenwagen-Armada ein Gesamtsieg in der Meisterschaft so gut wie ausgeschlossen war, betätigten sich viele 911-Piloten lieber in den attraktiveren internationalen GT-Rennen. So holte der Kölner Porsche-Tuner Erwin Kremer mit GT-Siegen in Monza, Spa, Nürburgring, Paris, Barcelona und Jarama den Porsche-Cup 1971. Er verfügte über zwei bestens präparierte 911 S sowie einen 914/6, einen Etat von mehr als 100.000 Mark und sechs seiner insgesamt zwölf Angestellten für den Service. Für Kremer dennoch eine sinnvolle Investition, weil jeder Erfolg Werbung für seinen Tuning-Betrieb bedeutete. Von den in der Deutschen Rundstrecken-Meisterschaft Aktiven schaffte es niemand auf einen der prämienberechtigten 22 Ränge der Abschlusswertung des weiterhin hochdotierten Porsche-Cups.

Mit der Saison 1972 änderte sich der Rundstreckensport in Deutschland ganz gewaltig. Die schon lange beklagte Klassen- und Hubraumvielfalt der Deutschen Rundstrecken-Meisterschaft war plötzlich Vergangenheit. Drei Männer standen hinter diesem Wandel: Hugo Emde, Chef des Motorsportdienstes von Bilstein, Jochen Neerpasch, damals Ford-Rennleiter, und Fritz Jüttner, Leiter des Bosch Motorsportdienstes. Ihr Vorschlag war ebenso einfach wie genial: Die Deutsche Rennsport-Meisterschaft, so der Name, sollte nur noch in zwei Divisionen (bis und über zwei Liter Hubraum) ausgetragen werden. Die Punktvergabe sollte nach dem CanAm-System (20-15-12-10-8-6-4-3-2-1 Punkte pro Division) erfolgen. Rennsportmeister sollte der Fahrer mit den meisten Punkten werden. Es gab also 1972 nur noch zwei Rennen für Spezial-Tourenwagen der Gruppe 2 und Serien-GT der Gruppe 3. Einbezogen waren 1972 noch zwei Berg-

Hockenheim 1972: Günther Steckkönig

GT Race Norisring 1971

150 DAS HEIMSPIEL FEST IM GRIFF

For the numerous privateer drivers, the factory had come up with something new: instead of the usual discount on spare parts, the Porsche Cup was founded in 1970 for the first time and has survived to date. Every driver competing with a Porsche at national or international level was eligible to score points, but factory-backed efforts weren't being considered. Moreover, there was a rating system for the various championships, depending on the level of competition. In 1970, the prize fund included a total of 200,000 DM, with 50,000 DM at stake for the overall winner. Gijs van Lennep became the inaugural Porsche Cup winner.

For the 1971 season, there were only few changes in German circuit racing. Alfa, BMW and Ford battled it out for touring car honours, both at the track and at the green table. Meanwhile, in the GT categories that were relevant for Porsche-drivers, only the names of the successful drivers changed. Helmut Hinse and Eckart Gutowski were the top 911-drivers in the class of up to 2 litres, which became more and more difficult against the strong 914/6s. In the class above 2 litres, Dieter Fröhlich was missing, having switched to an Opel Commodore. Next to Schickentanz, Frank Gerlach and Helmut Henzler were now the fastest 911-drivers.

Because none of the drivers stood out, winning the title against the mostly works-supported touring car armada was nigh impossible. Therefore, many 911-drivers preferred to compete in the more attractive international GT-races. For instance, Cologne-based Porsche-tuner Erwin Kremer claimed the Porsche Cup in 1971 with GT race wins at Monza, Spa, Nürburgring, Montlhery, Barcelona and Jarama. He had two well-prepared 911 Ss and a 914/6, a budget of over 100,000 DM and six of his twelve employees on duty in the service crew. For Kremer, the investment paid out nonetheless, because every success was promotion for his tuning company. From the drivers competing in the German circuit racing championship, no one managed to finish among the first 22 drivers in the well-funded Porsche Cup, who were entitled to a share of the prize money.

For the 1972 season, circuit racing in Germany would see dramatic changes. The variety of categories and engine capacities of the German circuit racing championship, criticised by many, was abandoned. Three men were responsible for this turnaround: Hugo Emde, boss of Bilstein's racing service, Jochen Neerpasch, at the time Ford's motorsport director, and Fritz Jüttner, head of Bosch's racing service. Their

Hockenheim 1972: Eberhard Sindel (29), Wolfgang Siegle (52)

proposal was both simple and ingenious: the German racing championship (Deutsche Rennsport Meisterschaft) would only have two categories, under and above 2 litres. The points scheme would be the same as in Can-Am (20-15-12-10-8-6-4-3-2-1 points for each category), with the title of Rennsportmeister (racing champion) awarded to the driver with the most points at the end of the season. As a result, in 1972, every event had just two races for special touring cars of Group 2 and production GT cars of Group 3. The Nürburgring 1000 km, the "Großer Preis der Tourenwagen" at the Eifel-circuit (6-hour race) and the Nürburgring 500 km were counted as additional races with double points at stake.

The calendar of the 1972 season also included two hill-climbs. The Division 1, the only category that was of interest for Porsche, attracted a total of 13 competitors for the season opener, the Eifelrennen at the Nürburgring, with only two 911 Ss. While Dieter Fröhlich, third in qualifying, retired following an accident right after the start, Franz-Josef Rieder scored the first two points for Porsche by finishing ninth. The works Ford Capris set the pace in the class (among others with eventual champion Hans-Joachim Stuck). Porsche failed to score one race win throughout the season. The 911 S 2.5s with slightly enlarged 2.4 litre engines and 270 hp just weren't powerful enough. Jürgen Barth, who scored the first podium of the season by finishing third at Hockenheim in August, still did fairly well with his seventh place in the season's final standings, having racked up 71 points.

The huge popularity of the series made things go forward at Porsche for 1973. The new Carrera RSR, a Porsche 911 that weighed a little more than 900 kg and had an output of 300 hp, finally allowed Porsche-drivers to battle it out for top positions in the Division 1 against the Ford Capris and the BMW 3.0 CSLs. Podium places for Clemens Schickentanz and Günther Steckkönig at the Nürburgring and Mainz-Finthen already gave a hint of things to come soon. At the airfield race of Diepholz on July 15, 1973, Rolf Stommelen brought Porsche its maiden victory in the German racing championship, with a range of more victories still to come. Clemens Schickentanz and Günther Steckkönig kept their title hopes alive until well into the month of August, but their respective hopes were destroyed by engine and gearbox failures at Kassel-Calden and the Norisring.

At the Sauerland hill-climb, Reinhardt Stenzel and Swiss Paul Keller claimed a double victory for Porsche with their Carreras, but the title of German racing champion went to Dieter Glemser with his Ford Escort from the so-called small division. The fact that team principal Erich Zakowski had brought an original sauna to the Sauerland in order to heat up the tyres for his racing cars was an indication of how professional the series had become. The best-placed Porsche

POPULAR ON HOME GROUND 151

rennen und als Zusatzrennen mit doppelter Punktzahl wurden die 1000-Kilometer Nürburgring, der Große Preis der Tourenwagen auf dem Eifelkurs (6-Stunden-Rennen) und die 500 Kilometer Nürburgring gewertet.

Die für Porsche allein interessante Division 1 startete bei der Premiere, dem Eifelrennen am Nürburgring, mit insgesamt 13 Teilnehmern, darunter nur zwei 911 S. Während der Trainingsdritte, Dieter Fröhlich, gleich zu Beginn durch Unfall ausschied, holte Franz-Josef Rieder mit Rang neun die ersten zwei Punkte für Porsche. Den Ton in der Division gaben die Werks-Ford Capri (u.a. mit dem späteren Meister Hans-Joachim Stuck) an, einen Porsche-Sieg gab es das ganze Jahr nicht. Dafür waren die 911 S 2.5 mit leicht aufgebohrtem 2,4-Liter-Motor und 270 PS nicht leistungsstark genug. Mit Jürgen Barth, der im August in Hockenheim mit Rang drei die erste Podiums-Platzierung holte, schnitt aber ein Porsche-Pilot mit insgesamt 71 Punkten auf Gesamtrang sieben sehr achtbar ab.

Die große Popularität der Deutschen-Meisterschaft sorgte es 1973 auch bei Porsche für richtig Schub. Mit dem neuen Carrera RSR, ein gut 900 Kilo schwerer und 300 PS starker Porsche 911, konnten nun auch die Porsche-Piloten den Kampf um Spitzenplatzierungen gegen die Ford Capri und BMW 3.0 CSL in der Division 1 aufnehmen.

Podestplätze für Clemens Schickentanz und Günther Steckkönig am Nürburgring und in Mainz-Finthen ließen schon erkennen, was bald darauf folgen sollte. Beim Flugplatzrennen in Diepholz am 15. Juli 1973 sorgte Rolf Stommelen für den ersten Porsche-Sieg in der Deutschen Rennsport-Meisterschaft, dem noch eine ganze Reihe weiterer Erfolge folgen sollten. Bis in den August hinein hatten Schickentanz und Günther Steckkönig noch intakte Meisterschaftschancen, ehe ein Motor- bzw Getriebeschaden in Kassel-Calden bzw. am Norisring, den Hoffnungen ein Ende machte.

Beim Sauerland-Bergpreis gelang Reinhardt Stenzel und dem Schweizer Paul Keller mit ihren Carrera ein Porsche-Doppelsieg, den Titel des Deutschen Rennsportmeisters aber holte sich Dieter Glemser mit seinem Ford Escort aus der sogenannten "kleinen" Division. Wie professionell die Serie inzwischen geworden war, illustrierte wohl am besten die Tatsache, dass Teamchef Erich Zakowski für seine Renner zum Aufheizen der Reifen eine Original-Sauna mit ins Sauerland gebracht hatte. Für die Porsche-Piloten – Günther Steckkönig und Clemens Schickentanz – blieben mit 99 bzw. 91 Punkten die Platzierungen fünf und sechs in der Gesamtwertung, doch war der Abstand zum Titelträger mit 31 bzw. 39 Punkten nicht mehr so schrecklich groß wie noch 1972, als der Rückstand noch volle 130 Punkte betrug.

Deutsche Rennsport Meisterschaft 1973: Paul Keller

Die Popularität der Deutschen Rennsport-Meisterschaft sorgte in der Saison 1974 für vollbesetzte Starterfelder und spannende Zweikämpfe. So traten in der Division 1 meist 25 Piloten an, beim Rennen um den Großen Preis von Europa (zugleich GT-Europameisterschaft) auf dem Nürburgring waren es sogar rekordverdächtige 33 Starter. Aber trotz zahlreicher Porsche Carrera im Feld dominierte die Zuffenhausener Marke in diesem Jahr keineswegs. Weil die Meisterschaft so populär war, schickte Ford zwei Werks-Capris mit Spitzenfahrern wie Rolf Stommelen und Toine Hezemans (obwohl als Niederländer nicht punktberechtigt) ins Gefecht. Sie konnten sich bei ihrem Unternehmen Titelgewinn auf einen neuen 400 PS starken Cosworth-Motor stützen. Schützenhilfe sollte Klaus Ludwig leisten, der mit einem Capri von Ford-Tuner Grab antrat.

BMW konterte sporadisch mit den 3,5 CSL-Coupés und Hans-Joachim Stuck oder auch Niki Lauda am Steuer. Für die privaten Porsche-Piloten wie Reinhardt Stenzel (Max Moritz Team) oder Hans Heyer und Clemens Schichentanz (Porsche Kremer) hingen die Trauben unter diesen Umständen meist zu hoch.

Beim Saisonauftakt, dem traditionellen Eifelrennen, musste Stenzel, der überraschend die zweitschnellste Trainingszeit markiert hatte, aufgrund einer gebrochenen Sitzhalterung in der dritten Runde aufgeben. Die Werks-Capris und Werner Schommers im BMW Coupé von Faltz ließen den übrigen Carrera keine Chance auf Spitzenplätze. In Abwesenheit der Werks-Autos holte sich Stenzel in Mainz-Finthen dafür den verdienten Sieg. Viel Aufregung gab es beim Rheinpokal-Rennen in Hockenheim, wo Stommelen klarer Favorit war. Doch Zündaussetzer bremsten den Kölner ein, so dass Hans Heyer die Spitze übernehmen konnte. Die Show lieferte jedoch Stenzel, der mit Intermediates auf abtrocknender Strecke alle in Grund und Boden fuhr. Wegen Frühstarts bekam er jedoch anschließend eine Strafminute aufgebrummt und fiel auf Rang drei hinter Heyer und Stommelen zurück. In Diepholz waren wieder die großen Namen am Start: BMW schickte Stuck, Ford setzte auf Stommelen. Für Kremer griff John Fitzpatrick ins Lenkrad, während Schickentanz zu Loos wechselte. Doch Stuck war nicht zu schlagen, auf den Plätzen liefen Fitzpatrick, Stommelen und Heyer ein. Beim vierten Lauf auf dem Nürburgring war auch die internationale GT-Elite am Start, Regen an einigen Abschnitten der Strecke machte das Rennen zum Poker. Das nutzten die Ring-Spezialisten Stommelen und Ludwig zum Ford-Doppelsieg vor den Carrera-Piloten Paul Keller (CH) und Stenzel. Mit Blick auf den Punktestand sorgte die Ford-Stallregie in Hockenheim dann für den umgekehrten Einlauf an der Spitze. Hans Heyer musste sich mit dem dritten Rang begnügen. Am Norisring machten die prominenten Gaststarter die Sache unter sich aus: Stuck siegte vor Hezemans. Erst

Deutsche Rennsport Meisterschaft 1972: John Fitzpatrick

152 DAS HEIMSPIEL FEST IM GRIFF

Deutsche Rennsport Meisterschaft: Clemens Schickentanz

drivers, Günther Steckkönig and Clemens Schickentanz, were classified fifth and sixth in the final championship standings with 99 and 91 points respectively. But with a gap of 31 and 39 points for the two of them, they were not so far behind as the year before, when they were 130 points down on the champion.

In 1974, the popularity of the German racing championship (DRM) attracted huge grids and provided exciting battles. For instance, the Division 1 usually had 25 competitors and during the race for the European Grand Prix (also counting towards the European GT championship) at the Nürburgring, there were 33 participants, probably a record. But in spite of having numerous Porsche Carreras in the field, the brand from Zuffenhausen didn't dominate proceedings in this year. Given the popularity of the championship, Ford entered two works-Capris with top drivers like Stommelen and Hezemans, although the latter wasn't eligible to score points as he was Dutch. In their fight for the title, they could rely on a new 400 hp Cosworth engine. Ludwig, who drove a Capri entered by Ford-Grab, would provide additional support.

BMW struck back only sporadically with its 3.5 CSL coupes, driven by the likes of Hans-Joachim Stuck and Niki Lauda. Privateer Porsche-drivers like Reinhardt Stenzel (Max Moritz Team) or Hans Heyer and Clemens Schickentanz (Porsche Kremer), usually couldn't play a role of any significance in these conditions.

During the season opener, the traditional Eifelrennen, Stenzel had to retire on the third lap after the mounting of his seat had broken. He had been a surprising second in qualifying. The works Capris and Werner Schommers with the Faltz-BMW Coupé didn't leave the remaining Carreras any hope for a top result. In absence of the works-cars, Stenzel then scored a well-deserved win at Mainz-Finthen. The Rheinpokal-Rennen at Hockenheim, where Stommelen was the clear favourite, caused a lot of controversy. Misfires slowed down the driver from Cologne, so that Hans Heyer was able to take the lead. However, it was Stenzel who put on the best show, outpacing everyone else with intermediates on a drying track. After the race however, he got a one minute's time penalty for jumping the start and was relegated to third behind Heyer and Stommelen. At Diepholz, the big shots were back again: BMW entered Stuck, Ford relied on Stommelen. John Fitzpatrick was signed to drive for Kremer, while Schickentanz switched to Loos. But nobody could stop Stuck, who beat Fitzpatrick, Stommelen and Heyer. Leading international GT drivers joined in the action for the fourth round at the Nürburgring, where rain at some sections of the track turned the race into a lottery. Ring-specialists Stommelen and Ludwig benefited and secured themselves a double victory for Ford, ahead of Carrera-drivers Paul Keller (CH) and Stenzel. Bearing the championship points in mind, Ford team orders led to a reversed order out in front at Hockenheim, while Hans Heyer had to make do with third place. At the Norisring, the famous guest drivers battled it out for victory: Stuck won from Hezemans and the three Porsche drivers Herbert Müller (CH), Heyer and Stommelen could only finish behind these two. During the season final at Hockenheim, the focus was on the battle for the title between Glemser and Obermoser in the small division. Reinhardt Stenzel's fantastic performance was put a little bit in the shadow: on a rain-soaked track, he defeated Klaus Ludwig and his Capri and scored a fine win.

Thus, Stenzel had two victories to his tally (Mainz-Finthen and Hockenheim), but in the final standings, his 66 points only brought him sixth place, because he also had three retirements. Hans Heyer scored points more consistently and, as a result, he was the best-placed Porsche-driver in fifth place with 87 points. At the Rheinpokal-Rennen at Hockenheim, he had won one race, too.

For the 1975 season, the works teams in the German racing championship reduced their efforts a little bit. Ford sold an ex-works-Capri to Werner Schommers at a friendly price and BMW supported the Schnitzer and Faltz-teams, each of then running a 3.5 litre CSL Coupé for Albrecht Krebs and Harald Grohs respectively. Porsche was again represented by customer teams, Kremer with Helmut Kelleners, Loos with John Fitzpatrick, Max Moritz with Reinhardt Stenzel, and Tebernum with Clemens Schickentanz. The 1975-spec Carreras had an output of circa 345 hp, but at least they were able to make up for some of their lack of power against the BMWs by means of a weight advantage of 145 kg.

Fitzpatrick set the fastest time in qualifying for the season opener at the Eifelrennen, but he retired with a broken gearlever in the race. Newcomer Harald Grohs took the chance and went on to win from Porsche drivers Clemens Schickentanz and Reinhardt Stenzel. The second round at Hockenheim saw the BMW Coupés and the Capri dominate proceedings out in front. After an exciting race, Krebs won ahead of Schommers, followed by the three Carreras of Kelleners, Stenzel and Bertrams. In the airfield race at Mainz-Finthen, the Porsche Carreras set the pace, rather than the BMWs, that had been considered as the favourites. Reinhard Stenzel made the most out of his fastest qualifying time and led from lights to flag, scoring a never challenged victory. Helmut Kelleners secured himself second place after Albrecht Krebs had spun. At the Norisring, the huge prize money of over 100,000 Deutschmarks also attracted the works-teams: the battle was Stuck (BMW) against Mass (Ford), much to the excitement of the spectators. Only after Stuck had retired

Nürburgring 1974: Herbert Müller (5), Reinhard Stenzel (19)

Deutsche Rennsport Meisterschaft 1975: Helmut Kelleners

dann folgten die drei Porsche-Fahrer Herbert Müller (CH), Heyer und Stommelen. Beim Finale in Hockenheim konzentrierte sich der ganze Rummel auf den Titelkampf zwischen Glemser und Obermoser in der kleinen Division. Dadurch ging die fantastische Leistung von Reinhardt Stenzel ein wenig unter, der auf regennasser Bahn Klaus Ludwig und seinen Capri niederrang und einen schönen Erfolg feierte.
Damit konnte sich Stenzel insgesamt zwei Laufsiege sichern (Mainz-Finthen und Hockenheim), doch reichte das in der Endabrechnung mit 66 Punkten „nur" zum sechsten Meisterschaftsrang, weil drei Ausfälle einfach nicht zu kompensieren waren. Ein konstanterer Punktesammler war Hans Heyer, der in der Endtabelle der Meisterschaft dann auch als bestplatzierter Porsche-Fahrer mit 87 Punkten den fünften Rang belegte und beim Rheinpokal-Rennen in Hockenheim auch einen Laufsieg feiern konnte.
In der Saison 1975 traten die Werksteams in der Deutschen Rennsportmeisterschaft etwas kürzer. Ford hatte Werner Schommers einen Ex-Werks-Capri zum Freundschaftspreis überlassen. BMW unterstützte die Teams von Schnitzer und Faltz, die jeweils ein bis zu 480 PS starkes 3,5-Liter CSL-Coupé für Albrecht Krebs beziehungsweise Harald Grohs einsetzten. Porsche war wiederum durch die Kundenteams Kremer mit Helmut Kelleners, Loos mit John Fitzpatrick, Max Moritz mit Reinhardt Stenzel sowie Tebernum mit Clemens Schickentanz vertreten. Die Carrera des Jahrgangs 1975 leisteten rund 345 PS, konnten ihr PS-Manko gegenüber dem BMW aber durch ein Mindergewicht von 145 Kilogramm wenigstens einigermaßen kompensieren.
Beim Eifelrennen, dem Saisonauftakt, fuhr Fitzpatrick zwar Trainingsbestzeit, doch im Rennen musste er mit defektem Schalthebel die Segel streichen. Newcomer Harald Grohs nutzte die Chance und siegte vor den Porsche-Piloten Clemens Schickentanz und Reinhardt Stenzel. Beim zweiten Lauf in Hockenheim bestimmten die BMW-Coupés und der Capri das Geschehen an der Spitze. Nach spannendem Rennverlauf siegte Krebs vor Schommers, gefolgt von den drei Carrera von Kelleners, Stenzel und Bertrams. Nicht wie erwartet die BMW-Coupés, sondern die Porsche Carrera gaben beim Flugplatzrennen in Mainz-Finthen den Ton an. Reinhardt Stenzel nutzte seine Trainingsbestzeit und fuhr einen klaren Start-Ziel-Sieg heraus. Weil Albrecht Krebs einen Dreher produzierte, konnte sich Helmut Kelleners noch den zweiten Rang sichern. Am Norisring lockte das enorme Preisgeld von über 100.000 Mark auch wieder die Werksteams an: Stuck (BMW) gegen Mass (Ford) hieß das Duell, das die Zuschauer von den Sitzen riss. Erst als Stuck wegen Bremsproblemen aufgeben musste, konnte Mass entspannt ins Ziel fahren. Die beiden weiteren Podiumplätze gingen an die Porsche-Fahrer Stenzel und Kelleners. Der Diepholzer Flugplatzkurs brachte Stenzel, der im Zwischenklassement den zweiten Rang in der Meisterschaft einnahm, kein Glück. Der Max Moritz-Pilot verschlief den Start und flog im Bemühen, verlorenen Boden gutzumachen, in der Startkurve von der Strecke. Da ein Reifen beschädigt war, gab er auf. Den Sieg sicherte sich Porsche-Fahrer Bob Wollek, Kelleners wurde Dritter. Zu einer richtigen Hitzeschlacht wurde der Lauf im Rahmen des Großen Preises von Deutschland auf dem Nürburgring. Gegen die PS-starken BMW-Coupés von Krebs und Grohs mussten sich Kelleners und Stenzel mit den Plätzen drei und vier zufrieden geben. In Kassel-Calden tauchte Meisterschaftanwärter Klaus Ludwig plötzlich mit einem Capri in der großen Division auf. Er fuhr Trainingsbestzeit, verlor aber mit einem defekten Gasgestänge alle Chancen. Nach der Reparatur versuchte er allerdings den Titelrivalen Albrecht Krebs einzubremsen, was aber nicht gelang. Viel Unmut zog Teamchef Georg Loos auf sich, der seine drei Carrera allesamt nicht punktberechtigten Ausländern (Hezemans, Fitzpatrick, Schenken) anvertraute. Obendrein setzte Lokalrivale Kremer den Franzosen Bob Wollek auf sein bestes Auto. Krebs siegte vor Wollek, Schenken, Schickentanz und Hezemans. Beim Preis der Nationen in Hockenheim erfüllte Ludwig im Capri seine Aufgabe mit einem Sieg optimal. Krebs minderte selbst seine Titelchancen durch ein Gerangel mit Fitzpatrick, das den BMW-Piloten auf den fünften Rang zurückwarf, während der Brite Zweiter wurde. Und auch das Finale an gleicher Stelle endete mit einem Ludwig-Sieg, aber Kelleners schaffte mit dem zweiten Platz wenigstens noch den vierten Schlussrang in der Meisterschaft.
Nach mehr oder minder sieglosen Jahren und bescheidenen Platzierungen in der Meisterschaft, holten die Porsche-Kunden in der Saison 1976 zum Gegenschlag aus. Mussten sie bisher bei der Motorleistung den Underdog spielen, so sollte der neue Porsche 934 mit dem 480 PS leistenden 3-Liter-Turbotriebwerk und einem Gewicht von 1130 Kilogramm den BMW-Coupés und Ford Capri zeigen, was eine Harke ist. Doch der Schlagabtausch fand gar nicht erst statt. Ford und BMW verzichteten auf weitere Einsätze in der großen Division, die Porsche-Kunden blieben meist unter sich.
So warteten beim Eifelrennen auf dem Nürburgring zehn der brandneuen 934 auf den ersten Renneinsatz. Max Moritz bot Kelleners und Stenzel auf, für Kremer trat Bob Wollek an, Rivale Georg Loos setzte auf Hezemans und Schickentanz. Der Franzose und der Holländer (ebenso wie viele andere Ausländer) starteten übrigens mit deutscher Lizenz und waren damit auch in der Meisterschaft punktberechtigt. Beide wechselten sich anfangs in der Führung ab, mussten jedoch bald feststellen, dass ihr 120-Liter-Tank nicht für die Distanz von 182 Kilometern reichte. Während sie dem Durst ihrer Turbo-Triebwerke mit einem Tankstopp Tribut zollen mussten, fuhren Kelleners und Stenzel (ohne Stopp!) vor

Deutsche Rennsport Meisterschaft 1975: Bob Wollek

154 DAS HEIMSPIEL FEST IM GRIFF

Deutsche Rennsport Meisterschaft 1976: Reinhard Stenzel

Deutsche Rennsport Meisterschaft 1976: Clemens Schickentanz

with brake problems, could Mass comfortably cruise to victory. The remaining podium slots were taken by Porsche-drivers Stenzel and Kelleners. The airfield track at Diepholz didn't bring any luck for Stenzel, who was in second place of the championship standings. The Max Moritz-driver missed the start and in his attempt to make up for ground lost, he came off the track on the first corner. He retired with a damaged tyre. Porsche-driver Bob Wollek claimed victory, Kelleners came home third. The race on the support bill of the German Grand Prix at the Nürburgring turned into a battle in the heat. Kelleners and Stenzel had to make do with third and fourth place against the powerful BMWs driven by Krebs and Grohs. At Kassel-Calden, title candidate Klaus Ludwig suddenly raced a Capri in the big division. He was fastest in qualifying, but was deprived of his chances by a broken throttle linkage. After the repair, he tried to slow down his rival for the title, Albrecht Krebs. Team principal Georg Loos didn't receive any sympathy for putting three foreign drivers (Hezemans, Fitzpatrick, Schenken) in his three Carreras, none of them being eligible to score any points. Moreover, local rival Kremer put Frenchman Bob Wollek into his best car. Krebs won from Wollek, Schenken, Schickentanz and Hezemans. At the Preis der Nationen at Hockenheim, Ludwig did a perfect job winning with his Capri. Krebs reduced his title chances all by himself in a fight with Fitzpatrick, which made the BMW driver drop back to fifth, while the Briton came second. The final at the same venue brought another win for Ludwig, but second place was enough for Kelleners to claim fourth position in the final standings of the championship.

After more or less winless years and rather weak results in the championship, Porsche customer teams struck back in 1976. In earlier years, they had a disadvantage when engine power was concerned, but the new Porsche 934 with its 480 hp three litre turbo engine and its weight of 1130 kg would show the BMW Coupés and the Ford Capris the way. But the battle never materialised. Ford and BMW refrained from further efforts in the big division, leaving it to the Porsche teams to fight it out amongst themselves.

Thus, ten brand-new 934s were waiting for their first race during the Eifelrennen at the Nürburgring. Max Moritz had entered Kelleners and Stenzel, Bob Wollek drove for Kremer, while rival Georg Loos relied on Hezemans and Schickentanz. Just like many other foreigners, the Frenchman and the Dutchman were driving with a German licence and therefore were eligible to score championship points. The lead changed between the two of them in the early stages, but they soon found out that their tank of 120 litres wasn't enough for the entire distance. They had to pay for the thirst of their turbo engines with an additional stop for refuelling, while Kelleners and Stenzel (without stopping) scored a double victory for the Max Moritz team, ahead of Wollek. The Frenchman then scored a lights-to-flag win after 50 demanding laps at Mainz-Finthen ahead of Schenken and Stenzel. Co-favourite Hezemans had to make do with tenth place due to brake

Deutsche Rennsport Meisterschaft 1976: Bob Wollek

Deutsche Rennsport Meisterschaft 1976: Toine Hezemans

Deutsche Rennsport Meisterschaft 1976: Kelleners (5), Bertrams (6)

POPULAR ON HOME GROUND **155**

Wollek zu einem Doppelsieg für das Max-Moritz-Team. Der Franzose holte sich dafür nach 50 anstrengenden Runden in Mainz-Finthen einen unangefochtenen Start-Ziel-Sieg vor Schenken und Stenzel. Mitfavorit Hezemans musste sich nach Bremsproblemen mit dem zehnten Rang begnügen. In Hockenheim konnte der Holländer dann allerdings den Spieß herumdrehen. Er siegte nach spannendem Rennverlauf vor Wollek. Kelleners, Stenzel und Bertrams landeten auf den folgenden Plätzen.

Das prestigeträchtige Norisring-Rennen konnte wiederum Bob Wollek für sich entscheiden. Trotz heftiger Attacken von Toine Hezemans führte Wollek 14 Runden lang vor dem Trainingsschnellsten, erst dann kam der Holländer vorbei. Aber er war vom Pech verfolgt: Ein Elektrikschaden warf ihn wenige Runden vor Schluss aus dem Rennen. So sicherten sich Stenzel und Schickentanz die weiteren Plätze auf dem Podium. Dafür gewann Hezemans beim Flugplatzrennen in Diepholz den Spieß wieder herum. Ein Unfall zur Halbzeit warf den Elsässer Wollek aus dem Rennen, so dass Hezemans mit großem Vorsprung siegte. Auf den zweiten Platz schob sich überraschend der Australier Tim Schenken in einem Saugmotor-Carrera RSR vor den 934 von Stenzel und Gaststarter Claude Haldi. Beim folgenden Lauf auf dem Nürburgring startete das Feld wegen des Lauda-Unfalls erst nach 18 Uhr. Da die Sauger beim stehenden Start besser wegkamen als die Turbos, kam es in der Südkehre zum großen Durcheinander in der Wiese, dem Wollek und Stenzel zum Opfer fielen. Das Rennen gewann Hezemans vor Kelleners.

Da immer mal wieder ein anderer Porsche siegte, hatte auch in dieser Saison kein Porsche-Pilot mehr Meisterschaftschancen. Ein ganz skuriles Ergebnis ergab sich in Kassel-Calden mit dem Sieg von Jürgen Neuhaus vor Edgar Dören, beide in einem Sauger-Carrera RSR. Die Profiteams traten nämlich in den Streik, weil der Veranstalter das geforderte Start- und Preisgeld nicht zahlen wollte. Die restlichen drei Saisonläufe sahen zwei Siege von Tim Schenken und einen von Bob Wollek, der den zweiten Schlussrang in der Meisterschaft nur um einen Punkt verpasste.

Mit dem Beginn der Saison 1977 erreichte die Aufrüstung in der Deutschen Rennsportmeisterschaft ganz neue Dimensionen. Erstmals wurde nach dem Reglement der Gruppe 5 gefahren, die Autos wurden noch spektakulärer, stärker und selbstverständlich teurer. In keinem anderen Land wurde eine nationale Meisterschaft auf einem derartigen Niveau ausgetragen, aber das Interesse des Publikums gab den Machern recht. In der „Porsche-Division" bedeutete die Änderung den Umstieg vom Typ 934 auf den Typ 935, das Auto, mit dem sich das Werk 1976 die Marken-Weltmeisterschaft gesichert hatte. Die offiziellen Daten: 640 PS, 970 Kilogramm Gewicht und 160.000 Mark Kaufpreis machten Eindruck.

Zum Auftakt in Zolder stellten sich allerdings nur 11 Autos dem Starter. Das Team von Georg Loos (mit Rolf Stommelen) fehlte, für Max Moritz fuhr Manfred Schurti, Bob Wollek trat für Kremer an, Jürgen Neuhaus vertrat die Farben von Brambring und bei Kannacher fuhren der Chef und Franz Konrad je einen 935. Den Sieg sicherte sich der Liechtensteiner TÜV-Beamte Schurti nach spannenden Kampf mit Wollek, der bis eine Runde vor Schluss geführt hatte. Am Nürburgring (vor 100.000 Zuschauern!) beherrschte Stommelen die Konkurrenz klar, Schurti, Wollek und Mass (für Brambring) belegten die folgenden Plätze. Auch der nächste Lauf fand auf dem Ring statt. Kremer tauchte dort erstmals mit einem aerodynamisch selbst modifizierten 935 auf, den Wollek prompt zum Sieg fuhr. Stommelen, Neuhaus und Tim Schenken (im zweiten Loos-935) belegten die Plätze. Das Flugplatzrennen in Kassel-Calden sah einen spannenden Dreikampf zwischen Stommelen, Wollek und Schurti, bei dem der Liechtensteiner mit Motorschaden die Segel streichen musste. Wollek holte sich seinen zweiten Sieg und führte die Punktewertung an. In Mainz-Finthen drehte Stommelen den Spieß wieder herum und sicherte sich die volle Punktzahl vor Wollek, Schenken und Schurti.

Am Norisring starteten erstmals in beiden Divisionen Fahrzeuge von Porsche, denn das Werk war es leid, sich nachsagen zu lassen, man könne nur gegen sich selber siegen. Während in der „Porsche-Division" Stommelen mit viel Glück vor Schurti (Plattfuß) und Gaststarter Peter Gregg aus den USA siegte, lief es für Jacky Ickx und den sogenannten Baby-Porsche (935 mit 1,4 Liter Hubraum) nicht so rund. In einem denkwürdigen Rennen, in dem die drei BMW-Junioren Surer, Cheever und Winkelhock alles daransetzten, den Ford Escort von Hans Heyer in seine Einzelteile zu zerlegen, schied Ickx bei Temperaturen von über 30 Grad nach einem Schwächeanfall aus. In Diepholz regnete es dagegen zeitweise in Strömen. Favorit Bob Wollek drehte sich zweimal, so dass Stommelen vor dem Elsässer und Tim Schenken gewann. Da sich in der kleinen Division alle Fahrer gegenseitig die Punkte abnahmen, führten Stommelen und Wollek in der Meisterschaft.

In den drei noch ausstehenden Rennen ließen beide nichts mehr anbrennen: zweimal siegte Wollek, einmal Stommelen, was für den Kölner als ersten Porsche-Piloten den Titel in der Meisterschaft bedeutete. Und auch das Werk feierte noch ein Erfolgserlebnis: Vor der Formel 1-Kulisse in Hockenheim fuhr Ickx das „Baby" beim zweiten Einsatz zum unangefochtenen Start-Ziel-Sieg. 51,4 Sekunden betrug sein Vorsprung im Ziel und Porsche stellte das Auto anschließend sofort ins Museum: Mission erfüllt, Beweis erbracht.

Zwölf 935 und ein einsamer Toyota Celica Turbo bildeten das Feld zum Auftakt der Saison 1978 in Zolder. Die Sensation aber war, dass am Lenkrad des schon 1977 von Schnitzer erstmals eingesetzten Toyota der amtierende Meister Rolf Stommelen saß. Für das Team von Georg Loos fuhren jetzt John Fitzpatrick und Toine Hezemans. Kremer setzte weiterhin auf Bob Wollek sowie Dieter Schornstein und „John Winter", bei Max Moritz blieb Manfred Schurti an Bord, für Konrad starteten der Chef und Volkert Merl und Reinhold Joest fuhr im 935 des eigenen Teams. In Zolder gab es für alle nur einen Kurzeinsatz, denn das Rennen musste nach nur 14 Runden wegen Regens abgebrochen werden. Hezemans siegte vor Wollek und Fitzpatrick.

Die große Überraschung beim zweiten Lauf auf dem Nürburgring präsentierte Georg Loos: Klaus Ludwig, nach fehlgeschlagenem Formel 2-Abenteuer arbeitslos, startete als

Deutsche Rennsport Meisterschaft 1977: Start Norisring

Deutsche Rennsport Meisterschaft 1977: Rolf Stommelen

Deutsche Rennsport Meisterschaft 1978: Bob Wollek

problems. At Hockenheim, it was the Dutchman's turn. After an exciting race, he won from Wollek. Kelleners, Stenzel and Bertrams followed suit.

The prestigious Norisring race brought another victory for Bob Wollek. In spite of fierce attacks by Toine Hezemans, Wollek had the lead over the fastest qualifier for 14 laps. Only then, the Dutchman found a way past. But luck wasn't on his side: electrical problems forced him to retire with only a few more laps to go, so Stenzel and Schickentanz claimed the remaining podium slots. Hezemans won again at the airfield circuit of Diepholz, by a huge margin after Wollek retired due to a collision halfway into the race. Surprisingly, second place wento to Australian Tim Schenken with an atmospheric Carrera RSR ahead of the 934s of Stenzel and guest driver Claude Haldi. During the following round at the Nürburgring, the race would only start after 6 pm due to Lauda's accident. Because the cars with atmospheric engines had a better getaway than the turbos, there was mayhem in the south bend with Wollek and Sten-zel as the main casualties. Hezemans won from Kelleners and Bertrams.

As every time, a different Porsche would win, none of the Porsche drivers had any chance of winning the title. The race at Kassel-Calden brought quite an extraordinary result, with Jürgen Neuhaus winning from Edgar Dören, both of them with an atmospheric Carrera-RSR. The professional teams were on strike, because the race promoter refused to pay the starting and prize money that they wanted. The remaining three season rounds brought two wins for Tim Schenken and one for Bob Wollek, who was only one point short of second place in the final points' standings.

With the start of the 1977 season, the technical battle in the German racing championship got into new dimensions. For the first time, Group 5 regulations were being used. The cars became even more spectacular, more powerful and, of course, more expensive. In no other country was there a national championship at such a high level, but the interest of the spectators proved the organisers to be right. In the "Porsche division", the change resulted into a switch from the 934 to the 935, the car with which the factory had won the 1976 world championship for manufacturers. The official figures: 640 hp, 970 kg of weight and a list price of 160,000 Deutschmarks. Quite impressive indeed.

However, the opening round at Zolder attracted only eleven cars. The team of Georg Loos (with Rolf Stommelen) was missing. Manfred Schurti was racing for Max Moritz, Bob Wollek drove for Kremer, Jürgen Neuhaus represented the Brambring-colours and at Kannacher, the team boss and Franz Konrad each raced a 935. Schurti from Liechtenstein won the race after a fierce battle with Wollek, who had been in the lead until the penultimate lap. At the Nürburgring (in front of a 100,000 strong crowd), Stommelen clearly dominated proceedings, with Schurti, Wollek and Mass (for Brambring) following suit. The next round also took place at the 'Ring. For the first time, Kremer ran a 935 with aerodynamics that had been modified by the team itself. Wollek took the car to victory right away, followed by Stommelen, Neuhaus and Tim Schenken (with the second Loos-935). The Kassel-Cal-den airfield race was marked by an exciting three-way fight between Stommelen, Wollek and Schurti, in which the driver from Liechtenstein had to give with engine failure. Wollek took his second win and the lead in the championship. At Mainz-Finthen, it was Stommelen's turn again, taking the total score ahead of Wollek and Schenken.

At the Norisring, Porsche cars competed in both divisions for the first time, because the factory had had enough of the perpetual criticism of "only being able to beat itself". While the "Porsche division" saw Stommelen taking a lucky win from Schurti (puncture) and guest driver Peter Gregg from the USA, things didn't go that well for Jacky Ickx and the so-called baby-Porsche (935 with an engine capacity of 1.4 litres). In a memorable race, during which the three BMW-juniors Surer, Cheever and Winkelhock did everything to Heyer's Ford Escort to pieces, Ickx retired because of exhaust in the temperatures of over 30 degrees. At Diepholz, rain came pouring down at stages. Favourite Wollek spun twice, so that Stommelen won ahead of him and Tim Schenken. As in the small class, all drivers were taking points off each other, Stommelen and Wollek led in the championship.

In the three remaining races, the two of them made no mistakes: Wollek won twice, Stommelen once, which made the driver from Cologne the first Porsche driver to win the title. And the factory had a success, too: in front of the Formula 1 crowd at Hockenheim, Ickx drove the "Baby" to an unchallenged lights-to-flag win on only its second outing. At flagfall, his margin was 51.4 seconds and after that, Porsche parked the car in the museum right away: mission accomplished, duties fulfilled.

Deutsche Rennsport Meisterschaft 1978: Toine Hezemans

POPULAR ON HOME GROUND

Rolf Stommelen

Bob Wollek

Fahrer Nummer drei fürs Gelo-Team und bewies auf Anhieb, dass er nichts verlernt hatte. Hinter Wollek und Hezemans belegte er den dritten Platz. Den sicherte er sich auch beim Eifelrennen, wo er beim Dreifach-Sieg für das Loos-Team den Stallgefährten Hezemans und Fitzpatrick den Vortritt lassen musste. Hatte es in der Eifel noch 22 Starter gegeben, so wollten nur zehn Fahrer die Avus unter die Räder nehmen. Wieder gab es mit Hezemans einen Sieger aus dem Loos-Lager, der Schurti ganz knapp niederhalten konnte, allerdings vom letzten Startplatz gekommen war. In Mainz-Finthen hatten dann beide kein Glück, je ein schleichender Plattfuß warf sie auf die Plätze vier und fünf zurück. Es siegte Bob Wollek vor Fitzpatrick und Ludwig.

Das Rennen in Zandvoort ähnelte eher einer Regatta, denn es regnete in Strömen. Wieder feierte Georg Loos einen Dreifachsieg. Für Lokalmatador Hezemans erwies sich allerdings Regenkönig Fitzpatrick als uneinholbar. Wollek donnerte in der Gischt von Hezemans ins Grüne, Pechvogel Schurti schied mit defektem Radlager aus. Zum dritten Mal hintereinander erwies sich Wollek in Kassel-Calden als unschlagbar, auf den Plätzen folgte das Loos-Trio in der Reihenfolge Hezemans, Fitzpatrick und Ludwig. Der Bonner glänzte dafür beim F1-Rahmenrennen in Hockenheim mit einem makellosen Start-Ziel-Sieg vor Schurti, Hezemans und Fitzpatrick. In Zolder krachte es dann im Loos-Team: Vor allem der Chef und Nummer 1-Fahrer Hezemans, der noch gute Titelchancen hatte, gerieten heftig aneinander. So siegte Schurti nach langer Zeit wieder einmal vor Fitzpatrick, die restliche Loos-Truppe mit Ludwig (9.) und Hezemans (15.) rangierte unter ferner liefen.

Am Norisring – diesmal im September – schaltete sich Porsche in den Hauskrach bei Loos ein. Obwohl der Kölner Immobilien-Tycoon Porsche-Kunde war (seine Autos wurden von der Werksreparatur gewartet und an den Strecken betreut) sicherte Porsche Hezemans mit Blick auf die Meisterschaftschancen einen Werkswagen zu, falls er von Loos kein gutes Auto bekommen sollte. Das Auto war da, aber Hezemans schied mit Motorschaden aus. Schurti siegte vor Ludwig und Wollek, aber der Titel war für Porsche weg.

Viel Aufregung gab es bereits vor der Saison 1979 in der Deutschen Rennsportmeisterschaft, denn das Wechselfieber grassierte bei Teams und Piloten. Georg Loos holte sich ausgerechnet Bob Wollek vom Kölner Erzrivalen Kremer sowie Manfred Schurti von Max Moritz, nachdem dieses Team wegen der ständig steigenden Kosten das Handtuch geworfen hatte. John Fitzpatrick blieb im Gelo-Team. Kremer konnte seinerseits die Verpflichtung von Klaus Ludwig vermelden, der bisherigen Nummer drei bei Loos. Sein Teamkollege bei Kremer wurde Axel Plankenhorn. Schließlich war Stommelen nach seinem Toyota-Abenteuer zurück im Porsche-Lager und fuhr den von Liqui Moly gesponsorten 935.

Der Saisonauftakt in Zolder sah mit Klaus Ludwig und der Eigenentwicklung Kremer-935 K3 die absolut überlegene Kombination dieser Saison als Sieger. Stommelen wurde Zweiter, die Loos-Piloten litten unter einer falschen Reifenwahl. Auch beim zweiten Lauf in Hockenheim machte Ludwig kurzen Prozess und gewann mit 18 Sekunden Vorsprung. Bei Loos ging eine beabsichtigte Stallregie in die Hose: Als der zweitplatzierte Schurti weisungsgemäß vor der Ziellinie stoppte, um Wollek vorbeizulassen, kam Fitzpatrick angeschossen, weil sich Wollek eingangs des Motodroms gedreht hatte. Das Eifelrennen auf dem Nürburgring ging deshalb in die Geschichte dieser Saison ein, weil es das einzige Rennen werden sollte, das Ludwig nicht gewann. Weil er in der dritten Runde auf einen langsameren Wagen der kleinen Division auflief, konnte Wollek vorbeischlüpfen und zehn Sekunden Vorsprung ins Ziel retten. Das Porsche-Einerlei in der Division unterbrach BMW mit dem Einsatz eines noch nicht homologierten M1, den Marc Surer auf Rang neun steuerte, einen Platz hinter dem Ford Capri Turbo von Toine Hezemans aus dem Stall von Erich Zakowski, eine weitere Premiere in der großen Division.

Die Ludwig-Show ging auch in Salzburg, Mainz-Finthen und am Norisring unverändert weiter. In Nürnberg sorgte allerdings BMW mit fünf M1 für Abwechslung, vor allem weil die Top-Stars Niki Lauda, Clay Regazzoni und Hans-Joachim Stuck mit den spektakulären weiß-blauen Flundern am Start waren. An der holländischen Küste in Zandvoort platzte Georg Loos ob der aussichtslosen Situation für seine drei Top-Piloten im Kampf mit Seriensieger Ludwig der Kragen und Porsche, wo seine Autos ja vorbereitet wurden, bekam sein Fett weg. Das änderte freilich nichts an den Gegebenheiten. Ludwig setzte seine Siegesserie auch in Diepholz und Zolder unbeeindruckt fort und sicherte sich beim vorletzten Lauf auf dem Kleinen Kurs in Hockenheim auch offiziell vorzeitig den Titel. Dort deutete sich übrigens an, dass es mit dem Porsche-Einerlei in der Division schon bald ein Ende haben könnte. Erich Zakowski brachte für Hans Heyer einen Turbo Capri mit etwas größerem Motor an den Start, weil er sich auf dem winkeligen Kurs Chancen gegen die Porsche ausrechnete. Tatsächlich fuhr Heyer auf den dritten Rang hinter dem Kremer-Duo Ludwig und Plankenhorn, aber klar vor den Loos-Piloten Schurti und Wollek, vor. Zakowski machte sich seinen eigenen Reim darauf und bereitete gemeinsam mit Ford im Verborgenen seinen „Porsche-Killer" für die kommende Saison vor.

Selten war eine Meisterschaftssaison so sehr von Politik und Grabenkämpfen der unterschiedlichsten Akteure bestimmt, wie die Saison 1980 in der Deutschen Rennsportmeisterschaft. Was sich 1979 schon angedeutet hatte, wurde Wirklichkeit: Erich Zakowski brachte seinen Super-Capri für die große Division als Gegner der Porsche 935 an den Start,

Winner Deutsche Rennsport Meisterschaft 1979: Klaus Ludwig

158 DAS HEIMSPIEL FEST IM GRIFF

Toine Hezemans    Klaus Ludwig

Twelve 935s and a solemn Toyota Celica Turbo were on the starting grid for the 1978 season opener at Zolder. The sensation was, however, that reigning champion Rolf Stommelen was behind the wheel of the Toyota that already had been entered for the first time by Schnitzer in 1977. John Fitzpatrick and Toine Hezemans were now racing for the team run by Georg Loos. Kremer continued with Bob Wollek and the pairing of Dieter Schornstein and "John Winter". Manfred Schurti remained at Max Moritz while the boss and Volkert Merl were driving for Konrad and Reinhold Joest drove the 935 run by his own team. At Zolder, the action was only brief for all of them, as the race had to be stopped after only 14 laps due to rain. Hezemans won ahead of Wollek and Fitzpatrick. Stommelen had already retired after two laps with an overheated engine.

Georg Loos came up with the biggest surprise for the second round at the Nürburgring: Klaus Ludwig, who was out of a job after his still-born Formula 2 adventure, was the third driver in the Gelo-team and proved right away that he had lost nothing of his skill. He came home third behind Wollek and Hezemans. And he did the same at the Eifelrennen, where he had to let team-mates Hezemans and Fitzpatrick past to secure the threefold win for the Loos-team. While the Eifel-event still attracted 22 competitors, only ten drivers turned up at the Avus, Hezemans scored another win for Loos, just managing to maintain the upper hand over Schurti, in spite of having started last on the grid. At Mainz-Finthen, both drivers were unlucky, a puncture for each of them made them drop back to fourth and fifth respectively, while Bob Wollek won ahead of Fitzpatrick and Ludwig.

The Zandvoort round was more like a regatta, as rain kept pouring down. Once again, there was a threefold win for Georg Loos. Local hero Hezemans however failed to pass rain man Fitzpatrick, although he stayed ahead of Ludwig. Wollek spun into the grass in the spray swirled up by Hezemans. Unlucky Schurti retired as a wheel bearing broke. For the third time in a row, Wollek proved to be unbeatable at Kassel-Calden, the Loos trio following suit with Hezemans ahead of Fitzpatrick and Ludwig. The driver from Bonn shone in the F1 support race at Hockenheim with an impeccable lights-to-flag victory ahead of Schurti, Hezemans and Fitzpatrick. At Zolder, there was mayhem in the Loos-team, the boss and number one-driver Hezemans, who still had chances of winning the title, had a big argument. Schurti won again after a long time ahead of Fitzpatrick, while the remaining Loos drivers were well down the order with Ludwig in ninth and Hezemans in fifteenth place.

At the Norisring, this time in September, Porsche interfered in the dispute within the Loos-team. Although the real estate tycoon from Cologne was a Porsche customer (his cars were maintained and looked after at the track by the factory's service department), Porsche promised Hezemans a factory car to keep his title hopes alive in case Loos wouldn't provide him with a decent car. The car was there all right, but Hezemans retired with a blown engine. Schurti won ahead of Ludwig and Wollek, but for Porsche, the title was gone.

Before the start of the 1979 season there was already plenty of action in the championship, because there were many changes among teams and drivers. Georg Loos hired Bob Wollek from his Cologne-based arch rival Kremer as well as Manfred Schurti from Max Moritz, after the latter team had closed down because of the increasing costs. John Fitzpatrick stayed with the Gelo-team. Kremer signed Klaus Ludwig, who had been number three at Loos before. At Kremer, Plankenhorn became Ludwig's team-mate. And last but not least, Stommelen was back in the Porsche camp after his Toyota adventure, driving the Liqui Moly-sponsored 935.

With Klaus Ludwig and the self-developed Kremer-935 K3, the season opener at Zolder saw the dominating combination of this season taking the first win. Stommelen came second while the Loos drivers suffered from the wrong tyre choice. At the second round at Hockenheim, Ludwig didn't take long either and won with an 18 seconds' margin. For Loos, a plan-ned team-order didn't work out: as second-placed Schurti stopped ahead of the finish line as he had been told in order to let Wollek past, it was Fitzpatrick who showed up, be-cause Wollek had spun while entering the Motodrom. The Eifelrennen at the Nürburgring made it into the history books because this was to become the only round of that particular season that Ludwig didn't win. As he caught a slower car from the small category on the third lap, Wollek could go past and he saved a ten seconds' advantage to the finish. BMW broke Porsche's authority in the category by entering a still non-homologated M1, driven to ninth place by Marc Surer, one place behind the Ford Capri Turbo of Erich Zakowski's team, driven by Toine Hezemans, another premiere in the big division.

Deutsche Rennsport Meisterschaft 1979: Rolf Stommelen

911 Carrera RSR - Deutsche Rennsport Meisterschaft 1975 Norisring: John Fitzpatrick (1), Toine Hezemans (2)

934 - Deutsche Rennsport Meisterschaft 1976 Norisring: Reinhard Stenzel

Kremer 935 K2 - Deutsche Rennsport Meisterschaft 1977 Nürburgring: Bob Wollek

Kremer 935 K3 - Deutsche Rennsport Meisterschaft 1981 Hockenheimring: Bob Wollek

POPULAR ON HOME GROUND

eine Rohrrahmen-Konstruktion, die das Gruppe 5-Reglement bis an seine äußersten Grenzen auslotete – wie Norbert Singer mit dem „Moby Dick". So sahen es zumindest Thomas Ammerschläger von Ford und Erich Zakowski, die auch bei der Besetzung des Cockpits mit einer faustdicken Überraschung aufwarten konnten. Am Lenkrad des Capri drehte mit Klaus Ludwig der Meister und Porsche-Seriensieger des Vorjahres. Georg Loos, der eigentlich gar nicht mehr mitmachen wollte, brachte überraschend doch noch ein Auto für Bob Wollek an den Start. Für Kremer sollte Axel Plankenhorn die Siegesserie von Ludwig mit dem K3 fortsetzen, unter Regie von Liqui Moly-Chef Henle traten Rolf Stommelen und Volkert Merl an – die Zahl der Sieganwärter in der Division war überschaubar geworden.

Den Auftakt in Zolder gewann Stommelen, aber Ludwig im Capri wurde Zweiter vor Wollek, Plankenhorn und Edgar Dören, ein deutliches Warnsignal an das Porsche-Lager, zumal Ludwig auch die schnellste Runde des Rennens markierte. Beim Zakspeed-Heimspiel auf dem Nürburgring fuhr Ludwig Trainingsbestzeit und belegte im Rennen den fünften Rang hinter Manfred Winkelhock, Volkert Merl, Stommelen und Helmut Kelleners, der wie Winkelhock einen BMW M1 steuerte. Doch über dem Super-Capri schwebte das Damokles-Schwert der Sport-Funktionäre und das Sportgericht des Verbandes disqualifizierte den Bonner nachträglich für die beiden ersten Rennen wegen eines überdimensionierten Heckflügels. Weil auch Winkelhock der Sieg am Nürburgring nachträglich aberkannt wurde, erhielt Merl die volle Punktzahl. Die Antwort von Ludwig war standesgemäß: Trotz nunmehr gestutztem Heckflügel siegte er in Hockenheim, nachdem Wollek noch in der letzten Runde zurückfiel. Die weiteren Podiumsplätze belegten Plankenhorn und Merl. Auch beim Eifelrennen musste sich die Porsche-Armada dem Capri von Ludwig beugen. Der Bonner führte vom Start bis ins Ziel und hatte auf seiner Hausstrecke nach sieben Run-den einen Vorsprung von unglaublichen 1.05,97 Minuten. Diesmal gingen die weiteren Plätze auf dem Podest an Bob Wollek und Manfred Schurti mit einem BMW M1.

Deutsche Rennsport Meisterschaft 1980 Hockenheimring

Wollek vor Merl und Dören lautete der Einlauf in Mainz-Finthen, wo Ludwig, Stommelen und Plankenhorn vorzeitig ausschieden. Das führte zur ersten Runde im Fahrer-Karussell der Porsche-Teams: In Spa musste Axel Plankenhorn das Cockpit des Kremer-Porsche für John Fitzpatrick räumen. Begründung wie im Fußball: Erfolglosigkeit. Überhaupt ging Spa unrühmlich in die DRM-Geschichte ein: Dort beharkte man sich mit einstweiligen Verfügungen, Gerichtsbeschlüssen, Vertragsannullierungen und Verleumdungen. Spektakulärer Sport dafür am Norisring: Das Rennen musste nach Regenunterbrechung in zwei addierten Läufen gewertet werden, Fitzpatrick gewann vor Merl und Jürgen Lässig. Der nächste Knall war damit programmiert: Sponsor und Teamchef Henle beförderte in Salzburg Stommelen aus dem Cockpit und setzte Manfred Winkelhock hinein. Der Schwabe bedankte sich mit dem Sieg vor Fitzpatrick, Wollek und Merl. In Diepholz gewann zur Abwechslung mal wieder Ludwig nach spannendem Kampf mit Winkelhock, der sich beim Zieleinlauf auch noch Wollek beugen musste. Die restlichen Laufsiege teilten sich Fitzpatrick (2), Winkelhock und Ludwig, der ohne die Flügel-Affäre seinen Titel sehr wahrscheinlich hätte verteidigen können.

Mit dem Auslaufen des Gruppe-5-Reglements zeichnete sich 1981 für die Deutsche Rennsportmeisterschaft eine Art Übergangs-Saison ab. Der bislang dominierende 935 wurde nicht mehr gebaut, aber die starken Privatteams von Kremer und Joest brachten immer noch tadellos präparierte Fahrzeuge an den Start, während Georg Loos nicht mehr mit von der Partie war. Die Porsche-Speerspitzen Bob Wollek (Kremer) und Jochen Mass (Joest) sahen sich in der großen Division auch durchaus ernsthafter Konkurrenz in Gestalt von Manfred Winkelhock mit einem Ford Capri Turbo von Zakspeed in Liqui-Moly-Farben sowie Hans-Joachim Stuck mit einem von Schnitzer eingesetzten BMW M1 Turbo gegenüber. Weitere starke 935 wurden von Volkert Merl, Dieter Schornstein und Jürgen Lässig pilotiert.

Deutsche Rennsport Meisterschaft 1980 Norisring

162 DAS HEIMSPIEL FEST IM GRIFF

The Ludwig-show continued in identical manner at Salzburg, Mainz-Finthen and the Norisring. In Nuremberg, however, BMW added some variation with five M1s, especially because top stars like Niki Lauda, Clay Regazzoni and Hans-Joachim Stuck were driving the white-blue sports cars. At the Dutch seaside resort of Zandvoort, Georg Loos was fed up with the hopeless situation of his three top drivers in the bat-tle with regular winner Ludwig and it was Porsche that got the blame. Of course, that didn't change the situation. An un-affected Ludwig continued his winning streak at Diepholz and Zolder and won the title early in the penultimate round at the short circuit of Hockenheim. There, it already became clear that Porsche's dominance of the category would soon be over. Erich Zakowski entered a Capri Turbo for Hans Heyer with a slightly bigger engine, because he expected to have some chances against the Porsches at the twisty track. And indeed, Heyer got all the way up to third behind Kremer team-mates Ludwig and Plankenhorn, but clearly ahead of Loos-drivers Schurti and Wollek. For Zakowski, it was clear and together with Ford, he started preparing his "Porsche killer" for the forthcoming season.

Only seldom had a championship season been dominated in such a way by politics and tactics from the various actors, like the 1980 season of the German racing championship. What already could be foreseen in 1979, became reality: Erich Zakowski brought his Super-Capri for the big division as an opponent for the Porsche 935. His car had a tubular frame construction and stretched the Group 5 regulations to their limits, like Norbert Singer had done with "Moby Dick". At least, that was how Ford's Thomas Ammerschläger and Erich Zakowski saw it. And their line-up was yet another huge surprise: behind the wheel was Klaus Ludwig, the champion and Porsche's serial winner from the year before. Georg Loos, who originally no longer wanted to take part at all, still entered a car for Bob Wollek after all in a surprise move. Axel Plankenhorn was meant to continue Ludwig's winning streak for Kremer with the K3. Rolf Stommelen and Volkert Merl raced under the guidance of Luiqi Moly boss Henle. The number of potential winners in the class had become smaller.

The season opener brought victory for Stommelen, but Ludwig finished second with his Capri ahead of Wollek, Plankenhorn and Edgar Dören, a clear warning for the Porsche fraction, and even more so, as Ludwig set the fastest race lap. Ludwig was then fastest in qualifying for Zakspeed's home race at the Nürburgring. In the race, he finished fifth behind Manfred Winkelhock, Volkert Merl, Stommelen and Helmut Kelleners, who drove a BMW M1, just like Winkelhock. But the stewards cast their clouds over the Super-Capri and the sporting court of the motorsport federation disqualified the driver from Bonn from the first two races because his rear wing was too big. As Winkelhock was also deprived of his Nürburgring-victory in retrospect, Merl scored maximum points. Ludwig's answer was appropriate: in spite of having a smaller rear wing, he won at Hockenheim after Wollek dropped back on the final lap. Plankenhorn and Merl filled the remaining podium slots. At the Eifelrennen, the Porsche-Armada once again had to bow to Ludwig's Capri. The driver from Bonn led from lights to flag and after seven laps at his home circuit, he had an incredible advantage of 1.05.97 minutes. This time round, the remaining podium places went to Bob Wollek and Manfred Schurti, who drove a BMW M1.

At Mainz-Finthen, the order was Wollek ahead of Merl and Dören, while Ludwig, Stommelen and Plankenhorn had retired. This led to the first action in the driver merry-go-round: at Spa, Axel Plankenhorn had to leave his Kremer-Porsche to John Fitzpatrick. Like in football, lack of success was the official reason. Spa was a blot on the copy-book of the DRM by all means: there were loads of law suits, accusations, court decisions and contracts were declared void. The Norisring showed spectacular racing: after an interruption because of rain, the race was split up in two heats and the results were accumulated. In the addition, Fitzpatrick won ahead of Merl and Jürgen Lässig. That paved the way for the next blow: at Salzburg, sponsor and team principal Henle left Stommelen sidelined and put Manfred Winkelhock into the cockpit. The latter duly won the race ahead of Fitzpatrick, Wollek and Merl. At Diepholz, Ludwig won for a change after an exciting battle with Winkelhock, who was also beaten by Wollek at flagfall. The remaining races were won by Fitzpatrick (2), Winkelhock and Ludwig, who most probably would have successfully defended his title, had it not been for the rear wing affair.

Deutsche Rennsport Meisterschaft 1980: Dieter Schornstein

POPULAR ON HOME GROUND 163

Deutsche Rennsport Meisterschaft 1981: Bob Wollek

Zum Auftakt der 13 Läufe umfassenden Saison im nassen Zolder gab Winkelhock auch gleich mal Wollek und Mass das Nachsehen, nachdem er schon das Training dominiert hatte. Auf der Betonschleife des Nürburgrings holten die Porsche-Fahrer dann allerdings den Löwenanteil der Punkte: Wollek siegte ganz knapp vor Mass und Stuck, während der Capri diesmal nicht ins Ziel kam. Ganz knapp ging es auch in Hockenheim zwischen den Porsche-Stars zu: Dort hatte Mass die Nase vorn vor Wollek, Winkelhock und Schornstein, während Stuck seinen M1 Turbo mit Motorschaden abstellen musste. Beim Eifelrennen auf der Nordschleife des Nürburgrings war Mass, der nur noch sporadisch auftauchte, nicht dabei. Auf der Zakspeed-Hausstrecke ließ sich Winkelhock den Sieg nach Trainingsbestzeit und schnellster Rennrunde nicht nehmen. Auf dem Podium flankierten ihn Bob Wollek und Hans-Joachim Stuck. Doch schon beim folgenden Lauf in Mainz-Finthen ging der Schnitzer-Pilot wieder leer aus, während Wollek einen weiteren Sieg vor Winkelhock und Merl feierte. Weil aber in der kleinen Division bisher jeder Lauf von Ludwig im Zakspeed-Capri gewonnen wurde, war bereits klar, dass der Meister nicht aus der umkämpfteren großen Division kommen würde.

In Wunstorf gab es ein Überraschungs-Podium mit den drei M1-Fahrern Manfred Henzler, Kurt König und Hans-Christian Jürgensen vor Dieter Schornstein. Bob Wollek wurde nur Fünfter, Winkelhock und Stuck gingen völlig leer aus. Auch beim prestigeträchtigen Norisring-Rennen verpassten die Porsche-Piloten den Sieg. Stuck triumphierte mit seinem M1 Turbo vor Gaststarter Gianpiero Moretti mit dem 935/81 „Moby Dick" und Winkelhock im Capri-Turbo. Fitzpatrick und Wollek in den Kremer-935 landeten nur auf den Rängen fünf und sechs. Nur noch zehn Starter traten zum Lauf am Nürburgring an, der auf der Betonschleife stattfand. Wollek gewann vor Winkelhock und „John Winter", der in einem 935 K3/81 von Kremer antrat. Beim Heimspiel am Salzburgring ließ sich das Schnitzer-Team von Hans-Joachim Stuck den Sieg nicht nehmen. Bob Wollek, neben Franz Gschwender einziger der nur 16 Starter mit einem Porsche, sicherte sich die Punkte für den zweiten Rang. Volles Haus konnte die große Division dagegen in Hockenheim melden: 25 Autos stellten sich beim Gold-Pokal-Rennen dem Starter. Der Sieg ging an Winkelhock vor Stuck, Mass und Merl. Auch in Zolder, in Hockenheim und beim Finale am Nürburgring siegte Winkelhock, der Zweitplatzierte hieß jedes Mal Bob Wollek, der sich damit noch punktgleich mit Hans Heyer die Vize-Meisterschaft sichern konnte. Mit der Saison 1981 endete die Ära der auf dem Porsche 911 basierenden Rennfahrzeuge in der Deutschen Rennsportmeisterschaft, die ab 1982 mit Blick auf das künftige Gruppe C-Reglement für Sportwagen ausgeschrieben war.

Nach mehr als einem Jahrzehnt feierte der GT-Sport in Deutschland mit dem ADAC GT Cup 1993 ein Comeback. Allerdings war die Definition dieser Fahrzeugklasse (GT = nur eine Tür pro Fahrzeugseite) doch recht grob, so dass sich in dieser Serie eine ganze Reihe von Fahrzeugen tummelte, die der früher üblichen Vorstellung von einem reinrassigen GT kaum entsprachen. In der für Porsche relevanten Division 1 sollte ein vorgeschriebenes Leistungsgewicht von 4 kg/PS und ein Tankinhalt von maximal 40 Litern für die Renndistanz von 100 Kilometern für Chancengleichheit sorgen, was allerdings nicht so recht gelang.

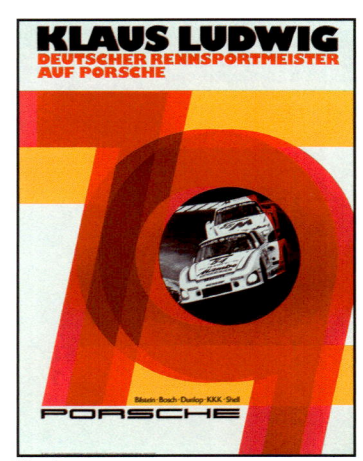

Poster

Start Deutsche Rennsport Meisterschaft 1981 Norisring

Harald Grohs

ADAC GT Cup 1993 Zolder: Jürgen von Gartzen

With the Group 5 regulations coming to an end, 1981 would be a year of transition for the German racing championship (DRM). The 935 that had been dominating was no longer being built, but the strong privateer teams of Kremer and Joest still entered immaculately prepared cars, while Georg Loos competed no longer. Porsche-spearheads Bob Wollek (Kremer) and Jochen Mass (Joest) faced stiff opposition in the big category with Manfred Winkelhock with a Zakspeed Ford Capri Turbo in Liqui Moly livery and Hans-Joachim Stuck with a BMW M1 Turbo, entered by Schnitzer. Additional strong 935 were being driven by Volkert Merl, Dieter Schornstein and Jürgen Lässig.

At the season opener at a rain-soaked Zolder, the first of 13 season rounds Winkelhock had the edge over Wollek and Mass, having already dominated qualifying. At the Nürburgring-Betonschleife, the Porsche-drivers then took the best share of the points: Wollek only just won from Mass and Stuck, while the Capri didn't make it to the finish this time. At Hockenheim, it was a close affair for the Porsche stars once more, with Mass winning from Wollek, Winkelhock and Schornstein. Stuck had to park his M1 Turbo with engine failure. At the Eifelrennen on the Nordschleife, Mass was absent, driving only selected races. At Zakspeed's home track, there was no way of stopping Winkelhock on his way to victory after he had already been fastest in qualifying and had set the fastest race lap. He was joined on the podium by Bob Wollek and Hans-Joachim Stuck. But the next round at Mainz-Finthen would be a non-score for the Schnitzer-driver, while Bob Wollek claimed another win from Winkelhock, Merl and Schornstein. In the small category, every race so far had been won by Klaus Ludwig with the Zakspeed Capri, so it had already become clear that the champion wouldn't come from the big category, that was more competitive.

At Wunstorf, there was a surprising podium with the three M1-drivers Manfred Henzler, Kurt König and Hans-Christian Jürgensen ahead Dieter Schornstein. Bob Wollek came only fifth and Winkelhock and Stuck didn't score any points at all. The Porsche drivers also missed out on victory in the prestigious Norisring race. Stuck won with his M1 Turbo ahead of guest driver Gianpiero Moretti with the 935/81 "Moby Dick" and Winkelhock with the Capri Turbo. Fitzpatrick and Wollek came only fifith and sixth respectively with their Kremer-935s. The round at the Nürburgring, which took place at the Betonschleife-circuit, attracted only ten cars. Wollek won from Winkelhock and "John Winter", who drove a Kremer-935 K3/81. Hans-Joachim Stuck's Schnitzer team won its home race at the Salzburgring. Bob Wollek, together with Franz Gschwender the only one with a Porsche on the 16 car grid, took the points for second place. At Hockenheim, there was a full house in the big category with 25 cars being entered for the Gold Pokal Rennen. Victory went to Winkelhock from Stuck, Mass and Merl. Winkelhock also won at Zolder, at Hockenheim and at the Nürburgring final, with Bob Wollek in second place every time, scoring enough points to claim runner-up position in the championship, tied with Hans Heyer. The 1981 season brought an end to the racing cars in the German championship that were derived from the Porsche 911. From 1982 onwards, the series was reserved for sports cars, with an eye on the future Group C regulations.

After more than a decade, GT racing made a comeback in Germany in 1993 with the ADAC GT Cup. However, the definition of the vehicle type (GT = only one door on each side of the car) was quite liberal, so that a range of car could be found in this series that hardly lived up to the expectations people would have of GT cars in the past. In the Division 1, that was relevant for Porsche, a required performance to weight ratio of 4 kg per bhp and a fuel tank capacity of 40 litres for the race distance of 100 kilometres were meant to guarantee equal chances, but that didn't really work out.

With nine cars, Porsche had the largest contingent for the opening round at the Avus in Berlin. The factory kept a low

ADAC GT Cup 1993: Harald Grohs

POPULAR ON HOME GROUND 165

Beim Auftaktrennen auf der Berliner Avus stellte Porsche mit neun Fahrzeugen das größte Kontingent. Das Werk hielt sich zurück und überließ den Kundenteams von Wehmeier & Castrup, Roock Racing, Obermaier und Joest das Feld. Es dominierte der neue 911 Carrera RSR 3.8, den Jürgen von Gartzen, Harald Grohs, Wolfgang Land, Fred Müther, Friedrich Leinemann und Ronnie Meixner fuhren. Franz Konrad startete mit einem älteren RS 3.6, während Peter Mamerow einen Carrera 2 fuhr. Mit von der Partie war auch ein von Manuel Reuter gefahrener 968 Turbo RS. Weitere Porsche-Fahrzeuge kamen im Verlauf der Saison noch hinzu.

Schon beim zweiten Lauf in Zolder stellte sich das Spritlimit für die Porsche als zu eng heraus. Gegen Ende blieben Autos reihenweise stehen oder schlichen nur noch um den Kurs, so dass zwei Honda vor Jürgen von Gartzens RSR 3.8 siegten. Ähnliches Bild auch am Nürburgring, wo die BMW M3 GTR von Cecotto und Nissen die Porsche von Grohs und von Gartzen auf die Plätze verwiesen. Erst beim vierten Lauf – wiederum auf dem Eifelkurs – gelang der erste Porsche-Doppelsieg für Bruno Eichmann und von Gartzen.

Um für mehr Chancengleichheit zu sorgen, genehmigten die Reglement-Macher den Porsche-Fahrern Gewichtserleichterung, 50 Kilogramm durften ausgeladen werden. Doch das Bild der ersten Saisonhälfte änderte sich nicht: gegen die BMW M3 GTR blieben für die Porsche-Treter bestenfalls dritte oder vierte Plätze. Vor allem Jürgen von Gartzen erwies sich als konstant, am Ende allerdings blieb ihm auch nur der vierte Meisterschaftsrang, weil er sich beim Finale in Zandvoort zwei selbstverschuldete Dreher leistete.

Mit einem deutlich dünneren Feld ging der ADAC GT-Cup 1994 in seine zweite Saison. Roock setzte zwei Carrera RSR 3.8 ein, die von Ralf Kelleners und Kris Nissen gesteuert wurden. Nissen fuhr allerdings nur ein Rennen, danach ga-

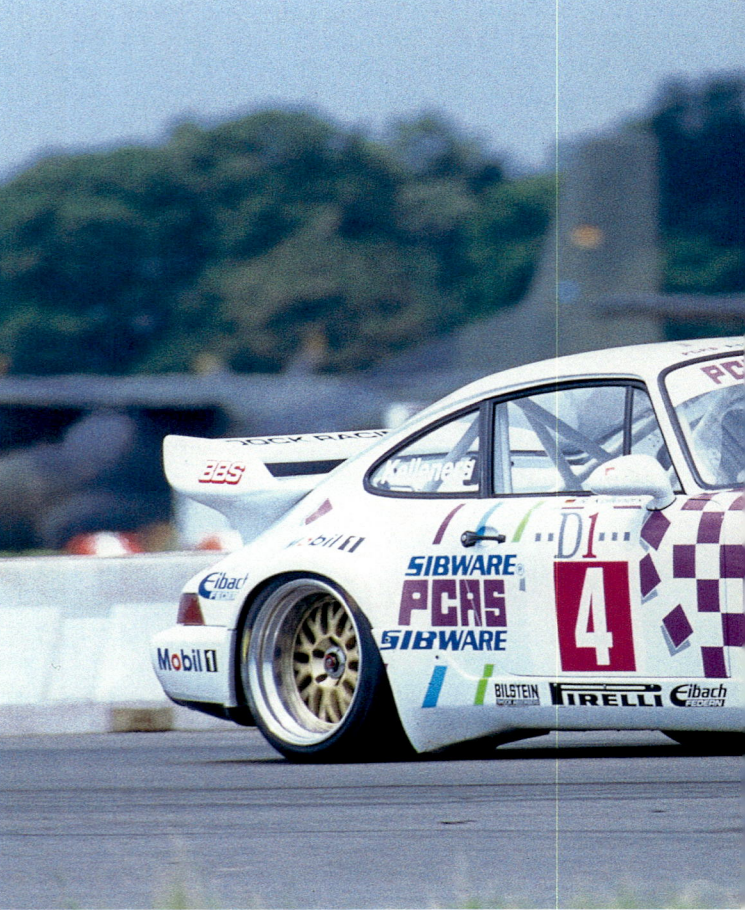

Winner ADAC GT Cup 1994: Ralf Kelleners

ben sich Uwe Alzen, Wolfgang Land, Mike Hezemans und Bernd Mayländer das Lenkrad dieses Autos in die Hand. Für Wehmeier & Castrup startete Harald Grohs als Solist, ebenfalls mit einen Carrera RSR 3.8. Auf eine Eigenkonstruktion auf Basis des neuen Typs 993 setzte Peter Mamerow, der dieses Schmuckstück dem routinierten Klaus Niedzwiedz anvertraute und selbst in die Rolle des Teamchefs schlüpfte. Den ungewöhnlichsten Porsche steuerte Wolfgang Schrey. Sein flacher gelber Strosek-Spyder mit Dach litt allerdings unter einem schwachbrüstigen Ersatzmotor, nachdem sein Turbotriebwerk gleich zu Saisonbeginn zu Bruch gegangen war. Ohne Siegchancen waren Dieter Köll im einzigen 968 Turbo RS und Oliver Mayer mit einem 911 RS.

Den Kampf um den Titel machten Kelleners, Grohs und Honda-Pilot Armin Hahne unter sich aus. Auf der Avus siegte Kelleners ganz knapp vor Grohs, in Wunstorf ging der Sieg an Uwe Alzen. Einen Dreifach-Triumph gab es in Zolder, wo Kelleners, Grohs und Niedzwiedz gemeinsam aufs Podium stiegen. Dank des zweiten Saisonsieges hatte Kelleners bereits einen deutlichen Vorsprung, den er in Zandvoort mit einem ungefährdeten dritten Sieg weiter ausbauen konnte. Zwar gab es keine weiteren Porsche-Siege mehr, aber für Kelleners reichte das Polster, um bereits nach dem vorletzten Lauf in Spa den Titel feiern zu können. Beim Finale auf dem Nürburgring begnügte sich der neue Meister dann mit einem zweiten Rang vor Niedzwiedz, der Sieg dort ging an das Kremer-Honda-Team mit Armin Hahne.

Zahlreiche Änderungen kennzeichneten die dritte Saison des ADAC GT Cup im Jahre 1995. Es gab wieder mehr Autos und es gab ein neues Rennformat: Die Rennen dauerten jetzt eine Stunde plus zwei Runden, wobei ein Reifenstopp mit möglichem Fahrerwechsel vorgeschrieben war. Es gab aber auch ein ganz neues Auto, nämlich den neuen Porsche

ADAC GT Cup 1994 Avus: Ronny Meixner

Poster

Jürgen von Gartzen

ADAC GT Cup 1994 Zandvoort: Klaus Niedzwiedz

profile and left it to its customer teams, Wehmeier & Castrup, Roock Racing, Obermaier and Joest. The new 911 Carrera RSR 3.8, driven by Jürgen von Gartzen, Harald Grohs, Wolfgang Land, Fred Müther, Friedrich Leinemann and Ronnie Meixner, dominated proceedings. Franz Konrad had entered an older RS 3.6, while Peter Mamerow drove a Carrera 2. A 968 Turbo RS was also in the race, driven by Reuter. Further Porsche cars would join in the action during the season. For the second race at Zolder, the limited amount of fuel would already turn out to be too small for the Porsches. Towards the end of the race, many cars stopped at the track or just cruised at low speed, so that two Hondas won, ahead of Jürgen von Gartzen's RSR 3.8. More of the same at the Nürburgring, where the BMW M3 GTRs of Johnny Cecotto and Kris Nissen beat the Porsches of Grohs and von Gartzen. Only the fourth round, again at the Eifel track, would bring the first double victory for Porsche, with Bruno Eichmann finishing ahead of von Gartzen.

In order to guarantee equal chances, those in charge of the regulations allowed the Porsche drivers to drop off weight, the minimum weight being lowered by 50 kilograms. But the situation from the first half of the season didn't change much: the Porsche-drivers couldn't match the BMW M3 GTRs and had to make do with third or fourth places at the best. Especially von Gartzen showed a consistent performance, but he, too, only became fourth in the championship standings after spinning twice all by himself in the season final at Zandvoort. In 1994, the grid was clearly down for the second season of the ADAC GT Cup. Roock entered two Carrera RSR 3.8s, driven by Ralf Kelleners and Kris Nissen. However, Nissen would only drive one race, after which the car was alternately driven by Uwe Alzen, Wolfgang Land, Mike Hezemans and Bernd Mayländer. Harald Grohs drove the singleton Wehmeier & Castrup entry, also a Carrera RSR 3.8. Peter Mamerow entered its own construction, based on the new 993 model range. Mamerow hired experienced driver Klaus Niedzwiedz to drive the car while concentrating on his duties as team principal himself. Wolfgang Schrey drove the most unusual Porsche. His flat yellow Strosek spyder with hard top was slowed down with a rather weak replacement engine, after the original turbo machinery had failed right at the start of the season. Köll in the solemn 968 Turbo RS and Oliver Mayer had no chance of winning with a 911 RS.

The fight for the title was a three-way affair, involving Kelleners, Grohs and Honda driver Armin Hahne. At the Avus, Kelleners just won ahead of Grohs, while Uwe Alzen was victorious at Wunstorf. There was a three-way victory at Zolder, with Kelleners, Grohs and Niedzwiedz had a clean sweep of the podium places. With his second win of the season, Kelleners already had a significant margin in the title race, which he extended even further by taking his never-threatened third victory at Zandvoort. Admittedly, there were no further victories for Porsche, but Kelleners had enough points to claim the title at Spa-Francorchamps with one race to go. In the season final at the Nürburgring, the newly-crowned champion made do with second place ahead of Klaus Niedzwiedz, while victory was taken by the Kremer Honda team with Armin Hahne.

Many changes marked the third season of the ADAC GT Cup in 1995. There were more cars and a new race format was put in place, races now running over one hour plus two

ADAC GT Cup 1994 Nürburgring: Harald Grohs

POPULAR ON HOME GROUND 167

ADAC GT Cup 1994 Nürburgring: Wolfgang Land

911 GT2, dessen Leistung vom ADAC-Reglement allerdings mittels zweier Luftmengenbegrenzer auf rund 420 PS reduziert wurde. Auf dieses Modell setzen die Teams von Roock Racing mit Uwe Alzen und Bruno Eichmann sowie Wehmeier & Castrup mit Vorjahresmeister Ralf Kelleners, der damit das Lager gewechselt hatte. Als reiner Privatier steuerte Herbert Zwack-Wandrey ebenfalls einen 911 GT2. Die bisherigen Carrera RSR 3.8 waren gegen das neue Modell chancenlos, so sehr sich Sandro Angelastri und Ernst Palmberger auch mühten. Olaf Pleuger, im jetzt mit Biturbo-Motor ausgerüsteten Vorjahres-Auto von Niedzwiedz unterwegs, konnte ebenfalls nicht mithalten. Zwei Porsche-Tuner wagten sich gar mit eigenen Konstruktionen in den ADAC GT Cup: Aus Österreich kam ein Cetoni-RSR Turmat mit mechanischer Auflagerung, aus Bayern ein Herberth GT auf Basis eines Carrera 2 Cup-Chassis und dem Kompressormotor wie im Cetoni. Vor allem der Herberth GT bewies gutes Potenzial, ohne an der Dominanz der GT2 aus Weissacher Produktion kratzen zu können.

So lösten sich denn bei den ersten drei Rennen die Porsche-Stars munter an der Spitze ab. Kelleners gewann vor Alzen und Eichmann in Zolder, Alzen vor Kelleners und Eichmann lautete der Zieleinlauf in Spa-Francorchamps. Auch in Zeltweg hatte Kelleners die Nase vorn, doch profitierte Alzen entscheidend vom Entgegenkommen seines Teamkollegen

Winner ADAC GT Cup 1995: Uwe Alzen

Bruno Eichmann. Weil das Fahrzeug des Betzdorfers nach einem Unfall im Freien Training zerstört war, teilte er sich im Rennen den Platz hinter dem Lenkrad mit dem Schweizer, so dass beide Punkte für Rang zwei gutgeschrieben erhielten. Die Rennen in Hockenheim (Kleiner Kurs) und Nürburgring (GP-Strecke) gewann Audi-Pilot Jürgen Hohenester, der sein Potenzial bereits mit einer Trainingsbestzeit in Spa-Francorchamps angedeutet hatte. Am Salzburgring siegte dann erneut Alzen vor Eichmann und Christian Abt, Kelleners kam nur auf den vierten Rang. Eine Vorentscheidung im Meisterschaftskampf schien in Berlin gefallen, als Kelleners siegte, während Alzen mit ABS-Ausfall nur Zweiter wurde. Doch die Sportkommissare entdeckten einen nicht gekennzeichneten Reifen am schwarzen Kelleners-Auto und entschieden auf Wertungsausschluss. Das Team ging in Berufung, unterlag aber letztlich in der zweiten Instanz. Da Alzen zuvor das Finale am Nürburgring vor Kelleners für sich entschieden hatte, gewann der Westerwälder ein Jahr nach seinem Titelgewinn im Porsche Supercup auch den ADAC GT Cup. Den dritten Meisterschaftsrang sicherte sich der Schweizer Bruno Eichmann.

Während der ADAC GT Cup noch bis 1997 ausgefahren wurde, schrieb der Veranstalter die Division 1 mangels Interesses anderer Hersteller als Porsche ab 1996 nicht mehr aus. Damit entfiel für die Porsche-Piloten und -Teams nach nur drei Jahren dieses Betätigungsfeld auf nationaler Ebene.

ADAC GT Cup 1994 Zolder: Ernst Plamberger

DAS HEIMSPIEL FEST IM GRIFF

Spa-Francorchamps 1995 (l.-r.): Bruno Eichmann, Uwe Alzen, Ralf Kelleners

ADAC GT Cup 1995 Nürburgring: Ralf Kelleners

laps with a mandatory pit stop for tyre change and a possible driver change. There was an all-new car, too: the Porsche 911 GT2, but the ADAC regulations reduced its output to approx. 420 hp with two air restrictors. This car was entered by the teams Roock Racing with Uwe Alzen and Bruno Eichmann as well as Wehmeier & Castrup with Ralf Kelleners, the champion of the previous season, who had switched to the other camp. Another 911 GT2 was raced by Herbert Zwack-Wandrey, a true privateer. The Carrera RSR 3.8s of previous years had no chance against the new model, no matter the efforts put in by Sandro Angelastri and Ernst Palmberger. Olaf Pleuger, who was driving the car used by Niedzwiedz in the year before, also failed to keep the pace, even though the car now had a biturbo engine. Two Porsche tuners entered their own constructions for the ADAC GT Cup. A Cetoni-RSR Turmat with a supercharger came from Austria, while a Herberth GT, based on a Carrera 2 Cup-chassis with a supercharged engine like in the Cetoni arrived from Bavaria. Especially the Herberth GT showed good potential, yet without being able to affect the domination of the GT2s from the factory in Weissach.

Porsche stars alternately took the top places in the first three rounds of the season. At Zolder, Kelleners won ahead of Alzen and Eichmann. In Spa-Francorchamps, Alzen finished first, with second and third places for Kelleners and Eichmann. At Zeltweg, Kelleners was in front again, but Alzen benefited from the help provided by team mate Bruno Eichmann. Because Alzen's car had been damaged in a crash in free practice, he shared driving duties in the race with the Swiss driver, so that both of them got the points for second place. The races at the short circuit of Hockenheim and the Grand Prix circuit of the Nürburgring were won by Audi driver Hohenester, who had already shown his potential by taking pole position at Spa-Francorchamps. At the Salzburgring, Alzen won again from Eichmann and Christian Abt, while Kelleners only finished fourth. The race in Berlin appeared to be an early decision in the title race as Kelleners won, with Alzen only second after troubles with his ABS. But the scrutineers discovered an unmarked tyre on Kelleners' car and the stewards decided to exclude him from the results. The team appealed, but the appeal was turned down. Because meanwhile, Alzen had won the final at the Nürburgring ahead of Kelleners, the driver from the Westerwald region won the title in the ADAC GT Cup, one year after his victory in the Porsche Supercup. Third place in the final standings was taken by Swiss Bruno Eichmann.

Although the ADAC GT Cup lasted until the end of 1997, the promoter pulled the plug on the Division 1 from 1996 onwards due to lack of interest from manufacturers other than Porsche. Thus, Porsche drivers and teams were deprived of this area of activity at national level after only three years.

POPULAR ON HOME GROUND **169**

IN TOP-FORM AUF JEDEM GELÄUF

SUPERB IN SNOW AND MUD

Author: John Davenport

BESCHEIDENE ANFÄNGE

Unbestritten feierte Porsche die meisten Erfolge im Motorsport bei Rundstreckenrennen, doch sollte nicht vergessen werden, dass die Autos aus Zuffenhausen auch im Rallyesport eine beachtliche Größe waren. Tatsächlich, betrachtet man die Karriere von Dr. Ferdinand Porsche, so stellt man fest, dass er höchstpersönlich dem Rallyesport verbunden war. Zu Beginn seiner Laufbahn, er war Chefentwickler bei Austro-Daimler, hat er nicht nur deren 22/80PS entworfen, sondern diesen auch selbst bei der Prinz Heinrich Fahrt 1910 pilotiert. Er gewann diese Veranstaltung auf Anhieb, zwei weitere Austro-Daimlers folgten auf den Podestplätzen. Auch bei der zweiten österreichischen Alpenfahrt triumphierte er mit dem kleineren 16/18PS, was Austro-Daimler zur Produktion eines 16/25PS Alpine veranlasste, der zum Verkauf an die breite Öffentlichkeit gedacht war.

Als Dr. Porsche und sein Sohn Ferry 1949 begannen, Autos unter ihrem eigenen Namen zu produzieren, war es nur zu erwarten, dass bald Privatleute den neuen 356 bei Rallyes einsetzten. Es war ebenfalls keine Überraschung, dass schnell ansehnliche Erfolge gefeiert werden konnten. So entschied Helmuth Polenski 1953 die erstmals ausgeschriebene Europäische Rallyemeisterschaft für sich, Hans-Joachim Walter wiederholte diese Leistung 1961. Dieses kleine Auto, in allen seinen Varianten, war erfolgreich bei Asphalt-Veranstaltungen wie dem Coupe des Alpes oder der Tour de Corse, bei Schotter-Rallyes wie der Rally to the Midnight Sun in Schweden und auch bei Langstrecken-Veranstaltungen wie Lüttich-Rom-Lüttich.

Als der Elfer im Jahr 1964 auftauchte, war die Frage nicht "wird er Rallyes bestreiten?", sondern nur "wann?". Die Antwort ließ nicht lange auf sich warten, denn das Werk selbst meldete ihn, und das bei einer Rallye, bei welcher der 356 noch kein Top-Ergebnis hatte einfahren können. Der erste bei einer Rallye eingesetzte 911 wurde von Herbert Linge, Obermeister der Versuchsabteilung, und Beifahrer Peter Falk bei der Rallye Monte Carlo 1965 an den Start gebracht. Der Elfer war seit dem 1. Januar für internationale Wettbewerbe homologiert und stellte vor allem eine unbekannte Größe dar.

Huschke von Hanstein, einer der höchst charismatischen Männer seiner Zeit, stand damals an der Spitze von Porsches Öffentlichkeitsarbeit und war gleichzeitig Sportchef. Er war besonders erpicht darauf, einen 911 bei der Rallye Monte Carlo zu sehen, hauptsächlich, um ihn Prinz Rainier

Monte Carlo 1966: Hans Joachim Walter, Werner Lier

Monte Carlo 1965: Herbert Linge, Peter Falk

Monte Carlo 1965: Herbert Linge, Peter Falk

FROM SMALL BEGINNINGS

The majority of Porsche success in motor sport has been on the racetrack, but it should not be forgotten that Zuffenhausen cars have also been a formidable force in rallying. Indeed, if one looks at the career of Dr. Ferdinand Porsche, one discovers that he has been personally linked with rallying. At the outset of his career, when he was chief designer at Austro-Daimler, he not only designed but also drove their 22/80PS on the Prinz Heinrich Fahrt of 1910. He won that event outright with two further Austro-Daimlers behind him. He also triumphed on the second Austrian Alpenfahrt with the smaller 16/18PS which led to Austro-Daimler producing a 16/25PS Alpine for sale to the general public.

When Dr. Porsche and his son Ferry started producing cars under their own name in 1949, it was only to be expected that private owners would soon start rallying the new 356. It was no surprise either that they soon enjoyed considerable success with Helmuth Polenski winning the first ever European Rally Championship in 1953 and Hans-Joachim Walter repeating the feat in 1961. The little car, in all its variants, was equally happy winning asphalt events like the Coupe des Alpes or Tour de Corse, gravel rallies like the Rally to the Midnight Sun in Sweden, or endurance events like the Liège-Rome-Liège.

Thus when the 911 emerged during 1964, the question was not 'Would it do a rally ?' but 'When ?'. The answer was not long coming and, surprisingly, it came from the factory and on a rally where the 356 had not yet managed to claim the top prize. The first 911 to be rallied was driven by Herbert Linge and Porsche engineer, Peter Falk, on the 1965 Monte Carlo Rally. The 911 had been homologated for international competition on January 1st and was very much an unknown quantity. But that most charismatic gentleman, Huschke von Hanstein was the top Porsche publicist as well as controlling the factory's sports activities. He was keen to have a 911 in the Monte Carlo Rally mainly because he wanted to show it off to Prince Rainer and other opinion-formers in Europe. He told Falk, at that time a chassis engineer working under Helmuth Bott, that Linge and he could drive the car in the rally but they were to remember why it was there and ensure that they brought it to the finish undamaged.

As it happened, the Porsche factory had a greater interest in the 1965 Monte Carlo Rally than this lone 911. They had entered two of their 904 GTS sports models for Eugen Böhringer and Pauli Toivonen, respectively European Rally

Monte Carlo 1966: Jean-Louis Schlesser, Robert Buchet

und anderen Meinungsbildern in Europa vorzuführen. Er sicherte Falk zu, der zu dieser Zeit als Karosserie-Ingenieur unter Helmuth Bott arbeitete, dass er und Linge das Auto bei der Rallye fahren könnten. Aber er schärfte ihnen auch ein, sich immer daran zu erinnern, warum der 911 eingesetzt wurde und dass er auf jeden Fall unbeschädigt ins Ziel zu bringen sei.

Als dies geschah, hatte das Porsche Werk jedoch ein noch größeres Interesse an der 65er Rallye Monte Carlo, als diesen einsamen 911. Sie hatten zwei ihrer 904 GTS Sportmodelle für Eugen Böhringer und den Finnen Pauli Toivonen, den Europameister und Sieger der 1000-Seen-Rallye 1962, gemeldet. So wussten Linge und Falk, dass sie auf die Unterstützung der Porsche Servicemobile zählen konnten, sie wussten aber auch, dass die spezielle Vorbereitung des aus der Versuchsabteilung stammenden 911 minimal war. Zu den wenigen Veränderungen gehörten Koni-Stoßdämpfer, die die serienmäßigen von Boge ersetzten. Eine weitere Vorsichtsmaßnahme war der Einbau von Weber 40 IDA Vergasern, da die standardmäßigen Solex-Vergaser den Nachteil eines Leistungslochs im mittleren Drehzahlbereich hatten. Im Ganzen war es ein recht geringer Aufwand, die Versorgung mit anständig bespiketen Schneereifen der Marke Hakkapellitas aus Finnland war jedoch ordentlich.

Dies erwies sich als besonders wichtig, da sich die Rallye durch fast permanente Schneestürme auf dem ganzen Weg von der Jura bis hinunter zur Riviera zu einem Winterklassiker entwickelte. An der Spitze war es ein dramatischer Kampf zwischen Böhringers 904 GTS und Timo Mäkinens Mini Cooper, dahinter überstand der grüne Linge- 911 mit der Start-Nummer 147 dieselben grausamen Bedingungen und erreichte das Ziel auf Rang fünf. Es war eine bemer-

Monte Carlo 1966: Henri Perrier, Piere de Pasquier

kenswerte Leistung, die von der Presse größtenteils unbeachtet blieb. Und Prinz Rainier kam in den Genuss, den unbeschädigten 911 zu sehen, als Linge und Falk zur traditionellen Siegerehrung vor dem monegassischen Palast vorfuhren.

Diejenigen, die erkannten, was passiert war, waren Leute wie Falk selbst und von Hanstein. Im Laufe des Jahres 1965 bestritt das Werk weitere Rallyes mit dem 904 und dem 904/6, allerdings weniger erfolgreich. Hinter den Kulissen jedoch wurde der 911 für eine Hauptrolle im Motorsport vorbereitet. Porsche homologierte, und erhielt Bestätigungen von der Federation Internationale d´ Automobile (FIA), für alle seine Modelle, ganz egal, ob das Werk oder jemand anderes ein Interesse daran hatte, Wettbewerbe zu bestreiten. So war selbst die 60 PS-Version des 356 in den 50er-Jahren homologiert.

Was allerdings von Hanstein und sein neuer technischer Assistent Jürgen Barth bemerkt hatten, war, daß der 911 unter den neuen internationalen Bestimmungen - Anhang J des FIA Sport-Kodex – auch als Gruppe 2-Tourenwagen durchging. Bis zu diesem Punkt war der Elfer lediglich als GT-Fahrzeug in der Gruppe 3 homologiert gewesen. Aber die Tatsache, dass er in jährlichen Stückzahlen von mehr als 1.000 hergestellt wurde und daß seine Innenmaße groß genug waren, qualifizierte ihn zum Tourenwagen.

Ebenso fiel ihnen auf, dass der 912, die Vierzylinder-Version des 911, in ausreichender Stückzahl produziert wurde, um als Gruppe 1-Tourenwagen eingestuft zu werden. Tatsächlich jedoch waren hier die Innenmaße um den Bruchteil eines Zentimeters, genau genommen betraf es die senkrechte Fläche der Rücksitze, zu klein. Die Einführung eines

Rolf Wütherich, Günther Klass (r.)

174 BESCHEIDENE ANFÄNGE

Champion and winner of the 1000 Lakes Rally in 1962. So Linge and Falk knew that they could count on using the Porsche service vans, but the detailed preparation of the car, a vehicle from the test department, was minimal. One thing they did change were the dampers, replacing the standard Boge with Konis while they also took the precaution of fitting Weber 40 IDA carburettors in place of the standard Solex that, at that time, caused the engine to suffer from a mid-range flat spot. On the whole, it was pretty low-key effort but they did have an adequate supply of decent studded snow tyres, Hakkapellitas from Finland. This was just as well since the rally turned out to be a winter classic with an almost continuous blizzard from the Juras all the way to the Riviera. At the front, it was an epic struggle between Böhringer's 904 GTS and Timo Mäkinen's Mini Cooper S, but behind them, the 911 went through all those same terrible conditions, and emerged fifth overall. It was remarkable achievement that went largely unsung in the international press. And Prince Rainier did get to see a 911 that was undamaged when Linge and Falk drove it up to the traditional prize giving outside Monaco's Palace.

Those who realised what had happened were people like Falk himself and von Hanstein. The factory did further rallies during 1965 with the 904 and 904/6 but with much reduced success while, behind the scenes, the 911 was being groomed for a principal role in motor sport. Porsche always homologated – obtained recognition forms from the Federation Internationale d'Automobile – for all their models no matter whether the factory or anyone else had an intention to compete with them. For instance, even the 60 bhp version of the 356 was homologated during the 1950s. But what von

Monte Carlo 1966: Rolf Wütherich, Günther Klass

Hanstein and his new technical assistant, Jurgen Barth, had noticed was that, under the new international regulations – FIA's Appendix J to its Sporting Code – that were introduced in the beginning of 1966, the 911 could pass as a Group 2 saloon car. Up until this point, the 911 had been homologated as a GT car in Group 3. But by virtue of the fact that it was produced in annual quantities of more than 1,000 and that its internal dimensions were large enough, it was able to qualify as a saloon. They also noticed that the 912, the four-cylinder version of the 911, was made in sufficient numbers to qualify as a Group 1 saloon car. In fact, the internal dimensions failed by the merest fraction of a centimetre on the vertical plane of the rear seat. By introducing a small wedge on all production 911s and 912s, this could be overcome and so their plans went ahead. By the time 1967 came around, they had the 912 homologated in Group 1, the 911 and 911L in Group 2 and the 911T and 911S in Group 3. The implications were favourable for rallying but it also enabled the 911 to gain some impressive results in saloon car racing.

The problem in rallying was that with the new rules came a positive effort to keep highly tuned saloon cars – Group 2 – and powerful GT cars – Group 3 – out of the top spot. This was immediately evident on the 1966 Monte Carlo Rally. Porsche had hired Gunter Klass as their driver for the year and the first event in which he was entered was the Monte. His co-driver was Rolf Wütherlich who just over ten years earlier had been a passenger in the 550 Spyder when

Austrian Alpine 1966: G Wallraberstein, Müller

FROM SMALL BEGINNINGS 175

kleinen Keils bei allen Produktions-911 und 912 schaffte Abhilfe und so gediehen die Pläne weiter. Zu Jahresbeginn 1967 war der 912 in der Gruppe 1 homologiert, der 911 und der 911L in Gruppe 2 und der 911T sowie der 911S in Gruppe 3. Die Auswirkungen waren günstig für den Rallyesport, aber sie befähigten den Elfer auch, einige eindrucksvolle Erfolge in Tourenwagen-Rennen herauszufahren. Das Problem des Rallyesports nach Einführung der neuen Bestimmungen waren verstärkte Bemühungen, die hoch gezüchteten Tourenwagen der Gruppe 2 und die starken GT-Fahrzeuge der Gruppe 3 weitestgehend aus der Spitzengruppe fernzuhalten. Dies wurde sofort augenscheinlich bei der Rallye Monte Carlo 1966. Porsche hatte Gunter Klass für dieses Jahr verpflichtet und seine erste Veranstaltung war die Monte. Sein Beifahrer Rolf Wütherich übrigens hatte zehn Jahre zuvor als Mitfahrer in dem 550 Spyder gesessen, in dem James Dean starb. Die monegassischen Veranstalter waren angehalten, hoch gezüchtete Fahrzeuge nicht aufs Podium kommen zu lassen. Die von den Autos der Gruppe 2 und 3 gefahrenen Zeiten wurden daher mit einem Strafzuschlag von 18% belegt.

So kam es, dass der 911, obwohl er drei Bestzeiten gefahren war, davon eine auf dem Col de Turini, und er die GT-Klasse gewonnen hatte, nur Gesamtrang 16 belegte, selbst nach dem Ausschluss der drei Werks-Mini Cooper, der zwei Werks-Ford Lotus Cortina und eines Werks-Hillman Imp. Glücklicherweise waren die Veranstalter der anderen großen Rallyes weniger strikt gegenüber den GT-Fahrzeugen und so ließ sich Klass auf ein beschränktes europäisches Rallyeprogramm ein, in welchem er so gute Ergebnisse einfuhr, dass diese zum Gewinn der GT-Wertung der Europäischen Rallyemeisterschaft ausreichten.

Tatsächlich war er der erfolgreichste Punktejäger, und hätte es schon einen Einzeltitel gegeben, er hätte ihn gewonnen. Wie dem auch sei, bei der österreichischen Alpen Rallye war er der Unglücksrabe, dem in Führung liegend die Antriebswelle abriss, und ein gerissener Gaszug ließ ihn bei der Genfer Rallye die Führung verlieren und Klassenzweiter hinter einem Triumph Spitfire werden. Im September 1966 gewann Klass beim Coupe des Alpes die GT-Klasse und wurde Gesamtsechster, obwohl er nach einem Unfall mit einem Zweirad auf einer Verbindungsetappe Zeit verloren hatte. Bei derselben Veranstaltung hatte Vic Elford in seinem Werks-Lotus Cortina vorn gelegen, ehe ein Motorschaden für das Aus sorgte.

Seine Unzufriedenheit mit Ford führte zu Gesprächen mit von Hanstein, der ihm ein 911-Cockpit für die Rallye Korsika anbot. Da diese damals kein Meisterschaftslauf war, gab es auch keine Probleme mit seinem Ford-Vertrag. Klass hatte einen Unfall am ersten Tag, verlor dadurch 40 Minuten und seine Siegchancen. Elford fuhr etwas beständiger aber kaum langsamer, was ihm im Ziel einen dritten Rang, sieben Plätze vor Klass, einbrachte. Mit einem erweiterten Programm, das für 1967 geplant war und Klass, der zur Rundstrecke wechselte, wurde entschieden, dass Elford Ford verlassen und die neue Porsche- Speerspitze bilden sollte.

Coupe des Alpes 1966: Rolf Wütherich, Günther Klass

Winner Polish 1967: Sobieslaw and Eva Zasada

Tour of Corsica 1966: Vic Elford, David Stone

176 BESCHEIDENE ANFÄNGE

Winner Geneva 1967: Vic Elford, David Stone

James Dean was killed. The Monegasque organisers were determined to keep highly tuned cars away from the podium and had put a penalty of eighteen percent on the times set by cars from Groups 2 & 3. Thus, despite making some of the best times over the special stages – three fastest times including one on the Col de Turini – and winning the GT category, the 911 was classified sixteenth overall even after the exclusion of three works Mini Coopers, two works Ford Lotus Cortinas and a works Hillman Imp. Fortunately, the other major rallies were not quite so tough on GT cars and Klass embarked on a restricted European programme in which they got sufficiently good results to win the GT section of the European Rally Championship. In fact, Klass was the highest points scorer and if there had been a single title he would have won it. As it was, he was the victim of bad luck on the Austrian Alpine when he snapped a driveshaft while leading while a broken throttle cable on the Geneva Rally saw him lose the lead and finish second in class to a Triumph Spitfire.

In September of 1966, Klass did the Coupe des Alpes where he won the GT category and finished sixth overall despite losing time on the road section after an accident with a cyclist. On that same event, Vic Elford had been leading in his factory Lotus Cortina before the engine broke. His dissatisfaction with Ford led him to talk with von Hanstein and he was offered a 911 for the Tour of Corsica, at that time a non-championship event and thus presenting no problem with his Ford contract. Klass had an accident on the first test, losing forty minutes and any chance of a win, but afterwards set some very fast times. Elford was a bit steadier and not much slower and finally finished third, seven places ahead of Klass. With a slightly bigger programme planned for 1967 and Klass showing more enthusiasm for going racing, it was decided that Elford would leave Ford and spearhead the Porsche attack.

FROM SMALL BEGINNINGS 177

Winner Lyon-Charbonnieres 1967: Vic Elford, David Stone

Pauli Toivonen, Martti Kolari (r.)

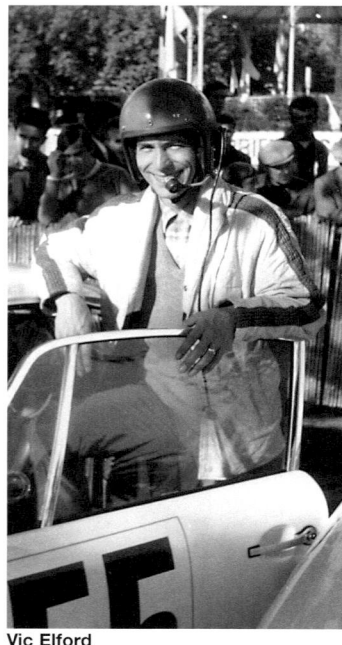

Vic Elford

Acropolis 1968: Pauli Toivonen, Martti Kolari

Die erste Veranstaltung, die einige Handikaps für die Gruppen 2 und 3 gebracht hatte, war die Rallye Monte Carlo. Stattdessen gab es nun eine neue Bestimmung, die ein Limit von acht Reifen pro Veranstaltungsetappe verhängte. Das war schwierig für den 911 und es war nicht überraschend, dass leichtere Autos wie der Mini Cooper oder der Lancia Fulvia besser in der Lage waren, ihre Reifen zu schonen, speziell in der verschneiten letzten Nacht, der so genannten Nacht der langen Messer. Am Ende der gewöhnlichen Schleife lag Elford in Führung vor drei Werks-Mini Coopern und zwei Werks-Lancias, wenige Sekunden dahinter fuhr Klass bei einem seiner letzten Auftritte bei einer größeren Rallye. Dann jedoch auf der Gebirgsschleife kam der Schnee und das beste, was Elford am Ende der Nacht erreichen konnte, war Gesamtrang drei hinter einem Mini Cooper und einer Fulvia. Klass fühlte sich auf bereits benutzen Reifen in frischem Schnee wenig heimisch, überschritt die Karenzzeit, nachdem er in der Nacht einen falschen Abzweig genommen hatte und fiel somit aus.

Elfords nächste Veranstaltung war die Schweden-Rallye, bei der sogar noch mehr Schnee lag. Hier fuhr er einen 911 in der Gruppe 2 und es war keine Veranstaltung, die er als einfach empfand. Einige Zeit verbrachte er abseits der Strecke damit beschäftigt, seinen 911 aus den Schneewehen wieder auszugraben. Bei derselben Rallye bestritt ein junger Bursche namens Björn Waldegård seinen ersten Wettbewerb in einem Elfer. Nach einer langen Lehrzeit bei VW war ihm der Porsche vom schwedischen Importeur Scania-Vabis angeboten worden und Waldegård nutzte die Chance und zeigte auf Anhieb allen das Heck, bis ihm kurz nach Halbzeit die Strecke ausging. Er konnte weiterfahren und war noch immer in den Top-Drei, als schließlich eine gebrochene Antriebswelle die Fahrt beendete.

Aber, wie auf Korsika Elford, so hatte von Hanstein wieder einen talentierten Fahrer ausgemacht. Während Waldegård sein Skandinavien-Programm mit Scania-Vabis absolvierte, wurde für ihn ein Werkswagen für die holländische Tulpen Rallye aufgetrieben und dem jungen Schweden jede Gelegenheit gegeben, seine Rallyeerfahrung auf europäischer Ebene auszuweiten.

Währenddessen gewann Vic Elford die Rallye Deutschland, die Tulpen Rallye, die Rallye Genf und das 84-Stunden-Rennen „Marathon de la Route" auf dem Nürburgring gemeinsam mit Jochen Neerpasch und Hans Hermann. Auf Korsika

178 DAS TEAM ENTSTEHT

Safari 1968: Edgar Herrmann, Gerd Elvers

The first event was the Monte Carlo Rally that had got rid of the handicap for Groups 2 and 3 but instead had created a regulation that imposed a restriction of eight tyres per leg of the event. This was difficult for the 911 and, not surprisingly, lighter cars like the Mini Cooper and the Lancia Fulvia were able to conserve their tyres much better especially on the last night when it snowed. At the end of the Common Route, Elford led ahead of three works Coopers and two works Lancias with Klass on one of his last appearances in a major rally just a few seconds behind in seventh place. But then on the Mountain Loop came the snow and the best Elford could do by the end of the night was third overall behind one Mini Cooper and one Fulvia. Klass was not completely at home on worn tyres in fresh snow and, after taking a wrong turning in the night, he ran out of time and retired.

Elford's next event was the Swedish Rally where there was even more snow. Here he was using a 911 in Group 2 but it was not an event at which he felt at ease and he spent quite some time off the road digging the 911 out of snowdrifts. On the same event, a young chap called Bjorn Waldegård was having his first drive in a 911. After serving a long apprenticeship in VWs. he had been offered a Porsche by the Swedish importers, Scania-Vabis and used it to show a clean pair of heels to everyone until he too went off just after the halfway point. He got back on the road and was still in the top three but finally a drive shaft broke and he was out. But, as in Corsica with Elford, von Hanstein had spotted a useful driver and, while Waldegård continued his own Scandinavian programme with Scania-Vabis, a works car was found for the Tulip Rally and every opportunity given to the young Swede to widen his experience of European rallying. Meanwhile, Elford won the West German, Tulip and Geneva rallies plus the 84 Hours of Nürburgring (Marathon de la Route) with Jochen Neerpasch and Hans Hermann. In Corsica, he was third again but his ultra-light 911R did not last the Alpine Rally, retiring with a broken cam follower high on the Col de Pennes. At this stage of the 911's development for rallying, the engine was pretty reliable and it was normally the transmission that gave trouble with the drive shafts a particular source of problems.

The other driving recruit to the 911 "family" at this time was the Polish driver, Sobieslaw Zasada. For many years he had driven a diminutive Steyr-Puch and astounded people with the performance he could get from the little 650cc car, win-

Winner Swedish 1968: Bjorn Waldegard, Lars Helmer

RAC 1968: Bjorn Waldegard, Lars Helmer

THE TEAM IS BUILT

Winner Swedish Rally: Lars Helmer, Björn Waldegard (r.)

wurde er wieder dritter, die Alpen Rallye überstand sein ultra-leichter 911R nicht, mit einem gebrochenen Ventilstößel schied er hoch auf dem Col de Pennes aus. In diesem Stadium der Rallyeentwicklung des 911 war der Motor recht zuverlässig und es war normalerweise die Kraftübertragung, die einige Probleme machte, speziell die Antriebswellen waren eine Fehlerquelle.

Der andere Fahrerneuling in der 911-Familie war der Pole Sobieslaw Zasada. Einige Jahre war er einen winzigen Steyr-Puch gefahren und hatte für Verblüffung gesorgt mit der Leistung, die er aus dem kleinen 650ccm-Auto herausgeholt hatte, so auch der Gewinn der Gruppe 2-Europameisterschaft 1966. Nun trat er mit Sponsoren im Rücken an Porsche heran und pilotierte einen 911S bei einigen Veranstaltungen, beginnend mit der Rallye Lyons-Charbonnières.

Bei der Eröffnungsprüfung am Solitude Ring brach jedoch die Benzinpumpe und die Zeit, die beim Wechsel verloren ging, führte dazu, dass er die Rallye vom 73. Startplatz aus in Angriff nehmen musste. Er schaffte es, daraus bis ins Ziel den dritten Gesamtrang zu machen, direkt hinter Elford im anderen 911S und Jean-Pierre Hanrioud. Seine nächste Veranstaltung war die Alpen-Rallye in Österreich, die er auf Anhieb gewann. Daraufhin bot man ihm an, für den Rest der Saison einen 912 zu fahren, um den Titel in der Gruppe 1 zu erobern, eine Aufgabe, die er mit Leichtigkeit vollendete. Er siegte bei der Rallye Polen in einem Jahr, in dem sie so hart war, das nur drei Autos das Ziel sahen. Dann nahm er mit einem 911 in Argentinien am Grand Premio de Turismo teil, um nach 3.600 absolvierten Kilometern als Erster von 367 Teilnehmern einzulaufen.

Das Jahr 1967 verlief extrem gut für Porsche und seine Elfer-Rallyeautos. Vic Elford und Sobieslaw Zasada gewannen ihre Kategorien in der Europameisterschaft mit einer eindrucksvollen Siegesbilanz bei größeren Veranstaltungen. Währenddessen lernte Björn Waldegård alles über den 911 unter skandinavischen Bedingungen und gewann auf Anhieb die schwedische Meisterschaft. Leider war es ihm und Elford nicht vergönnt, ihre Stärken bei der RAC-Rallye am Jahresende unter Beweis zu stellen, denn ein Ausbruch der Maul- und Klauenseuche führte zur Absage dieser Veranstaltung.

1968 bei der Monte waren sie dann Teamkollegen neben dem dritten Piloten, Pauli Toivonen. Toivonen war der Schützling des finnischen VW/Porsche-Importeurs und war während der Saison 1965 bereits für Porsche einen 904 bei der Rallye Monte Carlo und der Alpine-Rallye gefahren. Danach war er zu Citroën, dem Hersteller, mit dem er 1962 bei der 1000 Seen Rallye siegreich war, gewechselt und gewann prompt die Rallye Monte Carlo für die Franzosen.

Diese drei Fahrer zeigten schnell, dass sie und der 911 das Maß der Dinge waren. Und ihre Wettbewerbsfähigkeit wurde von der Tatsache unterstützt, dass die Veranstalter alle vorgetäuschten Handicaps, wie limitierte Reifenanzahl oder andere künstliche Vorrichtungen, die Ergebnisse zu beeinträchtigen, verworfen hatten. So konnte Porsche den Gruppe 3-911T in direkter Konkurrenz zu den anderen Gruppen einsetzen. Der 911T war ein Leichtbau-Auto mit ebenso minimaler Schalldämpfung wie Innenausstattung, dazu eine gewichtsmäßig erleichterte vordere Stoßstange und dem Motor aus dem 911S, allerdings mit einer auf mehr als 200 PS gesteigerten Leistung.

Zur selben Zeit räumte die Commission Sportive Internationale (CSI) bei ihren Homologations-Regeln auf, indem die Innenabmessungen erhöht wurden, die für die Einstufung in den Gruppen 1 und 2 benötigt wurden. Somit konnte der Basis-911 und der 912 an reinen Tourenwagenveranstaltungen nicht mehr teilnehmen.

Mit nun klaren technischen Vorgaben und dem besten Auto für alle Ansprüche, gewann Elford prompt die Rallye Monte Carlo 1968, mit Toivonen knapp geschlagen dahinter auf Platz zwei. In diesem Jahr gab es keinen Wintereinbruch in letzter Minute und der 911T konnte auf einigen Wertungsprüfungen mit Rennreifen mit nur wenigen Spikes gefahren werden. Seine Kraft und sein Handling waren etwas, auf das die Mini Coopers und Lancia Fulvias keine Antwort fanden.

Waldegård gewann in Schweden, während Toivonen, mit der Jagd auf den EM-Titel beauftragt, seine Siege in San Remo, bei der Deutschland sowie der DDR-Rallye, in Ungarn und in Genf genoss. So hatte Porsche zur Saisonmitte die Dinge gut unter Dach und Fach, Toivonen war bereits Europameister und, trotz mittelmäßiger Ergebnisse gegen Jahresende, wurde Porsche dritter der Herstellerwertung. Während des Jahres gab es noch weitere Entwicklungen: Edgar Herrmann setzte bei der East African Safari Rallye einen privaten 911 ein und war gut unterwegs, ehe er durch Überschreiten der Karenzzeit ausfiel. Es war das Jahr der heftigen Regenfälle, in dem nur sieben Autos ins Ziel kamen. Porsche sah sich nun veranlasst, diese Veranstaltung im Folgejahr genauer zu betrachten.

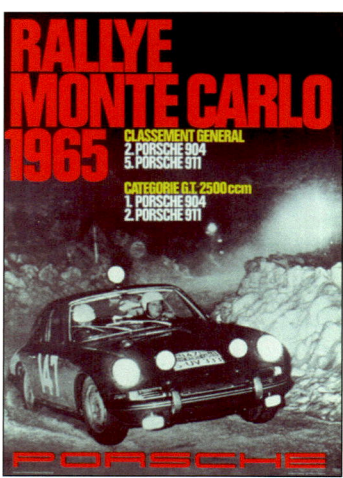

Poster

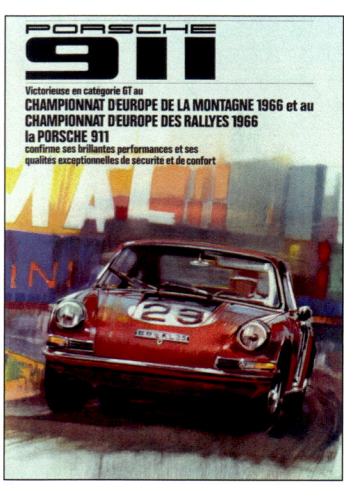

Poster

Poster

Poster

DAS TEAM ENTSTEHT

ning the European Championship in Group 2 with it in 1966. Now he approached Porsche with some sponsorship and drove a 911S on several rallies starting with the Lyons-Charbonnières. On the opening test at the Solitude Ring, he suffered a broken petrol pump and the time lost changing it meant that started out on the rally in 73rd place. He was able to convert that to third overall at the finish behind the other 911Ss of Elford and Jean-Pierre Hanrioud. His next event was the Austrian Alpine where he won outright. Then came the offer to drive a 912 for the rest of the season to capture the Group 1 title a task that he accomplished with some ease. He won the Polish Rally outright in a year when it was so tough that only three cars finished and then took a 911 to Argentina for the Grand Premio de Turismo where he won again over a route of some 2,250 miles [3,600km] and 367 competitors.

Thus 1967 went extremely well for Porsche and its 911 rally cars. Vic Elford and Sobieslaw Zasada won their categories in the European Championship with an impressive list of wins in major events while Bjorn Waldegård learnt all about the 911 in Scandinavian conditions. Sadly both he and Elford were denied the chance to show their pace on the RAC

Monte Carlo 1967: Vic Elford, David Stone

Rally at year's end when it was cancelled due to an outbreak of Foot & Mouth Disease, but 1968 started with them as team mates on the Monte Carlo alongside a third driver, Pauli Toivonen. Toivonen was the protégé of the Finnish VW-Porsche importer and had already driven 904s for Porsche on Monte Carlo and Alpine Rallies during the 1965 season. After that, he had gone to Citroen, the make with which he had won the 1000 Lakes in 1962, and promptly won the Monte Carlo Rally for them. These three drivers quickly showed that they and the 911 meant business. And their competitivity was helped greatly by the fact that the rally organisers abandoned all pretence of handicaps, limited number of tyres or other artificial contrivances to affect the result of their events, and thus Porsche were able to use their Group 3 911T in direct competition with the other Groups. The 911T was a lightweight car with minimal sound deadening and interior trim, a lightened front bumper and the 911S engine upgraded to give over 200 bhp. At the same time, the CSI, the international rule makers for motor sport, "tidied up" their homologation rules by increasing the internal dimensions required to qualify in Groups 1 and 2 thus removing the basic 911 and the 912 from events only open to saloon cars.

Anyway, with a clear technical field and the best car for the job, Elford promptly won the 1968 Monte Carlo Rally with Toivonen close behind him. This time there was no last minute delivery of snow and the 911T was able to use lightly studded racing tyres for some of the special stages. Its power and handling were something to which the Mini Coopers and Lancia Fulvias had no answer. Waldegård won in Sweden, while Toivonen with the remit to chase the European Rally Championship title tasted victory in San Remo, both German rallies, Hungary and Geneva so that by mid-season, Porsche had things pretty well wrapped up. Toivonen emerged as the new European Champion and, despite "average" results towards the end of the year, Porsche still finished third in the newly created European Manufacturer's Championship. There were other developments during the year for Edgar Herrmann took a private 911 on the East African Safari Rally and did well enough with it before running out of time – it was the year of the heavy rains when only seven cars finished – that caused Porsche to look more closely at the event for the following year.

Winner Monte Carlo 1968: Vic Elford, David Stone

THE TEAM IS BUILT 181

IM RALLYESPORT GANZ VORN

Veränderungen in der Porsche Führungsriege zum Jahresende 1968 führten dazu, daß Huschke von Hanstein seine direkte Kontrolle über die Wettbewerbsaktivitäten aufgeben mußte, um spezielle Aufgabengebiete für Ferry Porsche selbst zu übernehmen. Sein Nachfolger als Sportchef war Rico Steinemann, ein Motorsportjournalist mit Interesse sowohl an Rundstreckenrennen als auch an Rallyes.

Vic Elford hatte im Laufe des Jahres 1968 Geschmack gefunden an Sportwagenrennen und auch an der Formel 1 und sich nun entschieden, ganz zum Rundstreckensport zu wechseln. So wurde Björn Waldegård verpflichtet, neben dem Schweden gehörten Pauli Toivonen und Sobieslaw Zasada sowie der Neuling Gerard Larrousse, der vom Team Alpine-Renault gekommen war, zum Werkskader. Der Radstand des 911S war verlängert worden und theoretisch konnte sowohl mit einer Bosch Direkteinspritzanlage als auch mit zwei Weber Dreifach-Vergasern 46 IDA3 gefahren werden. Zunächst jedoch führten Homologations-Probleme dazu, dass bei der Rallye Monte Carlo die 911S in der Gruppe 3 schwerer waren und vielleicht sogar über 20 PS weniger verfügten als die 911T, die 1968 dominiert hatten.

Für Steinemann war diese erste große Rallye eine wahre Feuertaufe. Nicht weniger als vier 911S hatte er an den Start gebracht, um sicherzugehen, dass der Sieg von 1968 wiederholt werden könnte. Auch Elford in seinem letzten großen Rallyeauftritt für Porsche war dabei. Die Rallye begann schlecht, als Toivonen auf der ersten Prüfung von der Strecke abkam und sich die Aufhängung verbog führte Waldegård vor Elford, Larrousse lag an Position vier.

Auf der Gebirgsschleife verhörte sich Waldegård bei den Anweisungen eines Mechanikers beim Service und trat aufs Bremspedal, als die Bremsbeläge herunter genommen waren. Tatsächlich hatte der Mechaniker gesagt: "Nicht bremsen", aber der Schwede hatte nur das letzte Wort gehört! Die Kolben fielen aus dem Bremssattel und das darauf folgende Chaos kostete ihm vier Minuten auf der Verbindungsetappe. Nun führte Elford, doch eine kurze Unaufmerksamkeit auf einer vereisten Straße Richtung Sospel ließ seinen 911 gegen einen Baum rutschen und ausfallen. So siegte Waldegård während Larrousse Platz zwei heimfuhr, nachdem er sich die ganze Nacht hindurch einen Kampf mit seinem alten Teamkollegen von Alpine-Renault, Jean Vinatier, geliefert hatte.

East African Safari 1969: Sobieslaw Zasada, Marek Wachowski

Winner Tour de Corse 1969: Gerard Larrousse, Maurice Gelin

Winner Acropolis 1969: Pauli Toivonen, Martti Kolari

Winner Swedish 1970: Bjorn Waldegard, Lars Helmer

NEW LEADERSHIP

Changes within the Porsche Company at the end of 1968 saw von Hanstein relinquish his direct control over competition activities and take up special assignments working directly for Ferry Porsche. His replacement on the sporting side was Rico Steinemann, a motor sport journalist with an interest in both racing and rallying through his editorship of Powerslide magazine. Vic Elford had already developed a taste for both Sports Car racing and Formula One during 1968 and now decided to go full time racing so Bjorn Waldegård was elevated to the Porsche factory squad with a recruit from the Alpine Renault team, Gerard Larrousse alongside him and with Toivonen and Zasada as long-stops. Now they had the new longer wheelbase 911S and in theory could use it either with Bosch plunger pump fuel injection or on two triple-choke Weber 46 IDA3 carburettors. But initially, homologation problems meant that for the Monte Carlo, the Group 3 911Ss were heavier and with perhaps 20bhp less than the 911Ts that had dominated in 1968.

For Steinemann, this first major rally was a baptism of fire. He had entered no less than four 911S to be sure of repeating the 1968 victory including Elford in almost his last rally appearance for Porsche. The rally started badly as Toivonen went off on the first stage and bent the suspension, but back in Monaco after the Common Route, Waldegård led from Elford with Larrousse fourth. On the Mountain Loop, Waldegård misheard one of the mechanics at service and pressed the brake pedal when the brake pads had been removed. The mechanic actually said "nicht bremse" and Waldegård only heard the last word ! The pistons popped out of the calliper and the ensuing chaos cost him four minutes on the road section. Now Elford led, but a moment of inattention coming down an icy road into Sospel saw him crash the 911 into a tree and retire. Thus Waldegård won while Larrousse took second after a nightlong battle with his old team mate from Alpine Renault, Jean Vinatier.

Success continued to follow the 911 as, after the 1-2 on the Monte Carlo Rally, Waldegård won his home event in Sweden for the second time. New challenges were needed and it was decided to send a 911 from Stuttgart to the East African Safari Rally to be driven by Zasada. For a first attempt, it was pretty good with the car running well in a dry year except for petrol pump trouble in Uganda which dropped the Poles from second to sixth at the finish. Actually the 911 very nearly did not start the rally as Alitalia lost it on the

East African Safari 1970: Sobieslaw Zasada, Mike Sochacki

NEW LEADERSHIP 183

Die Erfolgsserie des 911 hielt an als Waldegård seine Heimrallye in Schweden zum zweiten Mal gewann. Neue Herusforderungen waren nötig und so wurde entschieden, dass ein 911, der von Zasada gefahren werden sollte, von Stuttgart nach Kenia zur East African Safari Rallye geschickt wurde. Für den ersten Anlauf lief es zufriedenstellend mit einem zuverlässig laufenden Auto in einem trockenen Jahr. Nur Probleme mit der Benzinpumpe in Uganda warfen den Polen von Rang zwei auf sechs im Ziel zurück. Tatsächlich wäre der 911 fast gar nicht gestartet, weil Alitalia ihn auf dem Flughafen in Rom "vergessen" hatte. Verzweifelt auf die Ankunft wartend hatte Zasada und sein Sponsor Castrol einen vor Ort vorbereiteten Peugeot 404 gemietet, um die Rallye zu bestreiten. Glücklicherweise traf der Porsche nach elf Stunden ein, so dass die Rallye wie geplant bestritten weren konnte.

Zurück in Europa, konnte Toivonen endlich die Rallye Akroolis mit einer überlegenen Vorstellung seines Könnens und seiner Ausdauer gewinnen. War ihm der Sieg im Vorjahr noch durch einen Reifenschaden in einer Wertungsprüfung verwehrt worden, so fuhr er nun seinen mit Direkteinpritzung ausgestatten 911S ganz nach vorne. Während seine Teamkollegen Waldegård und Larrousse hingegen

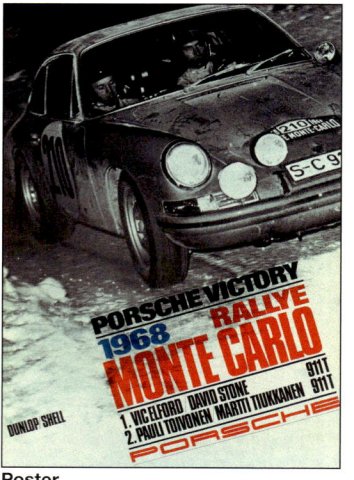

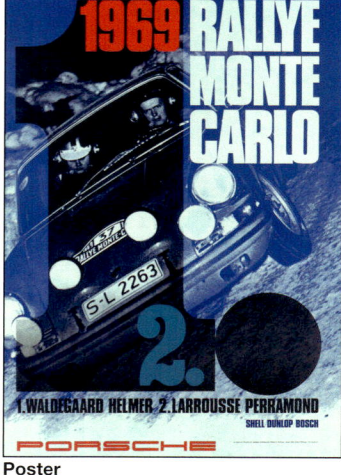

Poster

Poster

diversen Problemen bei dieser harten und rauen Veranstaltung erlagen, kam er durch, schlug Roger Clarks Ford Escort TC und erhielt so seine Revanche für 1968.

Der 911 zeigte brilliant seine Vielseitigkeit bei Rallyes. Als 911R konnte er klassische Asphalt-Veranstaltungen wie die Tour de France Automobile oder die Rallye Korsika gewinnen. Im nächsten Moment hatte er bei gemischten Straßenbelägen wie in Polen die Nase vorn. Die Rallye, bei der Zasada gemeinsam mit seiner Frau Eva als Beifahrerin triumphierte. Auch bei schnellen Schneesprints, wie bei der Schweden-Rallye, siegte er. Diese Vielseitigkeit wurde mit einem zweiten Platz für Porsche in der Europäischen Markenmeisterschaft gebührend honoriert.

Nach dem gleichen Muster ging es 1970 weiter, zumal Waldegård und Larrousse nun über einen 2,5 Liter Motor mit 230 PS verfügten. Zur selben Zeit homologierte Porsche Plastiktüren für den 911S in der Gruppe 4, so dass die Fahrzeuge nicht nur stärker, sondern auch leichter waren. Der Schwede und der Franzose belegten die Plätze eins und zwei bei der Rallye Monte Carlo und verhalfen Porsche somit zum Hattrick. Dieses war bei dieser Veranstaltung noch keinem anderen Werk zuvor gelungen und es wurde einmal mehr untermauert, was für ein höchst wettbewerbsfähiges Auto der 911 war.

Porsche hatte großes Interesse, die neu geschaffene Internationale Meisterschaft für Marken (IRCM), die acht europäische Top-Rallyes und die East African Safari einschloss, zu gewinnen. Der Sieg bei der Monte Carlo war ein guter Anfang und dann gewann Waldegård, wie gewöhnlich, die Schweden-Rallye und fügte später im Jahr noch einen Sieg bei der österreichischen Alpine hinzu. Diese drei Erfolge waren nahezu genug, um die neue Meisterschaft zu Gunsten von Porsche zu gewinnen. Tatsächlich jedoch wurde die IRCM erst bei der letzten Veranstaltung, der RAC-Rallye, entschieden.

Porsches Rivale im Titelkampf war Alpine-Renault und beide Teams traten stark an. Der Verlust von Waldegård und seinem schwedischen Landsmann Åke Andersson, die mit geborstenem Getriebe im 911S ausgefallen waren, ließ alle Stuttgarter Hoffnungen auf Larrousse ruhen. Als die letzten Prüfungen in Süd-Wales bevorstanden, hatte er jedoch drei Alpines vor sich. Doch zuerst fing die Alpine von Jean-Pierre Nicolas Feuer und brannte aus, dann brach auf der letzten Prüfung bei Jean-Luc Thérier eine Antriebswelle. So kam Larrousse als sechster ins Ziel und das war gerade ausreichend, den Titel für Porsche zu entscheiden.

Zasada startete wieder und als einziger Porsche-Vertreter bei der Safari-Rallye. Allerdings traf er eine falsche Entscheidung schon vor dem Start, die schließlich seinen Ausfall verursachen sollte. Die Vorjahres-Rallye war außergewöhnlich trocken, doch 1970 sollte es sehr nass werden und mit einer Menge Schlamm dabei. Er befürchtete mit einem zu großen Motorenunterschutz zu oft im Schlamm stecken zu bleiben. So entschied er sich nur für das nötigste, kleinste Schutzblech, wechselte jedoch die Ölwanne nicht gegen eine stärkere aus Magnesium. Während der Rallye traf er dann ein zu hartes Stück Ostafrika, zerriss sich dabei die Ölwanne und fiel an zweiter Stelle liegend aus.

Porsche war erfreut, die IRCM gewonnen zu haben, doch der Erfolg - speziell die drei dominanten Siege in Monte Carlo - bedeuteten nun in eine gänzlich andere Art von Wettbewerb einzutreten. Dies war nun ein Entwicklungswettlauf unter den Fahrzeugherstellern. Der Rallyesport veränderte sich, gerade in jenem Moment in dem der 911 gezeigt hatte, dass er ein Serienauto war, dass über ausreichend Schnelligkeit, Stärke und Zuverlässigkeit verfügte, um bei nahezu jeder Rallye auf der Welt gut zu sein, begann der Aufstieg des spezialisierten Rallyeautos.

Alpine-Renault hatte Schritt für Schritt das Modell seines zierlichen Fiberglas-A110 verbessert und war nun bereit, die neue Version mit einem 1600ccm Motor in einem Auto, das nicht viel mehr als 750 kg auf die Waage brachte, zu homologieren. Lancia war am Ende des Wegs mit seinem Fulvia Coupé, obwohl dieses einen Überraschungssieg bei der Rallye Monte Carlo 1972 einfuhr. Aber man hatte revolutionäre Pläne für ein Auto, das nicht nur die neue Alpine, sondern auch den Porsche 911 ausbeschleunigen sollte. Und Ford bugsierte seinen 16-Ventil BDA-Motor in den bereits konkurrenzfähigen Escort. 1971 sollte die Luft viel dünner werden.

Winner Monte Carlo 1970: Bjorn Waldegard, Lars Helmer

ground at Rome airport and, despairing of its arrival, Zasada and his sponsor, Castrol, had hired a locally prepared Peugeot 404 in which to do the rally. Fortunately, the Porsche arrived at the eleventh hour and they were able to do the rally as planned. Back in Europe, Toivonen at last won the Acropolis Rally in a drive of considerable skill and patience. Denied outright victory the previous year by a mid-stage puncture, this time he drove his fuel-injected 911S to perfection and, while his team mates, Waldegård and Larrousse succumbed to various problems on this hard, rough event, he came through to beat Roger Clark's Ford Escort TC and thus reap revenge for 1968.

The 911 was certainly showing its versatility in rallies. One moment, as a 911R, it could be winning classic tarmac events like the Tour de France Automobile or the Tour of Corsica. The next minute, it could be winning mixed surface events like the Polish Rally where Zasada triumphed with his wife, Eva, who had for so many years navigated him in the Steyr-Puch. Then it could win sprint snow rallies like the Swedish. This versatility was duly rewarded with a second place for Porsche in the European Makes Championship.

The same pattern continued in 1970 though now Waldegård and Larrousse had the use of the 2.25litre engine that gave them 230 bhp. At the same time, Porsche homologated plastic panels for the 911S in Group 4 so the cars were not just more powerful but they were lighter as well. The pair finished first and second on the Monte Carlo Rally thus giving Porsche its hat trick and hammering home the lesson that the 911 was a very competitive rally car. Porsche were keen to win the newly created International Championship for Makes that comprised the top eight European rallies plus the East African Safari. They got off to a good start with the Monte Carlo victory and then Waldegård, as usual, won the Swedish and added a win on the Austrian Alpine to their total later in the year. With the cancellation of the Alpine Rally that year thanks to funding problems, those three wins were almost enough on their own to grab the new championship for Porsche. In fact, the IRCM was only decided at the very last event, the RAC Rally. Porsche's rival for the title was Alpine and both teams were there in strength. The loss of both Waldegård and fellow Swede, Åke Andersson, with cracked gearboxes in their 911Ss meant that all Stuttgart's hopes rested with Larrousse. Going into the last stages in South Wales, he had three Alpines ahead of him. But first Jean-Pierre Nicolas had his Alpine catch fire and burn out and then Jean-Luc Thérier broke a drive shaft on the very last test. Larrousse made it home in sixth place that was just sufficient to clinch the title for Porsche.

On the Safari, Zasada had gone back and drove again with a lone entry, but made a wrong technical decision that eventually caused his retirement. The previous year had been exceptionally dry but 1970 was going to be wet with plenty of mud. He knew that if he fitted the full-sized protection plate under the car at the rear, it would "belly out" in deep mud and get stuck. So he opted for the more slender guard but did not change the sump for the stronger magnesium one. During the rally, he hit a piece of East Africa a bit too hard and split the sump thus retiring from what could have been another second place.

Porsche were delighted to win the International Championship but their success – and particularly their three dominant wins in Monte Carlo – meant that they were now entered in a different kind of race. This was a development race between the car manufacturers. Rallying was changing and, just at the very moment when the 911 was showing that it was a production car that had sufficient speed, strength and reliability to do well on almost any rally in the World, the rise of the specialised rally car was just beginning. Alpine Renault had been gradually improving the specification of their diminutive, fibreglass A110 and was now poised to homologate their new version with a 1600cc engine in a car weighing not much more than 750kg. Lancia were at the end of the line for their Fulvia Coupé, though this was going to win a surprise Monte Carlo for them in 1972, but they had revolutionary plans for a car that would outperform both the new Alpine and, most importantly, the Porsche 911. And Ford was about to shoehorn their 16-valve BDA engine into the already competitive Escort.

The pace in 1971 was going to be a lot hotter.

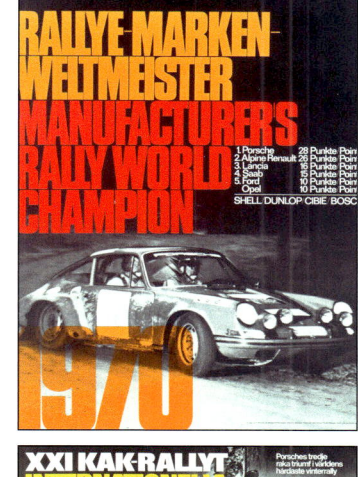

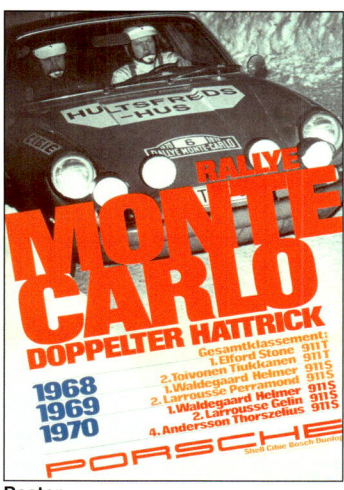

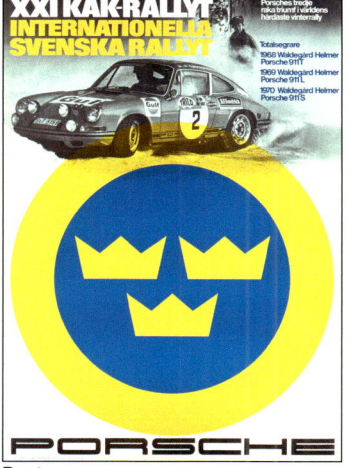

Winner Monte Carlo 1969: Bjorn Waldegard, Lars Helmer

911 S Monte Carlo 1969

Lyon-Charbonnieres 1969: Gerard Larrousse, Maurice Gelin

Bjorn Waldegard, Lars Helmer (r.)

911 S Monte Carlo 1969

186 IM RALLYESPORT GANZ VORN

Winner Monte Carlo 1970: Bjorn Waldegard, Lars Helmer

Monte Carlo 1969

NEW LEADERSHIP 187

DER SCHWARZE KONTINENT LOCKT

Für die Rallye Monte Carlo wurde entschieden, dass Porsche mit drei Exemplaren des 914/6 antreten sollte, um den Verkauf dieses neuen Modells, mit dem von Hanstein nun betraut war, zu forcieren. Wie auch immer der Effekt auf den Absatz des als VW-Porsche bekannten 914 war, diese Entscheidung brachte dem Elfer und Porsche im Allgemeinen keinen Vorteil. Waldegård mochte das Handling des Mittelmotor-Wagens nicht, der weit weniger zugänglich für seinen übersteuernden Fahrstil war als sein geliebter 911. Gerard Larrousse und Åke Andersson mühten sich ebenfalls ab, und alle drei beklagten mangelnde Kraftentfaltung.

Waldegård versuchte sein Möglichstes, aber die Konkurrenz war etwas stärker als im Jahr zuvor. Alpine hatte den A110 mit einer 1600ccm-Maschine homologiert und die Dienste von Ove Andersson erworben. Diese Kombination war nicht aufzuhalten und Waldegård fand nicht nur eine, sondern drei Werks-Alpines vor sich. Er schaffte es an Jean-Claude Andruet dranzubleiben, und diese beiden lagen schließlich punktgleich auf dem dritten Platz, aber für die breite Öffentlichkeit sah es aus wie ein glatter Dreifachsieg der Alpines.

Wer kann schon sagen, ob es nicht Waldegårds persönlicher Hattrick geworden wäre, hätte er in einem 911 gesessen? Aber was auch immer gewesen wäre, Tatsache war, dass die Franzosen einen überlegenen Sieg eingefahren hatten, der sie motivierte, den A110 weiterzuentwickeln. Renault stellte dafür die nötigen finanziellen Mittel bereit. Das Ergebnis war, dass Ove Andersson die Akropolis, die San Remo und die österreichische Alpine Rallye gewann und die Franzosen somit Ende Juli bereits die neuen IRCM-Meister waren.

Es war eine Zeit, in der die Rallyeautos sich veränderten und viel stärker spezialisiert wurden. Der 911 war bereits ein ziemlich spezielles Renn-Fahrzeug und hatte daher so viele Rallyes und Titel in den späten 60er-Jahren gewonnen, aber nun war man nicht mehr konkurrenzfähig. Trotz ihrer besten Bemühungen kamen Björn Waldegård und Åke Andersson bei der Schweden-Rallye über einen vierten und sechsten Platz hinter einem Saab, einem BMW und einem Lancia nicht hinaus. Sicher profitierte der von Lars Nyström gefahrene BMW von einer hohen Startnummer 52, die dazu führte, dass er mehr auf Schotter als auf Eis fuhr. Doch ebenso sicher war das Gefühl, dass der 911S deklassiert wurde.

RAC 1971: Bjorn Waldegard, Lars Helmer

Poster

Safari 1971: Sobieslaw Zasada, Marian Bien, Ake Andersson, Hans Thorselius, Bjorn Waldegard, Lars Helmer

East African Safari 1973: Bjorn Waldegard, Hans Thorselius

POWER STRUGGLE AND INTO AFRICA

For the 1971 Monte Carlo Rally, it was decided that Porsche should enter three examples of the new 914/6 model to promote sales of the Volkswagen-based variant with which von Hanstein was now involved. Whatever the effect of that decision on 914 sales, it did the 911 and Porsche in general no favours. Waldegård did not like the handling of the mid-engined car, which he found far less amenable to his oversteering style than his beloved 911. Gerard Larrousse and Åke Andersson also struggled and all three complained at the power output. Waldegård tried his best but the opposition was a bit sharper than the year before. Alpine had homologated their A110 with a 1600cc engine and acquired the services of Ove Andersson. The combination was irresistible and Waldegård found not just one but three works Alpines ahead of him. He did manage to hang on to Jean-Claude Andruet and these two were eventually tied for third place, but to most people it looked as if Alpine had got a straight 1-2-3.

Who can tell whether Waldegård might not have got his own personal hat trick if he had been 911 mounted. But whatever might have been, the fact that was that the French had won a considerable victory and were motivated – and thus funded – to continue. The result was that Ove Andersson won Acropolis, San Remo and the Austrian Alpine for them and, by the end of July, they were the new IRCM champions.

This was a time when rally cars were changing and becoming much more specialised. The 911 was a pretty special car already which is why it had won so many rallies and titles in the late 1960s but now it was beginning to feel left behind. Despite their best efforts, Bjorn Waldegård and Åke Andersson could do no better than finish fourth and sixth on the Swedish Rally behind a Saab, a BMW and Lancia. Certainly the BMW driven by Lars Nyström benefited from a very low start number – number 52 – so that it was able to run on gravel rather than ice in the stages, but there was certainly the feeling that the 911S was being outclassed.

With three works supported cars on the Safari Rally run by Jurgen Barth, great things were expected after Zasada's exploratory trips. But Åke Andersson retired and then Waldegård, trying to get past his team mate Zasada in the dust, was the victim of a misunderstanding. He thought that Zasada had pulled over after a radio request only to find that the Polish driver was taking a sharp right turn. Waldegård hit a bank and retired while Zasada went on to finish fifth. In Por-

Poster

East African Safari 1972: Sobieslaw Zasada, Marian Bien

Von den drei werksunterstützten Autos, die bei der Safari Rallye von Jürgen Barth eingesetzt wurden, konnte man nach Zasadas Forschungsfahrten gute Ergebnisse erwarten. Aber Åke Andersson fiel aus und dann wurde Waldegård, beim Versuch, seinen Teamkollegen Zasada durch eine Staubwolke zu überholen, Opfer eines Missverständnisses. Er dachte, Zasada würde nach seiner Funkbitte zur Seite fahren, stellte dann aber fest, dass der Pole nur einen scharfen Rechtsabzweig nahm. Waldegård traf eine Böschung und fiel aus während Zasada weiterfuhr und Platz fünf erreichte. In Portugal musste Waldegård mit einer gebrochenen Antriebswelle aufgeben, bei der RAC-Rallye hingegen fuhr er ein herausragendes Ergebnis ein, als er Platz zwei hinter Roger Clarks Ford Escort RS belegte.

Für die Rallye Saison 1972 beschloss Porsche, mit noch weniger Aufwand an die Sache heranzugehen. Immerhin zwei 911S starteten mit Larrousse und Waldegård am Steuer bei der Rallye Monte Carlo. Gemeinhin wurden diese Autos mit 2,5 Liter Hubraum und 260 PS als Favoriten gehandelt, ganz egal wie die Bedingungen waren. Wie auch immer, beide Piloten wurden von plötzlich einsetzendem Schneefall in der Ardeché eiskalt erwischt. Waldegård war auf Slicks gestar-

East African Safari 1973

tet und litt fürchterlich, als er in den tiefen Schnee kam. Er stoppte im Service, um auf Reifen mit Spikes zu wechseln, hatte aber bereits viele Strafpunkte erhalten. Larrousse hatte zwar Spikereifen aufgezogen, doch geriet er beim Service so in Zeitnot, dass er entschied, die Reifen hinten nicht zu wechseln, was ihm zehn Minuten auf der Verbindungsetappe einsparte.

Später streifte Waldegård, nun wieder auf Slicks unterwegs, eine Mauer und zerstörte einen Querlenker. Die Porsche-Mechaniker kamen samt Schweißausrüstung zur Unfallstelle, schafften es aber nicht, innerhalb der Karenzzeit den Querlenker zu reparieren und der Schwede war somit draussen. Vor der letzten Nacht waren alle führenden Autos Renault Alpines, doch dann fielen alle überraschend aus und spülten Sandro Munari in dem Lancia Fulvia auf Platz eins. Auf den zweiten Platz kam Larrousse, der eine ungeheuerliche Aufholjagd in dieser letzten Nacht gezeigt hatte, aber dennoch 10.50 Minuten hinter Munari zurück lag.

Der Lancia-Sieg war auf Dauer betrachtet eine schlechte Nachricht. Da Lancia nun endlich nach acht Jahren erfolgloser Versuche die Rallye Monte Carlo gewonnen hatte, bekamen sie grünes Licht für den Lancia Stratos. Porsches Hoffnungen für seine Rallye-Zukunft ruhten auf dem Carrera RS, der auf dem Pariser Autosalon Ende 1972 vorgestellt wurde. Anfänglich hatte er einen 2,8 Liter Motor mit Doppelzündung und mechanischer Benzineinspritzung, ein Jahr später war der Hubraum auf drei Liter erhöht worden, mit nun über 300 PS.

Zasada fuhr wieder die Safari Rallye mit einem 911S aus dem Vorjahr und zeigte in diesem Jahr, in dem es weitgehend trocken blieb, mit einer mitreißenden Fahrt und einem zweiten Platz, was mit dem Auto noch zu erreichen ist. Zusammen mit Gesamtsieger Hannu Mikkola stellte er einen neuen Rekord auf: Es war das erste Mal, dass nicht afrikanische Fahrer vor allen Afrikanern in Ziel kamen.

Der Carrera RS feierte sein Debüt bei der Rallye Korsika im November, mit je einem Fahrzeug für Waldegård und Larrousse. Zu den stärksten Gegnern zählten sechs Alpine A110 mit 1800ccm-Motoren, der neue Lancia Stratos, zwei Ligier JS2, zwei Simca-CG Prototypen und ein Ford GT70. Es waren weiterhin die Alpines, die sich als die stärksten Gegner herausstellten, auch wenn der Simca von Fiorentino ebenfalls das Tempo der Spitze mitgehen konnte. Larrousse verlor einige seiner Zusatzscheinwerfer, war aber kurz vor Mitternacht noch immer vierter, Waldegård direkt hinter ihm. Allmählich fingen die Porsches an, sich nach vorne zu fahren, als Waldegård von der Strecke abkam und sich zweifach in einer Schlucht überschlug. Später beklagte Larrousse einen Antriebswellenschaden und war ebenfalls draußen.

Dieses war tatsächlich das letzte Mal, dass Werks-911 bei europäischen Rallyes gesehen wurden. Aber es gab genügend Privatfahrer, die die Rallyequalitäten des Carrera RS zu schätzen wussten, während das Werk sein Hauptaugenmerk auf die Safari-Rallye richtete.

1973 schickten sie Waldegård und Zasada mit zwei neuen Carrera RS in Afrika an den Start. Barth selbst hatte viele Tests durchgeführt, von denen die Autos sehr profitiert hatten. Es war ein Jahr mit gemischten Wetterverhältnissen wie frühem Regen in Tansania, der seinen Preis forderte. Zasada kämpfte mit Mikkolas Escort, überschlug sich und konnte noch Usumbaras erreichen. Er wechselte Front- und Heckscheibe in Daressalam, doch dann gab sein Getriebe auf. Waldegård hatte Probleme mit der Aufhängung, kämpfte aber weiter, ehe sich am Morgen des letzen Tages der Ölkühler losrappelte, schließlich das ganze Öl verlor und somit für den Ausfall sorgte.

Einige Lektionen hatte man gelernt und bei der Rückkehr 1974 hatte man drei Autos im Gepäck. Waldegård war noch immer die Nummer eins, komplettiert wurde die Mannschaft von den Ex-Safari-Siegern Bill Fritschy und Edgar Hermann, die mit Unterstützung privater Sponsoren, zwei weitere Fahrzeuge pilotierten. Alle drei überstanden die grausam nassen Abschnitte der ersten Rallyenacht. Doch dann ereilten Fritschy Probleme an Zündung und Batterie, die am Ende zu seinem Ausfall führten, während bei Hermann eine Strebe an der vorderen Aufhängung brach und die Lenkstange von der Karosserie riss.

Inzwischen führte Waldegård die Rallye an, obwohl in der ersten Nacht eine Strebe an der hinteren Aufhängung gebrochen war. Doch als er gerade aus Taita Hills kam und nicht mehr weit vom Ziel in Nairobi entfernt war, trat das gleiche Problem erneut auf. Die Reparatur an Chassis und Aufhängung dauerte eine Stunde und zwanzig Minuten. Wie auch immer, war das nicht lange genug, um ihm und dem Carrera auch noch den zweiten Gesamtrang zu rauben.

Monte Carlo 1972: Gerard Larrousse

tugal, Waldegård retired with a broken drive shaft but had a superb result on the RAC Rally when he finished second to Roger Clark's Ford Escort RS.

For the 1972 rally season, Porsche decided to take a more low-key approach. Two 911S started the Monte Carlo Rally in the hands of Larrousse and Waldegård and these 2.5 litre, 260bhp cars were generally considered as favourites no matter what the conditions. However, both drivers were caught out by a sudden snowfall in the Ardeche. Waldegård was using slicks to start with and suffered terribly when he hit the deep snow. He stopped at service to change for studded tyres but was already heavily penalised. Larrousse who had chosen studs was so short of time that he decided not to change for new rears and lost ten minutes on the road sections. Later Waldegård, on slicks again, clipped a wall and broke a wishbone. The Porsche mechanics gamely carried their welding kit down the road to him but could not repair it in time and he was out. Before the last night, all the leading cars were Alpine Renaults but then they dropped out like flies leaving the Lancia Fulvia of Sandro Munari in a clear lead. In second place was Larrousse who had made a formidable recovery during the last night but still finished ten minutes and fifty seconds behind Munari.

The Lancia victory was bad news in the long term. With Lancia finally winning the Monte Carlo after eight years of trying, they were able to get the green light for the Lancia Stratos. Porsche's hopes for its future in rallying rested with the Carrera RS that was launched at the Paris Salon d'Automobile towards the end of 1972. This initially sported a 2.8 litre engine with a twin-spark head and mechanical fuel injection but a year later the capacity was increased to 3.0 litres with over 300bhp available.

Zasada did the Safari using a 911S from the previous year and, in a year that was largely dry, he showed what the car could achieve by a stirring drive to second overall. Together with the overall winner, Hannu Mikkola, he created a new record as this was the first time that overseas drivers had finihed ahead of all the locals. The Carrera RS made its debut on the Tour of Corsica in November with two of the new cars entered for Waldegård and Larrousse. It was something of an historic event since their opposition, apart from the six Alpine A110s now fitted with 1800cc engines, included the new Lancia Stratos, two Ligier JS2, two Simca-CG prototypes and a Ford GT70. It was the Alpines that proved the most worthy opponents though Fiorentino Simca CG was also running at the front. Larrousse lost some of his auxiliary lights but was still fourth overall just ahead of Waldegård shortly before mid-night. Gradually, both Porsches started to move up but then Waldegård went off and rolled twice into a ravine. Finally Larrousse had a drive shaft fail and he was out as well.

This was effectively the last time that factory 911s were seen on European rallies. But there were still plenty of private owners to appreciate the rallying abilities of the Carrera RS while, for the factory, they had their eye on the Safari Rally. For 1973, they sent out two new Carrera RS for Waldegård and Zasada. Barth had done a lot of testing himself and the cars had benefited greatly. It was a mixed year with early rain in Tanzania taking its toll. Zasada rolled coming away from the Usumbaras while racing with Mikkola's Escort. He replaced both front and rear screens in Dar es Salaam but then his gearbox gave out. Waldegård kept going despite problems with his suspension but car eventually retired on the very last morning when the oil cooler worked loose and dumped all the oil.

Many lessons were learned about the Carreras on this Safari and, when they returned in 1974 it was with three cars. Waldegård still had the lead role but backing him up in two cars with private sponsorship were ex-Safari winners, Bill Fritschy and Edgar Hermann. All three survived the awful wet sections that featured during the first night of the rally but then Fritschy had ignition and battery problems that eventually put him out, while Hermann had a front suspension strut break which tore the steering rack away from the body. Waldegård meanwhile was leading the rally despite breaking a rear suspension arm during the first night. But then the same problem occurred coming out of the Taita Hills not long before the finish in Nairobi. The repair, which involved the chassis as well as the suspension, took an hour and twenty minutes. It was not, however, enough delay to rob him and the Carrera of second place overall.

1000 Lakes 1973: Leo Kinnunen, Atso Aho

911 S Monte Carlo 1972

East African Safari 1971: Ake Andersson, Hans Thorselius

POWER STRUGGLE AND INTO AFRICA 191

Swedish Rally 1972: Bjorn Waldegard, Lars Nystrom

Hans Thorselius

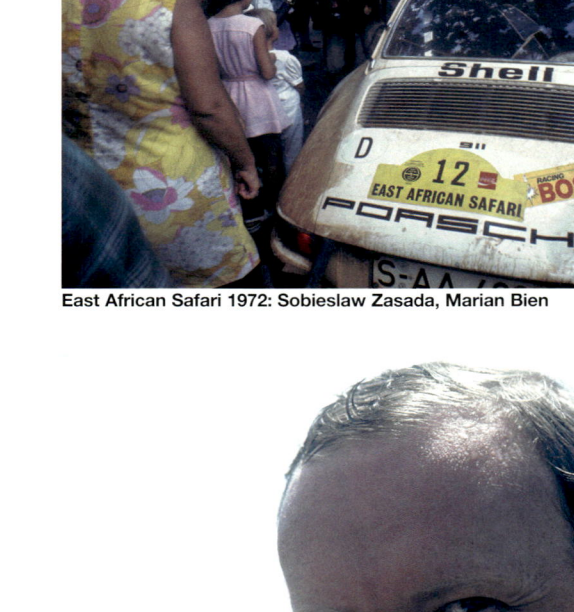

East African Safari 1972: Sobieslaw Zasada, Marian Bien

East African Safari 1974: Bill Fritschy, Sir Peter Moon

Bjorn Waldegard

192 DER SCHWARZE KONTINENT LOCKT

East African Safari 1974: Bjorn Waldegard, Bo Thorselius

Monte Carlo 1972: Bjorn Waldegard, Hans Thorselius

FRANKREICH IST EIN GUTES PFLASTER

Die Safari-Autos wurden verkauft und eines fand seinen Weg nach Amerika, wo Zasada es bei der härtesten US-Veranstaltung, der Press on Regardless-Rallye in Michigan, fuhr. 1974 kam er als siebter ins Ziel, 1975 siegte der Pole. Danach verkaufte er den Wagen an John Buffum, der bis dahin zwischen einem älteren 911 und einem Ford Escort wechselte, um 1975 die SCCS-Rallyemeisterschaft zu gewinnen. Buffum war kein Unbekannter für Porsche, seine erste große Veranstaltung war die Rallye Monte Carlo im Jahr 1969, die er am Steuer eines 911T bestritten und auf Gesamtplatz zwölf beendet hatte. Mit seiner neuen Errungenschaft war er nun nicht mehr zu bremsen, 1976 räumte er richtig ab, indem er sowohl die US-Rallyemeisterschaft als auch eine kombinierte amerikanisch-kanadische Meisterschaft gewann.

Zeitgleich in Europa, genoss der Carrera ein hohes Ansehen als Einsatzwagen für Privatfahrer. Jacques Almeras erwies sich als einer der besten Fahrer und - in Verbindung mit seinem Bruder Jean-Marie - einer der besten Vorbereiter für Rallyeautos. Beide Brüder waren seit den späten 60er-Jahren selbst aktiv, ehe 1975 ihr Tuning-Geschäft für Rennsport-Fahrzeuge richtig begann und sie anfingen, Top-Fahrer in ihre Autos zu setzen.

Jacques hatte als Fahrer zweimal die Rallye Korsika auf den vorderen Rängen beenden können, 1976 als fünfter und 1977 als sechster. Im gelang es, Jean-Pierre Nicolas zu überzeugen, den Almeras-Drei Liter-Carrera bei der Rallye Monte Carlo 1978 zu fahren. Es war ein enormer Aufwand, der überhaupt erst möglich wurde durch den Sponsor Gitanes, der in letzter Minute gewonnen werden konnte. Das Fiat-Werksteam mühte sich im Schnee ab, der viele Streckenabschnitte bedeckte, während der 911 problemlos durchfuhr, um mühelos zu gewinnen. Es war ein krönender Zufall, dass Porsches Geschäftsleitung, angeführt von Professor Dr. Ernst Fuhrmann, zur gleichen Zeit in Monaco weilte, um den „Car of the Year Award" aus den Händen von Prinz Rainier zu erhalten.

Zu jener Zeit als der 911SC ins Spiel kam, beschloss Porsche - mit finanzieller Unterstützung von Martini - einen letzten Anlauf bei der Safari-Rallye zu nehmen. Prof. Dr. Ernst Fuhrmann hatte ein großes Interesse daran, sich schließlich doch eine Safari-Sieger-Trophäe an die Wand hängen zu können. Dass Mercedes drei Werksautos an den Start brachte, hatte ihren Kampfgeist zudem geschärft. Zwei

East African Safari 1978: Bjorn Waldegard, Hans Thorselius

East African Safari 1982: Sandro Munari, Ian Street

Monte Carlo 1976: Guy Freauelin, Jacques Delaval

Winner Monte Carlo 1978: Jean-Pierre Nicolas, Vincent Laverne

CARRERA HAS GOOD FRENCH CONNECTION

The Safari cars were disposed of and one found its way to America where Zasada drove it in the toughest US event, the Press on Regardless Rally in Michigan, where he finished seventh in 1974 and won outright in 1975. He promptly sold the car to John Buffum who, up until that point, had been alternating between an older 911 and his Ford Escort to win the 1975 SCCS Rally Championship. Buffum was no stranger to Porsches since his first major event had been back in 1969 at the wheel of 911T on the Monte Carlo Rally where he finished twelfth overall. With his new acquisition, there was no stopping him and in 1976 he cleaned up by winning both the US Rally championship and a combined US/Canadian championship.

Back in Europe, the Carrera was seen as being a good bet for private owners and Jacques Almeras emerged as one of the better drivers as well as, in conjunction with his brother, Jean-Marie, one of the better preparers of the car for rallying. Both brothers had been actively competing since the late 1960s but in 1975, their Porsche business took off and they started to have top drivers in their cars. Following up his own success in twice finishing the Tour of Corsica among the top places – fifth in 1976 and sixth in 1977 – Jacques persuaded Jean-Pierre Nicolas to drive their 3-litre Carrera on the 1978 Monte Carlo Rally. It was an amazing effort with last minute sponsorship from Gitanes making it all possible. The Fiat works team struggled in the snow that affected much of the route while the 911 just sailed through to win outright. It was a nice touch that Porsche's management team, headed by Professor Fuhrmann, just happened to be in Monaco at the time to collect the Car of the Year Award from the hands of Prince Rainer.

It was the this point that the 911SC came into play and Porsche, with financial help from Martini, decided to have one last proper go at the Safari Rally. Professor Fuhrmann and Jurgen Barth were both keen to finally nail a Safari winner's trophy to their wall and the fact that Mercedes were entering works cars may have also sharpened their sense of competition. Two 911SCs were prepared with three litre engines developing 250bhp, a ground clearance of 28cm, and an all up weight of some 1,180kg. Bjorn Waldegård was invited to drive one of them and Vic Preston Junior joined him in the second car. Porsche's Monte winner, Nicolas was driving a

Tour de Corse 1977: Jacques Almeras, 'Tilber'

911SC wurden vorbereitet, die Motoren leisteten 250PS aus drei Litern Hubraum, die Bodenfreiheit lag bei 28cm, das Leergewicht bei etwa 1.180kg. Björn Waldegård wurde ans Steuer des einen Wagens gebeten, im zweiten nahm Vic Preston jr. Platz. Porsches Monte-Sieger Nicolas hingegen fuhr einen Peugeot und Zasada einen Mercedes 280E. Der Wettkampf sollte also äußerst spannend werden, mehr noch, zog man die Wetterbedingungen in Betracht. Während des Trainings hatte es viel geregnet und auch die eigentliche Rallye sollte nicht trocken bleiben.

Am Ende der ersten Etappe führte Waldegård mit komfortablen 43 Minuten vor einer Horde von Datsuns. Preston war durch einen Defekt an der hinteren Aufhängung gebremst worden, konnte aber weiterfahren und lag am Ende der zweiten Etappe auf Gesamtrang drei. Schlechte Nachrichten kamen dann von Waldegård, der einen Bruch eines hinteren Stoßdämpfers erlitten hatte und beim Wechsel eine halbe Stunde verlor. Auf der letzten – vornehmlich trockenen - Etappe bliesen die 911 zur Aufholjagd, aber der Schwede verlor weitere 45 Minuten aufgrund eines gerissenen Gaszuges. Bei Preston brachen zwei Antriebswellen, die er beide selbst wechselte. Trotzdem erreichten sie die Plätze zwei (Preston) und vier (Waldegård). Nur eine halbe Stunde trennte Preston vom Sieger, der niemand anderes als Nicolas war. Einmal mehr hatte diese so schwer zu bezwingende Rallye ihre Tücken deutlich gezeigt.

Auch bei anderen Events hatte der 911SC im Jahr 1978 begonnen, seine Qualifikation mit soliden Ergebnissen von Privatfahrern in San Remo oder auf Korsika zu beweisen. Die 1000-Seen-Rallye beendete Per Eklund auf einem 911SC als vierter, dank diesem sowie der Ergebnisse der Monte und Safari wurde Porsche vierter in der Herstellerwertung der Rallyeweltmeisterschaft. Im folgenden Jahr hatte Nicolas keine Chance, seinen Monte-Sieg zu wiederholen. Das Team Almeras musste sich mit den Gesamträngen sechs und neun zufrieden geben.

Auf nationaler Ebene feierte der 911SC ganze Siegesserien. Allen voran Bernard Beguin, der die französische Meisterschaft gewann, und Franz Wittmann, der in der österreichischen triumphierte. In den nächsten vier Jahren war der 911SC ein gewohnter Anblick bei europäischen Rallyes mit Fahrern wie Marc Duez, Antonio Zanini, Per Eklund, Jean-Luc Thérier, Manfred Hero, Francis Vincent, Patrick Snyers und Tony Zanussi, die alles - von Gesamtsiegen bei einzelnen Veranstaltungen bis hin zum Gewinn weiterer nationaler Meisterschaften - sammelten. Für einen weiteren Sieg in der Rallye-WM sorgte Thérier 1980, der mit einem Almeras-911 die Rallye Korsika für sich entschied.

Poster

Portugal 1982: Jean-Luc Therier, Michel Vial

1000 Lakes 1978: Per Eklund, Bjorn Cederberg

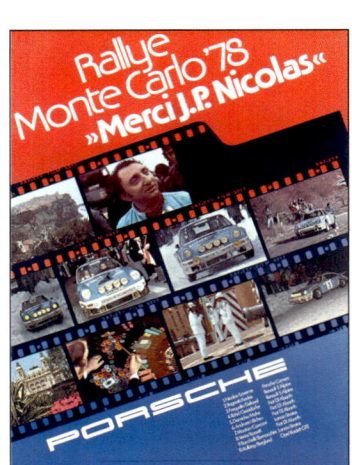

FRANKREICH IST EIN GUTES PFLASTER

East African Safari 1978: Bjorn Waldegard, Hans Thorselius

Monte Carlo 1982: Guy Frequelin, J.-F. Fauchille

Poster

Peugeot and Zasada had been retained to drive a Mercedes 280E so the contest was going to be very interesting and more so when the weather conditions were taken into account. It had rained a lot during practice and now it rained on the rally.

At the end of the first leg, Waldegård led by a massive forty-three minutes from a brace of Datsuns. Preston had been delayed with a rear suspension failure but was still in the running. and by the end of the second leg was up to third overall. The bad news was that Waldegård had suffered a broken rear shock absorber and had lost half an hour replacing it. On the final leg, which was mainly dry, the Porsches had the chance to catch up but Waldegård lost another 45 minutes while his throttle linkage was sorted out and Preston broke, and changed himself, two drive shafts. Nevertheless, their speed gave Preston second and Waldegård fourth place at the finish, only a matter of half an hour separating Preston from the winner, who was none other than Nicolas. But the elusive win had proved to be just that once again.

Elsewhere in 1978, the 911SC began to make its mark with solid results from private owners on rallies like San Remo and Corsica. On the 1000 Lakes Rally, Per Eklund finished fourth in a 911SC and thanks largely to this plus the Monte and Safari results, Porsche finished fourth in the WRC for Manufacturers. The following year, Nicolas found he could not repeat his Monte victory and the Almeras team had to be content with sixth and ninth overall, Nicolas coming home ahead of his patron. But at a national level, the 911SC was starting to dominate with Bernard Beguin winning the French championship and Franz Wittmann the Austrian championship. Over the next four years, the 911SC was a very familiar sight in European rallies with drivers like Marc Duez, Antonio Zanini, Per Eklund, Jean-Luc Thérier, Manfred Hero, Francis Vincent, Patrick Snyers and Tony Zanussi collecting everything from outright wins on individual events to more national championships. And it also showed that it was capable of winning WRC events when Thérier, driving for Almeras, won the 1980 Tour of Corsica.

San Remo 1981: Walter Röhrl, Christian Geistdörfer

CARRERA HAS GOOD FRENCH CONNECTION 197

DER 911 AUF ALLEN VIEREN

Zu Beginn der 80er-Jahre nahm der Rallyesport eine rasante Entwicklung, weg von dem Amateursport, in welchem Huschke von Hanstein 1965 in Monte Carlo den 911 vom Stapel hatte laufen lassen. 1981 kam Audi mit dem Quattro und urplötzlich hatte jeder, der Siegambitionen hegte, ein Allrad-Fahrzeug in der Hinterhand. Die Meßlatte wurde höher gelegt. Die FIA versuchte, die Kosten niedrig zu halten, gleichzeitig aber den Fortschritt nicht schon im Keim zu ersticken. Nach Beratung mit den Herstellern war das Resultat die Gruppe B.

Für diese neue Kategorie mussten nur 200 Fahrzeuge gebaut werden, ausgerüstet mit Allradantrieb, einem Turbomotor oder was auch immer für Erfolge als notwendig erachtet wurde. Ferner war es möglich, eine höhere Entwicklungsstufe des Basismodells zu bauen, von dem nur zehn Prozent der anfänglichen Produktion hergestellt werden mussten. Bei Porsche wurde entschieden, diese Möglichkeit zu nutzen und eine Rallyeversion des SC zu homologieren, die als 911 SC-RS bekannt werden sollte.

Zu den treibenden Kräften avancierte das britische Prodrive-Team, die zwar einen Sponsor (Rothmans) und den Fahrer Henri Toivonen hatten, aber noch ein wettbewerbsfähiges Auto brauchten, um in der Rallye Europameisterschaft gegen die Lancia 037, Audi Quattro und Renault 5 Turbo bestehen zu können. Ebenso stand der äußerst wettbewerbsfähige Saeed al Hajri aus Katar in ihren Diensten, der darauf aus war, die Middle East Rallye Meisterschaft (MERC) zu gewinnen.

Die zwanzig Autos verfügten über einen drei Liter Motor mit mechanischer Benzineinspritzung, der 225 PS in der Standardversion und bei Bedarf 290 PS für Rallyeeinsätze zur Verfügung hatte. Alle zwanzig Evolutionsmodelle wurden mit einer Differentialsperre ausgestattet und alle nicht tragenden Karosserieteile waren aus Aluminium oder leichten Verbundstoffen gefertigt.

Toivonens erster Einsatz war die Rallye Garrigues 1984 und er belegte auf Anhieb Platz drei. Schnell lief es für ihn bei einer Reihe von Läufen zur Europäischen Rallyemeisterschaft noch besser: Er siegte bei der Rallye Costa Smeralda, der Rallye Ypern und der Rallye Madeira. Diese Erfolge sicherten ihm Platz zwei in der Meisterschaft, obwohl ihn eine Rückenverletzung für den größten Teil der zweiten Saisonhälfte zum Zuschauen verurteilte. Al Hajiri hatte mehr Glück, er bestritt die komplette MERC, gewann drei der sechs Läufe und errang den Meistertitel.

David Richards, (li.) Henri Toivonen (re.)

Poster

Tour de Corse 1985: Bernard Beguin, Jean-Jacques Lenne

Paris – Dakar 1984: Jacky Ickx, Claude Brasseur

ALL-WHEEL DRIVE AND GROUP B

At the start of the 1980s, rallying was changing fast away from the amateur sport into which von Hanstein had launched the 911 on the Monte Carlo of 1965. In 1981, Audi came with their Quattro and, all of a sudden, everyone had to have a four-wheel drive car if they wanted to win. The stakes were getting higher and, in an attempt to keep costs down and not stifle innovation, the FIA, advised by the car manufacturers, devised Group B. For this new category, just 200 cars needed to be built featuring 4WD, a turbocharged engine or whatever was deemed necessary for success. And it was possible to evolve a higher performance version of that base car with just 10% of the initial production. At Porsche, it was decided to use this opportunity to homologate a rally version of the SC that would be known as the 911 SCRS. To a certain extent this was done at the behest of Prodrive who had a sponsor (Rothmans) and a driver (Henri Toivonen) but needed a competitive car to go up against the Lancia 037, Audi Quattro and Renault 5 Turbo in the European Rally Championship. They also had the ultra-competitive Saeed al Hajri from Qatar who was keen to win the Middle East Rally Championship.

The twenty cars featured the now familiar 3-litre engine with mechanical fuel injection giving 255bhp in standard form and in excess of 290bhp for rallying. All twenty evolution cars were fitted with a limited slip differential and they gained performance from their bodywork since most of the unstressed panels were made from aluminium or composite materials.

Toivonen first appeared on the Garrigues Rally in 1984 where he was third but he soon went on to do better on a string of ERC events eventually winning the Costa Smeralda, Ypres and Madeira rallies. Sadly a back injury forced him to rest up for most of the second half of the season but those results were enough to place him second in the championship. Al Hajri was more fortunate and he went the full distance in the MERC winning three of the six events and claiming the title. In Belgium, both Patrick Snyers and Robert Droogmans got their hands on 911SCRS and went head-to-head for the national title with Snyers getting the decision with four outright wins. In Germany, Manfred Hero campaigned a 930 Turbo and took second overall in the German Rally Championship. The 911SCRS was equally effective in 1985 with al Hajri winning the MERC again and privateers like Billy Coleman winning the Donegal Rally and finishing fourth on the Tour of Corsica just behind Bernard Beguin's similar car.

911SC 4WD Paris – Dakar 1984

In Belgien lieferten sich Patrick Snyers und Robert Droogmans in ihren 911SC-RS ein Kopf-an-Kopf-Rennen um die nationale Meisterschaft. Am Ende hatte Snyers mit vier Siegen die Nase vorn. In Deutschland war Manfred Hero mit einem 930 Turbo unterwegs und belegte Rang zwei der Deutschen Rallyemeisterschaft. 1985 war der 911SC-RS gleichermaßen erfolgreich: Al Hajiri gewann wieder die MERC und Privatfahrer sorgten für weitere Highlights. So Billy Coleman, der bei der Rallye Donegal siegte und bei der Rallye Korsika als vierter ins Ziel kam, direkt hinter Bernard Beguin, der ebenfalls einen 911SC-RS pilotierte.

Bevor jedoch der SC-RS die Rallyeszene eroberte, sorgte ein noch interessanteres Projekt für Aufsehen. Im Jahre 1983 stellte Porsche auf der Frankfurter Automobilausstellung eine Gruppe B-Studie vor. Es war ein 911 mit einem hoch entwickelten Allradantrieb, Sechsganggetriebe, doppelter Querlenkeraufhängung und einer atemberaubenden Karosserie aus Kevlar. Verfeinert wurde das Ganze mit einem 2,85 Liter-Vierventilmotor, wassergekühlten Zylinderköpfen und zwei Turboladern, um bei Bedarf 400 PS zu entwickeln. Der Preis wurde mit "um die DM 400.000,-" angegeben, und als Liefertermin für die 200 Fahrzeuge war Ende 1985 geplant. Tatsächlich wurden die ersten für Autos aber erst zwei Jahre nach diesem Termin fertig.

Dieses neue Auto wurde als 959 bekannt. Als er dann, verfügbar war, war bereits das Ende der Gruppe B in Sicht.

Doch zum Glück für alle jene Menschen, die unter der Führung von Manfred Jantke gearbeitet hatten, gab es eine Veranstaltung, bei der dieses neue Auto seine Fähigkeiten noch vor der Homologation unter Beweis stellen konnte. Diese Veranstaltung fand größtenteils in Afrika statt und war noch härter als die Safari: Es war die Paris-Dakar. Als Jackie Ickx und Rothmans 1983 mit dem Vorschlag auf Porsche zukamen, den 911SC mit der Technik und dem Allradantrieb des neuen Autos einzusetzen, stießen sie bei den Porsche Ingenieuren auf offene Ohren.

Schließlich wurden drei Fahrzeuge, gesponsert von Rothmans, Texaco und Dunlop, eingesetzt. Sie waren dem 911 SC-RS sehr ähnlich, mit 3,2 Liter Saugmotoren und einem Allradsystem mit einem mechanischen Zwischendifferential ausgestattet. Es wurden Fünfganggetriebe eingebaut und die Motoren durch Zurücknehmen der Verdichtung auf 225 PS gedrosselt, um der geringeren Benzinqualität Rechnung zu tragen, das Tankvolumen wurde auf 260 Liter erhöht.

Die Fahrer waren Ickx, Sieger des Vorjahres mit einem Mercedes G-Modell, René Metge, der 1981 in einem Range Rover erfolgreich war und Roland Kußmaul. Der Porsche-Versuchsingenieur steuerte den dritten Wettbewerbswagen als „fliegenden Service". Zwei in Rothmans-Farben lackierte LKW waren mit Porsche-Mechanikern besetzt und standen für den großen Service während der 20 Tage dauernden Veranstaltung bereit.

Am dritten Tag bewahrten sie Ickx vor dem Ausfall. Ein Stein hatte ein Kabel beschädigt und einen Kurzschluss mit folgendem Kabelbrand ausgelöst. Ickx war schon an dem Punkt aufzugeben, als einer der LKW auftauchte und es der Mannschaft gelang, die Notreparatur durchzuführen. Ickx verlor vier Stunden, konnte aber in Tamanrasset die Rallye von Platz 139 wieder aufnehmen. Metge hatte keine Probleme und lag in Führung. Ickx gelang später eine Reihe von Bestzeiten und war schnell zurück in den Top Ten. Metge gewann schließlich die Rallye mit fast zweieinhalb Stunden Vorsprung, Ickx wurde sechster und Kußmaul, der oft anhalten mußte, um seinen Teamkollegen zu helfen, kam auf Platz 26.

Im nächsten Jahr kam das Team zurück mit dem Ziel, noch

Winner Oman-Rallye 1984: Saeed Al Hajri, John Spiller

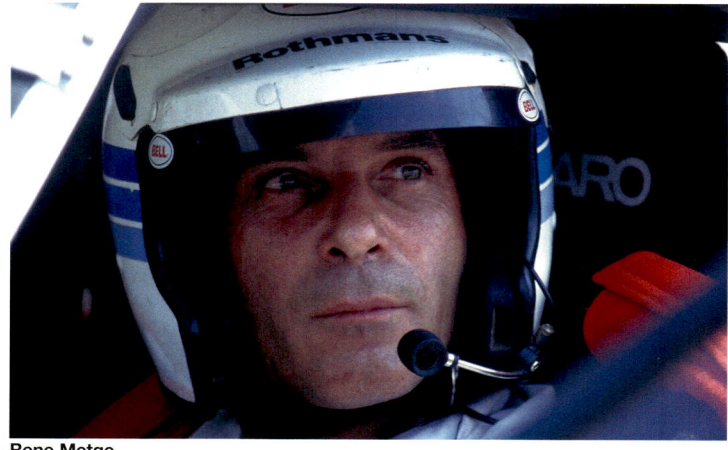

Rene Metge

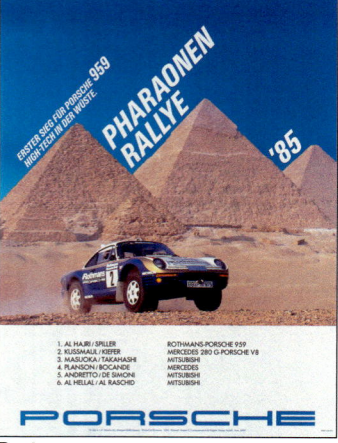

Poster

Paris – Dakar 1985: 911 SC 4WD

Poster

Paris – Dakar 1985: Rene Metge, Dominique Lemoyne

But before the SCRS entered the rally scene, an even more interesting project had come to light. At the Frankfurt Motor Show of 1983, Porsche exhibited a "Group B Studie" which was a 911 with a sophisticated four wheel drive system, six speed gearbox, double wishbone suspension, a stunning body executed in Kevlar and the whole thing powered by a 2.85 litre engine featuring four valve, water cooled cylinder heads and twin turbochargers compounded to develop in excess of 400bhp. The price was announced as being "about" DM400,000 and the original delivery date for the 200 was quoted as towards the end of 1985. In fact, the first cars destined for private consumption were not delivered until two years after that date.

But it was a car to get the world talking. Audi had the Quattro but no one could call its 4WD system sophisticated. This new Porsche lifted 4WD technology and the control of turbo-charged engines to stratospheric levels of electronic elegance. The sad thing was that it was this very complexity and its futuristic design that delayed it for so long and, by the time that it was a fully available concept, refined to the high standards that Porsche set for itself, Group B rally cars had been consigned to the dustbin by the fatalities that occurred during the 1986 season.

But happily for all the people working under the passionate guidance of Manfred Jantke, there was an event in which this new car could show its capabilities prior to homologation. The event was largely in Africa and in some respects it was even tougher than the Safari: it was the Paris-Dakar. When Jackie Ickx and Rothmans approached Porsche during 1983 with the suggestion that they should run 4WD 911 SCs based on the running gear of the new car, the Porsche engineers were very much in favour. Eventually three cars were entered carrying the sponsorship of Rothmans, Texaco and Dunlop. They were pretty much 911SCRS with 3.2 litre normally aspirated engines and with an early 4WD system featuring a mechanical central differential capable of being locked. They were fitted with five speed gearboxes, the engines were detuned to 225bhp to handle the low-octane fuel and the tank capacity was increased to 260 litres.

The drivers were Ickx himself, winner the previous year in a Mercedes G-wagen, and René Metge who had won in 1981 with a Range Rover while Porsche engineer, Roland Kussmaul, drove the third car in support. A pair of MAN trucks decked out in Rothmans livery and crewed by Porsche mechanics provided major service during the twenty-day event. As it turned out, they saved Ickx from retirement on the third day when a stone hit a wiring loom and created a short circuit. He was on the point of giving up when one of the trucks came along and its crew were able to effect a temporary repair. He rejoined the rally at Tamanrasset having lost four hours and was lying 139th overall. No such problem for Metge who, despite the occasional puncture, was over 45 minutes in the lead. As the days passed, he continued to extend that while Ickx, by setting a string of fastest times in the desert, was soon up into the top ten. Metge won the rally by almost two and half hours while Ickx came sixth and Kussmaul, after stopping many times to help out his team mates, came 26th.

It was a very rewarding effort and spoke highly of Porsche's

Oman 1984: Saeed Al Hajri, John Spiller

Paris – Dakar 1985: Jacky Ickx, Claude Brasseur

Paris – Dakar 1984: Rene Metge, Dominique Lemoyne

Winner Mille Piste 1986: Rene Metge, Jean-Marc Andrie

ALL-WHEEL DRIVE AND GROUP B

mehr zu erreichen. Sie wollten wieder gewinnen und sie wollten noch mehr über das Auto lernen. Peter Falk, Porsches Renndirektor jener Zeit, nannte die Paris-Dakar "den effektivsten Weg, um ausgiebige Tests vor Produktionsbeginn durchzuführen".

Neben Ickx und Metge saß bei der 85er-Auflage Jochen Mass in einem der drei Allrad-911. Beim Motor hatte es keine Veränderung gegeben, es kam noch immer das 3,2 Liter Aggregat zum Einsatz. Beim Fahrwerk hingegen wurde von der jüngsten Allradentwicklung und neuen 16-Zoll-Rädern profitiert. Roland Kußmaul war auch wieder unterwegs, um die drei mit Ersatzteilen und Serviceleistungen zu versorgen, wann immer es nötig würde.

Und Hilfe wurde schon bald benötigt für Mass, der vom Start weg mit Aufhängungsprobleme haderte und nach einem Überschlag frühzeitig aufgeben musste. Ickx lag an zweiter Stelle, als er in einer Sanddüne einen großen Stein traf. Zur Halbzeit lief es gut für Metge und er schloss zu den Führenden auf, nachdem er anfängliche Probleme überwunden hatte. Doch dann brach ein Ölschlauch und bereitete seinem Motor das vorzeitige Aus.

Der eigentliche Zeitplan war, die 200 zu produzierenden Wagen im Laufe des Jahres 1985 fertig zu stellen. In den USA hatte der Senat inzwischen Gesetze verabschiedet, die strengere Emissionskontrollen aller Neufahrzeuge ab 1988 vorsahen. Das Ergebnis war, dass Unternehmen wie BMW und Mercedes begannen, den gemeinsamen Lieferanten Bosch unter Druck zu setzen, Entwicklung und Produktion von Hunderttausenden von Motorsteuerungen, die zu den neuen Lambdasonden passten, zu beschleunigen. Porsche hatte somit abzuwarten, bis sie an der Reihe waren und so verschob sich der Zeitplan von Entwicklung und Produktion des 959 und seiner Homologation in der Gruppe B.

Der von Mass gefahrene 911 wurde wieder aufgebaut und an Prodrive übergeben, wo er komplett auf eine 959-Version umgebaut wurde. Im Oktober 1985 pilotierte Al Hajiri diesen dann bei der Pharaonen-Rallye in Ägypten, wie die Paris-Dakar eine Wüstenveranstaltung. Ickx startete dort ebenfalls, jedoch in einem 959, der in Weissach gebaut worden war. Bedauerlicherweise erlitt Ickxs Wagen in der allerersten Wertungsprüfung ein Ölleck, fing Feuer und brannte aus. Das Prodrive Auto lief perfekt und Al Hajiri führte zur Halbzeit bereits mit mehr als einer Stunde. Er gewann komfortabel und gab Porsche die Zuversicht, einen kompletten Einsatz bei der 86er-Paris-Dakar in Angriff zu nehmen.

Oman 1986: Saeed Al Hajri, John Spiller

Der 959 hatte einen wassergekühlten Vierventil-Sechszylinder-Motor mit Registeraufladung durch zwei KKK-Turbolader und 400 PS. Zudem gab es neue Sechsganggetriebe, die bei 6.000 Umdrehungen pro Minute eine Kraft von 210 Newtonmetern entwickelten, während als Spitzenwert im Extremfall 260 Newtonmeter bei 7.800 Umdrehungen zur Verfügung standen. Die Differentiale waren elektronisch gesteuert, auch das Lamellendifferential, welches die Kraft zwischen Vorder- und Hinterachse verteilte. Dies konnte, bei insgesamt vier möglichen „Fahrprogrammen", vom Cockpit aus auf Vollelektronik eingestellt werden.

Das Tankvolumen lag nun bei 340 Litern. Diesmal erhielt wieder Kußmaul den dritten Wagen, in den anderen beiden saßen erneut Metge und Ickx am Steuer. Alle drei kamen ohne größere Probleme durch die Wüste und Metge errang seinen dritten Paris-Dakar Sieg, Ickx wurde zweiter und Kußmaul sechster. Es war ein glanzvoller Sieg mit gemischten Gefühlen, da seit Beginn der Rallyesaison 1986 der Traum der Gruppe B ausgeträumt war. Die Ankündigung ihres Verbots kam vor Jahresmitte.

Metge fuhr dann beim 24 Stunden-Rennen von Le Mans einen 961 zusammen mit Claude Ballot-Lena, Kußmaul war dort Teammanager. Metge hatte einen letzten Einsatz in einem 959 bei der Rallye Mille Pistes, die auf einem Militärgelände im Süden Frankreichs ausgetragen wurde. Der 959 enttäuschte nicht und gewann wieder auf Anhieb. Er sollte nun nie in der Gruppe B homologiert werden, aber er hatte gezeigt, wozu die ultimative Rallyeentwicklung des 911 fähig war.

Winner Jordan 1986: Saeed Al Hajri, John Spiller

Paris – Dakar 1986: Rene Metge, Dominique Lemoyne

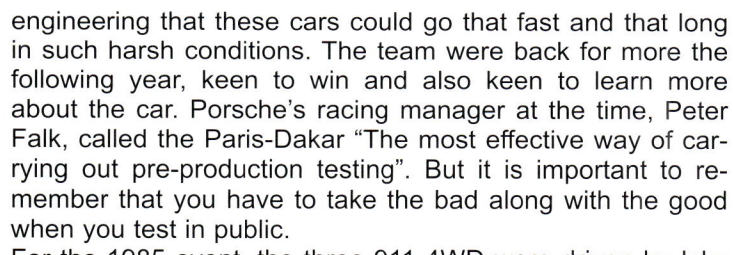

engineering that these cars could go that fast and that long in such harsh conditions. The team were back for more the following year, keen to win and also keen to learn more about the car. Porsche's racing manager at the time, Peter Falk, called the Paris-Dakar "The most effective way of carrying out pre-production testing". But it is important to remember that you have to take the bad along with the good when you test in public.

For the 1985 event, the three 911 4WD were driven by Ickx and Metge plus Jochen Mass. They were still powered by the de-tuned 3.2 litre engine but benefited from the latest 4WD development and 16 inch wheels. Kussmaul was given a Mercedes G-wagen to chase them with spares and help if needed. And help was needed for Mass was in suspension problems right from the start and finally crashed. Ickx was lying second and then put himself beyond rescue when he crested a dune and hit a very large rock. At halfway, Metge was running well and catching the leaders after some initial problems but then an oil pipe to the timing chain tensioner fractured and his engine was finished.

The original schedule was to complete the 200 production cars during 1985 but a problem arose that was not under Porsche's control. In America, the Senate had passed laws requiring stricter emission controls on all new cars by 1988. The result was that companies like BMW and Mercedes all started pressuring their common supplier, Bosch, for development and eventual production of hundreds of thousands of engine management kits to work with the new lambda exhaust probes. As minnows in this sea of commercialism, Porsche had to wait its turn and thus the timetable for development and production of the road-going 959 – and its homologation into Group B – slipped backwards.

The 911 driven by Mass was recovered and sent to Prodrive who completely re-built it as a 959 and sent it in October 1985 for al Hajri to drive in the Pharaohs Rally in Egypt – a sort of mini Paris-Dakar – where Ickx was also entered in a Stuttgart built 959. Sadly, the Ickx car had an oil leak onto one of the twin-turbos on the very first stage, caught fire and burnt out. The Prodrive car ran perfectly and, by halfway, al Hajri already had a lead of more than one hour. He won easily and this was enough to give the factory the confidence to make a full entry in the 1986 Paris-Dakar.

The cars they used were the Real McCoy, 2.8 litre, twin-turbo 959/961s with 400bhp. They were fitted with six speed transmissions chosen to give 210kph at 6,000rpm though in extremis, 260kph at 7,800rpm could be used. The differentials were all electronically controlled including the central multi-plate fluid clutch that split the torque between front and rear wheels on demand. The fuel capacity was 340 litres. About the only feature of the final 959 production car that they did not have was the ride-height control. This time Kussmaul was given the third car with Metge and Ickx in the other two. All three ran without major problems to give Metge his third Paris-Dakar win with Ickx taking second place and Kussmaul fifth.

It was a win tinged with sadness since it was during the early part of the 1986 rally season that the Group B dream fell apart and the announcement banning them was made before mid-year. Metge drove a 961 at the Le Mans 24 Hour race with Kussmaul as his team manager and sharing the driving with Claude Ballot-Lena. It was a Porsche that won the race but not the 961. Thanks to its weight of 1,169kg it had only qualified 26th and spent the entire race catching up to finish seventh overall and first in the IMSA GTX category. Metge had one last outing in a 959 when he entered the Mille Pistes rally, held on Army land in the south of France. The 959 did not disappoint and won outright. It was now never to be homologated in Group B but it had shown what the ultimate rally development of the 911 could do.

REICHER LORBEER IN AMERIKA

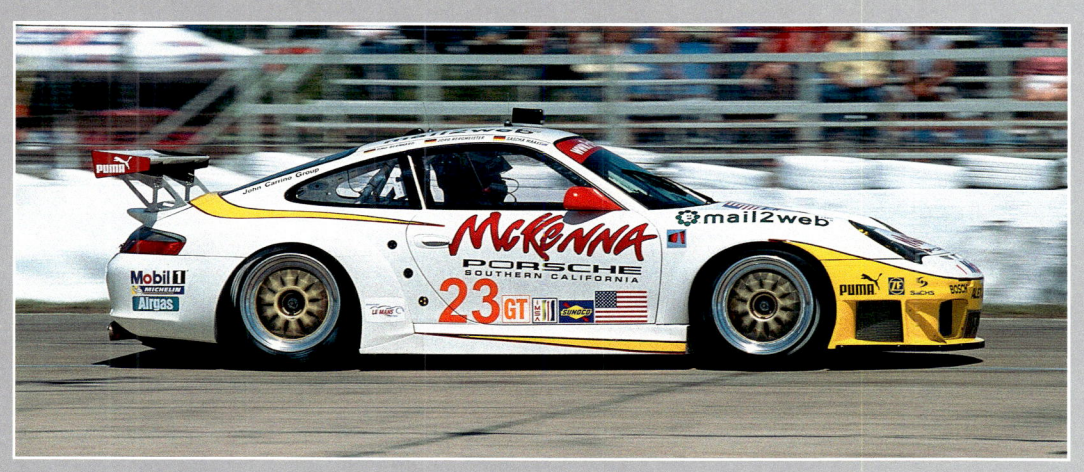

A BATTLEGROUND IN AMERICA

Author: Bill Oursler

207

DER 911 MARKIERT SEIN REVIER

Die Motorsport-Karriere des 911 begann bei der Rallye Monte Carlo 1965 und erfolgte nahezu zeitgleich mit dem Produktionsbeginn des Serienmodells. Es dauerte rund ein Jahr, ehe auch in Nordamerika Porsches neueste Modellreihe in einem Wettbewerb auftauchte. Für das Debüt sorgten die Privatfahrer Jack Ryan, Linley Coleman und Bill Bencker bei den 24 Stunden von Daytona 1966. Mit ihrem Sechszylinder stand das Trio allerdings im Schatten der zahlreichen Werks-Ford GT 40 MkII und des neu entwickelten Porsche 906, der ebenfalls zum ersten Mal an den Start ging.

Ryan, Coleman und Bencker siegten auf Anhieb in der Klasse bis zwei Liter Hubraum und belegten Platz 16 im Gesamtklassement. Und das obwohl die drei Piloten mit einem nahezu serienmäßigen Fahrzeug an den Start gegangen waren. In der Division der Serienwagen musste man sich nur der hubraumstarken Chevrolet Corvette von Roger Penske geschlagen geben. Nach diesem eindrucksvollen Abschneiden nahmen Ryan, Coleman und Bencker auch die 12 Stunden von Sebring in Angriff. Kleinere Probleme verhinderten den erneuten Klassensieg, aber hinter einem MGB fuhr das Trio immerhin auf den zweiten Platz. Der Mythos der motorsportlichen Erfolgsgeschichte des 911 war auch in Nordamerika geboren.

Zwei Männer, die ebenfalls hierzu beigetragen haben, waren der Porsche-Händler Vasek Polak aus Los Angeles und der Motorsportjournalist Jerry Titus. Polak, der jahrzehntelang eine der wichtigsten Schlüsselfiguren für Porsche Motorsport war, bat Titus, seinen 911 zu steuern. Denn dieser war ein besserer Rennfahrer als Schreiber. Die beiden entschieden sich für die Nationale Meisterschaft des Sports Car Club of America (SCCA). Ihr 911 wurde in der Serienwagen-Klasse D homologiert.

Die SCCA-Finalläufe des Jahres 1966 fanden auf dem Riverside Raceway in der Nähe von Los Angeles statt. Ein Vorteil für Titus, denn er kannte die Strecke wie seine Westentasche. Sein Klassensieg war keine Überraschung, umso mehr die 30 Sekunden Vorsprung, die Titus auf den Sieger der leistungsstärkeren Klasse C herausfahren konnte. Dieser Sieg war der erste für den Elfer in Nordamerika, viele weitere sollten im nächsten Vierteljahrhundert folgen. Erfolge, die sich natürlich positiv auf den Absatz in den USA und Kanada auswirkten.

24 Hours Daytona 1966: Jack Ryan, Linley Coleman, Bill Bencker

24 Hours Daytona 1966: Jack Ryan, Linley Coleman, Bill Bencker

911 MAKES ITS MARK

Although the 911's career in motorsport started almost as soon as it began rolling off the production line with its debut at the 1965 Monte Carlo Rally, it didn't enter the North American competition arena until nearly a year later.

Privateers Jack Ryan, Linley Coleman and Bill Bencker gave the six-cylinder car its US debut at the season opening 24 Hours of Daytona. It was overshadowed not only by the massive factory Mark II GT40s, which dominated the event, but also by Porsche's new 906, which was itself running for the first time.

Ryan, Bencker and Coleman brought the coupe home 16th overall, and first in the GT 2-liter category. In fact the Porsche, which had seen service as a demonstrator before being turned into a racer, was the second production car to cross the finish line, headed only by a Roger Penske entered Corvette. At the end of March Ryan, Bencker and Coleman were back with their 911, this time for the annual Sebring 12-Hour classic. Unfortunately, a down-on-power engine left them second in their class behind a MGB. Even so, the trio had started something that would not go unnoticed, as the 911 began to make its mark in American motorsport.

Two men who helped in that cause were Los Angeles Porsche dealer Vasek Polak and automotive journalist Jerry Titus. In the spring Polak, one of the key players in Porsche motorsport for many decades, hired Titus, who was not just a good writer and editor, but a superb driver, to run his 911 in the D-Production category of the Sports Car Club of America's National Championship tour. This comprised a series of local title chases, ending in Runoffs between the various divisional class winners each fall.

For 1966 the SCCA held its Runoffs at Riverside Raceway, about 60 miles east of Los Angeles, and Titus' home track. It was an advantage Titus put to good use, smoking his D-Production opposition in a runaway performance that saw him also finish ahead of the supposedly faster C-Production field, which had been flagged off 30 seconds earlier.

Titus' win was the first of many for the 911 over the next quarter of a century in the SCCA National Championship, a tradition that greatly helped the sales of the model in the United States and Canada.

As important as that D-Production triumph was, it would be soon overshadowed by success in another SCCA series, the Trans-Am. Created in 1966, the SCCA decided to change the championship's regulations for its second season, choo-

24 Hours Daytona 1968 (l.-r.): Sten Axelson, Peter Gregg

Siege in der Trans-Am-Serie, die ebenfalls vom SCCA organisiert wurde, hatten einen noch höheren Stellenwert. Diese Serie wurde beherrscht von Hubraum- und PS-Protzen aus Detroit, angeführt vom Ford Mustang. Für 1967 wurde aber zusätzlich eine Zweiliterklasse ins Leben gerufen. Während das Reglement der großen Klasse in den Händen der Detroiter lag, war für die Division bis zwei Liter die FIA zuständig. Kleine, wendige europäische Mittelklassewagen wie der Ford Lotus Cortina oder Alfa Romeo GTV sollten hier um Punkte und Pokale kämpfen. Zum Glück für Porsche, homologierte die FIA trotz der Innenraumdimensionen den 911 ebenfalls für diese Klasse, sehr zum Missfallen des SCCA.

Der 911 dominierte die Zweiliterklasse von 1967 bis 1969 so sehr, dass der SCCA die deutschen Sportwagen nicht als Divisionssieger anerkannte. Erst im Jahr 1973 folgte das Umdenken, als das Trans-Am-Reglement komplett überarbeitet wurde und den Porsche-Teams die Erfolge im Nachhinein anerkannt wurden.

Mit Beginn der Saison 1967 wechselte auch Peter Gregg, der mit den Modellen 904 und 906 große Erfolge gefeiert hatte, zum Elfer. Gregg und einige andere private Porsche-Teams erhielten wenig Unterstützung aus Weissach, wo zu jener Zeit die Weiterentwicklung von Prototypen Priorität genoss. Mit einem nahezu serienmäßigen 911 trat Gregg daher an. Nur ein Überrollbügel, Koni-Stoßdämpfer, andere hintere Stabilisatoren und sechs Zoll breite Felgen mit Goodyear-Reifen waren montiert worden. Die einzige Modifikation des Motors bestand in der Bearbeitung der Einlasskanäle.

24 Hours Daytona 1967 (l.-r.): Jack Ryan, Bill Bencker, George Drolsom, Harold Williamson

24 Hours Daytona 1968: Sten Axelson, Peter Gregg

Tony Adamowicz brachte die Überlegenheit auf den Punkt: "1967 pilotierte ich einen Ford Lotus Cortina, mit dem ich sehr zufrieden war. Ich dachte, es gäbe nichts Besseres. Als ich dann in Kalifornien einen Porsche 911 von Fred Opert fahren durfte, wusste ich, was ich für 1968 wollte!" Während den 24 Stunden von Daytona 1967 war Adamowicz Zuschauer, als der 911 zwei Klassensiege feierte. Jack Ryan, Bill Bencker hatten in der GT 2-Liter die Nase vorn, George Drolsom, Harold Williamson in der Klasse T2000.

Einen Samstag vor den 12 Stunden von Sebring hatten Peter Gregg, Sam Posey mit dem Brumos-911 ebenfalls einen Klassensieg gefeiert. Bei dem eigentlichen Sebring – Klassiker zeigten dann Bob Kirby und Alan Johnson mit ihrem 911S der Zweiliter-Konkurrenz den Auspuff und wurden Gesamtneunte. Zwei Plätze vor ihnen sahen Gregg, Buzetta im 906 das Ziel.

Bert Everett, seit Jahren mit einem Speedster bei Rennen des SCCA unterwegs, kaufte im Frühjahr 1967 dem damaligen Fahrer und heutigen Porsche-Händler Bob Holbert einen im Werk aufgebauten 911 ab. Sohn Al Holbert sollte in den 70er Jahren zu den erfolgreichsten Piloten gehören. Everett und sein Partner Steve Smith gingen erstmals beim Trans-Am-Lauf in Lime Rock an den Start, wo die versammelte Porsche-Meute vor allem auf den hochmotivierten Alfa-Fahrer Horst Kwech traf.

Die leichtgewichtigen GTA hatten bereits beim Rennen zuvor in Green Valley eine empfindliche Niederlage hinnehmen müssen, als Bill Bowman und Fred Baker für einen 911-Doppelsieg sorgten. Doch in Lime Rock sollte Kwech nochmals die Oberhand behalten vor Everett und Smith. Und auch in Mid-Ohio siegten mit Kwech und Jim Baker zwei Alfa vor Everett.

Beim nächsten Rennen in Bryar war dann der Bann gebrochen: Es regnete fast ohne Unterlass und Everett dominierte die Zweiliter-Klasse nach Belieben. Erst in der Schlussphase, als die Idealline abtrocknete, musste sich Everett dem Mercury Cougar von Peter Revson im Gesamtklassement geschlagen geben. Hinter einem ebenfalls hubraumgewaltigen Ford Mustang kam ein weiterer Zweiliter-Porsche mit John Kelly auf Gesamtrang vier. Everett und Jerry Titus siegten dann auch auf dem Marlboro Speedway vor ihren Markenkollegen Herb Wetanson und Bruce Jennings und Peter Gregg, Sam Posey.

Horst Kwech und Monty Winkler sorgten beim Rennen in Castle Rock für einen Alfa-Doppelsieg vor Bert Everett. Und auch in Crow´s Landing musste sich der Porsche-Pilot Winkler knapp geschlagen geben. In Riverside freuten sich die 911-Teams über den ersten Vierfachsieg der Saison, einmal mehr angeführt von Everett. Ein Sieg von Kwech in Las Vegas verschob die Titelentscheidung auf das Saisonfinale in Kent. Gary Wright und Mike Everly siegten vor zwei weiteren Porsche-Teams und Bert Everett und Porsche gewannen vor Kwech den Titel.

Keine 90 Tage später standen die 24 Stunden von Daytona des Jahres 1968 auf dem Programm, die dieses Mal auch zur Trans-Am zählten. Und standen in den Anfangsjahren

Trans-Am Champion 1967: Bert Everett

sing to add a separate 2-liter division below the homegrown, headlining Detroit Pony Car class led by Ford's classic Mustang. While the rules governing the Detroiters were of the SCCA's making, those defining the 2-liter class were not. Instead, they came from the FIA, a not inappropriate situation since the new class was expected to be a haven for the hot, small displacement European sedans like Ford's Lotus Cortina and Alfa Romeo's GTV.

Unfortunately for the SCCA, but happily for Porsche, the FIA had decreed that the interior dimensions of the 911 were such that they qualified the Porsche as an A-class sedan.

From 1967 through 1969, Porsche 911 drivers would dominate the 2-liter Trans-Am category to such an extent that the SCCA would eventually bar the German sports car from its sedan title chase, not re-admitting it until the sanctioning body revamped the Trans-Am's entire rules package in 1973. By that time, the 911 had found other arenas to conquer. When the Trans-Am opened up for business at Daytona in 1967 it was a driver name new to the series, and new to the 911 which started the first Porsche era rolling. That individual was Peter Gregg, who up to that point had raced 904s and 906s, and wasn't all that sure he really liked the 911S he put in the winner's circle in the Friday preliminary to that year's 24-hour affair.

In an interview some years ago in Porsche Panorama, the Porsche Club of America magazine, Gregg was blunt in his assessment of the 911 as a racer. "The 911 is my favorite road car in the world, but as a race car it leaves much to be desired. The road holding strikes me as only fair, not excellent, and the brakes can be overstressed when really pushed." Nevertheless, Gregg gave everyone a peek into the future when he borrowed back a 911 he had sold to one of his Brumos customers, modified it, and took it fifth overall in the race.

Like other 911 competitors, Gregg had little help from the factory, which at the time was almost completely focused on its line of ever more potent prototypes. It was not surprising therefore that Gregg's 911 was not fault free, especially since it was nearly standard when it ran at Daytona.

Indeed, other than adding a rollover bar, Koni shocks, a rear anti-swaybar and six-inch wide American Racing wheels fitted with Goodyear tires, the only other thing the Brumos crew did to improve performance was to polish the intake manifolds.

At a shade under 3300 pounds, and with around 145 horsepower, the white Porsche with its red and blue striping was, for the time, quite capable of running at the front of the 2-liter Trans-Am field.

As Tony Adamowicz, who would make a name for himself in the 911, put it: "I spent most of the 1967 season running a Lotus Cortina in the Trans-Am for Bob Tullius' Group 44 team, and thought it was a pretty good car.

24 Hours Daytona 1967: Jack Ryan, Bill Bencker

"Then later in the season I raced in California for Fred Opert, who had a 911. Although it wasn't all that well prepared, it really opened my eyes to what I wanted to have for 1968, which is why I went with Milestone Racing when they offered me a ride in their 911 for the coming year."

At the 1967 24 Hours, Adamowicz was a spectator as Jack Ryan and Bill Bencker won the GT 2-liter class with their 911S while George Drolsom and Harold Williamson claimed the victory in T2000 with their 911, the two Porsches finishing 10th and 11th overall.

Peter Gregg, partnered by Sam Posey, made it two in a row, winning the 2-liter honors with his Brumos-entered 911 in the Trans-Am show that preceded Saturday's annual Sebring 12-Hour. In that endurance event, Bob Kirby and Alan Johnson added to the Porsche coupe's growing reputation by taking a class win in their 911S, crossing the line in ninth overall, just two places behind the 906 of Gregg and Buzetta.

It was on the Trans-Am tour that the Porsche would gain the most attention, this coming largely through the efforts of Pennsylvanian Bert Everett. A former amateur SCCA Porsche Speedster competitor, Everett joined the Porsche ranks in the spring of 1967 after purchasing a 911 from the factory via former Porsche star, now turned Porsche dealer, Bob Holbert. Located in the Philadelphia suburb of Warrington, Holbert, whose own son Al would join the ranks of successful 911 drivers in the 1970s, took charge of the preparation of the blue Porsche, which had been partially prepared by Porsche in Germany.

Everett and his partner, Car&Driver magazine editor Steve Smith, joined the Trans-Am at Lime Rock, Connecticut over the Memorial Day weekend, where they and the rest of the Porsche contingent would run into the Alfa Romeo of a determined Horst Kwech.

The reign of the lightweight Alfa GTA seemed nearly over. At Green Valley, Texas, the third round in the series, Bill Bowman and Fred Baker finished one-two in the 2-liter class with their 911s, Bowman claiming seventh in the outright standings, and Baker ninth.

Lime Rock would be different, as it was Kwech who came away with the first place honors in the smaller Trans-Am division, finishing fourth overall, two places ahead of Everett and Smith. Things didn't get much better for Everett the next time out at Mid-Ohio where he crossed the line third behind the GTAs of Kwech and Jim Baker.

Peter Gregg: Winner Trans-Am Daytona 1967

die hubraum- und zylinderstarken Boliden einheimischer Produktion im Mittelpunkt des Interesses, so hatten sich die Zweiliterfahrzeuge allmählich zu Publikumslieblingen gemausert. In der großen Klasse wurde allerdings auch mächtig aufgerüstet, denn Ford und Chevrolet unterstützen ihre Teams in einem bis dahin nicht gekannten Umfang. Somit wuchs auch das Interesse der Zuschauer und Medien an der Trans-Am im Allgemeinen.

Porsche feierte in Daytona mit dem 907 Langheck einen unerwarteten dreifachen Gesamtsieg. Und auch die 911 waren in der Klasse bis 2000 ccm nicht zu schlagen. Die Gesamtneunten Peter Gregg und Sten Axelson siegten mit dem Brumos-911T vor den Markenkollegen Robert Stoddard, George Drolsom und Mary Gifford.

Tony Adamowicz musste nach einem Unfall mit dem Milestone Racing-911 aufgeben. Das Fahrzeug wurde so stark beschädigt, dass der weitere Saisonverlauf in Frage gestellt wurde. Adamowicz Teamchef Marvin Davidson kaufte allerdings wenige Tage später bei einer Versteigerung der New York City Police eine 912-Rohkarosse, die binnen weniger Tage zu einem Rennwagen aufgebaut wurde. Bei den 12 Stunden von Sebring schob Milestone Racing dann diesen bildschönen 911 in Rennspezifikation aus dem Transporter, der sogar über eine – damals – revolutionäre Hinterachsenkonstruktion mit verstärkten Buchsen verfügte. Ein Vorteil gegenüber den Wettbewerbern, den Adamowicz auch zu nutzen wusste.

Im Trans-Am-Rennen am Freitag vor den 12 Stunden endete die Fahrt für Adamowicz und Richard nach einem Motorenplatzer bereits in der 28. Runde. Der amtierende Meister Bert Everett siegte somit vor John Moore, beide im 911T. Einzig Alfa-Pilot Horst Kwech verhinderte als dritter einen Siebenfach-Sieg. Im 12 Stunden-Rennen wiederholten Bob Kirby und Alan Johnson ihren Vorjahreserfolg, zweite wurden Gregg Loomis, Jack Ryan und Pete Harrison. Beide 911S-Teams kamen im Gesamtklassement auf die hervorragenden Ränge sieben und acht.

Bei den sechs Stunden von Watkins Glen 1968, einem Lauf zur FIA-Marken-Weltmeisterschaft, sorgten Peter Gregg und Bert Everett für Porsches dritten Langstreckensieg der Saison. Mit ihrem 911 fuhren sie darüber hinaus auf den neunten Gesamtrang. Beim nächsten Trans-Am-Rennen in War Bonnet war es dann allerdings Horst Kwech, der mit seinem Alfa vor Adamowicz und Everett siegte.

Auf ihrer Heimstrecke Lime Rock durfte das Milestone-Team dann wieder richtig jubeln. Porsche belegte die ersten fünf Plätze und Tony Adamowicz führte vom ersten bis zum letzten Meter das Zweiliterfeld an. Mit 19 Runden Rückstand sah der Volvo 122S von Dick Bauer und Bob Huber als bester Nicht-Porsche das Ziel.

In Mid-Ohio war es dann wieder Everett, der vor Adamowicz und Ross Norburn siegte. Mit fünf Siegen in Folge – Bridgehampton, Meadowdale, St. Jovite, Bryar und Watkins Glen – hatte Adamowicz den Rest der Saison im Griff und wurde neuer Trans-Am-Meister in der Klasse bis zwei Liter. Für den Höhepunkt einer perfekten Saison sorgten die beiden 911-Klassensiege beim SCCA-Saisonfinale 1968 in Riverside.

Zumeist handelte es sich bei den im Motorsport eingesetzten Boliden - wie dem Milestone 912 und 911 – um umgebaute Straßenfahrzeuge. Bert Everett gehörte zu den wenigen, die einen Semi-Werkswagen mit spartanischer Innenausstattung und dünneren Scheiben gewichtsreduziert hatten. Diese Modelle erhielten die Bezeichnung 911L für „lightweight". Es wurden aber auch rund 10.000 Stück 911L als Straßenfahrzeuge importiert, wobei hier das L "luxury" bedeutete. Was auch immer das "L" bedeutete: Beide Versionen waren sowohl alltags- wie auch motorsporttauglich.

Der SCCA wollte für 1969 mehr Eigenständigkeit der Trans-Am-Serie, so dass Daytona und Sebring nicht mehr zur Meisterschaft gewertet wurden. Auch Milestone Racing und Tony Adamowicz waren nach dem Wechsel in die Formel 5000 nicht mehr mit von der Partie, ihren Porsche hatten sie an Herb Wetanson verkauft. Dennoch endete der Saisonauftakt in Michigan mit einem 911-Doppelsieg durch Fred Baker und Dick Smothers vor Gary Wright.

24 Hours Daytona 1969: Jacques Duval, George Nicholas (911T)

Bei den 24 Stunden von Daytona erreichten Wetanson, Adamowicz und Bruce Jennings das bis dahin beste Ergebnis eines seriennahen 911 in der Marken-Weltmeisterschaft. Das Trio freute sich nicht nur über einen souveränen Sieg in der Klasse bis zwei Liter, sondern auch über den vierten Gesamtrang. In Sebring lenkten dann Gerard Larrousse, Jean Sage und Andre Wicky dessen 911 zum Sieg in der GT-Klasse.

Ein weiterer Klassensieg folgte dank Greggs und Haywoods fehlerfreier Fahrt bei den sechs Stunden von Watkins Glen. Hierbei kam der 911B mit längerem Radstand zum Einsatz. Zum Jahresende 1968 waren die ersten B-Modelle vom Band gelaufen und Gregg feierte während der Saison 1969 zahlreiche Erfolge mit dieser Weiterentwicklung.

Ungeachtet seiner anderen Ergebnisse, wurde Gregg beim Trans-Am-Lauf in Lime Rock nur siebter. Tony Adamowicz holte somit für Porsche die Kohlen aus dem Feuer und siegte mit seinem Vorjahres-911 vor Gaston Andrey im Alfa und Bert Everett in einem weiteren 911.

Trans-Am Champion 1968: Tony Adamowicz

3 Hours Sebring 1968: Tony Adamowicz

At Bryar, New Hampshire, now the site of the NASCAR New Hampshire Motor Speedway, but then just a small, tight 1.5-mile road course, Everett came into his own. Driving through a rain storm, Everett shook the Detroiters by nearly winning outright. However as the rain passed and the track started to dry, he was forced to settle for second overall, one lap down from Peter Revson's Mercury Cougar, but two laps ahead of Dick Thompson's third-placed Mustang. Fourth overall, and second in class was John Kelly in yet another of the 911s.

Everett then added to his victory string when he teamed with Jerry Titus to win the 2-liter class of the Trans-Am double-header at Marlboro Speedway, an impossibly tight 1.7-mile circuit on the outskirts of Washington, D.C.

Porsches came away with the top six places, second going to Herb Wetanson and local hero, Bruce Jennings, with Gregg and Posey behind them in third.

At the following round in Castle Rock, Colorado the Alfas were again ascendant, Kwech winning and Monty Winkler second, with Everett taking third in the 2-liter class. Winkler would then lead Everett home on flat Modesto airport circuit at Crow's Landing, California.

From Modesto the series moved to Riverside Raceway, 60 miles east of Los Angeles, where Everett headed a one-through-four Porsche sweep. Then came Las Vegas at the old Stardust International Raceway just outside of town. There, Kwech put on a strong first place performance while Everett failed to finish.

The Porsche driver skipped the Kent, Washington, season finale where Gary Wright and Mike Everly topped a one-through-three 911 parade. When the points were finally tallied, Everett and Porsche were the champions, starting a trend for Zuffenhausen and its bread and butter sports car, turned 'sedan' that would continue through the next two seasons. Less than 90 days later the 911 brigade would return to Daytona for the 1968 season-inaugurating FIA 24-Hours, an event which this time would include the Trans-Am opener as well.

The SCCA sedan tour was about to get a big boost during the 1968 season, one that would benefit the interests of Porsche, even though it was aimed primarily at increasing the public's attention for the domestically-produced 'Pony Car' entrants.

Roger Penske and his driver Mark Donohue had spent the better part of 1967 racing their Camaro against the factory-backed Shelby Team Mustangs and the Dearborn-supported Mercury Cougars of Parnelli Jones and Dan Gurney. Not until nearly mid-season did GM engineers take any serious notice of Penske and Donohue.

For 1968 GM jumped in with its full backing, even if it did its best to disguise the fact. With Ford versus Chevrolet and the American Motors Javelins playing a supporting role, the Trans-Am had now reached the 'Big League' of professional road racing in North America. The result was not only a larger spotlight being focused on the Pony Cars, but a similar spotlight being focused on Porsches in the 2-liter category.

The 1968 Daytona 24-Hours was a Porsche show all the way, with a trio of factory 907 longtails taking the top three positions. The Brumos entered 911T of Gregg and Sten Axelsson finished ninth, the pair topping the Under 2-liter Trans-Am division in the process, ahead of the similar 911 driven by Robert Stoddard, George Drolsom and Mary Gifford, which was 11th overall.

Adamowicz, who had signed on with Marvin Davidson's Connecticut-based Milestone Racing Team after running Fred Opert's 911 near the end of the '67 Trans-Am campaign, was left without a car following a Daytona smash, a situation which made the future more than a little uncertain.

Fortunately, although Davidson decided to retire after the crash, he managed to acquire a stripped 912 shell purchased at a New York City Police auction. By Sebring, the now orange-painted Porsche had been transformed into a full race 911 with the secret advantage of having the standard suspension bushings replaced by solid units.

Nowadays solid bushings are a normal part of production car racing but back then they were virtually unheard of, and with them, the Milestone 911 had a true edge over its rivals in handling that Adamowicz would exploit to the fullest.

At Sebring, in the Friday Three-Hours Trans-Am, Adamowicz and Richard became early spectators when their engine blew after 28 laps. Reigning champion Bert Everett took victory with his 911T over John Moore's nearly identical Porsche in an event totally dominated by Zuffenhausen's coupe. Indeed, only Kwech's Alfa, which came home third, broke a one-through-seven sweep of the standings.

Bob Kirby and Alan Johnson repeated their previous year's GT triumph in the 12-Hours with their 911S, followed across the line by Gregg Loomis, Jack Ryan and Pete Harrison, also in a 911S, the two Porsches crossing the line in seventh and eighth overall.

Later that year, at the July Watkins Glen Six-Hour FIA Makes round, Gregg joined Everett to garner the 911's third North American long distance win of the season, placing ninth outright.

For American Porsche enthusiasts it was the Trans-Am which held their attention, and at War Bonnet, Oklahoma, Kwech and his Alfa were first at the checkered flag. Following him to the line, though, was Adamowicz, both six laps ahead of Everett in third place.

If the Milestone Team had reason to cheer in Oklahoma, they had reason to shout at their home track of Lime Rock Park where Adamowicz finished fourth, leading the 2-liter field home for the first, but not the last time.

In all, 911s claimed the first five positions in the smaller displacement Trans-Am, Adamowicz finishing more than 19 laps over the 1.5-mile course ahead of the first non-Porsche, the Volvo 122S of Dick Bauer and Bob Huber.

Everett returned to the winner's circle at Mid-Ohio, beating Adamowicz and Russ Norburn in what was another top three Porsche showing.

For the next five races it was all Adamowicz and his unique 911, the Milestone driver taking Bridgehampton, Meadowdale, Illinois, St Jovite, Quebec, Bryar and Watkins Glen. With his six victories Adamowicz had wrapped up the 2-liter

Trans-Am Champion 1969: Peter Gregg

In Mid-Ohio gewann dann Gregg vor Baker und Pete Harrison, in Bridgehampton lautete die Reihenfolge Gregg vor Harrison. Die nächsten beiden Rennen in Brainerd und Bryar entschied Everett für sich, Gregg wurde jeweils Zweiter.

Danach war St. Jovite jenseits der kanadischen Grenze Schauplatz des vermutlich dramatischsten Trans-Am-Rennens aller Zeiten. Nachdem am Ford Mustang von George Follmer der Motor geplatzt war und eine riesige Ölspur die Folge war, flogen nicht nur die anderen drei Werks-Ford ab, sondern auch ein Grossteil der Zweiliterfahrzeuge. Unter ihnen auch Tony Adamowicz, der wieder mit Wetansons 911 unterwegs war. Bis auf ein paar Prellungen und Verstauchungen blieben alle involvierten Fahrer unverletzt. Doch das Rennen musste gestoppt werden, um die havarierten Fahrzeuge zu bergen. Nach dem Neustart setzte sich Peter Gregg sofort in Führung und gab diese nicht mehr ab. Lokalmatador Roger Barrel wurde im Mini Cooper S mit Rundenrückstand Zweiter.

In Watkins Glen war Gregg erneut das Maß der Dinge und siegte vor den Markenkollegen Bob Bailey und Jim Netterstrom. Der fünfte Saisonsieg folgte in Laguna Seca vor Elliott Forbes-Robinson. Letztgenannter drehte in Sears Point den Spieß um, nachdem sich an Greggs 911 ein Rad selbständig gemacht hatte. Beim Finalrennen in Riverside wurde Gregg dann dritter hinter den beiden Markenkollegen Alan Johnson und Pete Harrison. Diese Position reichte, um überlegen Meister der Zweiliterklasse zu werden. Porsche landete in der Markenwertung einen lupenreinen Hattrick.

Beim SCCA-Saisonfinale gewann Gregg darüber hinaus den Titel in der Klasse B, während Alan Johnson und Milt Minter in der Klasse C sogar für einen Porsche-Doppelsieg sorgten. Es sollten die letzten Erfolge von Porsche in der Trans-Am sein, denn das Reglement änderte sich und der 911 war für die kommenden drei Jahre nicht mehr startberechtigt. Erst 1973 kehrte das Erfolgsmodell – als Carrera RSR – in die Serie zurück.

Für Porsche änderten sich nicht nur die motorsportlichen Rahmenbedingungen. Volkswagen USA avancierte zum Nordamerika-Importeur. Diese Maßnahme war ein Teil der weltweiten Umstrukturierungen zur optimalen Ausnutzung der Synergieeffekte. Volkswagen vertrieb ab sofort den Vierzylinder-914, während Porsche weiter für den Absatz der Sechszylinder verantwortlich zeichnete. Der neue Rennleiter Josef Hoppen verhandelte mit dem SCCA über die Zulassung des 914. Denn der SCCA lehnte strikt die Rückkehr des 911 ab, die Zweiliter-Klasse sollte, wie ursprünglich angedacht, die Plattform für Tourenwagen sein.

Hoppen wollte mit Einsätzen in den nationalen Meisterschaften die Promotion des 914 forcieren, so dass beide Parteien sich auf ein Abkommen einigten. Der 911 bleibt aus der Trans-Am verbannt, dafür startet der 914 auf regionalem Level nicht in der B-Klasse, sondern mit größeren Erfolgsaussichten in der C-Klasse. Die Aussichten für die nächsten Jahre erschienen gut, doch die Realität sah schon bald anders aus. Andere Umstände sorgten bald für die komplette Neustrukturierung des nordamerikanischen Motorsports. Und im Zentrum des Geschehens sollte der 911 sein.

24 Hours Daytona 1969: Tony Adamowicz, Herb Wetanson, Bruce Jennings

crown. As icing on Porsche's North American cake, 911s once again won the C-Production and B-Sedan honors in the SCCA's National Championship Runoffs, held back out west at Riverside, with Alan Johnson repeating his C-P victory of the year before.

For the most part, the cars that participated in the SCCA and the Trans-Am were, like the Milestone 912/911, converted street cars, although a few, such as Everett's came from the factory with semi-stripped interiors and thinner glass to reduce their weight.

These were given the designation 911L, the same as applied to the 10,000 or so "luxury" 911s imported to the United States by Porsche Cars of America during 1967 and 1968. Even so, these special 911s, while fully roadworthy, were intended primarily for competition use, a role many would play during their lifetimes.

For 1969, the Trans-Am was strictly a 'stand-alone' championship, eschewing the two long distance affairs at Daytona and Sebring for a mid-May start at the Michigan International Speedway. Unlike Daytona, Michigan's road course, while using part of its tri-oval, actually extended beyond the speedway's confines to wander through the wooded area behind the track's backstretch.

Winning the messy event in the 2-liter category was Baker's 911, co-driven by television star Dick Smothers, one of only two 911s to finish, the other being Gary Wright's which took second in class.

Adamowicz and Milestone had moved on to the single-seat Formula 5000 series, selling their Porsche to the New Yorker Herb Wetanson at the end of 1968. In an astute move, Wetanson's deal included the uprating of his original Trans-Am 911 to the same specification as the Milestone entry he had just purchased.

It was with this car that he, Adamowicz and Bruce Jennnings won the 2-liter GT category in the Daytona 24 Hours, finishing a superb fourth in the outright standings, the highest placing up to that point for a production 911 in the World Manufacturers title chase.

Later in March, at Sebring, Gerard Larrousse, Jean Sage and Andre Wicky won the small displacement GT class trophy in Wicky's 911. Rounding off the 911's endurance record for the year, Gregg and Hurley Haywood piloted their 911 to eighth in the outright finishing order in the Watkins Glen 6-Hours, and first in the 2-liter GT standings.

Gregg's mount at the Glen was one of the new, longer wheelbase 911 "B" bodies which had gone into production in the latter part of 1968, and which would carry Gregg to much success during the course of the '69 season.

Regardless of the eventual outcome, Gregg could do no better with his new car when the Trans-Am came to Lime Rock over the Memorial Day weekend for its second race of the year. While Gregg struggled home seventh, Adamowicz, driving his old '68 911, won the race from Gaston Andrey's Alfa, Everett taking third a lap back.

Things were different, however, at Mid-Ohio where Gregg beat Baker to claim his first class victory of the season. Gregg followed this with a second straight triumph at Bridgehampton, topping Pete Harrison, who had been third at Mid Ohio.

At Brainerd, Minnesota, Gregg was forced to settle for second as Everett turned in another first place performance, Everett again besting Gregg at Bryar in the following Trans-Am race.

The series then moved across the Canadian border to St. Jovite for what was, and still is, one of the most dramatic Trans-Ams ever. A huge multi-car pile up, triggered by a blown engine in George Follmer's factory Mustang, eliminated not only the other three factory Fords but a large portion of the remaining pony car set, as well Adamowicz, back driving Wetanson's original 911.

Fortunately, other than a few bruises and some scrapes there were no serious injuries, but the race did have to be stopped to clear the wreckage. When it restarted Gregg was out front, a position he maintained to the end, beating, of all things, the Mini Cooper S of local hero Roger Barrel by more than a lap.

Gregg won his fourth Trans-Am at Watkins Glen in mid August, taking the checkered flag ahead of the 911 of Bob Bailey and Jim Netterstrom. At Laguna Seca, Gregg's next 'victim' was Elliott Forbes-Robinson's 911 as the Jacksonville, Florida resident posted his fifth triumph.

He lost a wheel and retired at Sears Point, where the victory honors would go to a determined EFR. Gregg's fortunes improved, if only slightly, at the Riverside finale where he was third behind Johnson and Harrison.

Gregg clinched the season 2-liter honors, as Porsche won its third consecutive Manufacturers crown. Later in the SCCA Runoffs at Daytona, Gregg also claimed the B-Sedan National Championship, while Johnson finished second to teammate Milt Minter in C-Production.

It would be the final 2-liter title for Zuffenhausen in the Trans-Am, the political winds forcing Porsche to miss the next three seasons before the 911, this time in Carrera RSR form, was welcomed back under a new series format.

Circumstances were not only changing for Porsche with the SCCA, but with its corporate structure, as Volkswagen of America became its North American importer. That deal was part of an overall re-structuring in which VW AG and Porsche joined forces to market all of Zuffenhausen's products worldwide, VW to sell the four-cylinder 914 and Porsche the six-cylinder.

Porsche's new racing chief, Josef Hoppen, negotiated with the SCCA over where 914 would be allowed to compete. The SCCA wanted the 911 out of its sedan series, so that the 2-liter division could return to what series officials had originally intended it to be.

Hoppen wanted to promote the 914 through the club's National Championship arena, so the two struck a compromise. The 911 would depart the Trans-Am, and the 914/6 would be placed in C-Production, rather than B-Production where it had a much better chance at being competitive against its neighbors.

It was a situation that looked more promising than it turned out to be. Circumstances were about to transform North American road racing in a way no one could have expected at the time. And in the middle of that change would be the 911.

SCCA Champion 1968: Alan Johnson

911 MAKES ITS MARK

IMSA ZEIGT DIE ROTE KARTE

Seit Ende der fünfziger Jahre war John Bishop der Vorsitzende des Sports Car Club of America (SCCA). Doch Querelen innerhalb der Organisation sorgten im Winter 1969 dafür, dass Bishop abdanken mußte. Aus Bishops Sicht absolut unverständlich, denn der SCCA hatte es in erster Linie ihm zu verdanken, dass aus einem kleinen Amateur-Verein eine der bedeutendsten Motorsportorganisationen der USA geworden war. Seit 1963 oblag ihren Händen die United States Road Racing Championship Tour.

Außerdem hatte der SCCA den Canadian-American Challenge Cup – besser bekannt als Can-Am – und die Trans-Am Sedan Series ins Leben gerufen, in deren Zweiliterklasse der Porsche 911 drei Jahre lange dominierte. Auch die Formula 5000 wurde vom SCCA ausgerichtet, der sich somit auch weltweit einen guten und einflussreichen Ruf erworben hatte. Aber: Umso mehr Macht zur Verfügung steht, umso größer ist auch die Einflussnahme von Lobbyisten. Bishop wurde Opfer der differenzierenden Strömungen und wurde auf dem SCCA-Winterkongress 1969 abgewählt.

Doch John Bishop sollte nicht lange arbeitslos sein. Bill France sr., der Gründer der sehr erfolgreichen NASCAR-Serie, fand zunehmend Gefallen an internationalen Großereignissen wie den 24 Stunden von Daytona. France konnte Bishop von seinen Ideen überzeugen und beide schmiedeten den Plan, unabhängig vom SCCA eine neue Organisation auf die Beine zu stellen. France sorgte für die Finanzierung während Bishop die Strukturen aufbauen sollte. Im Sommer 1969 war es soweit: Die International Motor Sports Association (IMSA) bezog ihr neues Hauptquartier in Bridgeport, unweit entfernt vom SCCA-Sitz in Westport.

Im Oktober 1969 erlebte dann die IMSA ihre Feuertaufe: Formel Ford und kleinere Tourenwagen starteten auf dem Pocono International Raceway. Weitere Veranstaltungen folgten und die Formel Vau sowie die Formel Super Vau wurden zu einem festen Bestandteil. Doch auf Dauer wollten Bishop und France den Zuschauern und Teilnehmern mehr bieten, Sportwagen standen auf der Wunschliste ganz oben. Ende 1969 stand dann das erste IMSA-Rennen für GT's auf dem Programm. Schauplatz war der Talladega Super Speedway, der France's Familie gehörte.

Weitere eineinhalb Jahre vergingen, ehe es die erste GT-Meisterschaft im Rahmen der IMSA-Events gab. Das Verhältnis zwischen Bishop und seinem früheren Arbeitgeber war mehr als angespannt. Der SCCA rief daher seine Mit-

Josef Hoppen – Porsche Motorsport

12 Hours Sebring 1970: Peter Gregg, Pete Harrison

12 Hours Sebring 1970: Bruce Jennings, Bob Tullius

REBUFF FROM IMSA

John Bishop, a former engineer with Martin Aircraft who had changed career paths to become the Executive Director of the Sports Car Club of America near the end of the 1950s, was forced to resign his post in the winter of 1969 in a political wrangle over control of the SCCA's highly successful professional road racing division. The irony was inescapable from Bishop's viewpoint, for it was he who had moved the club from its strictly amateur focus into the pro ranks with the establishment of the United States Road Racing Championship tour in 1963.

From the USSRC, Bishop and the SCCA had gone on to create not only the Canadian-American Challenge Cup, better known as the Cam-Am, for unlimited capacity sports cars, but also the Trans-Am sedan series, the 2-liter division of which had become a playground for Porsche's 911.

These two championships, along with the open-wheel Formula 5000 single seaters, had transformed the SCCA, making it one of the most powerful and visible sanctioning organizations in the world. Unfortunately, with that visibility came the struggle for control, a struggle which Bishop lost at the SCCA's '69 winter convention.

Bishop was not to be out of a job for long, though. Within weeks he was invited to visit NASCAR founder Bill France Sr. Although the world of oval track stock car racing was the foundation for France's success he had branched out, taking an interest in the international scene with the establishment of Daytona 24-Hour Manufacturers event on the combined high-banked tri-oval and infield road courses of the Daytona International Speedway.

With Bishop's enforced departure and his subsequent availability, France saw an opportunity to create some leverage with the club, if not a large degree of independence from it by financing a new sanctioning organization headed by the former SCCA leader. By mid-summer Bishop was in business, the new president of the fledgling International Motor Sports Association headquartered in Bridgeport, Connecticut, less than five miles distant from the SCCA in Westport.

Initially, Bishop's stated goal for IMSA was to run small bore formula cars, such as Formula Fords, and small imported sedans on the ovals under France's control. It was a modest aspiration which became a reality in October, 1969, when IMSA staged its first event, a Formula Ford race, on the now defunct quarter mile oval at the then still uncompleted Pocono International Raceway.

24 Hours Daytona 1970: James Patterson, Paul Stanford

glieder und Teilnehmer auf, die IMSA-Rennen zu boykottieren. Doch der Grossteil der Aktiven interessierte sich nicht für politische Intrigen, sie wollten einfach nur Rennen fahren. Jo Hoppen stand weiterhin zu seinem Wort gegenüber des SCCA, keine Elfer mehr in der Trans-Am einzusetzen, wenn im Gegenzug dafür der 914/6 für die Serienwagenklasse C homologiert würde. Aber der Rennleiter erlebte eine herbe Enttäuschung, als der SCCA seine ursprüngliche Zusage zurückzog und dem amerikanischen Publikum Porsches neuester Roadster vorenthalten blieb. Wie France war nun auch Hoppen auf der Suche nach einer motorsportlichen Alternative.

IMSA-Präsident Bishop bat Hoppen um ein Engagement in der für Frühjahr 1971 geplanten GT-Meisterschaft und dieser stimmte bedingt zu. Sollte das IMSA Regelwerk auf der FIA-Gruppe 4-Homologation basieren, würde Porsche die Serie mit Fahrzeugen, Teilen und Ehrenpreisen unterstützen. Der in den Kinderschuhen befindlichen Rennserie konnte fast nichts Besseres passieren, als die prestigeträchtige Marke mit im Boot zu haben. Mit der Einteilung in vier Klassen erlebte die IMSA dann ihre Premiere: Sportwagen der FIA-Gruppe 4 und Tourenwagen der FIA-Gruppe 2, jeweils bis und über 2,5 Liter Hubraum.

Im Jahr 1970 hatten die 911-Piloten unter den Nachwirkungen der Trans-Am-Verbannung zu leiden. Ihnen blieb nur mehr die Möglichkeit, an FIA-Veranstaltungen teilzunehmen. Bei den 24 Stunden von Daytona feierten Ralph Meaney, Gary Wright und Bill Bean einen Sieg in der Klasse T2000. Als Gesamtachte und ebenfalls Klassensieger beendeten Peter Gregg und Peter Harrison mit ihrem 911 die 12 Stunden von Sebring. Bruce Jennings feierte zusammen mit Bob Tullius einen weiteren Klassensieg bei den sechs Stunden von Watkins Glen.

24 Hours Daytona 1970: Ralph Meaney, Gary Wright, Bill Bean

IMSA GT 1971: Martin Steger, George Smith

While IMSA would continue to sanction such events, adding Formula Vees, and eventually Super Vees to the mix into the early 1980s, the real objective of IMSA was revealed within a month when Bishop's organization put on its first GT race. This was at the newest France family Super Speedway, Talladega, on a combined infield and banked tri-oval circuit based on the one at Daytona.

It would be a year and a half before IMSA would launch its own GT series but the SCCA, which tried to prevent its members from staffing or running in IMSA events, got the message. Relations between Bishop and his former employer were soured, except when it came to the underground war between the two for the hearts of those interested in US road racing.

Jo Hoppen agreed to take the 911 out of Trans-Am in return for the 914/6 being accepted for C-production, but he was soon disappointed when the SCCA refused to permit the upgraded 914/6GT to run competitively in the National arena, frustrating Hoppen's plans to further promote Porsche's new entry-level roadster with the American public.

Like France, Hoppen was looking for alternatives when Bishop came to see him, asking for his support. What the IMSA president wanted was a commitment from Porsche to participate in the proposed IMSA GT championship, which he wanted to start in the spring of 1971.

Hoppen agreed to make the commitment, both in terms of cars and parts, as well as contingency awards, if Bishop would use the FIA's international Group 4 production car regulations as a basis for the series. Given the prestige that Porsche's presence would generate, never mind the financial benefits to IMSA, Bishop agreed.

Although the series would consist of four categories, for sports cars and sedans under and over 2.5-liters, all would

12 Hours Sebring 1970: Ralph Meaney, Bill Bean

Watkins Glen 1970: Bob Tullius, Bruce Jennings

be prepared to FIA rules, Group 4 for the sports cars, Group 2 for the sedans.

The 911's profile was still low in 1970 in the wake of its banishment from the Trans-Am. At Daytona that year Ralph Meaney, Gary Wright and Bill Bean captured the T2000 category in the 24-Hours, finishing 15th overall.

At Sebring, Gregg and Peter Harrison were class winners in their orange-painted 911 with an eighth overall performance. Porsche SCCA stalwart Bruce Jennings and Bob Tullius, better known for the British Leyland connections with his Group 44 National Championship team, rounded out the 911's FIA season in America with a class victory at the Watkins Glen 6-Hours in July. Other than that the 911 was absent from the headlines of the sport in North America.

With Hoppen's support in place, and the inauguration of what would become the Camel GT series, the 1971 season saw the 911's return to the production car spotlight. At Daytona the best placed 911 in the 24-Hours was driven by Bert Everett, Jim Netterstrom and Jim Lock, who finished third in the 2-liter GT class behind a pair of 914/6GTs. Happily for Everett and Locke they improved on that at Sebring where they beat the 914s to win their class.

It was the story of the season as the 911 had to play second fiddle to the mid-engined 914/6, especially that of Gregg and Haywood who came away with five GTU class and three overall wins in the six-race series to become joint champions. The 914/6 was on the wane, though, as the importer decided to drop the slow selling six-cylinder version in favor of the cheaper 914/4. Once again the 911 became the primary Porsche production racer in America.

Hoppen arranged for Gregg to purchase one of the 911ST lightweights from the Porsche Salzburg team in Austria, one of 35 or so lightweight shells produced by the factory in the

REBUFF FROM IMSA 219

Dank des Einsatzes von Jo Hoppen und der Einführung der IMSA-Sportwagen-Meisterschaft mit dem Titel Camel GT Series im Jahre 1971 kehrten auch die Elfer in den US-Produktionswagensport zurück. In Daytona belegten Bert Everett, Jim Netterstrom und Jim Locke nach 24 Stunden den dritten Rang in der Klasse bis 2500 ccm hinter zwei 914/6. In Sebring drehten Everett und Locke den Spies um und behielten gegenüber den 914 die Oberhand. Trotzdem sollte der 911 in diesem Jahr nur die zweite Geige spielen, zu überlegen war der 914/6 in der sechs Rennen umfassenden Serie. Vor allem der von Gregg und Haywood, der drei Gesamt- und fünf Klassensiege in der GTU – unter 2500 ccm – feiern durfte.

Mit Ablauf der Saison 1971 hatte der 914/6 sein motorsportliches Rentenalter erreicht. Zumal gleichzeitig der US-Importeur entschied, aufgrund der geringen Absatzzahlen zukünftig stärker den 914/4 zu forcieren. Die Elfer rückten somit wieder ins Rampenlicht des US-Sports.

Jo Hoppen vermittelte für Peter Gregg den Erwerb eines 911 ST-lightweight vom österreichischen Team Porsche Salzburg. Insgesamt waren nur 35 dieser gewichtsreduzierten Karossen im Werk vom Band gelaufen. Genügend, um bis Ende 1972 die wichtigsten Kundenteams für Rallye- und Rundstreckensport zu versorgen. In den Brumos-911 war erstmals ein 2,5 Liter-Boxermotor anstelle des 2,4 Liter-Triebwerkes eingebaut worden. Porsche offerierte diesen Motor auch für den Straßen-Elfer ab 1972.

IMSA GT 1971: Michael Keyser, Bob Bailey

Der neue Bolide debütierte beim IMSA Camel GT-Saisonauftakt 1972 in College Station. Peter Gregg und Hurley Haywood bewiesen vom ersten Meter an das Potenzial des neuen ST-lightweight, siegten in der GTU und mussten sich im Gesamtklassement nur einem Ford Mustang aus der großen Klasse geschlagen geben. Da das nächste IMSA-Rennen erst wieder im April folgen sollte, stand als nächstes die FIA-Langstrecken-WM in Daytona auf dem Programm. Die Renndistanz war auf sechs Stunden verkürzt worden, damit die lightweight-Ferrari 312PB überhaupt eine Chance hatten, das Ziel zu sehen. Gregg und Haywood waren einmal mehr das Maß der Dinge in der 2,5 Liter-Klasse und wurden Gesamtsiebte. Wenige Wochen später in Sebring folgte der nächste Sieg für das Fahrer-Duo.

In Watkins Glen krachte Haywood in die Leitplanken, so dass Mike Keyser und Bob Beasley im Keysers-911ST den Klasse gewannen. Zwei Wochen später stellten Gregg und Haywood in Virginia die alte Rangordnung wieder her und führten vor Keyser, Beasley einen Porsche-Fünffachsieg an. In Lime Rock siegten dann Locke, Bailey vor Klaus Bytzek in einem weiteren 911. Keyser und Beasley freuten sich in Mid-Ohio sogar über einen Gesamtsieg vor Haywood und Sam Posey, der den zeitgleich mit einem 917/10 in der Can-Am fahrenden Gregg vertrat.

12 Hours Sebring 1972: Peter Gregg, Hurley Haywood

12 Hours Sebring 1972: Bill Bean, Michael Keyser

220 IMSA ZEIGT DIE ROTE KARTE

latter part of 1969, and used as the basis for both rally and circuit racing 911s through 1972. The Brumos 911 was fitted with a new 2.5-liter six based on the 2.4-liter engines introduced by Porsche for its 1972 911 street cars.

The new Porsche, barely reconverted to pavement racing, made its debut at the 1972 IMSA Camel GT season opener held in College Station, the Texas International Speedway. Gregg and Haywood started the season off on a good footing, coming home second overall and first in GTU behind a Ford Mustang which was able to stretch its legs on the banked tri-oval portion of the Texas track.

IMSA's '72 campaign would not resume until April, back at Daytona. Before that was the FIA Championship race at Daytona, its length reduced to six hours in deference to the lightweight Ferrari 312PB prototypes that would dominate.

At Daytona Gregg and Haywood put in a near perfect performance to win the 2.5-liter class, taking an outright seventh in the final standings. They moved up two places in the overall finishing order to fifth at Sebring, where they gave Porsche its second straight FIA GT class victory of the young season. The duo was less fortunate in the Watkins Glen 6-Hours when Haywood backed the 911 into a guardrail and was forced to retire, leaving the class honors to Mike Keyser and Bob Beasley in Keyser's 911ST. Two weeks later the series headed north to Virginia International Raceway where Gregg and Haywood led a 911 sweep of the top five positions, Keyser and Beasley finishing second.

At Lime Rock on Memorial Day, Locke and Bob Bailey were outright victors their 911 ahead of Klaus Bytzek's similar car. Beasley's good fortunes continued at Mid Ohio's Six-Hour, where he was joined at the top of the overall podium by Keyser, the pair finishing more than a lap ahead of Haywood, who was partnered by Sam Posey as Gregg was away racing his 917/10 in the Can-Am.

In September Haywood and Gregg returned to the Glen for IMSA's first stand-alone weekend at the upstate New York circuit, and there they dominated the proceedings with an overall win.

From the Glen, the series moved to Bryar Motorsport Park in New Hampshire where George Stone drove his 911ST to second place and the top of the GTU lists. Keyser and Beasley, still seeking the GTU championship, went to the Daytona finale well prepared with two cars.

Beasley did what he had to do, winning the class with the help of Keyser. Unfortunately for Beasley, Haywood's second place performance in GTU was enough not only to make him class champion, but the overall IMSA Camel GT crown winner for 1972.

That Daytona event marked the end of an era. From the mid 1960s when the 911 made its competition debut, through 1972 the factory had done little serious development with their best selling coupe other than the unique 911R project, except to offer stripped and lightened versions to those who wanted to race them.

That was to change when Dr. Fuhrmann took over as head of the company in late 1971, with the philosophy that Porsche should run what it sold the public, and assigned Norbert Singer to transform the 911 into a world class GT contender. The Carrera RS and RSR would dominate the GT scene through 1975 before deferring to Singer's new line of turbos, the 934 and its more sophisticated brother, the 935.

The 1973 season was to be crucial not only for Camel GT and the Trans-Am, but for their organizers as well. Trans-Am was in trouble, having lost the support of the Detroit manufacturers, leaving the SCCA in a quandary over how to reverse its fortunes. The SCCA's solution was to open the

12 Hours Sebring 1972: Erwin Kremer, Günther Huber, Juan Carlos Bolanos

Watkins Glen 1972: Michael Keyser, Bob Bailey

IMSA GT 1972: Peter Gregg, Hurley Haywood

REBUFF FROM IMSA 221

Winner 24 Hours Daytona 1973: Peter Gregg, Hurley Haywood

Zurück in Watkins Glen, dieses Mal im Rahmen der IMSA Camel GT, stand Peter Gregg wieder zur Verfügung und landete mit Hurley Haywood einen weiteren Gesamtsieg. In Bryar ging dann der GTU-Sieg an George Stone und dessen 911ST. Keyser und Beasley führten weiterhin die Tabelle an und brachten zum Saisonfinale nach Daytona sogar zwei Elfer mit. Beasley erreichte zumindest das, was er erreichen musste: Einen Klassensieg in der GTU. Aber Haywoods zweiter Platz reichte nicht nur aus, GTU-Meister zu werden, sondern er war auch IMSA Camel GT-Gesamtsieger des Jahres 1972.

Dieses Rennen bedeutete gleichzeitig das Ende einer Ära. Seit den ersten Motorsporteinsätzen Mitte der 60er Jahre hatte Porsche den 911 kaum weiterentwickelt. Doch das sollte sich mit dem neuen 911R ändern.

Ende 1971 hatte Prof. Dr. Ernst Fuhrmann die Firmenleitung übernommen. Für ihn war das Motorsportengagement sehr wichtig und er übertrug Norbert Singer die Leitung, den 911 zu einem weltweit erfolgreichen GT-Renner zu entwickeln. Von 1973 bis 1975 sollten die Carrera RS und RSR die GT-Szene nach Belieben dominieren. Erst mit Einführung der turbogeladenen 934 und des großen Bruders 935 erfolgte die Wachablösung.

Die Saison 1973 sollte nicht nur für die IMSA Camel GT und die Trans-Am, sondern auch für deren Organisatoren wegweisend sein. Die Trans-Am geriet zunehmend in Probleme, da die Detroiter Hersteller den SCCA verlassen hatten. Als Rettung in letzter Sekunde verabschiedete der SCCA ein neues Reglement, welches nahezu jedem Wagen mit vier Rädern die Startberechtigung ermöglichte. Hiermit wollte man nicht nur die Porsche-Teams, sondern auch andere europäische Hersteller wie BMW anlocken. Das Regelwerk der Trans-Am mutierte somit zum Spiegelbild der IMSA.

Wie gut die Rennabteilung ihre Hausaufgaben erledigt hatte, zeigten die 24 Stunden von Daytona im Februar 1973. Peter Gregg und Hurley Haywood nahmen am Volant des Brumos-911 Carrera RSR Platz, Mark Donohue und George Follmer lenkten Roger Penskes Sunoco-Modell. Optisch sahen beide wie RSR aus, doch unter der Haube war noch der 2,7 Liter statt der neue 2,8 Liter-Motor eingepflanzt worden. Da Porsche die für die Homologation erforderlichen Mindeststückzahlen an Straßenfahrzeugen noch nicht gefertigt hatte, wurden die 911 RSR als Prototypen eingestuft.

Die reinrassigen Prototypen bestimmten zunächst das Tempo, doch nach Sonnenaufgang lagen dann beide Porsche an der Spitze des Gesamtklassements. Aus dem Doppelsieg wurde allerdings nichts, nachdem Donohue und Follmer aufgeben mussten. Der Carrera von Gregg und Haywood lief bis zum letzten Meter absolut problemlos und überquerte mit 22 Runden Vorsprung auf einen Ferrari 365 GTB den Zielstrich. Es war der erste Gesamtsieg für einen Porsche im Rahmen der FIA-Langstrecken-Weltmeisterschaft. Für den totalen Triumph sorgten Bob Bergström und Jim Cook mit ihrem 911S als Sieger der GT-Klasse bis zwei Liter.

Daytona 1973 (l.-r.): Hurley Haywood, Peter Gregg

Trans-Am to any and all foreign competition, thus bringing not only Porsche back to the series, but other European manufacturers such as BMW as well. Effectively this transformed the Trans-Am into a mirror image of Bishop's Camel GT championship, a situation in which Trans-Am would prove to be unsustainable.

Just how well Porsche had done their homework with the 911 Carrera RSR became clear at the Daytona 24-Hours in February 1973 when two factory owned examples took part, one for Gregg and Haywood in the colors of the Brumos team, and the second for Mark Donohue and George Follmer in the blue of Roger Penske's primary sponsor, Sunoco. While both appeared to be the full-race RSRs, in fact they were classified as RSs because they were powered by the 2.7-liter flat six, rather than the 2.8-liter units used by the outright competition models. Actually the two Porsches were classified as prototypes since not enough had yet been constructed to qualify them for homologation as production machines.

This meant that the Brumos and Penske entries would have to run against the 3-liter sports prototypes, which did not have the stamina for the 24-Hours and left the Carreras at the front of the field from the early morning hours of Sunday on. Any hopes of a one-two Porsche sweep were dashed shortly after dawn when Donohue and Follmer were forced to retire, leaving Gregg and Haywood far enough in front to cruise home 22 laps ahead of the second place Ferrari 365 GTB, to record the 911's first-ever overall FIA World Manufacturers triumph.

It was an historic moment for the Porsche factory, reinforced by the performance of Bob Bergstrom and Jim Cook whose 911S won the 2-liter GT category.

Winner 24 Hours Daytona 1973: Peter Gregg, Hurley Haywood

PRESSE-MITTEILUNG

PORSCHE

PORSCHE ÜBERRASCHUNGSSIEGER IN DAYTONA

Sensationelles Debut des Carrera RS

Das erste von elf Rennen um die Markenweltmeisterschaft brachte Porsche einen Sieg, mit dem selbst Optimisten im Stuttgarter Werk nicht gerechnet hatten. Bei seinem ersten Renneinsatz überhaupt behielt der neue Carrera RS, ein designierter GT-Wagen, die Oberhand über die hoch favorisierten Prototypen von Gulf-Mirage, Matra und Lola. Zwei im Porsche Werk vorbereitete und von den amerikanischen Teamchefs Peter Gregg und Roger Penske eingesetzte Carreras übernahmen schon nach 10 von 24 Rennstunden die Führung im Gesamtklassement, nachdem die schnelleren Prototypen von Gulf-Mirage (Getriebeschäden) und Matra (Motorschaden) ausgefallen waren. In der 15. Stunde musste auch der führende Porsche, gefahren von Penske's CanAm-Piloten Mark Donohue und George Follmer, aufgrund eines Kolbenschadens die Segel streichen. Der danach in Front rückende Carrera unter Peter Gregg / Hurley Haywood konnte seinen Vorsprung vor dem folgenden Ferrari GTB 4 von Minter / Migault zeitweilig 25 Runden ausbauen und trotz dem Verlust der Windschutzscheibe durch Steinschlag in den letzten Rennstunden mit rund 140 km Vorsprung gewinnen. Nicht nur der siegreiche Carrera RS (Porsche-Entwicklungsleiter Bott: "Eigentlich wollten wir in Daytona nur einen Motoren-Dauerversuch absolvieren"), sondern auch eine Reihe gut placierter Porsche 911 S stellten in dem amerikanischen 24 Stunden-Rennen ihre Standfestigkeit unter Beweis, darunter vor allem die viertplacierten Stone / Jennings (Porsche 911 S) und Fitzpatrick / Kremer (911 S) auf Platz 6 des Gesamtklassements. Von 52 gestarteten Wagen beendeten 20 das Rennen.

ERGEBNIS

1. Gregg/Haywood (USA) Porsche Carrera RS 4.100 km = 170,5 km/h
2. Minter/Migault (USA/F) Ferrari GTB 4 22 Runden zurück
3. Heinz/McClure (USA) Chevrolet Corvette 26 Runden zurück
4. Stone/Jennings (USA) Porsche 911 S 32 Runden zurück
5. Chinetti/Grossmann (USA) Ferrari GTB 38 Runden zurück
6. Fitzpatrick/Kremer (GB/D) Porsche 911 S 40 Runden zurück
7. Kessler/Pickett (USA) Chevrolet Camaro 78 Runden zurück
8. Keyser/Beasley (USA) Porsche 911 S 83 Runden zurück
9. Greger/Schmid (D) Porsche 911 S 96 Runden zurück
10. Bergström/Cook (USA) Porsche 911 S 99 Runden zurück

TSOP No.2a 5.2.1973

7 STUTTGART 40   PORSCHESTRASSE 42   TELEFON 0711/8203-1   TELEX PORSCHEAUTO 07-22406

PRESSE-MITTEILUNG

PORSCHE

PORSCHE'S SURPRISING VICTORY IN DAYTONA

A Sensational Debut of the Carrera RS

The first of 11 races for the World Championship of Makes was unexpectedly won by a Porsche. Even for the optimists in the factory in Stuttgart this victory was a surprise, coming as it did in the first competitive event for the new Carrera RS and gained with a future GT car against the higly favored prototypes of Matra, Gulf-Mirage and Lola. Two factory-prepared Carreras given to the American teams of Peter Gregg and Roger Penske took the overall lead already after 10 of the 24 hours, when the faster prototypes run into gearbox-troubles (as did the Gulf-Mirages) or engine-breakdown (Matra). In the 15th hour the leading Porsche, driven by Porsche's CanAm winners George Follmer and Mark Donohue, was forced to retire due to a burnt piston. Thereafter the leading Carrera of Gregg/Haywood increased its lead up to 25 laps to the following Ferrari GTB 4 of Minter/Migault. Even a smashed windshield during the last hours of the race (hit by a stone) could not hinder the winning Carrera to hold a distance of 140 km to the 2nd placed Ferrari. Not only the surprising Carrera RS (Porsche development director Helmuth Bott: "Actually in Daytona we only wanted to absolve a long distance-test of our engines.") but also the number of Porsches finishing the American 24 hour race in the upper standings indicate the durability and competitiveness of Porsche's GT cars; 4th place to the 911 S of Stone/Jennings and a 6th place finish of the 911 S of Fitzpatrick/Kremer. Of the 52 cars which started the race only 20 finished.

FINAL STANDINGS

1. Gregg/Haywood (USA) Porsche Carrera RS 4.100 km = 170,5 km/h
2. Minter/Migault (USA/F) Ferrari GTB 4 22 laps back
3. Heinz/McClure (USA) Chevrolet Corvette 25 laps back
4. Stone/Jenrings (USA) Porsche 911 S 32 laps back
5. Chinetti/Grossmann (USA) Ferrari GTB 38 laps back
6. Fitzpatrick/Kremer (GB/D) Porsche 911 S 40 laps back
7. Kessler/Pickett (USA) Chevrolet Camaro 78 laps back
8. Keyser/Beasley (USA) Porsche 911 S 83 laps back
9. Greger/Schmid (D) Porsche 911 S 96 laps back
10. Bergström/Cook (USA) Porsche 911 S 99 laps back

TSOP No.2b 5.2.1973

7 STUTTGART 40   PORSCHESTRASSE 42   TELEFON 0711/8203-1   TELEX PORSCHEAUTO 07-22406

Da die FIA Sebring nicht mehr für zeitgemäß erachtete, gehörte der Flugplatz-Kurs nicht mehr zur WM. Und auch IMSA-Boss John Bishop hatte eigentlich nicht die Absicht, dort einen Lauf auszurichten. Corvette-Pilot John Greenwood bot allerdings die Vermarktung eines solchen Events an und Bishop stimmte zu. Rückblickend betrachtet eine richtige Entscheidung, denn Sebring hat der IMSA in der Folgezeit zum heutigen Stellenwert mitverholfen.

Für Sebring 1973 hatte Porsche drei brandneue Carrera RSR 2,8 genannt. Brumos kümmerte sich um den Wagen für Dr. Dave Helmick, Peter Gregg und Hurley Haywood. Die anderen beiden Duos bildeten Greg Egerton und Elliott Forbes-Robinson und Michael Keyser und Milt Minter. Zu den größten Wettbewerbern zählten eine Horde Corvettes, unter anderem pilotiert von Promotor John Greenwood. Im Vergleich zu den RSR waren die Rundenzeiten der Corvettes etwas schneller, dafür war aber die Technik nicht so standfest. Mit Rundenvorsprung sollten Helmick, Gregg, Haywood vor Keyser, Minter, deren Fahrzeug nach dem Verlust des Öleinflussstutzendeckels kurzfristig brannte, gewinnen. Greenwoods Chevy wurde dritte vor Egerton und Forbes-Robinson.

Beim nächtlichen drei Stunden-Sprint in Daytona siegten erneut Gregg und Haywood, Keyser wurde dieses Mal Dritter. Beim Paul Revere 250 beendeten die ersten fünf das Rennen in der gleichen Runde, angeführt von Gene Feltons Camaro, Michael Keyser kam im besten 911 auf Rang vier. Aufgrund der Vorbereitungen für die FIA-Sechs Stunden von Watkins Glen trat Peter Gregg nicht in Mid-Ohio an. Keyser und Beasley gewannen somit locker mit Rundenvorsprung. Das 100 Meilen-Rennen in Lime Rock, aufgeteilt in zwei Läufe, wurde von vielen Unfällen überschattet. Michael Keyser hatte im ersten Teil die Nase vorn, Gregg im zweiten.

IMSA GT Daytona 1973: Bob Hagestad

IMSA GT 1973: Pete Harrison, Gregg Loomis

IMSA GT 1973: Peter Gregg

IMSA GT 1973: Ludwig Heimrath

IMSA GT Daytona 1973: Peter Gregg, Hurley Haywood

Eine Woche später in Road Atlanta war Gregg Schnellster, Keyser belegte Platz drei. Und auch auf dem Indianapolis Raceway Park, nur ein paar Meilen entfernt vom berühmten Speedway, ging das Duell der beiden Piloten weiter. Nach 260 Meilen siegte Peter Gregg mit einer Runde Vorsprung auf Keyser, so dass die Titelentscheidung auf das Finale in Daytona vertagt wurde. Dort ließ Gregg zusammen mit Hurley Haywood nichts mehr anbrennen und feierte einen überlegenen Sieg sowie seinen zweiten Camel GT-Titel vor Keyser, der beim letzten Rennen dritter wurde. Unter den ersten acht der Jahreswertung 1973 lagen nicht weniger als sieben 911. Nur wenige Tage später sicherte sich Gregg auch den Titel der Trans-Am.

Nach 1970 war die ehemals sehr erfolgreiche Rennserie auf dem absteigenden Ast. Für 1973 hatte der veranstaltende SCCA das Reglement der IMSA angepasst, und nicht nur die amerikanischen Hubraumriesen, wie Camaro oder Corvette, sondern auch Porsche, BMW und Datsun standen nun am Start.

Für den Saisonauftakt in Road Atlanta hatte Peter Gregg einen brandneuen Brumos-RSR genannt, Al Holbert hatte seinen Penske-911 nun ebenfalls mit einem 2,8-Liter-Triebwerk ausgestattet. Beide Piloten lieferten sich ein spannendes Rennen, wobei Gregg knapp gewann. Beim zweiten Rennen in Lime Rock sah es lange Zeit nach dem zweiten Sieg für Peter Gregg aus, doch dessen Teamkollege Sam Posey wurde in der letzten Runde vom Markenkollegen Milt Minter überholt. Beim nächsten Rennen in Watkins Glen profitierte Camaro-Fahrer Mo Carter vom Abbruch wegen Regens und Nebels, denn er hätte noch einen Boxenstopp absolvieren müssen. Peter Gregg wurde erneut zweiter und baute seine Tabellenführung weiter aus.

Sebring was removed from the FIA calendar since, following the 1972 event, the airfield track was deemed unsuitable for a world championship race.

Even so the the Sebring 12-Hours was run as an IMSA event starting off the 1973 Camel GT season.

Initially Bishop had no intention of going to Sebring but when one of his competitors, Corvette driver John Greenwood, suggested to the IMSA president that he would be willing to promote the annual long distance race as part of the Camel GT series, Bishop gave him a positive response. In retrospect taking advantage of the opportunity was one of the best decisions he made because Sebring that year helped give IMSA the stature of a major player in professional motorsport.

If Daytona was a preview of what was to come for Porsche's GT aspirations in America, then Sebring was the opening act. Three new 2.8-liter Carrera RSRs were entered, the Gregg-Haywood Daytona entry having been returned to the factory and the Penske example sold to Al Holbert for the upcoming SCCA Trans-Am season.

Of the three, the most visible was the one delivered to Dr Dave Helmick a week before the Sebring 12-Hours. This yellow-painted 911 was prepared by Brumos for Helmick, who would have the services of Gregg and Haywood as his co-drivers.

The other two RSRS were also painted yellow, one belonging to Greg Egerton who was partnered by Elliott Forbes-Robinson, and the other was bought by Michael Keyser whose Toad Hall Racing team had entered it for himself and Milt Minter. Against the three new Porsches were arrayed a number of well prepared Corvettes, among them Greenwood's, who would be joined for the 12-Hour by Mike Brockman and Ron Grable.

IMSA GT 1973: Jim Cook

The Corvettes were slightly faster but they proved less durable than the Carreras. Gregg, Haywood and Helmick took the win by a lap over Keyser and Minter, who were second despite a mid-race fire caused by a loose filler cap. Third went to Greenwood, Grable and Brockman, with Egerton and EFR claiming fourth.

From Sebring the IMSA series headed back to Daytona for a three-hour night-time sprint in April. Gregg and Haywood won again, this time in Gregg's new Carrera RSR which had been delivered earlier in the month for the Trans-Am season inaugural at Road Atlanta. Second went to Dave Heinz's Corvette, and Keyser finished third with his RSR.

The third round of the Camel GT, the Paul Revere 250, was also a night time event, run at Daytona as a preliminary to the NASCAR stock race held during the daylight hours of July Fourth. This time Gregg and Haywood were forced to settle for second behind Gene Felton's Chevrolet Camaro, Keyser taking fourth in a race that saw the top five all finish on the same lap.

With Gregg away preparing for the FIA Watkins Glen 6-Hours, Keyser became the favorite at IMSA's own Mid-Ohio 6-Hour Camel GT event and he made the most of it, winning with Bob Beasley by more than a lap over the rest of the field. In the twin Lime Rock Labor Day weekend 100 milers Keyser and Gregg exchanged victories, Keyser winning the first half of the doubleheader, and Gregg the second. It was an incident filled afternoon that pleased the fans, but not those who had to rebuild the bodywork after the "crash and bang" frolics.

Gregg finished ahead of the field at a steamy Road Atlanta event a week later, Keyser crossing the line third at the end of the 200 miler. The Gregg-Keyser duel continued at the Indianapolis Raceway Park, just a few miles from the famed Speedway.

Gregg beat Keyser by a lap after 260 miles, leaving the championship points decision to the November Daytona finale, where Gregg and Haywood finished first ahead of Warren Agor's Camaro. Keyser was no higher than third, so that gave Gregg his second Camel GT crown. Agor's Chevrolet was the only non-Carrera to break into the top eight.

For Gregg, who had turned his 917/10 Can-Am Turbo over to Haywood after the end of the 1972 season, the IMSA title was only half of his championship season, as the Jacksonville driver also claimed the year-end Trans-Am honors.

Trans-Am, conceived largely as a showcase for Detroit's sporty Pony Car set, had hit hard times after 1970 as the American manufacturers turned away from racing and focused instead on meeting new government-mandated environmental and safety regulations. With public interest waning as well, the SCCA revamped the championship for 1973 to embrace both the domestically-produced muscle machinery, such as the Corvette and Camaro, and their European and Asian counterparts from Porsche, BMW and Nissan.

IMSA GT 1973: George Dickinson

Winner IMSA GT Daytona 1973 (l.-r.): Hurley Haywood, Peter Gregg, Miss Camel GT

REBUFF FROM IMSA 225

Die Überlegenheit des Carrera RSR – auch resultierend aufgrund des günstigen Kraftstoffverbrauches im Vergleich zu den heimischen Produkten – war dem SCCA erneut ein Dorn im Auge. Beim nächsten Lauf wurden statt einem Langstreckenrennen mit Boxenstopps zwei Läufe von je einer Stunde absolviert. In Montreal kamen somit Al Holbert und Peter Gregg nicht über die Plätze vier und sechs hinaus. Bei den 500 Kilometern von Road America stieg Holbert wenigstens als Dritter auf das Podium. Zum Saisonfinale in Edmonton verfügte Gregg erstmals über einen Drei-Liter-Motor in seinem RSR. Dank Platz zwei vor Al Holbert triumphierte Gregg in der Fahrerwertung, nur in der Markenwertung musste sich Porsche knapp geschlagen geben.

Als Saisonausklang hatte Roger Penske die erfolgreichsten Rundstrecken- und Ovalpiloten eingeladen, in der IROC-Serie – International Race of Champions – auf identischen Carrera RS 3,0 an den Start zu gehen. Mark Donohue beendete seine beeindruckende Rennfahrerkarriere mit einem Sieg. Im Anschluss wurden die Elfer vornehmlich an IMSA-Teams verkauft, die die Fahrzeuge in RSR-Ausführung 1974 einsetzen sollten.

226 IMSA ZEIGT DIE ROTE KARTE

For the 911 it was a rebirth of sorts, the SCCA having barred the Porsche from the series after it won three straight 2-liter class titles between 1967 and 1969. Now the 911 was back in the much more potent guise of the Carrera RSR, and the SCCA quickly found itself right where it was when it closed the door on Zuffenhausen's best seller in 1970.

Gregg arrived at the April Road Atlanta Trans-Am opener with a brand new RSR. Squaring off against him were several other RSRs including that of Al Holbert, which had raced at Daytona under the Penske organization banner with a 2.7-liter flat six. Now fitted with a full 2.8-liter RSR powerplant, but still painted in the blue of Penske sponsor Sunoco, Holbert's car would prove to be a potent challenger to Gregg.

At Atlanta young Holbert challenged the Brumos driver, but ultimately settled for second place. At Lime Rock on Memorial Day Monday, Gregg, teamed with local hero Sam Posey, seemed to have a second straight triumph in hand before Posey was surprised by Milt Minter's RSR on the final lap, Minter sweeping into the lead with less than a mile to go.

The second place points boosted Gregg's position in the championship standings as the series headed to Watkins Glen in June, where in a race shortened by rain and fog, Canadian Mo Carter's Camaro crossed the line in front of the Porsche, Gregg settling for second once again.

By this time the SCCA had had enough of the Carrera, the competitiveness of which depended as much on its better fuel economy as it did its new found horsepower in its battle against the domestics. As a result the SCCA decided the Trans-Am would go to a two-heat format start with the tight Sanair event which came next. Located about an hour due east of Montreal, the road circuit was built around the #facility's drag strip, incorporating the twisting return road as part of the complete circuit.

It should have been a Porsche walkaway, but the new regulations handed the affair to the US products, the best placed Porsche being Holbert's in fourth overall, two places ahead of Gregg. Road America, which hosted the fifth round of the championship, was considered a horsepower track, so the SCCA dropped the two-heat scheme in favor of a single 500 kilometer event. At the checkered flag Greenwood's Corvette led Warren Agor's Camaro, with Holbert's third placed RSR the top Porsche in the field.

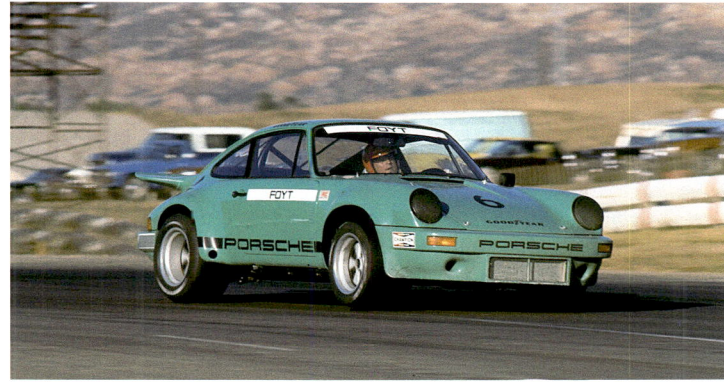

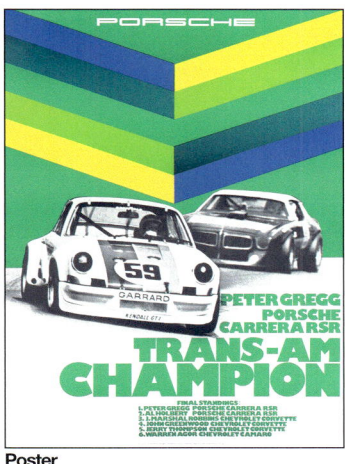

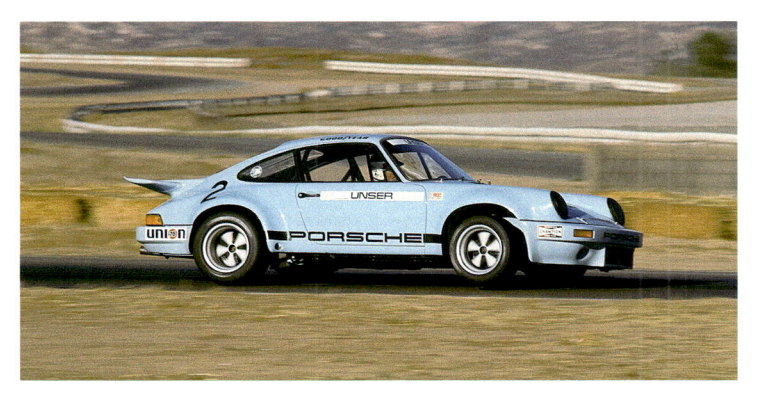

The series finale was held at another fast track, the Edmonton, Alberta, course in western Canada where Greenwood won again. This time Gregg, whose RSR was now powered by a full 3-liter flat six, was second with Holbert third.

Although Porsche didn't win the Manufacturers' honors, Gregg came away with the Drivers' crown for what was ultimately, a perfect year, at least so far as the points championships were concerned.

A postscript to the season came in the form of Roger Penske's made-for-television International Race of Champions tour (IROC), the bulk of which was held at Riverside, California as part of the Can-Am weekend.

Using identically prepared lightweight whale-tail 1974 Carrera RSs fitted with full race 3-liter engines, the series pitted champions from both the oval and road course arenas against each other. A multi-race, two-day framework was adopted with the finale to be held the following February at Daytona Speedweeks, just prior to the stock car 500.

Donohue took home the top prize at the Daytona shootout in his last event before his official, but short-lived retirement from the sport as a driver. After the television show the cars were sold off, mainly to IMSA Camel GT competitors, most +of whom upgraded them to full '74 RSR specifications.

DER RSR KOMMT IN FORM

Am 6. Oktober 1973 brach der Jom-Kippur-Krieg aus, der vierte seit 1945 zwischen arabischen Staaten und Israel. Erneut waren die Israelis siegreich und als eine hieraus resultierende Konsequenz verhängten die arabischen Ölförderstaaten ein Lieferembargo gegenüber der westlichen Welt. Innerhalb kürzester Zeit hatte dieses auch dramatische Auswirkungen auf den Motorsport, viele Veranstalter waren gezwungen, die Renndistanzen zu kürzen oder ihre Events sogar abzusagen.

Hiervon betroffen waren auch die traditionsreichen 24 Stunden von Daytona und 12 Stunden von Sebring, die der Ölkrise zum Opfer fielen. Der IMSA-Startschuss für die Saison 1974 erfolgte somit erst im April beim Sechs-Stunden-Rennen in Road Atlanta. Die 911 Carrera galten einmal mehr als große Favoriten nicht nur in der IMSA, sondern auch in der Trans-Am, die allerdings nicht mehr den Stellenwert der 60er Jahre hatte. Der SCCA hatte sogar eine Absage der Trans-Am in Erwägung gezogen, drei Rennen – Lime Rock, Watkins Glen und Road America – fanden dann aber doch statt. Alle drei Rennen wurden einmal mehr eine sichere Beute #der Carrera RSR, die mit neuer Aerodynamik und verbesserten Drei-Liter-Motoren ausgerüstet waren. Zum Wahrzeichen des Carrera wurde der Heckspoiler, den der Volksmund Enten-Bürzel taufte, und der in Kombination mit dem Frontspoiler für spürbare Verbesserungen des Fahrverhaltens sorgte.

In Lime Rock schied Peter Gregg früh nach einem Unfall aus, so siegte Al Holbert vor Ludwig Heimrath. Der Kanadier wurde in Watkins Glen erneut zweiter, dieses Mal hinter Gregg und Haywood. Dank einem fünften Platz in Road America wurde Heimrath Trans-Am Vizemeister. Peter Gregg gewann das Trans-Am-Finale und verteidigte somit seinen Titel erfolgreich.

Im Vergleich zur IMSA Camel GT hatte die Trans-Am bei weitem nicht mehr die Bedeutung und den Bekanntheitsgrad, so dass die Verantwortlichen des SCCA für 1975 beschlossen, das Niveau der Trans-Am zu senken und diese den reinen Amateuren zu überlassen. Als bester Porsche schloss John Bauer die Saison als zehnter ab. Nach den Differenzen zwischen Porsche und IMSA am Ende der Saison 1975 sollte die Trans-Am ab 1976 - Dank Porsche - zu neuer Blüte kommen.

Peter Gregg

SCCA Trans-Am Champion 1974: Peter Gregg

IMSA GT 1974: Milt Minter (81), Paul Spruell (16)

THE RSR MATURES

In October 1973 the Mid East erupted in yet another Arab-Israeli war, and while Israel again proved victorious, the consequences of the conflict extended far beyond the region as the oil producing nations imposed an oil embargo that was to have effects both immediate and long-lasting. Politics aside, racing in North America was drastically affected in 1974, with many events either shortened or cancelled altogether.

Among the latter were the traditional Daytona 24 and Sebring 12-Hour endurance classics, thus pushing the start of the '74 road racing calendar back to the third week of April when IMSA opened the Camel GT campaign with a six-hour event at Road Atlanta. In spite of the fact that makes other than Porsche had visited the winner's circle in 1973, it was clear that the 911 Carrera was becoming the dominant machine both in IMSA and in the SCCA's Trans-Am which, without major sponsorship, had fallen far down the ladder from the days when it was one of the premier American professional motorsport attractions. Indeed, there were worries that given the times and circumstances, the SCCA might simply decide to terminate the Trans-Am and cut its losses. However, in the end the SCCA staged three events, the first coming at Lime Rock in the spring, the second at Watkins Glen in early summer, and the last at Road America. As one might expect, all three were Carrera RSR festivals, the Porsches now featuring upgraded aerodynamics, including the whaletail spoilers and improved front air dams, as well as the 3-liter engines developed by the factory the previous year, and used by Gregg late in '73 in the Trans-Am. At Lime Rock, Gregg was put out early with an accident, leaving Al Holbert to lead Canadian Ludwig Heimrath to the flag for his first series win. Heimrath would again finished second in the Glen Six-Hours behind Gregg and Haywood, and fifth at Road America to garner second in the standings. Gregg would complete his Trans-Am run with another first at the Wisconsin track, this giving him two Trans-Am titles in two years. Even so, the Trans-Am was a relatively meaningless exercise in 1974, presenting the image of a poor first cousin to the Camel GT, leaving the SCCA in a quandary about what to do for 1975. After much thought, the club decided to change the format, transforming the Trans-Am into a minor league series for the top four classes running in its largely amateur National Championship arena. In a season long forgotten, the highest placed Porsche in 1975 was John Bauer's, which took tenth in the standings, this after Gregg

IMSA GT Laguna Seca 1974: Hurley Haywood

IMSA-Boss John Bishop hatte wegen der Porsche-Überlegenheit seit einiger Zeit ein flaues Gefühl im Magen. Vor allem, nachdem die Mannschaft rund um Norbert Singer den RSR weiter verbessert hatte, fürchtete Bishop eine Fortsetzung des Elfererfolges. Bishop wünschte sich viele verschiedene Siegermarken, doch gegen Porsche war nicht viel zu gewinnen. Er erlaubte im ersten Schritt Corvette-Pilot John Greenwood, seine Karosserie nach eigenen Wünschen zu modifizieren. Außerdem wurde eine Klasse eingeführt, die American GT oder kurz AAGT genannt, in der heimische Piloten ihre Boliden sehr freizügig verändern durften.

"Das Problem ist, dass die US-Hersteller im Gegensatz zu Porsche keine Lust haben, ihre Fahrzeuge den FIA-Regeln anzupassen und somit zu homologieren", sagte Bishop. "Aber wir brauchen diese Hersteller, wollen wir auch in Zukunft eine spannende und expandierende Rennserie haben." Mit der neuen Silhouetten-Klasse AAGT umging Bishop die Homologationspflicht in den Gruppen zwei und vier für die Camel GT. "Das Reglement dieser Klasse liegt in unserer Hand und wir ersparen uns vor allem die zeitaufwendigen Verhandlungen mit der FIA."

Es sollte allerdings noch mehr als ein Jahr dauern, ehe der erste echte AAGT am Start stand, ein werksunterstützter Chevrolet Monza von Horst Kwech. Und weitere 12 Monate vergingen, ehe die schnellsten AAGT ernsthafte Gegner der RSR wurden. Die Saat von 1974 sollte bald zu einem blühenden Garten werden, Porsche zur nächsten – turbogeladenen – Generation des 911 veranlassen und das Bild der IMSA-Serie nachhaltig verändern.

Aber das alles war noch Zukunftsmusik, als in Road Atlanta der Auftakt zur Camel GT 1974 auf dem Programm stand. Die einzige ernsthafte Porsche-Konkurrenz waren zwei ehemalige Werks-BMW CSL Coupé mit den Piloten John Buf-

IMSA GT 1974: George Stone, Mike Downs

IMSA GT 1974: Bob Harmon

fum, Steve Behr, Brett Lunger und Andy Petery. Beide Marken kämpften zwar um den Gesamtsieg, die BMW´s starteten allerdings in der Tourenwagen-Klasse und die Elfer bei den GT´s.

Die Bayern sollten eine große Enttäuschung erleben während die Corvette zwar schnell, aber nicht standfest war. Road Atlanta, als materialmordende Strecke bekannt, sorgte auch im Porsche-Lager für Enttäuschungen, nachdem die lange Zeit führenden Gregg und Haywood ihren RSR mit defektem Ventiltrieb abstellen mussten. Die Markenkollegen Al Holbert und Elliott Forbes-Robinson siegten somit in ihrem Entenbürzel-911 vor Michael Keyser und Milt Minter im Toad Hall-RSR.

In Laguna Seca fanden zwei Läufe von je 50 Runden statt. Im ersten gewann Forbes-Robinson vor Kwech im Chevrolet und Gregg. Nach dem Start zum zweiten Rennen übernahm Gregg die Führung, büßte nach einem Boxenstopp dann aber alle Chancen ein. Minter hatte somit die Nase vorn vor Kwech, Forbes-Robinson und Holbert. Für einen Porsche-Fünffachsieg sorgten eine Woche später in Ontario Gregg, George Dyer, Bob Bondurant, Keyser, Minter, Bob Bergström, John Morton sowie Bob Hagestad, Skip Barber.

Im verregneten Fünf-Stunden-Rennen von Mid-Ohio sahen Gregg und Holbert als erste die Ziellinie vor Haywood und Bill Webbe in dessen Apple Jack Racing-Carrera. Bei diesem Fahrzeug handelte es sich um eines der IROC-Chassis aus dem Vorjahr, der von Webbe aber auf den aktuellsten RSR-Stand gebracht wurde. Keyser und Minter belegten Platz drei, während die beiden BMW die Top Fünf komplettierten.

Vor dem nächsten Camel GT-Lauf in Talladega, gingen viele IMSA-Teams bei den alljährlichen FIA-Sechs Stunden von Watkins Glen an den Start. Keyser, Minter peilten einen

DER RSR KOMMT IN FORM

IMSA GT 1974: Charlie Kemp

Poster

IMSA GT 1974: Michael Keyser, Milt Minter

had led the RSR clan to a one-through-five sweep of the points the previous year. Porsche would return, and do so with great determination in 1976 as a result of a political squabble between Zuffenhausen and IMSA. Bishop had long been uneasy with his relationship with Porsche, especially given the focused nature of Hoppen. As Singer perfected the RSR, the IMSA president's discontent grew with the increasing lack of variety in terms of his winners. What Bishop wanted was a host of different nameplates. What he got was one: Porsche.

Already for 1974 he had permitted Zora Arkus Duntov, the Corvette's father figure, to develop radical new bodywork for his offspring, which Greenwood wasted little time applying to his car, and which made that car look like nothing so much as a train locomotive. If Hoppen was unhappy, he was about to become even more displeased when Bishop launched a new homegrown category, the American GT division. While not quite an "anything goes" class, the AAGT rules could best be described as "liberal," a fact which didn't bother Bishop at all.

Indeed, even before the '74 season had begun Bishop had started thinking about ways to loosen Porsche's grip on his series. "The problem," said Bishop, "was that the Detroit manufacturers had no interest in jumping through the hoops needed to achieve FIA homologation. Without that there was no way for them to be competitive in our series, and frankly we needed them if we were grow in the future."

Ever innovative, Bishop eliminated the problem of homologation, by creating a new homegrown class, basically 'silhouette', where the approval to race would be IMSA's alone. Thus came into existence the All American GT division, the intellectual origins of which could be found in NASCAR.

"We knew that Detroit would never go through the hoops required by the FIA to homologate special performance versions of their cars. However, we wanted and needed to have a winning domestic presence in our series if it were to grow and continue its success. Therefore, we decided to create a set of rules which eliminated the problems and expense of dealing with the FIA."

It would take a year before the first true AAGT entry, the factory-assisted Chevrolet Monza of Horst Kwech, appeared on the scene, and another year before an ever increasing AAGT fleet truly began to challenge the RSRs. However, the seeds planted in 1974 would become a mighty orchard that would eventually reconfigure the face of IMSA and set the stage for a new generation of Porsche-built 911 turbos. That, though, was in the future when the IMSA teams set up camp at Road Atlanta on a hot spring weekend in 1974. As the teams laid out their equipment the only immediate challenge to the Porsche brigade came from a pair of ex-factory BMW CSL coupes run by John Buffum for himself, Steve Behr, Brett Lunger and Andy Petery. In fact, under IMSA's class system the BMWs would run in the large touring category, while the Porsches and Greenwood's rebodied Corvette would compete in the headlining GT division, although all were expected to battle for overall honors. Ultimately the BMWs would prove a disappointment, while the Corvette would be fast, but not necessarily reliable. At Atlanta, also proving to have durability problems were Gregg and Haywood whose new 3.0-liter, whaletail RSR retired with engine valve train woes after leading much of the six-hour affair. That left the similar, blue-painted Porsche of Holbert, teamed on this occasion with Elliott Forbes-Robinson, to take the win ahead of Keyser and Minter in the former's '74 spec Toad Hall RSR. From Atlanta, and after the majority of the teams had stopped over at Lime Rock for the season

THE RSR MATURES 231

Hattrick in der GT-Klasse an, aber 1974 war gegen den Brumos-RSR von Gregg, Haywood nichts zu gewinnen. Auffallend: Der Brumos-Bolide hatte eine vordere Stossstange, die der an den Werks-Turbos zum Verwechseln ähnlich sah und die den Neigungswinkel der Fronthaube verringerte. Sowohl die FIA- als auch die IMSA-Regeln erlaubten dieses, denn nur die vordere Kante der Stossstange musste die gleichen Konturen aufweisen wie das Serienfahrzeug.

Es hatte den Anschein, als ob Gregg seine guten Verbindungen zu Porsche genutzt hatte, um sich eine solche – revolutionäre – Spoilerstossstange aus dem Ersatzteil-Reservoir der Werksmannschaft, die mit Gijs van Lennep und Herbert Müller im Carrera Turbo hinter einem Matra V12 Gesamtzweite wurde, auszuleihen.

In Talladega hatte Gregg wieder auf die ursprüngliche Form zurückgerüstet. Aber es lag nicht nur an der normalen vorderen Stossstange, dass er hinter Minter, Keyser und Dyer nur vierter wurde. Nur eine Woche später sorgten Gregg, Haywood und Behr in Charlotte für einen weiteren RSR-Dreifachsieg. Am ersten Montag im September, siegte Gregg im ersten der beiden 100-Meilen-Rennen. Ein defektes Gasgestänge sorgte im zweiten für einen Ausfall, so dass Keyser triumphierte.

Einen unglaublichen Elffachsieg feierte der Elfer – davon acht RSR auf den ersten acht Plätzen – beim nächsten Rennen in Mexico City. Hector Rebaque, Guillermo Rojas, Freddy van Beuren wurde als erste abgewunken vor Behr, Loomis, Sprowls. Beim Saisonfinale in Daytona sorgte John Greenwood für einen Chevrolet-Sieg vor Holbert, während Jerry Thompson und Dave Heinz mit ihrem 911 dritte wurden. Obwohl Gregg Mexico ausgelassen hatte und in Daytona nur achter wurde, feierte er seinen dritten IMSA-Titel in vier Jahren. Für Porsche war es einmal mehr ein optimaler Saisonverlauf, nicht so für Bishop, der nach wie vor eine Serie mit nur einer Siegermarke hatte.

Mit dem Ende der Ölkrise kehrte der Motorsport zu seinem gewohnten Umfang zurück. Die 24 Stunden Daytona und Sebrings 12 Stunden bildeten (nach der Absage von 1974) den Auftakt zur IMSA Camel GT. Die Veranstalter von Daytona hatten endgültig die Seiten gewechselt, von einem Lauf zur FIA-Markenweltmeisterschaft hin zum alljährlichen Auftakt der IMSA-Serie. Während Prototypen nicht mehr zugelassen waren, standen nun die GT´s im Vordergrund.

Und neben den erfolgsverwöhnten Porsche Carrera zählte das BMW-Werksteam mit der letzten Entwicklungsstufe des CSL Coupé zu den Favoriten. Hans-Joachim Stuck, Ronnie Peterson, Brian Redman und Sam Posey griffen für die Weiß-Blauen ins Lenkrad, die in den Jahren zuvor zahlreiche Siege in Europa feiern durften. Nicht zu vergessen die Silhouetten-Fahrzeuge der AAGT.

Doch kaum war die Jagd zweimal rund um die Uhr eröffnet, waren die Porsche-Teams bei der Vergabe des Gesamtsieges einmal mehr unter sich. Die AAGT-Boliden waren zwar schnell, aber sehr anfällig. Und auch die BMW-Werksmannschaft verfehlte ihre Ziele, da man die vorzügliche Arbeit der nordamerikanischen Porsche-Teams unterschätzt hatte.

Dieses gab auch BMW-Rennleiter Jochen Neerpasch zu: "Wir haben einen Fehler gemacht. Wir dachten es wäre einfach, die privaten US-Teams zu besiegen, da wir es von Europa gewohnt sind, dass Werks-Teams den privaten überlegen sind. Aber die Realität sah anders aus. Fahrer oder Teams wie Peter Gregg arbeiten auf einem sehr hohen Level, vielleicht sogar auf einem höheren als wir. Das ist uns eine Lehre!" Josef Hoppen war klar, dass man für die Zukunft gegen BMW bestens gerüstet sein muss. "1975 kön-

IMSA GT Daytona 1974: Eddie Wachs

IMSA GT Daytona 1974: Milt Minter

Road Atlanta winner 1974: Al Holbert

opening Trans-Am, the series moved west to Laguna for a pair of 95-mile, 50-lap sprints, the first won by Elliott Forbes-Robinson in a Carrera over Horst Kwech's Capri and Gregg's immaculate Porsche. Gregg moved into the front spot in the second sprint at the start, but later dropped from contention after pitting for mechanical repairs. This left Minter in Keyser's second RSR to earn top honors, followed across the line by Kwech, EFR and Holbert. A week later at the old Ontario Motor Speedway, 60 miles east of Los Angeles, Gregg led a five-car Porsche sweep in the four-hour Camel race held on the combined infield and oval courses, George Dyer and Bob Bondurant finishing second, followed by Keyser and Minter with Bob Bergstrom and John Morton fourth, and Bob Hagestad and Skip Barber fifth. A month and a half later the IMSA set returned to action at a rainy Mid-Ohio, where Gregg joined Holbert in the latter's Carrera to beat Haywood and Bill Webbe in Webbe's Apple Jack Racing Carrera in the five-hour event. The Apple Jack car was one of the Penske IROC Porsches, sold to Webbe after the series and then brought up to full RSR specifications. It would be Haywood's mount for the majority of the season, and he would do well with it. Third at Mid Ohio went to Keyser and Minter, while the two BMWs rounded out the top five. Before The Camel series' next event at Talladega in early August came the annual FIA Watkins Glen Six-Hour Manufacturers event, in which Keyser and Minter had won the GT honors in both 1972 and 1973. In 1974 it was the turn of Gregg and Haywood in their Brumos entry, the affair marking the return, at least temporarily, of Haywood to the Brumos fold. Interestingly, The Brumos RSR wore a new front bumper, the top edge of which matched the slope of the front bonnet, very similar in shape that used by the factory's 911 Turbo Carreras.

The American RSR entrants had all modified the front bumpers to give them flat vertical surfaces, this being perfectly legal under both IMSA and FIA regulations. So modified, the bumpers improved the aerodynamics over the RSRs which retained the standard indented front bumpers. However, supposedly the top edge of the component had to match the contours of the standard road unit, which the Brumos RSR's bumper did not at the Glen. It seems probable that Gregg's close ties to Porsche allowed him to "borrow" a spare bumper from the factory Turbo Carrera prototype which was brought to the upstate New York track for the Six-Hour, Gijs

IMSA GT 1974: Adrian Gang, Jim Cook

IMSA GT Daytona 1974: Al Holbert

van Lennep and Herbert Muller taking it to second overall behind the winning Matra V-12. At Talladega, Gregg, whose Porsche was now fitted with the more standard bodywork, found he could do no better than fourth behind the Carreras of Keyser and Dyer, both of whom were beaten by Minter, who had a "one off" drive in a Greenwood Corvette and made the most of it. Eight days later the Camel GT regulars were at the Charlotte Motor Speedway where Gregg led Haywood and Behr to a one-through-three RSR sweep on the combined infield and tri-oval circuit under a steamy August sun. Labor Day Monday saw the series at Lime Rock for another twin 100-mile double feature, the opener going to Gregg who led all the way, and the nightcap to Keyser who inherited the victory after Gregg retired with throttle linkage troubles. Following a long layoff, almost two months, the Camel GT circus travelled to Mexico City for a 1000 kilometer race. The majority of the contenders opted to make the trip south, but Gregg did not. After almost six and three-quarter hours, local heroes Hector Rebaque, Guillermo Rojas and Freddy van Beuren beat Behr, Loomis and Billy Sprowls in yet another dominating Porsche performance that saw the RSR contingent sweep the first eight places. In fact the highest non-911 finisher was Ray Walle's Mazda RX-3 sedan in 12th. At the Daytona finale, John Greenwood demonstrated that Minter's Talladega triumph wasn't a fluke as his Corvette beat Holbert's Carrera, with Jerry Thompson and Dave Heinz finishing third. Despite missing Mexico and doing no better than eighth at Daytona, Gregg wrapped up his third IMSA crown in four seasons.

It had been a good year for Porsche, but not for Bishop since his task was to sell a show that generally had only a single manufacturer winning.

With the oil crisis solved, at least for the moment, racing began to return to normal in 1975. For Camel GT enthusiasts that meant a return to the traditional long-distance Daytona 24 and Sebring 12-Hour season openers. Although both had been cancelled in 1974, IMSA had taken over the Sebring date making it the inaugural round of the Camel series. Now, as 1975 approached Daytona likewise switched allegiances, transforming itself from an FIA World Manufacturers event to a dedicated Camel affair.

While the prototypes had gone, in their place was a strong GT entry that included not only the traditional Porsche Carreras, but a full factory BMW squad, consisting of star

THE RSR MATURES 233

nen wir die CSL Coupés und die AAGT noch hinter uns halten, aber danach brauchen wir etwas Neues. Deshalb nehme ich meine wichtigsten Ingenieure im April mit nach Road Atlanta, damit diese sich selbst ein Bild davon machen können, was wir in Zukunft brauchen!"

Mit Hochdruck arbeiteten Norbert Singer und seine Mannschaft an der Entwicklung der turbogeladenen 934 und 935, die beide 1976 ihre Premiere erleben sollten. Während der 935 ausschließlich vom Werk in der Marken-Weltmeisterschaft eingesetzt werden sollte, wurde mit dem 934 die Ablösung des RSR in der Gruppe vier anvisiert.

Doch zunächst zurück zu den 24 Stunden von Daytona 1975: Die Werks-BMW mit Posey, Stuck und Redman, Peterson gehörten schnell zu den Ausfällen, so dass Gregg und Haywood ihren 73er Erfolg wiederholten und einen 911-Sechsfachsieg anführten. So erfolgreich der Saisonauftakt für Porsche auch war, so ernüchternd waren die 12 Stunden von Sebring. Redman und Allan Moffat, unterstützt von Posey und Stuck, nachdem deren BMW früh ausgefallen war, siegten vor vier Porsche-Teams.

Horst Kwech stellte den Chevrolet Monza in Road Atlanta auf die Pole-Position, doch im Rennen siegte Holbert vor Gregg und Haywood. In Laguna Seca freuten sich Peter Gregg und Hans-Joachim Stuck über jeweils einen 100 Meilen-Laufsieg. Bei den Sechs Stunden von Riverside hatte BMW mit Stuck, Quester und Posey, Redman erneut die Nase vorn während Gregg und Haywood dritte wurden. Die BMW hatten mittlerweile vor allem hinsichtlich der Motorleistung die RSR überholt.

Nicht ungelegen kam den Porsche-Teams das nächste Rennen auf dem kleinen und winkligen Kurs von Lime Rock, wo Handling wichtiger war als reine Motorleistung. Peter Gregg gewann vor Stuck, Holbert und Posey den ersten Durchgang. Im zweiten Rennen sorgten Holbert und Gregg für einen RSR-Doppelsieg vor Stuck und Posey. In Mid-Ohio

24 Hours Daytona 1975: Ramon de Izaurieta, Sergio Tabec, Fidel Martinez

12 Hours Sebring 1975: Bob Harmon, Jon Woodner

24 Hours Daytona 1975: Charlie Kemp, Carson Baird

234 DER RSR KOMMT IN FORM

drivers such as Hans Stuck, Ronnie Peterson, Brian Redman and Sam Posey, all equipped with the latest version of Munich's potent CSL coupe. Although technically, under IMSA's rules in a separate class from the Carrera RSRs, the BMWs were serious challengers for overall honors.

Not only would the 911 competitors have to come to grips with the new band of AAGT homebreds, but also from the well-developed BMWs, whose performance had been amply demonstrated for several seasons in Europe. Even so, Porsche would continue to claim an edge, particularly since the American entries were at the beginning of their development cycle and lacked any consistent reliability, while the Munich manufacturer made the mistake of under-estimating the standard of preparation which was the norm in North American motorsport.

As BMW's racing boss, Jochen Neerpasch put it, "We made a mistake. We thought it would be easy to win against the private teams in the United States because in Europe the factories generally have an edge. However, here we found it quite different. People such as Peter Gregg are every bit at our level, if not even a little bit higher. It has been a real lesson for us."

Yet, Hoppen and Porsche were worried. "I knew," said Hoppen, "that while we might be able to keep the BMWs and the cars in John's new class at bay for 1975, we would have to have something better for the future. To emphasize that point I brought the engineers to Road Atlanta in April to see first hand what was going on."

Singer and his engineering team were already developing the 934 and 935 turbos for their twin introductions in 1976. While the 935 was intended to be a "factory only" item for the '76 FIA Manufacturer's series, Hoppen fully expected to have the Group 4 934 as a replacement for the RSR. That, however, wouldn't come until the end of the '75 season. Meanwhile, the opening Daytona 24-Hour had to be faced.

24 Hours Daytona 1975: Mike Tillson, Dieter Oest

IMSA GT 1975: Hurley Haywood

24 Hours Daytona 1975: Rusty Bond, George Rollin, John Belperche

There, the only truly serious opposition facing the Carrera RSRs were the two factory BMWs, one for Posey and Stuck, the other with Redman partnered by Formula One ace Ronnie Peterson. Ultimately, the CSLs faded away as the Porsches swept the top six positions, Gregg and Haywood repeating their 1973 victory despite Gregg tangling with another car and damaging his rear bodywork.

If Daytona was a promising start, Sebring was the opposite. While Carreras occupied four of the first five spots, the victory went to the factory BMW of Redman and Allan Moffat, who were joined in the latter stages by Posey and Stuck after their CSL had retired.

The first serious AAGT contender, the Dekon Chevrolet Monza of Horst Kwech, made its inaugural Camel appearance at the April Road Atlanta twin 100-mile sprints. Although fast enough to garner the pole, Kwech failed to finish after a minor accident, leaving the show to Holbert, Gregg and Haywood. The spring Laguna Seca event saw Gregg win the first 100-miler with Stuck's CSL second, while in the companion affair it was Gregg slipping to fourth as Stuck took the win trailed by the RSRs of Mike Keyser and Elliott Forbes-Robinson.

From Laguna the championship traveled to Riverside for a Six-Hour event that was dominated by the factory BMWs, Stuck and Dieter Quester beating Posey and Redman, with Gregg and Haywood finishing third. At this point there were worries in the Porsche ranks because the CSLs had achieved their sweep on the basis of horsepower, something the Carreras could not match.

Happily for the Porsche teams the next race came on Memorial Day weekend at the short, tough 1.5-mile Lime

THE RSR MATURES 235

stand dann nur ein 100 Meilen-Rennen auf dem Programm, dessen Ergebnis aber die Basis für die Startaufstellung des nächsten Sechs-Stunden-Rennens bilden sollte. Nachdem sowohl Stuck als auch Gregg mit defekten Radlagern vorzeitig aufgeben mussten, gewann Holbert vor Posey.

In kanadischen Mosport folgten zwei 50 Meilen-Sprints ein 100 Meilen-Finale. Im ersten Sprint siegte Redman vor Gregg, im zweiten Holbert vor George Dyer in einem weiteren RSR. Im Finale sah Redman lange Zeit wie der Sieger aus, ehe der BMW-Motor platzte. Clark Shafer übernahm mit seinem AAGT-Camaro die Spitze. Bei der Verfolgung von Shafer kam Gregg von der Strecke ab und verbog am Porsche die Radaufhängung. Holbert sollte schließlich gewinnen und Gregg kam wenigstens noch als vierter ins Ziel.

Das Paul Revere 250-Meilen Rennen in Daytona wurde um Mitternacht gestartet. Stuck nutzte den Leistungsvorteil im BMW CSL und wurde vor Haywood und Holbert abgewunken, Gregg musste nach Motorproblemen vorzeitig aufgeben. In Mid-America siegte Holbert in beiden Läufen vor Gregg. Stuck schlug dann in Talladega zurück, als der Deutsche vor Gregg, Haywood und Holbert siegte. Peter Gregg wollte erneut mit einer veränderten Aerodynamik für Aufsehen sorgen, denn das PS-Defizit versuchte der Amerikaner auf anderen Wegen wieder auszugleichen und ersuchte daher Weissach um Hilfe.

Die Mannschaft rund um Norbert Singer bot Gregg ein neues hinteres Seitenteil – welches 1976 an den Werks-935 Berücksichtigung finden sollte - anstelle des normalen Kotflügels samt der Verbreiterung an. Obwohl die AAGT-Boliden mit teilweise abenteuerlichen und seltsam anmutenden Konstruktionen an die Rennstrecken kamen, fanden Greggs neue Seitenbleche nicht die Zustimmung von Bishop. Der IMSA-Boss hatte Einwände gegen diese Modifikation, die auch Holberts RSR bald aufweisen sollte. Bishop ordnete an, dass die neuen Seitenteile unverzüglich gegen ihre Vorgänger wieder ausgetauscht werden müssten.

24 Hours Daytona 1975: Michael Keyser, Billy Sprowls, Andres Contreras

24 Hours Daytona 1975: George Dyer, Jacques Bienvenue

In Mid-Ohio hatte Greggs RSR noch immer die neuentwickelten Seitenteile montiert, denn der Amerikaner konnte glaubhaft versichern, dass er noch nicht zu Hause gewesen sei, um den entsprechenden Brief der IMSA zu lesen. Gregg und Haywood führten vier Stunden lang das Rennen an, ehe die Kollision mit einem Nachzügler für das Aus sorgte. Holbert und Forbes-Robinson wurde somit erste vor John O´Steen und Dave Helmick in einem weiteren RSR.

Beim Saisonfinale in Daytona hielt Greenwoods Chevrolet länger als üblich und siegte vor den beiden BMW von Redman und Posey sowie Gregg, dieses Mal wieder mit alten Kotflügeln, und Haywood. Rang vier reichte Peter Gregg für seinen dritten Titel in Folge – und vierten insgesamt – in der Camel GT Series.

Für Gregg war die Angelegenheit mit den Kotflügeln eigentlich abgehakt, denn im Reglement sei nirgendwo der Punkt enthalten, dass er nicht das modifizieren dürfte, was andere auch machen würden. Aber für Bishop und die IMSA was das Thema noch lange nicht erledigt. Am Ende einigten sich beide Parteien doch.

Im Sommer 1975 hatte Josef Hoppen Bishop überzeugen können, dass der neue 934 ab der kommenden Saison in der Camel GT startberechtigt sei. Mit diesen Perspektiven vor Augen, wurden Gregg und Holbert in das Entwicklungsteam integriert. Die beiden besuchten mehrfach die Werkstätten in Weissach, um den Testträger auf Herz und Nieren zu prüfen sowie Verbesserungen vorzuschlagen.

Während einem dieser Testtage im November, erhielt Hoppen einen Anruf von Bishop. Es sollte ein kurzes Telefonat sein in dessen Verlauf der IMSA-Boss mitteilte, dass er nach

Park course in northwestern Connecticut, where handling was more important than power. Even so Stuck made a good showing finishing second to Gregg, Holbert crossing the line third and Posey claiming fourth in the opener, while Holbert beat Gregg, Stuck and Posey in that order in the second 100 miler.

Mid Ohio, which followed, was a somewhat unusual affair in that the weekend consisted of only a single 100-mile sprint, the finishing order of which would determine the grid upon IMSA's return to the track for a six-hour long distance event. Although both Stuck and Gregg led they both retired with wheel bearing failures, leaving Holbert in the lead over Posey at the checkered flag. Mosport, outside of Toronto, featured two 50-mile heats and a 100-mile finale. Redman won the first heat ahead of Gregg, Holbert besting George Dyer's RSR in the second. Redman led the final in his BMW until its engine blew; then Clark Shafer, a farmer who raced for fun, took over in his AAGT Camaro. When Gregg tried to get by the Chevrolet Shafer put him off the track, damaging the Porsche's suspension and leaving him fourth at the finish in a race won by Haywood in his own RSR.

The July Fourth weekend Paul Revere 250, a race that started at midnight over the combined high-banked and infield Daytona Speedway circuit, saw Stuck use the BMW's power to beat Haywood and Holbert, after Gregg was sidelined by a sick engine. The twin 100-mile format made its return at Mid-America Raceway later that month just west of St. Louis. With the BMW team skipping the trip it was all Porsche, Holbert beating Gregg and Haywood, and then winning again over his Jacksonville, Florida rival after Haywood's transmission failed in the summer heat.

That brought the Camel GT to the high-banked Talladega Speedway for a rain-shortened preliminary to the NASCAR stock car feature. Once again Stuck found himself in the winner's circle with Gregg, Haywood and Holbert taking the next three position. However there was a difference, one that involved the bodywork on Gregg's car. Knowing that there was virtually nothing that could be done to improve the horsepower output of his RSR, Gregg turned to Weissach for some aerodynamic help.

What Singer and his colleagues came up with was a rear fender shape not far removed from that which would appear on the factory's 935s in 1976. Although the AAGT set, led by the Corvettes of John Greenwood, had pioneered some of the wildest bodywork seen in racing to that time without objection from Bishop, when Gregg's Carrera appeared with its new fenders, and was later joined by the similarly clothed Holbert RSR, Bishop took an entirely different view, ordering the offending fiberglass to be replaced by its less radical predecessor.

At Mid-Ohio Gregg Porsche's again had the factory-inspired rear fenders, Gregg claiming he hadn't been home to read the official letter sent to him by IMSA on the matter. The Florida driver, with Haywood as his partner, handily led for four hours until he collided with a slower car and putting himself out of the event. The beneficiary of all this was Holbert, who with Elliott Forbes-Robinson as his co-driver, beat John O'Steen and Dave Helmick.

The season finale came back to Daytona on the last day of November. Greenwood survived long enough to claim the victory, the BMWs of Redman and Posey taking second and third with Gregg fourth and Haywood fifth. That performance was more than enough to earn Gregg his third straight, and fourth Camel driver's crown in five years.

For this event Gregg's Carrera had reverted back to its 'normal' state, the offensive rear fenders having been left at

24 Hours Daytona 1975: Al Holbert, Elliot Forbes-Robinson

Winner 24 Hours Daytona 1975: Peter Gregg, Hurley Haywood

24 Hours Daytona 1975: John Graves, Dave Helmick, John O'Steen

THE RSR MATURES 237

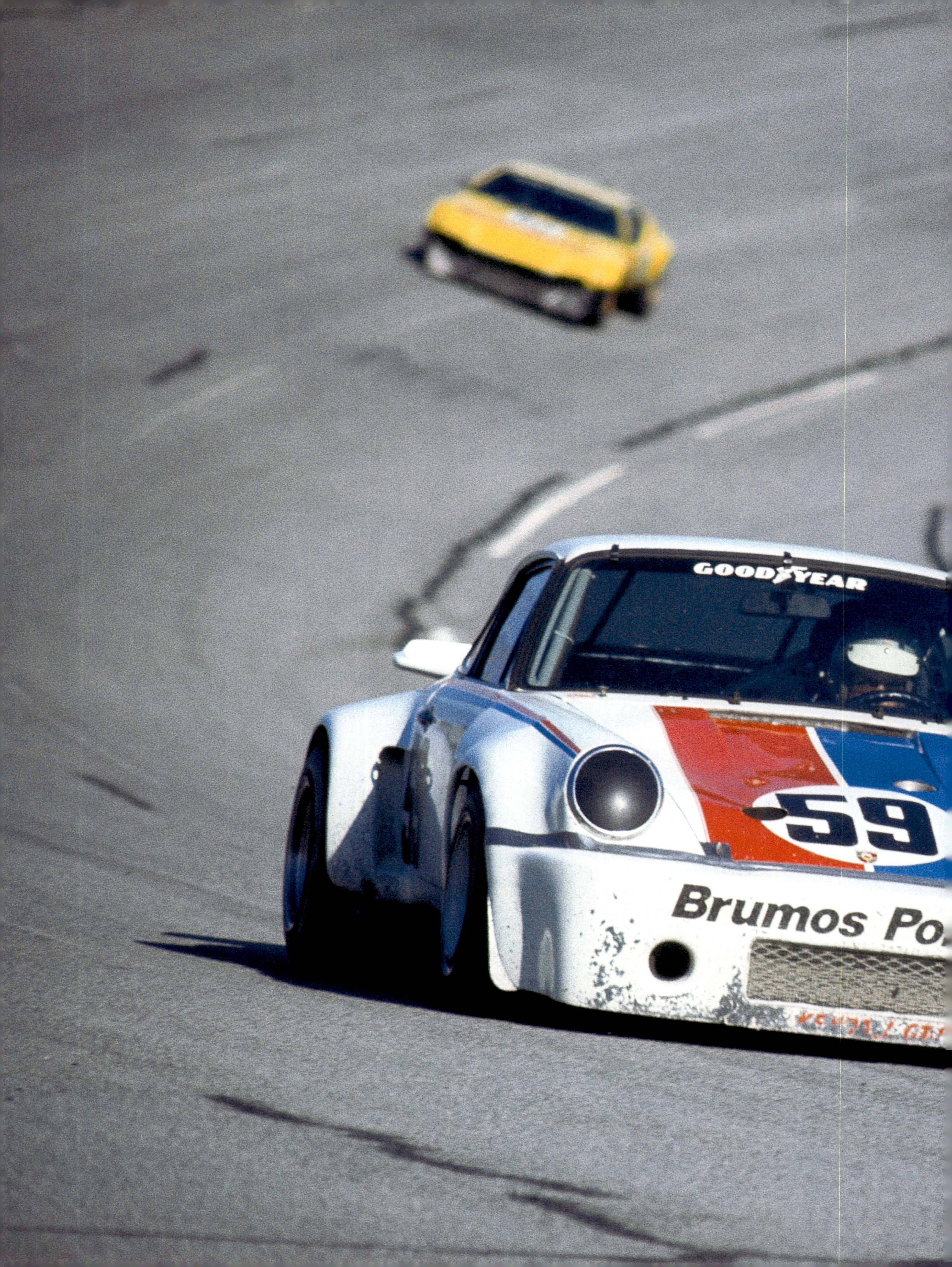
GOODYEAR
59
Brumos Po

Triumph
der Zuverlässigkeit:
24 Stunden
Daytona
USA
PORSCHE
Triumph of
Reliability:
24 Hours of
Daytona
USA
PORSCHE
IMSA CAMEL
GT-CHALLENGE
CUP
1975
1. Peter Gregg Porsche Carrera RSR
2. Hurley Haywood Porsche Carrera RSR
3. Al Holbert Porsche Carrera RSR
4. Hans Stuck BMW CSL
5. John O'Steen Porsche Carrera RSR
6. George Dyer Porsche Carrera RSR
7. Charly Kemp Porsche Carrera RSR
8. Mike Keyser Porsche Carrera RSR
9. Sam Posey BMW CSL
10. Elliot Forbes-Robinson Porsche Carrera RSR
11. Brian Redman BMW CSL
Goodyear
Champion
Brumos Porsche
59
PORSCHE
che

Rücksprache mit einigen Mitbewerbern seine Meinung geändert habe. Der 934 dürfe 1976 nicht in der Camel GT starten! "Ich war schockiert und bat John, das Thema noch einmal zu diskutieren, wenn ich zurück in Amerika wäre", sollte Hoppen später sagen. "Ich hatte schon ein halbes Dutzend bestellt und nun hatte ich keine Serie, wo die Fahrzeuge starten konnten und auch keine Kunden, die diese gebrauchen konnten!" Auch ein weiteres Gespräch zwischen Hoppen und Bishop erbrachte kein neues Ergebnis.

Hoppen: "John bewegte sich keinen Millimeter, es ging einfach nicht weiter. Unsere Situation war festgefahren." Aber Jo Hoppen war kein Typ, der so schnell die Flinte ins Korn warf. Er kontaktierte seinen alten Freund Cameron Argetsinger, damals Chef der SCCA ProRacing, und sprach mit ihm über die Reaktivierung der leblosen Trans-Am-Serie. Hoppen stellte den gegenseitigen Nutzen in den Mittelpunkt der Verhandlungen und schaffte es, Argetsingers Bedenken auszuräumen. Die beiden einigten sich auf eine Meisterschaft mit zwei Divisionen.

Die Division 1 sollte weiterhin das Sammelbecken für die nationalen SCCA-Fahrzeuge sein. In der Division 2 waren der 934 und alle anderen Camel GT-Boliden startberechtigt. Diese Klasseneinteilung sollte bis 1979 Bestand haben. Und, was noch viel wichtiger war, die Trans-Am überlebte und Hoppen fand einen Ausweg aus seinem 934-Dilemma.

Hatte Bishop geglaubt, mit dem Startverbot für den 934 zum Wohle seiner Teilnehmer, und vor allem der Nicht-Porsche-Teams, gehandelt zu haben, musste er bald einsehen, dass er auf dem falschen Weg war. Mit der Trans-Am-Freigabe des 934 Turbo und bekannten Fahrernamen wie Holbert, Haywood, dem ehemaligen Can-Am-Sieger George Follmer oder dem aufstrebenden Paul Miller, geriet die Camel GT in den Hintergrund des allgemeinen Interesses.

Mehr noch: Josef Hoppen setzte alle Hebel in Bewegung, um die PR-Maschine der Trans-Am so richtig in Fahrt zu bringen. Bishop sollte später eingestehen: "Es ist nicht gut, Porsche nicht auf deiner Seite zu haben!" Der einzige, schwache Trost für den IMSA-Boss war die Tatsache, dass Holbert für die Camel GT einen Chevrolet Monza gekauft hatte. Und das Gregg am Volant eines ehemaligen Werks-BMW CSL der Serie erhalten blieb.

24 Hours Daytona 1975: Mandy Alvarez, Juan Montalvo

24 Hours Daytona 1975: Charlie Kemp, Carson Baird

24 Hours Daytona 1975: George Drolsom, Bob Nagel

240 DER RSR KOMMT IN FORM

home. However, the issue was far from settled as Gregg filed suit against Bishop and IMSA, claiming there was nothing in the rules book that prohibited him from doing what his rivals had done.

In the end, the parties settled their issues. Even though the outcome remained secret, never again did Bishop single out Porsche for a "remedial" rules change not covered in the printed regulations. On the other hand, the Daytona finale was the final time Gregg would drive an RSR in anger, a situation which had a great deal to do with Bishop's continuing desire to eliminate what he perceived as Porsche's on-going domination of his series.

By the summer of 1975, Hoppen had persuaded Bishop to allow the 934s to take part in the next season's Camel championship. With that in mind, he involved both Gregg and Holbert in the development of the car, sending them to Weissach to test and make recommendations about how to improve the prototype.

During one of those sessions in November, Hoppen took a telephone call from Bishop in Helmuth Bott's office (Bott then being the head of Research and Development for Porsche). The conversation was short as Bishop told Hoppen that he had changed his mind after "talking to some of the Porsche Camel GT regulars" and would not permit the 934 to participate in the Camel Series for 1976.

"I was shocked, " said Hoppen later. "However I simply told John that I would discuss the matter further when I returned to North America. It put me in a tremendously difficult position because I had already ordered more than a half a dozen 934s which had to be paid for, and conversely had no place to race them, and thus no customers for them." Things did not improve after a subsequent meeting with Bishop, when the IMSA president maintained his negative stance toward the 934.

"I tried to reason with him, but John would not budge. There was no negotiating with him. We were stuck." However, Hoppen was not an individual to be stymied for long. Within days he had contacted his old friend Cameron Argetsinger, then head of SCCA ProRacing, to talk about reviving the moribund Trans-Am, and what Hoppen viewed as a mutually beneficial move from all concerned.

24 Hours Daytona 1975: Gregg, Haywood (59), Townsend, Thomas, Papke (13)

24 Hours Daytona 1975: Guillermo Rojas, Hector Rebaque, Fred van Beuren

What Hoppen proposed, and what Argetsinger accepted, was a two-tier title chase. Category I would continue to be the home for the SCCA National machinery, while the newly formed Category II would embrace the orphaned 934s and anything else the Camel competitors might want to enter. It was a formula that would not only remain in place until 1979, more importantly it was a formula that saved the Trans-Am and provided Hoppen with a way out of what could have been a career-ending problem.

If at first Bishop had believed he had made his competitors happy and levelled the Camel playing field for the non-Porsche entrants, he quickly discovered he was wrong. With Trans-Am now accepting the Group 4 turbo 934, the 1976 series would boast the presence of Holbert, Haywood, 1972 series and Can-Am titlist George Follmer, and the up-and coming Paul Miller as regulars with their 934s.

Moreover, Hoppen, using all the promotional means he could muster, made sure that as many people as possible knew they were there. As Bishop later remarked, "It isn't good to have Porsche angry with you." About the only saving grace was the fact that Holbert had purchased a Dekon Monza to campaign in IMSA from Road Atlanta on, and that Gregg had chosen to stay full time in the Camel series behind the wheel of an ex-factory BMW CSL.

THE RSR MATURES 241

TURBOS EROBERN DIE NEUE WELT

1976 sollte für die Camel GT und John Bishop ein interessantes Jahr werden, zumal der 934 vom IMSA-Boss persönlich – zumindest am Saisonbeginn – nicht zum Start zugelassen worden war. Mit 70 Fahrzeugen versprachen die 24 Stunden von Daytona zu einem spannenden und ereignisreichen Saisonauftakt zu werden. Allerdings konnte niemand ahnen, welches Drama sich in der Morgendämmerung abspielen sollte.

Gleich reihenweise steuerten die Piloten mit stotternden oder nicht mehr funktionierenden Motoren die Boxenstraße an. Schnell wurde festgestellt, dass im Verlauf der Nacht Wasser anstelle von Benzin den Weg in die Bodentanks gefunden hatte und die Teams Zug um Zug bei den Boxenstopps Wasser getankt hatten. Unverzüglich wurde das Rennen mit der roten Flagge abgebrochen. In den Erdtanks der Boxenanlage wurde das Wasser wieder gegen Treibstoff ausgetauscht und auch die Teams hatten alle Hände voll zu tun, die Motoren instandzusetzen oder auszutauschen.

Kurz nach Mittag wurde neu gestartet und Gregg, Redman, Fitzpatrick im BMW CSL als Sieger abgewunken, vor Holbert, Ballot-Lena, Busby und Haywood sowie zwei weiteren RSR-Teams. Vier Fahrzeuge unter den ersten fünf waren einmal mehr ein Beweis für die Stärke des Carrera. Bei den 12 Stunden von Sebring fuhren die 911er dann alles in Grund und Boden. Holbert und Keyser siegten mit ihrem RSR und nicht weniger als zehn Porsche-Teams landeten unter den ersten Elf. Lediglich Gregg und Haywood verhinderten im BMW als siebte den zehnfachen Porsche-Sieg.

Dass der RSR noch lange nicht zum alten Eisen gehörte, bewiesen die beiden Langstreckenklassiker zu Saisonbeginn. Doch würden die Carrera-Teams auch bei den folgenden Sprintrennen Chancen haben? Beim 100 Meilen-Rennen in Road Atlanta dominierte der neue Chevrolet Monza das Geschehen, Holbert und Keyser siegten vor Gregg im BMW. Bob Hagestad, als bester RSR nur Sechster, hatte bereits eine Runde Rückstand.

Auch in Laguna Seca sollte es kaum besser laufen: Holbert hatte erneut die Nase vorn, vor Gregg und Keyser. George Dyer hielt als vierter die Porsche-Flaggen hoch. Eine Woche später in Ontario kam Dyer als Dritter aufs Treppchen. Und auch der erste Camel GT-Sieg folgte schon bald für Dyer in Lime Rock, wo Keyser und Jim Busby das Nachsehen hatten. In Mid-Ohio zeigte dann Keyser im Chevrolet der Konkurrenz wieder den Auspuff und überquerte als Erster die Ziellinie vor Holbert.

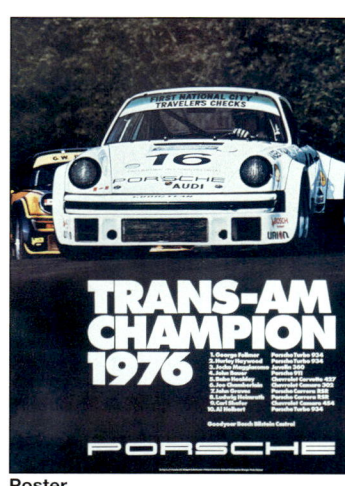

IMSA GT 1976: Dave White, Fritz Hochreuter

Poster

SCCA Trans-Am 1976: Al Holbert

Trans-Am Champion 1976: George Follmer

934 PRECEDES 935

Clearly, 1976 would be an interesting year for IMSA and John Bishop, even though he had banished, if only temporarily, Porsche's new 934 from his popular Camel GT championship. With a field of over 70, the Daytona 24-Hours promised to be memorable. It is best remembered, though, not for the racing but for the fuel. As dawn approached on Sunday more and more of the competitors were struggling back to the pits with their engines either sputtering or silent altogether. It was soon determined to be water in the gasoline supply, forcing IMSA officials to red flag the event while a new batch of untainted fuel was brought in.

During the halt, which lasted until the lunch hour, teams up and down the pitlane worked furiously either to make repairs or replace the damaged powerplants completely. Ultimately Gregg, Redman and Fitzpatrick prevailed in their BMW CSL over Holbert and Ballot-Lena in their Carrera RSR, with Busby and Hurley Haywood taking third in the Brumos Carrera. Daytona was another case of the Carreras dominating the top five, but not quite having the steam to win.

That situation changed at the Sebring 12-Hours where Holbert and Keyser teamed up in Holbert's RSR to claim the victory, ten of the first eleven positions being claimed by Carreras. Indeed only Gregg, now with Haywood as his co-driver, broke the Porsche chain, finishing seventh in his BMW. Despite all the politics and all the promises, Porsche's Carreras seemed to have kept the upper hand in the two long distance Camel rounds. That illusion would be shattered at Road Atlanta, where the first of the single 100-mile format race weekends took place. There the new Chevrolet Monzas dominated, Holbert beating Keyser, while Gregg's BMW took third, the only other car to complete the full 100-mile distance. Such was the dramatic change that the best-placed RSR was Bob Hagestad's, which was sixth, one lap off the pace.

Things improved little for Porsche when the series headed to Laguna Seca for the second sprint of the year, Holbert beating Gregg with Keyser third. George Dyer, a relative newcomer who was on the verge of becoming a top Camel contender, brought his RSR home fourth. Dyer would finish third the following week at Ontario, California, in the desert about 60 miles to the East of Los Angeles. However, he got little attention because of the battle up front that saw Busby defeat Gregg's abandoned Carrera.

IMSA GT 1976: Norm Ridgely

Watkins Glen 1976: John Graves, Dave Helmick, John O'Steen

Watkins Glen 1976: John Bauer, Walt Maas

Mit dem bisherigen Saisonverlauf konnte John Bishop mehr als zufrieden sein. Die Einführung des Chevrolet Monza, Peter Greggs starker BMW CSL sowie die Nichtzulassung des 934 hatte für abwechslungsreichen und spannenden Motorsport mit vielen verschiedenen Siegern gesorgt. Gleichzeitig hatte die Trans-Am wieder an Bedeutung gewonnen, nicht nur Dank dem 934 Turbo, auch viele AAGT-Teams starteten in beiden Serien.

In der Trans-Am Division II gingen mit Hurley Haywood, George Follmer, Al Holbert und Paul Miller regelmäßig vier 934 an den Start. Das Quartett kontrollierte mühelos das Geschehen, gleich beim Saisonauftakt in Pocono sorgten Haywood, Holbert und Follmer für einen Dreifachsieg. Letztgenannter siegte dann beim nächsten Rennen in Nelson Ledges. Follmer gewann schließlich auch den Meistertitel vor Haywood und Dank drei Siegen und sechs zweiten Plätzen gewann Porsche die Markenwertung.

Trotz der Erfolge waren die Piloten mit dem 934 nicht so richtig zufrieden. Holbert machte sogar kein Geheimnis daraus, dass er lieber den Monza bei der IMSA als den Porsche in der Trans-Am fahre. "Es sind weder der Motor noch die Bremsen", versuchte Holbert zu erklären. „Es ist das Handling, genauer gesagt fehlender Grip. Der Porsche hat sehr schmale Hinterräder, nur einen kleinen Heck- und keinen Frontspoiler. Und auch das Turboloch ist sehr gewöhnungsbedürftig. Eine optimale Runde ist sicherlich kein Problem, aber kontinuierliche Rundenzeiten sind mit dem Turbo nur schwer möglich."

Der Turbo-Porsche wurde dennoch schnell zum Publikumsmagneten. Und auch Bishop war nicht entgangen, dass er sich nun das Rampenlicht mit der Trans-Am teilen musste. Somit kam es im Sommer 1976 zum Umdenken in der IMSA-Chefetage und der 934 war ab sofort auch in der Camel GT willkommen. Dass dieses Fahrzeug nicht so überlegen war wie befürchtet, hatten nicht nur die Trans-Am-Rennen bewiesen, sondern es zeigte sich auch beim nächsten Camel GT-Lauf in Mid Ohio.

Follmer belegte mit dem 934 nur Rang 14, mit neun Runden Rückstand auf Busby im siegreichen RSR. Die von Holbert angesprochenen Probleme mit dem Handling und dem Turboloch sorgten dafür, dass der 934 dem RSR noch nicht das Wasser reichen konnte. Erst einige Reglementsveränderungen sollten dieses im Jahre 1977 bewirken. Für Siege war der RSR weiterhin gut, auch wenn Holbert mit dem Chevrolet beim Paul Revere 250 gewinnen konnte. In Sears Point triumphierten mit Busby und Dyer zwei RSR vor Gregg im BMW und Holberts Monza.

Eine wahre Meisterleistung vollbrachte Jim Busby bei den Sechs Stunden von Mid Ohio: Seine Alleinfahrt im RSR wurde mit dem Gesamtsieg belohnt vor Gregg und Haywood im BMW und Holbert im Chevrolet. Beim Road Atlanta 500 drehte Holbert den Spieß vor Busby um, der wiederum in Laguna Seca erneut gewann, vor BMW-Pilot Gregg und Haywood in einem weiteren RSR.

Die IMSA-Saison endete wie gewohnt in Daytona, wo Keyser im Monza knapp vor Charlie Kemp (Ford Mustang) gewann. Dritter wurde Danny Ongais mit dem Interscope-934. Peter Gregg war mit dem Saisonverlauf natürlich nicht zufrieden. Nicht nur, dass Al Holbert Camel GT-Meister wurde, sondern dass er auf Anraten von Hoppen den Carrera gegen einen BMW getauscht hatte. Für 1977 sollte dieser Fehler korrigiert werden.

Greggs Entscheidung, zu Porsche zurückzukehren, wurde maßgeblich vom BMW-Werk beeinflusst. Für die 77er-Saison gaben die Münchener dem McLaren-Team mit dem Piloten David Hobbs den Vorzug für den Einsatz des 320i Turbo, nicht zuletzt auch aufgrund der jahrelangen und guten Beziehungen zwischen Gregg und Weissach.

Im Gegensatz zur Vorsaison hatte Hoppen dieses mal Planungssicherheit, da der 934 sowohl in der IMSA Camel GT als auch in der Trans-Am startberechtigt war. Allerdings musste sich der Deutsche noch mit Bishop einigen, unter welchen Bedingungen die Teilnahme erfolgen durfte. "Dank Johns Einsatzes waren die AAGT absolut ebenbürtig und er hatte natürlich kein Interesse, dass diese gegenüber uns wieder ins Hintertreffen gerieten", sagte Hoppen.

"Auf der anderen Seite war der 934 noch unterlegen, im Gegensatz zum RSR waren wir sogar benachteiligt. Das mussten wir natürlich schnellstens ändern und ich bat Peter Gregg und Al Holbert, uns bei der Weiterentwicklung zu helfen. Beide bestanden auf breitere Räder und aerodynamische Hilfsmittel, so dass ich bei Bishop für diese Modifikationen anfragte."

Der IMSA-Chef stimmte vorläufig zu und der 934 durfte mit dem Heckflügel des 935, einer geänderten Frontspoilerstoßstange und 15 Zoll breiten Felgen an der Hinterachse antreten. Allerdings wollte Bishop noch die Testfahrten im Vor-

Watkins Glen 1976: Al Holbert, Jim Busby

Dyer finally claimed his first win at the tight Lime Rock track on Memorial Day Monday, beating Keyser and Busby after Holbert crashed his Monza into one of the earthen banks that surrounded the Connecticut track. Somehow Holbert had his badly damaged Chevrolet ready six days later for Mid Ohio where he was second to Keyser, with Busby taking third in the RSR and Gregg fourth in the CSL.

At this point John Bishop should have been smiling. The introduction of the Chevrolet Monza spaceframe cars, added to the presence of Gregg's highly competitive BMW CSL, had transformed the Camel GT from a one-marque series into a vastly entertaining and often unpredictable championship battle. However the Trans-Am series had sprung back to life, thanks in large measure to the new Porsche 934 turbos and their occasional AAGT rivals that jumped back and forth between the SCCA and IMSA tours.

There were four of Porsches which could be counted on as regulars. Vasek Polak, the southern Californian Porsche dealer, entered two for Haywood and George Follmer, Al Holbert campaigned his own 934 and the fourth belonged to New York Porsche dealer and racer Paul Miller.

Porsche drivers were easily beating their new category II opposition. Their dominance was evident from the start when Haywood, Holbert and Follmer swept the first three places with their 934s in the Pocono opener. Follmer won the next time out at Nelson Ledges in Eastern Ohio, with Haywood placed second. In all the 934s scored three victories and six seconds as Zuffenhausen won the manufacturers crown in Category II, and Follmer won the drivers honors with Haywood earning the runner up spot.

Despite the success the 934 wasn't necessarily beloved by the men who drove it. Holbert for one was clear about preferring the Monza to the Porsche. "It wasn't so much a difference in power, or even braking, even though the Monza has the edge in both," said Holbert. "Rather it's the handling. With the 12-inch (wide) rear tires and a very small spoiler, not to mention the lack of any real kind of front splitter, there's very little grip. Add in the problems of turbo lag and it's almost impossible to be consistent. I can put in one good lap, but I can't put in two in a row. It just won't happen."

People were turning out in large numbers to see the new Porsches, a fact not lost on Bishop who now found he had to share the spotlight with the Trans-Am. By midsummer Bishop threw in the towel and reversed his decision, allowing the 934s to compete in the Camel GT.

Watkins Glen 1976: George Follmer, John Morton (16), John Gunn, Carson Baird (5)

Winner 12 Hours Sebring 1976: Al Holbert, Michael Keyser

Their much anticipated debut at Mid Ohio turned out to be something of a disappointment, Follmer's Polak 934 finishing 14th, nine laps off the winning pace of Busby's Carrera RSR. Indeed, the handling and throttle lag woes described by Holbert would blunt any thoughts of the 934 displacing the RSR from its perch as a front line IMSA contender during the latter part of 1976. Only after rules concessions were made for 1977 was the 934 in a position to win.

Winning was exactly what the venerable RSR was still doing. Although Holbert's Chevrolet Monza won the Midnight Paul Revere 250 at Daytona, Busby and Dyer went out ahead at Sears Point with Gregg's BMW third and Holbert fourth. The Talladega race, on a horsepower track, was won by Gregg over his Detroit rivals without a single Porsche in the top five. Matters didn't improve much at Pocono where Busby's fourth place represented the highest finish for Porsche.

Driving solo, Busby redeemed his and Zuffenhausen's honor in a brilliant performance at the Mid Ohio Six-Hours, Gregg and Haywood finishing second in Brumos' BMW. Holbert, who had finished third, returned to the winner's circle at the Road Atlanta 500 kilometre race in his Monza. However, less than a minute behind was Busby, who returned to his winning ways at IMSA's Laguna Seca round, again beating Gregg and Haywood, the latter once again in an RSR.

That left only the November Daytona finale on the schedule, won by Keyser's Chevrolet Monza ahead of Charlie Kemp's AAGT Ford Mustang II. Third went to Danny Ongais in his Interscope 934, more than two laps behind Keyser at the end of the nearly 250-mile distance. The year was a less than happy one for Gregg as he saw Holbert claim his first Camel GT driving crown while he struggled not only to beat the Monzas, but the Carreras he had forsaken on the advice of Hoppen before the start of the year. Gregg was determined to rectify that error for the next season.

In making his choices for '77, Gregg had help from the BMW factory which announced that it would re-enter the Camel GT with a factory-backed Citicorp-sponsored 320i Turbo run by McLaren, featuring David Hobbs as its lead driver. The fact that BMW had cast Gregg aside in favor of McLaren for the program represented in some measure the manufacturer's concerns over Gregg's close ties to Porsche, bonds that the Jacksonville driver was quite ready to renew.

Hoppen was in a far better position as he prepared for the 1977 season than in '76 when he was forced to negotiate a place for the 934s to race. Even so, his plans were compli-

Dave Cowart, Charles Mendez    IMSA GT 1977: Wayne Lambert    IMSA GT 1977: Hurley Haywood

IMSA GT 1977: Jim Busby    **IMSA GT 1977: Dennis Aase**

feld der 24 Stunden von Daytona abwarten, um eine endgültige Entscheidung zu fällen. Um mögliche Differenzen bereits im Vorfeld auszuschließen, bestand Bishop außerdem darauf, dass der 934 in der Trans-Am in identischer Spezifikation startet. Zukünftige Veränderungen benötigten die Zustimmung von IMSA und SCCA.

Hoppen: „Diese Kröte mussten wir erst einmal verdauen, aber wir haben diese akzeptiert und die ersten Fahrzeuge an die Kundenteams ausgeliefert." Gregg kaufte sowohl einen 934 als auch einen 935, Jim Busby, Ludwig Heimrath sr., Ted Field, Danny Ongais und Teamchef Vasek Polak legten sich ebenfalls einen 934 zu. Bob Hagestad kaufte einen Gruppe 4-RSR.

Es sollte eigentlich eine große Porsche-Familie sein, doch Peter Gregg, oder besser gesagt sein Porsche, sorgten für Missstimmung. Immer auf der Suche nach der entscheidenden Zehntelsekunde versuchte Gregg, Bishop zu überlisten. Dem Porsche-Piloten war klar, dass ein konkurrenzfähiger 934 den baldigen Start eines 935 verhindern würde. Also brauchte er einen besonders guten 934 und verbaute etliche Teile – vor allem im Bereich der Radaufhängungen – vom Porsche 935.

Da die Absprache zwischen Bishop, Hoppen und dem SCCA erst ab Sebring zum Tragen kam und Gregg zusammen mit Busby in dessen 934 dort startete, hatte er rund drei Monate Zeit bis Road Atlanta im April für seinen außergewöhnlichen Plan. Gregg glaubte, dass er clever genug sei, die anderen an der Nase herumzuführen. Doch er lag gänzlich falsch und die Folgen dieses Vergehens hatten nicht nur Einfluss auf seinen Saisonverlauf, sondern auch auf die – bis in die Gegenwart anhaltenden – Beziehungen zwischen amerikanischen Organisationen und der FIA.

IMSA GT Daytona 1977: Johnny Rutherford, Dick Barbour

246   TURBOS EROBERN DIE NEUE WELT

cated since he continued to do battle with Bishop over the terms under which the Porsches would compete.

"John had invested a great deal in his All American GT category and was reluctant to do anything which might put his AAGT competitors behind our cars. On the other hand, it was obvious that the 934 not only did not have an edge when it came to the AAGT class, it was actually at a disadvantage. At this point, I had talked to Peter (Gregg), who was going to race our cars again, and to Al (Holbert) about what was needed. They both agreed that bigger tires at the rear and better downforce would go a long way towards improving matters, so that's what I asked for."

The agreement between Bishop and Hoppen allowed the 934s to use the 935's rear wing, 15-inch wide rear rims and a new front splitter. Even then, Bishop would not give his final approval until he had seen the revised 934 in action during a test prior to the Daytona 24-Hour round in January. To further complicate matters, Bishop insisted that not only would these be the sole modifications allowed, but that the SCCA maintain an identical policy with respect to the 934s running in the Trans-Am's Category II title chase. In short, the 934s would have to race as they came from the factory, with any future developments having to be approved on a case-by-case basis after review by IMSA and the SCCA.

"It was a bit harsh," recalled Hoppen, "but, it gave us a chance, and at that point I was willing to agree to John's stipulations if it would allow me to sell cars to our customers." And sell is what Hoppen did, Gregg purchasing both a 934 and a 935, while Busby, now back on his own, took another 934. Others acquiring 934s were Canadian Ludwig Heimrath Sr, and Ted Field's Interscope team which had Field himself and Danny Ongais as drivers. Also adding to his 934 fleet was Vasek Polak, while Bob Hagestad, for whom Haywood had been driving in 1976, likewise bought one of new Group 4 Porsches.

It should have been one big happy family, but it wasn't and Gregg's preparation was the reason why. Always looking for an edge, and knowing that while Bishop might give in when it came to improving the 934's performance, he wouldn't even think of allowing the 935 to participate in that year's Camel GT, Gregg came up with a plan to strip the 935, one of a dozen or so replicas of the 1976 factory entry made available to Porsche privateers, of its suspension and incorporate it in his new 934.

Because the agreement between Bishop, Hoppen and the SCCA didn't take effect until Sebring, and because at Sebring Gregg would run with Busby in the latter's new 934, he had three months to do the work before the April sprint race at Road Atlanta. Gregg figured if he was clever enough no one would notice he had breached the "no modifications" rule. In that he was wrong, and the resulting furore would not only affect his season, it would change the relationship between the American sanctioning organizations and the FIA forever.

If racing in general, and the IMSA Camel GT in particular were in a transition period, that fact was never more clear than at Daytona which counted for the IMSA title chase and the FIA manufacturer's series as well. Present were no fewer than three 935s running as part of the international entry, one a factory entry for Jacky Ickx and Jochen Mass which would retire with accident damage, and the other two run by privateers. Of these the ex-factory Jolly Club entry of Martino Finotto and Romeo Camathias was second, while the "homemade" Kremer entry of Albrecht Krebs, Bob Wollek and Reinhold Joest was third.

24 Hours Daytona 1977: Peter Gregg, Jim Busby

Poster

Poster

IMSA GT 1977: Gary Belcher

Trans-Am Champion 1977: Peter Gregg

Der GT-Sport war in einer Umbruchphase und dieses wurde nachhaltig bei den 24 Stunden von Daytona untermauert, die sowohl zur IMSA Camel GT als auch zur FIA-Sportwagen-WM zählten. Gleich drei 935 hatten den Weg nach Florida gefunden, einer vom Werk eingesetzt für Jacky Ickx und Jochen Mass, dessen Fahrt nach einem Unfall allerdings zu Ende war. Besser schnitten die beiden Privaten ab. Martino Finotto und Romeo Camathias wurden im Jolly Club-935 zweite und das Fahrzeug der Kremer-Brüder lenkten Albrecht Krebs, Bob Wollek, Reinhold Joest auf Rang drei.

Mit einem Ex-Gregg-RSR freuten sich Dave Helmick, John Graves, Hurley Haywood jedoch mächtig über den Gesamtsieg, denn es sollte gleichzeitig auch der letzte große internationale Triumph für dieses Modell sein. Wenige Wochen später gewann Haywood zusammen mit Ickx und Jürgen Barth am Volant eines 936 Spyder auch in Le Mans und der Amerikaner sollte somit zum ersten Piloten avancieren, der beide Rennen in einem Kalenderjahr gewann.

Die 12 Stunden von Sebring endeten erneut mit einem Triumphzug für Porsche: George Dyer und Brad Frisselle siegten vor Diego Febles, Hiram Cruz und Rio Piedras in einem weiteren ehemaligen Brumos-RSR, mit Peter Gregg und Jim Busby, Gary Belcher und John Gunn, Danny Ongais und Hurley Haywood folgten drei 934.

Für den nächsten Lauf in Road Atlanta wurden die Karten neu gemischt. George Dyer startete erstmals mit dem 934 und Al Holbert sorgte für das Debüt des 77er Monza. Ebenfalls vor Ort der McLaren-BMW 320i turbo von David Hobbs, dem nach den Kinderkrankheiten von Daytona ebenfalls gute Chancen eingeräumt wurden. Im Allgemeinen wurde ein großer Kampf vorausgesagt, doch kaum jemand ahnte, dass dieser bereits vor dem ersten Training anfangen würde. Im Mittelpunkt des Geschehens stand – wie nicht anders zu erwarten – Peter Gregg mit seinem ganz speziellen 934. Auch wenn der Amerikaner seine Unschuld beteuerte, so glaubten ihm nur wenige, unter ihnen allerdings Hoppen und Polak. Fakt war jedoch auch, dass noch vor dem Samstagtraining Gregg samt seinem Renntransporter aus dem Fahrerlager abgereist war. Das 100 Meilen-Rennen gewann Holbert vor Shafer im Camaro, Dyer wurde dritter vor Hobbs im BMW.

Gut im Rennen lag lange Zeit auch Danny Ongais, doch bei einem leichten Abflug zerstörte er sich in der Auslaufzone sowohl den Wasser- als auch den Ölkühler, die beim 934 in

24 Hours Daytona 1977: Reinhold Joest, Bob Wollek, Albrecht Krebs

24 Hours Daytona 1977: Richard Weiss, Bill Alsup, Raymond Gage

24 Hours Daytona 1977: John Higgins, Chip Mead, Dave White

Winner 24 Hours Daytona 1977: Hurley Haywood, John Graves, Dave Helmick

At the head of the finishing order, however, was an ex-Gregg RSR driven by Dave Helmick, John Graves and Hurley Haywood. That would be the last major triumph by an RSR in international competition. For Haywood the victory was the first part of a two race triumph that would see him win Le Mans in a 936 Spyder with Ickx and Juergen Barth, the Florida driver being the first ever to accomplish first-place finishes at Daytona and Le Mans in the same calendar year.

Sebring presented a different picture, for the 12-Hour race marked the debut of the 1977 934s, all of which arrived late enough that they raced in white. If anyone expected a 934 victory on the old airport course they were disappointed as George Dyer, stretching his well-worn RSR to the limit, claimed the win with Brad Frisselle, the pair followed home by Diego Febles, Hiram Cruz and Rio Piedras in another ex-Brumos RSR.

Gregg was entirely out of the picture as he and Busby finished third in Busby's new 934, with the similar 934 of Gary Belcher and John Gunn fourth. Rounding out the top five were Ongais and Haywood in Interscope's somewhat battered 934 with which Ongais had explored the real estate surrounding the track.

24 Hours Daytona 1977: Ted Field, Jon Woodner, Danny Ongais

After Sebring came the start of IMSA's "sprint season" at Road Atlanta, where the paddock looked like a new car lot as Dyer introduced his new 934 and Holbert his '77 spec Monza. Also present was yet another interesting car, the McLaren BMW 320i turbo with David Hobbs behind the wheel. Although first seen at Daytona where it retired with teething problems, the still virgin 320i looked completely ready to take on its Porsche and AAGT opposition. Everyone was anticipating a battle royal; they just didn't expect it to start before the first practice.

At the heart of the conflict was Peter Gregg's 934 with its obviously modified front spoiler and lower stance. Although Gregg maintained his innocence few accepted his position, especially Hoppen and Polak. By the end of the Saturday practice and qualifying sessions, Gregg and the Brumos transporter were gone. As for the 100-mile race, that went to Holbert, with Dyer's 934 third behind Carl Shafer's Camaro, and ahead of Hobbs' fourth placed BMW. None of the other 934s played an immediate role in the event although one, the Interscope entry of Ongais, would affect the shape of things in the long term.

The reason for that was Ongais' penchant for knocking both the front mounted oil and water coolers off his car during agricultural excursions, one of which caused his retirement at Atlanta. The fact that he could damage the car so easily was far less important to IMSA's management than the oil and water trails he left behind on his way back to the pits.

To reduce slipping and sliding, Bishop agreed that the 934s could be retrofitted with 935 rear fenders that incorporated the coolers in their leading edges. Within a short period, almost all the turbo Porsches sported the new bodywork creating what has since become to be known as the "934 and half" look. One of those taking advantage of this was Gregg. However, his car would not run again in IMSA but in Trans-Am.

Trans-Am administrator and long time SCCA technical guru John Timanus was facing a difficult year. With IMSA, no matter how reluctantly, having given in to Hoppen, the Porsche man had switched much of his attention away from the Trans-Am to the Camel GT and only Heimrath had signed on as a regular for Zuffenhausen. Monte Shelton, Hagestad, Haywood and Paul Miller would venture into the series later on in various 934s but what Timanus needed was a "name," and shortly after Road Atlanta he got Peter Gregg with his modified 934.

It was at best a pragmatic decision and it infuriated Heimrath, who saw his chances of winning the series disappearing. Although the Canadian won the opening round at Seattle and Gregg the second event in Westwood, British Columbia, Heimrath would claim just two more victories, while Gregg, who had been forced to withdraw from the opener because of crash damage, would take four more wins. That should have been enough for Gregg to secure the Category II crown, but it was not. Heimrath went home with the title, but only months after the series had ended. The problem was the Mosport Trans-Am round, which was combined with the FIA Makes Series.

From the start Heimrath had protested the legality of Gregg's car, and from the start Timanus had turned down those protests. At Mosport the Canadian had appealed to the FIA, and their officials agreed with him. Timanus accepted the ruling, making Gregg modify the rear wheel wells to conform to FIA specifications. He also ordered Gregg to add seven pounds of ballast to the front of the Porsche to compensate for the removal of the 934's front bumper brackets, this having been done so that Gregg could use a 935 nose the following weekend for a special IMSA Mid-Ohio Camel event.

Gregg beat Heimrath at Mosport and the Canadian protested again, claiming the removal of the brackets constituted an "illegal chassis modification." The FIA agreed and disqualified Gregg, the decision being upheld by the international body's appeal board in Paris later that winter. The shift in points was enough to hand Heimrath the championship.

24 Hours Daytona 1977: Carlo Facetti, Martino Finotto, Romeo Camathias

IMSA GT Road Atlanta 1977: George Dyer (30), Ted Field (00)

IMSA GT Paul Revere 250 Daytona 1977: Bob Bergstrom (01), George Dyer (30)

IMSA GT Lime Rock 1977: John Paul sr. (38), Diego Febles (58)

IMSA GT Sears Point 1977: Clif Kearns

der vorderen Stossstange montiert waren. Ongais setzte die Fahrt zu den Boxen fort und sorgte auf der Strecke natürlich für eine kilometerlange Ölspur, die einigen Wettbewerbern zum Verhängnis wurde. Um solche Probleme zukünftig zu vermeiden, erlaubte Bishop den 934-Teams ab dem nächsten Lauf, die Heckschürzen vom 935 zu verwenden. Somit wanderten beide Kühler von der Fahrzeugfront zum Heck.

Damit wurde eine der Veränderungen, die Gregg an seinem Fahrzeug vorgenommen hatte, legalisiert, doch eine Starterlaubnis für die Camel GT erhielt er noch immer nicht. SCCA Technik-Chef John Timanus buhlte um Gregg, denn außer Heimrath hatte kein anderer 934 eine komplette Trans-Am-Saison geplant. Außerdem fehlten Timanus bekannte Fahrerpersönlichkeiten und Gregg war eine solche.

Heimrath sah dieses natürlich anders und fürchtete um seine Meisterschaftschancen. Der Kanadier siegte beim Auftakt in Seattle und landete zwei weitere Siege, während Peter Gregg insgesamt fünfmal die Nase vorne hatte. Genug, um Heimrath in der Trans-Am-Jahreswertung hinter sich zu lassen. Zumindest vorläufig, denn Monate später sollte der Kanadier den Titel doch noch am grünen Tisch gewinnen.

Solange Timanus für das Regelwerk der Trans-Am alleinverantwortlich war, biss sich Heimrath die Zähne aus und protestierte vergeblich gegen Greggs 934. Doch das Rennen in Mosport zählte gleichzeitig auch zur FIA-Markenweltmeisterschaft. Bei den dort anwesenden FIA-Kommissaren fand Heimrath Zustimmung, dass Gregg sein Chassis illegal modifiziert hatte. Auch das FIA-Gericht in Paris kam zu diesem Ergebnis, Sieger Gregg wurde disqualifiziert und Heimrath somit Meister der Trans-Am Division 2.

Dieses gerichtliche Nachspiel sollte auf einem anderen Gebiet für noch erheblichere Veränderungen sorgen. Sowohl die IMSA als auch der SCCA minimierten den Einfluss der FIA bei ihren Serien und Veranstaltungen. Sie wollten in Eigenregie bestimmen, nach welchem Reglement die Fahrzeuge vorbereitet werden. Einzig bei den von der FIA ausgeschriebenen und ausgerichteten Veranstaltungen sollten auch deren Regeln in Anrechnung kommen.

Während der 934 das überlegene Fahrzeug der Trans-Am war, hingen die Trauben in der Camel GT wesentlich höher. Allerdings nicht zu hoch, denn in Laguna Seca sorgten Ongais, Busby und Follmer für einen Dreifachsieg des Turbos. In Mid America und Lime Rock war dann Holbert mit dem Chevrolet nicht zu stoppen während Hobbs für den ersten BMW-Sieg in Mid Ohio sorgte. Dyer, Haywood und Busby landeten konstant unter den ersten Fünf.

In Brainerd freute sich Ongais über seinen zweiten Saisonsieg, dieses Mal vor Haywood in Hagestads-934. Gleich einen Dreifachsieg für Porsche landeten Dyer, Haywood und Belcher beim Paul Revere 250, welches wie gewohnt erst um Mitternacht gestartet wurde. In Sears Point siegte Hobbs im BMW, Chevrolet-Pilot Holbert dann in Pocono vor Teamkollege Tom Franks und Haywood im 934.

12 Hours Sebring 1977: John Gunn, Gary Belcher

12 Hours Sebring 1977: Gary Hirsch, Fritz Hochreuter, Rainer Brezinka

12 Hours Sebring 1977: Diego Febles, Hiram Cruz

Für IMSA's Rückkehr nach Mid Ohio hatte sich Promotor Les Griebling etwas Besonderes ausgedacht. Einmalig durften die von Bishop nicht zugelassenen 935 teilnehmen. Der IMSA-Chef hatte sich bis dahin erfolgreich gegen Hoppens Wunsch gewehrt, diesen Gruppe 5-Boliden zuzulassen. Auf der anderen Seite hatte Bishop bei diesem 935-Gastspiel die Möglichkeit zu sehen, wie leistungsfähig Porsches neueste Entwicklung wirklich ist, um für 1978 eine endgültige Entscheidung zu fällen.

Ironie des Schicksals war der Sieg von Peter Gregg in seinem Eigenbau-934, der nun mit dem kompletten Aerodynamikpaket vom 935 ausgestattet war. Jacky Ickx, Skeeter McKitterick und Jim Busby, John O´Steen folgten im Original-935. Im besten 934 wurden Haywood und Hagestad Vierte. In Road Atlanta kam Haywood auf Rang drei hinter Hobbs und Holbert. BMW vor Chevrolet lautete auch in Laguna Seca die Reihenfolge, wo George Dyer als bester Porsche-Pilot nur Sechster wurde. Hurley Haywood war dann bei den Daytona 250 nicht zu bremsen und triumphierte in Hagestads 934.

Aus heutiger Sicht gibt es nicht wenige, die die 1977er Saison als "Goldenes Zeitalter" titulieren. Drei verschiedene Hersteller sorgten für spannende und abwechslungsreiche Rennen, die vielleicht besten in der Geschichte der Camel GT. Erst 1992, nach dem Ende der GT-Prototypen, sollte sich eine ähnliche Dramaturgie abspielen. Doch zuvor begann mit der Saison 1978 einmal mehr eine Dominanz der Porsche 935.

Unfortunately for Heimrath, Porsche had already printed its Trans-Am poster declaring Gregg the title holder, and the manufacturer would not remake it in the aftermath of the FIA ruling. The result of this was a move by IMSA and the SCCA, as well as other sanctioning organizations in North America with ties to the Paris-based governing body, that limited the FIA's decision-making powers with regards to their own series. From then on, the North American groups would decide for themselves who won and who didn't regardless of how the FIA saw it. The only power the international group maintained was over its own championships, a situation that has been maintained to this day.

While the 934 established itself as the car to beat in the Trans-Am, it was far less secure on the Camel GT tour. After Road Atlanta there was a moment of glory at Laguna Seca where Ongais led Busby and George Follmer, the latter in one of Polak's cars, to a one-two-three 934 sweep.

After that Holbert reeled off two in a row at Mid America and Lime Rock before Hobbs added to the Porsche camp's disappointment with his first victory of the season at Mid Ohio.

12 Hours Sebring 1977: George Dyer, Brad Frisselle

IMSA GT Mid Ohio 1977: George Drolsom

IMSA GT Road Atlanta 1977: Ted Field

Although the likes of Dyer, Haywood and Busby had been able to keep themselves in the top five, and often the top three, it was a different story in Ohio, where the BMW was followed home by a string of AAGT entries led by Holbert in second place.

Porsche's mood improved greatly at Brainerd where Ongais won for the second time with Haywood second, driving Hagestad's 934. This was followed by the midnight July Fourth Paul Revere 250, in which Dyer led Haywood and Belcher to a sweep of the top three places. Back on the West Coast at Sears Point there was yet another reversal of fortunes as the Porsches were shut out by Hobbs' BMW, ahead of Holbert. Things didn't get better at Pocono where Holbert won once more, Haywood taking third behind the Monza of Tom Franks. That brought the IMSA circus to Mid Ohio for a three-hour enduro that would feature Porsche Group 5 935s.

Mid Ohio promoter Les Griebling wanted something different for IMSA's return visit to this track, and negotiated a "one-off" event that would include the production-based silhouette prototypes. For Bishop, who had resisted Hoppen's moves to make the 935s eligible for the Camel series, and who was feeling pressure from the Camel camp to relent in his opposition to the cars, this was a chance to size up the situation before committing himself to their presence in 1978.

Ironically, the race was won by Gregg in his controversial 934, dressed in full 935 bodywork. Second were Ickx and Skeeter McKitterick in a 'real' 935, followed by Busby and John O'Steen in a similar turbo. Haywood and Hagestad brought their 934 home fourth, just a lap behind the winners. Haywood finished third in Hagestad's 934 when the series returned to Road Atlanta in September, behind Hobbs and Holbert. The top two would repeat their performances at Laguna Seca in October, where the best placed 934 was Dyer's, which finished sixth.

Haywood put in a perfect race with the Hagestad 934 in the Daytona 250-mile finale to garner the victory, and cap what had been the most diverse year in Camel GT history. Later, many would look back at 1977 as a "golden age", the likes would not come again until 1992 near the end of the GT Prototype. In between it was almost all Porsche, with Zuffenhausen's new domination starting with the official introduction of the 935 at the beginning of 1978.

IMSA GT Mid Ohio 1977: Dick Barbour

DER 935 RÄUMT ALLES AB

Was die Chancengleichheit und die Spannung betrifft, so sind selbst heute viele Menschen der Überzeugung, dass die Camel GT Saison 1977 das wahre Highlight der IMSA-Geschichte war. Es war ein klassischer Fall, in der die heimische All-America-GT-Gemeinde den Kampf gegen die herbeiströmenden Porsche und BMW aufnahm. Und die Erfolge gingen sowohl an die einen als auch an die anderen.

R.J. Reynolds Zigarettenmarke Camel war zwar bereits Hauptsponsor der IMSA, doch die Geschäftsleitung war nun der Meinung, dies sei nicht genug. Für Reynolds war es genauso wichtig, Sportwagentechnologie in höchster Vollendung zu sehen. Und ohne die Aufnahme der auf dem 911 basierenden 935er fand Reynolds, dass der Serie die Hauptzutat für langfristigen Erfolg fehle.

IMSA-Präsident John Bishop hingegen war naturgemäß ein vorsichtiger Mann, wenn es um neue, hochentwickelte Automobile ging. Sicherlich mögen Porsche-Enthusiasten anderer Meinung gewesen sein, dennoch war nicht zu leugnen, dass Bishops Furcht vor der Einführung des 935 in der Camel-Serie gute Gründe hatte.

Anfang der 70er Jahre nahm Bishop Kontakt mit Josef Hoppen auf, dem Porsche-Beauftragten in den USA, damit dieser bei der Gründung der Camel GT hilft. Wie dem auch sei, standen während der kommenden Jahre Porsche's und Hoppen's Ziel, schnell Siege herauszufahren, im Gegensatz zu Bishops Wunsch nach vielen siegfähigen Marken. Ein Interessenskonflikt, der einmal mehr zu einer Hassliebe zwischen den beiden Männern führte und an dessen Ende Hoppen sich durchsetzen konnte.

Bishop hatte die Dominanz der Porsche RSR kennen gelernt und selbst den Boden bereitet für das Nachfolgemodell 934. Im 935 sah er eine Gefahr für seine an Interesse gewinnende Serie, an deren Chancengleichheit er hart gearbeitet hatte. Sicherlich hatten die BMW 320i Turbo das nötige Potential, es fehlte ihnen jedoch an Zuverlässigkeit. Auch die Weiterentwicklungsstufen der Monzas und Corvettes aus der AAGT-Klasse waren zwar schnell, Norbert Singers neueste Entwicklung war jedoch schneller. Den 911-Privatteams stand darüber hinaus der Porsche-Service-Truck mit Rat und Tat im Fahrerlager bei allen IMSA-Rennen zur Verfügung.

Einige Privatiers hatten sich für 1978 mit 935-Jahreswagen – Haupterkennungsmerkmal nur ein Turbolader – eingedeckt. Da im Datenblatt des 934 die gleichen Eckdaten notiert waren wie bei seinem großen Bruder, rüsteten viele ihren Grup-

12 Hours Sebring 1978: Bob Hagestad, Hurley Haywood

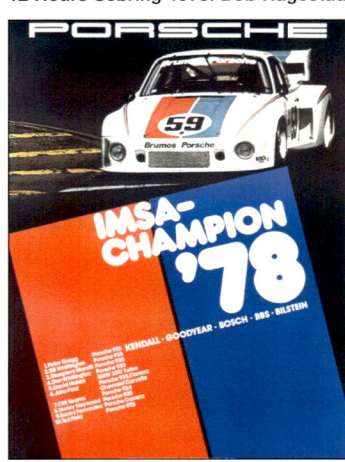

Poster

24 Hours Daytona 1978: Franz Konrad, Reinhold Joest, Volkert Merl

Winner 12 Hours Sebring 1978: Brian Redman, Charles, Mendez, Bob Garretson

935 SWEEPS THE BOARD

Even today many people believe that the Camel GT season of 1977 was one of the true highlights in the history of IMSA, in terms of the equality of competition and excitement to be found. It was a classic case of the homebred All-America GT community pitted against the invading Porsches and BMWs, with success shared between them. Yet, for the management of the R.J. Reynolds company, whose Camel cigarette brand was IMSA's primary sponsor, it was not enough.

What RJR wanted most was to be in the forefront of sports car technology, and without the inclusion of Porsche's 911-based 935 they felt the series lacked the key ingredient for long term success. By nature, though, IMSA president John Bishop was a cautious man when it came to new, high tech automobiles, especially when they bore the Porsche crest. And while Porsche enthusiasts may have had a different view, there was no denying that Bishop had good reason to fear the introduction of the 935 into the Camel series.

Initially, he had gone to Porsche through the offices of its American representative, Josef Hoppen, for help in launching what became the Camel GT Challenge. However, Hoppen's and Porsche's focus on winning soon ran counter to Bishop's need for a variety of successful nameplates, a clash of interests which led to a love-hate relationship between the two men.

Having experienced the domination of Zuffenhausen's Carrera RSR, and having negotiated the minefield that was its successor, the 934, Bishop saw in the 935's performance figures a vehicle which could destroy the on-track equality he had worked so hard to achieve, and thus endanger the growing interest popularity of his main series. The product of the inventive mind of Porsche engineer Norbert Singer, the man behind those RSRs, the 935 was more than a step ahead of its opposition in the World Championship.

Certainly the BMW 320i turbo had the potential, but it lacked the reliability to be a consistent winner. As for the AAGT Monzas, Corvettes and the other homebreds, the depth of engineering which had gone into their designs did not in any way match the engineering efforts of Porsche. Simply put, the 935 was a better car than its opposition.

Further, it was a much easier vehicle for IMSA's private teams to maintain, given the parts support and technical assistance offered by Porsche to its customers. A parts supply truck attended all the Camel weekends, and could supply anything the customers needed for the weekend.

Winner 24 Hours Daytona 1978:
Rolf Stommelen, Toine Hezemans, Peter Gregg

pe 4-934 in einen 935 um. Oder auch umgekehrt, welches zu Konfusionen bei allen Beteiligten führte. Aber die Mehrheit legte sich neue 935-Doppelturbolader zu, ein Fahrzeug, wie es sich Reynolds und die Teams gewünscht hatten.

Kaum waren die ersten echten 935 ausgeliefert, begannen die US-Teams ihre eigenen Ideen in die Weiterentwicklung einfließen zu lassen, um sich gegenüber den Markenkollegen einen Vorteil zu verschaffen. Besonders beliebt waren Karosserieteile und Antriebskomponenten des von den Kremer-Brüdern zu Beginn des Jahres 1979 entwickelten K3. Die Boliden aus dem Team von Reinhold Joest basierten auf den Fiberglas-Konstruktionen des Werks-935 aus dem Jahre 1977.

Zu den ersten Teams, die mit einer Mixtur aus Teilen vom 934 und 935 an den Start gingen, gehörte die Mannschaft rund um Peter Gregg. Seine Umbaumaßnahmen an einem 934 hatten zu Beginn der Saison 1977 dazu geführt, dass die IMSA ein Startverbot verhängte und Gregg in die Trans-Am umstieg. Bei seinem einzigen Camel GT-Start, den drei Stunden von Mid-Ohio, gab es prompt einen Gesamtsieg.

Am Ende der Saison hatte Gregg das Fahrzeug wieder zu einem echten Gruppe 4-934 zurückgerüstet und an den bis

24 Hours Daytona 1978: Dick Barbour, Manfred Schurti, Johnny Rutherford

24 Hours Daytona 1978: Rolf Stommelen, Toine Hezemans (r.)

dahin unbekannten Bruce Leven verkauft. Die 935-Komponenten wanderten wieder in einen echten zurück. Bei den 24 Stunden von Daytona lenkten Gregg, Claude Ballot-Lena und Brad Frisselle das Fahrzeug auf den neunten Gesamtrang. In Sebring endeten die 12 Stunden vorzeitig in einem Sandhaufen. Gregg und Frisselle siegten dann bei den sechs Stunden von Talladega, ehe auch der 935 an Leven verkauft wurde, den dieser in der Trans-Am einsetzte.

Zu Saisonbeginn waren die einfach turbogeladenen 935 sowohl in der Camel GT als auch in der Trans-Am konkurrenzfähig, doch schon bald sollten die Doppellader ihren Siegeszug antreten. Die 1978er Kundenversion basierte auf dem 1976er-Werksstand, allerdings mit dem Hauptunterschied, dass zur Erzielung einer besseren Aerodynamik zwischen dem vorderen und hinteren Kotflügel Seitenschweller montiert waren. Bishops Bedenken wurden jedenfalls Realität. Bis zum Erscheinen des 956/962 im Jahre 1983 sollte der 935 das Geschehen diktieren und etliche Kundenteams für viele Jahre an Porsche binden.

Die Weiterentwicklung des 935 legte das Werk in die Hände der Teams. Hierbei waren federführend die Brüder Erwin und Manfred Kremer, die Fabcar-Mannschaft von Dave Klym, Alwin Springers Andial-Truppe und der ehemalige Werksfahrer Reinhold Joest. Peter Gregg und sein Team hatten in den Jahren 1978 und 79 auch vielen Rennen den Stempel aufgedrückt, doch ihm Verlauf der Zeit geriet die Mannschaft ins Hintertreffen. Zu lange hatte man an der Verbesserung von Werksteilen festgehalten, anstatt eigene Wege zu gehen. Gregg war nicht mehr siegfähig, ein Horror für den Mann mit dem Spitznamen „Peter Perfect".

"Er überließ nichts dem Zufall, wenn ich seinen Wagen pilotierte wusste ich, dass die Vorbereitung bestmöglich war", erinnert sich sein langjähriger Weggefährte Hurley Haywood. Mit 41 Siegen liegt Gregg bis heute auf dem zweiten Platz in der ewigen IMSA-Liste. Gleichzeitig baute Peter in den 70er Jahren Brumos zu einem der größten Porsche-Händler in den USA aus. Die meisten respektierten sein Können und seine Erfolge, aber beliebt war er nicht.

"Peter wurde krank wenn er wusste, dass er nicht gewinnen kann", fügt Haywood hinzu. "Nicht vielen Menschen war bekannt, dass Peter sehr depressiv war. Seine Stimmung wechselte innerhalb von Minuten und das musste man in Kauf nehmen, wollte man sein Freund sein." In Le Mans 1980 verletzte sich Gregg am Auge und musste für einige Monate aussetzen. "Er war ein lieber Ehemann und ein toller Vater. Aber irgendwie sind ihm die Dinge über den Kopf gewachsen." Ende des Jahres nahm sich Gregg das Leben.

Für die 24 Stunden von Daytona 1978 hatten sich Brumos und Georg Loos verbündet. Rolf Stommelen, Antoine Hezemans und Peter Gregg lenkten den ausnahmsweise weiß lackierten 935 – GELOs Hausfarbe war eigentlich rot – zum Gesamtsieg vor sechs weiteren Porsche. Johnny Rutherford, Manfred Schurti und Dick Barbour wurden zweite vor dem Sieger der GTO-Klasse, Diego Febles und Alec Poole in einem Ex-Gregg-RSR.

Nach halbjähriger Verletzungspause kehrte Brian Redman ins Cockpit zurück und landete auf Anhieb zusammen mit Bob Garretson und Charlie Mendez in einem Barbour-935 den Gesamtsieg bei den 12 Stunden von Sebring. Mit ihrem zum 935er umgebauten 934 mussten sich Bob Hagestad und Hurley Haywood knapp geschlagen geben. In Talladega siegte dann Peter Gregg vor Bill und Don Whittington mit ihrem neuen BiTurbo. In den folgenden eineinhalb Jahren sollten die Brüder in den USA mit dem in Le Mans siegreichen Kremer-K3 für Furore sorgen.

256 DER 935 RÄUMT ALLES AB

Peter Gregg

Some of IMSA's Porsche customers bought the single turbo 935s built and sold by the factory in 1977 on the used market, but the majority were attracted to the better performing twin turbos Porsche had developed for sale in 1978. Bishop may not have wanted to, but between the wishes of his sponsor, RJR, and the desires of his teams, he was forced to give in and accept the 935 with the start of the '78 season. Because the 934 had the same basic engineering parameters, converting the Group 4 turbo to full Group 5 spec was not a difficult task to undertake, and many American 934 owners chose to do just that. In fact, throughout the heyday of the Porsche turbo's reign a good number of cars switched identities, both up and down, confusing the experts and those in charge of keeping track of their numbers.

Further complicating matters was that a number of the Americans built their own 935s, first from factory supplied shells, then moving into locally developed tubeframe-based designs. And, as if that weren't enough, many cars were built up using the Kremer brothers' K3 bodywork and mechanical components. Those from Reinhold Joest were based on the fiberglass pieces used to make up the factory's 1977, raised roof twin-turbo entry.

That fluidity first became apparent in 1977 when Peter Gregg not only purchased a 934, but a companion 935 as well. Even before its first race the 934 had acquired the 935's suspension, later adding its unique rear fenders before finally being fitted with the 935's nose for the special Camel Three-Hour event at Mid Ohio in late August, where the bastardised car won as a Group 5 entry. Normally used in the Trans-Am that year by Gregg, at the end of the SCCA season the car was stripped of the majority of its 935 pieces and sold to then little-known Bruce Leven.

The components were re-installed on the still virgin 935 which Gregg took to the Daytona IMSA finale, where he used it to set several speed records. Subsequently Gregg entered the car at the first three Camel GT rounds in 1978, driving it to ninth at Daytona with Claude Ballot-Lena and Brad Frisselle, before flipping it into a sand bank and recording a DNF at Sebring. In its final appearance in Gregg's hands it won the six-hour at Talladega with Frisselle as co-driver before being sold to Leven to run in the '78 Trans-Am championship.

Although single turbo 935s played a role both in IMSA and Trans-Am, the future belonged to the factory-built customer twin turbos produced for 1978. Visually similar to the 1976 factory 935s, but fitted with "running boards" between the front and rear fenders to improve aerodynamics, the new twin turbos proved the nightmare for Bishop, just as he had believed they would.

In the longer term, the 935s attracted customers who would stay with Porsche through the 956/962 decade of the 1980s. In the process they reshaped the IMSA championship, and even reshaped the sport as a whole on a worldwide basis. Peter Gregg and his Brumos team were at the top in 1978, a position they would confirm both that season and the next.

Gregg was the epitome of success in IMSA, even though he was strongly challenged, in particular by Al Holbert. Yet until his last two full seasons, those challenges had more to do with Bishop's and the SCCA's often-fluid rules structure and the cars they produced than any loss of internal focus on the part of the Brumos camp.

The continued development of the 935 switched from the Porsche factory to the teams themselves, with men like the Kremer brothers, Fabcar's Dave Klym, Alwin Springer's Andial operation and even factory stalwart Reinhold Joest going their own way. Much of this work was fueled by the ambitions of Porsche's new privateers who included New York industrialist Bob Akin, who would turn to Klym and others for homegrown 935 variants every bit as potent as those from Weissach.

Unfortunately for Gregg and Brumos, they were less attuned to the evolving 935 scene, preferring to perfect what Porsche gave them. In the end, even though they had joined the new parade with a modified 935 built at the factory loosely based on Weissach's 1977 FIA contender, they were out of their element. As a result Gregg, whose mindset was such that he couldn't live with failure, took his own life in 1980.

The 1978 season opened at Daytona where Gregg and Brumos teamed up with Georg Loos' Gelo team 935 of Rolf Stommelen and Toine Hezemans. The Gelo car, normally red, was repainted white with the blue and red trim used by Brumos for the occasion, Gregg being added to the team as a third driver. Indianapolis winner Johnny Rutherford and Manfred Schurti joined Dick Barbour in the latter's single turbo. The 935s performed well, and at the checkered flag Stommelen, Hezemans and Gregg led the Barbour entry in a Porsche sweep of the first seven places. Included in that number was the ex-Gregg RSR of Diego Febles and Alec Poole, who finished third overall and took the GTO production class honors.

24 Hours Daytona 1978: Jim Busby, Howard Meister, Hal Shaw

935 SWEEPS THE BOARD

IMSA GT Champion 1979: Peter Gregg

IMSA GT 1979: Howard Meister

IMSA GT 1978: Dave White

6 Hours Watkins Glen 1978: George Follmer, Jacky Ickx

IMSA GT 1978: Gianpiero Moretti

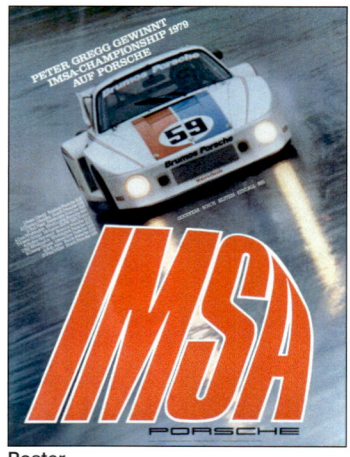

Poster

Winner 12 Hours Sebring 1979: Bob Akin, Rob McFarlin, Roy Woods

Brian Redman returned to racing at Sebring following his serious crash the previous summer at St. Jovite's Formula 5000 Can-Am car series. Joining Redman was newcomer Bob Garretson, whose west coast Porsche operation would soon become a force in its own right, and Floridian Charlie Mendez, then the promoter of Sebring, in a Barbour 935.

The trio came home ahead of Bob Hagestad and Hurley Haywood in Hagestad's 934, now fully converted to 935 single turbo spec. Following Gregg home at Talladega were Bill and Don Whittington in their new twin turbo 935. Within a year and a half the two brothers would begin the revamping of IMSA when they brought their ex-Kremer K3 Le Mans winning 935 to America, making themselves a powerhouse on the Camel tour in the process.

After that it was on to Road Atlanta to begin the traditional IMSA sprint race season, where Gregg introduced his new twin turbo 935 along with the similar, but black-painted Interscope entry for Danny Ongais. Gregg beat Ongais across the line in a one-two sweep for the new cars. Such was the advantage of the 935 that at Laguna the best David Hobbs could in his factory McLaren BMW 320i turbo was fourth, a lap behind George Follmer's Vasek Polak Porsche, Haywood in the Hagestad machine and Gregg.

Even though Hobbs enjoyed an unusual victory at Hallett, the Porsche juggernaut was back in charge at Lime Rock with Gregg winning. He swept to victory at Brainerd, the Paul Revere 250 and Portland before Bill Whittington and Jim Busby claimed the 350 miler at Mid Ohio. Gregg then swept the final rounds of the series at Road Atlanta and Daytona to regain the Camel driver's title.

Only the BMW turbos had an outside chance of standing up to the Porsche 935s, and by the end of the season the All American GT category just about disappeared, despite Bishop's decision to allow the AAGT competitors to run rear-mounted transaxles to cure their chronic drive train woes.

IMSA GT 1979: Chales Mendez

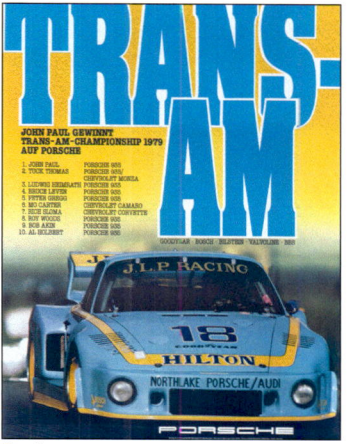

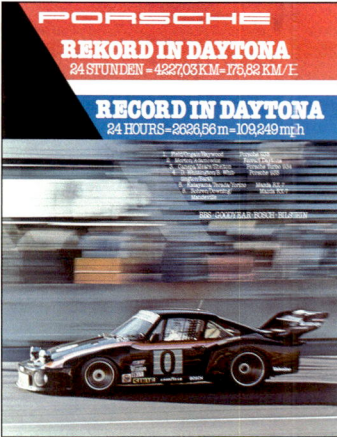

Poster

Poster

Although the 935s were holding sway in IMSA they were having trouble in the Trans-Am, where many of the AAGT set had chosen to race. Of the top ten Category II cars at season's end just four were 935s. The highest placed of these was Ludwig Heimrath who finished third in the points with two victories, just ahead of Hal Shaw's similar turbo with one win to its credit. Monte Shelton's 935, with two first place finishes, was fifth in the standings.

Things would improve for Porsche in 1979 as John Paul, Sr claimed the Category II crown in his '77 single turbo 935 with no fewer than seven wins. Gregg went moonlighting at Road America to score a one-off victory, while Roy Woods and Akin joined forces in Akin's 935 to win at Watkins Glen.

It was an impressive season, but it was the last for the Category II division and the 935 as the SCCA revamped its regulations to have a single class format in 1980. That decision might have eliminated the Porsche 935s, but it did little to change the overall picture as John Bauer piloted his 911 SC to that year's Trans-Am crown on the strength of four winning performances. In subsequent years various 911s and 934s would appear in the Trans-Am, none making any great impression on the results.

In IMSA, meanwhile, Bishop was reviewing his options, trying to find a way to break the 935's stranglehold on Camel GT. In the short term, the only solution he could find was to add a weight penalty to the twin turbo variants, thereby encouraging the teams to switch back to single turbo engines. This was supposed to degrade throttle response and slow the cars down a bit, but in reality it had little effect other than to raise costs as most teams now had both single and twin turbo engines, using whichever one was most appropriate for the track being raced on.

Don (l.) and Bill Whittington

Dick Barbour

24 Hours Daytona 1979: Rusty Bond, Ren Tilton

Für Road Atlanta brachten Gregg und Danny Ongais neue BiTurbo-935 mit und feierten prompt einen ungefährdeten Doppelsieg. Auch in Laguna Seca wurde die Porsche-Überlegenheit einmal mehr deutlich: George Follmer siegte in Vasek Polaks Fahrzeug vor Hagestad-Pilot Haywood und Gregg. David Hobbs sah im Werks-BMW 320i Turbo mit Rundenrückstand die Zielflagge als vierter. In Lime Rock und Brainerd siegte dann Gregg, ehe Bill Whittington und Jim Busby in Mid-Ohio die Nase vorn hatten. Mit zwei weiteren Erfolgen in Road Atlanta und Daytona zementierte Gregg dann den erneuten Camel GT-Titelgewinn. Während die BMWs wenigstens Außenseiterchancen aufwiesen, hatten noch vor Saisonende die letzten AAGT-Teilnehmer das Handtuch geworfen. Und das, obwohl Bishop erlaubt hatte, zur besseren Gewichtsverteilung der kopflastigen Fahrzeuge Antriebsteile im hinteren Bereich zu platzieren.

Die AAGT-Teams waren überwiegend in die Trans-Am Division zwei abgewandert und waren harte Wettbewerber für die dort startenden Porsche-Teams. Ludwig Heimrath und Monte Shelton erzielten jeweils zwei Laufsiege, Hal Shaw einen. In der Jahreswertung rangierten Heimrath, Shaw und Shelton auf den Rängen drei bis fünf. 1979 war John Paul senior mit sieben Siegen der überlegene Fahrer in der Trans-Am und wurde Meister. Gregg war nur in Road America mit von der Partie, siegte aber. Und Roy Woods und Bob Akin standen ganz oben auf dem Podium in Watkins Glen. Es sollte die letzte Saison der Division zwei im Rahmen der Trans-Am sein, ehe der SCCA 1980 eine Einheitsklasse einführte. Diese Entscheidung tangierte zwar den 935, aber John Bauer sicherte sich am Volant seines 911 SC Dank vier Siegen den Titel.

Die Überlegenheit des 935 veranlasste John Bishop einmal mehr zu Gedankenspielen zur Wiederherstellung der Erfolgsmöglichkeiten anderer Hersteller. Doch außer einem Zusatzgewicht für die Doppelturbo-Variante kam er zu keiner Lösung. Sicherlich wurden diese Boliden hierdurch etwas eingebremst. Auf der anderen Seite erhöhten sich aber auch die Kosten für die Teams, die nun je nach Streckencharakteristik und Erfolgsaussichten entweder einen schweren BiTurbo oder einen leichten Einfach-Turbo aus dem Transporter schoben.

Das IMSA-Jahr 1979 begann für Porsche, wie das alte aufgehört hatte. Danny Ongais, Ted Field und Hurley Haywood hatten bei den 24 Stunden von Daytona mit dem Interscope-935 elf Runden Vorsprung, und das, obwohl sie bereits 20 Minuten vor Schluss in Sichtweite der Ziellinie geparkt hatten. In Sebring war dann das Garretson-Trio mit Rob Mc Farlin, Bob Akin und Roy Woods erfolgreich, gefolgt von elf weiteren Porsche-Teams.

Mit Ausnahme von Hallet und Road America, wo David Hobbs im BMW siegte, dominierten die 935 auch den Rest der Camel GT-Saison. Allen voran Peter Gregg, der nicht weniger als achtmal triumphierte und erneut Titelträger wurde. Für weitere Siege sorgten Charlie Mendez und Hurley Haywood beim Paul Revere 250 sowie Bill und Don Whittington bei den sechs Stunden von Riverside. Die Brüder gehörten bald zu den Stars der IMSA, auch wenn die US-Behörden ihnen unterstellten, den Motorsport aus Drogengeldern zu finanzieren.

Dass sie aber auch mit jeder Menge Talent ausgestattet waren, bewiesen die 24 Stunden von Le Mans, wo die beiden zusammen mit Klaus Ludwig im Kremer-K3 vor Rolf Stommelen, Dick Barbour und Paul Newman mit einem Garretson-935 gewannen. Beide Boliden sollten in der Folgezeit noch einige IMSA-Sträuße ausfechten.

Watkins Glen 1979: Rolf Stommelen, Dick Barbour, Paul Newman

260 DER 935 RÄUMT ALLES AB

No matter what IMSA did, the 1979 Camel GT season promised to be 'more of the same', a conclusion in no way diminished by the 11-lap triumph at Daytona by the Interscope 935 twin turbo of Ongais, team owner Ted Field and Haywood. This overwhelming victory came after the Interscope Porsche had sat motionless for the last 20 minutes in front of the finishing line before moving forward the last few feet to take the checkered flag.

Tony Adamowicz and John Morton scrambled to second place at Daytona with their ancient Ferrari Daytona 365 GTB coupe, but Sebring was an all Porsche show. Rob McFarlin, Bob Akin and Roy Woods won in their Garretson Team 935, and such was Zuffenhausen's domination that the first 12 finishing positions were filled by Porsches, including the Carrera RSR of Bonky Fernandez and Tato Ferrer which garnered the GTO class honors.

Other than David Hobbs' two victories, at Hallett in the spring and Road America in late summer, the rest of the season belonged to the 935 teams with Gregg leading the way on most occasions in his 1978 spec 935. He easily won what would be his final Camel drivers championship, winning twice at Road Atlanta, at the Laguna Seca spring stopover, Lime Rock, Brainerd, the July Mid Ohio round, Sears Point, and Portland. In between, Charlie Mendez and Haywood came away with a rare first place at the Daytona Paul Revere 250, Bill and Don Whittington having done the same in the spring Riverside Six-Hour.

The South Florida-based brothers were quickly turning into new stars on the IMSA circuit, fuelled by their talents, and by money the US government would claim was earned in the drug trade. No matter how they got there, it was clear that the Whittingtons were every bit as good as Gregg, both in terms of their abilities, as well as in the team's standard of preparation.

Brian Redman **Paul Newman**

IMSA GT 1979: Bill Whittington

Winner 24 Daytona 1980: Ted Field, Danny Ongais, Hurley Haywood

Just how good the Whittington brothers were was seen in June at Le Mans where, driving with Klaus Ludwig in a Kremer K3, they won the 24-Hours beating Rolf Stommelen, Dick Barbour and actor Paul Newman. The second-place car was a standard body 935 twin turbo built in California from a shell by Bob Garretson's organization. Both cars would go on to have a tremendous impact on IMSA.

The short-term effect came when the Whittingtons purchased the Le Mans winner and brought it to America for the Camel GT. Until the arrival of their Kremer-built and designed K3 at Sears Point in July, the American Porsche teams had largely raced with cars that Porsche had supplied. Even the cars built by the teams from shells used largely standard factory components in their construction.

The K3 was different. Although its aerodynamic package with its raised rear roof was clearly attributable to Singer's work, its execution with its unique wing fences was something done by the brothers outside of the factory's influence. Perhaps even more important, the Kremers had figured a way to re-install an air-to-air intercooler for the turbo system, this having the advantage over its water cooled counterpart in that it allowed the engine to maintain its boost longer, because it was better able to keep the air temperatures lower for greater periods of time.

What with better aerodynamics and an engine able to produce better horsepower figures over the long haul, the K3 had a distinct advantage over its 935 rivals, though not until September when the Camel GT returned to Road Atlanta did this become truly apparent. Until the final lap, when he ran out of gas, Don Whittington led Gregg in a manner that made it clear that in the future those who wanted to win had better have a K3 or else be out to lunch.

The Le Mans winner would race just once more, in the Daytona finale where Bill Whittington used it to claim victory. However, it was a triumph which saw the car destroyed in the process. Whittington, in the lead at the time, was caught up in a late stage backstretch mess that left several vehicles, including his and John Paul Sr's single turbo Trans-Am champion, total wrecks. IMSA officials red flagged the race and did not restart it, so the results were based on the last complete lap, the one on which Whittington was ahead.

Even though the K3 was gone, it encouraged the purchase of many new Kremer 935s, and the conversion of many existing Porsche turbos to K3 standards. One of these conversions was the Garretson second-place finisher at Le Mans, perhaps the most successful and certainly well-travelled 935s to race.

935 SWEEPS THE BOARD 261

Der von den Brüdern Manfred und Erwin Kremer entwickelte K3 war das Maß der Dinge und den anderen 935 überlegen. Viele kleine, sowohl optische als auch mechanische Veränderungen sorgten für die entscheidenden Vorteile. Im Bereich der verlängerten hinteren Dachpartie hatten sich die Kölner noch an Norbert Singers Werks-Version anno 1977 orientiert, doch die seitlich hochgezogenen Kotflügel mit integrierten Luftleitlippen entstammten ihrer Idee.

Für höhere Motorleistung und mehr Langlebigkeit sorgte die Abkehr von der Wasserkühlung des Ladeluftkühlsystems. Durch die Karosserieveränderung im Bereich des Heckfensters gewannen die Kremers dort soviel Raum, dass sie eine sehr effektive Luftzuführung erreichten. Der Vorteil: Während sich das Kühlwasser bis zu 40 Grad erhitzt, bleibt die Luft in ihrer Temperatur immer konstant, was sich natürlich positiv auf die Leistungsausbeute auswirkt. Weitere Vorteile sind das für das Kühlwasser eingesparte Gewicht und eine Handvoll PS, die übrig bleiben, wenn keine Wasserpumpe angetrieben werden muss.

Trotz der weltweiten Erfolge des K3 sollte es bis zum September 1979 dauern, ehe das Fahrzeug auch dem US-Sport den Stempel aufdrückte. Don Whittington führte in Road Atlanta bis in die letzte Runde hinein vor Peter Gregg, ehe ihm der Kraftstoff ausging. Doch die bis zum Ausfall gezeigte Überlegenheit hatte verdeutlicht, dass in Zukunft der K3 der 911 war, den es zu schlagen galt.

Wie dicht Glück und Pech beieinander liegen können, mußte Bill Whittington beim Daytona-Saisonfinale erleben. Er führte das Rennen überlegen an, geriet dann aber in eine Massenkarambolage gemeinsam mit zu überrundenden Teilnehmern. Sowohl Whittingtons K3 als auch der 935 von Trans-Am-Champion John Paul sr. hatten nur noch Schrottwert. Es war der erste US-Sieg für den K3, gleichzeitig aber auch das letzte Rennen der siegreichen Le Mans-Karosse.

IMSA GT 1980: John Fitzpatrick

Poster

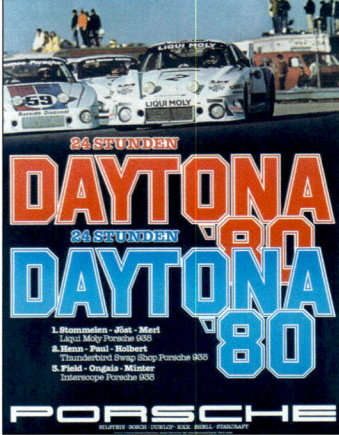

Poster

24 Daytona 1980: J. Paul, A. Holbert, P. Henn

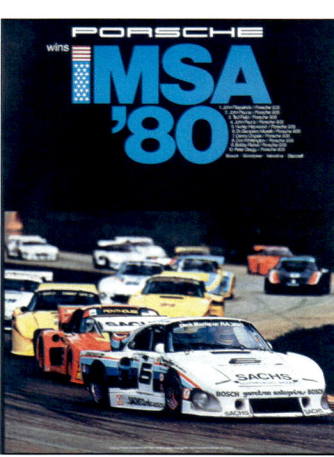

Poster

Winner 24 Hours Daytona 1980: Reinhold Joest, Rolf Stommelen, Volkert Merl (2), Peter Gregg, Hurley Haywood, Bruce Leven (59)

Für 1980 kauften einige Teams neue K3 in Köln oder rüsteten ihre vorhandenen 935 mit entsprechenden Teilen um. Zu den letztgenannten gehörte Bob Garretsons in Le Mans 1979 zweitplazierter BiTurbo, der mit Jim Trueman, Brian Redman, Bobby Rahal und dem Teamchef die 24 Stunden von Daytona 1981 gewinnen sollte. Ende 1982 übernahm Wayne Baker dieses Fahrzeug und rüstete es auf den Stand eines 934 GTO zurück. Baker wurde hiermit nicht nur Divisionssieger, sondern sorgte auch zusammen mit Jim Mullen und Kees Nierop in Sebring für den ersten IMSA-Gesamtsieg eines GTOs.

Während sich das Werk auf die Einführung des 956 konzentrierte, war für die US-Teams die Entwicklung des 935 noch nicht am Ende. Natürlich waren keine Quantensprünge – und erst recht nicht ohne Weissach – mehr möglich. Die Kremer-Brüder hatten aber gezeigt, zu welchen Leistungen auch ein Privatteam im Stande sein kann. Für viele hatte der 935/78, auch bekannt unter dem Kosenamen „Moby Dick", eine Vorbildfunktion. Wenn überhaupt, hatte der 935 nur einen Schwachpunkt: den nichtwassergekühlten Zylinderkopf, der die Ursache für einige Kolbenschäden war.

Die Teams erwarben im Werk lediglich einige Bauteile wie die Rohkarosse, Dach, Türholme, Innenverkleidungen, Motorabdeckungen oder Scheiben. Alle anderen Karosserieteile wurden nach eigenen Vorstellungen aus Carbon oder Kevlar gegossen. Nebenbei präsentierten die Kremers den K4, ein 911, dessen Gene eindeutig beim „Baby" getauften 935 mit dem 1,4 Liter-Turbomotor lagen. Der Wettbewerb unter den Teams führte dazu, dass der 935 noch besser und noch schneller wurde. Und zum Überflieger der frühen 80er Jahre. Nur zwei K4 verließen die Hallen in Köln-Longerich. Mit dem ersten fuhr Bob Wollek im Rahmen der Deutschen Renn-

In 1981 it won the Daytona 24 Hours with Jim Trueman, Brian Redman, Bobby Rahal and Bob Garretson, remaining as a K3 until it was sold in late 1982 to Californian Wayne Baker who transformed it into a single turbo GTO class 934. In that configuration it not only earned Baker the division title, but also a stunning upset victory at Sebring with Jim Mullen and Kees Nierop, the first time a GTO car had won that prestigious classic outright. Baker later converted the car back to a 935 K3, racing it the following season at the Daytona opener before selling it to Chester Vincentz, who changed it back to a 934, racing in that configuration for a number of years thereafter.

From now on the Americans would take matters into their own hands, building a number of unique versions of Porsche's now venerable turbo without any significant influence from the factory. If it wasn't exactly a new day for the 935, it was clearly a new afternoon with plenty of sunshine.

The 935 takes a new direction. Until the appearance of the Kremer brothers' K3, most 935 customer teams had run cars developed and produced by the factory, even though in America, several teams, namely Bob Garretson's central California-based organization and the JLP Racing team in Georgia were constructing standard single and twin-turbo factory customer versions from basic 930 shells on their own. However, with the K3 that changed. Now, teams began to think about building their own cars, a number of which were based on the factory's spectacular 935/78 tubeframe entry, better known to the world as 'Moby Dick'.

About the only production 935 pieces used for the 935/78 were the roof, cowl, door jambs, engine compartment opening, and part of the rear quarter sections containing the windows. Everything else was custom-built from carbon composites, Kevlar and other lightweight materials.

Regardless of its limited factory career, the 935/78 was the inspiration for the fleet of 935 'Specials' which would come to dominate the Camel GT scene during the early 1980s. In fact, there are many who believe that if the K3 grew in the minds of the Kremer brothers from the 935/77 and its 1.4-liter sibling, better remembered as the 'Baby,' then its successor, the K4 clearly owed its origins to the Moby Dick.

Like its factory progenitor, the K4 was a tubeframe vehicle with fully enclosed, or covered doors and a raised rear fiberglass roof built over the steel original. Unlike Moby Dick, the K4 retained the wing fences around the fenders, as well as much of the rest of the K3's nose profile. Only two K4s were built, the first used by the Kremers themselves with Bob Wollek, who had considerable success in the German National Championship before being sold in 1981 to John Fitzpatrick to campaign in IMSA, again with success. The second was constructed for Ted Fields' Interscope, and although tested by Danny Ongais at Road Atlanta, was never raced before the team disbanded. If the K4 was based on the 935/78, the two Reinhold Joest 'super' turbos were exact replicas, constructed in his shops by ex-factory mechanics from Porsche's own plans. The first of the two, with completely uncovered doors, was run by Joest in the German series with Klaus Ludwig before being sold in '81 to Dr. Gianpiero Moretti, who raced it extensively on the Camel tour through 1984. The second of the Joest replicas, which did use Singer's bodywork that had been rejected by the FIA, went to Fitzpatrick.

Debuting at Le Mans in 1982 Fitzpatrick and David Hobbs claimed fourth overall, and first among the production car set in the 24-Hour classic. Unfortunately, the car's career was short, being destroyed the following April at the Riverside Camel GT round in an accident that tragically took the life of Rolf Stommelen. The two Moby Dick replicas were but a small part of a parade of Joest homebuilt 935s that would make their mark during the 1980s in IMSA. The others, collectively described by insiders as '935Js', were based on the factory 935/77 but incorporated the front and rear space frame sections found on the 1.4-liter version of that car.

The potential of the 935J became immediately apparent when it won the 1980 Daytona 24-Hour Camel GT opener in Joest colors with Volkert Merl, Stommelen and Joest himself aboard. Immediately after the race it was sold to Moretti, who ran it alongside his own 935 throughout the rest of that year and into 1981 before moving on to his 935/78 replica.

Two other 935Js eventually appeared, each featuring slightly modified bodywork with elongated noses. One of these was

IMSA GT 1980: Howard Meister

Watkins Glen 1980: John Paul Jr. and Sr.

Watkins Glen 1980: Don and Dale Whittington

Watkins Glen 1980: Harald Grohs, Randolph Townsend

IMSA GT 1981: John Fitzpatrick

Winner 24 Hours Daytona 1981: B. Garretson, B. Rahal, B. Redman

Daytona 1981 (l.-r.): Bob Garretson, Bobby Rahal, Brian Redman

24 Hours Daytona 1981: William Koll, Jeff Kline

sportmeisterschaft (DRM) allen um die Ohren, ehe das Fahrzeug mit John Fitzpatrick in der Camel GT erfolgreich an den Start ging. Das Interscope-Team von Ted Fields hatte den zweiten bekommen, doch noch vor dem ersten Rennen hatte sich die Truppe aufgelöst.

Für exakte Kopien des 935/78 sorgten Reinhold Joest und seine – teilweise – aus ehemaligen Werksmechanikern bestehende Mannschaft. Klaus Ludwig griff für Joest in der DRM 1980 ins Lenkrad, ehe Gianpiero Moretti dieses Fahrzeug bis Ende 1984 in der IMSA pilotierte. Den zweiten Joest-935 kaufte John Fitzpatrick, der zusammen mit David Hobbs bei den 24 Stunden von Le Mans 1982 Gesamtvierter und Klassensieger wurde. Wenige Wochen später wurde der Bolide bei Rolf Stommelens tödlichem Unfall in Riverside irreparabel zerstört.

Neben den beiden Moby Dick-Replicas entstanden bei Joest in Absteinach auch zahlreiche andere Gruppe 5-Varianten, die 935J genannt wurden. Gleich zu Beginn der 80er Saison sorgten Volkert Merl, Rolf Stommelen und Reinhold Joest für einen Gesamtsieg bei den 24 Stunden von Daytona, dem Auftakt der IMSA Camel GT. Gianpiero Moretti übernahm das Chassis, startete hiermit bis Ende 1981 und baute es dann zu einem 935/78 um.

Bruce Levens Bayside Disposal Team erwarb bei Joest einen 935J mit verlängerter Fronthaube, mit welchem der rennfahrende Teamchef, Al Holbert und Hurley Haywood Sebrings 12 Stunden 1981 gewannen. Nur einige Läufe später brannte das Fahrzeug nach einem Unfall von Haywood in Sears Point aus.

Mit der Einführung der IMSA GT-Prototypen zu Beginn des Jahres 1981 erhielten die Porsche-Teams ernsthafte Konkurrenten. Doch beim Saisonauftakt gab es das gewohnte Bild, als Brian Redman, Bob Garretson und Bobby Rahal bei der Jagd zweimal rund um die Uhr mit Garretsons 935 in K3-Optik siegten. In Sebring zeigten dann Holbert, Haywood und Leven dem Rest des Feldes den Auspuff. John Fitzpatrick war in Road Atlanta und Riverside erfolgreich, ehe Redman mit dem Lola in Laguna Seca die Oberhand behielt. Es dauerte bis zum Paul Revere 250, ehe Mauricio DeNarvaez für den nächsten Porsche-Sieg sorgte. Beim Saisonfinale knöpfte John Paul jr. im JPL-935 Redman noch in der letzten Runde den Sieg ab.

Während die Kremer-Brüder ihren K3 auf einer Rohkarosse aufbauten, diente dem JLP-Team und dessen Konstrukteur Chuck Gaa ein Gitterrohrrahmen für den äußerlich sehr ähnlichen 911. Das Vater und Sohn-Team John Paul sr. und jr. triumphierte mit dem JLP-935 im Jahre 1982 sowohl bei Daytonas 24 Stunden als auch bei den 12 Stunden von Sebring. In Road Atlanta und Laguna Seca gewann der Sohn, ehe beim Sieg in Charlotte der Vater wieder mit von der Partie war. Am Jahresende durfte sich der Sohn IMSA-Gesamtsieger nennen und sein Vater hatte in der Camel GT-Langstrecken-Sonderwertung die Nase vorn. Für drei weitere Laufsiege sorgten Fitzpatrick und Hobbs in einem 935 K4.

JLPs Chuck Gaa baute 1982 den 935L1 genannten Nachfolger des JLP-935. Die Piloten Bob Akin und Derek Bell beklagten allerdings ein miserables Fahrverhalten. Nach einem Bell-Unfall in Daytona beim Saisonfinale war das L1-Projekt beendet und Akin aktivierte seinen 935 K3.

Dave Klym übernahm die Reste des L1 und baute hieraus einen komplett neuen Gitterrohrrahmen-911 mit der Bezeichnung 935-84. Im Herbst 1983 debütierte der vermutlich letzte komplett neu aufgebaute 935 für den professionellen Motorsport. Bob Akin und John O´Steen wurden beim Daytona-Saisonfinale zweite hinter dem March-Porsche von Al Holbert und Jim Trueman. Optimistisch ging Akin in die 84er

sold by Joest to Bruce Leven's Bayside Disposal team, in whose employ it won the 1981 12 Hours of Sebring driven by Al Holbert, Hurley Haywood and Leven himself. As with the Fitzpatrick Moby Dick replica, this car had a short life, burning to the ground at Sears Point later that summer after Haywood went off course with it and spun it in the grass.

The one thing the 935s did not have, of course, was the engine with water cooled cylinder heads, which was not released by the factory despite its efficiency in solving an increasingly alarming number of heat-related piston failures. John Bishop, in any case, wanted no part of giving the Porsche an even stronger advantage over its immediate opposition. It was Bishop's staunch anti-Porsche position, in fact, which actually drove the creation of the American-built 935 'specials' that would join their European counterparts in IMSA over the coming three-year period before the emergence of the 962.

Regardless of labels, the homegrown brand of Porsche 'specials' was coming. While they might be enough to stem the opposition through 1980 and into 1982 it was an ever increasingly difficult task. One of the first to recognize this was California's Andial company, a group of three ex-Vasek Polak employees engaged in helping Porsche street racing customers get the most from their cars.

In 1981, Andial converted a standard twin turbo 935 into a modified version of the K3, using slightly different aerodynamics and suspension pieces, as well as the air-to-air intercooled 3.2-liter engine which was the heart and soul of the K3's success. Driven by Stommelen and Harald Grohs, the Andial 935 won three straight events, Mosport, Road America and Mid Ohio in the late summer of 1981, beating not only rival Porsches but also Brian Redman's new Chevrolet-powered Lola T600. The Lola, the first of the successful IMSA GT Prototypes, was the car which would help carry Redman to the Camel driving championship at the end of the season. Building on the success of the converted 935, Meister commissioned Andial to build an entirely new car based on the Moby Dick's sweeping tubeframe design, but drafted entirely in Andial's Costa Mesa shops. Under the direction of Glen Blakely, the basic dimensions of the car were laid out on the floor using string and what Blakely had determined to be the pick up points as references as a guide, the construction of its space frame proceeding from there without the use of any blueprints. Although Meister withdrew from the deal, Andial finished the car in time for Holbert and Grohs to race it at Riverside, where they finished second behind the Lola T600 of Ted Field and Bill Whittington. Later, it was sold to South Florida's Preston Henn, who dressed it up in the colors of his highly profitable T-Bird Swap Shop operation and entered it for the 1983 Daytona 24 Hours, where in the hands of Claude Ballot-Lena, Bob Wollek and A.J. Foyt, it won the rain swept event. In July Foyt and Wollek repeated their winning performance at the Paul Revere 250, and the pair then returned to Daytona the following February to finish second in the 24 Hour behind the Kreepy Krauly ex-Holbert '83 championship March 83G Porsche. Indeed, what made the performance of the Andial 935 so impressive was that its success came against the ever more potent GT Prototypes, cars supposedly far superior to the agricultural 935. Also impressive during this same period were the American built JLP team 935s of the Pauls, John, Sr. and John, Jr. The most significant of these were the tubeframe K3 built by Chuck Gaa, and its successor, built by Dave Klym's Fabcar organization,

Winner 12 Hours Sebring 1981: Hurley Haywood, Al Holbert, Bruce Leven

24 Hours Daytona 1982: Mauricio de Narvaez, Bob Garretson, Jeff Wood

Daytona 1982: Hurley Haywood, Al Holbert, Bruce Leven

IMSA GT 1982: John Paul Jr.

IMSA GT 1982: Bob Akin, Craig Siebert

IMSA GT 1981: John Fitzpatrick

Poster

12 Hours Sebring 1982: Ray Ratcliff, Grady Clay, Skeeter McKitterick

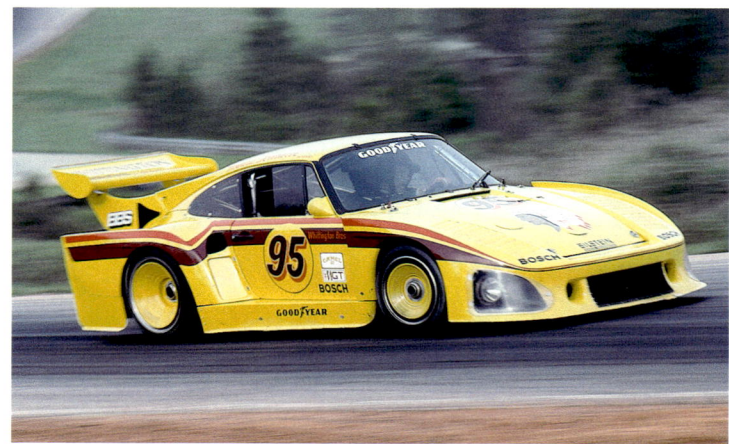

Poster

Poster

IMSA GT 1981: Dale Whittington

12 Hours Sebring 1982: Marty Hinze, Bill and Don Whittington

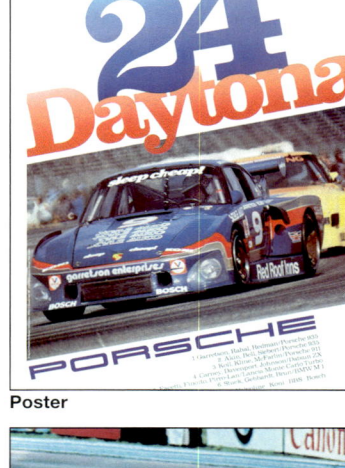

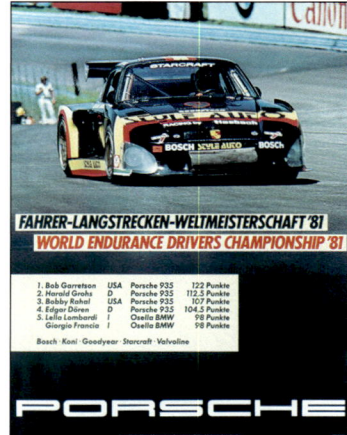

IMSA GT 1981: Gianpiero Moretti (30), Hurley Haywood (86)

266 DER 935 RÄUMT ALLES AB

both in 1981-82. It was with these two Porsches that John Sr won the Camel GT endurance title, and his son the Camel driving honors, the pair claiming both the Daytona 24 and Sebring 12-Hour events along the way.

During this same period, Gaa constructed the monocoque 935L1 for Akin's Coca Cola-backed team as a replacement for Akin's now venerable K3. Appearing in 1982, the L1 was a fast, but miserable handling machine that Akin hated. When Derek Bell crashed the car at the Daytona season finale, the remains were parked, Akin returning the K3. However by late spring he realized he needed something better if he were to have any chance against the new GT Prototypes. He then sent the L1's remains to Klym, who used some the undamaged bits and pieces to create yet another Moby Dick-K4 style tubeframe car, this one labeled as a 935-84. Finished in the fall of 1983, Akin and John O'Steen debuted what was to be the last serious 935 ever built at the Daytona finale with a strong second-place performance, nearly beating the March Porsche of Holbert and Jim Trueman. Akin began the 1984 season with his new 935 but much of its promise remained unfulfilled because of mechanical failures, the car posting a rather dismal record before being replaced by Akin's new 962 at Charlotte in the spring. O'Steen continued to race it for a while, but eventually the car faded from the scene as the era of the 962s took hold. At the 1980 Daytona season opener, the American 'specials' and their GTP opposition were still largely a part of the future. Most expected that Peter Gregg would continue to enhance his glittering IMSA record, this in spite of the 24-Hour victory by the Joest 935J. John Fitzpatrick was setting himself up as the challenger, though, joining forces with Dick Barbour's San Diego-based team to run an

IMSA GT Daytona 1981: Bobby Rahal, Bob Garretson

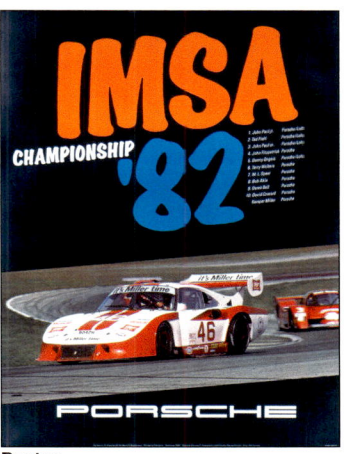

Poster   Poster

extremely fast 935 K3 with backing from Europe's Sachs Corporation. Fitzpatrick and Barbour brought their Porsche home ahead of the field at Sebring. They won again at Riverside, the Englishman going on to claim victories at Laguna Seca, the Paul Revere 250, Sears Point, Portland, Mosport (where he shared the car with Redman) and the Road Atlanta September event to garner the year-end driving honors. Other winners included Bill Whittington, who won at Atlanta in the spring, the Pauls, who took Lime Rock and Road America, and Moretti, who drove his 935J to victory at the Daytona finale in November. Unhappily, the latter affair saw Peter Gregg's last competive appearance. While the Jacksonville resident had found himself in the top three on several occasions in the spring, he was forced to sit out much of the season because of a road mishap at Le Mans, which left him with double vision until late in the fall. He withdrew from the November Daytona event after disappointing practice results with his brand new 935J. Said to blame himself for the car's problems, Gregg then took his own life at gunpoint the following month, bringing to a close one of the fabled careers in American motorsport. It was a time of change for IMSA in 1981 as the first of the IMSA prototypes, the Lola T600 was introduced to the Camel GT for Redman by Cook-Woods racing, along with the first of the March GTPs, a BMW version for veteran David Hobbs. Redman, who would go on to secure the Camel crown, began the year by winning Daytona with Garretson and Bobby Rahal in Garretson's long-lived 1979 935, then bodied as a K3. Holbert, Haywood and Leven then added to Porsche's record with their Sebring triumph, Fitzpatrick joining in the Zuffenhausen party by winning Road Atlanta in the second of his K3s, also garnering first place at Riverside, before

935 SWEEPS THE BOARD 267

IMSA GT Riverside 1982: Harald Grohs, Al Holbert

IMSA GT 1982: John Fitzpatrick (2), John Paul Jr. (18)

Harald Grohs

Saison, doch zahlreiche technische Defekte verhinderten gute Ergebnisse und er war froh, im Frühsommer auf den 956 umsteigen zu dürfen.

Zu denen, die sich ebenfalls die konsequente Weiterentwicklung des 935 auf die Fahnen geschrieben hatten, gehörte der kalifornische Porsche-Spezialist Andial. Deren Kerngeschäft war eigentlich die Veredelung und Betreuung von Straßenfahrzeugen. Im Jahre 1981 nahm Howard Meister mit Andial Kontakt auf, mit der Bitte, aus seinem BiTurbo-935 eine K3-Replica zu bauen, inklusive einem luftgekühlten 3,2 Liter-Motor.

Im Sommer 1981 debütierte der Andial-935 und Rolf Stommelen und Harald Grohs hatten keine Probleme, die IMSA-Rennen in Mosport, Road America und Mid Ohio zu gewinnen. Auch Brian Redman im Lola T600 mit Chevrolet-Motor hatte keine Chance. Der Lola war einer der ersten Vertreter der IMSA-Prototypen-Generation und Redman sollte sich hiermit auch 1981 den Fahrertitel sichern.

Meister war klar, dass normale 935 zukünftig gegen die Prototypen keine Chancen mehr hätten. Er beauftragte Andial, auf Basis des Moby Dick-Rohrrahmens ein völlig neues Fahrzeug zu kreieren. Obwohl Meister noch vor Vollendung des Projektes ausstieg, wurde das Fahrzeug rechtzeitig fertig gestellt und das Duo Holbert/Grohs belegte in Riverside auf Anhieb Rang zwei hinter dem Lola von Ted Field und Bill Whittington. Preston Henn kaufte ein Jahr später den Boliden, den seine Piloten Claude Ballot-Lena, Bob Wollek und A.J. Foyt zum Gesamtsieg bei den verregneten 24 Stunden von Daytona 1983 lenkten.

Im Juli 1983 standen Foyt und Wollek beim Paul Revere 250 erneut auf der obersten Stufe des Podiums. In Daytona 1984 verpassten die beiden nur knapp die Titelverteidigung und mussten sich dem March 83G-Porsche von Kreeply Krauly geschlagen geben. Der Andial-935 war so etwas wie die letzte Entwicklungsstufe des 935, der mit seinen Urahnen, die den GT-Prototypen mittlerweile unterlegen waren, nur noch wenige Gemeinsamkeiten hatte.

Im Rahmen der 24 Stunden von Daytona 1983 hatten sich der neue Porsche-Chef Peter Schutz und Josef Hoppen zusammen mit den Kundenteams an einen Tisch gesetzt. Die Prototypen aus der GTP-Klasse hatten die 935 nicht nur eingesondern auch überholt. Schutz versprach, dass Porsche alle Hebel in Bewegung setzen würde, damit der Gruppe C-956 auch in der IMSA startberechtigt wäre. Außerdem würden Al Holbert und Jim Trueman einige Läufe in einem March 83G mit 935-Motor bestreiten.

Den letzten Camel GT-Sieg durfte der 935 im März 1984 in Sebring feiern. Mauricio DeNarvaez, Stefan Johansson und Hans Heyer hatten am Volant des 935J Platz genommen und mit zwei Runden Vorsprung auf einen March-Chevrolet die Oberhand behalten. Ein stolzer Moment für Reinhold Joest, aber gleichzeitig auch ein trauriger. Auch wenn der 935 noch etliche Jahre aktiv am Renngeschehen partizipierte, war seine Zeit abgelaufen. Die Zeit war reif für den 956 und andere GTP-Boliden. Es sollte rund ein Jahrzehnt dauern, ehe Porsche-Fahrzeuge auf Basis des 911 wieder Aufsehen erregten.

Redman's onslaught on the title with his Lola began at Laguna Seca. Not until the Paul Revere 250 did a 935 again emerge with a victory, this time through the good efforts of Mauricio DeNarvaez. After that came the three-race run of Stommelen and Grohs, with JPL Racing ending the season on a twin set of high notes, the father and son duo winning at Pocono, followed by John Jr's first place performance at the Daytona season finale over Redman in a thrilling last second, last lap sprint to the finish.

The Pauls started the 1982 season as they had finished in 1981, winning at both Daytona and Sebring, the younger Paul going on to claim Road Atlanta and Laguna solo before rejoining his father at Charlotte for yet another victory. Fitzpatrick would further the 935 cause with back-to-back triumphs at Lime Rock and Mid Ohio in his Kremer K4, later returning to Mid-Ohio with David Hobbs for another big success. In between, Paul the younger improved his record, winning three times, the last occasion with his father at Brainerd, Portland and Mosport. The two concluded the championship season with a win at Road Atlanta before giving way to Ted Field and Danny Ongais' Lola in the last two Camel rounds of the year. It was becoming increasingly obvious that the GTPs were taking over, a fact recognized by new Porsche president Peter Schutz at a meeting with Hoppen and Porsche's racing customers in Daytona for the 1983 24-Hour event. Schutz promised that Porsche would work to make its Group C 956 legal in whatever form it might take for IMSA, while also putting together an interim program with Holbert that would see him and Jim Trueman team together in a new 935-powered March 83G starting at the spring Charlotte race. Holbert meanwhile helped his cause by winning the rain-shortened Miami street race with a March-Chevy, the Porsche marque regaining the top after the performance of Wollek, Foyt and Ballot-Lena at Daytona. Wayne Baker pulled off a coup as he won the Sebring 12-

Winner 24 Hours Daytona 1982: Rolf Stommelen, John Paul Jr. and Sr.

Hours in his ex-Garretson 935, temporarily converted to a 934. He would race the car through the remainder of the year in Group 4 spec, eventually winning the GTO crown before converting it back to a 935 K3 for the Daytona season closer.

Fitzpatrick and Hobbs, in the wake of Stommelen's death, took their K4 to a sorrowful win at Riverside, this and the return Paul Revere triumph by Foyt and Haywood in Henn's Porsche being the swan song victories for the 935 in 1983. Those triumphs were among the last for a 935 in Camel competition. The final victory came at Sebring the following March when Joest brought his veteran 935J out of retirement at short notice and shipped it to Sebring for DeNarvaez, Stefan Johansson and Hans Heyer to drive. They rewarded him with a two-lap triumph over the March-Chevrolet of Randy Lanier, Bill Whittington and Marty Hinze.

It was a proud moment for Joest, but, ultimately a sad one. Even though the 935 would remain active for a while longer, its day as an outright contender was over. It was time for the 962s and their GTP opposition to take center stage. Not for a decade would a 911-based Porsche make a serious impression on the North American racing scene.

Winner 24 Hours Daytona 1983: Bob Wollek, Preston Henn, Claude Ballot-Lena, A. J. Foyt

DER 911 BEGINNT VON VORN

Von dem weltweiten Ende der Gruppen eins bis acht und der Einführung der Gruppen A, C oder N zu Beginn der 80er Jahre blieben natürlich auch die Camel GT-Teams nicht unberührt. Der langjährige Wunsch von IMSA-Präsident John Bishop nach Beendigung der Porsche-Dominanz schien – aus seiner Sicht – zum Greifen nah. Seit mehr als zehn Jahren hatten die 911 der Serie ihren Stempel aufgedrückt, doch selbst die GT-Prototypen konnten nur aufschließen, aber nicht vorbeiziehen. Die nächste GTP-Generation und die ähnlich konzipierten Gruppe C-Boliden, wie der 956, sollten die Gruppe 5-Porsche an der Spitze der Ergebnislisten ablösen.

Im März 1984 sorgten Mauricio DeNarvaez, Stefan Johansson und Hans Heyer am Volant eines 935J für den letzten Sieg. Nahezu gleichzeitig wurden die ersten 956 an die Kunden ausgeliefert. Ein Fahrzeug, welches die nächsten Jahre die IMSA ähnlich beherrschen sollte wie der 935.

Zwar standen die GTP und Gruppe C-Boliden im Focus des Interesses, aber auch auf Serienproduktion basierende Fahrzeuge sorgten immer wieder für Farbtupfer in der Camel GT. Einer von diesen war der 961, ein allradgetriebener 911, der eine Weiterentwicklung des bei der Rallye Paris-Dakar 1986 siegreichen 959 war. Der 961 debütierte 1986 bei den 24 Stunden in Le Mans und stand beim IMSA-Saisonfinale des gleichen Jahres erstmals in den USA am Start.

Die Achillesferse des 961 waren unbestritten die viel zu schmalen Dunlop-Reifen, die vor allem auf der Vorderachse den starken Belastungen, speziell in der Steilkurve, nicht gewachsen waren. Nach zahlreichen Reifenplatzern endete dann nicht nur dieses Rennen vorzeitig, sondern auch die Karriere dieses Fahrzeuges. Und niemand würde sich heute noch an den 961 erinnern, hätte nicht Audi 1988 und 1989 mit allradgetriebenen Tourenwagen den US-Sport dominiert, denn die Ingolstädter hatten aus Porsches Problemen die richtigen Rückschlüsse gezogen.

Weil der 961 weder schnell noch standfest war, gab es in der Trans-Am vor dem Saisonbeginn 1988 keine Bedenken gegen den Start des Audi 200 Quattro. Kaum einer glaubte an einen Vorteil des Allradantriebs. Falsch gedacht, denn 1988 fuhren die Audis in der Trans-Am alles in Grund und Boden. Die logische Konsequenz dieser Überlegenheit war das Allradverbot für beide Serien ab 1990.

Poster

24 Hours Daytona 1989: Terry Wolters, Peter Kraft, Rusty Bond

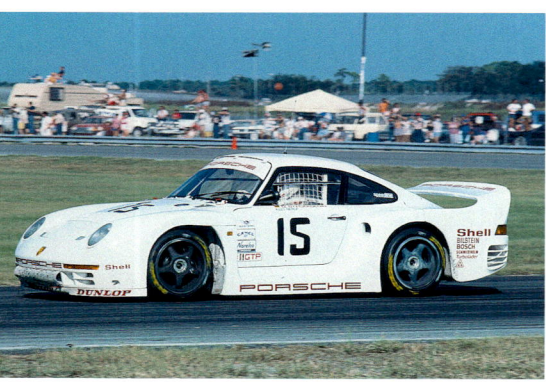

IMSA GT Daytona 1986: Günther Steckkönig, Kees Nierop

IMSA Supercar Champion 1991: Hurley Haywood

FRESH START FOR 911

For IMSA and its Camel GT competitors, the first part of the 1980s was a period of change. As IMSA president John Bishop had intended, the previously dominant Porsche 935 Turbos were now being supplanted by the recently introduced power-to-weight based GT Prototypes. Like their similar Group C counterparts, these were enclosed, traditional sports racing vehicles, the origins of which could be found in the Porsche 917s and Ferrari 512s of a decade earlier. Starting in 1981, the GTP contenders, led by the Chevrolet-powered Lola T600s from the Cooke-Woods Racing and Interscope teams, pushed their way to the front, although their 935 opposition continued to find success as well. Not until the spring of 1984, when the first of the customer Porsche 962s arrived, was the age of the Zuffenhausen silhouette Group 5 car brought to a close, the remaining 935s being put under dust covers in favor of their newly-minted successors. With the bulk of the 1980s reserved for prototypes the 911 sometimes which crept into the spotlight at, or at least near the top. One such production Porsche, in fact, possibly the most visible, was the all-wheel-drive 961. Developed from the 959 Paris-Dakar rally car program, the 961 made its first appearance at Le Mans in 1986 and came to America later that fall for the IMSA Daytona finale.

It was unimpressive, its narrow Dunlops tires being unequal to the task of dealing with Daytona's high-banked speedway section. The poor performance of that lone 961 at Daytona might have been forgotten were it not for Audi, then in the preliminary stages of planning their own assault on the American production car scene. Audi attacked first in the 1988 Trans-Am with the Audi 200 Turbo Quattro, then later with the all-wheel-drive Audi 80/90 sedans in the IMSA Exxon GTO category.

Because the 961 seemed unable to keep up with, much less out perform, its IMSA GTO production car rivals, few gave any real thought to the implicit advantages all-wheel-drive would give the Audis. This was a mistake only rectified after the Quattros had dominated the SCCA series, then done nearly the same thing in the IMSA championship. Ultimately, the solution was to ban the Audis and all-wheel-drive completely from both title chases. But that two year grace period in '88 and again in '89 might not have been given Audi had the 961 been able to explore its full potential at Daytona with better developed tires. Non-turbo 911s could still be found in some of IMSA's lower classes, where Larry Schumacher ru-

24 Hours Daytona 1990: Alex Job, Peter Kraft, Tommy Johnson

24 Hours Daytona 1992: Joe Pezza, Alex Padilla, John Sheldon

12 Hours Sebring 1993: Walter Röhrl, Hans-Joachim Stuck, Hurley Haywood

Mitte der 1980er Jahre waren einige Saugmotor-911 in diversen regionalen IMSA-Klassen unterwegs. Zu den erfolgreichsten Piloten dort zählte Larry Schumacher mit seinem Carrera RSR 3,8. Von 1991 bis 1993 schrieb die IMSA den Bridgestone Super Cup aus, den Hurley Haywood und Hans Joachim Stuck mit ihrem Brumos-911 S dominierten.

Ebenfalls Anfang der 90er Jahre spielte Porsche Cars North America mit dem Gedanken, den in Europa überaus erfolgreichen Carrera-Cup auch in den USA auszutragen. Nachdem die Fahrzeuge beim kalifornischen Kooperationspartner Andial angekommen waren, zwangen rechtliche Bedenken zur Absage des Markenpokals. Die 911 wurden von Andial auf Serienstandard zurückgerüstet und veräußert, wobei einige Käufer wieder die Rennsportspezifikationen verbauten und erfolgreich Motorsport betrieben.

Europäische Veranstaltungen sowie der gleichzeitige Untergang der FIA-Sportwagen-Weltmeisterschaft, die mit ihren 3,5 Liter-Saugmotoren in eine Sackgasse geraten war, sorgten für die Rückkehr des 911 ins internationale Rampenlicht. Norbert Singer und seine Mannschaft entwickelten den 911 Turbo S LM-GT, der im Frühjahr 1993 sein Roll-out erlebte. Vorhandene Fahrzeugkonzepte und Reglements legt der Ingenieur bis heute ebenso genial und unkonventionell wie erfolgsorientiert aus. Und der LM-GT gehörte zweifelsfrei zu den besten Konzepten Singers.

Um für die 24 Stunden von Le Mans 1993 gut gerüstet zu sein, wurden Sebrings 12 Stunden als Test unter Rennbedingungen ausgesucht. Brumos setzte den Turbo ein und Hans-Joachim Stuck, Walter Röhrl und Hurley Haywood teilten sich das Cockpit. Startberechtigt war das Trio in einer Sonderklasse, dessen Reglement mit dem des ACO identisch war. Nach zwölf zumeist verregneten Stunden sah der Brumos-911 als Gesamtfünfter und Klassensieger das Ziel. Obwohl der LM-GT den Grossteil seines Lebenszyklus auf europäischen Strecken verbrachte, entstanden bei Champion Racing und bei Brumos Schwesterfahrzeuge.

IMSA Supercar Championship 1992: Hurley Haywood (59), Hans-Joachim Stuck (58)

272 DER 911 BEGINNT VON VORN

led the GTU category during the mid 1980s with his 3.8-liter Carrera RSR. Later, IMSA created the Bridgestone Super Car Cup, which for three straight years from 1991 through 1993 was ruled by the Brumos 911S Turbos through the efforts and talents of Hurley Haywood and Hans Stuck.

During this time Porsche Cars North America decided it would try to emulate the successful Carrera Cup in Europe. However, after the cars were delivered and converted by southern California's Andial corporation, legal issues forced the abandonment of the idea and the cars were converted back to full road-going specifications before being sold off (many then being converted back to racing trim by their new owners.)

Events in Europe were influential in the return of the 911 to American circuits. When it was clear that the 3.5 liter sports car formula was doomed, Porsche signalled its renewed interest by handing Ing. Singer the task of creating a new 911 production contender. What he produced by the late winter of 1993 was the 911 Turbo S LM-GT, a 3.2-liter twin turbo version of Porsche's street coupe.

Perhaps one of the cleverest of Singer's long list of competition 911 creations, the LM-GT was more of a "proof of concept" prototype, intended to run in the new GT category established by the organisers of Le Mans for their 24-Hour event that June. As a test, the 911 Turbo was brought to Sebring, where it was officially entered by Brumos for Hans Stuck, Walter Rohrl and Hurley Haywood. Running in the specially designed Invitational GT division, whose rules mirrored those of the ACO, the 911 survived the rainy 12-Hour to finish seventh overall and first in class, the third production car across the line behind a Nissan 300ZX turbo and a Ford Mustang. Although the 911 S Turbo LM-GT would spend the bulk of its career in Europe and in the Far East, it did spawn two 'look alike' siblings, one from south Florida-based Champion Racing and the other from Brumos. The latter was built up from the second 1993 Brumos Bridge-

IMSA Supercar 1992: Hurley Haywood

12 Hours Sebring 1993: Justin Bell, Mike Peters, Oliver Kuttner

24 Hours Daytona 1994: G. Döbler, K.-H. Wlazik, D.-R. Ebeling, U. Richter

12 Hours Sebring 1993 (l.-r.): Hurley Haywood, Hans-Joachim Stuck, Walter Röhrl

24 Hours Daytona 1994: H. Haywood, H.-J. Stuck, W. Röhrl, D. Sullivan

FRESH START FOR 911 273

12 Hours Sebring 1994: Hurley Haywood, Hans-Joachim Stuck, Walter Röhrl

Poster

Poster

12 Hours Sebring 1994: Charles Slater, Peter Uria, Joe Cogbill

World Challenge Cup 1994: Price Cobb

24 Hours Daytona 1995: Enzo Calderari, Lilian Bryner, Renato Mastroprieto, Ulrich Richter

Poster

24 Hours Daytona 1995: Joe Cogbill, Jack Lewis, Monte Shelton, Charles Slater

Winner IMSA Supercar Championship 1993: Hans-Joachim Stuck

24 Hours Daytona 1994: B. Adam, J. M. Fangio II, B. Redman, M. Peters

World Challenge Cup 1995: David Murry

FRESH START FOR 911 **275**

Letztgenannter basierte auf einer der beiden Karossen aus dem Brigdestone Super Cup 1993 und beide LM-GT debütierten in Daytona im Februar 1994. Während optisch keine Unterschiede zum europäischen Stammvater zu erkennen waren, vertrauten beide US-Teams nicht auf den ursprünglichen 3,2 Liter-BiTurbo-Motor. Brumos implantierte ein 3,6 Liter-Triebwerk, Champion einen 3,3 Liter-Motor jeweils mit einem Turbolader.

Während der Champion-911 früh nach einem Motorbrand ausfiel, konnten Stuck, Röhrl und Haywood, verstärkt durch Danny Sullivan, sogar zeitweise die Gesamtführung übernehmen. Ein defekter Keilriemen sorgte dann aber für den Ausfall. Für Porsche war aber das Labre-Team erfolgreich, denn mit einem Original 911 S Turbo LM-GT wurden Bob Wollek, Dominique Dupuy, Jürgen Barth und Jesus Pareja-Mayo als Gesamtzweite abgewunken.

Seitdem John und Peggy Bishop sich 1989 aus der IMSA zurückgezogen hatten, war die von Bill France sr. gegründete Serie ins Trudeln geraten. Den diversen Nachfolgern gelang es nicht, die IMSA in ruhigen Fahrwassern zu halten. Sie hatten viele Ideen und bemühten sich auch, dass möglichst Beste für die IMSA und die Teams zu erreichen. Aber die meisten dieser Ideen standen in engem Zusammenhang mit der Fernsehberichterstattung. Niemandem der neuen Besitzer war die vorteilhafte Umsetzung gelungen. Die IMSA Serie, als Camel GT groß geworden und später in Exxon GT umbenannt, erlebte in den 90er Jahren ihren Abgesang.

1995 kaufte Andy Evans, ein früherer Bill Gates-Berater und selbst Hobby-Rennfahrer, die IMSA-Organisation und gab der Rennserie den neuen Namen: Professional Sports Car Racing (PSCR). Evans war nicht unumstritten, einmal änderte er sogar während den 12 Stunden von Sebring das Reglement zu Gunsten seines eigenen Teams. Er haderte mit den

24 Hours Daytona 1995: H.-J. Stuck, B. Adam, H. Grohs, D. Schroeder

World Challenge Cup 1995 (l.-r.): Jochen Rohr, David Murry

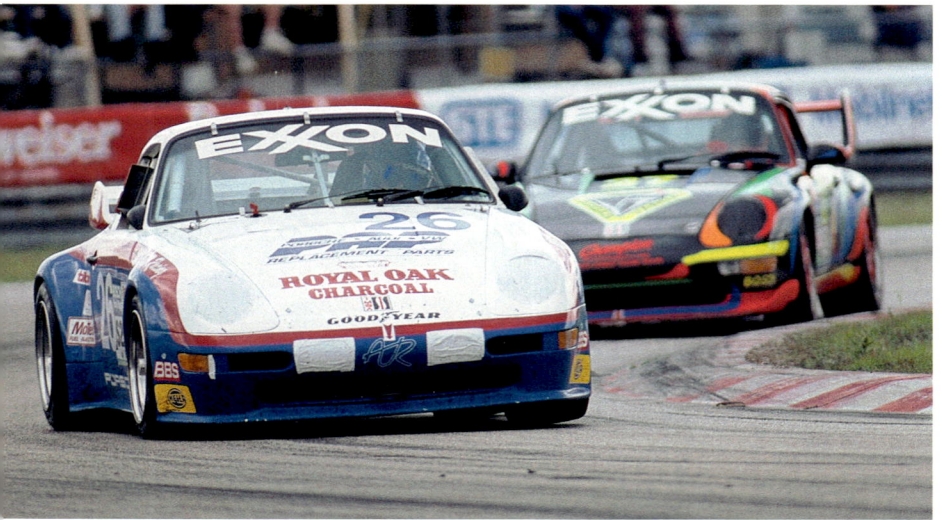

12 Hours Sebring 1995: Bill Auberlen, Charles Slater, Joe Cogbill

gleichen Problemen wie seine Vorgänger und geriet Ende 1997 in finanzielle Schwierigkeiten, als er Sebrings PSCR-Rechnung nicht bezahlen konnte. 1998 übernahmen Mike Gue, Doug Robinson und Tim Milner die Geschicke der PSCR. Gleichzeitig reaktivierte der Sports Car Club of America (SCCA) die United States Road Racing Championship (USRRC), die zuletzt in den 60er Jahren ausgetragen worden war.

Ein neuer Name tauchte im Motorsport auf: Don Panoz, Chef der Pharmazeutika produzierenden Elan Corporation. Adrian Reynard hatte für Panoz die häufig als skurril bezeichneten Frontmotor-Prototypen entworfen und gebaut, die sowohl in der PSCR als auch in der USRRC an den Start gingen. Panoz gelang es, sehr zur Freude der US-Motorsportszene, mit dem ACO, dem Veranstalter der 24 Stunden von Le Mans, ein Abkommen zu erzielen. Die American Le Mans Serie (ALMS) war für 1999 geboren, eine Meisterschaft mit einem berühmten Namen und dem identischen Reglement wie der Klassiker an der Sarthe.

Mit Gründung der ALMS gehörte die USRRC nach drei Rennen im Jahre 1999 wieder der Geschichte an. Doch die von der France-Familie geführte International Speedway Corporation, eine Schwester der NASCAR, wollte die USRRC nicht so sang- und klanglos untergehen lassen, übernahm die Reste und gründete die Grand-American Racing Association im Jahr 2000. Bis 2002 waren die Regularien identisch mit der ALMS, ehe 2003 eigenständige eingeführt wurden. Diese beinhalteten unter anderem die Daytona Prototypen-Kategorie sowie die verschiedenen Produktionswagenklassen.

Einen solchen Verlauf der Entwicklung konnte 1994 noch niemand erahnen, als die IMSA versuchte, die Porsche-

World Challenge Cup 1995: Jochen Rohr

24 Hours Daytona 1996: Joe Cogbill, Ron Finger, John Rutherford

stone Super Car Cup entry, making its debut at Daytona along with its Champion rival at Daytona in February, 1994. While both American 'home-builts' featured the same smoothly-flowing body style of their factory progenitor, complete with the 'batmobile' rear wing, they eschewed the 3.2-liter twin turbo flat six, the Brumos coupe running a single turbo 3.6-liter powerplant, the Champion 911 being fitted with a similar 3.3-liter engine Champion's 911 was never a factor, dropping out early after an engine fire, but the Brumos example, with Stuck, Rohrl, Haywood and former Indy 500 winner Danny Sullivan, led before it retired on account of a fan belt problem. The original 911 S Turbo LM-GT, now in the hands of the Larbre team, crossed the line second overall with Bob Wollek, Dominique Dupuy, Jurgen Barth and Jesus Pareja-Mayo behind the wheel.

By this time, politics were again becoming a headline feature of the racing. IMSA had been sold several times since John Bishop and his wife Peggy bowed out of the organisation in 1989, and each succeeding owner had taken over the reins of the now-venerable sanctioning body with good intentions and many inventive ideas on how to improve both IMSA and its championships. Unfortunately, most of those ideas revolved around television coverage, which IMSA bought from the networks and which none of the new owners could really afford.

In 1995 Andy Evans, an IMSA competitor and former financial advisor to Microsoft's Bill Gates, bought the sanctioning group, renaming it Professional Sports Car Racing, Inc. The controversial Evans, who once changed the rules during the Sebring 12-Hour to the benefit of his team, eventually found himself facing the same problems as his predecessors. Ultimately he found the financial burden too much, selling out his interest in PSCR at the end of 1997 after refusing to pay the purse for PSCR's Sebring event that fall. PSCR struggled on in 1998 with Mike Gue, Doug Robinson and Tom Milner as interim owners, while the Sports Car Club of America revived its United States Road Racing Championship title, last used in the late 1960s, for a rival version of PSCR's title chase. It was during this period that a new name appeared on the scene, that of Don Panoz, a major player in the pharmaceutical business through his Elan corporation. He soon found himself hip deep in racing, running front engined cars designed by Adrian Reynard both in PSCR and in the USSRC. Courted by just about everyone, Panoz eventually put together an agreement with the organisers of Le Mans to use their rules and their name to start what became the American Le Mans Series in 1999, after staging the first Petit Le Mans event at Road Atlanta the previous October.

12 Hours Sebring 1995: John Fergus, Neto Jochamowitz, Mike Peters

24 Hours Daytona 1996: Derek Bell, John Fergus, Dorsey Schroeder

E. Calderari, F. de Lesseps, L. Bryner

C. Slater, R. Spenard, T. Hessert

24 Hours Daytona 1996 (l.-r.): Hans-Joachim Stuck, Thierry Boutsen

24 Hours Daytona 1997:
Jack Lewis, Edison Lluch, Kevin Buckler, Vic Rice (73), Rick Bye, Doug Trott, John Ruther, Phillip Kubik, Grady Willingham (45)

12 Hours Sebring 1997: Hans-Joachim Stuck, Bill Adam

Teams von der Ferrari- und Oldsmobile-Konkurrenz fernzuhalten. Die Turbo-911 mussten in der internationalen GT-Klasse antreten und trafen dort auf die starken GTS-Nissan 300 ZX. Dennoch konnte das Brumos-Team die IMSA-Langstreckenmeisterschaft Dank Stuck, Haywood und Röhrl und deren Siegen in Sebring und Watkins Glen gewinnen. Der Champion-911 fing in Sebring erneut Feuer und wurde danach nicht mehr eingesetzt.

Mit Einführung des 911 GT2 schickte auch Brumos seinen LM-GT in Rente. Aber es war vor allem das Champion-Team, welches von Januar 1995 bis 1997 mit dem vom 993 abgeleiteten Boliden große Erfolge feierte. Kaum hatte die Mannschaft ihren GT2 in Empfang genommen, wurde der Heckspoiler wesentlich höher montiert. Auch an der Fahrzeugfront wurde Dank größeren Spoilern mehr Abtrieb erzielt.

Porsche hatte dieses Fahrzeug nicht für die höchstmögliche Klasse angedacht, sondern wie der Name schon sagt, für die GT2. Aber wie schon beim 911 S LM-GT, befürchteten die IMSA-Verantwortlichen, daß Porsches neuestes Coupé zu dominant wäre. Die GT2-Teams wurden eine Klasse höher eingestuft und trafen dort auf die hubraumgewaltigen amerikanischen Boliden. Beim Saisonauftakt 1995, wie immer die 24 Stunden von Daytona, gab es dennoch zufriedene Gesichter, denn Hurley Haywood, Jochen Rohr, Bernd Mayländer und David Murry fuhren auf den zweiten Gesamtrang.

Das gleiche Ergebnis gelang Hans-Joachim Stuck und Bill Adam dann auch in Sebring und in Watkins Glen. Für das einzige weitere Podiumsergebnis in dieser Saison sorgte Stuck bei seiner Alleinfahrt zu Rang drei in Sears Point. Erst im folgenden Jahr gelang Stuck und Adam mit einem Champion-GT2 in Evo-Spezifikation ein GTS-Klassensieg und sechster Gesamtrang bei den 12 Stunden von Sebring. Es sollte allerdings auch der einzige Saisonsieg bleiben. 1997 begann dann mit einem Doppelsieg in Daytona: Ralf Kelleners, Patrice Goueslard, Claudia Hürtgen und André Ahrle siegten vor Axel Rohr, Andy Pilgrim, Harald Grohs und Arnd Meier. Im Folgemonat wurde das Rohr-Team ebenfalls zweiter in Sebring.

With the ALMS coming on line the USSRC faded to just three events, the Daytona 24 Hours, Lime Rock and Mid Ohio, before folding its tent and again becoming a part of history. In its place the France family-led International Speedway Corporation - the sister group to NASCAR – formed the Grand-American Racing Association in 2000, at first using similar regulations to those of the ALMS, but later in 2003 adopting its own rules. These created the unique Daytona Prototype category and the different single production car division which was inaugurated at the beginning of 2005. Even though much of this was in the future during 1994, IMSA's management was busy making sure that Porsche didn't offend its opposition, particularly Ferrari and Oldsmobile. While the Porsche turbos were given their own separate International GT class, they were actually forced to run with the GTS Cutlasses and the potent Nissan 300ZX turbos when it came to their official positions on IMSA's results sheets.

Ultimately, the Brumos 911 managed to claim the IMSA Endurance crown through the efforts of Stuck, Haywood and Rohrl at Sebring and Watkins Glen, although that success was so low key that few outside of Porsche knew anything about it. As for Champion's 911, it found a home in the back of the team's racing shops after again catching fire at Sebring, never to be seen again. The two 911 LM-GTs departed the scene when Porsche introduced its new production car challenger, the 911 GT2 Turbo. Champion Racing soon became the leading GT2 team, developing the first of the two such cars they would run through 1997 almost from the moment it left the Miami customs shed in January 1995. One of the first changes made by Champion was to raise the rear wing on a pair of extended struts. This moved the wing higher into the air stream, increasing the downforce, counterbalanced at the front by a revised, slightly enlarged splitter. Over the next several years, during the GT2's heyday, the wing itself would be modified, becoming forward curved in plan form, while the front air dam and splitter would also undergo modifications. Porsche had developed the 993-based GT2 to run in not the top production category, but as the name suggested, in the next class down. However, as

Winner SportsCar GT 1997: Andy Pilgrim, Allan McNish

(l.-r.): Claudia Hürtgen, Ralf Kelleners, Patrice Goueslard, Andre Ahrle

24 Hours Daytona 1997: J. Rohr, A. Pilgrim, H. Grohs, A. Meier

24 Hours Daytona 1997: D. Kitch, C. Bingham, C. Hanauer, C. Lyford (24), J. Purner, T. Lingner, R. Groff, C. Slater (25), A. Lozzaro, E. Bretzel, M. Conte, A. Cilli (26)

had happened with the 911 S Turbo LM-GT, IMSA saw things differently, preferring to prevent the new Zuffenhausen coupe from gaining a dominant foothold in what had now become the Exxon GT tour. Thus, the new GT2 owners racing in North America found themselves squaring off not against the smaller sports cars, but against the big stock block American muscle cars.

It was, as IMSA has intended, an unequal contest from the start, even though the GT2 of Haywood, Jochen Rohr, Bernd Maylaender and David Murry finished second in GTS at the '95 Daytona 24-Hour season opener. This placing was repeated by the Champion GT2 of Stuck and Bill Adam at Sebring and later Watkins Glen. The only other podium finish for a GT2 came at Sears Point where Stuck put in a solo third place performance. The first triumph for Porsche's new model didn't come until the following year when Stuck and Adam drove the Champion GT2, now in Evo form, to a sixth overall and first in GTS at the Sebring 12-Hours. This victory was the sole such performance for the Porsche turbo in the 1996 Exxon series.

Things began on a somewhat higher note in 1997 as Ralf Kelleners, Patrice Goueslard, Claudia Huertgen and Andre Ahrle took their GT2 to a class victory at the Daytona 24-Hour, followed home by Rohr, Andy Pilgrim, Harald Grohs

FRESH START FOR 911   **279**

24 Hours Daytona 1998: A. McNish, D. Sullivan, D. Müller, U. Alzen

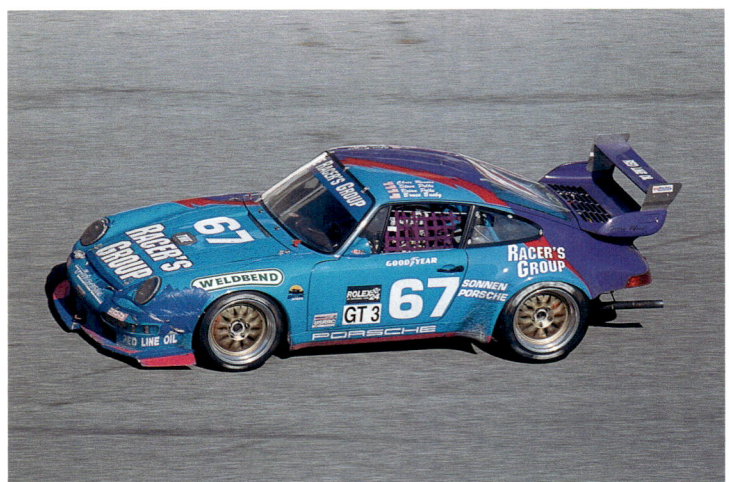

24 Hours Daytona 1998: C. Ronson, B. Pelke, B. Busby, S. Pelke

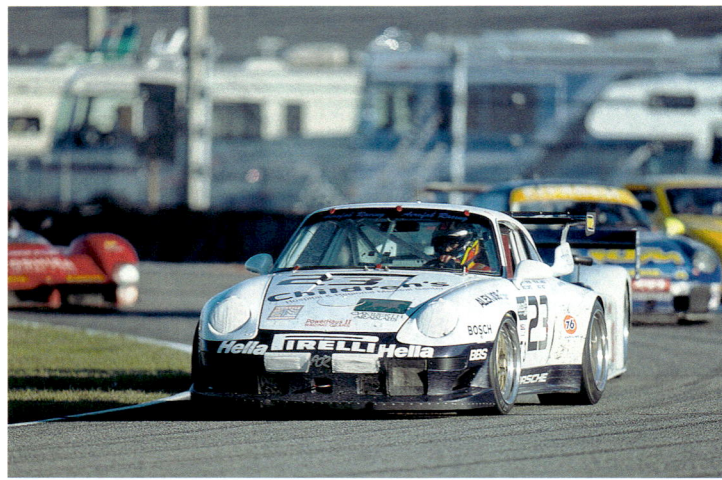

24 Hours Daytona 1998: M. Conte, B. Lambert, N. Holt, D. Havens

12 Hours Sebring 1998: Thierry Boutsen, Bob Wollek, Andy Pilgrim

Die Einführung des 911 GT1 stellte dann natürlich das Interesse am GT2 in den Schatten. Mit diesem Fahrzeug hatte Porsche die passende Antwort auf den McLaren F1-GTR. Der GT1 war ein gelungener Zwitter aus 993 und Prototyp. Reglementskonform wurden in Weissach zahlreiche Exemplare produziert, die an Rennsportteams, aber auch Privatpersonen verkauft wurden. In Le Mans 1996 feierte der GT1 einen Doppelsieg in der Klasse und musste sich im Gesamtklassement nur einem Joest-Prototypen mit Porsche-Motor geschlagen geben.

Auf einer US-Rennstrecke tauchte der 911 GT1 – dann bereits in Evo-Ausführung – erstmals im Herbst 1997 beim FIA GT-Event in Sebring auf. Yannick Dalmas und Bob Wollek wurden Dritte. Eine Woche später in Laguna Seca sorgten erneut Dalmas, Wollek sowie Allan McNish, Ralf Kelleners mit den Rängen zwei und drei für das beste Saisonergebnis. In der Zwischenzeit hatte Axel Rohr einen Vorjahres-GT1 im Werk erworben. Mit Platz zwei bei den 24 Stunden von Daytona schaffte Rohr das beste Ergebnis zusammen mit Allen McNish, Jörg und Dirk Müller, Uwe Alzen und Danny Sullivan.

1998 ging Champion mit einem GT1-Evo aus der letztjährigen FIA GT an den Start. In Daytona verhinderten kleinere Probleme das Duell mit dem Rohr-GT1. Für Sebring waren die Champion-Piloten Thierry Boutsen, Bob Wollek und Andy Pilgrim jedoch guter Hoffnung und sahen auch als erste die Zielflagge. Doch ein Regelverstoß beim Tanken ließ das Trio auf Rang drei zurückfallen. In Watkins Glen wurden Boutsen und Wollek immerhin GTS-Klassensieger und Gesamtdritte. Dank weiterer Topp-Fünf-Ergebnisse wurde Boutsen USRRC-Meister und Porsche siegte in der Markenwertung.

In der parallel ausgetragenen PSCR lief es für Champion nicht so gut, zu überlegen waren die Panoz Coupés mit dem Ford V8-Motor. Auch bei den FIA GT-Rennen in Homestead und Laguna Seca hatte Porsche das Nachsehen, dieses Mal gegenüber Mercedes. Ein Unglück kommt selten allein, und so passierte es beim Petit Le Mans 1.000 Meilen-Rennen 1998. Yannick Dalmas führte überlegen mit dem 911 GT1-98, als er in den Sog eines anderen Teilnehmers geriet, eine Rolle rückwärts hinlegte, aber mit den Rädern zuerst wieder landete und unverletzt blieb. Der Champion-Porsche rettete als Klassensieger und Gesamtdritter die Ehre und sicherte sich gleichzeitig einen Startplatz für Le Mans 1999.

Die ALMS wurde 1999 auf Anhieb ein großer Erfolg: Erstklassige Starterfelder, spannender Motorsport und eine üppige Berücksichtigung in den Medien. Nachdem das Werksengagement Ende des Vorjahres beendet worden war, konzentrierte sich Porsche auf die Produktion des für den Kundensport ausgelegten 911 GT3 auf Basis der Baureihe 996. Champion und Manthey Racing brachten für die 24 Stunden von Le Mans jeweils einen an den Start: Eine neue 911-Ära hatte begonnen.

Mantheys GT3 sah als überlegener Klassensieger die Zielflagge. Selbst von den wesentlich stärkeren GTS-Boliden waren nur zwei besser platziert als der 911 aus der Eifel. Bernd Mayländer, Bob Wollek und Dirk Müller sorgten im Champion-Cockpit für einen Doppelsieg, obwohl einmal das Getriebe gewechselt werden musste. Im September sorgte beim Petit Le Mans Alex Job für das US-Debüt des GT3. Fast schon eine logische Folge: Klassensieg von Cort Wagner, Dirk Müller und Sascha Maassen.

Probleme mit den Reifen verhinderten in Laguna Seca den neuerlichen Erfolg und Wagner, Müller mussten sich dem Reiser Callas-911 RSR von David Murry und Johnny Mow-

280 DER 911 BEGINNT VON VORN

12 Hours Sebring 1999: R.Pobst, M. Fitzgerald, D. MacNeil

12 Hours Sebring 1998: Kevin Buckler, Stephen Earle, Philip Collin

and Arnd Meier in second. Rohr and company also took a second in GTS at Sebring the following month. While the GT2 would continue to soldier on in an ever more chaotic environment, attention in America was now being focused on another, more potent Porsche turbo, the 911 GT1. Designed and developed by Porsche as their answer to the center-seat McLaren F1 GTR, the GT1 was part 993 and part pure prototype. In order to meet the production car regulations of the time, a run of 20 examples was built and sold to teams and public. First seen at Le Mans in 1996, where the two factory team entries swept the GT1 class and finished second and third overall behind a Joest Porsche-powered prototype, the GT1 became a customer racer in 1997.

The Americans got their first real look at the GT1 in its Evo factory guise when the newly-created FIA GT series came to Sebring that fall. The three-hour event was won by Mercedes with Yannick Dalmas and Bob Wollek third in their factory GT1. A week later, at Laguna Seca, Dalmas and Wollek chased the Bernd Schneider/Klaus Ludwig Mercedes to the line, followed home by McNish and Kelleners in third place. It was the Porsche team's best result of the entire season.

Meanwhile Rohr had taken delivery of a used customer GT1, based on the previous year's factory model, and was racing it with some success in the late season IMSA events. Rohr's effort faded from the scene after he, McNish, Jörg Muller and Danny Sullivan captured second overall and second in the top production class at the Daytona 24 Hours in 1998. That event marked the start of the USRRC's brief reappearance on the North American professional road racing stage.

The GT1 program then rested on Champion, who had purchased one of the two 1997 factory GT1 Evos. After a shaky start at Daytona, where problems prevented the team from challenging Rohr's car, the Champion GT1 went to Sebring with hopes of an outright victory. That was not to be however. Thierry Boutsen, Wollek and Andy Pilgrim led, but in the end a refuelling infraction left them third in the PSCR sanctioned event. For the most part, the Champion Porsche remained a strong but non-winning contender, both in PSCR and in the USRRC. The exception was at the latter series' summer Watkins Glen race where Boutsen and Wollek came home third overall and first in the GTS category. That effort, plus the South Florida team's string of consistent top five finishes, left Boutsen as the USRRC drivers champion and Porsche with the season-end manufacturer honors.

Unfortunately for Porsche and Champion, they fared less well in PSCR where they played second fiddle to Don Panoz' V8 Ford-powered coupes. That was also the case for the Porsche factory at the FIA Homestead and Laguna Seca rounds, where the revised GT1-98s were soundly defeated by their Mercedes rivals. That was bad enough. At the first Petit Le Mans 1,000 mile race, the progenitor to the ALMS, Dalmas, leading the race in a GT1-98LM, got caught in another car's turbulence and flipped over backwards, happily landing the right way up without injury to the driver. Porsche's honor was eventually upheld by the Champion GT1, which claimed the GTS class with an outright third, guaranteeing Champion an entry at the 1999 Le Mans 24 Hours.

The American Le Mans Series was fully established in 1999, marking a change of direction for endurance racing in the States and for Porsche, which scrapped its factory team in order to concentrate on the production of a new customer car, the 911 GT3.

The new era began at Le Mans when Champion Racing nominally ran one of two new GT3Rs in the LM-GT division. The Manthey Racing entry finished 13th overall, beating all but two of the GTS entries, while the Champion Racing GT3 driven by Bernd Maylaender, Bob Wollek and Dirk Muller finished 19th, and second in class after having its gearbox changed.

From there, one of the GT3Rs was released to Alex Job Racing and made its US debut at the Petit Le Mans in September. Cort Wagner, Dirk Muller and Sascha Maassen

12 Hours Sebring 1998: C. Slater, D. Kitch, A. Cilli, D. White, M. Petersen

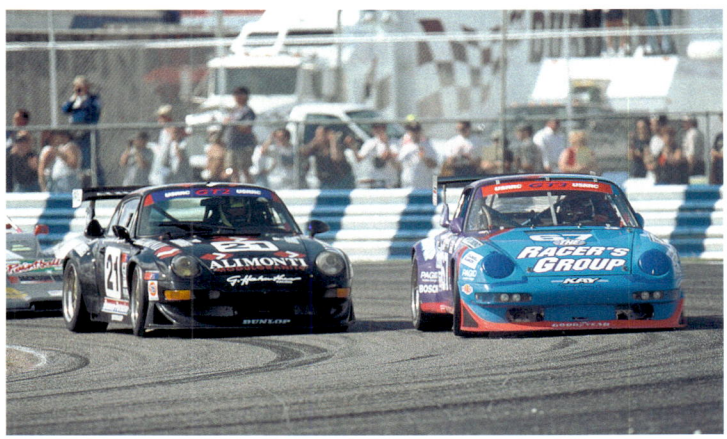

24 Hours Daytona 1999: G. Rosa, S. Zonca, F. Rosa, R. Mangifesta (21), S. Pelke, R. Herrerias, B. Pelke, P. di Giovanni (67)

ALMS 1999: Dirk Müller, Cort Wagner

Grand American Road Racing 2000: Darren Law, Mike Fitzgerald

24 Hours Daytona 2000: K. Buckler, D. Gaylord, D. Kitch, S. Miller

ALMS 2000: Dirk Müller, Lucas Luhr (5), Sascha Maassen, Bob Wollek (51)

ALMS 1999: Allan McNish, Ralf Kelleners

24 Hours Daytona 2000: Michael Petersen, Dale White, Philip Collin

ALMS 2000: Mike Fitzgerald, Bob Nagel

Speedvision GT Challenge 2001: Mike Fitzgerald

24 Hours Daytona 2000: R. Pobst, B. Lambert, M. Conte (23), P. Vuillaume, D. Faller, A. Munz (49)

Alex Job

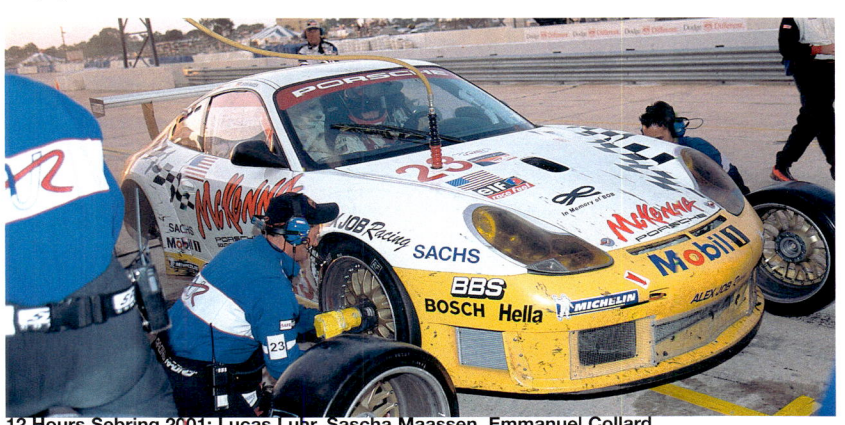

12 Hours Sebring 2001: Lucas Luhr, Sascha Maassen, Emmanuel Collard

ALMS 2001: Kevin Buckler, Tyler McQuarrie

12 Hours Sebring 2000: Michael Petersen, Dale White, Michael Lauer

Bob Wollek

FRESH START FOR 911 283

ALMS 2001: Bob Wollek, Johnny Mowlem

24 Hours Daytona 2002: J. Michaelian, R. Valentine, T. Hessert Jr.

24 Hours Daytona 2002: Leo Hindery, Marc Lieb, Kyle Petty, Peter Baron

12 Hours Sebring 2002: Michael Schrom, Vic Rice, Pierre Ehret

ALMS 2002: Jörg Bergmeister, Timo Bernhard (22), Lucas Luhr, Sascha Maassen (23)

lem geschlagen geben. Beim ALMS-Finale in Las Vegas war dann die alte Rangordnung wieder hergestellt. Das Jahr 2000 begann, wie das alte aufgehört hatte: Luca Drudi, Fabio Babini, Gabrio und Fabio Rosa wurden im GT3R Klassensieger bei den 24 Stunden von Daytona, dem ersten Lauf zur Grand-Am. Bis zum Jahresende konnten Mike Fitzgerald und Darren Law mit dem G&W Motorsports-996 in der GT-Klasse die meisten Punkte sammeln und wurden Meister.

Fitzgerald wechselte für 2001 zur White Lightning-Mannschaft und wurde mit Lucas Luhr, Randy Pobst und Christian Menzel als Klassensieger in Daytona abgewunken. Pobst und Kim Hiskey holten am Steuer des Fordahl-Crazy Redhead GT3-RS noch drei weitere Siege, in der Meisterschaft waren aber erneut G&W Motorsports und Darren Law eine Fronthaube voraus. Der angepeilte Hattrick misslang, da die Ferrari 360 für 2002 mächtig aufgerüstet hatten und sowohl die Marken- als auch Fahrerwertung für sich entscheiden konnten. Dass Porsche nicht sieglos blieb, dafür sorgten Kevin Buckler und seine Racer's Group bei zwei Rennen in Daytona. Neben Buckler griffen Timo Bernhard, Jörg Bergmeister und Michael Schrom ins Lenkrad.

2003 sollte dann die bislang erfolgreichste Saison für Kevin Buckler werden: Mit Schrom, Bernhard und Bergmeister siegte der rennfahrende Teamchef in Daytona beim 24 Stunden Rennen nicht nur in der GT-Klasse, sondern fuhr als sensationeller Gesamtsieger über die Ziellinie. Fast auf den Tag genau jährte sich zum dreißigsten Mal der erste 911-Sieg durch Peter Gregg und Hurley Haywood und deren Carrera RS im Jahre 1973. Im weiteren Grand-Am Saisonverlauf und auch während 2004 sollten die Daytona Prototypen und die Ferrari 360 bevorteilt werden, so dass die GT3-Teams nur zweimal erfolgreich waren.

Der erste Triumph – wie in den Jahren zuvor – kam erneut bei den Rolex 24 Stunden in Daytona. Mike Fitzgerald, Robin Liddell, Johnny Mowlem und die Brüder Joe und Jay Policastro zeigten mit dem Orbit Racing-GT3RS der Ferrari-Konkurrenz das Heck. Das Rennen in Homestead endete mit dem Erfolg von Kevin Buckler und Tom Nastasi im Racer's Group-996. In der SGS-Sonderwertung sorgten Marc Bunting, Andy Lally und Mike Levitas, Randy Pobst für einen Doppelsieg in der Meisterschaft.

had a textbook race to 15th overall, and the LM-GT class win, despite nursing an overheating gearbox in the latter stages.

The AJR Porsche GT3R did not win its class at Laguna Seca, strangely enough, as the Michelin tires uncharacteristically gave up. Wagner and Muller slid back to second in class, behind the Reiser Callas team's 911 RSR of David Murry and Johnny Mowlem. Order was restored at Las Vegas, the final round, as Wagner and Muller won the class with two laps to spare.

The Grand-Am series opened up for business at Daytona in 2000 and there, Luca Drudi, Fabio Babini and Gabrio and Fabio Rosa took their GT3R to eighth overall and first in the GT category. G&W Motorsports' Mike Fitzgerald and Darren Law topped the point standings in GT at the end of the season in their GT3R.

Driving the White Lightning GT3R, Fitzgerald started the 2001 season the way he left off in 2000 by claiming victory in the GT class at Daytona with Lucas Luhr, Randy Pobst and Christian Menzel.

Pobst, teamed with Kim Hiskey, won three more times in the Fordahl-Crazy Redhead GT3RS, the follow-on version of the GT3R, although the points title again went to G&W and Law. The next year, 2002, brought a nasty surprise to the Porsche camp in the form of the Ferrari 360 which garnered not only the GT title for the Italians, but the driving crown for Ferrari of Washington team's Bill Auberlen. Even so, the season was not without success for Zuffenhausen, thanks to Kevin Buckler's Racer's Group Porsche team. In what was a remarkable string of success Buckler, with Timo Bernhard, Jorg Bergmeister and Michael Schrom, won the GT class with a stunning performance at Daytona. Buckler and Schrom also won the California round of the Grand-Am title chase later that March.

However, that triumph faded almost into obscurity as Buckler and company also won the GT class trophy at Le Mans. The greatest reward for Buckler's team came at the 2003 Daytona 24 hours when he, Schrom, Bernhard and Bergmeister won that prestigious event outright on the 30th anniversary of Peter Gregg's and Hurley Haywood's similar performance with their 2.7-liter Carrera RS. The Grand-Am, with its restrictive rules, many of which were intended to protect the

12 Hours Sebring 2002: Kevin Buckler, Michael Schrom

Winner 24 Hours Daytona 2003 (l.-r.): Michael Schrom, Kevin Buckler, Jörg Bergmeister, Timo Bernhard

series' newly formed Daytona Prototype division, was not a Porsche-friendly place in 2003, the GT regulations tending to favor Ferrari. The pattern continued, at least in the GT category, in 2004 when Porsche scored just two GT successes. The first of these came at the Rolex Daytona 24 where Orbit Racing's GT3RS with Fitzgerald, Robin Liddell, Johnny Mowlem and the Policastros, Joe and Jay, claimed class honors. The second GT triumph belonged to Buckler and his Racer's Group partner Tom Nastasi, the pair coming home first in GT in the September Homestead round of the Rolex championship tour.

What the Porsche brigade lost in the GT wars, they more than made up for in the newly established SGS production classification, which will form the basis for the Grand-Am's assembly line division from 2005 on. There it was an all GT3 Cup show with TCP teammates Marc Bunting and Andy Lally eventually beating team owner Mike Levitas and Randy Pobst for the championship crown. If Porsche has struggled in the Grand-Am's GT universe, it has been far more successful in the ALMS' LM-GT arena. With the exception of 2001, when Tom Milner's Prototype Technology Group, topped the standings with a pair of lightweight V8-powered special BMW M3 coupes, the class has belonged to Zuffenhausen's 911.

That trend started in 2000, the first full season for the GT3R, with Dick Barbour's team leading the way, Dirk Muller winning eight of the 13 races he participated in, winning the main titles for himself, the Barbour team, and for Porsche. In part Barbour's success was attributable to his close association with Porsche Motorsport North America, ties which switched in 2001 to Alex Job Racing, the Orlando, Florida-

ALMS 2002:
Leo Hindery, Peter Baron

Im Gegensatz zur Grand-Am ist der 911 seit Einführung der ALMS dort das Maß der Dinge in der GT-Klasse. Bis auf 2001, wo Leichtbauversionen eines BMW M3 V8-Prototypen startberechtigt und siegreich waren, kam immer ein Porsche-Pilot zu Meisterehren. Den Anfang machten 2000 Dick Barbours Team und Dirk Müller, der acht der 13 Rennen gewann, auch Dank der Hilfe von Porsche Motorsport North America. Die Unterstützung wanderte im Folgejahr zu Alex Job Racing, deren Piloten Sascha Maassen und Lucas Luhr trotz der BMW-Überlegenheit bis kurz vor Saisonende Titelchancen hatten.

Nachdem für 2002 BMWs Prototyp ausgeschlossen wurde, machten die 911-Teams die Meisterschaft unter sich aus. Mit Lucas Luhr, Sascha Maassen, Jörg Bergmeister und Timo Bernhard lagen am Ende vier Alex Job-Fahrer vorn. Gemeinsame Titelehren dann in 2003 für Luhr und Maassen. In 2004 boten die Wettbewerber dem Job-Team bis zum letzten Rennen Paroli, allen voran Petersen Motorsport und Flying Lizard. Job-Pilot Bernhard sollte schließlich doch noch die Oberhand behalten. Denn auch 40 Jahre nach der Motorsport-Premiere ist der Porsche 911 noch immer das Maß der Dinge.

Lucas Luhr, Sascha Maassen (r.)

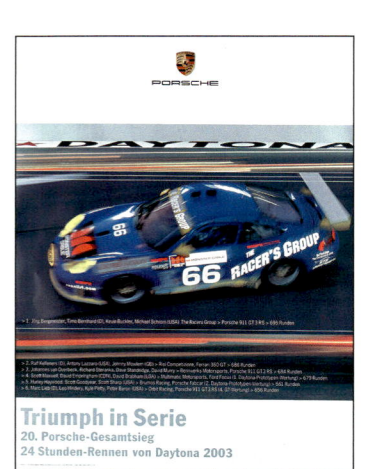

Poster

24 Hours Daytona 2003: L. Hindery, M. Lieb, K. Petty, P. Baron

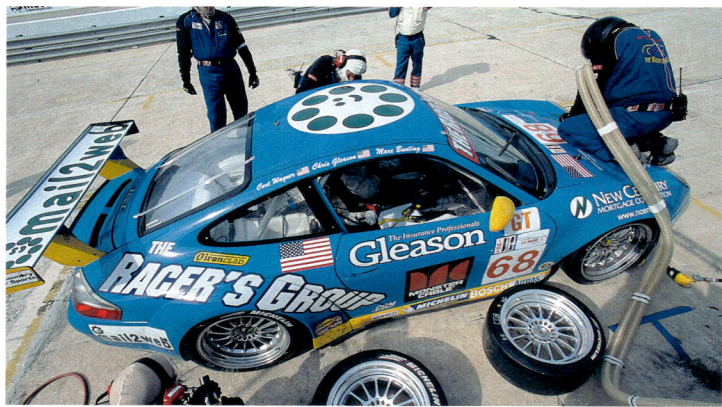

12 Hours Sebring 2003: C. Gleason, M. Bunting, C. Wagner

ALMS 2003: Michael Schrom, Pierre Ehret

12 Hours Sebring 2003: Lucas Luhr, Sascha Maassen

12 Hours Sebring 2003: Johnny Mowlem, Craig Stanton, Nic Jonsson

286 DER 911 BEGINNT VON VORN

ALMS 2003: Leo Hindery, Peter Baron, Marc Lieb

ALMS 2003: Timo Bernhard, Jörg Bergmeister

24 Hours Daytona 2004: Johannes van Overbeek, Seth Neiman, Lonnie Pechnik, Peter Cunningham, Mike Rockenfeller

based team maintaining that relationship ever since. Despite BMW's winning season, Job and his drivers, Sascha Maassen and Lucas Luhr did well enough to challenge for the crown.

When the rules makers sent the limited production BMWs packing for 2002, it was an all Porsche GT3 parade, Luhr beating out his partner Maassen for the title, with Bergmeister and Bernhard, in Job's second GT3RS, finishing third and fourth respectively. Things changed little in 2003 as Job's team continued to rule, although challenged by rival teams with Porsche GT3s. Luhr and Maassen emerged as co-champions, with Porsche claiming its third GT manufacturers crown in four seasons.

Job found it much harder in 2004, with strong challenges from Petersen Motorsport and the Flying Lizard GT3RSR teams. Even though the points chase went down to the last race at Laguna Seca, Bernhard came away with the crown, finishing second in the finale to the Job entry of Romain Dumas and Marc Lieb.

The 911 GT3 continued to build on its legend in 2004, apparently with no end in sight. That is a great tribute to a car whose origins and racing history go back 40 years.

FRESH START FOR 911 287

American Le Mans Series 2004: Timo Bernhard, Jörg Bergmeister

12 Hours Sebring 2004: Leo Hindery, Mike Rockenfeller, Peter Baron

12 Hours Sebring 2004: David Murry, Craig Stanton

American Le Mans Series 2004: Cort Wagner, Patrick Long

911 – IN LE MANS DAHEIM

911 FORMS FABRIC OF LE MANS

Author: Michael Cotton

Mehr als ein halbes Jahrhundert ist vergangen, seit Porsche zum ersten Mal in Le Mans am Start stand. In dieser Zeit wurde die von Ferdinand Porsche geschaffene Marke zum Synonym des 24 Stunden-Rennens in Frankreich. Porsche-Rennwagen haben die Veranstaltung bisher sechzehn Mal gewonnen, was an sich schon eine bemerkenswerte Leistung ist.

So waren zum Beispiel im Jahr 1970, als Porsche das Rennen zum ersten Mal gewann, fünf der sieben gewerteten Autos in Zuffenhausen gebaut worden. Die beiden anderen, die die Zielflagge sahen, waren Ferrari 512. Im folgenden Jahr wurden mehr Fahrzeuge gewertet, dreizehn insgesamt, davon zehn Porsche und drei Ferrari. Sieben von diesen zehn Porsche waren Elfer.

Die Reise begann mit einem 160 PS starken 911S, der 1966 von Jean Kerguen und Jacques Dewez, ebenfalls bekannt als „Franc", pilotiert wurde. Es gab nichts Besonderes an diesem Auto - mit der Ausnahme - dass es in Stuttgart zugelassen war und über ein Paar Zusatzscheinwerfer verfügte. Es startete von der 37. Position, lief wie ein Uhrwerk und kam auf Gesamtrang vierzehn und Sieger der 2-Liter GT-Klasse ins Ziel. Es hatte 3.821 Kilometer mit einer Durchschnittsgeschwindigkeit von 159,22 km/h absolviert.

1966 entschied Porsche drei Kategorien für sich: Die Klasse der 2-Liter Prototypen (Jo Siffert und Colin Davis in einem 906/6), die 2-Liter Sportwagenklasse (Rolf Stommelen und Günther Klass, ebenfalls in einem 906/6) und die 2-Liter GT-Klasse. Alle angetrieben von ähnlichen 1.991 ccm starken Sechszylinder-Boxermotoren aus dem 911.

„Franc" war im Jahr 1967 weniger glücklich, er sorgte sogar für den ersten Ausfall im Rennen, als seine Kupplung den Dienst quittierte. Herbert Linge und Robert Buchet kamen mit einem 911S sicher ins Ziel und gewannen wieder die 2-Liter GT-Klasse, gleichbedeutend mit Gesamtrang vierzehn. Mit den 4.158 absolvierten Kilometern stellten sie in ihrer Klasse einen neuen Distanzrekord auf.

1968 senkte Regen die Durchschnittsgeschwindigkeiten, dennoch gönnten Rolf Stommelen und Dieter Spoerry dem siegreichen Ford GT40 bis ins Ziel keine Verschnaufpause. In der 2-Liter GT-Klasse war der 911T die Wahl der Sieger. Jean-Pierre Gaban und Roger Vanderschrick wurden Zwölfte im Gesamtergebnis, gefolgt von einem weiteren 911T, gefahren von Claude Laurent und Jean-Claude Ogier.

1971: Sylvain Garant, Pierre Greub

1967: Pierre Boutin, Patrice Sanson

1971: Erwin Kremer, Nicolas Koob

Winner GT-2000 1968: Jean-Pierre Gaban, Roger Vanderschrick

1968: Claude Ballot-Lena, Guy Chasseuil

More than half a century has gone by since a Porsche first raced at Le Mans, and in that time the brand created by Ferdinand Porsche has become synonymous with the 24-Hour race in France. Porsche products have won the event outright 16 times, a remarkable achievement, and it is a sobering thought that if Porsche had made coffee pots instead of motor cars, the 24-Hours of Le Mans would barely have existed in key years.

For instance, in 1970, when Porsche won the classic race for the first time, five of the seven cars classified were made in Zuffenhausen; the other two finishers were Ferrari 512s. More cars were classified the following year, 13 in total, comprising 10 Porsches and three Ferraris. Of the 10 Porsches, seven were 911s, a huge testimony to the integrity of the production-line GT that dominated endurance racing in the last three decades of the 20th century.

The journey began with a 160 horsepower 911S that raced in 1966 in the hands of Jean Kerguen and Jacques Dewez, also known as 'Franc'. There was nothing special about the car, except that it was registered in Stuttgart and carried a pair of auxiliary spotlights, but it started in 37th position, ran like clockwork and finished in 14th position overall, winning the 2-litre GT category. They covered 3,821 kilometres at an average speed of 159.22 km/h.

Porsche won three categories in 1966, the 2-litre prototype (Jo Siffert and Colin Davis in a 906/6), the 2-litre Sports (Rolf Stommelen and Gunther Klass, also in a 906/6) and the 2-litre GT, all of course with similar 1,991 cc flat-six engines from the 911.

'Franc' was not so fortunate in 1967, in fact he was the first to retire when his Porsche's clutch failed. Porsche's own Herbert Linge got to the finish safely in a 911S shared with Robert Buchet, also winning the 2-litre GT class in 14th position, covering 4,158 kilometres.

Average speeds were sharply reduced by rain in 1968, when Rolf Stommelen and Dieter Spoerry gave the winning Ford a good run for its money, and the 911T was the choice of the winners of the 2-litre GT class, Jean-Pierre Gaban and Roger Vanderschrick. They finished 12th, followed by another 911T driven by Claude Laurent and Jean-Claude Ogier.

Porsche chased Ford even more strongly in 1969, providing the closest finish between rival makes as Hans Herrmann failed to beat Jacky Ickx's Ford by 70 metres (the official margin) or perhaps less. The 911S that won the 2-litre GT class, that of Gaban and Yves Deprez, was almost overlooked in all the excitement. It finished 10th, but failed by two laps to beat the class distance record set by Linge and Buchet two years previously.

1971: Jean Jacques Cochet, Jean Selz

1971: Paul Vestey, Richard Bond

911 FORMS FABRIC OF LE MANS

Porsches Jagd auf Ford war im Jahr 1969 sogar noch härter, heraus kam der knappste Zieleinlauf konkurrierender Marken. Hans Herrmann verpasste den Sieg über Jacky Ickx nur um 70 Meter. In all dieser Aufregung war der 911S von Jean-Pierre Gaban und Yves Deprez beinahe übersehen worden. Er gewann die 2-Liter GT-Klasse und wurde Gesamtzehnter, verpasste allerdings den Distanzrekord von Linge und Buchet um zwei Runden.

Auch strömender Regen konnte Porsche 1970 nicht den Erfolg verderben. Nicht nur, dass Hans Herrmann und Richard Attwood mit dem von Porsche Salzburg eingesetzten 917K zum ersten Mal die 24-Stunden von Le Mans gewannen, auch die ersten drei im Gesamtklassement und fünf der im Ganzen sieben, die gewertet wurden, waren Porsche. Durch eine Änderung in der Zweiliter GT-Klasse siegte dort der 914/6 mit Guy Chasseuil und Claude Ballot-Lena. Im Gesamtklassement belegte er Platz sechs, gefolgt von Erwin Kremer und Nick Koob im 911S. Es war bereits das fünfte Le Mans-Jahr des 911 und erst jetzt wurde der Motor bedeutend aufgewertet: Aus 2.253 ccm entwickelte Kremers Auto 240 PS.

1971 übernahm Martini Racing den Werkseinsatz. Mit dem 917K siegten Dr. Helmut Marko und Gijs van Lennep vor dem Gulf-917K von Richard Attwood und Herbert Müller. Ferrari belegte Rang drei bis fünf, in ihrem Kielwasser jedoch fanden sich auf den Gesamträngen sechs bis dreizehn allesamt Porsche. Sieben von ihnen waren 911, angeführt vom 2,4-Liter 911S, den Henri Cachia für Raymond Touroul und André Ansallem, auch bekannt als „Anselm", einsetzten. Der nächste Platz in der GTS-Klasse ging an den von René Mazzia und Jürgen Barth pilotierten 911E, dann folgte der 911S von Jean Mesange und Gerard Merlin („Gedehem") sowie der 911S von Erwin Kremer und Nick Koob.

1971: Jean Mesange, Gerard Merlin 'Gedehem'

Winner GT-2000 1971: Raymond Touroul, Andre Ansallem 'Anselme'

1972: John Fitzpatrick, Erwin Kremer

1972 war das erste Jahr der 3-Liter Klasse, die vom Matra Simca Team dominiert wurde. Porsche bekam gerade einen Fuß auf das Podium, der privat eingesetzte 908 von Reinhold Joest, Michael Weber und Mario Casoni kam auf Rang drei. Die 911-Mannschaften, deren Motoren nun mit 2.466 ccm Hubraum ausgestattet waren, kämpften mit mechanischen Problemen und nur einer von ihnen kam über die Distanz. Michael Keyser, Jürgen Barth und Sylvain Garant gewannen zwar die 2,5-Liter GTS-Klasse, hatten ihrem Motor hierfür jedoch auch das Letzte abverlangt.

Mit der Vorstellung des Carrera RS für die Saison 1973 begann ein neuer Lebensabschnitt des Elfer. Schon in der Straßenversion war es jetzt ein viel stärkeres Auto. Und der Renn-RSR hatte nun auch die Entwicklungsarbeit des Werks im Rücken. Sogar ein reines Werksteam wurde eingesetzt, dies jedoch direkt in der Prototypen-Klasse mit Gijs van Lennep und Herbert Müller am Volant. Die GTS-Klasse wurde den Kundenteams überlassen.

Ein Sieg bei den 24 Stunden von Daytona war eine Überraschung, danach kam der Erfolg bei der Targa Florio, doch auf die Wiederholung dieser Vorstellungen in Le Mans zu hoffen, war zu viel des Guten. Die Sportprototypen liefen wie Uhrwerke und sicherten sich die ersten Plätze. Van Lennep und Müller jedoch fuhren den 2.806 ccm starken, von Martini Racing gesponserten Werks-911 Carrera RSR auf den vierten Gesamtrang. Interessant ist, dass sie 100 Kilometer mehr absolvierten, als die Sieger der GTS-Klasse, Vic Elford und Claude Ballot-Lena im 4,4 Liter Ferrari 365 GTB/4. Zweiter in der GTS-Klasse war der Kremer Racing Carrera RSR mit Erwin Kremer, Clemens Schickentanz und Paul Keller, die den Ferrari Daytona von Alain Serpaggi und Jose Dolhelm hinter sich ließen. Auf Platz vier folgte mit Georg Loos und Jürgen Barth ein weiterer Carrera RS.

1972: Claude Haldi, Paul Keller, Gerard Merlin

Torrential rain in 1970 did not spoil the party for Porsche, which not only won the 24-Hours of Le Mans for the first time with the Salzburg entered 917K of Hans Herrmann and Richard Attwood, but claimed the top three positions overall and five of the seven finishing positions.

By way of a change the 2-litre GT class was won by the 914/6 of Guy Chasseuil and Ballot-Lena, sixth over-all, ahead of the 2,253 cc 911S of Erwin Kremer and Nick Koob. Only now, at the fifth appearance of the 911, was the engine significantly uprated, Kremer's car developing 240 bhp.

Porsche's baton passed to the Martini Racing team in 1971, their 917K winning the 24-Hours in the hands of Dr Helmut Marko and Gijs van Lennep, ahead of the Gulf Porsche 917K of Richard Attwood and Herbert Muller. Ferrari claimed the next three positions, third to fifth, and in their wake was a solid wall of Porsches, in sixth to 13th positions overall.

Seven of them were 911s, the squadron led by the 2.4 litre 911S entered by Henri Cachia for Raymond Touroul and Andre Ansallem, also known as 'Anselm'. Next in GTS was the 911E driven by Rene Mazzia and Juergen Barth, then a 911S driven by Jean Mesange and Gerard Merlin ('Gedehem') followed by the 911S of Erwin Kremer and Nick Koob.

Porsche just got a toe-hold on the podium in 1972, the first year of the 3-litre racing car formula dominated by the Matra Simca team. The privately entered 908 finished third, driven by Reinhold Joest, Michael Weber and Mario Casoni, but the 911 teams, usually with engines rated at 2,466cc, suffered mechanical carnage and only one completed the distance, that of Michael Keyser, Juergen Barth and Sylvain Garant. They did win the 2.5 litre GTS category, but a new engine was clearly needed.

The 911 model was given a new lease of life when the Carrera RS/RSR was introduced for the 1973 season. Not only was this a much more powerful car, in road trim, but the RSR now had factory development behind it, even a factory team which avoided the GTS class, which would be dominated by customers, and moved straight into the prototype group where Gijs van Lennep and Herbert Muller gave good account of themselves.

An outright victory in the Daytona 24-Hours was soon followed by another outright success in the Targa Florio, but a repeat performance at Le Mans was too much to hope for. The sports prototypes ran off with the race, claiming the top positions, but van Lennep and Muller drove the factory's 2,806 cc 911 Carrera RSR, sponsored by Martini Racing, to fourth place overall. As a matter of interest it finished 100 kilometres ahead of the GTS winner, the 4.4 litre Ferrari 365 GTB/4 of Vic Elford and Claude Ballot-Lena.

Second in GTS was the Kremer Racing Carrera RSR of Erwin Kremer, Clemens Schickentanz and Paul Keller, holding off the Ferrari Daytona of Alain Serpaggi and Jose Dolhelm, and fourth was another Carrera RS of Georg Loos and Juergen Barth.

Even more was expected of the Martini Racing Porsches at Le Mans in 1974, since they had the newly developed turbocharged engine which developed 480 horsepower, reliably, installed in cars that were down to 750 kilograms. The second 'works' entry was for Manfred Schurti and Helmuth Koinigg, and they were indeed an incredible machines, but still they could not compete on level terms with the four 650 kg Matra-Simca prototypes, nor the Ford Cosworth DFV powered Gulf-Mirages.

All the teams had a full quota of problems in 1974, even Porsche, as the Schurti/Koinigg Martini Turbo blew its engine up

1972: Dominique Bardini, Raymond Touroul, Fernand Sarapoulos

911 FORMS FABRIC OF LE MANS **295**

Noch mehr wurde von den Martini Racing-Porsches in Le Mans 1974 erwartet. Nun verfügten sie über neu entwickelte Turbomotoren, die standfeste 480 PS erzeugten und in Autos verbaut waren, die nur 750 kg wogen. Die zweite „Werksnennung" war für Manfred Schurti und Helmuth Koinigg. Die neuen Autos waren in der Tat unglaubliche Maschinen, doch auch sie waren nicht in der Lage, ebenbürtig zu konkurrieren mit den vier 650 kg leichten Matra Simca-Prototypen oder den Gulf-Mirages mit Ford Cosworth DFV-Motoren.

Alle Teams hatten ihre Probleme im Jahr 1974, auch Porsche, als am Samstagabend der Motor von Schurti und Koinigg streikte. Zwei Matras, einer gefahren von Bob Wollek, erlitten Motorschäden noch vor Mitternacht, und beide Gulf Mirages haderten mit technischen Problemen. So war am Sonntagmorgen das Rennen ein Kampf zwischen dem Matra von Henri Pescarolo und Gerard Larrousse und dem Martini-Porsche von Gijs van Lennep und Herbert Müller.

Pescarolo lag meilenweit vor dem Porsche, war aber auch weit entfernt von seinem französischen Team, als der blaue Prototyp auf der Mulsanne-Geraden ausrollte. Pescarolo schaffte es langsam zurück in die Box, wo die Getriebe-

1973: Peter Gregg, Guy Chasseuil

1973: Gijs van Lennep, Herbert Müller

Winner GT-3000 1973: Erwin Kremer, Clemens Schickentanz, Paul Keller

reparatur eine ganze Stunde in Anspruch nahm. Ironie des Schicksals: Porsche hatte spezielle Getriebe für das Matra-Team entwickelt und geliefert. Bereitwillig stellte man nun ein inneres Bauteil zur Verfügung, das zur Reparatur dringend benötigt wurde. Mit einem auf nur eine Runde geschrumpften Vorsprung vor dem Martini-Porsche wurde Pescarolo schließlich wieder ins Rennen geschickt.

Es gab keine Chance für den Porsche, den Matra zu schlagen, auch wenn dieser zum Schluss ohne die Gänge drei und fünf von seinen Fahrern in Ziel getragen werden musste. Der zweite Rang jedoch wurde verteidigt gegen den Matra von Jabouille und Migault und den Gulf-Mirage von Bell und Hailwood. Starke Ferrari GTB Daytonas belegten die Plätze fünf und sechs, achter wurde der 911 Carrera RSR des Schweizer Porsche Club Romand mit Bernard Cheneviere und Peter Zbinden. Insgesamt erreichten fünf Carreras das Ziel, alle unter den ersten vierzehn des Gesamtklassements.

1975 nahm sich das Werk, in Erwartung des Erscheinens neuer technischer Regularien, eine Auszeit. Reinhold Joest bereitete seinen 908/3 Turbo vor und pilotierte ihn gemeinsam mit Mario Casoni und Jürgen Barth in Le Mans. Es war das Jahr, in dem der Automobile Club de l'Ouest von den Teilnehmern forderte, erst nach 20 absolvierten Runden nachzutanken, um Treibstoff zu sparen. Das Matra Team lehnte diese Herausforderung ab.

Der Sieg ging an Derek Bell und Jacky Ickx in ihrem Gulf-Mirage, wenn der sich auch mit einer gebrochenen hinteren Aufhängung ins Ziel schleppte. Guy Chasseuil und Jean-Louis Lafosse in einem Ligier JS2 wurden zweite vor Vern Schuppan und Jean-Pierre Jassaud in einem weiteren Gulf-Mirage. Joest, Casoni und Barth kamen auf Rang vier, nachdem sie fast 60 Minuten verloren hatten, um einen Unfallschaden von Casoni zu richten. Hinter ihnen liefen auf Platz fünf bis elf ausschließlich Drei-Liter Carrera RSR ein. Angeführt wurden diese vom ehemaligen Sieger Gijs van Lennep, der zusammen mit John Fitzpatrick und Manfred Schurti im Gelo Racing Team-Carrera die GT-Klasse gewann. Dahinter lag der RSR von Jean Blaton und den Briten Nick Faure und John Cooper.

spectacularly on Saturday evening. Two Matras, one driven by Bob Wollek, blew their engines up before midnight, both the Gulf Mirages had technical problems, and by Sunday morning the race had become a straight fight between the Matra of Henri Pescarolo and Gerard Larrousse, and the Martini Porsche of van Lennep and Muller.

Pescarolo was far ahead of the Porsche, and just as well for the French team because on Sunday morning the blue prototype rolled to a stop on the Mulsanne Straight. Pescarolo managed to reach the pits and the gearbox was rebuilt, a process that took a full hour. Ironically, Porsche had designed and supplied special gearboxes to the Matra team, and willingly supplied an internal component that was needed to get Pescarolo back on the track, just one lap ahead of the Martini Porsche.

There was no chance for the Porsche to beat Matra since the drivers had lost third and fifth gears, and were nursing the car to the finish while protecting second place from the overheating Matra of Jabouille and Migault, and the Gulf Mirage of Bell and Hailwood.

Strong Ferrari GTB Daytonas occupied fifth and sixth positions, and eighth was the Swiss Porsche Club Romand 911 Carrera RSR of Bernard Cheneviere and Peter Zbinden. A total of five Carreras reached the finish, all in the top 14 overall, a very satisfactory result for the private teams.

The Porsche factory took a break from racing in 1975, awaiting the introduction of new technical regulations, but Reinhold Joest prepared and raced his special 908/3 turbo (often dubbed 908/4), which he shared with Mario Casoni and Juergen Barth at Le Mans. This was the year of the fuel economy run, the ACO requiring competitors to complete 20 laps before refuelling, and the Matra team declined the challenge.

Victory went to Derek Bell and Jacky Ickx in their Gulf-Mirage, though almost crippled with broken rear suspension, ahead of Guy Chasseuil and Jean-Louis Lafosse in a Ligier JS2, and Vern Schuppan with Jean-Pierre Jaussaud in another Gulf-Mirage.

Joest, Casoni and Barth were fourth after a lengthy stop to rectify accident damage, and behind them was a solid wall of 3-litre Porsche Carrera RSRs, filling the fifth to 11th positions. At their head was the Gelo Racing Team Carrera driven by former winner Gijs van Lennep with John Fitzpatrick and Manfred Schurti, winners of the GT category, followed by Jean Blaton's RSR with Britons Nick Faure and John Cooper co-driving.

Poster

Poster

1974: Raymond Touroul, Henri Cachia, Denis Rua

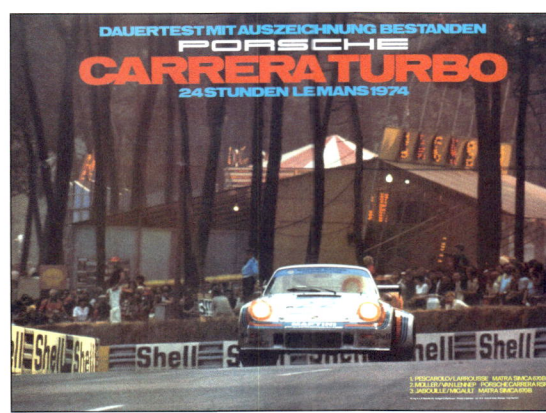

1974: Gijs van Lennep, Herbert Müller

1976: Bob Wollek, Didier Pironi, Marie-Claude Chamasson

1976: Hans Heyer, Juan Bolanos, Billy Sprowls, Lopez Negrete

1977: Rolf Stommelen, Manfred Schurti

1977: Hans Heyer, Tim Schenken, Toine Hezemans

Zum ersten Mal traten die Fahrzeuge der neuen Gruppen vier, fünf und sechs im Jahr 1976 in Le Mans gegeneinander an. Das Porsche-Werk hatte Autos für alle drei Gruppen vorbereitet. Die Speerspitze bildeten an der Sarthe die beiden Martini Racing 936 in der Gruppe sechs. Pilotiert wurden sie von Jacky Ickx und Gijs van Lennep beziehungsweise Reinhold Joest und Jürgen Barth. In der Gruppe fünf hatte das Martini-Team einen 935 für Rolf Stommelen und Manfred Schurti genannt. Eine Reihe von privaten 934 stand in der Gruppe vier am Start.

Die einzige Renault Alpine A446 im Feld war schnellste im Training. Jabouille, Tambay und Dolhem führten mit ihr auch die ersten Rennrunden an. Doch bereits um viertel nach vier lag Ickx vorn, konnte seine Führung konstant ausbauen und sollte diese bis ins Ziel nicht mehr abgeben. Es war der erste Sieg eines turbogeladenen Fahrzeugs überhaupt und für Porsche der dritte in Le Mans. Der zweite 936 lag lange direkt hinter den Teamkollegen, verlor am Sonntagmorgen aber an Leistung. Mit einem Getriebeschaden mussten Joest und Barth den Wagen schließlich abstellen. Ihr Ausfall sollte jedoch der einzige eines 936 in der ganzen 76er Saison bleiben.

Die 935 enttäuschten ein wenig bei ihrem Le Mans Debüt. Der Martini 935 von Stommelen und Schurti litt unter hohem Sprit-verbrauch und Elektrikproblemen. Trotz alledem sahen sie als Gesamtvierte das Ziel und gewannen ihre Gruppe. Zweiter in der Gruppe fünf und sechster im Gesamt wurde der 911 Carrera RSR von Raymond Touroul, Alain Cudini und René Boubet. Kremer Racing hatte in Köln einen 935 für Hans Heyer aufgebaut. Zusammen mit seinen mexikanischen Teamkollegen Carlos Bolanos, Billy Sprowls und Alfredo Negrete fuhr Heyer ein aussichtsreiches Rennen. Unglücklicherweise lösten sich alle ihre Hoffnungen in dem Rauch auf, den ein Feuer an ihrem 935 verursachte und zum Aufgeben zwang. Den dritten Rang in der Gruppe fünf holten sich Egon Evertz, Hartwig Bertrams und Heinz Martin mit einem verbesserten 934.

In der Gruppe vier hielten die Porsche-Kundenteams nahezu ein Monopol. Der Gelo 934 von Tim Schenken und Toine Hezemans war bis auf den sechsten Gesamtrang vorgefahren, ehe am Sonntag das Getriebe streikte und instand gesetzt werden musste. Die Reparatur kostete das Loos-Team zweieinhalb Stunden, dennoch konnten sie sich wieder bis auf den zweiten Platz in der Gruppe vier vorkämpfen. Auch Bob Wollek, Didier Pironi und Marie-Claude Beaumont haderten etwas mit der Technik. Ein Kupplungsschaden hatte sie bis auf den 19. Rang zurückgeworfen, bis ins Ziel schafften sie es jedoch, auf Rang vier vorzukommen. Der Sieg in der Gruppe vier ging somit an den 911 Carrera RS von Ouviere, Gahinet und Gadal.

1977: Jean-Louis Ravenel, Jean Detrin, Jacques Ravenel

Winner IMSA GTX 1978: Brian Redman, Dick Barbour, John Paul

Cars built to the new Groups 4, 5 and 6 categories raced together for the first time at Le Mans in 1976, and the Porsche factory had prepared cars for all three groups. At the forefront at Le Mans were the two Martini Racing Porsche System 936s (Group 6) for Jacky Ickx with Gijs van Lennep, and Reinhold Joest with Juergen Barth, backed by a Martini Racing Porsche System 935 (Group 5) for Rolf Stommelen and Manfred Schurti. There were a number of 934s (Group 4) in the field, in private hands.

The lone Renault Alpine A446 of Jabouille, Tambay and Dolhelm was fastest in practice and led the early laps, but Ickx soon swept past into the lead and drew away steadily, not headed again during the 24 hours. Joest and Barth followed, but their engine lost power on Sunday morning and the second 936 retired with simultaneous failures in the valve gear and gearbox input shaft. It was the one retirement posted by a 936 all season.

This was Porsche's third Le Mans victory and the first by any car with a turbocharged engine. The 935s were a little disappointing on their debut at Le Mans, the Martini entry of Stommelen and Schurti suffering from high fuel consumption, niggling electrical problems and damaged bodywork. Even so, it finished in fourth place overall and won its category, while in sixth position, second in Group 5, was the 911 Carrera RSR of Raymond Touroul, Alain Cudini and Rene Boubet.

Kremer Racing entered their 935, built in Cologne, and it raced well in the hands of Hans Heyer with Mexicans Carlos Bolanos, Billy Sprowls and Alfredo Negrete. Unfortunately it caught fire on Sunday afternoon, and was unable to finish. Third place in Group 5 was claimed by Egon Evertz with his uprated 934, with co-drivers Hartwig Bertrams and Heinz Martin.

Porsche's customers had a near monopoly in the Group 4 division and the Gelo Racing 934 of Tim Schenken and Toine Hezemans was up to sixth place overall when the gearbox failed on Sunday, and had to be rebuilt. This delay cost the Loos team two and a half hours, but they still recovered to second place in Group 4 behind the 911 Carrera RS of Marcel Ouviere, Andre Gahinet and Jean-Yves Gadal.

Bob Wollek, Didier Pironi and Marie-Claude Beaumont had the clutch fail on their Kremer Porsche 934 and dropped back to 19th place, though still managing fourth in the Group 4 category.

The 1977 edition of Le Mans had a fine entry and promised a major battle between Porsche, with 936 and 935 teams in strength, and Renault Alpine with a trio of A442s. Martini Porsche's two 936s were driven by Jacky Ickx and Henri Pescarolo, and Hurley Haywood with Juergen Barth, but the lead car was an early retirement on Saturday evening with a broken connecting rod.

1978: Rolf Stommelen, Manfred Schurti

Winner Group 5 1978: Jim Busby, Rick Knoop, Chris Cord

1978: Claude Haldi, Herbert Müller, Nik Mac Granger

911 FORMS FABRIC OF LE MANS 299

Die 1977er-Auflage von Le Mans beeindruckte durch eine hochkarätige Nennungsliste. Sie versprach packende Kämpfe zwischen starken 936 und 935-Teams und einem Trio von Renault Alpine A442. Die beiden 936 Martini wurden von Jacky Ickx und Henri Pescarolo sowie Hurley Haywood und Jürgen Barth gefahren. Der führende Wagen von Ickx und Pescarolo fiel jedoch am Samstagabend mit Motorschaden aus. Ickx wechselte ins Schwesterauto zu Haywood und Barth, die ihrerseits durch einen Wechsel der Benzinpumpe früh 30 Minuten verloren hatten. Im Kampf um den Anschluss an die Renaults fuhr Ickx vor allem in der Nacht ein grandioses Rennen, wenn nicht sogar das Rennen seines Lebens.

Von den Alpines erlitt eine nach der anderen einen Kolbenschaden. So lagen Haywood, Barth und Ickx gegen 15 Uhr mit 17 Runden Vorsprung vor dem mit einem Renault-Motor angetriebenen Mirage von Vern Schuppan und Jean-Pierre Jarier an der Spitze. Und diesen Vorsprung hatten sie auch bitter nötig, denn Haywood steuerte, in eine riesige Rauchwolke gehüllt, die Box an. Kolbenschaden war auch die Diagnose. Die Mechaniker entfernten eine Zündkerze, um den defekten Kolben stillzulegen und schickten Barth für drei langsame Runden zurück auf die Strecke und siegreich über die Ziellinie. Dieser dramatische vierte Porsche-Sieg in Le Mans sollte in die Geschichte eingehen.

Auch die vielen 935 waren nicht immun gegen technische Probleme. Der Gelo-Porsche von Tim Schenken und Toine Hezemans musste früh mit Motorschaden aufgegeben werden, schnell gefolgt vom Ausfall des Kremer 935 mit John Fitz-patrick, Guy Edwards und Nick Faure. Der Martini 935 von Rolf Stommelen und Manfred Schurti hatte eine defekte Zylinderkopfdichtung und fiel frühzeitig aus. Somit war der zweite 935 aus dem Team von Georg Loos der engste Verfolger für die Autos der Gruppe sechs. Doch Hans Heyer, Klaus Ludwig und Toine Hezemans blieben mit einer defekten Einspritzpumpe auf der Strecke liegen. Der Sieg ging an ihre stolzen Verfolger Claude Ballot-Lena und Peter Gregg im JMS 935. Ein gutes Rennen hatte hingegen Bob Wollek im Kremer 934, mit dem er zusammen mit Philippe Gurdijian und „Steve" (J.P. Wielmans) auf Gesamtrang sieben kam und seine Klasse gewann.

Die langen Vollgaspassagen, die ebenso Le Mans-typisch wie weltweit einmalig sind, wurden als Ursache für die Flut von Kolbenschäden angesehen. Also verbrachten beide – Porsche und Renault – die nächsten Monate mit einer entsprechenden Weiterentwicklung ihrer Motoren. Beide Werke stellten sehr starke Teams für das Jahr 1978 zusammen. Porsche führte für den 936 wassergekühlte Vierventil-Zylinderköpfe ein. Und der futuristisch anmutende 935-78, besser als „Moby Dick" bekannt, startete 1978 in der Gruppe fünf.

Dank noch leistungsstärkerer Motoren konnte Ickx 1978 die Pole Position vor dem Renault-Team ergattern. Und die Franzosen nahmen die neue Herausforderung an: Jabouille holte sich nicht nur die Führung schon in der Startrunde, als er aus dieser zurückkam, hatte er bereits elf Sekunden Vorsprung herausgefahren. Er war schon außer Sicht durch die Dunlop-Kurve enteilt, als die Verfolger erst die Ford-Schikane erreichten. Ickx geriet früh in Schwierigkeiten und steuerte am Ende seiner zweiten Runde die Box an, um das Benzindruck-Ventil neu einstellen zu lassen. Wieder einmal hatte er die Aufgabe, einen Rückstand aufzuholen. Doch am Samstagabend brach im Getriebe das Ritzel des fünften Gangs. Das gleiche Problem ereilte am Sonntagmorgen auch den 936 von Haywood, Gregg und Joest.

So war es diesmal für Renault an der Zeit zu siegen. Ickx, Wollek und Barth mussten sich mit dem zweiten Platz begnügen, gefolgt von Haywood, Gregg und Joest. Auch der 935 Moby Dick konnte die Erwartungen nicht erfüllen. Von Fehlzündungen geplagt sahen Rolf Stommelen und Manfred Schurti nur als Gesamtachte die Zielflagge. Die IMSA-Kategorie entschieden Dick Barbour, John Paul und Brian Redman für sich. Im Gesamtergebnis belegte das Trio Platz fünf. Gesamtrang sechs und den Sieg in der Gruppe fünf verbuchten die Amerikaner Jim Busby, Rick Knoop und Chris Cord im Kremer 935. Und in der Gruppe vier siegte der 911 Carrera RSR von Anny-Charlotte Verney, Xavier Lapeyre, Francois Servanin und Hubert Streibig.

1979 sah sich Porsche auf dem Höhepunkt des Langstreckensports. Der Kremer 935 K3 war eine hoch modifizierte Rennmaschine. Klaus Ludwig und die amerikanischen Brüder Bill und Don Whittington gewannen auf Anhieb die 24 Stunden. In diesem Jahr waren in Le Mans keine

1979: Bob Akin, Rob McFarlin, Roy Woods

Winner IMSA GTX 1979: Dick Barbour, Paul Newman, Rolf Stommelen

Winner 1979: Klaus Ludwig, Bill and Don Whittington

Poster

1979: Axel Plankenhorn, Philippe Gurdjian, John Winter

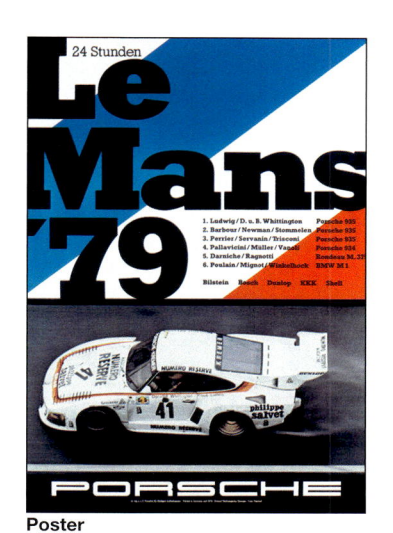

1980: Dick Lovett, John Cooper, Dudley Wood

Ickx then moved across to join Haywood and Barth, whose car had an early delay to change the fuel injection pump, and the Belgian then drove an epic race through the night to get on terms with the French Renaults.

Nor were the 935s immune, as the Gelo Porsche of Tim Schenken and Toine Hezemans was an early retirement with a blown engine, soon followed into retirement by the Kremer Racing 935 of John Fitzpatrick/Guy Edwards/Nick Faure.

Rolf Stommelen and Manfred Schurti, front runners in the Martini Porsche 935 with special bodywork for straight-line speed, had their turbocharged engine succumb to cylinder head gasket failure. Georg Loos' remaining 935 was the nearest challenger to the Group 6 cars, driven by Hans Heyer/Klaus Ludwig/Toine Hezemans, chased by the JMS Racing Team's 935 in the hands of Claude Ballot-Lena and Peter Gregg.

One by one the Renaults suffered piston failure, leaving Haywood, Barth and Ickx with a 17 lap lead over the Renault powered Mirage of Vern Schuppan and Jean-Pierre Jarier. They needed that margin, too, because on Sunday afternoon the Porsche also arrived at the pits in a huge cloud of smoke, denoting a collapsed piston. The pit crew removed a spark plug and sent Barth out to complete three slow laps to take the flag and claim a quite historic victory, Porsche's fourth at Le Mans.

The Loos 935 fell by the wayside with a broken injection pump, so third place overall was proudly claimed by the JMS Porsche 935 of Ballot-Lena and Gregg. Bob Wollek had a better run in the Kremer Racing Porsche 934, finishing seventh overall and class winner with co-drivers Philippe Gurdijian and "Steve" (J.P. Wielmans).

1980: Ted Field, Danny Ongais, Jean-Louis Lafosse (41),
Rolf Stommelen, Tetsu Ikusawa, Axel Plankenhorn (42),
Xavier Lapeyre, Anny Charlotte Verney, Jean-Louis Trintignant (43)

Long periods of full throttle motoring, unique at Le Mans, was held to be the reason for the spate of piston failures, and both Porsche and Renault spent the next few months developing their engines. Both factories mounted very strong teams in 1978, Porsche introducing the water-cooled, four-valve cylinder heads for the 936s and the futuristic 935-78, 'Moby Dick'.

The engines were more powerful and Ickx snatched pole position from the Renault team, a challenge that the French could not ignore. Jabouille not only led the opening lap, but pulled out a margin of 11 seconds, going out of sight through the Dunlop Curve before the pursuers reached the Ford chicane!

Ickx was already in trouble with a slow throttle return and stopped at the end of his second lap to have the fuel pressure valve regulated, so once again he had a big catch-up job to do. During Saturday evening, unfortunately, his 936 broke its fifth gear pinion a weak link, and the same thing happened to the Haywood/Gregg/Joest 936 on Sunday morning.

This time it was Renault's turn for victory, and afterwards the French company devoted its attention to Formula One, introducing the turbocharging technology to the formula dominated by the Ford Cosworth DFV. Ickx, Wollek and Barth finished second, Haywood, Gregg and Joest were third, then in fifth place Dick Barbour's Porsche 935 won the IMSA category, Barbour sharing his car with John Paul and Brian Redman.

'Moby Dick' did not live up to expectations, plagued by a misfiring engine, and finished eighth overall driven by Rolf Stommelen and Manfred Schurti.

The Group 5 honours fell to the Kremer Porsche 935 crewed by Americans Jim Busby, Rick Knoop and Chris Cord, sixth overall, and Group 4 went to the 911 Carrera RSR of Anny-Charlotte Verney, Xavier Lapeyre, Francois Servanin and Hubert Streibig.

One year later, 1979, Porsche's 935 reached the pinnacle of endurance racing when the Kremer Racing K3, a highly modified version inspired by Moby Dick, won the 24-Hours outright in the hands of Klaus Ludwig and the American brothers, Bill and Don Whittington.

There were no Renaults to set the pace and the two 'works' 936s, now sponsored by Essex Petroleum, were right out of luck with tyre problems and other difficulties which put them out of the race.

A thunderstorm on Saturday evening turned the race around in favour of the 935s and by nightfall the event was headed by a quartet of Group 5 cars. Two of them were from the

Renaults am Start, die das Tempo in die Höhe trieben. Die Franzosen widmeten nach ihrem Erfolg vom Vorjahr ihre Aufmerksamkeit der Formel 1. In die vom Cosworth DFV-Motor dominierte Serie führten sie die Turbo-Technik ein.

Doch zurück an die Sarthe, die beiden von Essex Petroleum gesponserten 936 litten unter Reifenschäden. Weitere Probleme führten schließlich zum Ausfall. Ein Gewittersturm am Abend wendete das Blatt zu Gunsten der 935. So führte ein Quartett von Gruppe fünf-Fahrzeugen das Feld in die Nacht. Zwei von ihnen kamen aus dem Gelo-Team: Hans Heyer, Manfred Schurti und John Fitzpatrick, Harald Grohs, Jean-Louis Lafosse kämpften mit dem Kremer 935. Auch der IMSA-935 von Dick Barbour, Rolf Stommelen und dem Schauspieler Paul Newman wollte noch ein Wörtchen mitreden. Die Morgendämmerung zog nur zögerlich auf, während der Stern der Gelo Racing-Porsche sank. Die Fahrer hatten die Anweisung, den Ladedruck zu erhöhen, um den Vorsprung auf Kremer zu vergrößern. Doch beide mussten mit Motorschaden aufgeben.

Somit verfügte der Kremer K3 über einen luxuriösen Vorsprung von zwölf Runden. Dieser löste sich jedoch auf, als unter Volllast auf der Mulsanne-Geraden der Zahnriemen der Einspritzpumpe riss. Don Whittington montierte den Ersatzriemen, doch auch dieser riss sofort. Don Whittington hatte die rettende Idee, den Ersatzriemen der Lichtmaschine einzusetzen und konnte so an die Box zurückkehren. Der 935 von Barbour stand mit einer verklemmten Radmutter ebenfalls länger beim Service. So war der Status quo wiederhergestellt und der Kremer K3 feierte einen verdienten Sieg mit sieben Runden Vorsprung vor dem Barbour 935. Rang drei ging an den zweiten Kremer 935 der Franzosen Laurent Ferrier, Francois Servanin und Francois Trisconi. Die Porsche-Dominanz setzten Herbert Müller, Angelo Pallavicini und Marco Vanoli mit Rang vier fort. Mit ihrem Lubrifilm 934 entschieden sie auch die Gruppe vier für sich.

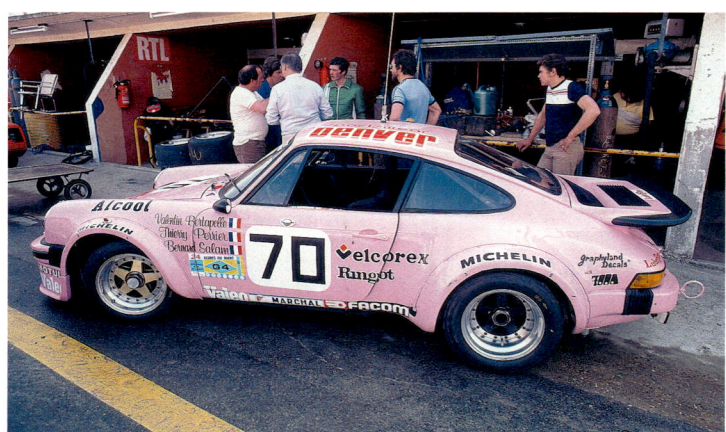

Winner IMSA GTX 1980: John Fitzpatrick, Dick Barbour, Brian Redman

Winner Group 4 1981: Thierry Perrier, Valentin Bertapelle, Bernard Salam

1981: Mauricio de Narvaez, Kemper Miller, Günther Steckkönig

Die Weiterentwicklung des 935 wurde 1978 eingestellt, die des 936 im Jahr 1979 nach dem enttäuschenden Abschneiden in Le Mans. Denn für 1980 ordnete Dr. Fuhrmann einen Taktikwechsel an: Mit verringertem Aufwand sollten drei 924 Carrera GT eingesetzt werden, um dem Interesse an dem Vierzylinder Auftrieb zu geben. Selbst intern war diese Entscheidung umstritten, doch Norbert Singer nahm die Herausforderung an, den 924 in einen Langstrecken-Rennwagen zu verwandeln. Über den von Volkswagen stammenden Motor sagte Helmuth Bott später: „Wenn ich eine Schwarzwälder-Kirschtorte backen wollte, würde ich nicht mit einem Eimer Sand anfangen!" Zwei der 924 Carrera GT schleppten sich mit verbrannten Ventilen ins Ziel. Barth und Schurti entgingen diesem Schicksal und sahen als Gesamtsechste das schwarz-weiß karierte Tuch.

Am Martini 936 von Reinhold Joest und Jacky Ickx musste am Sonntagmorgen das Zahnradpaar des fünften Gangs erneuert werden. Dennoch kam das Duo auf dem zweiten Platz ins Ziel. Dick Barbour trat zum dritten Mal in Le Mans an. Nach einem fünften und einem zweiten Platz kam der Amerikaner 1980 mit seinen Teamkollegen Brian Redman und John Fitzpatrick wieder auf Rang fünf. Was für den 935 gleichzeitig der Sieg in der IMSA GTX-Klasse war. Harald Grohs, Dieter Schornstein und Götz von Tschirnhaus fuhren ihren 935 auf den achten Gesamtrang und siegten in der Gruppe fünf. Ein ungewöhnliches Fahrzeug startete in der Klasse vier: Ein 911SC, dessen Sechszylinder mit einem Kraftstoffgemisch aus Alkohol und Benzin angetrieben wurde, führte auf Einladung des A.C.O. einen Testlauf durch. Thierry Perrier und Roger Carmillet absolvierten

Gelo stable for Hans Heyer/Manfred Schurti and John Fitzpatrick/Harald Grohs/Jean-Louis Lafosse, battling with the Kremer Porsche 935 and the IMSA class 935 of Dick Barbour, actor Paul Newman and Rolf Stommelen.

Dawn broke grudgingly, and then both the Gelo Racing Porsches retired with blown engines, the drivers instructed to increase the boost pressure to get away from the Kremer 935 K3. The Kremer car now had the luxury of a 12 lap lead, but this dissolved when the fuel injection system drive belt broke while Don Whittington was going at full speed on the Mulsanne Straight.

He fitted the spare belt but that broke, and finally he used his engineering skills to make the spare alternator belt do the job well enough to get the car back to the pits. Barbour's 935 was delayed, too, by a jammed wheel nut, so the status quo was maintained.

The Kremer Porsche claimed a thoroughly deserved victory seven laps ahead of the Barbour Porsche, and in third place was Kremer's second 935 driven by Frenchmen Laurent Ferrier, Francois Servanin and Francois Trisconi. Continuing Porsche's domination, fourth position was taken by the Lubrifilm Racing 934 of Herbert Muller, Angelo Pallavicini and Marco Vanoli, winners of the Group 4 category.

Development of the 935 model ceased in 1978 with 'Moby Dick', and of the 936 in 1979 after the disappointing appearance at Le Mans. Dr Fuhrmann ordered a switch of tactics for Le Mans in 1980, putting limited effort into a low-key entry of three 924 Carrera GTs, in order to boost interest in the four-cylinder line.

His decision was controversial even within the company, but Ing. Norbert Singer took on the task of turning the 924 into an endurance racing car. Of the Volkswagen derived engine, Professor Helmuth Bott later commented: "If I was to make a Black Forest gateau, I would not start with a bucket of sand!" Two of the 924 Carrera GTs limped home with burned valves, while that of Juergen Barth and Manfred Schurti avoided the same fate and crossed the line in sixth position overall.

Reinhold Joest and Jacky Ickx were able to claim second place in a 936 entered by Martini Racing, after having their fifth gear restored on Sunday morning, and for the third year running Dick Barbour was able to get a high placing with his 935 and win the IMSA GTX category. In 1980 the big man finished in fifth place, with Brian Redman and John Fitzpatrick sharing the driving. Fifth, second, and fifth again was a superb record for the American.

Harald Grohs, Dieter Schornstein and Goetz von Tschirnhaus drove their 935 to eighth place, winners of Group 5, and Thierry Perrier and Roger Carmillet won Group 4 in a 911 SC, in 16th position, an unusual entry in having a mixture of benzine and alcohol fuelling the flat-six.

Peter W. Schutz, the brash American, was appointed chief executive at Porsche on the first day of January, 1981, and he soon overturned some of Dr (lately Professor) Fuhrmann's decisions. The 911 line was to be extended into infinity, with heavy investment in its development, and as an adjunct the 936 was to be resurrected for another attempt to win Le Mans.

Professor Bott was a willing accomplice in all this, switching Ing. Singer to the 936 programme, and his first decision was to mate the old Can-Am box to the 936 engine, which was now based on the stillborn Indy project and uprated to 2.7 litres. The old Can-Am box might have been heavy, but it would never break!

Jacky Ickx and Derek Bell had a Le Mans to dream about in their 'Jules' sponsored 936, losing not a moment in the pits and winning handsomely, Porsche's sixth big success at Le Mans. Behind the two Rondeaus that filled out the podium positions came the Charles Ivey prepared 935 K3 of Claude Bourgoignie, Dudley Wood and John Cooper, winners of the Group 5 category, and sixth was the Cooke Woods Racing 935 K3 of Ralph Cooke, Bob Garretson and Anny-Charlotte Verney.

New Group C regulations came into force in 1982, heralding the debut of the Porsche 956 which was almost unbeatable over a five-year period, winning the 24-Hours of Le Mans each and every year between 1982 and 1987. In the first year, factory entered Rothmans-Porsche 956s filled the entire podium, first, second and third overall, and in fourth and fifth positions overall were two 935s entered in the IMSA GTX class.

1981: Dieter Schornstein, Harald Grohs, Götz von Tschirnhaus

diesen Test mit Bravour, dem Gewinn der Klasse und Gesamtrang 16.

Am ersten Januar 1981 wurde der Amerikaner Peter W. Schutz neuer Vorstandsvorsitzender. Schon bald kippte er einige von Dr. Fuhrmann getroffene Entscheidungen. Die 911-Serie wurde nahezu grenzenlos ausgeweitet, so stammte die Entscheidung, ein 911 Cabrio auf den Markt zu bringen, auch von Schutz. Für den Versuch, noch einmal in Le Mans zu gewinnen, wurde der 936 wiederbelebt. In Professor Bott fand sich ein Gesinnungsgenosse, der Norbert Singer mit in die 936-Mannschaft holte. Die erste Entscheidung war, den guten, alten Can-Am Motor in den 936 einzupflanzen. Das Alkohol-Triebwerk wurde zu einem 2,7 Liter starken Benzinmotor umgebaut. Der alte Can-Am Motor mag schwer gewesen sein, doch war er auch enorm standfest.

Jacky Ickx und Derek Bell fuhren in ihrem von Jules gesponserten 936 ein traumhaftes Rennen. Sie verbrachten nicht einen Augenblick länger als unbedingt nötig an der Box und feierten mit Leichtigkeit Porsches sechsten großen Erfolg in Le Mans. Hinter den beiden Rondeaus, die das Podium komplettierten, kam der von Charles Ivey vorbereitete 935 K3 ins Ziel. Für Claude Bourgoignie, Dudley Wood und John Cooper war dieser vierte Rang gleichzeitig der Sieg in der Gruppe fünf. Gesamtrang sechs ging an den Cooke Woods Racing 935 K3 von Ralph Cooke, Bob Garretson und Anny-Charlotte Verney.

1982 trat die neue Gruppe C die Nachfolge der Gruppe sechs an. Mit ihr kündigte sich auch das Debüt des 956 an, der für mehr als fünf Jahre nahezu unschlagbar sein sollte. Von 1982 bis 1987 gewannen diese Prototypen jede der 24 Stunden von Le Mans. Im ersten Jahr füllten die Werks-Rothmans-956 gar das ganze Podium. Als Abrundung des Erfolgs kamen auf den Gesamträngen vier und fünf zwei 935 aus der IMSA GTX Klasse ins Ziel. Hierbei lag John Fitzpatrick, der nun sein eigenes Team hatte, mit David Hobbs vor dem BP Cooke-Team um Danny Snobeck, René Metge und Francois Servanin.

1982: Anny Charlotte Verney, Bob Garretson, Ray Ratcliff

1983: Claude Haldi, Günther Steckkönig, Bernd Schiller

1984: Claude Haldi, Altfrid Heger, Jean Krucker

Wieder einmal hatte Charles Ivey das Siegerauto der Gruppe fünf vorbereitet. Für den 935 K3 von Claude Bourgoignie, John Cooper und Paul Smith war es zudem der achte Platz im Gesamtklassement. Mit dem, was sie selbst als den mit 600 PS wohl kraftvollsten 934 bezeichneten, der jemals gebaut wurde, siegten Richard Cleare, Tony Dron und Richard Jones in der Gruppe vier.

1983 ging die Reise des so außergewöhnlichen 935 zu Ende, zumindest bei FIA-Veranstaltungen. Der Automobile Club de l'Ouest ließ nur noch Fahrzeuge der Gruppen B und C zum Start an der Sarthe zu. So wurden die Turbo-Porsche als 930 genannt, was ihren Zeichnungsnummern entsprach. Zudem waren sie näher an der Serienversion als zuvor. In diesem Jahr feierte das Rothmans-Werks-Team einen Doppelsieg. Neun der Top-Ten-Platzierungen gingen an 956-Modelle. Auf Rang elf kam der Gruppe B-930 Turbo von John Cooper, Paul Smith und David Ovey heim. Teamchef Charles Ivey hatte damit den dritten Klassensieg in Folge errungen. Zwei Plätze dahinter nahm der 930 Turbo von Georg Memminger, Fritz Müller und Heinz Kuhn-Weiss die Zielflagge entgegen.

Für das Jahr 1984 hatte die FIA die bereits beschlossenen Vorschriften zur Verbrauchssenkung ausgesetzt. Technische Änderungen, in die Porsche und Lancia viel Geld gesteckt hatten, waren somit unnütz. Aus Protest zog das Porsche-Werksteam, mit Zustimmung des Sponsors Rothmans, seine Nennung zurück. Dennoch sah die Geschichte ähnlich wie im Vorjahr aus, nur das jetzt privat eingesetzte 956 das Geschehen dominierten. Klaus Ludwig und Henri Pescarolo im NewMan-Joest 956 entschieden das Rennen für sich. Auf Gesamtrang 16 musste sich der 930 Turbo von Claude Haldi, Altfrid Heger und Jean Krucker in der Gruppe B nur einem BMW M1 beugen. Einen Platz dahinter und als Sieger der IMSA GTO-Klasse kamen Raymond Touroul, Thierry Perrier und Valentin Bertapelle mit ihrem 911SC ins Ziel.

1985 überstand nur ein Gruppe B-Fahrzeug die 24-Stunden, ein BMW M1. Der einzige Porsche 911 SC, eingesetzt von Raymond Touroul, fiel in der Nacht mit einem Defekt an der Zylinderkopfdichtung aus.

John Fitzpatrick, who had now formed his own team, drove to fourth place with David Hobbs, and behind them was the BP Cooke team's 935 K3, also in the IMSA class, driven by Danny Snobeck, Rene Metge and Francois Servanin.

Charles Ivey again prepared the Group 5 winner, the 935 K3 of Claude Bourgoignie, John Cooper and Paul Smith, who were classified eighth, and another British based team, that of Richard Cleare, won Group 4 with what they claimed was the most powerful 934 ever built, with 600 horse-power. Cleare drove this car with Tony Dron and Richard Jones.

That was the end of the road for the fabulous Porsche 935 in FIA racing. The Automobile Club de l'Ouest accepted cars only from Groups B and C for Le Mans in 1983 so the Porsche Turbos were listed as 930, their drawing board numbers, and they were much closer to standard condition.

Porsche 956 models claimed nine of the top 10 positions at Le Mans in 1983, a 1-2 for the factory's Rothmans team, and in 11th position was the Group B Porsche 930 Turbo entered by Charles Ivey, class winner for the third year in succession, the 3.3 litre car driven by John Cooper, Paul Smith and David Ovey. Two places back was Georg Memminger's 3-litre Porsche 930 Turbo co-driven by Fritz Muller and Heinz Kuhn-Weiss.

It was a similar story in 1984, the year that Rothmans-Porsche withdrew their factory team in protest against the FIA's decision to delay the reduction in fuel consumption, a technical change for which Porsche and Lancia had prepared for at great expense. Even so, privately entered 956s dominated the 24-Hours with Reinhold Joest's New Man sponsored car taking victory.

Way back in 16th position, Claude Haldi, Altfrid Heger and Jean Krucker were second to a BMW M1 in the Group B category, driving a 930 Turbo, and in 17th place was the IMSA GTO class winner, the 911 SC of Raymond Touroul, Thierry Perrier and Valentin Bertapelle.

There was only one Group B finisher at Le Mans in 1985, a BMW M1, and the sole Porsche, a 911 SC entered by Raymond Touroul, retired on Saturday night with a broken cylinder head gasket.

1982: Danny Snobeck, Francois Servanin, Rene Metge

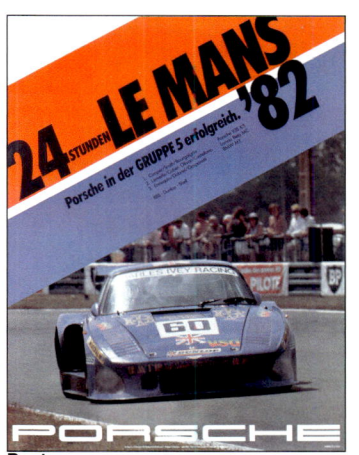

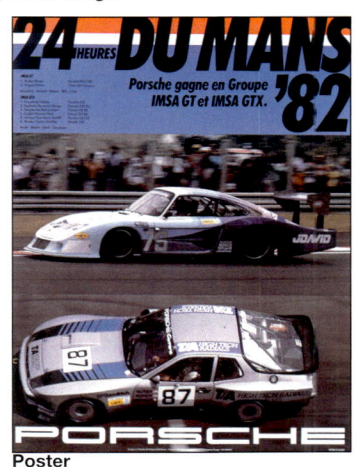

Poster

Poster

1983: Georg Memminger, Fritz Müller, Heinz Kuhn-Weiss

Winner IMSA GTO 1982: Raymond Touroul, Valentin Bertapelle, Thierry Perrier

911 FORMS FABRIC OF LE MANS

Im Januar 1986 hatte die Allrad-Version des 959 die Rallye Paris-Dakar gewonnen. Zur gleichen Zeit rauchten in Weissach die Köpfe über der Arbeit am 961, einer Gruppe B-Rundstrecken-Version. Norbert Singer war - als übergeordnetem Ingenieur - die Mitarbeit an diesem Projekt abgelehnt worden. Doch Singer war von Derek Bell, der 1969 den allradgetrieben McLaren MP9A-Formel Eins gefahren war, stark beeinflusst. Und Bell drängte Porsche, diese Entwicklung nicht weiterzuführen. „Ich sagte Professor Bott, was Derek Bell mir gesagt hatte, nämlich dass es nie funktionieren würde, aber er schaute mich nur finster an und sagte: Ich denke, Sie passen nicht zu diesem Projekt", erinnert sich Singer. „Ich entgegnete, das ist schade. Tatsächlich jedoch war ich sogar recht froh darüber. Schließlich gaben sie die Aufgabe an Roland Kussmaul."

Nach Singers Meinung war die Rennversion des 961 von Anfang an zum Scheitern verurteilt. „Ich saß in meinem Büro, als sie ihn aus der Halle schoben. Und ich dachte, dass er höher ist, als das Paris-Dakar Auto. Rolf Huber nahm ein Maßband und später machten wir Fotos. Es stellte sich heraus, dass er tatsächlich nur ein wenig niedriger war, als das Paris-Dakar Auto. Höher jedoch als ein Straßenauto."

Ein junger Ingenieur hatte entschieden, dass der Fahrzeugunterboden einen Anpressdruck erzeugen sollte. Allerdings nicht in dem Maße wie beim „Moby Dick", der sich regelrecht an den Boden saugte. Das Ergebnis war ein Wagen, der höher stand als das Serienauto und nicht niedriger, wie es wünschenswert gewesen wäre. Und somit auch einen extrem hohen Schwerpunkt hatte.

Von der Papierform her war der 961 ein gutes Auto, obwohl es trotz Leichtbauweise 1.180 Kilogramm auf die Waage brachte. Das komplexe Allradsystem sollte Vorteile im Regen bringen. Der wassergekühlte 2,85 Liter Sechszylinder Bi-Turbo Motor leistete 650 PS.

Winner IMSA GTX 1986: Rene Metge, Claude Ballot-Lena

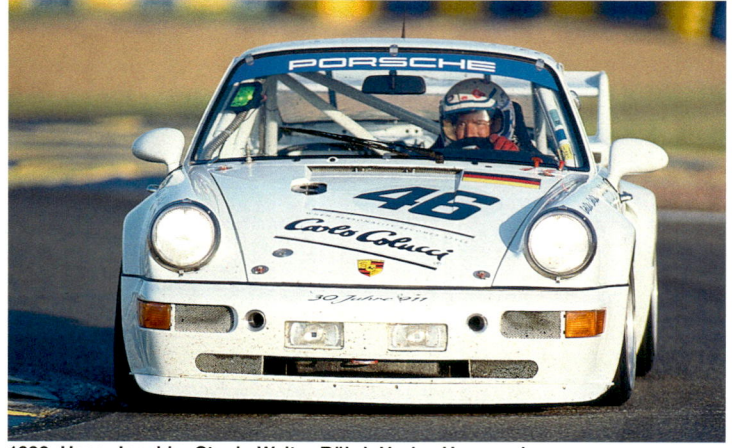

1993: Hans-Joachim Stuck, Walter Röhrl, Hurley Haywood

1987: Rene Metge, Claude Haldi, Kees Nierop

Ein ganz in weiß gehaltener Wagen wurde 1986 in Le Mans in der IMSA GTX-Klasse genannt. Pilotiert wurde der 961 von Paris-Dakar-Sieger René Metge und Claude Ballot-Lena. „Hat er eine Chance", wollte Kussmaul wissen. „Nur wenn es schneit", bekam er als Antwort. Natürlich schneite es in der Nacht vom 31. Mai zum 1. Juni in Frankreich nicht. Dennoch kam die französische Mannschaft bis auf zwei außerplanmäßige Boxenstops gut durch die 24 Stunden und auf den siebten Gesamtrang. In ihrer Klasse siegten sie.

Vermutlich glaubte Professor Bott, der 961 hätte schon genug erreicht, um das Interesse von Kunden zu wecken. Die Entscheidung jedoch, den Wagen bei den 250 Meilen in Daytona einzusetzen, war ein Fehler. Die Kombination des engen Innenfelds der Strecke mit den unter Höchstgeschwindigkeit gefahrenen Überhöhungen stellte hohe Anforderungen an die Dunlop-Reifen. Zu hohe sogar, denn die Reifen neigten zum Platzen, wenn der Wagen mit Höchstgeschwindigkeit durchs Oval gefahren wurde. Günther Steckkönig und Kees Nierop fuhren so, dass die Reifen 45 Minuten hielten und beendeten das Rennen auf Platz 24. Sie beeindruckten niemanden, mit Ausnahme der Fotografen.

Der dritte und letzte Auftritt des 961 in einem Wettbewerb war in Le Mans im Juni 1987. Nun in Rothmans-Farben lackiert wurde er von Metge, Nierop und Claude Haldi gefahren. Diesmal hatten sie ein schwieriges Rennen und mussten am Sonntagmorgen ganz aufgeben. Das Getriebe machte Probleme und Nierop ging die Strecke aus.

Was auch immer die Vorzüge des Allrad-Antriebs unter Off-Road-Bedingungen sind, sein Beitrag zum Rundstreckensport ist umstritten.

Zwischen 1988 und 1992 waren keine auf Serienwagen basierenden Porsche in Le Mans gestartet. Doch der unvermeidbare Zusammenbruch der Sportwagen-Weltmeisterschaft am Ende der Saison 1992 hinterließ eine Lücke im Langstreckensport. Und die Hersteller, allen voran Porsche, hegten großes Interesse, diese zu füllen.

The Porsche 959 four-wheel drive model won the Paris-Dakar Raid in January 1986, when Porsche's brains at Weissach had already set to work on the 961, a Group B racing derivative. As senior engineer, Ing. Singer was given first refusal on developing the 961 but he was heavily influenced by Derek Bell, who had raced the McLaren MP9A 4-wd Formula One car in 1969 and urged Porsche not to pursue this line of development.

"I told Mr Bott what Derek Bell had told me, that it would never work, and he frowned at me and said ? I think you are not suitable for that project' " recalls Singer. "I said that was a pity, but in fact I was quite happy. They gave it to Roland Kussmaul instead."

In the opinion of Singer, the 961 race car was not right from the beginning. "I was sitting in my office when they pushed it out of the workshop, and I thought it was higher than the Paris-Dakar car! Rolf Huber got out a tape measure and we took photographs, and it was just a little bit lower than the Paris-Dakar car, but higher than a road car."

A young engineer had decided that it should have underfloor venturi, but without the benefit of being able to lower the floor, as they had with Moby Dick. The result was a machine that stood higher than the standard product, not lower as would have been desirable, with a consequent high centre of gravity.

The 961 was a good car on paper although it weighed-in at 1,180 kg despite having composite bodywork. It had a complex 4-wd system which ought to be a benefit if it rained (it did not), and a 2.85-litre, water cooled, twin-turbo flat-six developing 650 horsepower.

One car, in white, was entered in the IMSA GTX class for Paris-Dakar winner Rene Metge with Claude Ballot-Lena. "Does it stand a chance?" I asked Kussmaul. "Only if it snows" he replied. It did not snow, but the French crew had a clear run through the 24-Hours and finished up in seventh position overall, winners of the IMSA class.

Possibly Professor Bott believed that the 961 had done enough to interest customers of the racing department, but the decision to enter it in the Daytona 250 later in the year was a mistake. The combination of the twisty infield and the loadings of the high-speed banking placed high demands on the Dunlop tyres, which were prone to blow-outs if the car was driven at full speed on the bowl. Gunther Steckkonig and Kees Nierop drove to make the tyres last 45 minutes and finished 24th, impressing no-one but the photographers who waited, like vultures, for the next tyre blow-out!

The third, and final appearance of the 961 in competitions was at Le Mans in June 1987, when it was smartly dressed in Rothmans livery and driven by Metge, Nierop and Claude Haldi. This time it had a troubled race and retired on Sunday morning when the gearbox started jamming, and Nierop crashed off the track. Whatever the merits of 4-wd in off-road conditions, its contribution to circuit racing was contentious although Audi had considerable success in racing with its A4 Quattro. Was the success due to 4-wd, or did Audi simply have the best team?

No production based Porsches raced at Le Mans between 1988 and 1992, but the inevitable collapse of the World Sportscar Championship at the end of the 1992 season left a vacuum in endurance racing, and manufacturers led by Porsche were keen to fill the gap.

The 3.5 litre sports-prototypes were still welcome at Le Mans in 1993, and Peugeot and Toyota dominated the results with their V10 engined racers. Porsche prepared a 930 Turbo (the S Le Mans) for Hans Stuck, Walter Rohrl and Hurley Haywood, and after an early delay it ran well until Rohrl had an unfortunate accident with Yojiro Terada's Mazda at a chicane, and retired with a broken oil radiator.

Jack Leconte's Larbre Competition team competed for the first time at Le Mans and scooped up the Grand Touring category with a pair of FAT sponsored 911 Carrera RSRs, beautifully prepared and well driven. Dominique Dupuy, Juergen Barth and Joel Gouhier finished 15th overall, one place ahead of Leconte with Jesus Pareja and Pierre de Thoisy. Third in the GT class was the Heico Motorsports 911 Carrera RSR of Ulli Richter, Dirk Rainer Ebeling and Karl-Heinz Wlazik.

Porsche's total of outright Le Mans victories rose to 13 in June 1994 when the Dauer Porsche 962 GT narrowly beat a Group C Toyota. Larbre Competition again excelled in what was now called the GT2 category as Dupuy, Pareja and Carlos Palau drove the 911 Carrera RSR to eighth place overall, ahead of Lilian Bryner, Enzo Calderari and Renato Mastropietro in their Ecurie Biennoise 911 Carrera Cup car.

1993: Franz Konrad, Jun Harada, Antonio de Hermann

1994: Cor Euser, Patrick Huisman, Matjaz Tomle

Die 3,5 Liter Sportprototypen waren noch immer willkommen in Le Mans 1993. Peugeot und Toyota dominierten diese Klasse mit ihren V10 Boliden. Porsche hatte einen 930 Turbo (den S–Le Mans GT) für Hans-Joachim Stuck, Walter Röhrl und Hurley Haywood vorbereitet. Nach anfänglichem Zeitverlust durch einen gerissenen Gaszug lagen sie gut im Rennen, ehe Röhrl unglücklich mit dem Mazda von Yojiro Terada kollidierte. Die Folge war ein gebrochener Ölkühler, der zur Aufgabe zwang.

1993 war das Larbre Competition Team von Jack Leconte zum ersten Mal in Le Mans am Start. Auf Anhieb gelang ein Doppelsieg in der GT-Klasse mit den bildschönen, FAT-gesponserten 911 Carrera RSR. Dominique Dupuy, Jürgen Barth und Joel Gouhier wurden Fünfzehnte im Gesamt, direkt vor ihren Teamkollegen Jack Leconte, Jesus Pareja und Pierre de Thoisy. Den dritten Rang in der GT-Klasse belegten Ulli Richter, Dirk Rainer Ebeling und Karl-Heinz Wlazik im Heico Motorsports 911 Carrera RSR.

Im Juni 1994 wuchs Porsches Siegbilanz in Le Mans auf dreizehn an, als der Dauer-962 GT knapp einen Gruppe C-Toyota bezwang. Larbre Competition glänzte wieder in der nun GT2 genannten Kategorie. Gesamtplatz acht fuhren Dupuy, Pareja und Carlos Palau mit dem 911 Carrera RSR heraus. Direkt dahinter überquerte der 911 Carrera Cup von Lilian Bryner, Enzo Calderari und Renato Mastropietro die Ziellinie.

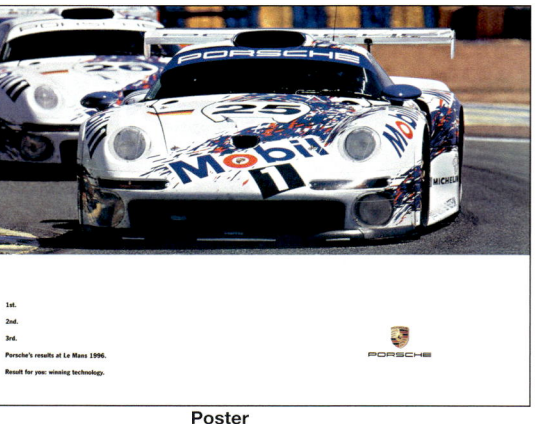

Poster

1994: Calderari, Bryner, Mastropietro

1995: Dominique Dupuy, Emmanuel Collard, Stephane Ortelli

Wenn der Dauer-962 tatsächlich ein GT-Fahrzeug war, so war er seiner Zeit um einige Jahre voraus und Alain Bertaut, der Sportdirektor des A.C.O., verschärfte die Regeln für die folgenden Rennen. Rechtzeitig für die 95er Auflage führte Porsche das turbogeladene GT2-Modell ein. Das Wetter war grausam nass und das Rennen für Porsche katastrophal. Die besten Fahrzeuge schieden noch vor Mitternacht durch Unfälle aus. Es war das Jahr des McLaren F1 GTR, der sein Debüt an der Sarthe siegreich beendete. Die GT2-Klasse gewann eine japanische Mannschaft mit einem Honda NSX. Am Ende war Peter Seikel mit Rang vier der bestplatzierte Porsche in dieser Klasse. Im Gesamt kamen er und seine Teamkollegen Guy Kuster und Karel Dolejsi auf Platz 15.

Natürlich hatte Porsche bereits eine Neuentwicklung parat: den Mittelmotor 911 GT1. Wieder einmal hatte Norbert Singer eine clevere Lösung gefunden. Man nehme die Front des Turbo- Monocoques, schweiße einen Schott hinter die Frontsitze und montiere einen neuen, wassergekühlten Bi-Turbo-Motor über der Hinterachse. Zwei Fahrzeuge wurden mit starker Unterstützung von Mobil und Michelin an den Start gebracht. Im einen nahmen Hans-Joachim Stuck, Thierry Boutsen und Bob Wollek am Volant Platz, im anderen Karl Wendlinger, Yannick Dalmas und Scott Goodyear. Die Hauptkonkurrenz, so schien es, würde von den Mc Larens sowie Reinhold Joest und dessen unabhängigem Porsche-Team kommen.

Joest setzte in der Prototypen-Klasse zwei Wagen mit TWR-Chassis ein. McLaren hingegen schien dem Geschehen ein wenig hinterherzuhinken. Am Sonntagmorgen hatte sich das Rennen zu einem offenen Kampf zwischen Joest Racing und den Werks-GT1 entwickelt. Siegreich war schließlich der dem Werk entliehene Joest-World Sports Car mit Davy Jones, Manuel Reuter und Alexander Wurz.

Beide GT1 mussten nach Besuchen im Kiesbett oder zu engem Kontakt mit hohen Kerbs unplanmäßig die Box ansteuern. Platz zwei und drei im Gesamt sowie der Doppelsieg in der GT-Klasse war ihnen aber nicht zu nehmen. Beim teaminternen Duell hatte das Trio um Wollek, Stuck und Boutsen die Nase vorn. In der GT2-Klasse debütierte die Roock Racing- Mannschaft. Ralf Kelleners, Bruno Eichmann und Guy Martinolle fuhren auf Anhieb den Klassensieg und zwölften Gesamtrang für die Brüder Michael und Fabian Roock ein. In der Klasse folgten die GT2-Schwesterautos von Parr Motorsport. Bill Farmer, Greg Murphy und Robert Nearn wurden zweite vor Stephane Ortelli, Andy Pilgrim und Andrew Bagnall.

Die 97er-Auflage des Klassikers war die einzige, die Porsche wirklich verwünschen könnte. Reinhold Joest holte mit dem schon im Vorjahr siegreichen TWR-Sportwagen die Kohlen aus dem Feuer. Für den 15. Porsche Gesamtsieg in Le Mans waren diesmal Michele Alboreto, Tom Kristensen und Stefan Johansson verantwortlich. Die Joest-Mannschaft holte somit ihren vierten Erfolg mit Porsche, davon zwei Siege mit dem gleichen 956 und zwei weitere mit dem gleichen TWR-Prototypen. Immer jedoch mit der glücklichen Startnummer sieben.

Die Evolutions-Modelle des GT1 fuhren mit raffiniert verbesserter Karosserie und waren höchst konkurrenzfähig. Doch am Sonntagmorgen schied Bob Wollek im Kampf um die Spitze unglücklich aus. Zur Mittagszeit führten Ralf Kelleners, Emmanuel Collard und Yannick Dalmas mit einer Runde vor dem Joest Porsche-Prototypen. Der Sieg war in greifbare Nähe gerückt, als Kelleners bei Höchstgeschwindigkeit auf der Mulsanne-Geraden der Ölwärmetauscher platzte. Der Unterboden des Porsche stand in Flammen als der junge Deutsche auf die Bremse trat und auf dem Seiten-

If the Dauer really was a GT car it was some years ahead of its time, and Alain Bertaut, the ACO's sporting director, tightened the rules for ensuing races. Porsche introduced the turbocharged GT2 model in time for the 1995 edition, but the weather was horribly wet and it was a disastrous race for Porsche, with all its best cars crashed out of the competition before midnight. This was the year of the McLaren F1 GTR, on its Sarthe debut, and the GT2 class was won by a Japanese crewed Honda NSX. Peter Seikel was the leading Porsche GT2 entrant at the end, his car classified fourth in category, 15th overall, driven by Seikel himself, Guy Kuster and Karel Dolejsi.

Of course, Porsche had a new development in the wings, the mid-engined 911 GT1 model. Once again Ing. Singer had

1995: Eric van de Vywer, Didier Ortion, Jean-Francois Veroux

1996: Karl Wendlinger, Yannick Dalmas, Scott Goodyear

come up with a clever solution, taking the front end of the Turbo monocoque, welding in a bulkhead behind the front seats, and installing a new water-cooled twin-turbo engine ahead of the rear wheels.

Two cars were entered for Le Mans with heavy sponsorship from Mobil and Michelin, one for Hans Stuck, Thierry Boutsen and Bob Wollek, the other for Karl Wendlinger, Yannick Dalmas and Scott Goodyear. The principal competition, it seemed, would come from the McLarens, which proved to be somewhat off the pace, and from Reinhold Joest's independent Porsche team, running two TWR chassis Porsches in the prototype category.

By Sunday morning the race had become a straight fight between Joest Racing and Porsche's factory GT1 team, and it was the factory loaned WSC that eventually won the 24-Hours in the hands of Davy Jones, Manuel Reuter and Alexander Wurz.

Both of the Porsche GT1s had made unscheduled pit stops after visits to the gravel traps or over the high kerbs, but were easily able to finish second and third overall, first and second in the GT1 category, with the class win going to Wollek, Stuck and Boutsen.

Roock Racing, run by brothers Michael and Fabian Roock, won the GT2 category with the Porsche GT2 turbo of Ralph Kelleners, Bruno Eichmann and Guy Martinolle, 12th overall, with a pair of Parr Motorsport GT2s in second and third positions. Bill Farmer, Greg Murphy and Robert Nearn were second in class, and third went to Stephane Ortelli, Andy Pilgrim and Andrew Bagnall.

Porsche could only rue the race that got away, Le Mans in 1997, although Reinhold Joest saved the day by winning outright with the same TWR WSC Porsche that had triumphed the year before. This time it was driven by Michele Alboreto, Tom Kristensen and Stefan Johansson, who clocked up the company's 15th Le Mans victory. Joest had won four times with Porsches, twice with the same 956 and twice with the same TWR prototype, always with lucky number 7 on the flanks.

Evolution versions of the Porsche GT1 raced with subtly improved bodywork, and were competitive with the best. Bob Wollek, unfortunately, crashed out of the race while duelling for the lead on Sunday morning, most likely due to a broken driveshaft which prevented him from getting back to the pits. Even so Ralf Kelleners, Emmanuel Collard and Yannick Dalmas were leading at lunch-time on Sunday with a lap in hand over the Joest Porsche prototype, and were beginning to think of the celebrations to come when a front oil cooler connection severed while Kelleners was going at full speed on

streifen zu stehen kam. Der GT1 war zu stark beschädigt, um das Rennen fortsetzen zu können.

Zwei McLaren und ein Courage-Porsche C41 liefen auf den Plätzen zwei, drei und vier ein. Die McLarens errangen damit einen Doppelsieg in der GT1-Klasse. Den dritten Rang in dieser Kategorie sicherten sich Pedro Lamy, Patrice Goueslard und Armin Hahne im Schübel Engineering-Porsche GT1. Im Gesamt wurden sie fünfte. Auf dem neunten Gesamtrang kamen die Klassensieger der GT2 ins Ziel, der schweizerische Elf Haberthur-Porsche mit Michel Neugarten, Jean-Claude Lagniez und Guy Martinolle.

Zugegebenermaßen verlief die Saison 1998 miserabel für Porsche. In der FIA GT-Meisterschaft wurden sie von Mercedes geschlagen. Doch es gab auch einen Lichtblick in jenem Jahr, ein brillantes Wochenende, das einige Enttäuschungen wiedergutmachte. Und das war der große Erfolg in Le Mans. Er fiel zusammen mit den Feierlichkeiten zu Porsches 50-jährigem Bestehen. Der vom Rennen gezeichnete 911 GT1-98 stand im Mittelpunkt des Interesses, als er am Montag danach nach Stuttgart zurückkam.

Allan McNish, Stephane Ortelli und Laurent Aiello hatten über eine mächtige Konkurrenz triumphiert. Da waren Werksmannschaften von AMG Mercedes, BMW, Toyota und Nissan – und nicht zu vergessen die beiden TWR-Porsche. Diese wurden zwar von Joest eingesetzt, waren aber vom Werk genannt worden. Vor dem Rennen konnte niemand einen Sieger vorhersagen, es hätte jeder der fünf Hersteller sein können.

Die Mercedes hatten nur einen kurzen Auftritt, einem defekten Servopumpenantrieb fielen beide Autos zum Opfer. Auch BMW erging es nicht besser. In den ersten vier Rennstunden mussten beide mit gebrochenen vorderen Radlagern aufgeben. Das Rennen war noch jung und vier deutsche Top-Autos schon nicht mehr mit von der Partie. Die TWR-Nissans konnten das Tempo an der Spitze nicht ganz mitgehen, der Toyota GT-One hingegen lag am Samstagabend in Führung. Doch dann kostete Thierry Boutsen, Ralf Kelleners und Geoff Lees ein Getriebewechsel 15 Minuten.

Um Mitternacht führten die beiden 911 GT1-98 mit zwei Runden vor dem Nissan R390 von John Nielsen. Der Vorsprung auf Boutsens Toyota betrug vier Runden, doch dieser konnte bis zum Sonntagmorgen wieder an die Spitze vorfahren. Die Morgendämmerung brachte nichts Gutes für Porsche: Joests besser platzierter TWR-Porsche-WSC wurde bei einem Dreher beschädigt, Jörg Müller setzte seinen GT1-98 auf einem hohen Kerb auf und beschädigte den Unterboden. McNish schließlich berichtete von einem überhitzenden Motor. Dreißig Minuten dauerte die Reparatur, was Boutsen reichte, die Führung zurückzuerobern. Doch kurz darauf zwang ein zweiter Getriebewechsel den Toyota für zehn Minuten an die Box.

Die 18-Stunden-Marke war gerade um eine Minute überschritten, als McNish wieder vorn lag. Genau in diesem Moment kam auch Boutsen ins Rennen zurück. Nur 24 Sekunden betrug sein Rückstand, und der Toyota fuhr etwas schnellere Rundenzeiten. Als an McNishs Wagen dann die Bremsbeläge gewechselt werden mussten, fiel die Mannschaft eine Runde zurück. Und nur eine Runde hinter ihnen lagen Jörg Müller, Bob Wollek und Uwe Alzen.

90 Minuten waren noch zu fahren, als Ortelli, jetzt 44 Sekunden hinter dem führenden Toyota, für den letzten Turn an McNish übergab. Ein Fotofinishs gab es nicht, denn Boutsens Wagen blieb in der Arnage-Kurve stehen. Wieder einmal war das Getriebe kollabiert und diesmal führte auch kein Weg an die Box zurück. Beide 911 GT1 gelang schließlich ein Doppelsieg.

Eine bunte Mischung von Nissans, McLarens und Panoz schaffte es in der GT2-Klasse ins Ziel. Der Sieg ging jedoch an die Oreca-Chrysler Viper von Justin Bell, David Donohue und Luca Drudi vor einer weiteren Viper mit Olivier Beretta, Tommy Archer und Pedro Lamy am Steuer. Bestes Porsche-Team wurde Roock Racing mit Claudia Hürtgen, Michel Ligonnet und Robert Nearn. In der GT2 wurden sie dritte hinter den amerikanischen Boliden, im Gesamtklassement kam das Trio auf Rang 17.

Winner 1998: Allan McNish, Stephane Ortelli, Laurent Aiello

1996: Stephane Ortelli, Andy Pilgrim, Andrew Bagnall

Winner LM GT2 1997: Michel Neugarten, Jean-Claude Lagniez, Guy Martinolle

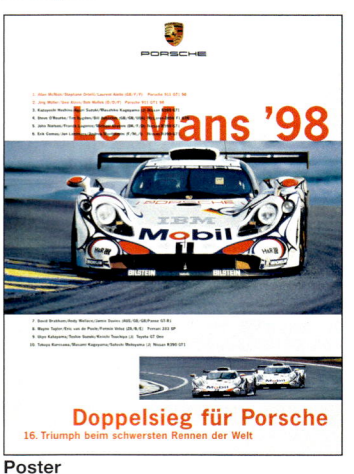

Poster

1998: Michel Nourry, Thierry Perrier, Jean-Louis Ricci

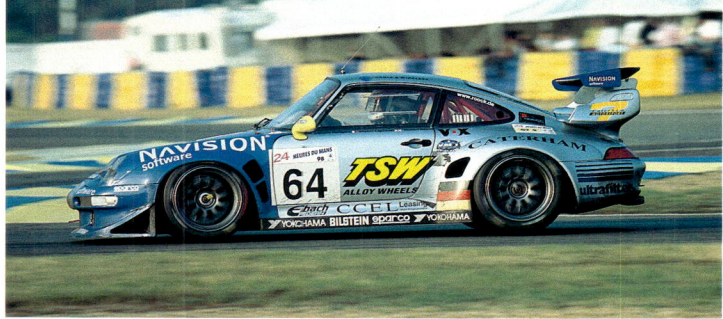

1998: Claudia Hürtgen, Michel Liconnet, Robert Nearn

the Mulsanne Straight. The underside of the Porsche was ablaze as the young German stamped on the brakes and headed for the side of the road, and the car was much too badly damaged to continue.

Two McLarens and a Courage Porsche C41 claimed second, third and fourth positions, the McLarens first and second in GT1, with third in GT1 going to the Schubel Engineering Porsche GT1 driven by Pedro Lamy, Patrice Goueslard and Armin Hahne, fifth overall.

The Swiss Elf Haberthur Porsche team claimed the GT2 prize, in ninth place overall, with their 911 driven by Michel Neugarten, Jean-Claude Lagniez and Guy Martinolle.

The 1998 season, it has to be said, was thoroughly miserable for Porsche as its factory team was trounced by Mercedes in the FIA GT Championship. There was one brilliant weekend, though, which helped to make up for some of the disappointments, and that was the great success at Le Mans.

It coincided with Porsche's 50th birthday celebrations, and the travel stained GT1-98 was centre of attraction when it was returned to Stuttgart on Monday. Allan McNish, Stephane Ortelli and Laurent Aiello triumphed over some formidable competition which included factory teams from AMG Mercedes, BMW, Toyota and Nissan, plus two TWR Porsches run by Joest but entered by the factory -- just to make sure! -- and prior to the event nobody could predict a winner. It could have been a car from any of five manufacturers.

The Mercedes had a short appearance, as it happened, with oil pump drive failures on both cars, then, within four hours, both BMW prototypes retired with broken front wheel bearings, so four top German cars were out while the race was young. The TWR prepared Nissans were not quite on the pace but the Toyota GT-One led on Saturday evening, handled by Thierry Boutsen, Ralf Kelleners and Geoff Lees, before losing 15 minutes having its gearbox changed.

Porsche's GT1-98s were first and second at midnight, two laps ahead of the Nissan R390 with John Nielsen leading the driver crew, and now four laps ahead of Boutsen's Toyota, which would return to the lead on Sunday morning.

Dawn brought nothing but bad luck to Porsche. Joest's better placed TWR Porsche WSC was spun and damaged, Joerg Muller launched his GT1-98 over a high kerb and damaged the underfloor, and McNish reported an overheating engine. It took 30 minutes to replace a fractured water pipe and in that time Boutsen regained the lead, only to stop for 10 minutes to have a new gear cluster installed.

A minute past the 18-hour mark McNish regained the lead just as Boutsen was driving from the garage, the Toyota now 24 seconds behind but lapping at a faster pace. A brake pad change put McNish's car a lap behind with Muller, Wollek and Uwe Alzen a further lap behind.

Ninety minutes from the end, Ortelli was 44 seconds behind the leading Toyota when he handed over to McNish for the final stint, but we were robbed of a photo-finish when Boutsen's car rolled to a stop at Arnage, off the road with a failed gearbox that would go no further. Some of his pit crew were in tears, but the only tears in Herbert Ampferer's eyes were of joy, because his two GT1s were first and second overall.

An assortment of Nissans, McLarens and Panoz packed the finishing order, but the GT2 category was won by the Team Oreca Chrysler Viper of Justin Bell, David Donohue and Luca Drudi, ahead of another Viper driven by Olivier Beretta, Tommy Archer and Pedro Lamy.

Third in GT2, but out-gunned by the American cars, was the Roock Racing Porsche GT2 of Claudia Huertgen, Michel Ligonnet and Robert Nearn, who were 17th overall.

Podium 1998 (l.-r.): Dr. Wolfgang Porsche, Laurent Aiello, Stephane Ortelli, Allan McNish

911 FORMS FABRIC OF LE MANS

Der 16. Porsche-Gesamtsieg in Le Mans sollte für einige Jahre der Letzte sein. Die Nachricht, das Werksteam würde aufgelöst, schlug bei der Porsche Cup-Feier im Dezember 1998 wie eine Bombe ein. „Wir brauchen eine Pause", sagte Horst Marchart, Vorstandsmitglied im Entwicklungszentrum Weissach.

Die gebündelte Weissacher Kraft sollte nötig sein, um dem Cayenne zu großem Erfolg zu verhelfen. Was schließlich auch gelang. Zur gleichen Zeit arbeitete die Rennabteilung an der Entwicklung des GT3. Dieser sollte in der vom Automobile Club de l' Ouest neu geschaffenen Kategorie antreten und diese dominieren können. Der GT3 verfügte über einen Saugmotor, der Auspufflärm dröhnte in Le Mans fast schmerzhaft in den Ohren. Er war kaum langsamer als das turbogetriebene GT2-Modell.

Zwei Fahrzeuge gaben im Juni 1999 ihr Le Mans-Debüt. Ein 911 GT3 vom Team Manthey Racing für Uwe Alzen, Luca Riccitelli und Patrick Huisman, der andere von Dave Marajs Champion Racing für Bob Wollek, Dirk Müller und Bernd Mayländer. Beide wurden anfangs von Werksmechanikern mitbetreut. Der Manthey-GT3 absolvierte ein völlig problemloses Rennen, kam auf den 13. Gesamtrang und gewann mit Leichtigkeit die Klasse. Bis auf zwei hatte er alle sieben gestarteten 8-Liter Chrysler Vipers hinter sich gelassen. Der Champion-GT3 folgte auf Platz zwei in der Klasse. Im Gesamtklassement wurden sie getrennt durch den Konrad GT2-Porsche, den neben Teamchef Franz Konrad auch Charles Slater und Peter Kitchak steuerten.

1999: Bernd Mayländer, Bob Wollek, Dirk Müller

Winner LM GT 2000: Hideo Fukuyama, Atsushi Yogo, Bruno Lambert

Mit einem neuen Stammbaum versehen, bot Porsche rechtzeitig für das Jahr 2000 eine Reihe von GT3 den Kundenteams in Europa, den USA und Japan an. Gleich sechs dieser Fahrzeuge dominierten in der GT3-Kategorie in Le Mans. Zunächst sah es nach einem Klassensieg für Dick Barbour Racing aus. Doch es wurde eine technische Nachuntersuchung angeordnet. Diese brachte ein leicht vergrößertes Tankvolumen ans Tageslicht. Vierzehn Tage nach der Veranstaltung wurden Lucas Luhr, Bob Wollek und Dirk Müller disqualifiziert. Der Sieg in der GT3-Klasse ging somit an den Taisan Advan-GT3 von Hideo Fukuyama, Atsushi Yogo und Bruno Lambert. Auf Rang zwei rückten Sascha Maassen, Johnny Mowlem und David Murry im australischen Rohan Skea-GT3 vor.

Die turbogeladenen GT2 Porsche traten zum letzten Mal in Le Mans an und mussten sich den Chrysler Vipern geschlagen geben. Konrad Motorsport kam mit Jürgen von Gartzen, Charles Slater und Tommy Kendall auf Rang sieben in der Klasse. Besonders bitter endete das Rennen für Wolfgang Kaufmann, Katsunori Iketani und Yukihiro Hane, die in der Arnage nur elf Minuten vor Schluss liegen blieben. Zwei oder drei Runden mehr hätten dem Freisinger-GT2 zum achten Klassenplatz gereicht.

Im Jahr 2001 sollte Porsche die GT3-Klasse unter sich ausmachen, zehn Fahrzeuge standen bereit und acht von ihnen wurden im Ziel gewertet. Siegreich war die Mannschaft von Peter Seikel mit den Piloten Luca Drudi, Gabrio Rosa und Fabio Babini. Mit nur einer Runde Rückstand folgten Gunnar Jeannette, Romain Dumas und Philippe Haezebrouck im Freisinger-GT3. Im Gesamtklassement belegten sie die Plätze sechs und sieben, ein beachtliches Ergebnis für Gruppe 3-Fahrzeuge mit etwas mehr als 400 PS.

2002 sah man neue Gesichter auf dem Podium. Kevin Buckler, Lucas Luhr und Timo Bernhard hatten im The Racers Group-GT3 ein packendes Duell für sich entscheiden

2002: Leo Hindery, Peter Baron, Tony Kester

2001: Max Cohen-Olivar, Andrew Bagnall, Tony Burgess

Porsche's 16th victory at Le Mans was the last for many years, as we now know. The bombshell was dropped at the Porsche Cup awards in December that the factory team would be disbanded. "We need a break" said board member Horst Marchart, head of R&D at Weissach. "We need time to take a breath!"

All the skills of Weissach would be required to make the Cayenne a big success, while the racing department worked on the GT3 model which would contest, even dominate, the GT3 category created by the Automobile Club de l'Ouest. It was naturally aspirated, the exhaust noise was almost painfully loud at Le Mans, and it was not much slower than the turbocharged GT2 model which would soon look obsolete.

Two cars made their debut at Le Mans in June 1999, one entered in the name of Manthey Racing for Uwe Alzen, Luca Riccitelli and Patrick Huisman, the other in the name of Dave Maraj's Champion Racing for Bob Wollek, Dirk Muller and Bernd Maylaender.

Both were run by factory personnel, initially, and Manthey's GT3 had a completely trouble-free run to 13th place overall, easily winning its class. It was ahead of all but two of the seven 8-litre Chrysler Vipers in the race, in fact, and the Champion Racing GT3 was second in class after having a faulty wheel bearing changed on Sunday morning. They were split in the finishing order by the Konrad Motorsport Porsche GT2 driven by Konrad with Charles Slater and Peter Kitchak.

With a new pedigree, Porsche released a batch of GT3s to customer teams in Europe, in America and in Japan in time for the year 2000...and surprise, six of these dominated the top positions in the GT3 category at Le Mans!

It seemed that the Dick Barbour Racing entry won the class with Lucas Luhr, Bob Wollek and Dirk Muller driving, but at post-race scrutineering, announced a fortnight later, the fuel tank was deemed to be slightly over-size, and the American entry was disqualified. The discrepancy was almost certainly of an accidental nature, perhaps caused by heat expansion in the tank, but no excuse is valid in cases like this.

The GT3 class victory was passed to the Team Taisan Advan Porsche driven by Hideo Fukuyama, Atsushi Yogo and Bruno Lambert, with Australian Rohan Skea's Porsche second driven by Sascha Maassen, Johnny Mowlem and David Murry.

The turbocharged GT2 Porsches competed at Le Mans for the last time, out-gunned by the Chrysler Vipers. Konrad Motorsport managed seventh in class with the GT2 driven by Juergen von Gartzen, Charles Slater and Tommy Kendall, but there was a bitter blow for Manfred Freisinger's team as the GT2 driven by Wolfgang Kaufmann, Katsunori Iketani and Yukihiro Hane broke down at Arnage just 11 minutes from the finish. It needed two or three more laps to be classified eighth in class.

Porsche was represented exclusively in the GT3 category at Le Mans in 2001 with a total of 10 cars, of which eight were classified. Peter Seikel's team came out on top with the GT3 driven by Luca Drudi, Gabrio Rosa and Fabio Babini, a single lap ahead of the Freisinger Motorsport GT3 of Gunnar Jeannette, Romain Dumas and Philippe Haezebrouck. They were sixth and seventh overall, not a bad result for Group 3 cars with little more than 400 horsepower.

There were new faces on the podium in 2002, those of Kevin Buckler, Lucas Luhr and Timo Bernhard, when their Racers Group Porsche GT3 came out best in a thrilling duel with the Freisinger Motorsport GT3 of Sascha Maassen, Romain Dumas and Joerg Bergmeister.

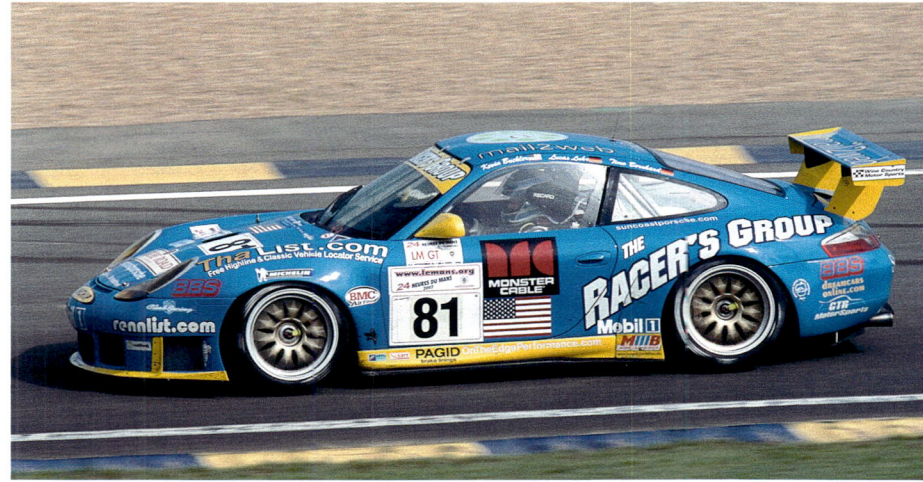

Winner LM GT 2002: Kevin Buckler, Lucas Luhr, Timo Bernhard

2003: Leo Hindery, Marc Lieb, Peter Baron

2003: Vanina Ickx, Patrick Bourdais, Patrick Berville

2003: Kevin Buckler, Jörg Bergmeister, Timo Bernhard

können. Das amerikanische Team hatte während der gesamten Distanz der 24 Stunden Stoßstange an Stoßstange mit den Freisinger-Markenkollegen im Formationsflug den Kurs umrundet. Auch in der deutschen Mannschaft saßen mit Sascha Maassen, Romain Dumas und Jörg Bergmeister Porsche-Werksfahrer am Steuer. Beim Fallen der Zielflagge waren sie nur durch eine Minute getrennt, wenn auch dem Racers Group-911 auf der Ergebnisliste eine Runde mehr gutgeschrieben wurde.

In diesem Jahr traf Porsche auf ernstzunehmende Konkurrenz von JMB Racing und deren Ferrari 360 Modena, dem ungewöhnlichen holländischen Spyker und dem veraltet wirkenden Morgan Aero 8 aus der Malvern-Mannschaft. Dennoch, das Ergebnis war vorhersagbar. Auf Platz drei in der Klasse fuhr der GT3 des japanischen Teams Taisan Advan mit Atsushi Yogo, Kenji Nishizawa und Akira Iida.

Für das Jahr 2003 bündelten Alex Job und Michael Petersens White Lightning Team ihre Kräfte, um eine Siegermannschaft auf die Beine zu stellen. Die beiden Teams,

Konkurrenten in der American Le Mans Serie, bekamen die Werksfahrer Sascha Massen, Lucas Luhr und Emmanuel Collard für ihr Projekt. Es sollte ein schwieriges Rennen werden, denn außergewöhnlich viele Trümmerteile auf der Strecke sorgten für Reifenschäden und zerschlagene Kühler. Dennoch waren ihre Bemühungen erfolgreich: Klassensieg und sechs Runden Vorsprung auf den Orbit Racing-911 von Leo Hindery, Peter Baron und Marc Lieb. Platz drei ging an Michel Neugarten, Nigel Smith und Ian Khan im Perspective GT3. In Führung liegend traf Kevin Buckler Racers Group 996 am Samstagabend ein Kupplungsschaden. Dank der entschlossenen Fahrweise von Buckler, Bernhard und Bergmeister waren sie im Ziel wieder auf den fünften Klassenrang vorgefahren.

2004 nahm die White Lightning Mannschaft die 24 Stunden auf eigene Faust in Angriff. Profitierend aus den Erfahrungen aus dem Vorjahr fuhr der GT3 mit Maassen, Bergmeister und Patrick Long, einem höchst talentierten amerikanischen Youngster, zum Klassensieg. Dieser geriet nur kurz in Gefahr, als ein defektes Kabel am Getriebe zu einem längeren Boxenaufenthalt zwang. Manfred Freisingers GT3 konnte die Führung übernehmen, doch Kelleners, Ortelli und Dumas wurden ihrerseits durch einen defekten Sensor der Kurbelwelle eingebremst. Die Freisinger-Mannschaft fiel zurück und kam hinter dem japanischen Choroq-GT3 von Haruki Kurosawa, Kazayuki Nishizawa und Manabu Orido auf Rang drei ins Ziel.

Somit endet zunächst die Geschichte des Porsche 911 in Le Mans. Eine nahezu ungebrochene Erfolgsgeschichte von siegreichen Einsätzen. Sie umfasst auch den Gesamtsieg des 935, des ersten und für lange Zeit einzigen Erfolgs eines aus der Serienproduktion stammenden Wagens.

2003 (l.-r.): Marc Lieb, Leo Hindery, Peter Baron

2003 (l.-r.): Jörg Bergmeister, Timo Bernhard, Kevin Buckler

The American and German teams, both with factory contracted drivers on loan, were neck-and-neck for the full 24 hours and at the flag no more than a minute separated them, although the American entry made an extra lap on the result sheet.

This time Porsche had some honest competition from the JMB Racing Ferrari 360 Modenas, the unusual Spyker from Holland and the antiquated Morgan Aero 8 from Malvern, but the result was predictable. Third in GT3 was the faithful Team Taisan Advan, the GT3 driven by Atsushi Yogo, Kenji Nishizawa and Akira Iida.

Another American team, that of Alex Job, finished on top in the GT3 class in 2003, although all the teams had a difficult race, with punctures and holed radiators resulting from an unusual amount of debris on the circuit. Kevin Buckler's Racers Group Porsche had its clutch fail on Saturday evening, while leading the class, and it took a lot of determined driving by Buckler, Bernhard and Bergmeister to climb back to fifth position at the end.

Alex Job joined forces with Michael Petersen's White Lightning Porsche team, rivals in the American Le Mans Series, to assemble the winning team, with factory loaned drivers Sascha Maassen, Lucas Luhr and Emmanuel Collard exercising their skills at the wheel. They finished six laps ahead of the Orbit Racing Porsche of Leo Hindery, Peter Baron and Marc Lieb, and third in the GT3 class was the Perspective Racing Porsche of Michel Neugarten, Nigel Smith and Ian Khan.

The White Lightning team made a solo run to victory at Le Mans in 2004, building on the shared experience of '03, so American teams were victorious in three successive years. Patrick Long, one of the most talented young drivers to come from America, joined Maassen and Bergmeister in the winning car, which had spent time in the pits having the gear selector cable replaced.

Manfred Freisinger's team snatched the lead, the GT3 crewed by Kelleners, Ortelli and Dumas, but this car was delayed by a broken crankshaft sensor and finished third in class, behind the Japanese Choroq Porsche driven by Haruki Kurosawa, Kazuyuki Nishizawa and Manabu Orido.

So ends, for now, the story of the Porsche 911 at Le Mans, a virtually unbroken succession of victorious competitions. It includes an outright victory for the 935, the first by a production based car for many years, and at times the Automobile Club de l'Ouest has had reason to be eternally grateful to the Porsche company for sustaining, and adding lustre to the classic 24-hour race.

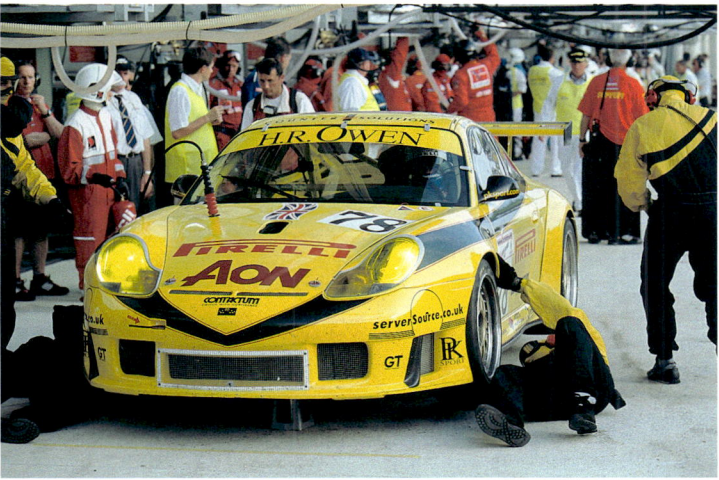

2003: Dave Warnock, Robin Liddell, Piers Masarati

Winner LM GT 2003: Sascha Maassen, Lucas Luhr, Emmanuel Collard

Winner LM GT 2004: Sascha Maassen, Jörg Bergmeister, Patrick Long

2004: Haruki Kurosawa, Kazuyuki Nishizawa, Manabu Orido

2004: Ian Donaldson, Gregor Fisken, Lars Nielsen

2004: Leo Hindery, Mike Rockenfeller, Marc Lieb

911 FORMS FABRIC OF LE MANS

911-MARKEN-POKALE EROBERN DEN GLOBUS

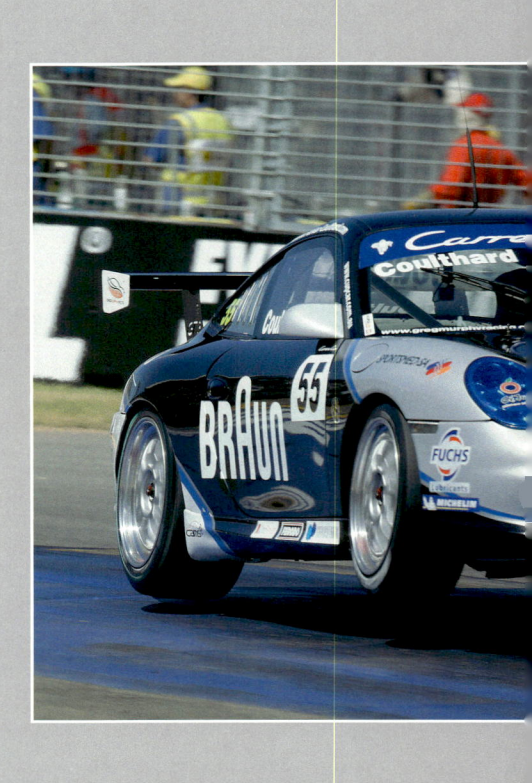

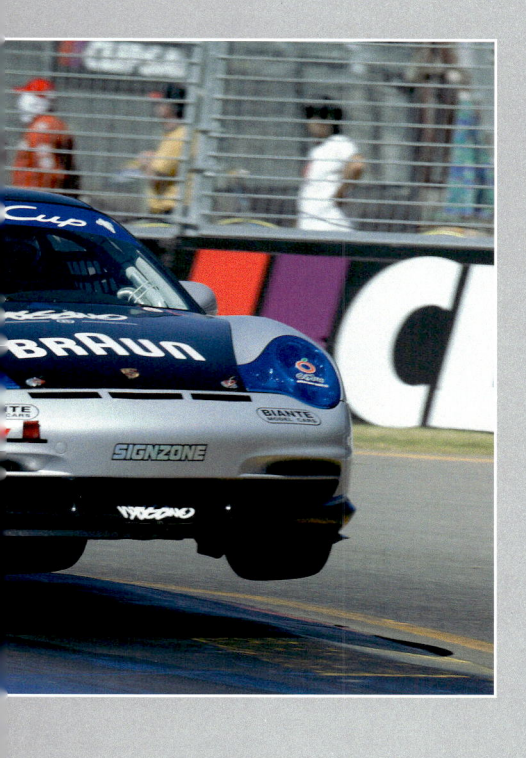

911 ONE-MAKE FASCINATES

Author: Wilfried Müller

Mit dem Jahr 1990 und dem „911 Carrera 2 Cup" beginnt die Geschichte der im Werk aufgebauten Cup-Neunelfer für die Markenpokale. Der 265 PS starke Urahn des GT3 Cup von 2005, der mit 400 Pferdestärken unterwegs ist, erlebt seine Premiere beim ersten Rennen des Carrera Cup im Motodrom von Hockenheim.

Die Philosophie hinter dem 911 für die Markenpokale bleibt über die Jahre unverändert: Alle Cup-Carrera sind identisch und nah an der Serie. Das Reglement erlaubt Einstellarbeiten am rennmäßig überarbeiteten Fahrwerk und am Heckflügel, hält aber den technischen Aufwand und die Kosten in engen Grenzen. Die Steigerung der Motorleistung bleibt im Vergleich zum Standard-911 moderat, sämtliche zentralen Komponenten entsprechen den straßenzugelassenen Modellen. Alle Teilnehmer rollen auf Einheits-Rennreifen an den Start.

Erst mit dem 911 GT3 Cup für das Jahr 2005 geht Porsche einen Schritt weg von der Seriennähe, hin zum kompromisslosen Renngerät: erstmals wird auf das ABS verzichtet, das Fahrwerk übernimmt Komponenten der Spezial-Entwicklung für den 911 GT3 RSR, das sequentielle Getriebe des GT3 Cup-2005 ist ebenfalls in der Serie nicht zu haben. Fast unverändert aber bleibt das Gewicht über die 15 Jahre: 1.120 Kilogramm brachte der Carrera 2 Cup Jahrgang 1990 auf die Waage, 1.150 Kilo sind es 2005 – trotz aller sicherheitsrelevanten Karosserieverstärkungen, die der 911 über die Jahre erhalten hatte.

Zwischen den Anfängen und dem letzten hier beschriebenen Modell von 2005 stehen zwei weitere Generation von Cup-Carrera: Im Jahr 1994 löst der 911 Cup 3.8 – zuerst im Porsche-Pirelli-Supercup, von 1995 an auch im Carrera Cup – als erste im Werk entstandene Rennversion der Baureihe 993 seinen Vorgänger ab. Der „Cup Dreiacht" bringt einen Leistungssprung auf 310 PS.

Ab 1998 kommt die erste Motorsportversion des wassergekühlten 911 (Baureihe 996) im Porsche-Pirelli-Supercup zum Einsatz. Es ist der 911 GT3 Cup, der mit 370 PS debütiert und ein Jahr später auch im Carrera Cup eingesetzt wird.

Der erste Cup-Carrera entsteht auf Basis des Carrera 2 bei Porsche Motorsport 1989. Dieser 911 Carrera 2 Cup verfügt für die Rennsaison 1990 über einen luftgekühlten Sechszylinder-Boxermotor mit Doppelzündung, der aus 3,6 Litern Hubraum 265 PS (195 kW) bei 6.100 Kurbelwellenumdrehungen abgibt. Als Höchstdrehzahl werden 6.800 Touren erreicht. Die Leistungssteigerung gegenüber dem Serienmodell beträgt lediglich fünf PS. Wie alle folgenden Cup-Carrera benötigt der Motor handelsüblichen Treibstoff und verfügt über geregelte Abgaskatalysatoren.

Porsche Carrera Cup Germany Team 1991

Poster

Poster

Winner Carrera Cup Germany 1991: Roland Asch

Winner Carrera Cup Germany 1993 and 1997: Wolfgang Land

Carrera Cup Germany 1991

The history of the first factory-built 911 for the Cup one-make series starts in 1990 with the "911 Carrera 2 Cup". The 265 hp strong ancestor of the GT3 Cup of 2005, that is running with 400 hp, celebrated its debut in the inaugural race of the Carrera Cup at Hockenheim.

The philosophy behind the 911 designated for one-make series has remained unchanged over the years. All Carrera Cup-cars are identical and their specifications are close to those of the road-going versions. Regulations allow for adjustments to the suspension that has been fine-tuned for competition use and to the rear wing, but there are strict limitations for technical effort and costs. The increase of the power output remains quite modest compared to the production version of the 911. All the main elements are identical to those of road-going cars. All competitors are racing on control competition tyres.

With the 911 GT3 Cup for the 2005 season, based on the latest type 997 chassis, Porsche is moving a step away from the production models for the first time, towards a thoroughbred racing machine without compromise. For the first time, ABS has been abandoned, the suspension includes parts that had been especially developed for the 911 GT3 RSR, and the sequential gearbox of the 2005-spec GT3 Cup isn't available for production cars either.

The weight, however, has remained almost unchanged in the course of the 15 years: the Carrera Cup of 1990 weighed 1120 kilograms, the weight in 2005 is 1150 kilograms, in spite of all the safety-driven bodywork enforcements that the 911 got over the years.

Between the early days and the latest model to be described here, the 2004-spec car, there are two more generations of Carrera Cup-cars. In 1994, the 911 Cup 3.8 replaced its predecessor as the first factory-built competition version of the 993 model range. Initially, it was racing in the Porsche Pirelli Supercup and, from 1995 onwards, also in the Carrera Cup. The "Cup three-eight" featured a power increase to 310 hp.

From 1998 onwards, the first motor sport version of the water-cooled Porsche 911 (model range 996) is being used in the Porsche Pirelli Supercup. It is the 911 GT3 Cup, that has an output of 370 hp at its debut and arrives in the Carrera Cup one year later.

Winner Carrera Cup Germany 1990: Olaf Manthey

Winner Carrera Cup Germany 1992: Uwe Alzen

911 ONE-MAKE FASCINATES

Winner Supercup 1993: Altfrid Heger   **Poster**

Ein Fünfganggetriebe mit verkürztem dritten, vierten und fünften Gang und ein Sperrdifferenzial übertragen die Kraft an die Hinterräder. Die abgeänderte Fahrwerkskinematik, härtere und kürzere Federn und einstellbare Querstabilisatoren gewährleisten rennmäßige Präzision. Der Cup-Carrera liegt 55 Millimeter tiefer als sein Serien-Pendant, verzögert wird er über groß dimensionierte, innenbelüftete und gelochte Bremsscheiben sowie ein angepasstes Serien-ABS. Porsche wird bis zum GT3 Cup - 2005 das ABS im Cup-Sport einsetzen. Die Lenkung ist direkter übersetzt und kommt, wie alle Nachfolger bis zum 911 Cup 3.8, ohne Servo-Unterstützung aus.

Ein Aluminium-Sicherheitskäfig, der für 1992 durch einen eingeschweißten Stahlkäfig ersetzt wird, schützt den Fahrer und sorgt zusammen mit einer vorderen Domstrebe für erhöhte Steifigkeit. Porsche gibt das Gewicht des ersten Cup-Carrera mit 1.120 Kilogramm an.

Als erster Meister des Carrera Cup schreibt sich Olaf Manthey aus Bonn in die Annalen der Markenpokale ein. 1991 folgt ihm Roland Asch, der später während insgesamt zehn Jahren in den Cups mit 30 Siegen, 32 Pole Positions und 21 schnellsten Rennrunden schwer zu brechende Rekorde aufstellt. Das Tourenwagen- und GT-Ass Jean-Pierre Malcher holt in Frankreich den ersten Gesamtsieg im Carrera Cup. Er wird 1995 auch den Porsche-Pirelli-Supercup gewinnen.

Nach den ersten beiden Jahren im Wettbewerb überarbeitet die Rennabteilung den Cup-Carrera, der 1992 in der Karosserie des RS an den Start rollt. Der Motor gibt jetzt 275 PS ab und benötigt Super-Plus Kraftstoff mit 98 Oktan. Dünnglasscheiben in den Türen und hinten tragen zur Gewichtsverringerung bei. Die Radnaben vorne bestehen aus Aluminium, dreiteilige Magnesium-Aluminium Rennfelgen ersetzen die Aluminium-Räder des Vorgängers. Erstmals werden 18 Zoll große Räder eingesetzt. Die Federbeindome hinten sind um 20 Millimeter abgesenkt.

In Frankreich macht sich Dominique Dupuy mit seinem ersten Gesamtsieg daran, eine einzigartige Titelsammlung einzurichten: Der sympathische Renn-Profi gewinnt den Carrera Cup seines Heimatlandes 1992, '93, '97, '98 und '99.

Erstmals ist 1992 auch in Japan ein Carrera Cup zu sehen, Satoshi Ikezawa sichert sich die begehrte Trophäe.

Ein Jahr später startet Porsche den Porsche-Pirelli-Supercup, einen Markenpokal im Rahmenprogramm der Formel 1. Der Deutsche Altfrid Heger ist der erste Supercup-Sieger.

Im Mai 1993 beginnt in Weissach die Entwicklungsarbeit am 911 Cup 3.8, der seriennahen Rennversion des neuen Typs 993. Im November zeigt sich bei letzten Tests in Mugello und Vallelunga, dass der Neue nicht nur deutlich schneller, sondern auch leichter kontrollierbar ist als sein Vorgänger. Der „Cup Dreiacht" kommt im Supercup ab dem Jahr 1994 zum Einsatz, die Akteure des Carrera Cup fahren den Wagen ab 1995. Aus 3,8 Litern Hubraum gibt der Sechszylinder bei 6.100 Touren 310 Pferdestärken ab, das maximale Drehmoment von 360 Nm steht bei 5.500 Umdrehungen an. Als höchstzulässige Drehzahl nennt Porsche 6.900. Der Ventiltrieb übersteht gelegentliches Verschalten und damit Hochdrehen bis zu 7.800 Touren klaglos – eine Sicherheitsmaßnahme, genau wie die stählernen Synchronringe des neuen, eng gestuften Sechsganggetriebes.

Mit 1.100 Kilogramm Gewicht ist der Rennsportwagen 20 Kilo leichter als sein Vorgänger. Heck- und Seitenfenster hinter der B-Säule aus Kunststoff, ein Aluminium-Gepäckraumdeckel, der Verzicht auf Dämmmaterial, auf Heizung, Servolenkung und ein ausgeräumtes Cockpit tragen zu dem Leichtgewicht bei. Der Überrollkäfig aus Stahlrohr umfasst jetzt Rohrkreuze in den Türausschnitten. Wie beim Serien-Pendant fährt der Heckspoiler geschwindigkeitsabhängig aus seiner Ruheposition hoch, um Motorkühlung und Abtrieb zu optimieren.

Die neue Mehrlenker-Hinterachse ähnelt in ihrer Präzision einer Doppelquerlenker-Konstruktion. Der Cup 3.8 liegt 70 Millimeter tiefer als sein Vetter für die Straße. Die Federrate ist doppelt so hart wie im Cup-Porsche von 1993. Das ABS bleibt weiter im Einsatz. Eine Dreistempel-Luftheberanlage ersetzt ab 1994 die herkömmlichen Wagenheber.

Für die Saison 1995 erhält der Cup 3.8 eine überarbeitete Aerodynamik mit dem großen, feststehenden Heckflügel, den Seitenschwellern und dem Bugspoiler des Carrera RS. Auf der Fahrwerksseite widmen sich die Ingenieure vor allem der Vorderachse, wo die Spur- und Sturzveränderungen beim Ein- und Ausfedern weiter minimiert werden. Ein verkürzter sechster Gang sorgt für Durchzugskraft auch bei hohen Geschwindigkeiten.

1996 rollt der Cup-Porsche mit einem modifizierten Ventiltrieb und fünf Mehr-PS an den Start. Geänderte Feder- und Dämpferkennlinien ermöglichen eine noch feinere Fahrwerksabstimmung des 911. Die neuen, starren Kunststofflager der Getriebe-Aufhängung machen das Getriebe leichter schaltbar.

Porsche Supercup 1995

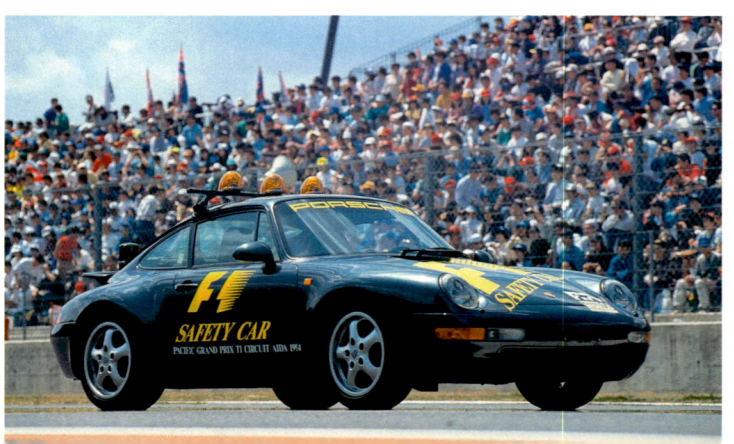

Official F1 Safety Car 1994

911-MARKENPOKALE EROBERN DEN GLOBUS

The racing department designs and builds the first Cup Carrera – dubbed 911 Carrera 2 Cup and based on the 964 – in 1989. The Carrera 2 Cup features an air-cooled six-cylinder boxer engine with twin ignition delivering 265 hp (195 kW) at 6,100 rpm from a capacity of 3.6-litres. Maximum revs are 6,800. Compared to the standard model, the performance increase of five horsepower is moderate. Like all subsequent Cup-Carreras, the engine runs on commercial petrol and features three-way catalytic converters.

A five-speed gearbox with shortened ratio for third, fourth and fifth gears, and a locking differential transfer the power to the rear axle. A modified suspension with harder and shorter springs and adjustable anti-roll bars guarantee racing precision. The Cup-Carrera lies 55 millimetres lower than its standard cousin.

Large internally ventilated and perforated brake discs combined with a standard ABS system modified for racing purposes ensure braking performances typical of Porsche.

Steering is more direct and without power-steering. An aluminium safety cage, which is replaced in 1992 with a welded-in steel cage, protects the driver, and increases the rigidity of the body. The first Cup-Carrera weighs in at 1120 kilograms. Olaf Manthey from Bonn has his name written in the history books of one-make racing as the inaugural winner of the Carrera Cup. In 1991, he is being followed by Roland Asch, who would go on to establish a series of records that will be hard to beat: in 10 years of Cup racing, he acquired 30 race wins, 32 pole positions and 21 fastest race laps. Touring car and GT stalwart Jean-Pierre Malcher becomes the inaugural winner of the Carrera Cup in France. In 1995, he also wins the Porsche Pirelli Supercup.

After the first two years, the Cup-Carrera receives fine-tuning touches. The 1992-spec rolls to the start sporting the RS body. The engine now delivers 275 hp and burns Super-Plus petrol with 98 Octane. Thinner glass panels in the doors and rear contribute to a lower weight. The front wheel hub consists of aluminium; three-part magnesium-aluminium racing rims replace the aluminium wheels. For the first time, 18 inch wheels are used.

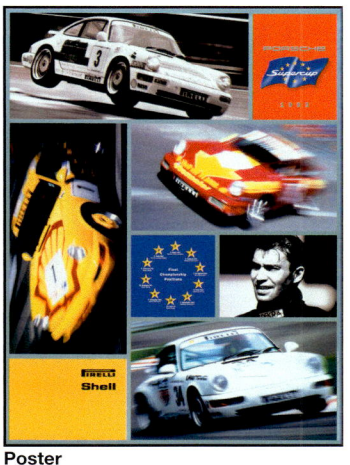

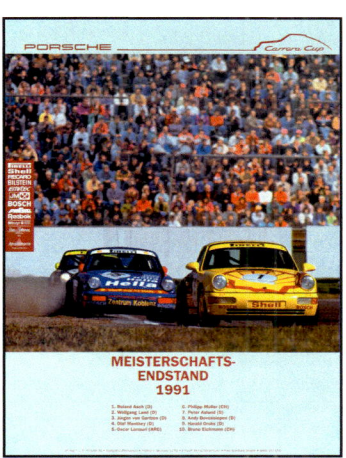

Poster **Poster**

Winner Supercup 1996: Emmanuel Collard

In France, Dominique Dupuy wins his first title, to be followed by an unique collection of titles. The amiable professional racing driver wins the Carrera Cup in his home country in 1992, 1993, 1997, 1998 and 1999.

In 1992, a Carrera Cup is being established in Japan as well. Satoshi Ikuzawa takes the coveted crown.

One year later, Porsche is establishing the Porsche Pirelli Supercup, a one-make series on the support package of Formula 1. German driver, Altfrid Heger, becomes the inaugural Supercup-winner.

In May 1993, Weissach starts development of the Porsche 911 Cup 3.8, the racing version of the new Carrera (993). In November that same year, tests at Mugello and Vallelunga confirm that the new Cup-Carrera is not only considerably faster than its forerunner, it is also easier to control. In 1994 the "Cup three-eight" lines up for the Supercup races, and can be seen in the national Carrera Cups the following season. With a capacity of 3.8-litres, the six-cylinder delivers 310 horsepower at 6,100 revs. Maximum torque of 360 Nm is reached at 5,500 rpm. Maximum revs are 6,900. The valve gear withstands up to 7,800 revolutions – a safety measure like the steel synchronizer rings of the new, narrowly staged six-speed gearbox.

Weighing 1,100 kilograms, the racing sportscar is 20 kgs lighter than its predecessor. The rear window and the side windows behind the centre post consist of plastic. An aluminium luggage compartment lid, the forfeiting of muffling material, as well as heating, power steering and a stripped down cockpit contribute to the light weight. The safety cage now features additional steel pipes in the door openings. At a certain speed the rear spoiler automatically rises from its resting position in the engine compartment lid in order to optimize engine cooling and downforce.

A true quantum leap takes place thanks to the new multi-link rear axle, which comes very close to the handling characteristics of a double wishbone construction. Compared to its road-going cousin, the Cup 3.8 lies 70 millimetres lower. The springs are twice as hard as in the 1993 Cup contender. Internally ventilated, perforated brake discs together with a standard ABS, modified for racing, ensure impressive deceleration. Thanks to a new, more service-friendly layout, adjustments to the camber of the front axle or the rear anti-roll bar can now be completed much quicker.

Winner Supercup 1994: Uwe Alzen

Winner Supercup 1997: Patrick Huisman

Winner Carrera Cup Germany 1998: Dirk Müller

Supercup 1993: Harald Grohs

Winner Supercup 1994: Uwe Alzen

Supercup 1994: Dominique Dupuy

324 911-MARKENPOKALE EROBERN DEN GLOBUS

Supercup 1996: Norberto Fontana, Fabio Santaniello

Supercup Monaco 1997: Matteo Maria Galimberti, Harald Grohs

Für 1997 nimmt die Rennabteilung an dem Cup-Sportler keine Änderungen vor. Auf der Fahrerseite macht der Niederländer Patrick Huisman mit seinem Gesamtsieg im Porsche-Pirelli-Supercup auf sich aufmerksam. Es ist der erste in einer bis dato unerreichten Serie von vier Meistertiteln en suite im Supercup, mit der sich der lange Niederländer für höhere Aufgaben im Tourenwagensport empfiehlt.

Der 911 GT3 Cup ist im Jahr 1998 das erste auf der Basis des neuen Carrera (Baureihe 996) aufgebaute Rennfahrzeug. Beim Supercup-Lauf im Rahmen des GP von San Marino im italienischen Imola ist dieser Rennsportwagen erstmals im Einsatz. Im deutschen Carrera Cup läuft der GT3 Cup ab der Saison 1999.

Der wassergekühlte 3,6-Liter-Boxer im Heck ist mit einer Bohrung von 100 und einem Hub von 76,4 Millimeter als drehfreudiger Kurzhuber ausgelegt, der in verschiedenen Entwicklungsstufen bis 2005 einschließlich als Antriebsquelle dienen wird. Der Sechszylinder mobilisiert 1998 zunächst 360 PS (265 kW) und ein Drehmoment von 360 Nm. Ab 1999 beträgt die Leistung 370 PS (272 kW) bei 7.200 U/min, das maximale Drehmoment ist bei 370 Nm und 6.250 Touren erreicht. Der Drehzahlbegrenzer regelt bei 8.000 U/min ab. Der Saugmotor verfügt über Titanpleuel, eine Öl-kühlung mittels Wasser-Öl-Wärmetauscher sowie eine Trockensumpfschmierung mit externem Öltank. Zwei geregelte Katalysatoren reinigen die Abgase.

Winner 1995: Jean-Pierre Malcher

Winner 1999: Patrick Huisman

Supercup Silverstone 1996

Winner Carrera Cup Germany 2002: Marc Lieb

Winner Carrera Cup Germany 1999: Lucas Luhr

Der Rumpfmotor ist in Sandwichbauweise ausgelegt: für die je drei Zylindereinheiten rechts und links sind Zylindergehäuse, Zylinderkopf und Nockenwellengehäuse im Sinne erhöhter Torsionssteifigkeit zu je einer Einheit zusammengefasst. In die Leichtmetall-Zylindergehäuse sind aus Aluminium gefertigte, mit Nikasil beschichtete Zylinderlaufbüchsen eingesetzt. Die Zylinderköpfe bestehen aus einer extrem temperaturbeständigen Leichtmetall-Legierung. Als Treibstoff wird handelsübliches Super Plus bleifrei in den 64-Liter-Tank gefüllt. Das Sechsgang-Schaltgetriebe entspricht im Prinzip dem Getriebe des stärkeren Porsche 911 GT2. Es wird über ein Gestänge betätigt.

Die McPherson-Federbeinachse vorn und die Mehrlenker-Hinterachse bieten mit verstellbaren Querstabilisatoren, höhenverstellbaren Feder-Dämpfereinheiten sowie Einstellmöglichkeiten von Sturz und Spur zahlreiche Abstimmungsvarianten. Der Einsatz von Unibal-Verbindungen an der Hinterachse (zur Spurstrebe, zu den Querlenkern) sowie in der Abstützung der Stoßdämpfer, und die Feinabstimmung in der Motorsportabteilung sichern rennmäßige Präzision.

330 Millimeter große, innenbelüftete Bremsscheiben und ein angepasstes Serien-ABS gewährleisten sichere Verzögerung. An der Vorderachse kommen Pirelli-Slicks der Dimension 245/645/18" zum Einsatz, hinten werden Pirelli-Rennreifen der Größe 305/645/18" aufgezogen. Eine Servolenkung erleichtert die Arbeit der Fahrer.

Der Heckdeckel mit verstellbarem Flügel, das Rückfenster und die Türen bestehen aus Verbundmaterial. Der verstellbare Heckflügel erzeugt bis zu 100 Kilogramm Abtrieb, Frontspoiler und Seitenschweller vervollkommnen die aerodynamischen Eigenschaften.

Der 911 GT3 Cup beschleunigt in weniger als vier Sekunden aus dem Stand auf 100 km/h, die Höchstgeschwindigkeit beträgt - übersetzungsbedingt - 286 km/h.

Im Jahr 2000 schreibt der 911 GT3 Cup ein Stück Motorsport-Geschichte, als am 23. September der Supercup-Lauf als erstes Rennen auf der neuen Grand Prix-Strecke von Indianapolis/USA ausgetragen wird.

Der 911 GT3 Cup des Jahrgangs 2001 rollt mit zahlreichen Detailverbesserungen an den Start. Neu ist ein großer, siebenfach verstellbarer Heckflügel, der den Abtrieb an der Hinterachse mehr als verdoppelt. Unsichtbar unter dem Heck verbessert eine vom 911 Turbo übernommene Getriebeverkleidung die Kühlung dieses Aggregats erheblich.

Die modifizierte Frontpartie gewährleistet eine ausgewogene aerodynamische Balance und die weitere Verringerung des Auftriebs an der Vorderachse. Sie leitet zudem die Abluft des hier befindlichen Mittelkühlers nach oben. Dadurch strömt keine Heißluft mehr unter dem Fahrzeug zum Motor.

Der erhöhte Abtrieb verringert das Rutschen des Fahrzeugs im Renneinsatz, was den Reifenverschleiß im Vergleich zum Vorgänger-Modell weiter vermindert.

Einen Fortschritt im Sinne des Cup-Sports, nämlich die Verringerung der Betriebskosten und die Steigerung der Leistungsdichte, macht eine weitere Modifikation möglich: Wie das Standardmodell 911 GT3 verfügt nun auch der Motor des 911 GT3 Cup über den Hydraulischen Ventilspiel Ausgleich (HVA). Betrug die Leistungsstreuung des 370 PS (272 kW) starken 3,6-Liter-Boxermotors beim Vorgängermodell unter Verwendung von Rennteilen noch bis zu drei Prozent, so wird sie dank der Komponenten aus dem stabilen Serien-Fertigungsverfahren jetzt auf ein Minimum reduziert. Zudem bedeutet der Einsatz von HVA eine Kostenreduzierung, da das Nachstellen der Ventile entfällt. Ansonsten bleiben Motor und Sechsgang-Getriebe unverändert.

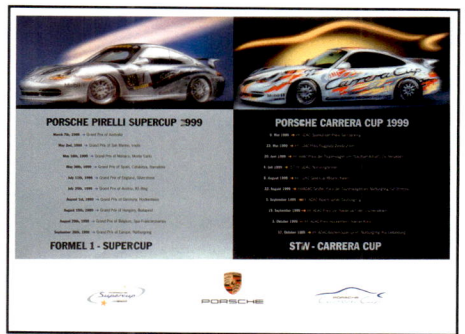

From 1994, a three-point air jack system replaces the usual car jack. For the 1995 racing season, the Cup 3.8 receives modifications to the aerodynamics, with the large fixed rear wing, the side sills and the front spoiler adopted from the Carrera RS. On the suspension side, the engineers concentrate primarily on the front axle, further minimising bump steer. The shortened ratio for the sixth gear ensures more "punch" at high speeds.

1996 sees the Cup 3.8 compete with changes to the valve gear and with five extra horsepower. Modified characteristics of the springs and shocks make a more precise suspension set up possible. The new rigid plastic gearbox bearings make gear shifting easier.

As far as drivers are concerned, Dutchman Patrick Huisman attracts the attention with his overall win in the Pirelli Supercup. It is the first in a range of four consecutive Supercup titles, an achievement that has not been equalled to date. It takes the tall Dutchman to higher echelons in touring car racing. In 1998, the 911 GT3 Cup becomes the first racing vehicle based on the new water cooled 911 Carrera (996). This sportscar makes its racing debut at the season-opening round of the Supercup at the Grand Prix of San Marino in Imola (I). In the German Carrera Cup, the GT3 Cup first lines up on the grid in 1999.

Starting with 360 hp (265 kW) and a torque of 360 Nm for the 1998 season, followed by 370 hp (272 kW) for 1999, the engine performance and power-to-weight ratio (4.19 kg/kW) surpasses all predecessors in the history of the Porsche makes cups. The water-cooled 3.6-litre boxer engine in the rear is a short-stroke unit (bore x stroke: 100 x 76.4 mm), reaching peak performance at 7,200 rpm. Maximum torque lies at 370 Nm with 6,250 revs. At 8,000 rpm the rev limiter kicks in. The normally aspirated engine features titanium connecting rods, oil cooling functions by means of an oil-to-water heat exchanger, as well as a dry sump lubrication with external oil tank. Two sensor-controlled catalytic converters clean the exhaust emissions. Fuel for the 64-litre tank is the customary unleaded Super Plus.

The six-speed gearbox shares main technical features with the transmission of the more powerful 911 GT2 (993). The McPherson struts in the front and the multi-link rear suspension feature adjustable anti-roll bars, as well as height adjustable spring and damper units. Track and camber can be adjusted. Unibal joints work at the rear axle (steering knuckle, control arm) as well as at the shock absorber mounts.

The inner ventilated discs measuring 330 millimetres in diametre are fitted with a modified standard ABS. 245/645/18 Pirelli tyres are fitted on the front axle, with 305/645/18 racing rubber at the rear. Power steering makes life at the limit easier. The body with its welded in safety cage is almost 30 percent stiffer than the GT class winning Le Mans Porsche of 1996 and 1997. The rear lid with an adjustable wing, the rear windows and doors are made of composite material. The rear wing generates up to 100 kgs of downforce, with the front spoiler and side sills completing the aerodynamic kit. The 911 GT3 Cup accelerates from zero to 100 kph in just under four seconds and reaches a top speed of 286 kph, depending on the gearbox ratio.

On 23 September 2000, the Porsche 911 GT3 writes a chapter in motorsport history. The Supercup race is the first race ever to be run on the new purpose-built Grand Prix track in Indianapolis (USA).

The 911 GT3 Cup rolls to the start of the 2001 season featuring improvements to numerous details. New is the larger rear wing, adjustable in seven positions, which more than doubles downforce at the rear axle. Under the rear, a gearbox cowling, adopted from the 911 Turbo, substantially improves the cooling of the 'box.

The modified front section ensures aerodynamic balance and reduces uplift. Hot air from the enlarged central radiator is channeled upwards. Thanks to this modification, the hot air no longer flows under the car to the engine.

The increased downforce reduces the skidding of the vehicle which results in less tyre wear. The adoption of the hydraulic valve-play compensation (HVA) from the production model, which replaces a racing component, has two effects: The performance range of the engine–which reached up to three percent–is further reduced. Moreover, with the adjustment of valves no longer necessary, the use of HVA reduces costs.

The well-proven suspension with McPherson struts in the front and a multi-link rear axle, the braking system with its adapted standard ABS, and the Pirelli racing tyres 245/645/18" (front) and 305/660/18" (rear) are taken from the predecessor without modifications.

Over the 2000/2001 winter Weissach built 114 units of the new racing sportscar: a new production record. One car stays in Weissach as a rolling lab, the others are sold world wide. For 2002, Michelin is supporting the Supercup as the new title sponsor whilst also supplying tyres for other one-make series.

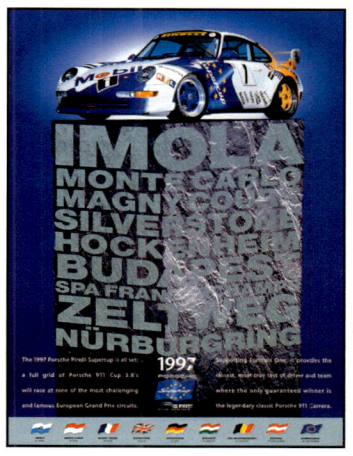

Poster

Winner Carrera Cup Germany 2000: Jörg Bergmeister

Das bewährte Fahrwerk mit McPherson-Federbeinachse vorn und Mehrlenkerhinterachse, die Bremsanlage mit dem angepassten Serien-ABS und Pirelli-Rennreifen der Dimension 245/645/18" (VA) bzw. 305/660/18" werden vom Vorgängermodell übernommen. Mit 114 im Winter 2000/2001 gebauten Exemplaren erreicht der 911 GT3 Cup einen neuen Produktionsrekord für Rennsportwagen in Weissach. Bis auf einen GT3 Cup, der als Versuchsträger in der Motorsportabteilung blieb, werden die Fahrzeuge in alle Welt verkauft. Für 2002 kommt mit Michelin ein neuer Titelsponsor des Supercup an Bord, der auch die anderen Markenpokale künftig mit Reifen versorgen wird.

Der GT3 Cup übernimmt für 2002 zahlreiche Detailverbesserungen von der zweiten Carrera-Generation (996), die im Sommer 2001 präsentiert wurde. Die Frontpartie zeigt jetzt das Scheinwerfer-Design des 911 Turbo. Das Bugteil mit seinen Lufteinlass-Öffnungen ist neu gestaltet und steigert die Kühlluft-Durchströmung der Front um 15 Prozent. Zudem konnte die Entlüftung der vorderen Radhäuser weiter optimiert werden. Bereits die neu gestylte Serienkarosserie zeichnet sich durch eine Verringerung des Auftriebs an der Vorderachse um 25 Prozent, an der Hinterachse um 40 Prozent aus. Die Rennabteilung übernahm die Modifikationen des Serienfahrzeugs und fügte im Windkanal den großen, siebenfach verstellbaren Heckflügel sowie renntypische Veränderungen in das Gesamtkonzept ein. Fahrversuche bestätigen die erwarteten Resultate, nämlich höhere Kurvengeschwindigkeiten, verringerten Reifenverschleiß und schnellere Rundenzeiten.

Während die Rohkarosse des 911 nach dem Generationenwechsel geringfügig schwerer wurde, bleibt das Gesamtgewicht des GT3 Cup konstant. Dies gelingt durch ein Bündel von Maßnahmen, wie beispielsweise die Erleichterung der Türen um insgesamt 2,5 Kilogramm, die Verringerung der Frontscheiben-Dicke um einen Millimeter sowie die Verwendung kleinerer und leichterer Außenspiegel. Im Zuge dieser Modifikationen wird auch die Gewichtsverteilung weiter verbessert, etwa durch die Verwendung einer kleiner dimensionierten Lichtmaschine (minus zirka ein Kilogramm) sowie einer kompakteren, leichteren Abgasanlage (minus zirka zwei Kilogramm).

Erstmals ist in den Markenpokalen die Aufzeichnung von Fahrzeugdaten per Elektronik während der Rennwochenenden erlaubt. Ein Achtkanal-Aufzeichnungsgerät an Bord des 911 ermöglicht jetzt die Datenerhebung und schnelle Abstimmung des Fahrzeuges. Eine moderate Leistungssteigerung um zehn PS auf 380 Pferdestärken (279 kW), die der 3,6-Liter-Motor bei 7.200 U/min abgibt, wird in erster Linie durch die Verwendung der Bosch-Motronic 3.1 erreicht, die bislang dem 911 GT3 RS vorbehalten war. Das maximale Drehmoment steigt um zehn Nm auf 380 Nm bei 6.250 U/min. Die neue Rennabgasanlage aus Edelstahl mit zwei integrierten Abgaskatalysatoren trägt zur Leistungssteigerung bei, spart Gewicht hinter der Hinterachse und liefert einen neuen Klang. Das Doppelendrohr mündet mittig unter der Heckschürze.

Neu im Bereich der Kraftübertragung ist die Kühlung des Getriebes durch eine Spritzkühlung mit Öl-Wasser-Wärmetauscher. Mit dieser Maßnahme trägt die Rennabteilung der Tatsache Rechnung, dass zahlreiche 911 GT3 Cup in Langstreckenwettbewerben eingesetzt werden. Das Sechsgang-Schaltgetriebe und die Übersetzungen bleiben unverändert. Die Bremsleistung des Cup-Carrera 2002 übertrifft nicht nur Dank der optimierten Entlüftung der vorderen Radhäuser die Performance aller Vorgänger: An der Vorderachse kommen erstmals Sechskolben-Festsättel zum Einsatz, die auf Bremsscheiben mit 350 Millimeter Durchmesser wirken (2001: 330 mm). Der Durchmesser der hinteren Bremsscheiben bleibt unverändert bei 330 mm. Auch das für den Motorsport angepasste Serien-ABS wird ohne Modifikation übernommen. Um Raum für die größere Bremse zu schaffen, ersetzen 9-Zoll-Felgen vorne die bisher verwendeten Räder der Dimension 8 1/2 Zoll. Das entsprechende Maß für die Hinterachse beträgt nun elf Zoll (2001: 10 1/2 Zoll).

Supercup Melbourne 1999

For the 2002 motorsport season the 911 GT3 Cup racing sportscar adopts numerous improvements from the second Carrera generation, introduced in summer 2001.

The front section displays the headlight design of the 911 Turbo. With its newly-shaped air-inlets, the cooling-air flow increased by 15 percent. The air extraction from the front wheel-houses underwent further optimization. The new standard body reduces uplift at the front axle by 25 percent, and at the rear axle by 40 percent. Based on the results of comprehensive wind tunnel work, the racing department added a large rear wing, adjustable in seven positions. Track tests confirmed the expected results: higher cornering speeds, reduced tyre wear and faster lap times.

Whilst the body shell of the latest generation 911 is marginally heavier than its forerunner, the total weight of the GT3 Cup remains the same. This was attained thanks to several weight-saving measures, for instance by lowering the weight of the doors by 2.5 kilograms, by reducing the front windscreen thickness by one millimetre as well as using smaller and lighter side mirrors. The weight distribution was improved in part thanks to the use of a smaller alternator (minus ca one kilogram) as well as a lighter, more compact exhaust system (minus ca two kilograms).

For the first time in the history of the makes cups data recording and the use of this data is allowed during the racing weekends. For this purpose an eight channel data recording device is on board.

A moderate 10 hp increase to 380 hp (279 kW), delivered by the 3.6-litre engine at 7,200 rpm, is predominantly reached through the use of the Bosch motronic MS 3.1 which by now was reserved for the stronger 911 GT3 RS. Maximum torque increased by ten Nm to 380 Nm at 6,250 rpm. The new stainless steel racing exhaust system with two integrated

(l.-r.): Renate Manthey, Patrick Huisman (Supercup winner 1997-2000), Olaf Manthey

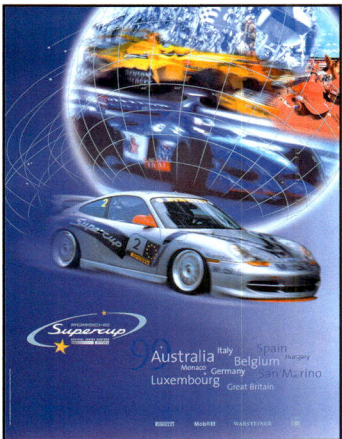

Poster　　　　Poster

catalytic converters contributes to the performance plus, whilst saving weight and lending the 911 a new sound.

With the cooling of the gearbox through a splash-oil cooling and an oil-to-water heat exchanger, the 2002-spec 911 GT3 Cup is well equipped for long distance racing. The six-speed manual gearshift and the transmission remain unchanged.

For the first time in Cup-car history, the front axle features six-piston fixed calipers, and brake discs measuring 350 mm in diameter (2001: 330 mm). The diameter of the rear brake discs remains unchanged at 330 mm. The standard ABS, modified for motorsport purposes, also stays the same. The larger discs and calipers together with the improved cooling of the brakes promise new records in the 2002 season. In order to provide space for the larger brakes, the front wheel grew from 8.5 inches to 9 inches. Correspondingly, the rear axle now sports eleven inch rims (2001: 10.5 inches). Thanks to tie rods from the GT3 RS fixed on the rear axle, teams can adjust the suspension quicker and more precisely to the characteristics of each track.

Due to the high worldwide demand, the racing department built 131 units of the new car – representing a record number of near-standard racing vehicles manufactured by Porsche AG for one season.

The 911 GT3 Cup, as the most popular of Porsche's near-standard racing sportscars, features a range of improvements for the new year. The Performance of the 3.6-litre six-cylinder engine increased by ten horsepower to 390 hp (287kW), which the power unit delivers at 7,300 rpm. The maximum torque rose by ten Nm and now reaches 390 Nm (6,300 revs). Power output was increased and optimised by the consistent reduction of moving masses. In this way the

Zu jedem Rennen lädt Porsche prominente Motorsportler, Schauspieler und Journalisten ein, in den VIP Carrera mit den Startnummern 1 und 2 gegen ein Feld von 911-Spezialisten anzutreten.

Die Gäste verfügen im Regelfall über geringe Erfahrung auf dem seriennahen 911 GT3 Cup und haben damit wenig Aussichten auf einen Podiums-Platz. Trotzdem kommen alle gerne zurück. Das spricht für ihren Sportsgeist. Bei 123 Rennen von 1993 bis 2004 siegten fünf VIP-Gastfahrer. Als erfolgreichster von ihnen gewann Mika Häkkinen 1993 in Monaco und Budapest. Auch Ralf Schumacher, Thierry Boutsen (Platz 4 in Silverstone 1997), Eddie Irvine, Jacque Laffite oder Jochen Mass stellten sich den Porsche-Routiniers. Genau wie die Rallye-Weltmeister Miki Biasion, Stig Blomqvist, Ari Vatanen, Walter Röhrl (Platz 3 in Monaco 1993), Björn Waldegard und Richard Burns. Jutta Kleinschmidt, die Siegerin der Rallye Paris-Dakar, ließ sich 2000 nicht lange bitten und klemmte sich in Spa hinter das 911er-Lenkrad.

Für die Motorrad-Fraktion übten Luca Cadalora, Giacomo Agostini, Ralf Waldmann, Wayne Gardner (Platz 3, Melbourne 1999) die schnelle Kurvenfahrt ohne Schräglage. Thomas Muster und Henri Leconte fuhren als Tennis-Asse. Das Showgeschäft wurde, sehr zum Vergnügen nicht nur der Motorsport-Fangemeinde, zum Beispiel von Chris Rea und Tobias Moretti vertreten.

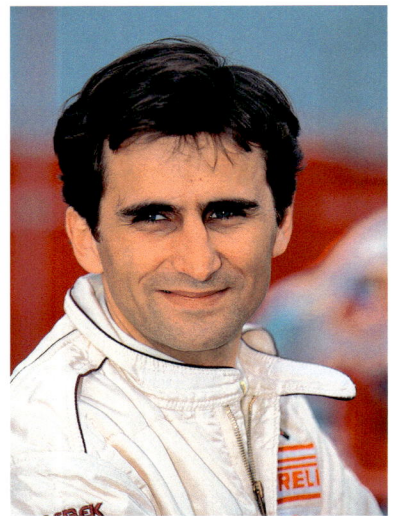

1995: Alessandro Zanardi

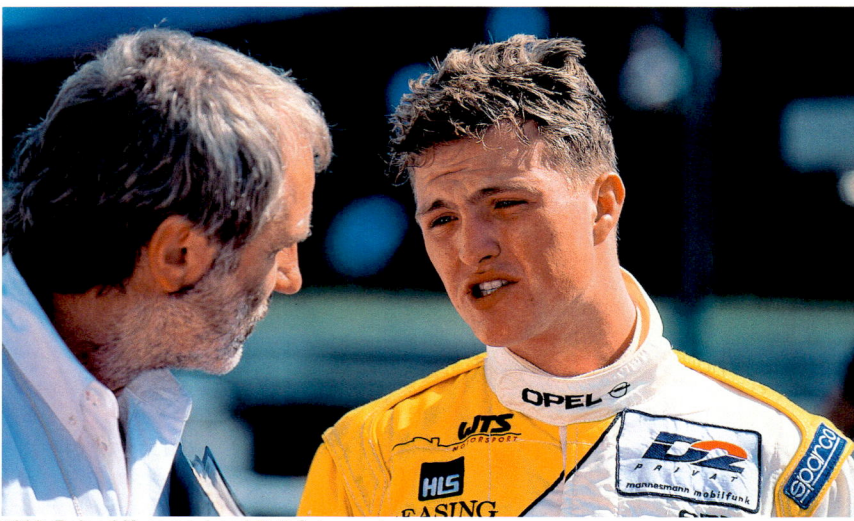

1996: Roland Kussmaul and Ralf Schumacher

1994: Chris Rea

1997: Ralf Waldmann

1996: Ralf Schumacher

1997: Loris Capirossi

330 911-MARKENPOKALE EROBERN DEN GLOBUS

2002: Jutta Kleinschmidt

1993: Mika Häkkinen

2002: Katja Poensgen

2002: Vanina Ickx

1994: Jochen Mass

For each race Porsche invites prominent motorsport personalities, journalists, showbiz and sport celebrities to drive the two VIP Carreras with starting numbers one and two against a grid of 911 specialists. Experience in the near-standard 911 GT3 Cup cars is something these guest drivers generally lack and hence have little chance of reaching the podium. Nevertheless, they are all keen to return – and that speaks volumes for their sporting spirit.

Of the 123 races from 1993 to 2004 only five guest drivers have won. Mika Häkkinen was the most successful with victories at Monaco and Bucapest in 1993. Ralf Schumacher, Thierry Boutsen (4th in Silverstone, 1997), Eddie Irvine, Jaques Laffite and Jochen Mass also pitted themselves against Porsche specialists. As did world rally champions Miki Biason, Stig Blomqvist, Walter Röhrl (3rd in Monaco, 1993), Ari Vatanen, Björn Waldegard and Richard Burns. Jutta Kleinschmidt, winner of Paris-Dakar rally, accepted the invitation without hesitation and joined the 911 action in 2000 at Spa.

Representing the motorbike faction, Luca Cadalora, Giacomo Agostini, Ralf Waldmann and Wayne Gardner (3rd in Melbourne, 1999) tried the unusual sensation of high speed cornering in a up-right position. Tennis aces Thomas Muster and Henri Leconte also took on the challenge. From show business, much to the delight of not only motorsport fans, Chris Rea, Tobias Moretti and Craig T. Nelson climbed aboard a Supercup Porsche.

911 ONE-MAKE FASCINATES

Durch die Verwendung der zweiteiligen Spurstange aus dem GT3 RS an der Hinterachse wird es den Teams möglich, die Spur noch präziser und mit geringerem Zeitaufwand auf die jeweiligen Streckenverhältnisse einzustellen.

Wegen der großen, weltweiten Nachfrage baut Porsche-Motorsport 131 Exemplare des Neuen, was einen weiteren Stückzahlrekord in der Fertigung der seriennahen Rennfahrzeuge darstellt. Der 911 GT3 Cup rollt 2003 mit einer Reihe von Detailverbesserungen an den Start, die großteils vom aktuellen 911 GT3 übernommen wurden, dem das Cup-Fahrzeug zu 90 Prozent entspricht.

Um zehn PS steigt im Vergleich zum Vorjahresmodell die Motorleistung auf 390 PS (287 kW), die das Triebwerk bei 7.300 U/min abgibt. Das maximale Drehmoment klettert um zehn Newtonmeter auf 390 Nm (6.300 U/min).

Die Steigerung und Optimierung der Leistungsabgabe erreicht Porsche unter anderem durch die konsequente Verringerung der bewegten Massen. So verlieren die Kolben neun Prozent ihres Gewichts, die Ventile werden 19 Prozent leichter. Auch die Pleuel und der gesamte Ventiltrieb erfahren grundlegende Optimierungen. Eine Riemenscheibe ersetzt den Schwingungstilger an der Kurbelwelle, was zwei Kilogramm an rotatorischer Masse einspart.

Die Gänge vier bis sechs werden kürzer ausgelegt. Mit dieser Veränderung reagiert Porsche auf den Wegfall der längsten Geraden im Rennkalender (alter GP-Kurs Hockenheim). Überdies wird die Beschleunigung in den höheren Gängen verbessert. Die Endgeschwindigkeit beträgt nun übersetzungsbedingt 271 Stundenkilometer.

Neue Sachs-Stoßdämpfer sind im Zug- und Druckbereich zweifach verstellbar. In Material (hochfester Stahl) und Profil neu ausgelegte Antriebswellen gewährleisten die hohe Zuverlässigkeit des GT3 Cup.

Winner Carrera Cup Germany 2003: Frank Stippler

Durch den Einsatz von Kohlefaser und anderen Kunststoffen gelingt es, das Gewicht bei 1.150 Kilogramm zu halten. So werden die Kunststoff-Türen mit Spiegeln, die 2002 noch 9.500 Gramm pro Stück wogen, auf 6.000 Gramm erleichtert. Fast acht Kilogramm werden durch die Verwendung einer Kohlefaser-Heckabdeckung eingespart. Der verstellbare Heckflügel kann jetzt 3 Grad steiler als 2002 justiert werden. Eine weiter verbesserte Innenraumbelüftung sorgt für ein optimales Arbeitsklima im Cockpit und für gute Sicht im Fall eines Regenrennens.

Supercup 2002: Katja Poensgen

Um den vielfältigen Einsatzmöglichkeiten des GT3 Cup im Sprint- und Langstreckensport Rechnung zu tragen, liefert die Renn-Abteilung das Modell für 2003 mit einem 89-Liter-Kraftstofftank (Vorgänger: 64 Liter) aus.

Porsche-Renningenieur Roland Kussmaul beschreibt die Charakteristik des 911 GT3 Cup für 2003 so: „Ein Wagen, der bewusst nah am Serienfahrzeug bleibt und auf exotisch-teure Technik verzichtet. Trotzdem ist dieser Porsche mit seinen 390 PS ein Rennwagen, der hohes Können erfordert und damit guten Fahrern die Möglichkeit gibt, sich zu profilieren." Im Winter 2002/03 entstehen bei Porsche 200 Exemplare des neuen 911 GT3 Cup. Noch nie in der Geschichte von Porsche wurde eine vergleichbar hohe Anzahl von Rennfahrzeugen während eines Winters gebaut.

Hintergrund dieser Produktionszahl ist zum einen der Boom bei den Porsche-Markenpokalen: Neben den lang etablierten Carrera Cups in Deutschland, Frankreich und Japan finden 2003 in Großbritannien und Australien erstmals Carrera Cups statt. Auch für den Carrera Cup Asien heißt es mit Veranstaltungen in Malaysia, Süd Korea, Thailand und der Volksrepublik China zum ersten Mal: „Start frei!"

Zum anderen setzen Kunden den 911 GT Cup nicht nur in den Cups, sondern auch bei GT-Rennen mit seriennahen Sportwagen ein. Der 911 GT3 Cup in Kundenhand gewinnt 2002 unter anderem den Fahrer- und Herstellertitel in der Grand American Cup Street Stock Series (Klasse GS1) in den USA sowie die Hersteller-Meisterschaft in der SCCA Speed World Challenge (Kl. GT). Auch in Australien (Nations Cup, GTP) und Frankreich (FFSA Coupe de France, GT) holen GT3 Cup-Fahrer Gran Turismo-Titel.

Eine in der 15jährigen Geschichte der Markenpokale von 1990 bis 2004 einzigartige Leistung vollbringt der deutsche Student Frank Stippler 2003, als er in einem Jahr den Porsche-Michelin-Supercup und den Carrera Cup Deutschland gewann. Im selben Jahr verlängert der in Neuseeland geborene Australier Jim Richards seine riesige Erfolgsliste um einen weiteren Titel: Richards ist der erste Gesamtsieger des Carrera Cup Australien; in Asien kommt diese Ehre Charles Kwan zuteil. Der Schotte Barry Horne erweist sich als bester Mann im Carrera Cup Great Britain, der erstmals unter der Ägide von Porsche Cars UK ausgetragen wird.

in Britain and Australia. And for the first time the Carrera Cup Asia brings Porsche fascination to Malaysia, South Korea, Thailand and the People's Republic of China.

There is also a considerable demand for 911 GT3 Cup cars from customers competing in GT racing series. In the USA during the 2002 season, the 911 GT3 Cup won the drivers' and manufacturers' title in the Grand American Cup Street Stock Car Series (GS1 class in the hands on customers as well as the manufacturers' championship in the SCCA Speed World Challenge (GT class). In Australia as well (Nations Cup, GTP) and France (FFSA Coupe de France, GT) GT3 Cup drivers carried off the Gran Turismo title.

A unique feat in the 15 years of one-make racing between 1990 and 2004 is being achieved by German student, Frank Stippler, in 2003. He becomes the first driver to win the Porsche Michelin Supercup and the German Carrera Cup in one year. In the same year, New-Zealand-born Australian Jim Richards adds another title to his already impressive achievement list: Richards becomes the winner of the inaugural Carrera Cup Australia. In Asia, this honour is being taken by Charles Kwan. Scotsman Barry Horne comes out on top in the Carrera Cup Great Britain, run by Porsche Cars UK for the first time.

pistons underwent a nine percent weight loss, the valves became 19 percent lighter. The con rods as well and the entire valve timing gear were subjected to fundamental optimization. A pulley replaces the crankshaft vibration damper, saving two kilos of rotating mass.

The new 911 GT3 Cup features a shorter fouth, fifth and sixth gear. With this modification Porsche reacts to the redesigning of the longest straight on the racing calendar at the old Grand Prix circuit of Hockenheim. At the same time, the acceleration in the higher gears became substantially better, with the top speed – depending on the ratio – now reaching 271 kph. New Sachs shock absorbers on the front and rear axle are adjustable in compression and rebound, and hence contribute to the precise set-up of the vehicle to suit each circuit. With new material (high tensile steel) and a new profile, the driveshafts ensure the high reliability of the GT3 Cup.

Through the use of carbon fibre and other plastics the weight of 911 GT3 Cup stays at 1,160 kilos. The plastic doors with mirrors, which weighed 9,500 grama in 2002, now weigh 6,000 grams. Almost eight kilograms were saved by using a carbon fibre rear body section.

A further improved cockpit ventilation allows an optimal working climate for the driver and for good visibility in the event of a rain race. The upholstery of the safety cage complies to the latest FIA requirements. As the 911 GT3 Cup is not only run in sprint events but increasingly in long distance sport, the racing department fitted the 2003 model with an 89 litre fuel tank (2002: 64 litres).

Porsche racing engineer, Roland Kussmaul, describes the characteristics of the 911 GT3 Cup for 2003 as: "A car that closely resembles a standard vehicle and avoids exotic and expensive technology. Nevertheless, with 390 hp, this Porsche is a race car which requires a great deal of ability and hence gives good drivers a change to show their skill."

Over the winter of 2002/03 Porsche built 200 units of the new 911 GT3 Cup car. Never before in the history of Porsche has such a large number of racing vehicles been built during a winter. The reason for increase in production is not least due to the boom of the Porsche one-make cups: Additional to the long-standing Carrera Cups in Germany, France and Japan, new Carrera Cup series get underway this year

Winner Carrera Cup Germany 2001: Timo Bernhard

Winner Supercup 2003: Frank Stippler

Winner Carrera Cup Great Britain 2003: Barry Horne

Winner Carrera Cup Japan 2003: Masayuki Yamamoto

Porsche Anniversary Cup 2002 (Carrera Cup Germany and Supercup) Spa-Francorchamps

Porsche modifiziert den 911 GT3 Cup für das Jahr 2004 vor allem mit Blick auf erhöhte passive Sicherheit und Vermeidung von Bedienungsfehlern. Eine Veränderung der Luftführung zum Motor bringt ein deutliches Leistungs-Plus und eine klare Verbesserung der Rundenzeiten.

Der Sechspunkt-Gurt und der Rennschalensitz ermöglichen jetzt den Einsatz des Head-And-Neck-Support-Systems (HANS), das Kopf- und Halsverletzungen vermeiden hilft. Der Sicherheitskäfig erhält ein zusätzliches Rohrkreuz und ein Querrohr hinter dem Sitz sowie eine A-Säulen-Versteifung. Die neuen Fondseitenscheiben aus Kunststoff mit Entlüftungsschlitzen gewährleisten beschlagfreie Fenster und tragen zur Gewichtsverminderung bei.

Winner Carrera Cup Australia 2003: Jim Richards

Drei kleinere Modifikationen erhöhen die Bedienungs-Sicherheit des GT3 Cup 2004: Eine Lampe im Cockpit signalisiert dem Fahrer das Erreichen der Schalt-Drehzahl. Der Speedlimiter stellt sicher, dass die in der Boxengasse vorgeschriebene Höchstgeschwindigkeit nicht überschritten wird. Die Wasserstands-Kontrolleuchte warnt bei zu niedrigem Kühlmittel-Level.

Der Sechszylinder-Boxer leistet wie im Vorjahr 390 PS. Das maximale Drehmoment beträgt unverändert 390 Nm. Neu für 2004 ist eine Ansaugluftabschottung auf dem Motor, die gewährleistet, dass keine heiße Luft aus der unmittelbaren Motor-Peripherie oder von der Fahrzeug-Unterseite in die Brennräume gelangt und eine Minderung der Leistungsabgabe hervorruft. Diese Abschottung erweist sich in der Praxis als äußerst wirksam: Bei ansonsten unveränderter Technik und gleichen Michelin-Reifen werden alle Rekorde teils deutlich unterboten. Das in Höhe, Sturz und Spur stufenlos einstellbare Fahrwerk mit in Zug- und Druckstufe zweifach justierbaren Sachs-Gasdruck-Stoßdämpfern und verstellbaren Querstabilisatoren bleibt unverändert, genau wie das Gesamtgewicht von 1.150 Kilogramm.

Der 911 GT3 Cup 2004 kommt in den Porsche-Markenpokalen sowie in zahlreichen weiteren Rennserien zum Einsatz. Vorjahres-Fahrzeuge können – mit Ausnahme des Sicherheitskäfigs – auf den Stand 2004 umgerüstet werden. Aufgrund der großen Nachfrage entstehen bei Porsche 150 Exemplare des Neuen für 2004.

Wieder ist die Liste der Carrera Cups um einen Neuzugang länger geworden: Nach Rennen in Dänemark, Finnland und Schweden ist der Schwede Robin Rudholm der erste Meister des Carrera Cup Skandinavien.

Drei Monate nach der Präsentation des neuen 911 Carrera (997) stellt Porsche die erste Rennversion des Sportwagens vor. Der 911 GT3 Cup 2005 ist der radikalste Cup-Carrera in der 15-jährigen Geschichte der Markenpokale. Er stellt mit der Porsche Ceramic Composite Bremse, die ohne ABS arbeitet, dem sequentiellen Sechsgang-Getriebe und der vom stärkeren RSR übernommenen Radaufhängung einen grossen Schritt in Richtung zum kompromisslosen Rennsportwagen dar. Hoher Abtrieb, niedriges Gewicht und eine bestmögliche Kühlung der Rennaggregate standen bei der Modifikation der klassischen Karosserie-Linie des 911 für den Einsatz auf der Rennstrecke im Vordergrund.

Winner Carrera Cup Germany 2004: Mike Rockenfeller

The 911 GT3 Cup features further improvements to driver safety and comfort in the 2004 specification. The six-point safety belt and racing bucket seat underwent modifications to integrate the Head and Neck Support System (HANS), which helps prevent head and neck injuries. The safety cage received an additional cross bar as well as a transversal bar behind the seat and reinforcement to the A-pillar. With this, the GT3 Cup meets the current FIA safety requirements. The new rear side windows of plastic safe weight and feature ventilation slots for an improved air exchange in the cockpit. Three minor modifications improve operational safety of the 2004 GT3 Cup: A light warns the driver when shifting revs are reached. The speed-limiter ensures that limits in the pit-lane are not exceeded. The water level control light warns the driver when the coolant level is too low.

As in 2003, the six-cylinder boxer engine with 3,598 cc capacity delivers 390 hp (287 kW) at 7,200 rpm. Maximum torque remains unchanged at 390 Nm (6,500 revs), with maximum revs reached at 8,000 rpm.

New for 2004 is an intake air shrouding on the engine preventing hot air from around the engine being taken in and causing power loss. The continuously variable adjustable height, camber and track of the suspension with Sachs gas-pressure shock absorbers adjustable in two position as well as adjustable anti-roll bars open possibilities for setting-up the car to suit each circuit. Through the use of carbon fibre the weight of the 911 GT3 Cup remains at 1,160 kilos. All windows, with the exception of the windscreen, consist of plastic, with the rear lid and doors made of carbon fibre.

The 2004 model of the 911 GT3 Cup competes in the Porsche makes cups as well as many other racing series. Older vehicles can – with the exception of the roll cage – be modified to 2004-spec. Due to the great demand for the GT3 Cup, Porsche built 150 new cars for 2004.

Once again, the list of Carrera Cups has been extended by a new entry: after rounds in Denmark, Finland and Sweden, Swede Robin Rudholm becomes the first overall winner of the Carrera Cup Scandinavia.

Three months after the presentation of the new 911 Carrera (997), Porsche introduces the first competition version of this sports car. The 911 GT3 Cup 2005 is the most radical Cup-Carrera in 15 years of one-make racing. With Porsche's Ceramic Composite Brake, working without ABS, its sequential six-speed gearbox and the suspension, adopted from the stronger RSR, it represents a big step towards a racing car without compromise. High downforce, low weight and the best possible cooling had priority with the classical body silhouette of the 911 was modified for racing.

Winner Carrera Cup Scandinavia 2004: Robin Rudholm

Porsche Carrera Cup Asia 2004

Nürburgring 2005: Porsche Michelin Supercup

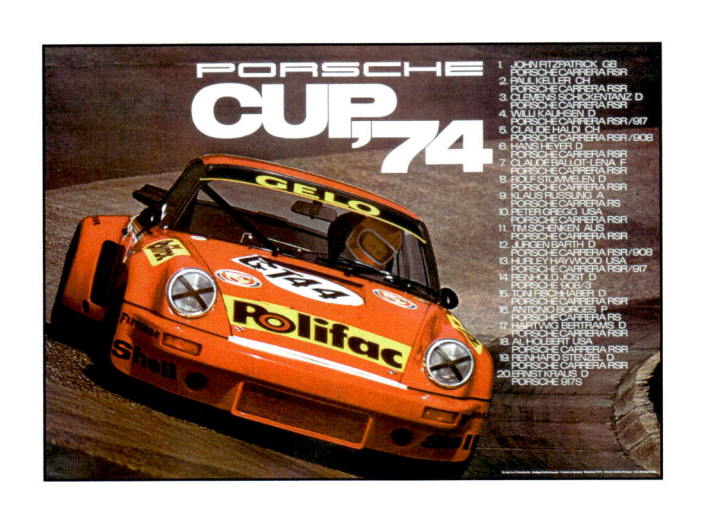

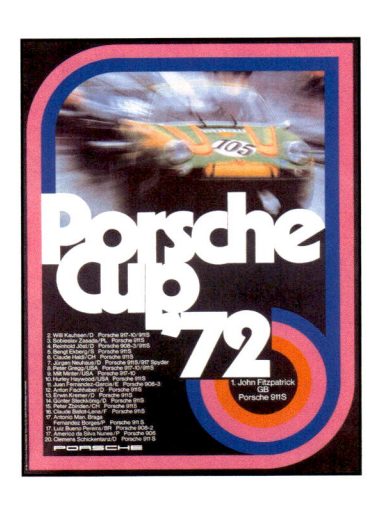

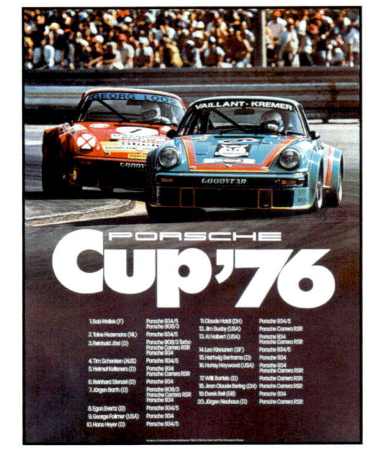

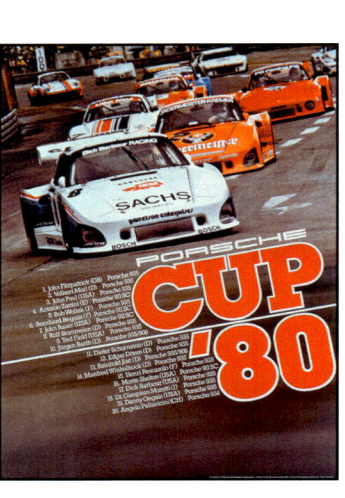

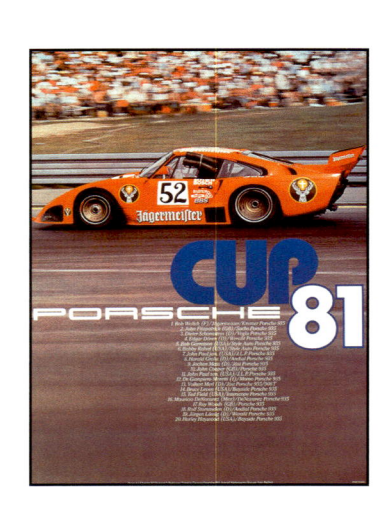

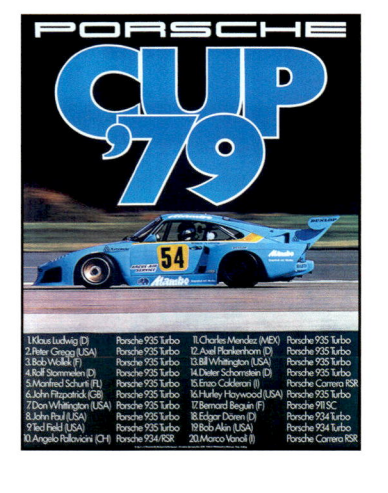

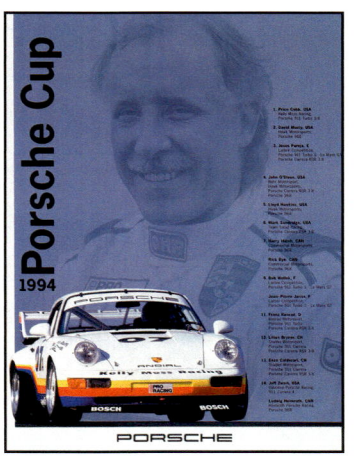

PORSCHE CUP POSTER

336

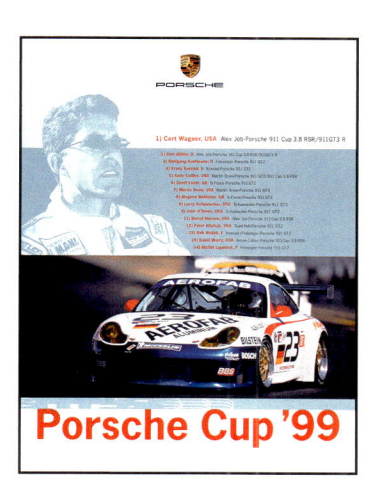

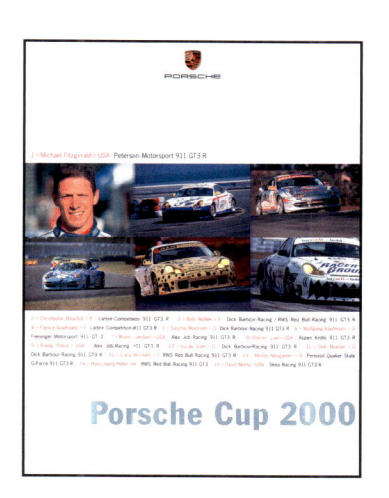

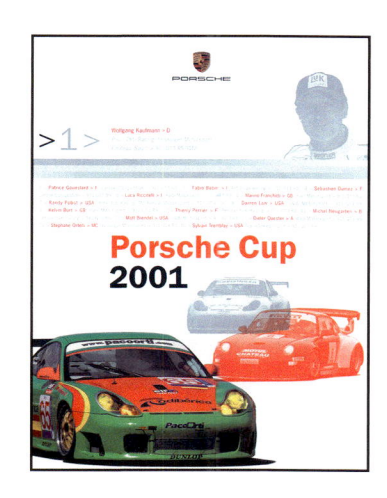

Porsche Cup Winners 1970 – 2004:

1970	Gijs van Lennep
1971	Erwin Kremer
1972	John Fitzpatrick
1973	Clemens Schickentanz
1974	John Fitzpatrick
1975	Claude Haldi
1976	Bob Wollek
1977	Bob Wollek
1978	Bob Wollek
1979	Klaus Ludwig
1980	John Fitzpatrick
1981	Bob Wollek
1982	Bob Wollek
1983	Bob Wollek
1984	Henri Pescarolo
1985	Jochen Mass
1986	Klaus Ludwig
1987	Volker Weidler
1988	John Winter
1989	Bob Wollek
1990	Bernd Schneider
1991	John Winter
1992	Oscar Larrauri
1993	Edgar Dören
1994	Price Cobb
1995	Lilian Bryner / Enzo Calderari
1996	Bruno Eichmann
1997	Franz Konrad
1998	Franz Konrad
1999	Cort Wagner
2000	Mike Fitzgerald
2001	Wolfgang Kaufmann
2002	Kevin Buckler
2003	Marc Lieb
2004	Stephane Ortelli

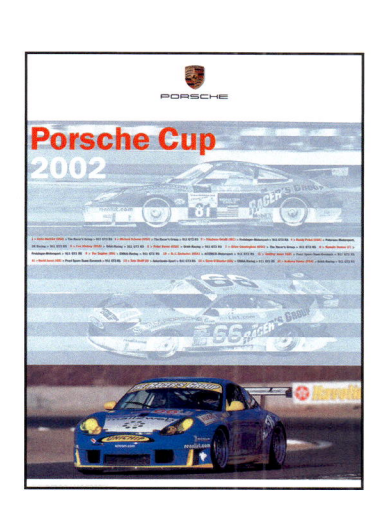

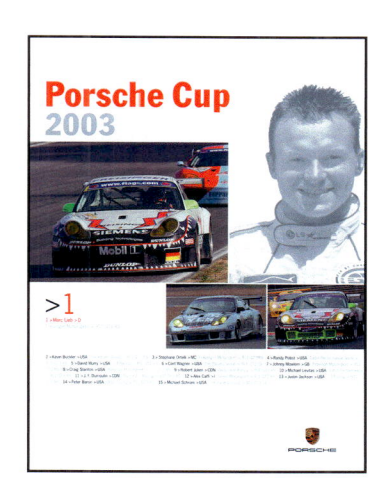

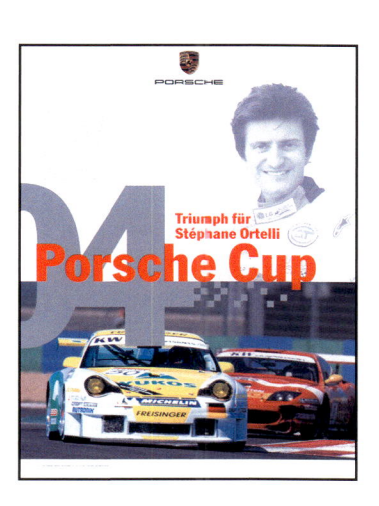

RESULTS STATISTICS

by Klaus Handermann

PRESENTED BY BAM!

NATIONAL AND INTERNATIONAL CHAMPIONSHIPS WON BY 911

YEAR	NATION	CHAMPIONSHIP	DRIVER - FAHRER	PORSCHE
1966	EUR	Rally GT Group 3	Günter Klass	911
	EUR	Hill climb GT	Eberhard Mitter	911
	A	Circuit racing, GT	Karl Egger	911
	E	Rally, GT	Juan Fernandez Garcia	911
	D	Circuit racing, GT	Günter Besier	911
1967	EUR	Rally, GT Group 3	Vic Elford, David Stone	911 S
	EUR	Hill climb, GT Cup	Toni Fischhaber	911 S
	EUR	Touring cars Cup, Div. 3	Karl von Wendt	911
	EUR	Rally, touring cars, Group 1	Sobieslav Zasada	912
	F	Circuit racing	Robert Buchet	911 S
	E	Touring cars	Juan Fernandez Garcia	911 S
	B	Rallye	Jean-Pierre Gaban	911 S
	S	Touring Cars, Group 5	Leif Hansen	911
	S	Touring Cars, Group 2	Boo Johansson	911
	S	Ice racing, GT	Anders Josephsson	911 S
	S	GT cars	Bjoern Rothstein	911 S
	S	Rally	Bjoern Waldegard	911
	A	Touring cars	Peter Peter	911
	NL	Touring cars	Ben Pon	911
	USA	Circuit racing, TransAm	Bert Everett	911
	P	Circuit racing	Americo da Silva Nunes	911 S
	B	Hill climb	Roger Vanderschrick	911
	A	Circuit racing	Günther Breyer	912
	FIN	Ice racing	Antti Aarnio Wihuri	911 S
	PL	Rally	Sobieslav Zasada	912
1968	EUR	GT Trophy	Porsche	911 S
	EUR	Hill climb Cup, GT cars	Holger Zarges	911 S
	EUR	Touring cars, 1601-2500 ccm	Helmut Kelleners	911 S
	EUR	Rally, driver	Pauli Toivonen	911
	CH	Touring cars	Artur Blank	911 S
	CH	GT cars	Jean-Jacques Cochet	911 S
	I	GT cars	Ennio Bonomelli	911 S
	S	Touring cars, Group 2	Helmut Brunner	911 S
	S	GT cars	Anders Josephsson	911 S
	S	Rally, group 2	Bjoern Waldegard	911
	CDN	Circuit racing	Jacques Duval	911
	F	Rally, class national	Jean Egreteaud	911
	DK	Touring cars, Group 5	Sven Engstrom	911 S
	I	Touring cars, 1600 ccm	Cesare Guzzi	911 S
	E	Circuit racing	Ben Heiderich	911 S
	E	Rally	Eladio Doncel	911
	P	Circuit racing	Americo da Silva Nunes	911 S
	USA	Sports Racing, class B	Scooter Patrick	911 S
	USA	Circuit racing, TransAm	Tony Adamowicz	911 S
	A	Hill climb	Peter Peter	911 S
	F	Circuit racing, class national	Raymond Touroul	911 S
	FIN	Circuit racing	Antti Aarnio Wihuri	911 S
	PL	Rally	Sobieslav Zasada	912

Deutsche Rennsport Meisterschaft 1974: Hans Heyer

Clemens Schickentanz

Vic Elford

Winner GT 1000 km Nürburgring 1971: Erwin Kremer, Jürgen Neuhaus

YEAR	NATION	CHAMPIONSHIP	DRIVER - FAHRER	PORSCHE
1969	EUR	Hill climb, GT Trophy	Porsche	911
	EUR	Hill climb, GT Cup	Sepp Greger	911 T
	EUR	Circuit racing, GT	Porsche	911
	USA	Trans-Am-Series	Peter Gregg	911 S
	USA	Trans-Am-Series	Porsche	911
	E	Rally	Jose Maria Palomo	911 S
	E	Touring cars	Jorge de Bagration	911 S
	S	Touring cars	Aake Andersson	911 S
	S	Auto cross	Boo Brasta	911
	S	Touring cars	Bengt Ekberg	911 S
	S	Touring cars, GT	Sten Frohde	911 S
	S	Touring cars, Super GT	Sven Gunarsson	911 S
	DK	Touring cars, GT	Sven Engstrom	911 S
	AUS	Touring cars, GT	Alan Hamilton	911 S
	NL	Touring cars, GT	Toine Hezemans	911 S
	A	Circuit racing, GT	Lambert Hofer	911 S
	F	Circuit racing, GT	Gerard Larrousse	911 S
	P	Circuit racing, GT	Americo da Silva-Nunes	911 S
	I	Circuit racing, GT	Everardo Ostini	911 S
1970		World Rally Championship	Porsche	911
	EUR	GT Trophy	Porsche	911
	E	Rally	Alberto Ruiz Giminez	911 S
	S	Auto cross	Roland Larsson	911
	S	Touring cars, GT	Sten Frohde	911 S
	S	Circuit racing, GT	Bengt Ekberg	911 S
1971	EUR	FIA Cup, GT cars	Porsche	911 S
	EUR	Hill climb, GT Cup	Wilhelm Bartels	911 S
	S	Circuit racing	Aake Andersson	911 S
	CDN	Circuit racing, class C	Jacques Bienvenue	911 S
	P	Rally	Giovanni Salvi	911 S
	I	GT cars	Giorgio Schon	911 S
	CH	GT cars	Florian Vetsch	911 S
1972	EUR	GT Trophy, GT cars	John Fitzpatrick	911 S
	EUR	FIA Cup, GT cars	Porsche	911 S
	P	Rally	Antonio Braga, Fern. Borges	911 S
	S	Touring cars	Bengt Ekberg	911 S
	USA	Circuit racing, IMSA GT	Hurley Haywood	911 S
	PL	Rally	Sobieslav Zasada	911 S
	CH	Circuit racing	Peter Zbinden	911 S

Norisring 1977: Bob Wollek

338 PRESENTED BY BAM

YEAR	NATION	CHAMPIONSHIP	DRIVER - FAHRER	PORSCHE
1973		Challenge Mondial de Vitesse	Porsche	Carrera RS
		FIA GT Cup	Porsche	Carrera RS
	EUR	GT cars	Clemens Schickentanz	Carrera RS
	EUR	GT cars	Claude Ballot-Lena	Carrera RS
	EUR	Hill climb, GT Cup	Sepp Greger	Carrera RS
	D	Rally	Gerd Behret, Willi-Peter Pitz	Carrera RS
	S	Touring cars	Bengt Ekberg	Carrera RS
	USA	Circuit racing, TransAm	Peter Gregg	Carrera RS
	USA	Circuit racing, IMSA GT	Peter Gregg	Carrera RS
1974		FIA GT Cup	Porsche	Carrera RSR
	EUR	GT cars	John Fitzpatrick	Carrera RSR
	EUR	Hill climb, GT cars	Toni Fischhaber	Carrera RSR
	USA	Circuit racing, IMSA GT	Peter Gregg	Carrera RSR
	USA	Circuit racing, TransAm	Peter Gregg	Carrera RSR
	F	Circuit racing	Claude Ballot-Lena	Carrera RSR
	S	GT cars	Bengt Ekberg	Carrera RSR
	CH	GT cars	Harry Blumer	Carrera RSR
	NL	GT cars	Kees Sievertsen	Carrera RSR
	A	Auto cross	Sepp Sommer	911 S
1975		World Championship GT Cup	Porsche	Carrera RSR
	USA	IMSA Camel Challenge Cup	Peter Gregg	Carrera RSR
	EUR	Hill climb GT Cup	Hartwig Bertrams	Carrera RSR
	EUR	Hill climb GT Cup, Group 3	Jean-Claude Bering	Carrera RS
	D	Hill climb Cup	Egon Evertz	Carrera RSR
	D	Rally	Rainer Altenheimer	Carrera RS
	F	Rally, Group 3	Jean-Francois Mas	Carrera RS
	F	Hill climb, Group 3	Jacques Almeras	Carrera RS
	F	Hill climb, Group 4	Jean-Marie Almeras	Carrera RS
	F	Circuit racing, Group 4	Claude Ballot-Lena	Carrera RS
	L	Hill climb	Nicolas Koob	Carrera RS
	A	Hill climb	Wilhelm Rabel	Carrera RS
	E	Rally	Mark Etchebers	Carrera RS
	GR	Rally	"Leonidas"	Carrera RS
	CH	Rally	Jean-Marie Carron	Carrera RS
	USA	SCCA Rally	John Buffum	911 Carrera
1976		Makes World Championship	Porsche	935
	EUR	GT cars	Toine Hezemans	934
	EUR	Hill climb, GT cars, division A	Jean Claude Bering	Carrera RS
	EUR	Hill climb, special GT cars	Willi Bartels	Carrera RSR
	USA	Circuit racing, TransAm	George Follmer	934
	USA	SCCA / NARA Rally	John Buffum	911 Carrera
	D	Rally	Heinz Walter Schewe	Carrera RS
	S	Rally cross	Björn Waldegaard	911

YEAR	NATION	CHAMPIONSHIP	DRIVER - FAHRER	PORSCHE
1977		Makes World Championship	Porsche	935
	EUR	Hill climb, group 3	Toni Fischhaber	Carrera RS
	D	Rennsport-Meisterschaft	Rolf Stommelen	935
	D	Rally	Ludwig Kuhn	Carrera RS
	USA	Circuit racing, TransAm	Peter Gregg	934
	USA	SCCA, B-production	Howard Meister	911
	I	GT cars, B-production	"Momo"	934
	I	GT cars, group 5	Mario Finotto	935
	CH	GT cars, group 5	Emil Brandenberger	Carrera RSR
	CH	Rally	E. Chappuis	Carrera RS
	L	Circuit racing	J. Lagodny	Carrera RSR
	L	Hill climb	J. Lagodny	Carrera RSR
	L	Rally	N. Demuth	Carrera RS
	A	Hill climb, division 3	W. Rabl	Carrera RS
	A	Auto Cross, division 3	R. Frommelt	Carrera RS
	NL	Touring cars, GT	H. v. Oorschot	934
	B	Touring cars, GT	H. v. Oorschot	934
	DK	Touring cars, group 5	P. Kristoffersen	Carrera RSR
	FIN	Circuit racing	J. Miettinen	Carrera RSR
	N	Rally cross	P. Engeseth	911
1978		Makes World Championship	Porsche	935
	EUR	Hill climb, category A, div. 2	Jacques Almeras	934
	EUR	Hill climb, category B	Jean-Marie Almeras	935
		FIA GT Cup	Andrea Palavicini	934
	USA	Circuit racing, IMSA GTX	Peter Gregg	935
	USA	Circuit racing, IMSA GT	Dave Cowart	Carrera RSR
	USA	Circuit racing, IMSA GTU	Dale White	911
	B	Circuit racing, group 5	Claude Bourgoignie	935
	B	Rally	H. Delbar	911
	DK	Circuit racing, group 5	John Poulsen	Carrera RSR
	DK	Rally cross, group 5	B. Soerensen	911
	F	Circuit racing	Henri Pescarolo	935
	F	Hill climb, group 5	Jean-Marie Almeras	935
	F	Hill climb, group 4	Jacques Almeras	934
	NL	Touring cars, group 5	H. v. Oorschot	935
	I	Touring cars, group 3 intern.	A. Brambilla	911
	I	Touring cars, group 5	C. Facetti	935
	I	Touring cars, group 3 nat.	C. Marchioli	911
	L	Hill climb, group 5	J. Lagodny	935
	L	Circuit racing, group 5	J. Lagodny	935
	A	Auto Cross, division 1	Siegfried Pfeifer	911
	S	Rally Cross	Anders Andersson	911
	E	Hill climb, group 1-4	J. Trabal	Carrera RSR

Winner Tour de France 1969: Gerard Larrousse, Maurice Gelin

NATIONAL AND INTERNATIONAL CHAMPIONSHIPS WON BY 911

Deutsche Rennsport Meisterschaft 1980: Rolf Stommelen (6), Bob Wollek (9)

YEAR	NATION	CHAMPIONSHIP	DRIVER - FAHRER	PORSCHE
1983	EUR	FIA Auto Cross	Peter Derber	911
	NL	Rally Cross	Rolf Nilsson	911
	CH	Rally	Eric Ferreux	911
	B	Rally	Patrick Snyers	911
	I	Hill climb, group B	Luigi Bormolini	911 turbo
	A	Auto Cross, division 2	Carl Woeber	911
	A	Auto Cross, division 3	Siegfried Pfeiffer	911
	F	Rally	Michel Teilhol	911
	USA	Circuit racing, IMSA GTO	Wayne Baker	934
	AUS	Circuit racing GT	Rusty French	935
	USA	IMSA GTO makes	Porsche	
1984		FISA Middle East Rally	Porsche	911 SC RS
		FISA Middle East Rally	Saaed Al Hajri	911 SC RS
	EUR	FIA Auto Cross	Peter Derber	911
	B	Rally	Patrick Snyers	911 SC
	S	Special production cars	Mats Linden	935
	A	Auto Cross, division 2	Siegfried Pfeiffer	911
	A	Auto Cross, division 3	Carl Woeber	911
	GB	Productions Sports	Bill Taylor	911
	E	Rally	Carlos Pizeiro	911
1985		FISA Middle East Rally	Saeed Al Hajri	911 SC RS
	EUR	FIA Rally Cross	Matti Alamaeki	935
	EUR	FIA Auto Cross, division 2	Jörg Felix	911
	D	Rally trophy	Reinhardt Schülein	911
	CH	Circuit racing	Antoine Salamin	935
	FIN	Drag racing	Leif Nylund	911
	DK	Rally Cross	Ole Carlson	911
	DK	Super Saloon cars	John Jensen	911 Carrera
	B	Rally	Pascal Gaban	911 SC RS
	L	Hill climb	Jean Welkenbach	911
	A	Auto Cross Cup	Siegfried Pfeifer	911
1986	EUR	FIA Auto Cross, division 2	Jörg Felix	911
	DK	Circuit racing	John Jensen	911 Carrera
	D	Rally Cross Cup	Adolf Heinz	911
	DK	Rally Cross Cup	Henrik Jacobsen	911
	YU	Rally	Vojko Podobnik	911
	A	Auto Cross, division 2	Siegfried Pfeifer	911
	A	Auto Cross, division 3	Carl Woeber	911
	B	Rally	Pascal Gaban	911 SC RS
	GB	Hill climb	Laura Keen	Carrera
1987	B	Rally	Marc Soullet	911 SC RS
	A	Circuit racing	Willi Rabl	911 turbo
	A	Auto Cross, division 2	Erwin Hofer	911
	A	Auto Cross, division 3	Werner Roesl	911
	DK	Rally Cross	A. Jörgensen	911 turbo
	D	Rally Cross Cup	H. Kirchhof	911

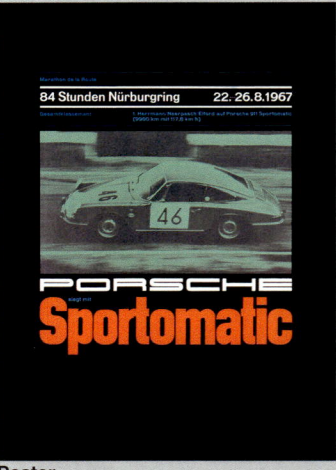

YEAR	NATION	CHAMPIONSHIP	DRIVER - FAHRER	PORSCHE
1979		Makes World Championship	Porsche	935
	EUR	Hill climb, category A, div. 2	Jacques Almeras	934
	EUR	Hill climb, category B	Jean-Marie Almeras	935
	EUR	Rally Cross	Olle Arnesson	911 SC
	D	Rennsport-Championship	Klaus Ludwig	935
	D	Rennsport-Trophy	Edgar Dören	934
	USA	Circuit racing, IMSA GTX	Peter Gregg	935
	USA	Circuit racing, IMSA GTO	Howard Meister	911
	USA	Circuit racing, TransAm, cat. 2	John Paul	935
	B	Rally	D. Moortgar	Carrera RS
	CH	Rally	Claude Haldi	934
	F	Rally	Bernard Beguin	911 SC
	NL	Rally	R. Guliker	911 SC
	S	Circuit racing	Jan Lundgarth	935
	L	Hill climb	J. Lagodny	935
	L	Circuit racing	J. Lagodny	935
	A	Rally	Franz Wittmann	911 SC
	A	Auto Cross, division 2	K. Singer	Carrera RS
	GB	Sports cars	B. Robinson	Carrera RSR
	GB	Hill climb	J. Sadler	Carrera RS
	AUS	Track Racing	R. Mathiesen	Carrera RS
1980		Makes World Championship	Porsche	935
		FIA World Endurance Driver	John Paul	935
	EUR	FIA Rally	Antonio Zanini	911 SC
	EUR	FIA Hill climb group 1 and 3	Roland Biancone	911 turbo
	EUR	FIA Hill climb group 4	Jacques Almeras	934
	EUR	FIA Hill climb group 5	Jean-Marie Almeras	935
	EUR	FIA Rally Cross, division 2	Olle Arnesson	911 SC
	USA	IMSA GTX and GTO makes	Porsche	
	USA	Circuit racing, IMSA GTX	John Fitzpatrick	935
	USA	Circuit racing, IMSA GTO	Charles Mendez	Carrera RSR
	USA	Circuit racing, TransAm	Jo Bauer	911 SC
	DK	Auto Cross, group 5	S. K. Hansen	911 SC
	L	Hill climb	J. Lagodny	935
	A	Auto Cross, division 1	Siegfried Pfeifer	911 SC
	A	Auto Cross, division 2	Karl Woeber	911 SC
	A	Rally	Franz Wittmann	911 SC
	E	Rally	A. Zanini	911 SC
	CH	Rally	J. P. Balmer	911 SC
	S	Circuit racing, group 5	Anders Olofsson	935
1981		FIA World Championship	Porsche (makes)	935
		FIA World Endurance, driver	Bob Garretson	935
	EUR	Hill climb, division 1	Karl Heinz Linnig	911 turbo
	EUR	FIA Rally Cross, division 2	Matti Alamäki	911
	EUR	FIA Auto Cross, division 1	Adolf Heinz	911
	USA	Circuit racing, IMSA makes	Porsche	
	AUS	Sports cars	Lotham	934
	DK	Rally Cross, group 5	Svanholt	911
	D	Auto Cross Cup	Eisen	911
	F	Rally Cross	Touroul	911
	I	Circuit racing, group 5	Coggiola	935
	CH	Rally	Carron	911
	NL	Rally Cross	van Ham	911
1982		FIA World Championship	Porsche	935
		FIA Endurance group B makes	Porsche	911 turbo
	EUR	FIA Hill climb, division 2	Jacques Guillot	911 turbo
	EUR	FIA Auto Cross, division 3	Peter Röhrig	911 SC
	USA	SCCA Pro solo makes	Porsche	935
	USA	IMSA GTP-GTX makes	Porsche	
	USA	Circuit racing, IMSA GTP	John Paul jr.	935
	USA	Circuit rac., IMSA Endurance	John Paul sr.	935
	AUS	Sport sedan series	Alan Jones	935
	B	Rally	Marc Duez	911 SC

Poster

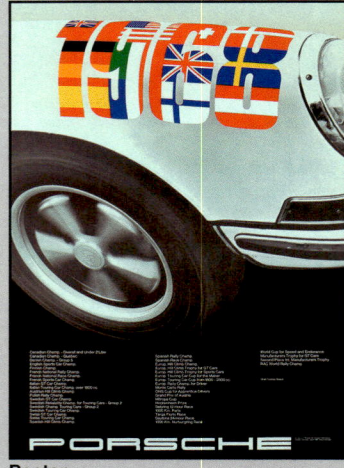

Poster

Deutsche Rennsport Meisterschaft 1979: Volkert Merl

340 PRESENTED BY BAM

Winner IMSA Camel GT Grand Prix Riverside 1983: John Fitzpatrick, David Hobbs, Derek Bell

Erwin Kremer

Herbert Müller (l.) and Norbert Singer

Bob Wollek

YEAR	NATION	CHAMPIONSHIP	DRIVER - FAHRER	PORSCHE
1990	GB	Circuit racing	Mike Burtt	911
	FIN	Circuit racing super stock	Leif Nylund	911
	A	Hill climb cup	Willi Rabl	935
	A	Circuit racing cup	Willi Rabl	935
	D	Carrera Cup	Olaf Manthey	Carrera 2 Cup
	A	Auto Cross	Siegfried Pfeifer	911
	B	Production car cup	Thierry van Dalen, Patrik Neve	Carrera 2
1991	GB	Pirelli Cup	Mike Jordan	911
	GB	Circuit racing	John Greasley	935
	F	Carrera Cup	Jean Pierre Malcher	Carrera 2 Cup
	D	Carrera Cup	Roland Asch	Carrera 2 Cup
	D	Carrera Trophy	Wolfgang Destree	Carrera 2 Cup
	D	Veedol Junior Trophy	Uwe Alzen	Carrera 2
	USA	IMSA Supercar driver	Hurley Haywood	911 turbo
	USA	IMSA Grand Sports makes	Porsche	911
	USA	IMSA Supercar makes	Porsche	911 turbo
	CDN	Circuit racing makes	Porsche	911
1992	EUR	Ferrari Porsche Challenge	Fred Spoor	911
	I	Circuit racing GT class	Angelo Zadra	Carrera RS
	N	Rally Cross, division 2	Raymond Petterson	911
	USA	IMSA Supercar	Brumos Racing	911 turbo
	D	Carrera Cup	Uwe Alzen	Carrera 2 Cup
	D	Carrera Trophy	Enzo Calderari	Carrera 2 Cup
	F	Carrera Cup	Dominique Dupuy	Carrera 2 Cup
	J	Carrera Cup	Satoshi Ikezawa	Carrera 2 Cup
1993	EUR	Supercup	Altfrid Heger	Carrera 2 Cup
	EUR	Ferrari Porsche Challenge	Lex Proper	911 SC RS
	USA	IMSA Supercar driver	Hans-Joachim Stuck	911 turbo 3.6
	USA	IMSA Supercar makes	Porsche	911 turbo 3.6
	D	Carrera Cup	Wolfgang Land	Carrera 2 Cup
	D	Touring car cup	Wolfgang Schrey	911 Carrera RS
	F	Carrera Cup	Dominique Dupuy	Carrera 2 Cup
	J	Carrera Cup	Koichi Kashiwabara	Carrera 2 Cup
	GB	Pirelli production	John Collins	911
	GB	Circuit racing	John Greasley	935
	S	Circuit racing cup	Örnulf Wirdheim	911 Carrera
	L	Circuit racing	Claude Schons	911 Carrera

YEAR	NATION	CHAMPIONSHIP	DRIVER - FAHRER	PORSCHE
1994	EUR	Supercup	Uwe Alzen	911 Cup 3.8
	USA	SCCA World Challenge driver	Price Cobb	911 turbo 3.6
	USA	SCCA World Challenge makes	Porsche	911 turbo 3.6
	USA	IMSA GT1 Endurance series	Hans-J. Stuck, Hurley Haywood	911 turbo 3.6
	USA	IMSA GT1 Endurance series	Porsche	911 turbo 3.6
	USA	IMSA GT2 Endurance series	Mark Sandridge	RSR 3.8
	USA	IMSA GT2 Endurance series	Porsche	RSR 3.8
	GB	Sports GT Challenge, class A	Ross Hyatt	935
	GB	Sports GT Challenge, class C	Nigel Barrett	911
	D	ADAC GT Cup	Ralf Kelleners	RSR 3.8
	D	Carrera Cup	Bernd Mayländer	Carrera 2 Cup
	F	Carrera Cup, division A	Christophe Bouchut	Carrera 2 Cup
	F	Carrera Cup, division B	Jean-Claude Lagniez	Carrera 2 Cup
	J	Carrera Cup	Koichi Kashiwabara	Carrera 2 Cup
	S	Circuit racing cup	Örnulf Wirdheim	911 Carrera
	GB	Pirelli production, class B	John Robinson	911
	GB	Pirelli production, class C	Peter Chambers	911
	AUS	Cup series	Wayne Park, Steve Webb	911
	NZ	Cup series, class B and C	Grah. Cameron, Clive Pilkington	911
	NZ	Circuit racing cup	Bruno Eichmann	911 turbo
		BPR Endurance GT series	Lilian Bryner, Enzo Calderari	911 Cup 3.8
1995	EUR	Supercup	Jean-Pierre Malcher	911 Cup 3.8
	EUR	Ferrari Porsche Challenge	Wolfgang Schrey	911
	USA	SCCA World Challenge driver	David Murry	911 GT2
	USA	SCCA World Challenge team	Rohr Motorsport	911 GT2
	USA	SCCA World Challenge makes	Porsche	911 GT2
	USA	IMSA Exxon GTS 2 driver	Jorge Trejos	911 RSR 3.8
	USA	IMSA Exxon GTS 2 team	Trexo Racing	911 RSR 3.8
	USA	IMSA Exxon GTS 2 makes	Porsche	911 RSR 3.8
	D	ADAC GT Cup driver	Uwe Alzen	911 GT2
	D	ADAC GT Cup team	Roock Racing	911 GT2
	D	Carrera Cup	Harald Grohs	911 Cup 3.8
	J	Circuit racing GT team	Team Taisan	911 GT2
	AUS	Circuit racing GT driver	Jim Richards	911 RS 3.6
	AUS	Circuit racing GT makes	Porsche	911 RS 3.6
	B	Carglass Endurance	Albert Vanierschot	Carrera RS
	I	Coppa GT special	Renato Mastropietro	911 turbo S
	HGK	Super Car	Alex Yan	911 Cup 3.6
	F	Carrera Cup, division A	Christophe Bouchut	911 Cup 3.8
	F	Carrera Cup, division B	Paul Gueslard	911 Cup 3.8
	S	Cup	Mats Linden	911 Cup 3.8
	NZ	Cup series, class B and C	Hamish Franklin, Owen Edwards	911 Carrera
	ZA	GT Challenge	Gary Dunkerley	911 Cup
	TW	Circuit racing	Chia Nung Wang	911 turbo

NATIONAL AND INTERNATIONAL CHAMPIONSHIPS WON BY 911   341

NATIONAL AND INTERNATIONAL CHAMPIONSHIPS WON BY 911

YEAR	NATION	CHAMPIONSHIP	DRIVER - FAHRER	PORSCHE
1996		BPR Endurance GT series	Bruno Eichmann, Gerd Ruch	911 GT2
	EUR	Supercup	Emmanuel Collard	911 Cup 3.8
	EUR	Ferrari Porsche Challenge	Wolfgang Schrey	911 turbo
	USA	IMSA Exxon GTS 2 driver	Larry Schumacher	911 GT2
	USA	SCCA World Challenge GTS 1	Martin Snow	911 turbo
	GB	ERF Intermarque	John Lock	911 RS
	GB	Cup	Robert Babikan	911 Carrera
	J	All Japan GT 300 team	Team Taisan	911 GT2
	AUS	Circuit racing GT driver	Cameron McConville	911
	AUS	Circuit racing GT makes	Porsche	911
	D	Carrera Cup	Ralf Kelleners	911 Cup 3.8
	F	Carrera Cup, division A	Christophe Bouchut	911 Cup 3.8
	F	Carrera Cup, division B	Christopher Campbell	911 Cup 3.8
	S	Special saloon	Koit Vertee	911 RS
	S	Cup	Mats Linden	911 Cup
	AUS	Cup	Geoff Morgan	911
	NZ	Circuit racing	Marc Fisk	911
1997	EUR	Supercup	Patrick Huisman	911 Cup 3.8
	USA	Exxon GT1 series driver	Andy Pilgrim	911 GT2 / GT1
	USA	Exxon GT1 series makes	Porsche, Rohr Motorsport	911 GT2 / GT1
	USA	Exxon GT2 series driver	Larry Schumacher	911 GT2
	USA	Exxon GT2 series makes	Porsche, Schumacher Racing	911 GT2
	D	Carrera Cup	Wolfgang Land	911 Cup 3.8
	GB	Privilege Insurance GT, div. 2	Steve O'Rourke	911 GT2
	GB	Privilege Insurance GT, div. 1	John Greasley	911 GT1
	F	FFSA GT	Patrice Gueslard	911 GT2
	F	Carrera Cup, division A	Dominique Dupuy	911 Cup 3.8
	F	Carrera Cup, division B	Alain Filhol	911 Cup 3.8
1998	EUR	Supercup	Patrick Huisman	911 GT3 Cup
	EUR	Ferrari Porsche Challenge	Daniel Schrey	911 GT2
	USA	USRRC GT1 team	Champion Porsche	911 GT1
	USA	USRRC GT1 driver	Thierry Boutsen	911 GT1
	USA	USRRC GT1 makes	Porsche	911 GT1
	USA	USRRC GT2 makes	Porsche	911 GT2
	USA	USRRC GT2 driver	Larry Schumacher	911 GT2
	USA	USRRC GT2 team	Schumacher Racing	911 GT2
	CDN	GT Challenge Cup	Klaus Bytzek	911 GT1
	AUS	GT production car	Domenic Beninca	911 RS
	NZ	Circuit racing GT driver	Tony Broad	911 RSR
	D	Carrera Cup	Dirk Müller	911 Cup 3.8
	L	Circuit racing	Daniel Schrey	911 GT2
	F	Circuit racing GT driver	Jean-Pierre Jarier	911 GT2
	F	Circuit racing GT serie, driver	Jean Bozzetti	911 RS
	F	Carrera Cup, division A	Dominique Dupuy	911 Cup 3.8
	F	Carrera Cup, division B	Alain Filhol	911 Cup 3.8

Winner BPR Endurance GT Series 1996: Bruno Eichmann, Gerd Ruch

Winner Carrera Cup Germany 1996: Ralf Kelleners

Winner USRRC GT1 Team and Driver Championship 1998: Champion Racing and Thierry Boutsen

Winner Japan GT 300 Team Championship 2001: Team Taisan

ALMS Sears Point 2002: Johnny Mowlem, Randy Pobst

YEAR	NATION	CHAMPIONSHIP	DRIVER - FAHRER	PORSCHE
1999	EUR	Supercup	Patrick Huisman	GT3 Cup
	EUR	Ferrari Porsche Challenge	Elmar Grimm	911 GT2
	USA	ALMS driver GT	Cort Wagner	911 GT3 R
	USA	ALMS makes GTS	Porsche	911 GT2
	USA	ALMS makes GT	Porsche	911 GT3 R
	USA	USRRC driver GT 2	Larry Schumacher, J. O'Steen	911 GT2
	USA	USRRC driver GT 3	Cort Wagner	911 RSR
	USA	USRRC team GT 3	Reiser / Callas	911 RSR
	USA	USRRC makes GT 2	Porsche	911 GT2
	USA	USRRC makes GT 3	Porsche	911 RSR
	USA	SCCA World Challenge makes	Porsche	911 RSR
	CDN	GT Challenge Cup GT 1	Klaus Bytzek	911 GT1
	F	GT series GT 2	Jean-Pierre Jarier	911 GT2
	F	GT series GT 3	Dominique Dupuy, Francois Fiat	911 Cup
	F	GT series GT	Joel Bozetti	911 RS
	F	Carrera Cup, division A	Dominique Dupuy	GT3 Cup
	F	Carrera Cup, division B	Louis Marques	GT3 Cup
	GB	Cup	Peter Chambers	911
	D	Special touring cars	Miguel Monte	911 GT2
	D	Carrera Cup	Lucas Luhr	GT3 Cup
	B	Belcar GT series	Paul Kumpen, Leonard Cohen	911 GT2
	S	GT series GT 2	Lennart Pehrson	911 GT2
	S	GT series GT 3	Niklas Loven	911 RSR
	AUS	GT production car	Jim Richards	911 RS
	AUS	Cup	Peter Brandbury	911 GT2
	J	All Japan GT 300 team	Team Taisan	911 GT3 R
2000		FIA N-GT driver	Christ. Bouchut, Pat. Gueslard	911 GT3 R
		FIA N-GT team	Larbre Competition	911 GT3 R
	EUR	Supercup	Patrick Huisman	911 GT3 Cup
	EUR	Ferrari Porsche Challenge A	Elmar Grimm	911 GT2
	EUR	Ferrari Porsche Challenge B	Edgar Althoff	911
	USA	ALMS driver GT	Dirk Müller	911 GT3 R
	USA	ALMS team GT	Dick Barbour Racing	911 GT3 R
	USA	ALMS makes GT	Porsche	911 GT3 R
	USA	Grand Am Series driver	Mike Fitzgerald	911 GT3 R
	USA	Grand Am Series team	G&W Motorsports	911 GT3 R
	USA	Grand Am Series makes	Porsche	911 GT3 R
	USA	Motorola GSP series driver	Al Worzman, Mike McCalmont	911 GT3 R
	GB	GT series GTO driver	Mark Sumpter	911 GT3 R
	F	FFSA GT Coupe driver	Thierry Perrier, Ger. Larrousse	911 RSR
	F	FFSA GT serie driver	Lionel Voucher	911 GT3 R
	F	Carrera Cup	Christophe Bouchut	911 GT3 Cup
	E	GT series driver	Jesus Diez Villar	911 GT 2
	J	All Japan GT 300 driver	Hideo Fujkuyama	911 GT3 R
	J	All Japan GT 300 team	Team Taisan	911 GT3 R
	NZ	Circuit racing GT driver	Nigel Caigou	911 SC
	NZ	Super Cup	Paul Higgins	911 RSR 3.8
	CDN	GT Challenge Cup	Klaus Bytzek	911 GT1
	D	Carrera Cup	Jörg Bergmeister	911 GT3 Cup
	GB	Cup	Peter Chambers	911 GT3 Cup
	AUS	GTP nation cup	Jim Richards	911 RS
	AUS	Cup	Simone Froude	911

342 PRESENTED BY BAM

YEAR	NATION	CHAMPIONSHIP	DRIVER - FAHRER	PORSCHE
2001	EUR	Supercup	Jörg Bergmeister	911 GT3 Cup
	EUR	ELMS GT driver	Robin Liddell, Mike Youles	911 GT3 RS
	EUR	ELMS GT team	Team PK Sport	911 GT3 RS
	EUR	Kumho Euro GT serie, cat. A	Klaus Abbelen	911 GT2
	EUR	Kumho Euro GT serie, cat. B	Krister Andersson	911 GT3 RS
	EUR	Kumho Euro GT serie, cat. C	Charles Brugmann	911 GT3
	USA	Grand Am Series GT driver	Darren Law	911 GT3 R
	USA	Grand Am Series GT team	D&W Motorsports	911 GT3 R
	USA	Grand Am Series GTS team	D&W Motorsports	911 GT2
	USA	Grand Am Series GT makes	Porsche	911 GT3 R
	USA	Grand Am Series GTS makes	Porsche	911 GT2
	GB	GT series GTO driver	Kelvin Burt, Marino Franchitti	911 GT3 RS
	F	FFSA GT serie driver	Nicola Fouchet	911 GT3 R
	F	FFSA GT Coupe driver	Sebast. Dumez, Herve Clement	911 GT3 Cup
	F	Carrera Cup, division A	Philippe Gache	911 GT3 Cup
	F	Carrera Cup, division B	Xavier Armanc	911 GT3 Cup
	B	Belcar GTA category driver	Patrick Schreurs, Kurt Thiers	911 turbo
	CDN	GT Challenge Cup	Klaus Bytzek	911 GT1
	D	Carrera Cup	Timo Bernhard	911 GT3 Cup
	J	All Japan GT 300 team	Team Taisan	911 GT3 RS
	J	Carrera Cup	Yasuo Miyagawa	911 GT3 Cup
2002		FIA GT, class N-GT driver	Stephane Ortelli	911 GT3 RS
		FIA GT, class N-GT team	Freisinger Motorsport	911 GT3 RS
	EUR	Michelin Supercup	Stephane Ortelli	911 GT3 Cup
	EUR	Euro GT serie, class B driver	Charles Brugmann	911 GT3 RS
	EUR	Euro GT serie, class C driver	Peter Wirichs	911 GT3 Cup
	USA	ALMS, GT driver	Lucas Luhr, Sascha Maassen	911 GT3 RS
	USA	ALMS, GT makes	Porsche	911 GT3 RS
	USA	IMSA Cup GT team	Alex Job Racing	911 GT3 RS
	USA	Grand Am Series GS1 driver	Scott Maxwell	911 GT3 Cup
	USA	Grand Am Series GS1 makes	Porsche	911 GT3 Cup
	USA	Grand Am Series GT makes	Porsche	911 GT3 RS
	USA	SCCA World Challenge GT	Porsche	911 GT3 Cup
	AUS	Nations Cup, class GTP driver	Jim Richards	911 GT3 Cup
	B	Belcar serie, class GTB driver	Rudi Penders, Marc Goossens	911 GT3 RS
	F	FFSA GT, driver	Philipp Soulan, Patr. Goueslard	911 GT3 RS
	F	FFSA Coupe, GT driver	Renato Dotta, Ivan Jacoma	911 GT3 Cup
	F	Carrera Cup, class A	Sebastien Dumez	911 GT3 Cup
	F	Carrera Cup, class B	Jean-Marc Mezzanotti	911 GT3 Cup
	S	Circuit racing, GT	Johan Stureson	911 GT3 RS
	J	JAF GT-300 serie, team	Team Tasian Advan	911 GT3 RS
	J	Carrera Cup	Takashi Inoue	911 GT3 Cup
	D	Carrera Cup	Marc Lieb	911 GT3 Cup
	GB	Cup	Mark Cole	911 GT3 Cup
	S	Cup, class 1, 2 and 3	P.Englund, J.Nystedt, T.Larson	911 GT3 Cup
	AUS	Cup	Matthew Coleman	911 GT3 Cup

Gijs van Lennep

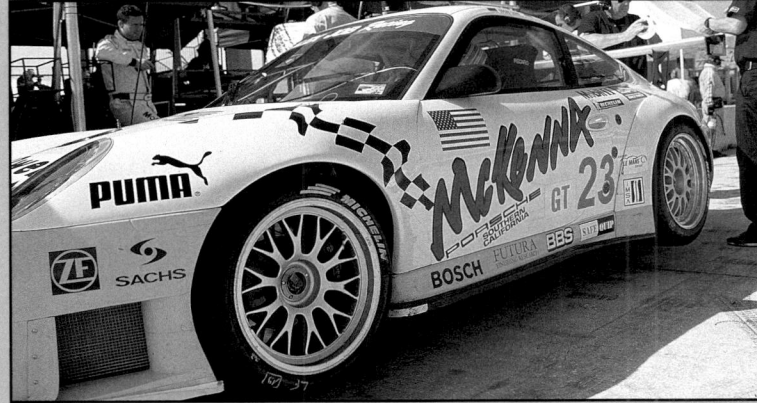

Reinhold Joest

Winner ALMS GT Team Championship 2003: Alex Job Racing

Winner ALMS Driver GT Championship 2004: Timo Bernhard

YEAR	NATION	CHAMPIONSHIP	DRIVER - FAHRER	PORSCHE
2003		FIA GT, class N-GT driver	Stephane Ortelli, Marc Lieb	911 GT3 RS
		FIA GT, class N-GT team	Freisinger Motorsport	911 GT3 RS
	EUR	Michelin Supercup	Frank Stippler	911 GT3 Cup
	USA	ALMS, GT driver	Lucas Luhr, Sascha Maassen	911 GT3 RS
	USA	ALMS, GT makes	Porsche	911 GT3 RS
	USA	ALMS, GT team	Alex Job Racing	911 GT3 RS
	USA	IMSA Cup GT team	Alex Job Racing	911 GT3 RS
	USA	Grand Am Series GS1 driver	Jean-F. Dumoulin, Robert Julien	911 GT3 Cup
	USA	Grand Am Series GS1 makes	Porsche	911 GT3 Cup
	USA	Grand Am Series GS1 team	Doncaster Racing	911 GT3 Cup
	USA	Grand Am Series GS2 driver	Joe and Wayne Nonnamaker	911 GT3 Cup
	USA	Grand Am Series GS2 makes	Porsche	911 GT3 Cup
	USA	Grand Am Series GS2 team	Planet Earth Racing	911 GT3 Cup
	B	Belcar serie, class GTB driver	Franz Lamot, Bart Couwberghs	911 GT3 RS
	GB	GT series, GT3 class	Matthew Griffin, Patrick Pearce	911 GT3 Cup
	GB	Carrera Cup	Barry Horne	911 GT3 Cup
	F	Carrera Cup, class A	Sebastien Dumas	911 GT3 Cup
	F	Carrera Cup, class B	Romain Bera	911 GT3 Cup
	F	Coupe de France FFSA GT	Jerome Miloe, James Ruffier	911 GT3 Cup
	F	Coupe de France, standard	Frederic Angel	911 GT3
	I	Campionato N-GT	Luca Riccitelli	911 GT3 RS
	J	JAF GT series, team 300	Team Taisan Advan	911 GT3 RS
	J	Carrera Cup	Masayuki Yamamoto	911 GT3 Cup
	S	GT Mästerskap Cup N-GT	Thomas Nystrom	911 GT3 RS
	S	GT Mästerskap GTC Cup	Anders Roos	911 GT3 Cup
	D	Carrera Cup	Frank Stippler	911 GT3 Cup
		Carrera Cup Asia	Charles Kwan	911 GT3 Cup
	AUS	Carrera Cup	Jim Richards	911 GT3 Cup
2004		FIA GT, class N-GT driver	Sascha Maassen, Lucas Luhr	911 GT3 RSR
		FIA GT, class N-GT team	Freisinger Motorsport	911 GT3 RSR
	EUR	LMES, GT team	Sebah Automobile	911 GT3 RS
	EUR	Divinol Europe Cup	Klaus Horn	911 GT2
	EUR	Michelin Supercup	Wolf Henzler	911 GT3 Cup
	USA	ALMS, GT makes	Porsche	911 GT3 RSR
	USA	ALMS, GT driver	Timo Bernhard	911 GT3 RSR
	USA	ALMS, GT team	Alex Job Racing	911 GT3 RSR
	USA	Grand Am Series GS driver	Craig Stanton	911 GT3
	USA	Grand Am Series GS makes	Porsche	911 GT3
	USA	Grand Am Series GS team	The Race Side.com Racing	911 GT3
	B	Belgian GTB championship	Christian Lambert, Yves Lefort	911 GT3 RS
	GB	GT championship	Tim Sugden, Jonathan Cocker	911 GT3 RSR
	GB	GT championship, N-GT driver	Tim Sugden, Jonathan Cocker	911 GT3 RSR
	GB	GT championship, N-GT team	Gruppe M-Racing	911 GT3 RSR
	GB	GT championship, Cup team	Tech 9-Motorsport	911 GT3 Cup
	GB	Carrera Cup	Richard Westbrook	911 GT3 Cup
	D	Special touring car trophy	Michael Irmgartz	911 GT3 R
	D	Carrera Cup	Mike Rockenfeller	911 GT3 Cup
	F	Trophy France FFSA N-GT	Moullin-Traffort, Rabineau	911 GT3 RS
	F	Coupe de France FFSA GT	Frederic Dedours, F.Makowiecki	911 GT3 RS
	F	Carrera Cup, class A	James Ruffier	911 GT3 Cup
	F	Carrera Cup, class B	Cyril Helias	911 GT3 Cup
	J	Super Taikyu Series, team	Falken Porsche	911 GT3 Cup
	HK	Hong Kong Supercar	Ray Li	911 GT3 RS
		Infineon Carrera Cup Asia	Mattwe Marsh	911 GT3 Cup
		Carrera Cup Scandinavia	Robin Rudholm	911 GT3 Cup
	AUS	Carrera Cup	Alex Davison	911 GT3 Cup

NATIONAL AND INTERNATIONAL CHAMPIONSHIPS WON BY 911 343

AUTOGLASS
PORSCHE
C. HALDI
R. METGE
K. NIEROP
203
Rothmans
PORSCHE
BILSTEIN
Shell
DUNLOP
MARTINI PORSCHE
1
MARTINI
Shell
CIBIE

961 Le Mans 1987 (203)
935/78 „Moby Dick" 1978 (1)
911 2.0 Coupe „Monte" 1965 (147)

OVERALL WINS BY 911 IN MAJOR NATIONAL AND INTERNATIONAL EVENTS

	EVENTS	DRIVERS - FAHRER	PORSCHE
1966	German Rally	Günter Klass, Rolf Wütherlich	911
	Rally Costa Brava	Juan Fernandez Garcia, Ribas	911
	"Westfalen-Lippe", Circuit	Mehn, Bökmann	911
	Hill climb Ceyreste	Clement	911
	Circuit racing Trier airport	Hans Kater	911
	German Hessen Rally	Wallrabenstein, Bretthauer	911
	Rally des Ardennes	Robert Barret, Chevin	911
	Rally de Lorraine	Robert Barret, Chevin	911
	100 miles Hockenheim, circuit	Hans Kistner	911
	Carrera en Vallividrera	Juan Fernandez Garcia	911
	Semperit Rally	Gass, Säckl	911
	Rally Bad Homburg-Frankf.	Gass, Dechert	911
	Hill climb von Arry	Robert Buchet	911
	Hill climb Vianden	Robert Barret	911
	Carrera en Corcavy	Juan Fernandez Garcia	911
	Rally Lazzaroni	Betto ja, Alicata	911
	Herst Rally	Buchet, Barthe	911
	Circuit racing de Jarama	Juan Fernandez Garcia	911

	EVENTS	DRIVERS - FAHRER	PORSCHE
1967	Rally Lyons-Charbonnieres	Vic Elford, David Stone	911 S
	ADAC Winterfahrt, circuit	Rosenberger, Küspert	911 S
	Austrian Alpine Rally	Sobieslaw Zasada, Jerzy Dobranski	911 S
	Rally de Maine	Robert Buchet, Benoit	911 S
	Polish Rally	Sobieslaw Zasada, Eva Zasada	912
	Protugal-Tour, rally	Americo da Silva-Nunes	911
	Rally Vaennaes	Bjorn Waldegard	911
	Tulip Rally	Vic Elford, David Stone	911 S
	4h Monza, circuit racing	Gerhard Mitter, F. von Wendt	911
	Rally de Invierno	Juan Fernandez Garcia	911
	Geneva Rally	Vic Elford, David Stone	911 S
	Course de Cote de Bourscheid	Fritz Leinenweber	911 S
	Fernandina Beach race	Peter Gregg	911
	6h Montjuich, circuit racing	Juan Fernandez Garcia, de Vilar	911 S
	Marathon de la Route	Vic Elford, Jochen Neerpasch, Hans Herrmann	911 R
	Coupe de Spa, circuit racing	Udo Schütz	911
	Magny-Cours, circuit racing	Robert Buchet, Benoit	911 S
	Hill climb Reisdorf	Fritz Leinenweber	911 S
	Grand Prix Imola, circuit	Pianta	911
	Rally Wiesbaden	Hans Schuller, Ulrich Jensen	911
	Hill climb Weser-Höxter	Christian Rötzel	911 S
	24h Spa-Francorchamps	Jean-Pierre Gaban, Pedro	911
	Scandiatrofen Rally	Bjorn Waldegaard	911
	Osceola Airport, circuit	Peter Gregg	911
	Trophy Baron de Villenfagne	Ben Pon	911
	Enduro at Westwood, circuit	Milt Davis, Wade Carter	911 S
	Grand Premio Argentina Rally	Sobieslav Zasada	911
	Race Double 300, circuit race	Bert Everett, Titus	911
	Rally Marokko	Jean Kerguen, Frank	911 S
	Touring cars Zandvoort	Ben Pon	911

Winner 4 hours Monza 1967: Gerhard Mitter, Freiherr von Wendt

	EVENTS	DRIVERS - FAHRER	PORSCHE
1968	Monte Carlo Rally	Vic Elford, David Stone	911 T
	4h Monza, circuit racing	Helmut Kelleners, Erwin Kremer	911
	San Remo Rally	Pauli Toivonen, Martti Tiukkanen	911 T
	East German Rally	Pauli Toivonen, Martti Kolari	911 T
	24h Spa-Francorchamps	Erwin Kremer, Willy Kaushen, Helmut Kelleners	911
	West German Rally	Pauli Toivonen, Martti Kolari	911 T
	Grand Prix Brno, circuit race	Erwin Kremer, Helmut Kelleners	911
	Marathon de la Route	Herbert Linge, Dieter Glemser, Willy Kaushen	911
	Swedish Rally	Bjorn Waldegard, Lars Helmer	911 T
	Geneva Rally	Pauli Toivonen, Urpo Vihervaava	911 T
	Castrol Danube Rally	Pauli Toivonen, Martti Kolari	911 T
	Firestone Rally	Eladio Doncel, Jaime Parejo	911 S

	EVENTS	DRIVERS - FAHRER	PORSCHE
1969	Monte Carlo Rally	Bjorn Waldegard, Lars Helmer	911 S
	Grand Prix Budapest, circuit	Gijs van Lennep	911
	Enduro Willow Springs	D. Pike, H. Miller	911
	Swedish Rally	Bjorn Waldegard, Lars Helmer	911 S
	6h Nürburgring, circuit race	Toine Hezemans, Gijs van Lennep	911
	Acropolis Rally	Pauli Toivonen, Martti Kolari	911 S
	Castrol Danube Rally	Walter Poltinger, J. Hartinger	911 T
	Tour de France	Gerard Larrousse, Maurice Grlin	911 R
	Polish Rally	Sobieslaw Zasada, Eva Zasada	911 S
	Tour de Corsica Rally	Gerard Larrousse, Maurice Grlin	911 R

GT European Championchip 1974: John Fitzpatrick

346 PRESENTED BY BAM

	EVENTS	DRIVERS - FAHRER	PORSCHE
1970	Monte Carlo Rally	Bjorn Waldegard, Lars Helmer	911 S
	Swedish Rally	Bjorn Waldegard, Lars Helmer	911 S
	Canadian Winter Rally	John Buffum, Vicki Buffum	911
	Austrian Alpine Rally	Bjorn Waldegard, Lars Helmer	911 S
	Bodensee Rally	Wilfried Gass, Frey	911
	Castrol Danube Rally	Gunther Janger, W. Wessiak	911 S

	EVENTS	DRIVERS - FAHRER	PORSCHE
1972	IMSA GT Virginia Danville	Peter Gregg, Hurley Haywood	911 S
	300km Nürburgring GT-EUR	John Fitzpatrick	911 S
	IMSA GT 200 Lime Rock	J. Locke, B. Bailey	911 S
	Coupe Montlhery GT-EUR	Claude Ballot-Lena	911 S
	IMSA GT 6 hours Mid Ohio	Bob Beasley, Michael Keyser	
	Zandvoort GT-EUR	Jürgen Neuhaus	911 S
	Nürburgring GT-EUR	John Fitzpatrick	911 S
	IMSA GT 500 Watkins Glen	Peter Gregg, Hurley Haywood	911 S
	Hockenheim GT-EUR	John Fitzpatrick	911 S
	Coppa Monza GT-EUR	John Fitzpatrick	911 S
	Gr. Prem. Estoril GT-EUR	John Fitzpatrick	911 S

	EVENTS	DRIVERS - FAHRER	PORSCHE
1973	24 hours Daytona	Peter Gregg, Hurley Haywood	Carrera RS
	IMSA GT 12 hours Sebring	Peter Gregg, Hurley Haywood, Dave Helmick	Carrera RS
	Targa Florio (WC)	Herbert Müller, Gijs van Lennep	Carrera RS
	Diepholz German Champion.	Rolf Stommelen	Carrera RS
	300km Nürburgring GT-EUR	Claude Ballot-Lena	Carrera RS
	Hill climb Sauerland	Reinhard Stenzel	Carrera RS
	Grand P. Montlhery GT-EUR	Claude Ballot-Lena	Carrera RS
	IMSA GT 3 hours Daytona	Peter Gregg, Hurley Haywood	Carrera RS
	4 hours Le Mans	Gijs van Lennep, Herbert Müller	Carrera RSR
	IMSA GT 6 hours Mido Ohio	Michael Keyser, Bob Beasley	Carrera RS
	Trans-Am 500 Road Atlanta	Peter Gregg	Carrrera RS
	IMSA GT Lime Rock	Michael Keyser	Carrera RS
	Benelux Nivelles GT-EUR	Clemens Schickentanz	Carrera RS
	IMSA GT 200 miles R. Atlanta	Peter Gregg	Carrera RS
	Trans-Am 500 Lime Rock	Milt Minter	Carrera RS
	IMSA GT 3 hours Indianapolis	Peter Gregg	Carrera RS
	Gr. Prem. Estoril GT-EUR	Paul Keller	Carrera RS
	IMSA GT Daytona 250	Peter Gregg, Hurley Haywood	Carrera RS
	Thruxton GT-EUR	Claude Ballot-Lena	Carrera RS
	6 hours Monza GT-EUR	Clemens Schickentanz, Paul Keller	Carrera RS

Winner IMSA GT 500 Watkins Glen 1972: Peter Gregg, Hurley Haywood

	EVENTS	DRIVERS - FAHRER	PORSCHE
1974	Mainz-Finthen German Champ.	Reinhard Stenzel	Carrera RSR
	300 km Nürburgring GT-EUR	Hans Bertrams	Carrera RSR
	IMSA GT 6 hours R. Atlanta	Al Holbert, Elliot Forbes-Robinson	Carrera RSR
	Hockenheim GT-EUR	John Fitzpatrick	Carrera RSR
	Hockenheim German Champ.	Reinhard Stenzel	Carrera RSR
	IMSA GT Laguna Seca	Elliot Forbes-Robinson	Carrera RSR
	Nürburgring GT-EUR	Paul Keller	Carrera RSR
	IMSA GT 4 hours Ontario	Peter Gregg	Carrera RSR
	Trophy Monza GT-EUR	Clemens Schickentanz	Carrera RSR
	IMSA GT 5 hours Mid Ohio	Al Holbert, Peter Gregg	Carrera RSR
	Österreichring GT-EUR	John Fitzpatrick	Carrera RSR
	IMSA GT 250 Daytona	Hurley Haywood	Carrera RSR
	Trans-Am Lime Rock	Al Holbert	Carrera RSR
	Coppa Pergusa GT-EUR	John Fitzpatrick	Carrera RSR
	IMSA GT Charlotte 300	Peter Gregg	Carrera RSR
	6 hours Monza GT-EUR	Rolf Stommelen, Toine Hezemans	Carrera RSR
	IMSA GT Lime Rock	Peter Gregg	Carrera RSR
	Trans-Am Elkhart Lake	Peter Gregg	Carrera RSR
	GT race Dijon circuit	Gerard Larrousse	Carrera RSR
	IMSA GT 1000 km Mexico	G. Rojas, H. Rebaque, F. van Beuren	Carrera RSR

Winner Marathon de la Route Nürburgring 1968:
Herbert Linge, Dieter Glemser, Willy Kaushen

OVERALL WINS BY 911 IN MAJOR NATIONAL AND INTERNATIONAL EVENTS

Targa Florio 1969: Corrado Ferlaino, Nino Todaro

750 km Paul Ricard 1974: Clemens Schickentanz, Jürgen Barth

(l.-r.): Jacky Ickx, Peter Falk, Norbert Singer

6 Hours Watkins Glen 1979: Dick Barbour, Rolf Stommelen, Paul Newman

6 Hours Watkins Glen 1976: George Follmer, John Morton

IMSA GT Sears Point 1979: Bob Harmon

Deutsche Rennsport Meisterschaft 1978 Zolder: Toine Hezemans (6), Manfred Schurti (5)

OVERALL WINS BY 911 IN MAJOR NATIONAL AND INTERNATIONAL EVENTS

OVERALL WINS BY 911 IN MAJOR NATIONAL AND INTERNATIONAL EVENTS

Winner Monte Carlo Rally 1978: Jean-Pierre Nicolas, Vincent Laverne

6 Hours Watkins Glen 1979: T. Field, D. Ongais (0) – L. Heimrath, C. Moran (7)

Jochen Mass

Klaus Ludwig

Winner Deutsche Rennsport Meisterschaft 1978 Norisring: Manfred Schurti

	EVENTS	DRIVERS - FAHRER	PORSCHE
1976	IMSA GT 12 hours Sebring	Al Holbert, Michael Keyser	Carrera RSR
	6 hours Mugello (WC)	Jochen Mass, Jacky Ickx	935
	Nürburgring German Champ.	Helmut Kelleners	934
	6 hours Vallelunga (WC)	Jochen Mass, Jacky Ickx	935
	Mainz-Finthen German Champ.	Bob Wollek	934
	IMSA GT 100 miles Ontario	Jim Busby	Carrera RSR
	Jim Clark race Hockenheim	Bob Wollek	934
	Hockenheim German Champ.	Toine Hezemans	934
	6 hours Watkins Glen (WC)	Rolf Stommelen, Manfred Schurti	935
	200 miles Norisring (GRM)	Bob Wollek	934
	IMSA GT 100 Lime Rock	George Dyer	Carrera RSR
	Trans-Am G. P. Pocono	Hurley Haywood	934
	Diepholz German Champion.	Toine Hezemans	934
	Österreichring GT-EUR	Toine Hezemans	934
	IMSA GT 100 Sears Point	Jim Busby	Carrera RSR
	Tour de France	J. Henry, Grobot	Carrera RS
	Nürburgring German Champ.	Toine Hezemans	934
	Cup Misano GT-EUR	Tim Schenken	934
	IMSA GT 6 hours Mid Ohio	Jim Busby	Carrera RSR
	6 hours Monza GT-EUR	Hans Bertrams, Clemens Schickentanz	Carrera RSR
	Kassel-Calden German Champ.	Jürgen Neuhaus	Carrera RSR
	IMSA GT 100 Laguna Seca	Jim Busby	Carrera RSR
	Giro d'Italia	Victor, P. Monticone	934
	Norisring Trophy GT-EUR	Toine Hezemans	934
	Hockenheim German Champ.	Tim Schenken	934
	6 hours Dijon (WC)	Jochen Mass, Jacky Ickx	935
	Trans-Am Nelson Ledges	George Follmer	934
	GT race Zolder, circuit	Edgar Dören	Carrera RSR
	Circuit race GT Sylt	Clemens Schickentanz	934
	Nürburgring German Champ.	Tim Schenken	934
	Coppa Imola GT-EUR	Bob Wollek	934
	Trans-Am Cup Portland	Mike Shelton	Carrera RSR
	Joisten Trophy Zolder	Egon Evertz	934
	Hockenheim GT-EUR	Toine Hezemans	934
	Trans-Am 200 Mosport	Ludwig Heimrath	Carrera RSR
	Hockenheim German Champ.	Bob Wollek	934
	Trans-Am Trios Rivieres	George Follmer	934
	Trophy GT race Monza	F. Bernbei	Carrera RSR
	Trohpy GT race Pergusa	G. Carducci	Carrera RSR
	Nordsee Cup Zandvoort	Edgar Dören	Carrera RSR
	4 hours GT CUP Nürburgring	Eberhard Sindel, Jürgen Kannacher	934
	Circuit race Ulm-Mengen	Volkert Merl	934
	GT Trophy Nürburgring	Bob Wollek	934

	EVENTS	DRIVERS - FAHRER	PORSCHE
1975	24 hours Daytona	Peter Gregg, Hurley Haywood	Carrera RSR
	IMSA GT Road Atlanta	Peter Gregg	Carrera RSR
	Canadian Winter Rally	John Buffum, Vicki Buffum	911 Carrera
	Mainz-Finthen German Champ.	Reinhard Stenzel	Carrera RSR
	Coppa Imola GT-EUR	John Fitzpatrick	Carrera RSR
	IMSA GT 100 Laguna Seca	Peter Gregg	Carrera RSR
	Twenty Stages Rally	John Buffum, Vicki Buffum	911 Carrera
	Diepholz German Champion.	Bob Wollek	Carrera RSR
	IMSA GT 6 hours Riverside	Peter Gregg, Hurley Haywood	Carrera RSR
	Österreichring GT-EUR	Clemens Schickentanz	Carrera RSR
	Norisring Trophy GT-EUR	John Fitzpatrick	Carrera RSR
	IMSA GT 100 Lime Rock	Peter Gregg	Carrera RSR
	200 miles Nürnberg Norisring	Toine Hezemans	Carrera RS
	Criterium of Quebec Rally	John Buffum, Vicki Buffum	911 Carrera
	IMSA GT 100 Mid Ohio	Al Holbert	Carrera RSR
	Joisten Trophy Zolder	Hans Heyer	Carrera RSR
	Hockenheim GT-EUR	Claudi Haldi	Carrera RSR
	IMSA GT 100 Mid-America	Al Holbert	Carrera RSR
	Tall Pines Rally	John Buffum, Vicki Buffum	911 Carrera
	IMSA GT 6 hours Mid Ohio	Al Holbert, Elliot Forbes-Robinson	Carrera RSR
	200 km Jarama GT-EUR	Tim Schenken	Carrera RSR
	Press on Regardiess Rally	Sobieslaw Zasada, Wojiek Schramm	911 Carrera

	EVENTS	DRIVERS - FAHRER	PORSCHE
1977	24 hours Daytona	John Graves, Hurley Haywood, Dave Helmick	Carrera RSR
	IMSA GT 12 hours Sebring	George Dyer, Brad Frisselle	Carrera RSR
	Zolder German Championc.	Manfred Schurti	935
	6 hours Mugello (WC)	Rolf Stommelen, Manfred Schurti	935/77
	Trans-Am Seattle Raceway	Ludwig Heimrath	934/5
	Gr. P. Stuttgart Hockenheim	Andre Pallavicini	934
	Nürburgring German Champ.	Rolf Stommelen	935
	IMSA GT Laguna Seca	Danny Ongais	934/5
	6 hours Silverstone (WC)	Jochen Mass, Jacky Ickx	935/77
	Nürburgring German Champ.	Bob Wollek	935 K2
	Jim Clark race Hockenheim	Bob Wollek	934
	IMSA GT Brainerd	Danny Ongais	934/5
	Trans-Am Westwood	Peter Gregg	934/5
	1000 km Nürburgring (WC)	Toine Hezemans, Tim Schenken, Rolf Stommelen	935
	Kassel-Calden German Champ.	Bob Wollek	935 K2
	100 miles GT Hockenheim	Dieter Schornstein	934
	IMSA GT 250 Daytona	George Dyer, Brad Frisselle	934/5
	Trans-Am Cup Portland	George Follmer	934/5
	6 hours Watkins Glen (WC)	Jochen Mass, Jacky Ickx	935/77
	Mainz-Finthen German Champ.	Rolf Stommelen	935
	200 miles Norisring (GRM)	Rolf Stommelen	935
	Trans-Am Nelson Ledges	Bob Hagestad	934/5
	Airport GT race Wunstorf	Heinz-Christian Jürgensen	934
	6 hours Mosport (WC)	Ludwig Heimrath, Paul Miller	934/5
	Diepholz German Champ.	Rolf Stommelen	935
	IMSA GT 3 hours Mid Ohio	Peter Gregg	934/5
	Trans-Am Hallett	Peter Gregg	934/5
	6 hours Brands Hatch (WC)	Jochen Mass, Jacky Ickx	935/77
	Giro d'Italia	Victor, P. Monticone	935
	Hockenheim German Champ.	Bob Wollek	935 K2
	Trans-Am Brainerd	Peter Gregg	934/5
	6 hours Hockenheim (WC)	Bob Wollek, John Fitzpatrick	935 K2
	Circuit race Düren Zolder	Franz Konrad	935
	Zolder German Championc.	Bob Wollek, John Fitzpatrick	935 K2
	Trans-Am Welkhart Lake	Ludwig Heimrath	934/5
	6 hours Vallelunga (WC)	Antonio Ferrari, Luigi Moreschi	935
	Trophy GT Misano	Gianpiero Moretti	934
	IMSA GT 250 Daytona	Hurley Haywood	934/5
	Trans-Am Mont Tremblant	Peter Gregg	934/5
	Nürburgring German Champ.	Rolf Stommelen	935
	Coppa Inter Europe Monza	M. Finotto	935
	Gran Premio Estoril circuit	R. Giannone	Carrera RSR
	Rheintal G. P. Hockenheim	Hubert van Oorschot	935

Winner Deutsche Rennsport Meisterschaft 1979: Klaus Ludwig

John Fitzpatrick

Rolf Stommelen

	EVENTS	DRIVERS - FAHRER	PORSCHE
1978	24 hours Daytona (WC)	Rolf Stommelen, Toine Hezemans, Peter Gregg	935
	IMSA GT 12 hours Sebring	Brian Redman, Charles Mendez, Bob Garretson	935
	6 hours Mugello (WC)	Toine Hezemans, John Fitzpatrick, Hans Heyer	935
	IMSA GT 6 hours Talladega	Peter Gregg, Brian Frisselle	935
	Zolder German Championc.	Toine Hezemans, John Fitzpatrick, Hans Heyer	935
	1000 km Dijon (WC)	Bob Wollek, Henri Pescarolo	935
	Benelux circuit Zolder	Claude Bourgoignie	935 K2
	300km Nürburg. Germ. Champ.	Bob Wollek, Henri Pescarolo	935
	IMSA GT Road Atlanta	Peter Gregg	935
	6 hours Silverstone (WC)	Jacky Ickx, Jochen Mass	935/78
	Nürburgring German Champ.	Toine Hezemans	935
	Coppa Torino Misano	V. Coggiola	935
	IMSA GT Laguna Seca	George Follmer	935
	Avus German Championchip	Toine Hezemans	935
	1000 km Nürburgring (WC)	Klaus Ludwig, Hans Heyer, Toine Hezemans	935
	Mainz-Finthen German Champ.	Bob Wollek	935
	IMSA GT 300 Lime Rock	Peter Gregg	935
	Zandvoort German Champ	John Fitzpatrick	935
	Nordzee Cup Zandvoort	Hubert van Oorschot	935
	6 hours Misano (WC)	Bob Wollek, Henri Pescarolo	935
	Kassel-Calden German Champ.	Bob Wollek, Henri Pescarolo	935
	IMSA GT Grand P. Brainerd	Peter Gregg	935
	Trans-Am Westwood Park	Ludwig Heimrath	935
	Coppa Enna Pergusa circuit	Carlo Facetti	935
	6 hours Watkins Glen (WC	Toine Hezemans, John Fitzpatrick, Peter Gergg	935
	Hockenheim German Champ.	Klaus Ludwig	935
	IMSA GT 250 Daytona	Peter Gregg	935
	Trans-Am Mont Tremblant	Mike Shelton	934/5
	Zolder German Campionchip	Manfred Schurti	935
	Airport circuit GT race Erding	Franz Gschwender	934
	IMSA GT Grand P. Portland	Manfred Schurti	935
	Norisring German Champ.	Manfred Schurti	935
	IMSA GT 250 Mid Ohio	Bill Whittington, Jim Busby	935
	Nürburgring German Champ.	Bob Wollek	935
	IMSA GT 100 Road Atlanta	Peter Gregg	935
	Joisten Trophy Zolder circuit	Claude Bourgoignie	935 K2
	200 miles Nürnberg Norisring	Bob Wollek	935
	Trans-Am Mexico-City	Ludwig Heimrath	935
	6 hours Vallelunga (WC)	Bob Wollek, Henri Pescarolo	935
	IMSA GT 250 Datyona	Peter Gregg	935
	Trophy Nappi Vallelunga GT	Carlo Facetti	935

OVERALL WINS BY 911 IN MAJOR NATIONAL AND INTERNATIONAL EVENTS 351

OVERALL WINS BY 911 IN MAJOR NATIONAL AND INTERNATIONAL EVENTS

Start 1000 km Nürburgring 1978

Deutsche Rennsport Meisterschaft Norisring 1978: Toine Hezemans

	EVENTS	DRIVERS - FAHRER	PORSCHE
1979	24 hours Daytona (WC)	Ted Field, Danny Ongais, Hurley Haywood	935-79
	IMSA GT 12 hours Sebring	Bob Akin, Rob McFarlin, Roy Woods	935
	6 hours Mugello (WC)	Manfred Schurti, John Fitzpatrick, Bob Wollek	935
	Zolder German Championchip	Klaus Ludwig	935 K3
	IMSA GT 6 hours Riverside	Don and Bill Whittington	935-79
	Trans-Am Autodr. Mexico	John Paul Sr.	935
	IMSA GT Road Atlanta	Peter Gregg	935-79
	Trophy GT Colmar Berg	Claude Bourgoignie	935 K2
	6 hours Silverstone (WC)	John Fitzpatrick, Bob Wollek, Hans Heyer	935
	Hockenheim German Champ.	Klaus Ludwig	935 K3
	1000 km Nürburgring (WC)	Manfred Schurti, John Fitzpatrick, Bob Wollek	935
	IMSA GT Laguna Seca	Peter Gregg	935-79
	24 hours Le Mans	Klaus Ludwig, Don and Bill Whittington	935 K3
	Trans-Am Westwood Park	John Paul Sr.	935
	Nürburgring German Champ.	Bob Wollek	935
	IMSA GT 350 Lime Rock	Peter Gregg	935-79
	6 hours Watkins Glen (WC)	Klaus Ludwig, Don and Bill Whittington	935 K3
	Salzburgring German Champ.	Klaus Ludwig	935 K3
	IMSA GT Grand P. Brainerd	Peter Gregg	935-79
	Grand Prix GT Hockenheim	Axel Plankenhorn	935 K3
	Trans-Am Cup Portland	John Paul Sr.	935
	Mainz-Finthen German Champ.	Klaus Ludwig	935 K3
	IMSA GT 250 Daytona	Charles Mendez, Hurley Haywood	935
	Trans-Am Elkhart Lake	Peter Gregg	935-79
	Norisring German Champ.	Klaus Ludwig	935 K3
	6 hours El Salvador (WC dr.)	Bill and Don Whittington, E. Molins	935
	IMSA GT 250 Mid Ohio	Peter Gregg, Hurley Haywood	935-79
	Trans-Am Watkins Glen	John Paul Sr.	935
	Zandvoort German Champ.	Klaus Ludwig	935 K3
	Ulm-Mengen Circuit GT race	Dieter Schornstein	935
	IMSA GT G.P. Sears Point	Peter Gregg	935-79
	200 miles Nürnberg Norisring	Rolf Stommelen	935 J
	IMSA GT Grand P. Portland	Peter Gregg	935-79
	Trans-Am Canadian Mosport	John Paul Sr.	935
	Diepholz German Championc.	Klaus Ludwig	935 K3
	Grand Prix Hockenheim	Axel Plankenhorn	935 K3
	Joisten Trophy Zolder	Claude Bourgoignie	935 K3
	Zolder German Championchip	Klaus Ludwig	935 K3
	IMSA GT Road Atlanta	Peter Gregg	935-79
	Coppa Carri Monza circuit	V. Coggiola	935
	Trans-Am Trois Rivieres	John Paul Sr.	935
	Giro d'Italia	Gianpiero Moretti, G. Schön, Radaelli	935-79
	Hockenheim German Champ.	Klaus Ludwig	935 K3
	IMSA GT 250 Daytona	Bill Whittington	935 K3
	Trans-Am Laguna Seca	Peter Gregg	935-79
	Production GT Magione cir.	V. Coggiola	935
	Nürburgring German Champ.	Klaus Ludwig	935 K3

Paul Newman

Deutsche Rennsport Meisterschaft 1979: Rolf Stommelen

Deutsche Rennsport Meisterschaft 1979: Jürgen Lässig

6 Hours Watkins Glen 1979: Peter Gregg, Hurley Haywood, Bruce Leven

OVERALL WINS BY 911 IN MAJOR NATIONAL AND INTERNATIONAL EVENTS

OVERALL WINS BY 911 IN MAJOR NATIONAL AND INTERNATIONAL EVENTS

Poster

Poster

Year	EVENTS	DRIVERS - FAHRER	PORSCHE
1980	24 hours Daytona (WC)	Rolf Stommelen, Reinhold Joest, Volkert Merl	935 J
	IMSA GT Road Atlanta	Bill Whittington	935 K3
	Zolder German Championship	Rolf Stommelen	935
	Rally Costa Brava	Antonio Zanini, Victor Sabater	911 SC
	IMSA GT Laguna Seca	John Fitzpatrick	935 K3
	SCCA Champion. Hallett	Jo Bauer	911 SC
	Nürburgring German Champion.	Volkert Merl	935/80
	Rally Montseny-Guillerias	Antonio Zanini, Victor Sabater	911 SC
	IMSA GT 12 hours Sebring	Dick Barbour, John Fitzpatrick	935 K3
	Internat. GT race Erding	Franz Gschender	935
	IMSA GT 400 Lime Rock	John Paul Jr. and Sr.	935 K3
	SCCA Champ. Elkhart Lake	Mike Shelton	911 SC
	Rally Criterium Alpin	Bernard Beguin, Jean-Jacques Lenne	911 SC
	Mainz-Finthen German Champ.	Bob Wollek	935
	IMSA GT Brainerd	Luis Mendez	Carrera RSR
	Rally Bulgarian	Antonio Zanini, Victor Sabater	911 SC
	IMSA GT 250 Daytona	John Fitzpatrick	935 K3
	Rally Quattro Regioni	Bernard Beguin, Jean-Jacques Lenne	911 SC
	200 miles Norisring German Ch.	John Fitzpatrick	935 K3
	Rally Antibes	Bernard Beguin, Jean-Jacques Lenne	911 SC
	IMSA GT Sears Point	John Fitzpatrick	935 K3
	Coppa Florio Enna Pergusa	Victor Coggiola	935
	SCCA Champion. Brainerd	Jo Bauer	911 SC
	IMSA GT Portland	John Fitzpatrick	935 K3
	6 hours Dijon (WC)	Henri Pescarolo, Jürgen Barth	935
	IMSA GT 5 hours Riverside	John Fitzpatrick, Dick Barbour	935 K3
	H.-P. Joisten Trophy Zolder	Dieter Schornstein	935
	IMSA GT Road Atlanta	John Fitzpatrick	935 K3
	SCCA Champion. Westwood	Jo Bauer	911 SC
	Rally Polish	Antonio Zanini, Victor Sabater	911 SC
	Rally Halkidikis	Antonio Zanini, Victor Sabater	911 SC
	Salzburgring German Champion.	Manfred Winkelhock	935
	IMSA GT 6 hours Mosport	John Fitzpatrick, Brian Redman	935 K3
	Rally OSAC	Franz Wittmann, Kurt Nestinger	911 SC
	Spanish Rally	Antonio Zanini, Victor Sabater	911 SC
	Zolder German Championship	John Fitzpatrick	935 K3
	Rally Catalunya	Antonio Zanini, Victor Sabater	911 SC
	Nürburgring German Champ.	Manfred Winkelhock	935
	IMSA GT 500 Elkhart Lake	John Paul Jr. and Sr.	935
	Rally Tour of Corsica	Jean-Luc Therier, Michel Vial	911 SC
	IMSA GT 250 Daytona	Gianpiero Moretti, Reinhold Joest	935 J
	Hockenheim German Champ.	John Fitzpatrick	935 K3
	EVENTS	DRIVERS - FAHRER	PORSCHE
1981	24 hours Daytona (WC)	Bob Garretson, Bobby Rahal, Brian Redman	935 K3
	IMSA GT Road Atlanta	John Fitzpatrick	935 K3
	Rally Wienerwald	Franz Wittmann, Husar	911 SC
	Nürburgring German Champ.	Bob Wollek	935 K3
	IMSA GT 12 hours Sebring	Bruce Leven, Hurley Haywood, Al Holbert	935
	Rally Criterium Alpin	Francis Vincent, Willy Huret	911 SC
	Hockenheim German Champ.	Jochen Mass	935/78
	1000 km Spa-Francorchamps	P. Bervoets, G. Trigaux	935
	1000 km Monza (WC)	Edgar Dören, Jürgen Lässig	935 K3
	Rally Metz	Manfred Hero, Hopfe	911 SC
	Mainz-Finthen German Champ.	Bob Wollek	935 K3
	Rally Rouerge	Jean-Pierre Ballet, Pluton	911 SC
	200 miles Norisring	Bob Wollek	935 K4
	Nürburgring German Champ.	Bob Wollek	935 K3
	Rally Tour de la Reunion	Bernard Beguin, Ozoux	911 SC
	IMSA GT 250 Daytona	Maurizio de Narvaez, Hurley Haywood	935 J
	1000 km Suzuka	Bob Wollek, Henri Pescarolo	935 K3
	3 hours Enna Pergusa	A. Guagliardo	911 turbo
	Rally Criterium Lucien Bianchi	Marc Duez, Willy Lux	911 SC
	IMSA GT 500 Mid-Ohio	Rolf Stommelen, Derek Bell	935
	IMSA GT 6 hours Riverside	John Fitzpatrick, Jim Busby	935 K3
	Rally Criterium Antibes	Francis Vincent, Willy Huret	911 SC
	IMSA GT 500 Pocono	John Paul Jr. and Sr.	935 K3
	6 hours Silverstone (WC)	Harald Grohs, Dieter Schornstein, Walter Röhrl	935 J
	Internat. Trofeo Cariplo Varano	Victor Coggiola	935
	IMSA GT 250 miles Daytona	John Paul Jr.	935
	SCCA Champ. Elkhart Lake	Mike Shelton	911 SC
	IMSA GT 1000 Mosport	Harald Grohs, Rolf Stommelen	935 K3
	IMSA GT 500 Elkhart Lake	Harald Grohs, Rolf Stommelen	935 K3

Winner 12 hours Sebring 1981: B. Leven, H. Haywood, A. Holbert

Winner 200 miles Norisring 1980: John Fitzpatrick

Hockenheim 1982: Dieter Schornstein

Winner Paris-Dakar 1986: Rene Metge, Dominique Lemoyne

Winner IMSA Mosport 1982: John Paul Jr. and Sr.

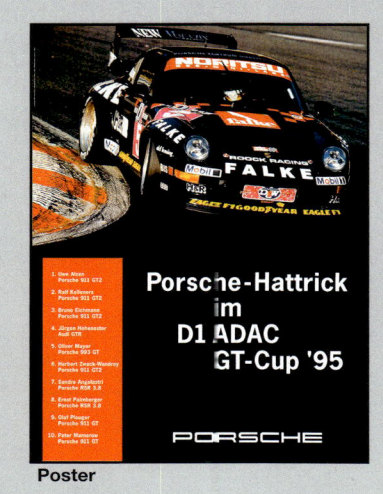

Poster

Poster

	EVENTS	DRIVERS - FAHRER	PORSCHE
1982	IMSA GT 24h Daytona	John Paul Jr. and Sr., Rolf Stommelen	935
	IMSA GT 12h Sebring	John Paul Jr. and Sr.	935
	Internat. GT race Magione	Victor Coggiola	934
	Rally Ypres	Marc Duez, Willy Lux	911 SC
	IMSA GT Road Atlanta	John Paul Jr.	935
	Australian GT Winton	Alan Jones	935
	Rally Criterium Lucien Bianchi	Marc Duez, Willy Lux	911 SC
	IMSA GT 500 miles Charlotte	John Paul Jr. and Sr.	935
	Australian GT Oran Park	Alan Jones	935
	Rally Criterium Antibes	Bernard Beguin, Jean-Jacques Lenne	911 SC
	IMSA GT Mid-Ohio	John Fitzpatrick	935 K4
	Australian GT Lakeside	Alan Jones	935
	Rally Three Cities	Manfred Hero, Muller	911 turbo
	IMSA GT 400 Lime Rock	John Fitzpatrick	935 K4
	Rally Condroz	Marc Duez, Willy Lux	911 SC
	Australian GT Wanneroo Park	Alan Jones	935
	IMSA GT Brainerd	John Paul Jr.	935
	Australian GT Calder Raceway	Alan Jones	935
	IMSA GT Gr. Prix Portland	John Paul Jr.	935
	Internat. Trofeo Magione	C. Tocci	Carrera RS
	Australian GT Surfers Paradise	Alan Jones	935
	IMSA GT Mosport	John Paul Jr. and Sr.	935
	Australian GT Baskerville	Alan Jones	935
	IMSA GT Elkhart Lake	John Fitzpatrick, David Hobbs	935 K4
	Internat. GT race Vallelunga	Victor Coggiola	934
	IMSA GT 6h Mid Ohio	John Fitzpatrick, David Hobbs	935 K4
	IMSA GT Road Atlanta	John Paul Jr. and Sr.	935
	EVENTS	**DRIVERS - FAHRER**	**PORSCHE**
1983	IMSA GT 24h Daytona	P. Henn, B. Wollek, C. Ballot-Lena, A.J. Foyt	935
	IMSA GT 12h Sebring	Wayne Baker, Jim Mullen, Kees Nierop	934
	Switzerland GT Dijon	Antoine Salamin	935
	Rally Saarland	Manfred Hero, Muller	911 turbo
	IMSA GT Gr. Prix Riverside	John Fitzpatrick, David Hobbs, Derek Bell	935 K4
	Switzerland GT Oberhallau	Antoine Salamin	935
	Rally Omloop van Vlanderen	Patrick Snyers, Dany Colebunders	911 SC
	Switzerland GT Hockenheim	Rene Madörin	Carrera RSR
	IMSA GT 250 Daytona	Hurley Haywood, A.J. Foyt	935
	Rally Condroz	Patrick Snyers, Dany Colebunders	911 SC
	EVENTS	**DRIVERS - FAHRER**	**PORSCHE**
1984	IMSA GT 12h Sebring	M. de Narvaez, Hans Heyer, Stefan Johansson	935 J
	Rally Paris - Dakar	Rene Metge, Dominique Lemoyne	911SC 4WD
	Interswiss GT Hockenheim	Antoine Salamin	935
	Rally Circuit des Ardennes	Patrick Snyers, Dany Colebunders	911 SC RS
	Interswiss GT Gurnigel	H. Hugentobler	Carrera RSR
	Rally Qatar	Saeed Al Hajri, John Spiller	911 SC RS
	Interswiss GT Champ. Dijon	Antoine Salamin	935
	Rally Wallonie	Patrick Snyers, Dany Colebunders	911 SC RS
	Interswiss GT Champ. Misano	Antoine Salamin	935
	Rally Costa Smeralda	Henri Toivonen, Juha Piironen	911 SC RS
	Interswiss GT Magny Cours	H. Hugentobler	Carrera RSR
	Rally Haspengouw	Robert Droogmans, Joosten	911 SC RS
	Rally Ypres	Henri Toivonen, Ian Grindrod	911 SC RS
	Rally Madeira	Henri Toivonen, Juha Piironen	911 SC RS
	Rally Criterium Lucien Bianchi	Robert Droogmans, Joosten	911 SC RS
	Rally Omloop van Vlanderen	Patrick Snyers, Dany Colebunders	911 SC RS
	Rally Oman	Saeed Al Hajri, John Spiller	911 SC RS
	Rally Dubai	Saeed Al Hajri, John Spiller	911 SC RS
	Rally Condroz	Robert Droogmans, Joosten	911 SC RS
	EVENTS	**DRIVERS - FAHRER**	**PORSCHE**
1985	Interswiss GT Champ. Misano	Antoine Salamin	935
	Rally Qatar	Saeed Al Hajri, John Spiller	911 SC RS
	Rally Yugoslavian	Quartesan, Vianello	911 SC RS
	Interswiss GT Magny Cours	H. Hugentobler	Carrera RSR
	Rally Jordan	Saeed Al Hajri, John Spiller	911 SC RS
	Interswiss GT Hockenheim	Antoine Salamin	935
	Rally Donegal	Billy Coleman, Roman Morgan	911 SC RS
	Switzerland GT Oberhallau	Antoine Salamin	935
	Rally Oman	Saeed Al Hajri, John Spiller	911 SC RS
	Interswiss GT Hemberg	Antoine Salamin	935
	Rally Pharoahs	Saeed Al Hajri, John Spiller	959 / 961
	EVENTS	**DRIVERS - FAHRER**	**PORSCHE**
1986	Interswiss GT Hockenheim	Antoine Salamin	935
	Rally Paris - Dakar	Rene Metge, Dominique Lemoyne	959 / 961
	Interswiss GT Varano	Antoine Salamin	935
	Interswiss GT Magny Cours	Antoine Salamin	935
	Interswiss GT Hemberg	A. Pfefferle	Carrera RSR
	Rally Mille Pistes	Rene Metge, Jean-Marc Andrie	959 / 961
	Interswiss GT Gurnigel	Antoine Salamin	935

NATIONAL AND INTERNATIONAL CHAMPIONSHIPS WON BY 911

OVERALL WINS BY 911 IN MAJOR NATIONAL AND INTERNATIONAL EVENTS

Winner Supercar Del Mar 1991: Hans-Joachim Stuck

Winner Porsche Cup 1995: Lilian Bryner

Winner GT Cup Zandvoort 1994: Ralf Kelleners

Winner BRDC GT Snetterton 1996: John Morrison, John Greasley

Winner 24 hours Zolder 1998: Patrick Huisman, Thierry Boutsen, Marc Goossens

	EVENTS	DRIVERS - FAHRER	PORSCHE
1988	Interswiss GT Dijon	A. Pfefferle	Carrera RSR
	24 hours Nürburgring	Edgar Dören, Günter Holup, Peter Faubel	Carrera RSR
	Interswiss GT Oberhallau	A. Pfefferle	Carrera RSR
	Interswiss GT Gurnigel	A. Pfefferle	Carrera RSR
	EVENTS	**DRIVERS - FAHRER**	**PORSCHE**
1991	Supercar Champ. Watkins Glen	Hurley Haywood	911 turbo
	Supercar Champ. Portland	Hurley Haywood	911 turbo
	Supercar Champ. Elkhart Lake	Hurley Haywood	911 turbo
	Supercar Champ. Del Mar	Hans-Joachim Stuck	911 turbo
	EVENTS	**DRIVERS - FAHRER**	**PORSCHE**
1992	Carglass Cup Zolder	F. Taels, P. Moonen	Carrera RS
	Supercar Champions. Miami	Hans-Joachim Stuck	911 turbo
	Carglass Cup Zolder	F. Taels, P. Simons	Carrera RS
	Supercar Champ. Watkins Glen	Hurley Haywood	911 turbo
	Carglass Cup 24 hours Zolder	Michael Beilke, P. Prosten, Edgar Dören	Carrera RSR
	Supercar Champ. Laguna Seca	Hurley Haywood	911 turbo
	Inter. GT 3 hours Hockenheim	Michael Beilke, P. Prosten	Carrera RSR
	Supercar Champ. Del Mar	Hans-Joachim Stuck	911 turbo
	Carglass Cup Zandvoort	F. Taels, P. Simons	Carrera RS
	EVENTS	**DRIVERS - FAHRER**	**PORSCHE**
1993	GT Cup Germany Nürburgring	Bruno Eichmann	Carrera RSR
	Supercar Champ. Lime Rock	Hans-Joachim Stuck	911 turbo
	BRDC GT Challenge Donington	John Greasley	935 K3
	24 hours Nürburgring	H.de Azevedo, F.Konrad, O.Wirdheim, F.Katthöfer	Carrera RS
	Italian Supercar GT Varano	G. Schenetti	Turbo S
	Carglass Cup GT Zolder	A. Vanierschot, J. Robberechts	Carrera 2
	Supercar Champ. Watkins Glen	Hans-Joachim Stuck	911 turbo
	24 hours Spa-Francorchamps	Christian Fittipaldi, Uwe Alzen, Jean-Pierre Jarier	Carrera RSR
	BRDC GT Challenge Oulton P.	R. Hyett	935
	Supercar Champ. Cleveland	Hans-Joachim Stuck	911 turbo
	BRDC GT Challenge Donington	R. Hyett	935
	Carglass Cup GT Spa-Franc.	A. Taels, P. Schreurs	Carrera RS
	Supercar Champ. Laguna Seca	Hans-Joachim Stuck	911 turbo
	BRDC GT Challenge Snetterton	John Greasley	935 K3
	Inter. GT 3 hours Hockenheim	Sandro Angelastri	Carrera RSR
	Supercar Champ. Portland	Hans-Joachim Stuck	911 turbo
	BRDC GT Challenge Silverst.	John Greasley	935 K3
	Supercar Champ. Phoenix	Hans-Joachim Stuck	911 turbo
	Carglass Cup 24 hours Zolder	K. Dujardyn, R. Maes, J.P. Herreman	Carrera RS
	Supercar Champ. Sebring	Hans-Joachim Stuck	911 turbo
	EVENTS	**DRIVERS - FAHRER**	**PORSCHE**
1994	BPR GT Serie Paul Ricard	Jean-Pierre Jarier, Jesus Pareja, Bob Wollek	Turbo S-LM
	Interswiss GT race Dijon	Froidevaux	Carrera RSR
	Carglass Cup Zolder	A. Vanierschot, P. Kumpen	Carrera RS
	GT Cup Germany Avus	Ralf Kelleners	Carrera RSR
	BPR GT Serie Jarama	Jean-Pierre Jarier, Jesus Pareja, Dominique Dupuy	Turbo S-LM
	BRDC GT Challenge Oulton P.	Nigel Barrett	Carrera RS
	GT Cup Germany Wunstorf	Uwe Alzen	Carrera RSR
	1000 miles Interlagos	Wilson Fittipaldi, Christian Fittipaldi	Carrera RSR
	Carglass Cup Zolder	A. Vanierschot, P. Kumpen	Carrera RS
	Interswiss GT Hockenheim	Enzo Calderari	Carrera RSR
	GT Cup Germany Zolder	Ralf Kelleners	Carrera RSR
	BPR GT Serie 1000km Suzuka	Jean-Pierre Jarier, Jesus Pareja, Bob Wollek	Turbo S-LM
	Carglass Cup 24 hours Zolder	K. Thiers, V. Dupont, A. Taels	Carrera RS
	Japan GT 2 hours Sugo	K. Takahashi, K. Tsuchiya	Carrera RSR
	GT Cup Germany Zandvoort	Ralf Kelleners	Carrera RSR
	Inter. GT 3 hours Hockenheim	Ernst Palmberger	Carrera RSR
	Italian Supercar GT Vallelunga	Bruno Rebai	Carrera RSR
	BPR GT Serie Zhuhai	Jean-Pierre Jarier, J. Laffite, Bob Wollek	Turbo S-LM
	Italian Supercar GT Misano	Bruno Rebai	Carrera RSR

356 PRESENTED BY BAM

1995

EVENTS	DRIVERS - FAHRER	PORSCHE
Interswiss GT race Dijon	A. Pfefferle	Carrera RSR
BRDC GT Champ. Silverstone	John Greasely	993 turbo
GT Cup Germany Zolder	Ralf Kelleners	911 GT2
Carglass Cup Zolder	A. Vanierschot, P. Kumpen	993
1000 miles Interlagos	Franz Konrad, Wilson Fittipaldi, Antonio Hermann	911 GT2
Japan GT Champ. Fuji	H. Matsuda, K. Iida	911 GT2
GT Cup Germany Spa-Franc.	Uwe Alzen	911 GT2
BPR GT Serie Montlhery	Stefan Oberndorfer, Dieter Hübner	911 GT2
Interswiss GT race Varano	A. Pfefferle	Carrera RSR
Italian GT Spec. Vallelunga	G. Tapparo	Carrera RSR
GT Cup Germany Österreichring	Ralf Kelleners	911 GT2
Italian GT Spec. Varano	Renato Mastropietro	Turbo S
Carglass Cup Spa-Francorch.	A. Vanierschot, P. Kumpen	993
Interswiss GT Hockenheim	Enzo Calderari	Carrera RSR
GT Cup Germany Salzburgring	Uwe Alzen	911 GT2
Italian GT Spec. Mugello	Renato Mastropietro	Turbo S
Interswiss GT race Oberhallau	A. Pfefferle	Carrera RSR
Carglass Cup 24 hours Zolder	A. Vanierschot, P. Kumpen, G. Cremer	993
GT Cup Germany Nürburgring	Uwe Alzen	911 GT2
Japan GT Championship Sugo	A. Reid, M. Kondo	911 GT2
Italian GT Spec. Imola	Renato Mastropietro	Turbo S
Inter. GT 3 hours Hockenheim	Enzo Calderari, Lilian Bryner	911 GT2
Japan GT Championship Mine	H. Matsuda, K. Suzuki	911 GT2
Italian GT Spec. Misano	Antonio de Castro	Carrera Cup

1996

EVENTS	DRIVERS - FAHRER	PORSCHE
Italian GT Spec. Magione	Antonio de Castro	Carrera Cup
Carglass Cup GT Zolder	A. Vanierschot, P. Kumpen	993
BPR GT Serie Brands Hatch	Hans-Joachim Stuck, Thierry Boutsen	911 GT1
24 hours Tokachi	Y. Yamada, E. Tajima, K. Mogi, H. Okada	911 GT2
Italian Supercar GT Monza	Angelo Zadra, P. Zadra	911 GT2
Carglass Cup GT Spa-Franc.	A. Vanierschot, P. Kumpen	993
BPR GT Serie Spa-Francorch.	Hans-Joachim Stuck, Thierry Boutsen	911 GT1
Carglass Cup Zolder	F. Taels, W. Daems	993
Italian Spec. GT 2 hours Misano	Alessandro Dazzan	Carrera RSR
World Challenge Elkhart Lake	Andy Pilgrim	911 GT2
BRDC GT Champ. Snetterton	John Morrison, John Greasely	993
Italian GT Spec. Varano	Renato Mastropietro	911 GT2
World Challenge Watkins Glen	Martin Snow	911 GT2
BPR GT Serie Zhuhai	Emmanuel Collard, Ralf Kelleners	911 GT1
World Challenge Reno	Andy Pilgrim	911 GT2
Carglass Cup 24 hours Zolder	V. Dupont, F. Bruynoghe, K. Dujardin	993
Italian GT Spec. Vallelunga	B. Corradi	Carrera RSR
World Challenge Sears Point	Martin Snow	911 GT2

1997

EVENTS	DRIVERS - FAHRER	PORSCHE
FFSA GT Serie Nogaro	Jean-Pierre Jarier	911 GT2
Cup Belcar GT Zolder	F. Taels, V. Dupont	911 GT2
SportsCar Champ. Mosport	Dorsey Schroeder, Andy Pilgrim	911 GT1
Canadian GT Cup Mosport	Harry Bytzek	Carrera RSR
Italian GT Spec. Varano	Luca Drudi	Turbo S
FFSA GT Serie Dijon	Christophe Bouchut, Patrice Goueslard	911 GT2
SportsCar Champ. Las Vegas	Alan McNish, Andy Pilgrim	911 GT1
3 hours GT race Zhuhai	John Greasley, Georg Lister, Marcus Wallinder	911 GT1
Italian GT Spec. Magione	G. Tapparo	Carrera RSR
SportsCar Champ. Pikes Peak	Andy Pilgrim, Alan McNish	911 GT1
FFSA GT Serie Val de Vienne	Christophe Bouchut, Patrice Goueslard	911 GT2
Cup Belcar GT Spa-Francor.	F. Taels, V. Dupont	911 GT2
Canadian Cup Shannonville	Scott Maxwell	911 GT2
SportsCar Champ. Sebring	Andy Pilgrim, Alan McNish	911 GT1
World Challenge Minneapolis	P. Kitchak	Carrera RSR
BRDC GT Champ. Silverstone	John Morrison, John Greasley	911 GT1
Canadian GT Shannonville	Harry Bytzek	911 GT2
FFSA GT Serie Paul Ricard	Patrice Goueslard, Andre Ahrle	911 GT2
Endurance Italia 12 h. Misano	G. Monforte, M. Monforte, D. Monforte	Carrera RSR
BRDC Champ. Brands Hatch	John Morrison, John Greasley	911 GT1
Cup Belcar GT Assen	Patrick Huisman, Vincent Vosse	911 GT2
FFSA GT Serie Albi	Christophe Bouchut, Patrice Goueslard	911 GT2
Cup Belcar 24 hours Zolder	Patrick Huisman, Vincent Vosse, Marc Goosens	911 GT2
Italian GT Spec. Misano	Angelo Zadra	Carrera RSR
BRDC GT Champ. Silverstone	John Morrison, John Greasley	911 GT1
Canadian GT Cup Mosport	Harry Bytzek	911 GT1
FFSA GT Serie Magny Cours	Christophe Bouchut, Patrice Goueslard	911 GT2

Winner GT Cup Zolder 1995: Ralf Kelleners

Winner FFSA GT Val de Vienne 1999: J. C. Lagniez, Patrice Goueslard

1998

EVENTS	DRIVERS - FAHRER	PORSCHE
BRDC GT Champ. Silverstone	Marcus Wallinder, John Greasley	911 GT1
Australian GT Calder Park	D. Beninca	911 RS
FFSA GT Serie Nogaro	Patrice Goueslard, Michel Sourd	911 GT2
Challenge Italia Paul Ricard	M. Beaverbrook, Geoff Lister, B. Williams	911 GT2
Australian GT Oran Park	P. Fitzgerald	911 RS
Belcar Trophy Spa-Francorch.	Patrick Huisman, Duncan Huisman	993
FFSA GT Serie Spa-Francor.	Jean-Pierre Jarier, F. Lafon	911 GT2
24 hours Le Mans	Alan McNish, Stephane Ortelli, Laurent Aiello	911 GT1 98
Canadian GT Cup Mosport	Klaus Bytzek	911 GT1
Scandinavian GT Mantorp Park	B Jonasson	Carrera RSR
BRDC GT Champ. Croft	John Nielson, T. Thyrring	911 GT1
Challenge Italia 6 hours Misano	Nigel Smith, R. Grassi, Michel Ligonnet	911 GT2
Canadian GT Cup Mosport	Klaus Bytzek	911 GT1
FFSA GT Serie Charade	Patrice Goueslard, Michel Sourd	911 GT2
GTR Euroserie 4 hours Misano	P. Kumpen, S. Cohen, C. Margueron	911 GT2
Belcar Trophy Spa-Francorch.	W. Daems, B. Leinders	993
Challenge Italia 2 hours A1 Ring	G. Dacco, Romoletto	Carrera RSR
FFSA GT Serie Dijon	Jean-Pierre Jarier, F. Lafon	911 GT2
BRDC GT Champ. Silverstone	Marcus Wallinder, John Greasley	911 GT1
Canadian GT Shannonville	Klaus Bytzek	911 GT1
GTR Euroserie 4h Nürburgring	Wolfgang Kaufmann, Michel Ligonnet	911 GT2
BRDC GT Champ. Donington	Marcus Wallinder, John Greasley	911 GT1
Canadian GT Mont Tremblant	Klaus Bytzek	911 GT1
GTR Euroserie 4h Spa-Franc.	Wolfgang Kaufmann, Michel Ligonnet	911 GT2
Belcar Trophy 24 hours Zolder	Patrick Huisman, Thierry Boutsen, Marc Goosens	993
FFSA GT Serie Le Mans	Patrice Goueslard, Michel Sourd	911 GT2
GTP race Surfers Paradise	Bob Forbes	911 RS CS
Showroom 3 hours Bathurst	P. Fitzgerald, Jim Richards	911 RS CS
FFSA GT Serie Magny Cours	Patrice Goueslard, Michel Sourd	911 GT2

1999

EVENTS	DRIVERS - FAHRER	PORSCHE
FFSA GT Serie Le Mans	J. C. Lagniez, Patrice Goueslard	911 GT2
Australian GT Eastern Creek	D. Beninca	911 RS CS
Belcar GT Trophy Zolder	A. Kumpen, S. Cohen	993 turbo
Australian GT Champ. Acelaide	Jim Richards	911 RS CS
FFSA GT Serie Ledenon	J. C. Lagniez, Patrice Goueslard	911 GT2
Spain GT Champ. Albacete	A. d'Orleans Bourbon, Ni Amorim	911 GT2
Swedish GT Mantorp Park	L. Pehrsson	911 GT2
Challenge GT Italia Magione	M. Pasini	911 turbo
Australian GT Phillip Island	D. Beninca	911 RS CS
Swedish GT Champ. Knutstorp	L. Pehrsson	911 GT2
Spain GT Champions. Jerez	E. Fernandez, Michael Irmgartz	911 GT2
Canadian GT Challenge Mosport	Klaus Bytzek	911 GT1
Swedish GT Champ. Karlskoga	L. Pehrsson	911 GT2
Speedvision GT Ch. Mid Ohio	P. Kitchak	Carrera RSR
Australian GT Hidden Valley	Jim Richards	911 RS CS
Canadian GT Shannonville	Klaus Bytzek	911 GT1
BRDC GT Champ. Silverstone	Marcus Wallinder, Geoff Lister	911 GT1
Australian GT Sandown Park	Jim Richards	911 RS CS
Challenge GT Monza	M. Frigerio, F. Babini	911 GT2
Challenge GT Italia Misano	M. Pasini	911 turbo
Australian GT Queensland	P. Fitzgerald	911 RS CS
FFSA GT Serie Nogaro	Jean-Pierre Jarier, L. Guitteny	911 GT2
Swedish GT Champ. Anderstorp	T. Johansson	Carrera RSR
Speedvision GT Trois Rivieres	P. Kitchak	Carrera RSR
Australian GT Champ. Winton	P. Fitzgerald	911 RS CS
FFSA GT Serie Val de Vienne	J. C. Lagniez, Patrice Goueslard	911 GT2
Speedvision GT West Michigan	P. Kitchak	Carrera RSR
Australian GT Champ. Oran P.	P. Fitzgerald	911 RS CS
Belcar GT Trophy Spa-Franc.	A. Kumpen, S. Cohen	993 turbo
Spain GT Champions. Jarama	J. Diez, Villarroel	911 GT2
FFSA GT Serie Valencia	F. lafon, Jean-Pierre Jarier	911 GT2
Internat. GT race Hockenheim	Uwe Sick, Axel Rohr	911 GT2
FFSA GT Serie Magny Cours	C. Chateau, Wolfgang Kaufmann	911 GT2
Speedvision GT Pikes Peak	P. Kitchak	Carrera RSR

NATIONAL AND INTERNATIONAL CHAMPIONSHIPS WON BY 911 357

OVERALL WINS BY 911 IN MAJOR NATIONAL AND INTERNATIONAL EVENTS

Poster

Poster

	EVENTS	DRIVERS - FAHRER	PORSCHE
2000	FFSA GT Serie Ledenon	C. Chateau, Wolfgang Kaufmann	911 GT2
	Coppa GT 2000 Vallelunga	M. Pasini	911 turbo
	24 hours Nürburgring	Uwe Alzen, Altfrid Heger, M. Bartels, B. Mayländer	911 GT3 R
	FIA GT Champ. Lausitzring	Wolfgang Kaufmann, Hubert Haupt	911 GT2
	Bilstein Cup Nürburgring	Ulrich Gallade, Olaf Manthey	996 turbo
	Canadian GT Chal. Mosport	Klaus Bytzek	911 GT1
	BRDC GT Champ. Oulton Park	T. Harvey, M. Youles	911 GT2
	Coppa GT 2000 Misano	M. Pasini	911 turbo
	Spain GT Champions. Valencia	J. Serra Bayona, E. de Aysa	911 GT2
	Swedish GTR Serie Knutstorp	L. Pehrsson	911 GT2
	Coppa GT 2000 Monza	Renato Mastropetro, C. Padovani	911 GT2
	Belcar GT Trophy Dijon	A. Vanierschot, Bert Longin	993 turbo
	FFSA GT Serie Dijon	C. Chateau, Wolfgang Kaufmann	911 GT2
	Canadian GT Shannonville	Klaus Bytzek	911 GT1
	Coppa GT 2000 Vallelunga	M. Pasini	911 turbo
	Nation's GT Cup Canberra	Jim Richards	911 GT3 R
	Swedish GTR Serie Mantorp P.	B. Jonasson	911 GT2
	Spain GT Champ. Albacete	J. Abia de la Torre, Ni Amorim	911 GT2
	Coppa GT 2000 Misano	M. Pasini	911 turbo
	Swedish GTR Oslo Speedw.	M. Ljungström	911 GT2
	Nation's GT Cup Oran Park	Jim Richards	911 GT3 R
	Speedvision GT Fort Worth	Mike Fitzgerald	911 GT3 R
	Spain GT Champions. Jarama	J. Diez Villarroel	911 GT2
	Nation's GT Cup Calder	Jim Richards	911 GT3 R
	Bilstein Cup Nürburgring	Ulrich Gallade, Olaf Manthey	996 turbo
	Speedvision GT Road Atlanta	Mike Fitzgerald	911 GT3 R
	Nation's GT Cup Gold Coast	P. Fitzgerald	911 GT3 R
	Inter. GT 3 hours Hockenheim	Uwe Sick, Axel Rohr	911 GT2
	Speedvision GT Laguna Seca	Mike Fitzgerald	911 GT3 R
	Spain GT Champions. Monmelo	Hubert Haupt, Andre Ahrle	911 GT2
	EVENTS	**DRIVERS - FAHRER**	**PORSCHE**
2001	Australian GT Cup Melbourne	Jim Richards	911 GT3 R
	FFSA GT Serie Le Mans	P. Soulan, Patrice Goueslard	911 GT2
	1000 miles Interlagos	M. Wilson, R. Schuch, A. L. Resende, F. Trindade	911 GT2
	Gr.Am SportsCar Tr. Rivieres	S. Pumpelly	911 GT3 R
	Euro GT Serie 1000 km Monza	Elmar Grimm	911 GT2
	Belcar Trophy GT Zolder	R. Penders, M. Goossens	911 GT2
	FFSA GT Serie Magny Cours	C. Chateau, Wolfgang Kaufmann	911 GT2
	GT Cup Spain Jarama	J. Diez Villarroel, M. Rosado	911 GT2
	Supercars serie Italy Monza	M. Spagnoli	911 GT3 R
	Australian GT Cup Wakefield P.	Jim Richards	911 GT3 R
	Euro GT Serie 1000 km Spa	Elmar Grimm	911 GT2
	Swedish GTR Mantorp Park	M. Linden	911 GT3 R
	Supercars serie Italy Imola	C. Pesenti	911 GT3 R
	GT Cup Canada Mosport	Klaus Bytzek	911 GT1
	Australian GT Cup 400 Canberra	P. Fitzgerald	911 GT3 R
	Supercars serie Italy Vallelunga	M. Spagnoli	911 GT3 R
	Swedish GTR Jyllandsringen	T. Björk	911 GT3 R
	Euro GT Serie Donington	Klaus Abbelen	911 GT2
	GT Cup Spain Estoril	N. Dalli, K. Zwart	911 GT2
	Speed World Chal. Sears Point	Johannes van Overbeek	911 GT3 Cup
	Swedish GTR Racway Rana	M. Erlandsen	911 GT3 R
	Euro GT Serie Zandvoort	Klaus Abbelen	911 GT2
	Belcar Trophy 24 hours Zolder	A. Vanierschot, F. van Roey, T. Verbergt	993 turbo
	Euro GT Serie Anderstorp	Elmar Grimm	911 GT2
	Supercars serie Italy Misano	M. Bompani	911 GT3 R
	FFSA GT Serie Val de Vienne	C. Chateau, Wolfgang Kaufmann	911 GT2
	Supercars serie Italy Varano	M. Spagnoli	911 GT3 R
	FFSA GT Serie Nogaro	P. Soulan, Patrice Goueslard	911 GT2
	Belcar Trophy Spa-Francorch.	K. Mollekens, S. Cohen	993 turbo
	Int. Race 100 miles Hockenheim	P. Zumstein, P. Hintermayer	911 GT2
	GT Cup Spain Barcelona	M. Sourd, E. de Aysa	911 GT2
	Australian GT Cup Oran Park	T. Quinn	911 GT3 R

Winner 24 hours Daytona 2003: K.Buckler, M.Schrom, T.Bernhard, J.Bergmeister

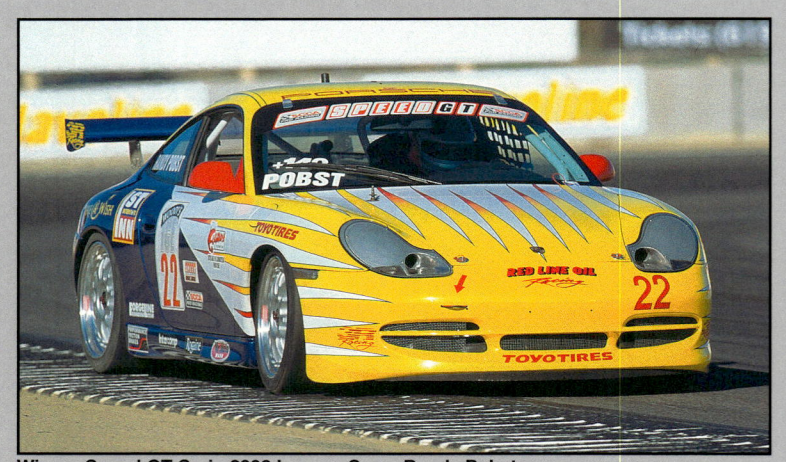

Winner Speed GT Serie 2002 Laguna Seca: Randy Pobst

Winner Speed World Challenge Sears Point 2001: Johannes van Overbeek

358 PRESENTED BY BAM

Winner 24 hours Nürburgring 2000: U.Alzen, A.Heger, M.Bartels, B.Mayländer

	EVENTS	DRIVERS - FAHRER	PORSCHE
2002	BFG Champ. Nürburgring	Wilhelm Kern, Olaf Manthey	911 GT3 MR
	FFSA GT Serie Nogaro	P. Soulan, Patrice Goueslard	911 GT2
	Supercars Serie Italy Magione	M. Spagnoli	911 GT3 RS
	Canadian GT Chal. Mosport	Klaus Bytzek	911 GT1
	BFG Champ. Nürburgring	Wilhelm Kern, Marcel Tiemann	911 GT3 MR
	FFSA GT Serie Ledenon	P. Soulan, Patrice Goueslard	911 GT2
	Swedish GTR Mantorp Park	J. Sturesson	911 GT3 RS
	Euro GT Serie Donington P.	Klaus Abbelen	911 GT2
	BFG Champ. Nürburgring	Jürgen Alzen, Arno Klasen, Timo Bernhard	911 GT3 RS
	GT Cup Spain Jarama	N. Dalli	911 GT2
	FFSA GT Serie Pau	M. Sourd, S. Hiesse	911 GT2
	BFG Champ. Nürburgring	Wolfgang Destree, Edgar Althoff, P. Hulverscheid	911 GT3 R
	Supercars Serie Italy Vallelunga	A. de Castro	911 GT3 RS
	Speed GT Champ. Lime Rock	Randy Pobst	911 GT3 Cup
	Czech Endurance 4 hours Brno	R. Machanek, J. Malcharek	911 GT3 RS
	BFG Champ. Nürburgring	Jürgen Alzen, Arno Klasen	911 GT3 RS
	Australian GT Cup Queensland	Jim Richards	911 GT3 R
	Speed GT Champ. Washington	Randy Pobst	911 GT3 Cup
	Remus RC Cup 6 hours Misano	F. Babini, M. Galimberti, E. Busnelli	911 GT3 RS
	Endurance 500 miles Interlagos	P. R. Bonifacio, D. Pires, M. Wilson	911 GT3 R
	Speed GT Champ. Trois Rivieres	Randy Pobst	911 GT3 Cup
	Supercars Serie Italy Misano	Renato Mastropietro, C. Padovani	911 GT2
	FFSA GT Serie Le Mans	C. Chateau, J. M. Thevenot	911 GT2
	Speed GT Champ. Laguna Seca	Randy Pobst	911 GT3 Cup
	Int. GT 3 hours Hockenheim	Wolfgang Kaufmann, T. Heutschi	911 GT3 RS
	Australian GT Surfers Paradise	Jim Richards	911 GT3 R
	EVENTS	**DRIVERS - FAHRER**	**PORSCHE**
2003	Gr.Am Serie 24 hours Daytona	K.Buckler, M.Schrom, T.Bernhard, J.Bergmeister	911 GT3 RS
	500 miles Interlagos	I. Hoffmann, X. Negrao, F. Nabuco, R. Etchenique	911 GT3 RS
	Gr.Am Cup Serie 250 Daytona	R. Julien, J. Dumoulin	911 GT3 Cup
	BFG Champ. Nürburgring	Jonathan Price, Frank Stippler	911 GT3 RS
	Supercars Serie Italy Imola	Luca Riccitelli, E. Busnelli	911 GT3 RS
	Gr.Am Cup Serie Homestead	Mark Levitas, Randy Pobst	911 GT3 Cup
	FIA GT Champ. 24h Spa-Franc.	Stephane Ortelli, Marc Lieb, Romain Dumas	911 GT3 RS
	BFG Champ. Nürburgring	Lucas Luhr, Emmanuel Collard	911 GT3 RS
	1000 km Brasilia Nelson Piquet	X. Negrao, L. Paternostro, P. Bonifacio	911 GT3 RS
	FFSA GT Serie Nogaro	M. Sourd, F. Dedours	911 GT2
	Gr.Am Cup Serie 250 Phoenix	D. Lacey, G. Wilkins	911 GT3 Cup
	Swedish GTR Falkenberg	M. Gustafsson, T. Nyström	911 GT3 RS
	BFG Champ. Nürburgring	Peter Mamerow, Klaus Niedzwiedz	911 GT3 RS
	Gr.Am Cup Serie 200 Barber P.	R. Julien, J. F. Dumoulin	911 GT3 Cup
	Dutch Supercar Chal. Assen	Bert Longin	993 turbo
	Speed GT Champ. Road Atlanta	M. Fitzgerald	911 GT3 Cup
	Gr.Am Cup Serie 250 Fontana	Mike Levitas, Randy Pobst	911 GT3 Cup
	Dutch Supercar Chal. Zolder	R. Snel	911 GT3 RS
	Gr.Am Cup Serie Watkins Glen	Mike Levitas, Randy Pobst	911 GT3 Cup
	Speed GT Champ. Elkhart Lake	M. Fitzgerald	911 GT3 Cup
	Gr.Am Cup Serie Mid Ohio	R. Julien, J. F. Dumoulin	911 GT3 Cup
	Swedish GTR Mantorp Park	M. Gustafsson, T. Nyström	911 GT3 RS
	Gr.Am Cup Serie Mosport	R. Julien, J. F. Dumoulin	911 GT3 Cup
	Int. GT race 500 Zandvoort	Mike and Sebastian Bleekemolen	996 GT3
	FFSA GT Serie Magny Cours	M. Palttala, R. Bera	996 turbo
	Gr.Am Cup Serie Daytona	R. Julien, J. F. Dumoulin	911 GT3 Cup
	EVENTS	**DRIVERS - FAHRER**	**PORSCHE**
2004	Grand-Am Cup 250 Daytona	Craig Stanton, Tony Borcheller	911 GT3 Cup
	British GT Champ. Donington	M. Jordan, M. Sumpter	911 GT3 RS
	Grand-Am Cup 250 Miami	Craig Stanton, Tony Borcheller	911 GT3 Cup
	Belcar World Serie Zolder	Vincent Vosse, F. Bouvy	996 turbo
	Grand-Am Cup 200 Phoenix	Craig Stanton, Tony Borcheller	911 GT3 Cup
	BFG Champ. Nürburgring	Arno Klasen, Timo Bernhard, Nicolas Leutwiler	911 GT3 RS
	British GT Champ. Mondello P.	Tim Sugden, Jonathan Cocker	911 GT3 RSR
	Gr.-Am Cup 250 Watkins Glen	Craig Stanton, David Murry	911 GT3 Cup
	FFSA GT Serie Dijon	O. Maximin, P.Prette	996 turbo
	British GT Ch. Castle Combe	Tim Sugden, Jonathan Cocker	911 GT3 RSR
	GT Cup Spain Estoril	M. Amaral, Pedro Couceiro	911 GT3 RS
	BFG Champ. Nürburgring	Marc Basseng, Patrick Simon	911 GT3 RS
	British GT Champ. Oulton Park	W. Hughes, Jonathan Cocker	911 GT3 RSR
	Speed World Ch. Sears Point	Wolf Henzler	911 GT3 Cup
	24 hours Tokachi	H. Takeuchi, T. Tanaka, S. Ara	911 GT3 Cup
	Nordic Supercar Valerbaren	J. S. Eidsvold	911 GT2
	BFG Champ. Nürburgring	Uwe Alzen, Michael Bartels, Jürgen Alzen	996 turbo
	Dutch Supercar Spa-Francorch.	R. Snel	911 GT3 RS
	Grand-Am Cup 250 Danville	Craig Stanton, David Murry	911 GT3 Cup
	British GT Champ. Brands Hatch	Tim Sugden, Jonathan Cocker	911 GT3 RSR
	Dutch Supercar Zandvoort	Michael Bleekemolen	911 GT3 RS
	Grand-Am Cup 250 Barber Park	Craig Stanton, David Murry	911 GT3 Cup
	Speed World Ch. Laguna Seca	Wolf Henzler	911 GT3 Cup
	BFG Champ. Nürburgring	Timo Bernhard, Lucas Luhr	911 GT3 MR

Winner BFG Nürburgring 2004: Marc Basseng, Patrick Simon

Poster

Poster

NATIONAL AND INTERNATIONAL CHAMPIONSHIPS WON BY 911   359

935 / 78 Moby Dick 1978

961 Le Mans 1987

Kunden-Motor / Customer engine 935 1977

935 / 78 Moby Dick 1978

964 IMSA Supercar 1992

361

TECHNISCHE DATEN – TECHNICAL DATA

Typ - Modell Type - Model	Baujahr Construction Year	Hubraum Displace- ment	Zylinder Cylinder	DIN-PS bei U / min. Power output	Gewicht Weight	Produktions - Stückzahlen Production figure
911 2,0 'Monte'	1965	1991	6	160 / 6600	1080	5 Werkswagen / 5 Factory cars
911 S 2,0 'Rallye'	1967	1991	6	170 / 7300	1080	3 Werkswagen / 3 Factory cars
911 R 2,0	1967	1991	6	210 / 8000	800	4 Versuchs-, 19 Kundenwagen / 4 Test, 19 Customer cars
911S 2,0 'London-Sydney'	1968	1991	6	160 / 660	1080	3 Werkswagen / 3 Factory cars
911 S 2,0 'Rallye'	1968	1991	6	170 / 7300	980	5 Werkswagen / 5 Factory cars
911 R 'Tour de France'	1969	1991	6	170 / 7300	800	1 Werkswagen / 1 Factory car
911 S 'Rallye'	1969	1991	6	170 / 7300	960	6 Werkswagen / 6 Factory cars
911 S 2,2 'Rallye'	1970	2247	6	230 / 7600	960	7 Werkswagen / 7 Factory cars
911 S 2,3 'Rallye'	1970	2247	6	240 / 7800	840	
911 S 2,4 'Tour de France'	1970	2395	6	260 / 8000	790	1 Werkswagen / 1 Factory car
911 S 2,2 'Safari'	1971	2195	6	180 / 6500	980	5 Werkswagen / 5 Factory cars
911 S 2,2 'Rallye'	1971	2195	6	180 / 6500	960	2 Werkswagen / 2 Factory cars
911 S 2,5 'Rallye'	1972	2466	6	270 / 8000	980	2 Werkswagen / 2 Factory cars
911 S 2,5 'Rennen/Race'	1972	2492	6	270 / 8000	960	21 Kundenwagen / 21 Customer cars
Carrera RS 2,8 'Corsica'	1972	2806	6	300 / 8000	960	2 Werkswagen / 2 Factory cars
Carrera RS 2,7 'Safari'	1973	2687	6	210 / 6300	980	2 Werks-, 1 Kundenwagen / 2 Factory, 1 Customer cars
Carrera 2,8 RSR	1973	2806	6	300 / 8000	900	57 Kundenwagen / 57 Customer cars
Carrera RSR	1973	2806	6	300 / 8000	850	8 Kundenwagen / 8 Customer cars
Carrera RSR Turbo	1974	2142	6	500 / 7600	750	4 Werkswagen / 4 Factory cars
Carrera RS 2,7 'Safari'	1974	2687	6	210 / 6300	980	2 Werks-, 1 Kundenwagen / 2 Factory, 1 Customer cars
Carrera RS 3,0	1974	2993	6	230 / 6200	900	56 Kundenwagen / 56 Customer cars
Carrera RSR 3,0	1974	2993	6	315 / 8000	920	42 Kundenwagen / 42 Customer cars
Carrera RSR 3,0 'Penske'	1974	2993	6	315 / 8000	920	15 Kundenwagen / 15 Customer cars

911 S 2,4 Tour de France 1970

911 S 2,2 Safari 1971

911 S 2,0 Rallye 1968

Das Buch „Porsche 911 in Racing" - für uns ein ganz besonderes Druckvorstufenprojekt.

PORSCHE
911 in Racing

www.LA-CONCEPT.de

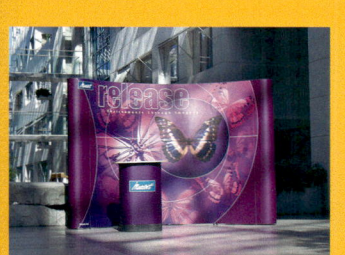

| Displaysysteme | Großformatdruck |  Werbemittel |  Textilien |  Personal |

LA CONCEPT GmbH • Robert-Perthel-Str. 5 • 50739 Köln
Tel.: +49 (0) 2 21 / 65 03 27 -0 • Fax: +49 (0) 2 21 / 65 03 27 -20
info@LA-CONCEPT.DE • www.LA-CONCEPT.de

TECHNISCHE DATEN – TECHNICAL DATA

934 turbo 1976

935 turbo 1976 Group 5

935 / 78 turbo Moby Dick 1978

Motor / Engine 935 / 77 2,0 Baby 1977

Typ - Modell Type - Model	Baujahr Construction Year	Hubraum Displace- ment	Zylinder Cylinder	DIN-PS bei U / min. Power output	Gewicht Weight	Produktions - Stückzahlen Production figure
Carrera RSR 3,0	1975	2993	6	330 / 8000	920	12 Kundenwagen / 12 Customer cars
934 Turbo	1976	2993	6	485 / 7000	1120	32 Kundenwagen / 32 Customer cars
935 Turbo 'Grp 5'	1976	2806	6	590 / 5400	970	2 Versuchs-, 2 Werkswagen / 2 Test, 2 Factory cars
934 Turbo USA	1977	2993	6	540 / 7000	1120	10 Kundenwagen / 10 Customer cars
935 / 77 Turbo	1977	2806	6	630 / 8000	970	3 Werkswagen / 3 Factory cars
935 / 77 Turbo	1977	2806	6	590 / 7900	970	17 Kundenwagen / 17 Customer cars
935 / 77 2,0 'Baby'	1977	1425	6	370 / 8000	750	1 Werkswagen / 1 Factory car
911 SC 'Safari'	1978	2993	6	250 / 6800	1300	3 Werks-, 1 Trainingswagen / 3 Factory, 1 Recce cars
935 / 78 Turbo 'Moby Dick'	1978	3211	6	650 / 8200	1025	2 Werkswagen / 2 Factory cars
935 / 78 Turbo	1978	3211	6	650 / 8200	970	19 Kundenwagen / 19 Customer cars
935 / 79 Turbo	1979	3124	6	680 / 8000	1025	17 Kundenwagen / 17 Customer cars
911 SC 'San Remo'	1981	2996	6	280 / 5600	1070	1 Werkswagen / 1 Factory car
935 'Joest', 'Kremer'	1981	3124	6	720 / 8000	1025	4 Kundenwagen / 4 Customer cars
953 'Paris-Dakar'	1984	3164	6	225 / 6000	1215	3 Werkswagen / 3 Factory cars
954 SC / RS	1985	2996	6	255 / 6500	960	21 Kundenwagen / 21 Customer cars
953 / 959 'Paris-Dakar'	1985	3164	6	230 / 5000	1185	3 Werkswagen / 3 Factory cars
959 'Paris-Dakar'	1986	2849	6	400 / 6500	1260	2 Werkswagen / 2 Factory cars
961 'IMSA GTX'	1986	2849	6	640 / 7800	1150	1 Werkswagen / 1 Factory car
959 RDW	1986	2850	6	450 / 6500	1450	113 Kundenwagen / 113 Customer cars
959 RDW	1987	2850	6	450 / 6500	1450	50 Kundenwagen / 50 Customer cars
959 USA	1988	2850	6	450 / 6500	1350	29 Kundenwagen / 29 Customer cars
953 'Foltene Paris-Dakar'	1988	3164	6	225 / 6000	1215	2 Kundenwagen / 2 Customer cars

911 SC Safari 1978

959 Paris-Dakar 1986

Typ - Modell / Type - Model	Baujahr Construction Year	Hubraum Displacement	Zylinder Cylinder	DIN-PS bei U/min. Power output	Gewicht Weight	Produktions - Stückzahlen Production figure
964 Carrera 4 'Leichtbau'	1990	3600	6	265 / 6720	1100	22 Kundenwagen / 22 Customer cars
964 Cup	1990	3600	6	265 / 6100	1210	50 Kundenwagen / 50 Customer cars
964 Turbo USA	1991	3299	6	320 / 5750	1470	1 Kundenwagen / 1 Customer car
964 Cup	1991	3600	6	265 / 6100	1210	120 Kundenwagen / 120 Customer cars
IMSA Super Car	1992	3299	6	381 / 6000	1290	1 Kundenwagen / 1 Customer car
964 Cup	1992	3600	6	265 / 6100	1210	112 Kundenwagen / 112 Customer cars
964 Cup USA	1992	3600	6	265 / 6100	1210	45 Kundenwagen / 45 Customer cars
964 Turbo S 'Le Mans'	1993	3164	6	474 / 6900	1000	1 Versuchs-, 1 Kundenwagen / 1 Test, 1 Customer cars
964 Cup	1993	3600	6	275 / 6100	1210	15 Kundenwagen / 15 Customer cars
964 RS 3,8	1993	3746	6	300 / 6500	1210	55 Kundenwagen / 55 Customer cars
964 RSR 3,8	1993	3746	6	325 / 6900	1200	50 Kunden-, 1 Versuchswagen / 50 Customer, 1 Test cars
993 Cup	1993	3746	6	315 / 6200	1120	40 Kundenwagen / 40 Customer cars
993 GT 2	1994	3600	6	450 / 5700	1100	43 Kundenwagen / 43 Customer cars
993 Cup	1994	3746	6	315 / 6200	1120	50 Kundenwagen / 50 Customer cars
993 GT 2 Evo	1995	3600	6	600 / 7000	1100	3 Kundenwagen / 3 Customer cars
993 Cup	1995	3746	6	315 / 6200	1120	57 Kundenwagen / 57 Customer cars
993 GT 2 Evo	1996	3600	6	550 / 6250	1100	5 Kundenwagen / 5 Customer cars
993 Carrera Cup	1996	3746	6	315 / 6200	1120	54 Kundenwagen / 54 Customer cars
911 GT 1 / 96	1996	3163	6	544 / 7000	1150	3 Werkswagen / 3 Factory cars
911 GT 1 / 97	1997	3163	6	600 / 7200	1050	3 Werkswagen / 3 Factory cars
911 GT 1 / 97	1997	3163	6	544 / 7000	1150	22 Kundenwagen / 22 Customer cars
993 GT 2	1997	3600	6	465 / 5750	1120	15 Kundenwagen / 15 Customer cars

911 GT 2 Evo 1997

961 Le Mans 1987

964 Cup 1990

953 Paris – Dakar 1984

954 SC / RS 1985

TECHNICAL DATA

TECHNISCHE DATEN – TECHNICAL DATA

996 GT 3 Cup 1999

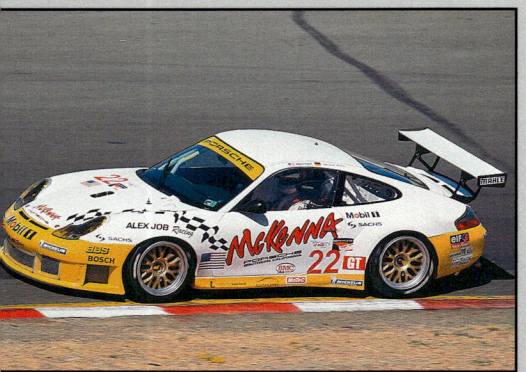

996 GT 3 RS 2001

996 GT 3 Cup 2003

996 GT 3 Rallye 2004

996 GT 3 RSR 2004

Typ - Modell Type - Model	Baujahr Construction Year	Hubraum Displace- ment	Zylinder Cylinder	DIN-PS bei U / min. Power output	Gewicht Weight	Produktions - Stückzahlen Production figure
993 Carrera Cup	1997	3746	6	315 / 6200	1120	15 Kundenwagen / 15 Customer cars
993 Cup 3,8 RSR	1997	3746	6	325 / 6900	1120	15 Kundenwagen / 15 Customer cars
911 GT 1 / 98	1998	3200	6	550 / 7200	950	5 Werkswagen / 5 Factory cars
993 GT 2	1998	3600	6	485 / 5750	1120	12 Kundenwagen / 12 Customer cars
996 Cup	1998	3387	6	370 / 7200	1140	30 Kundenwagen / 30 Customer cars
993 GT 2	1999	3800	6	550 / 6500	1120	1 Kundenwagen / 1 Customer car
996 GT3 Cup	1999	3598	6	370 / 7000	1145	81 Kundenwagen / 81 Customer cars
996 GT3 R	2000	3598	6	360 / 7200	1350	66 Kundenwagen / 66 Customer cars
996 GT3 Cup	2000	3598	6	370 / 7200	1150	71 Kundenwagen / 71 Customer cars
996 GT3 RS	2001	3598	6	360 / 7200	1350	51 Kundenwagen / 51 Customer cars
996 GT3 Cup	2001	3598	6	370 / 7200	1150	114 Kundenwagen / 114 Customer cars
996 GT3 RS	2002	3598	6	435 / 8250	1100	48 Kundenwagen / 48 Customer cars
996 GT3 Cup	2002	3598	6	380 / 7000	1150	138 Kundenwagen / 138 Customer cars
996 GT3 RS	2003	3598	6	435 / 8250	1100	20 Kundenwagen / 20 Customer cars
996 GT3 Cup	2003	3598	6	390 / 7300	1150	200 Kundenwagen / 200 Customer cars
996 GT3 RSR	2004	3598	6	435 / 8250	1100	27 Kundenwagen / 27 Customer cars
996 GT3 Cup	2004	3598	6	390 / 7300	1150	150 Kundenwagen / 150 Customer cars
996 GT3 'Rallye'	2004	3598	6	381 / 7400	1127	1 Kundenwagen / 1 Customer cars

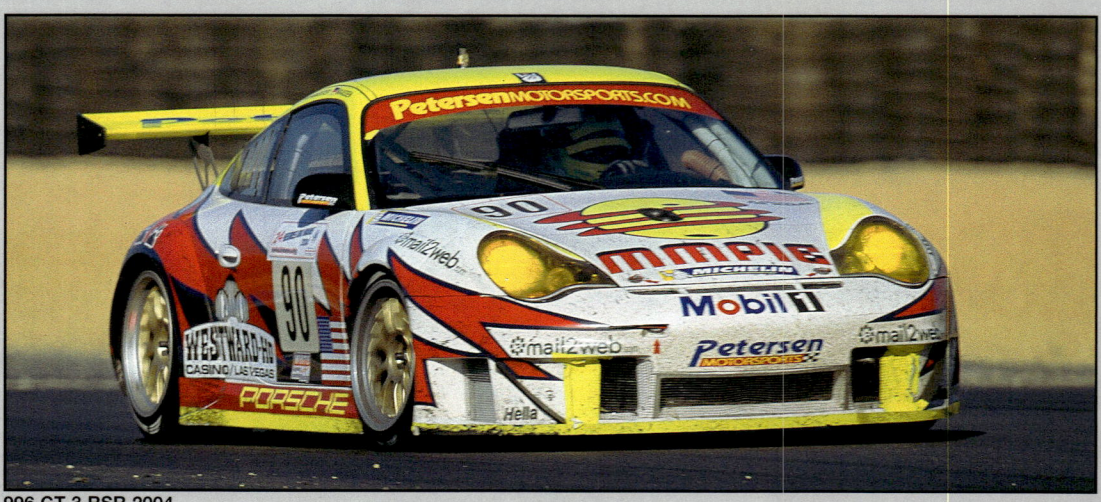

Druckpartner der Automobil-Industrie

HMB
print. medien. services.

Heining & Müller GmbH

Lahnstraße 30
45478 Mülheim/Ruhr

FON +49.208.999 26-0
FAX +49.208.999 26-26

EMAIL info@hmb-print.de
WEB www.hmb-print.de